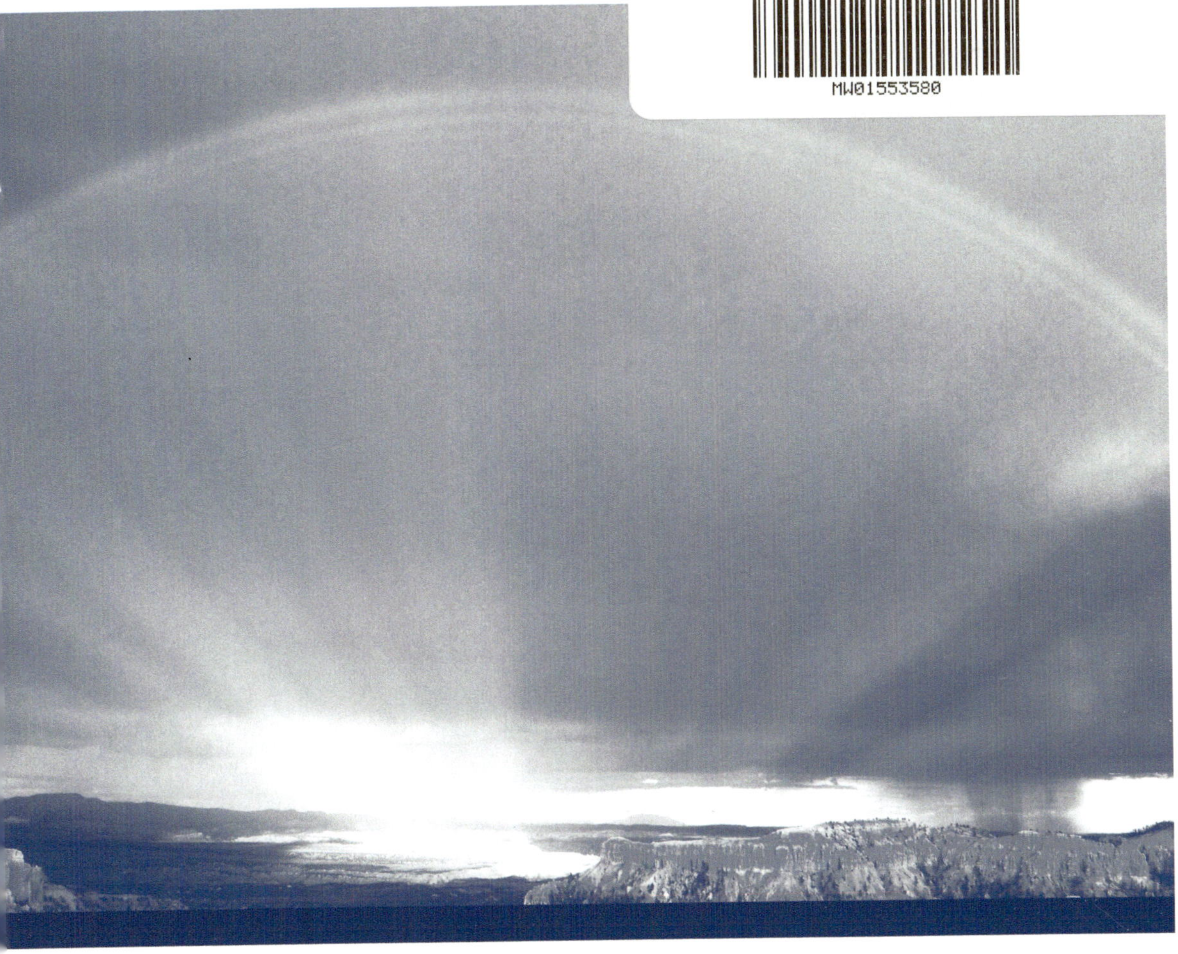

Interpreting Cultural and Natural Heritage

For A Better World

Larry Beck
Ted T. Cable
Douglas M. Knudson

©2018 Sagamore-Venture Publishing LLC
All rights reserved. No part of this book may be reproduced in any form or by any means without permission from the publisher.

Publishers: Joseph J. Bannon/Peter Bannon
Sales and Marketing Manager: Misti Gilles
Marketing Assistant: Kimberly Vecchio
Director of Development and Production: Susan M. Davis
Graphic Designer: Marissa Willison
Technology Manager: Mark Atkinson
Cover painting, "Old Point Loma Lighthouse," by Tina Christiansen

Library of Congress Control Number: 2017961081
ISBN print edition: 978-1-57167-865-2
ISBN ebook: 978-1-57167-866-9
Printed in the United States.

SAGAMORE VENTURE
1807 N. Federal Dr.
Urbana, IL 61801
www.sagamorepublishing.com

For interpreters of our cultural and natural heritage, champions of human integrity and natural beauty, who make the world a better place.

Contents

Frontispiece vii
Foreword ix
About the Cover and Artist... xi
Preface xiii

Section I: Introduction
1. What Is Interpretation? 3
2. Who Offers Interpretation? 17

Section II: Why Interpret?
3. Values to Individuals and Society 41
4. Values of Interpretation for Management 59

Section III: What Guides Us?
5. Guiding Principles of Interpretation 81
6. How People Learn.. 105
7. Serving Diverse Audiences 127

Section IV: How To Interpret
8. Interpreting to the Masses... 165
9. Personal Interpretation 185
10. Arts in Interpretation.. 215
11. Museums and Visitor Centers 233
12. Exhibits 259
13. Trails and Byways.. 283
14. Interpretation and the Written Word..................................... 303
15. Interpreting History 325

Section V: Managing Interpretation
16. A Business Approach to Interpretation................................. 347
17. Training and Professional Growth 377
18. Interpretive Planning... 395
19. Evaluating Interpretation 417

Section VI: Growth of the Profession
   20. Global Interpretation 435
   21. The Bright Future of Interpretation 457

Appendix A 479
Acknowledgments 480
About the Contributors 481
Photography Credits Key 484
Index 485

Finding beauty in a broken world…
is the work of daring contemplation that inspires action.
-Terry Tempest Williams

This is a new book, with a new title, and with a shift in authorship responsibilities, but with a foundation in two earlier versions of a text titled *Interpretation of Cultural and Natural Resources*. The new title reflects interpretation as a more deliberate process of communication and one that focuses on our *heritage*, rather than on *resources*. We have included a subtitle that we feel is critical for identifying why interpretation is offered at all—and at the most profound level. That purpose is something that most everyone could agree on, that interpreting cultural and natural heritage lends itself to a better world but is rarely put out front and center. In the title and throughout the book we have emphasized what we believe is at the root of interpretation: to make this world a better place through greater understanding, appreciation, and sense of stewardship for culture and nature. This seems to become increasingly important at this point in our history.

We are aware, as readers are aware, that problems exist throughout the world. The list is long. Yet the places interpretation takes place provide refuges where people can learn and be inspired about humanity in all its diversity, the landscape, and myriad other species we share the planet with. These places, and the people who interpret there, serve as beacons of hope.

Barry Lopez wrote, in the Introduction to a poem titled, *I, Snow Leopard,* by Jidi Majia, "We regularly forget what we want our lives to mean…We repeatedly lose touch with what we intend our lives to stand for. To protect us, the elders must constantly reacquaint us with our ideals." Those who interpret our cultural and natural heritage help us regain touch with what we intend our lives to stand for, by seeking to appeal to the better angels of our nature and reacquainting us with our ideals.

Foreword
By Eric Blehm

As a young man, my aspirations for what I wished to contribute to the world were limited. Back in the mid-80s, my dream was to become a professional snowboarder at a time when snowboarding was considered a renegade "activity," not even a sport. To better my chances of reaching stardom, I moved to Breckenridge, Colorado, a year after high school. One day, a man riding the chairlift with me began asking me all sorts of questions about the local scene. He explained that he was a journalist on assignment for a story about the area—and was actually getting paid for it. This seemed like a pretty good deal to me, making money off of travel adventures. I had discovered a new calling, and when the season ended, I headed to San Diego State University to pursue a major in journalism and a minor in outdoor resource management

Eventually I was able to combine aspects of my major and minor for my book, *The Last Season*, about Sequoia and Kings Canyon National Park Service Ranger Randy Morgenson. Although Morgenson was a search-and-rescue specialist, at heart he was a naturalist philosopher—an interpreter. Having grown up in Yosemite with mentors by the likes of Ansel Adams and Pulitzer Prize-winning author Wallace Stegner, he both loved the mountains and *knew* the mountains. He was enchanted by everything from the towering spires to the tiniest wildflowers, and he conveyed the magic of the Sierra mountains—through his knowledge, his passion, his experiences—to others. These are fundamental aspects of interpretation: to be an expert on the topic, to care deeply for the subject and those you share it with, and to be fully immersed in the place you work.

SDSU was where I first met the lead author of *Interpreting Cultural and Natural Heritage: For A Better World*. My former professor, Larry Beck, and his colleagues, Ted Cable and Doug Knudson, have devoted their long careers to not only learning as much as possible about our cultural heritage and the wonders of our natural world, but also how these things can be communicated to others in ways that will educate them, inspire them, and move them to new ways of thinking and doing.

Interpreting Cultural and Natural Heritage: For A Better World touches on what interpretation is, where it is performed, how to do it, why it is so important (especially now), and how it surrounds us. The 21 chapters of the book range from guiding principles, to arts in interpretation, to museums and visitor centers, to interpretive planning, to global interpretation, and the future of the profession. Although many books on interpretation exist, this is the only *comprehensive* text on the subject, in essence, a treatise for the interpretive profession. It will inspire interpreters and assist them in conducting more effective work, ultimately impacting the visitors to their interpretive sites.

One of Professor Beck's lectures particularly stuck with me through the years. He told us that there is your *job*, and there is your *work*. Your job pays your rent, and your work is what fulfills you. If you find work, you'll never have to "work" another day in your life—your job and your work will be the same thing. Within this book exists that same message. May the authors' words inspire readers on their own journeys to better understand the nuances of this fascinating profession and to conduct their work as a labor of love; not a job, but rather a calling and a joy. This solid interpretation of our natural and cultural heritage is essential to move us in ways that compel us to change the world.

Eric Blehm [www.ericblehm.com] is the *New York Times* bestselling author of *Fearless, The Only Thing Worth Dying For, Legend,* and the National Outdoor Book Award-winning *The Last Season*, which was also selected by *Outside* magazine as one of the 10 best adventure stories ever.

About the Cover and Artist

Lighthouse Metaphor

Lighthouses are beacons of guidance and hope. Interpretive sites are also beacons of hope that help people find their bearings and keep them on course—places such as national parks, nature centers, zoos, museums, aquariums, historic sites—where interpreters guide people to learn about and experience their cultural and natural heritage. Interpreters are stewards of areas that provide a sense of place and meaning. Each day it is the interpreter's responsibility, privilege, and joy to thus illuminate the world.

Lighthouses, in this broadest sense, provide authenticity for where we are in a complex world. Perhaps they are most needed in dark, stormy times to guide people away from danger and provide a sense of security and stability. Intimate relationship with our land and culture sustains us as a society. One such place is the Old Point Loma Lighthouse at Cabrillo National Monument in San Diego.

Cabrillo National Monument

The painting of the "Old Point Loma Lighthouse" at Cabrillo National Monument represents both our cultural and natural heritage. The lighthouse, built in 1855, was among the first eight lighthouses on the west coast as aids to ocean navigation. Because the lighthouse was at the *top* of Point Loma, some 400 feet above the Pacific, it was sometimes obscured by fog and not visible to sailors (note the fog creeping up the cliff face in the painting). Therefore, another lighthouse was built in 1891, nearby, at sea level, for greater visibility.

The cultural heritage of the site is also represented by the namesake of the monument, Juan Rodríquez Cabrillo, whose party sailed from Mexico in three ships to become the first Europeans to set foot on what is now the west coast of the United States, just 50 years after Columbus first sailed to the New World. Cabrillo weathered a bad storm by staying in the harbor he named San Miguel. Then in 1602, another explorer, Sebastián Vizscaíno, landed at the harbor and set up a chapel to celebrate the feast day of San Diego de Alcalá, a Spanish Franciscan who lived in the 15th century. Vizscaíno claimed that Cabrillo's observations didn't merit positive identification of the points he named, so Vizcaíno simply changed all the names. Hence his updated designation and what we know now as San Diego.

The natural heritage of Cabrillo National Monument includes the native coastal sage plant community. Coastal sage scrub habitat covered much of the surrounding area prior to the City of San Diego and this remnant shelters rare and sensitive plants and wildlife. The native peoples who lived here at that time lived off the resources of the land and sea, which served for shelter, food, and other necessities.

Nature is also featured in the splendor of the tidepools where, during low tides, visitors can explore and find octopuses, sea hares, chestnut cowries, owl limpets, bat stars, wavy turban snails, sand castle worms, and myriad other uniquely adapted organisms that live on the cusp of land and sea. Furthermore, Point Loma offers a vantage during winter months to witness the southbound migration of gray whales. The round-trip of some 10,000 miles is the longest migration of any mammal. The predictability of their migration made them easy targets for whale hunters, and they were hunted almost to extinction until protected by the International Whaling Commission. After a remarkable comeback, their current numbers are about the same as before hunting began. Advocacy for these magnificent creatures made a difference.

Finally, this painting was chosen because of strong personal connections and attachment to the place. Larry Beck worked at Cabrillo as a young interpreter and spent his entire academic career and adulthood working and living in San Diego. Ted Cable was born in Coronado within sight of the lighthouse and spent much time there as a child.

The Artist

Tina Christiansen is an accomplished artist who lives in Coronado, California, and Whidbey Island, Washington. She has enjoyed painting for 40 years, and many of her works are held in private collections. Tina is best known for her ocean paintings, beneath the deep, and for where the sea meets the sky. Tina's work is characterized by her emphasis on color, light, and form.

Tina's art inspires viewers to delve deeper into appreciating the dangers imposed upon our imperiled planet by focusing on the wondrous beauties of nature. Of course, early landscape paintings inspired protection of many of our national parks. Similarly, Tina paints with an interest in helping others to see the beauty and wonder of ocean, land, and sky, and to protect these for future generations.

Since Tina's home in Coronado is close to the Old Point Loma Lighthouse, she is aware of the various "moods" of the lighthouse, including the fog that often enshrouds the building. Her painting of the "Old Point Loma Lighthouse" is 36 inches by 60 inches, acrylic on canvas, and is held in a private collection.

Preface
Good Interpretation Is Worth A Million Dollars

In 2015, the *San Diego Union-Tribune* reported in a front-page story that the San Diego Museum of Art had acquired an important oil on canvas: "St. Francis in Prayer in a Grotto," 1655, by Francisco de Zurbarán. The background of the story reveals the power of good interpretation.

The director of the Museum of Art, Roxana Velásquez, had somehow convinced local philanthropist Conrad Prebys to give her one hour to show him around the museum. Prebys later reflected, "I went over there and it was the most exciting hour that I can remember. I'll never forget it. She took me to every painting. She pointed out what art was…Since that time I've thought, 'I've got to increase my horizons.'"

A short while after that meeting, Prebys agreed to give the museum $1.5 million to support its presentations during the centennial celebration (2015) of the Panama-California Exposition at Balboa Park where the museum is located. The gift from Prebys was used to purchase this masterpiece from the "golden age" of Spanish art. Prebys concluded, "So I'm delighted to do this, and I plan to continue to be a big supporter of the San Diego Museum of Art."

Interpretation, in sum, can change how people understand and perceive the world around them from art to nature. Even an hour can change someone's life. Furthermore, as we see in this story, that impact on one person could potentially influence the lives of many others. Indeed, interpretation is worth more than a million dollars.

Interpretation is Priceless

We believe that interpretation is priceless. More so than ever before, we see that it is essential to provide the public with important, factual information that is relevant to their lives and reveals essential meanings about the quality of the world we live in. Accurate interpretation can help people understand various complexities from social justice to energy to climate change to endangered species. With this in mind, the book is titled *Interpreting Cultural and Natural Heritage: For a Better World*. With reference to the subtitle, we strived to indicate in which ways this is true throughout the book. Because the bottom line is this: We believe that interpretation in its many different nuances makes the world a better place through its educational and inspirational qualities.

Roots of This Book

Some readers may be aware that a precursor of this book (*Interpretation of Cultural and Natural Resources*) was originally published in 1995. After its release, it was reviewed by Lowell Caneday in an academic journal. His book review began, "Occasionally a book, designed as a text, provides such a wealth of information that it crosses boundaries to become an invaluable resource outside of the academic community. [This] is such a book." At the end of the review, Dr. Caneday stated, "I predict with a high degree of certainty that [this book] will become the preferred source for information on interpretive services in recreation settings for the next decade."

In the beginning and conclusion of his review, Dr. Caneday captured our *intent* and our *hope* for the book. Our *intent* was to create a comprehensive text that would provide an overview of this growing and complex discipline and profession. Although we wanted the treatment of the material to be well rooted in the literature and scholarly, we also wanted the book to appeal to those outside of the university.

Our *hope* was that the book would continue to be useful to readers. In 2003 we wrote a second edition and are honored that for the past 20 years the book has been used throughout the U.S. and other English-speaking countries at various colleges and universities, and yet also by resource agencies and other interpretive sites in the United States and around the world. When the National Association for Interpretation began its certification program, this text was used as one of the resource books for various levels of professional certification. It is offered as one of five books in the Professional Certification Library Package. Recently, that book was translated into Chinese.

In each edition, we tried to make the book accessible to all readers and yet still demonstrate the research, philosophy, and theory so important to achieving interpretive goals. The studies and methods cited throughout the text verify the scholarly background that supports the discipline of interpretation.

Although many books have been written about various facets of interpretation since this volume was first published, we believe that it is still important to have a single source that provides a broad overview of the field. However, we also acknowledge the explosion of information now available and the challenges that presents. Seemingly countless essays, blogs, articles, speeches, TED talks, webinars, and books have come out on just about every conceivable aspect of the book. The literature on such separate topics as education, business, planning, evaluation, museums—each of which are chapter subjects in this book—is overwhelming. For that reason, our intent was not to attempt to cover everything out there (which of course isn't possible anyway), but rather to focus on those key things we felt our readers would find most useful, interesting, meaningful, and enlightening.

We strived to reveal a sense of the profession's roots, its vitality, and its lofty ideals for the future. Recent research, changes in technology, and international interest have also contributed to a different interpretive landscape. The greatest shifts have come from various technologies that can now be applied in the interpretive field. Digital advances over the past 20 years have transformed the way we live. However, we caution the reader as to the limits of technology and the importance of first-hand, authentic experience.

The authors have, collectively, more than 125 years of experience as front-line interpreters, researchers, authors of other interpretive books, professors teaching the subject at various universities, speakers at national and international conferences, and as consultants all over the country and all over the world. Nonetheless, we would be the first to acknowledge the complexity of this subject and our own limitations in regards to such a broad and deep discipline. Our approach is rooted in our own experiences and knowledge gained from so many others who have dedicated their lives to this profession. To supplement our perspectives, this book contains "boxes" that authorities have contributed within their areas of expertise.

An Interpretive Approach

In recognition of the history and philosophy of interpretation, in particular Freeman Tilden's Six Principles of Interpretation, we have strived to write this book with an "interpretive" approach in mind. This meant, first, to *relate the content* to our audience. This book has a broad potential audience that includes university students, instructors and trainers, front-line interpreters (who are permanent, seasonal, or volunteer), interpretive site managers and directors, and researchers. Others might merely want to know what interpretation is all about. We tried to keep this broad audience in mind throughout.

Second, we wanted to *reveal the deeper meanings* of interpretation and its power to make the world a better place. We hope *Interpreting Cultural and Natural Heritage* is a touchstone for readers, something *tangible* that serves as a companion, a familiar resource. In the realm of the *intangible*, our intent is that this book mobilizes the interpreter's dedication and purpose; and celebrates the creativity and integrity of this noble profession.

Third, we sought to *employ the use of story* to make our points. This preface begins with a story and we use a thematic story to begin *every* chapter. Stories from practicing interpreters are also woven throughout the text. Furthermore, we asked *New York Times* bestselling author Eric Blehm to share his story in his foreword to the book.

Fourth, we wanted to *provoke* readers to think differently and to do things differently. This is especially true for front-line interpreters who we encourage to be adventurous in thoughts and deeds. We counsel readers that, "If you want to get better, then you have to change. Everyone wants to get better, right? You can't get better if you don't change."

Fifth, we wanted the book to encompass a *"whole rather than a part"* of the broad discipline of interpretation. This is intended to be a *comprehensive* text in content and tone. The table of contents reveals the book's breadth. In tone, we strived to be pragmatic *and* philosophical; practical *and* poetic.

Sixth, we are aware that different audiences require different approaches to the subject matter. Although readers may come from different angles of interest toward interpretation, we chose to focus on the *student* of interpretation. Our intent was to engage the interests of *students* of interpretation, from whatever walk of life, not only college students, and inspire them to contribute to changing the world.

A final principle of interpretation is that love is the essential ingredient to effective interpretation. We, too, are students of interpretation. We love to learn and are fascinated by interpretation, what it is and its potential to change the world. We hope this passion shines through the pages and rubs off on readers too.

The Work of Interpreters

Collectively, *interpreters* produce, direct, and act in the greatest shows on earth. They do it every day. Each interpreter presents remarkable elements of our natural or cultural heritage. Millions of people enjoy and applaud the work of interpreters. However, even the word *interpretation* requires interpretation for most people. Here, it refers to a special type of communication and translation of historic, cultural, and natural phenomena so that people better understand and enjoy these special places and become more inclined to protect them.

The interpreter transforms bare facts into stories and experiences that stimulate understanding and wisdom. Interpreters serve as storytellers who transmit the essence and meaning of culture and nature to members of society. They tell their stories in many ways and in many places. Interpreters use media such as the printed word, exhibits, music, living history, websites, blogs, social media, radio, television, signs, walks in the woods, and weeklong experiences in nature. They work in some of the world's most beautiful and interesting places, both outdoors and indoors. Society usually regards interpreters as experts in their subject matter, charming and informative in their dealings with people, and fortunate in their choice of work.

This rewarding profession attracts people with solid academic backgrounds in cultural and natural resources (the social and natural sciences). Interpreters possess strong skills in communications, practical psychology, and program administration. They see things with new perceptions, finding hidden stories, discovering scientific details, using creative techniques…and weaving it all into fascinating presentations and programs. Interpreters possess a rare talent—often acquired—of perceiving and then translating for the rest of us. They have abilities to use creative imagination to help others understand and enjoy their cultural and natural environments. The best interpreters possess star quality.

Interpreters serve as the ambassadors of the employer (e.g., a museum or a wildlife organization). They need to understand the agency *and* the interpretive customers. The interpreters' work may include research, monitoring, writing, public speaking, building lifetime skills among the clients, planning, training, and evaluating.

Quality Interpretation

The ideas here will help equip the reader with the overall knowledge, as well as techniques and abilities, to work effectively as an interpreter. The reward for reading this book comes as you gain a *comprehensive* knowledge of the interpretive profession. A comprehensive treatment of interpretation considers the different fields from which interpreters draw their basic philosophy and operating procedures such as education, marketing, science, history, and communications.

Right now, we walk on the cutting edge of an emerging profession, worldwide. Interpretation in North America, Great Britian, Australia, and New Zealand has deep roots with many new sprouts. Other parts of the world have made new commitments, in places as diverse as Indonesia, China, Mexico, the Dominican Republic, Kenya, Russia, and Ghana.

To our readers from various nations of the world, we recognize our emphasis on the United States. Although we have lived, consulted, and observed interpretation in more than 50 nations, we take our examples and much of our inspiration from our home territories where we know the culture and practice the best. Still, the excellent work we have seen in many nations has affected the content and values that we express here and we have expanded in that arena. Ultimately, the principles and practices of this profession translate well when adjusted to any culture, economy, or tradition. A chapter toward the end of the book focuses on international interpretation.

The authors firmly believe in the need to challenge the interpreters of today, and the future, to perform with excellence and integrity. The growth of the profession responds to the critical need of urban society to understand our interdependence with the natural environment. This same society also needs to grasp the lessons of local, regional, national, and world human interdependence. To help inform and direct thoughts and behavior requires professional dedication, rigor, and enthusiasm to make interpretation an even more potent and constructive force in the face of today's challenges. The work of the interpreter is designed to broaden horizons in such ways that there may be change in people's thoughts and actions. The work of the interpreter is intentional.

A Dynamic Profession

Interpretation offers one of the most demanding, dynamic, and exciting fields of work anywhere. The profession needs bright, well-prepared people.

To build oneself into an excellent, effective interpreter requires command of the technical field. Interpreters need strong skills in communications and human relations; sensitivity toward people who seek interpretive services. In addition, interpreters benefit from an artistic sense. Design, photography, music, and drama all play a role in this work. One needs discipline to keep up on scientific and historic research. Then, all this needs to be translated to the public—a job that many researchers fail to do well. Interpreters never run out of subject matter nor new ways of presenting it. Interpretation is a creative endeavor.

One amazing phenomenon involves the range and diversity of the profession. Employment opportunities exist in many private sector businesses and services. Every level of government—city, county, state/province, and federal—has several agencies that employ or contract with interpreters. Some interpreters work in museums, zoos, aquariums, caves, and commercial attractions. Some work in forests, parks, wildlife refuges, camps, resorts, or on ships and trains. Others work for large industries. Many operate small businesses as freelance artists, planners, exhibit designers, and trainers. Several organize large groups of people to recreate the past for community historical events. The travel and tourism industry has awakened to the financial value of interpretation. In all, hundreds of thousands of people are involved in some way with interpreting our cultural and natural heritage and they are serving hundreds of millions of people who go to these places. Therefore, we can't help but sense the great hope there is for people, through the act of interpretation, to make the world a better place. As we noted in the beginning, good interpretation is priceless.

CHAPTER 1

What Is Interpretation?

Following a thorough orientation to the program content and logistics, the ranger told us a little bit about what we were going to learn and why it was important to know. As we walked to the first stop, he also taught us some basic facts about the progression of the war, how it came to this site, and some key players in the battles that were fought here. This was the extent of the "history lesson" about the Civil War. The real meat of the program was the story of one young man who lived in this town.

We stopped at the house where he grew up, sat in the schoolhouse where he learned to read and write as a child, and visited the blacksmith shop where he learned his trade as a young man. At each place we learned about daily life during the time period—how meals were prepared in the oppressively hot family kitchen, the walk to school and the cramped conditions inside the single room, the dangers of blacksmithing and the injuries that were regularly endured—all through the eyes of our main character. As such, we were able to frame the Civil War in a very tangible sense and see our character as a real person, similar to us, with real hopes, relationships, and struggles.

As we moved onto the historic battlefield, the interpreter described how the young man saw the fight coming over the hill and rushed out his front door to join the Union without enlisting in any official capacity. As we crossed the battlefield we saw the progression of the battle through the young man's eyes. We could feel his anxiety and excitement, his bravery and despair. As the tour neared its conclusion, we learned the young man's name. We also learned how he remained on the battlefield until the end, providing safe retreat for his Union Army comrades. His heroic actions saved the lives of many but cost him his own.

We entered the National Cemetery, and the interpreter told us of many of the young men who had been buried here. We stopped. The ranger quietly paused and seemed to take it all in. Then he looked down at his feet and pointed out a gravestone—the final resting place of the young man we had spent the past hour coming to know.

The audience's solemnity and sadness were palpable. The interpreter used few words to draw the connections between this young man's story and the magnitude of the Civil War's impact not only on our nation, but also on the people living so close to the battles. We had quite literally walked in this young man's footsteps as strong themes of sacrifice, beliefs, valor, and ordinary people unfolded. The audience stood in silence for quite some time after the program had ended. (Excerpted from Stern et al., 2013)

The preface provided an overview of interpretation and described it as a special type of communication and translation of historic, cultural, and natural phenomena. In this chapter we will delve deeper into what exactly interpretation is and survey some of the history of the profession.

People often associate interpretation with the translation of a foreign language. In the context of this book, interpretation refers to a communication process designed to inform and inspire people about culture and nature. Traditionally those seeking interpretation came to places such as parks, museums, historic sites, aquariums, zoos, and other areas that draw visitors. With digital advances, interpretation also occurs via websites, blogs, and social media, among other technologies. We will still refer to visitors in this book as those who receive interpretation, although they can also be referred to as guests, clients, or customers. The people who receive interpretation may be regarded as the audience. As suggested, interpretation may occur in many different ways from personal contact with visitors to interpretation through exhibits, signs, self-guiding tours, apps, podcasts, social media, virtual reality, and more.

Interpretation is diverse and complex. It can occur in different venues from arboretums to zoos. Various communication strategies can be personal *or* nonpersonal. Interpretation can involve personal interaction and the age-old wonders of storytelling or the newest technologies. It can last only a couple of seconds as someone surveys an interpretive sign, a few minutes through discussion with a park interpreter answering a question, a couple hours through a guided tour of a museum or historic site, or even over the course of a week as is the case for naturalist-guided loop hikes among the High Sierra Camps in Yosemite National Park (Beck, 2014). Indeed, with revolving programs based on different topics and updated as research continues, parks and museums can be a source of life-long learning and inspiration.

> "Interpretation is diverse and complex. It can occur in different venues from arboretums to zoos."

Interpretation can range from a few seconds to a lifetime. It can involve human interaction or the most advanced technologies. And it can take place almost anywhere!

Furthermore, the profession has continued to evolve. The field of interpretation traditionally focused on nature guiding (Mills, 1920) and field interpretation of cultural and natural resources (Tilden, 1957). As the interpretive field expanded in scope, it incorporated interpretation as a management tool (Sharpe & Gensler, 1978). For example, one study examined reducing theft of petrified wood at Petrified Forest National Park and understanding park visitors' responses to interventions to reduce petrified wood theft (Widner & Roggenbuck, 2003). Another study assessed interpretive communication focused on human-black bear conflict at Yosemite National Park (Lackey & Ham, 2003).

Knapp (2007) explored how visitors to various interpretive sites can embrace responsible environmental actions. Studies by Sam Ham and associates (Ham et al., 2008), have shown the efficacy of interpretation in assisting park administrators with various management issues and guiding strategic communication for protected area management.

Interpretation has also been applied in various venues for fund-raising to support park and other interpretive sites (Beck & Cable, 2011) and to target the behavioral impact of giving through Lindblad Expeditions' travelers' philanthropy programs (Ham, 2013).

Increasingly, interpretation is being considered as a tool to assist visitors to outdoor recreation settings to be safe and use proper actions to promote their health (Nelson, 2005). In a keynote speech, Jon Jarvis, former National Park Service Director, stated that a current focus [of the NPS] is "the role we play in public health" that includes addressing national health priorities such as heart disease, cancer, and depression (Jarvis, 2014). The evolution of the field suggests the primary emphasis of interpretation is that it is designed to make a difference on purpose (Ham, 2013).

> Many definitions of interpretation have been advanced over the years in an attempt to capture this complex phenomenon.

Definitions

Many definitions of interpretation have been advanced over the years in an attempt to capture this complex phenomenon. A widely quoted definition came from Tilden (1957):

> An educational activity which aims to reveal meanings and relationships through the use of original objects, by firsthand experience, and by illustrative media, rather than simply to communicate factual information.

Of course, one specific definition will never suit the breadth of the interpretive profession. Tilden (1957) understood as much when he wrote, "The true interpreter will not rest at any dictionary definition," and this has proved prophetic (Figure 1.1).

Canadian Yorke Edwards (1979) defined the essence of interpretive work as:

> The job of interpretation is to open the minds of people so they can receive—on the world's best receiver, the human brain—the interesting signals that the world is constantly sending. And the messages sent, when added up, tell what the world is all about.

The National Association for Interpretation definition is as follows:

Figure 1.1. Freeman Tilden offered the classic definition of interpretation but predicted new definitions would continue to evolve. (NPS-MWW)

Interpretation is a mission-based communication process that forges emotional and intellectual connections between the interests of the audience and meanings inherent in the resource.

Sam Ham (2013) captured much of the current thinking about what the term entails and is consistent with the National Association for Interpretation definition:

Interpretation is a mission-based approach to communication aimed at provoking in audiences the discovery of personal meaning and the forging of personal connections with things, places, people and concepts.

In other words, *interpretation* translates or brings meaning to people about cultural and natural heritage. Interpreters help their clients to better understand, connect to, and enjoy museums, industries, historical sites, botanical gardens, and natural resource areas such as national parks and forests. The term *interpretation* refers to a function long practiced in these and other places, more recently in places such as wineries and breweries.

These definitions (and many more) suggest that interpretation offers more than instruction through facts. It uses facts to pass on the meaning of something and to develop deep understanding. Through interpretation people connect with places. Interpretation stimulates interest and observation. It helps people to develop their skills, to read their landscape, to relive their history, and to feel their art. Ultimately, it helps them to further understand their home environment and the world around them.

Although interpreters use information they go beyond just repeating the facts—the names of trees and people, the dates of events, the numbers of the regiments. The interpreter must gather that type of information by study, experience, or instruction, but then put it in context to make it meaningful and relevant to the visitor. Information, then, is the raw material that the interpreter works, molds, and presents in ways that entice, engage, interest, inspire, and clarify what it all means.

Generally speaking, interpretation may assume a short, usually one-time exposure to the message and takes into account the current state of distracted and often time-constrained visitors, although it may also be far more complex. Regardless, interpreters strive to communicate the *significance* of cultural and natural resources by offering an array of informed choices on how to experience the resources.

Interpretation Roots

Early and vigorous efforts at interpretation in national and state parks helped make a stereotypical association between "interpretive rangers" and "parks." However, these efforts didn't start until private enterprises proved that interpretation was popular.

> "Interpreters strive to communicate the significance of cultural and natural resources."

Enos Mills owned a resort in Colorado on the edge of public land that now is Rocky Mountain National Park. He guided his clients on hikes along the creeks and up Long's Peak. He explained the stories of plants and animals that people saw along the way. At night in the lodge, his fireplace "lectures" made people feel at home. Soon Mills was interpreting nature on long national lecture tours. He regaled several U.S. presidents with his astute observations of nature as he sat before White House fireplaces, lobbying for national parks.

As Enos Mills' nature guiding became more in demand, he began training some of his guests to lead hikes. This training led to a book, *The Adventures of a Nature Guide* (Mills, 1920). It defined how nature guiding could best be done. His principles appear with modifications in most books that describe how to do interpretation (e.g., Tilden, 1957).

In the early years of Yellowstone and Yosemite, military troops had responsibility for protecting the parks. Some of them were college educated and felt compelled to interpret to the visitors. They gained considerable knowledge and skill in explaining botany and geology. Likewise, archaeologists who were excavating at Mesa Verde offered tours of the cliff dwellings and started a museum.

Stephen Mather, the first director of the National Park Service (NPS), initially rejected the suggestion of Mr. and Mrs. Charles M. Goethe to put nature guides on the NPS payroll. The Goethes were impressed with Swiss nature guides and decided to bring the idea home to California. They footed most of the bills and persuaded six Lake Tahoe resorts to try the idea of "nature lectures" in 1918. They had a full-blown program in 1919, with the support of the California Nature Study League and the California Fish and Game Commission. Dr. Harold C. Bryant, a University of California professor, and Dr. Loye Miller, a UCLA entomologist, built and marked trails around the resorts. They led nature lovers on hikes, provided evening campfire talks, gave slide ("magic lantern") talks on wildlife, and showed scientific movies.

Charles M. Goethe persuaded the doubting Director Mather to drop in on these resort programs. The enthusiastic public response Mather observed impressed him. In 1920, he added some of his fortune to Goethe's contributions to transfer the whole operation to Yosemite National Park. He put the two seasoned professors under a young full-time ranger trained in forestry. Ansel Hall, who had worked alone in 1919 as Yosemite's "Information Ranger," got a new title of "Acting Park Naturalist" in 1920. He also started a park museum (Figure 1.2). He collected Native American artifacts such as baskets, arrowheads, pictures, and oral history interviews with older American Indians still living in Yosemite. He built a scale model of the Yosemite Valley, tying it to rock and soil samples that illustrated glacial action. He collected and mounted flora and fauna, wrote guidebooks, and established the Yosemite Museum Association to raise funds for buildings. The president of the American Association of Museums took over the fund drive, eliciting a gift of $70,500 from the Laura Spelman Rockefeller Foundation.

The NPS interpretation/education work continued to expand, and in 1923–1924 Congress began to fund interpretation through public tax funds. By 1930, a Branch of Research and Education grew out of the chief naturalist's office. The stimulus for the growth of interpretation came partly from its ready acceptance and approval by the public. The visitors came and expressed

> "The stimulus for the growth of interpretation came partly from its ready acceptance and approval by the public."

their delight. Additionally, the Director's administrative support of "education" kept spirits high, as did donations from influential families such as the Goethes and Rockefellers. Mather, once won over, gave interpretive programs high priority and refused to divorce them from fun. This millionaire-turned-bureaucrat seemed delighted to leave Washington, D.C., behind for a while and immerse himself in the direct service of hosting and interpreting in several national parks (Figure 1.3).

Figure 1.2. The Yosemite Nature Guides at the Yosemite Museum. (NPS)

Principal Terms

Figure 1.3. Stephen T. Mather (left), NPS Director, joined in interpretive efforts as an enthusiastic leader. (NPS)

The terms *interpretation* and *interpreter* saw only occasional use a century ago. In the 1920s, western U.S. and Canadian national parks and private resorts referred to *lecturers,* which seemed appropriate because many of them were researchers and professors in universities during the school year.

Resort owner Enos Mills used the term *nature guiding* to describe his work in the Rockies. Mills was one of the first to use the term *interpret* to describe the work of *nature guides*. More recently, nature guiding has gained new prominence in the ecotourism industry. *Education* has been another synonym for interpretation, especially in many museums and zoos.

By the late 1930s, naturalists and historians worked together in the NPS, as historic sites came into the national park system. Their umbrella term, *interpretation*, was widely used but had little recognition by the public. By the 1950s, when Freeman Tilden (1957) first wrote *Interpreting Our Heritage*, the dominant term in the United States was *interpretation*, thus including those who explain history, art, archaeology, and nature.

In 1961, professionals in the field established the *Association of Interpretive Naturalists*. At about the same time, western professionals formed the *Western Interpreters Association*. When these two combined in 1988 as the *National Association for Interpretation*, the term was perpetuated.

Educators have published many articles arguing the distinctions between the terms *environmental education* and *interpretation*. Although these have some academic interest, it seems that the differences relate more to audience characteristics than to the ultimate purpose. Environmental educators generally have a captive audience with learning responsibilities and preparation plus follow-up time with teachers. Many field interpreters have a volunteer audience for only a few minutes to a few hours. Thus the techniques used with children in structured situations permit different methodologies than with drop-in visitors. Yet often the interpreter hosts school and camp classes and becomes by necessity an environmental educator.

Overall, the titles given to interpreters vary widely and include the following: art gallery director, curator of education, docent, ecotourism adventure travel operator, environmental educator, heritage education specialist, historian, museum floor interpreter, naturalist, outdoor recreation planner, park ranger, public engagement specialist, public information specialist, refuge ranger, and wildlife rehabilitator. One title, heritage interpreter, deserves special notice due to its current popularity. Heritage interpreter (and the term *heritage interpretation*) is often used in Europe and growing more frequent in the United States. There is greater use of the word "heritage" as a way to deal with the longstanding professional identity issue and to attempt to avoid the confusion associated with the word "interpretation" or "interpreter" when used without a modifier. The use of "heritage" can include nature (natural resource heritage) as well as interpretation of culture. Nonetheless, recognizing all the variety in titles, and for the sake of simplicity, this book refers to interpreters broadly to include all those with jobs that require that they interpret.

Purposes of Interpretation

Interpreters seek to add the essential elements of heightened appreciation, deeper understanding, and new ways of seeing the world. George Hartzog (1974), former Director of the National Park Service, noted:

> We who have spent our lives working in and for the parks should not expect other people to possess an instinctive knowledge of park values… A sensitive enjoyment and understanding of national parks does not come naturally to most persons.

Interpreters lead, enable, and encourage. Interpreters educate. Interpreters entertain. Interpreters inform. But most of all, interpreters enrich recreational experiences with substance and a sense of personal fulfillment.

Developing a Sense of Place

A *raison d'être* of interpretation is to help people to gain a sense of place and to respond to the beauty of their environment, the significance of their history, and their cultural surroundings. The interpreter helps visitors to recognize a location as more than just another mountain, river, arboretum, or pioneer settlement. The interpreter helps identify the special characteristics and the "big story" that the place represents in the overall scheme of things (Figure 1.4). The interpretation may expand to a broader horizon—relating a battlefield, for example, to the whole war and to the lasting effects on the current politics of the area.

Figure 1.4. Interpretation provides the "big picture" and a sense of place. (LB)

The interpretation of a place not only sets apart the unique attributes but also communicates the traits common to the human species and their societies. Visitors leaving an interpretive program should have a feeling for the familiar in the place, as well as what is different and special. They should feel stimulation to find out more and ways to carry on their own interpretive quest.

> A *raison d'être* of interpretation is to help people to gain a sense of place.

Enriching Experiences

> "These beautiful days must enrich all my life. They do not exist as mere pictures... but they saturate themselves into every part of the body and live always."
>
> –John Muir

Interpreters seek to enrich experiences. Interpretation adds value to leisure time and recreational activity. Interpreters may aspire to help provide what Maslow (1962) called *peak experiences*. These highly satisfying, joyful events often come from feeling at one with nature or from sensing as if temporarily transported into an historical period or an artistic moment of rapture.

However, interpreters do not directly produce those experiences. As Cable and Beck (2011) noted, "Interpretive professionals are in the business of creating and managing opportunities for enjoyment. They do not, however, produce that enjoyment. Only the visitor can do that."

Interpreters enrich experiences by expanding awareness and understanding of a museum, a forest, a marine sanctuary, a factory, or an agricultural landscape through personal interaction, informative exhibits, publications, blogs, social media, and other methods. As Jon Kohl (2017) suggested, "While we interpreters cannot provide amazing experiences to our audiences, we can pull a thousand different levers, many invisible, to coax them toward creating their own transformative, unforgettable, and amazing experiences."

Meeting Mandates

Management may have educational or interpretive mandates in their original bylaws or legislation. Historic societies and museums often list "education" as their primary end product, their purpose for being. That requires the services of interpreters.

Most conservation agencies seek to sustain the natural and cultural environment that they manage. Agencies such as the U.S. Fish and Wildlife Service and Environment Canada have nationwide responsibilities for wildlife and forests, respectively (Figure 1.5). This requires the agency to lead people to a greater concern and intelligent action, both during their visits and throughout the year. The use of interpretation in all of its forms—personal and nonpersonal—is a most productive means of encouraging stewardship. National and state forests, and parks, include public understanding as a key responsibility as well as an intelligent strategy for sustained political support.

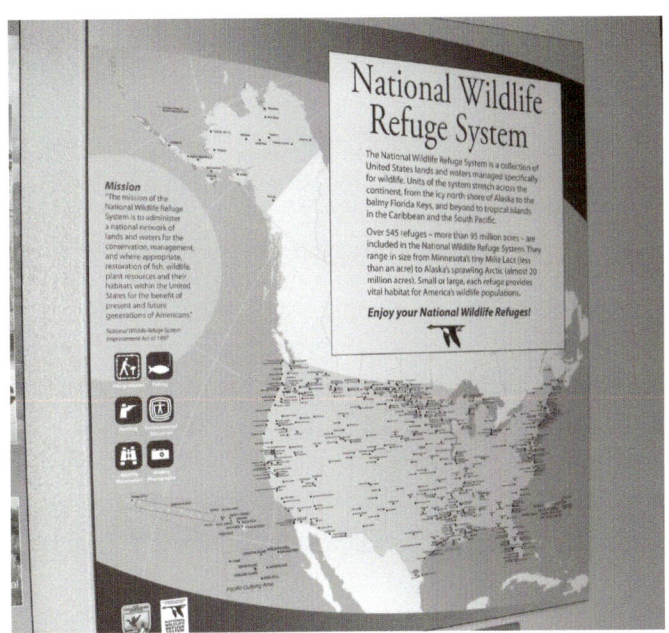

Figure 1.5. This interpretive sign communicates the mission of the U.S. Fish and Wildlife Service to the public. (TC)

Introducing Marketing and Management Benefits

Management supports interpreters as a part of making their property attractive to customers or the general public. Cruise lines, heritage tourism, and adventure and ecotourism companies attract customers by providing high-quality naturalists and historians to provide lectures and side trips to explain the places being visited. Thus, interpreters often serve as conspicuous marketing tools.

Chapter 1: What is Interpretation? 11

Land and water management agencies have learned that interpretation helps to lower costs of resource protection. By explaining the resource management policies and problems, interpreters often persuade visitors to behave in ways that prevent resource destruction and deterioration. Likewise, interpreters help the public to understand the scientific and economic bases of resource management. Therefore, interpreters and their managers do well to make interpretation a high priority at their sites.

> Interpreters help the public to understand the scientific and economic bases of resource management.

Serving the Visitor

The visitor gains a working understanding of the important meanings and relationships of a site as a result of the entire interpretive effort—exhibits, signs, talks, walks, brochures, audiovisual materials, computer reference sources, websites, apps, blogs, social media, and more. Exposure to many interpreters and many interpretive media on many occasions produces an alert, informed, observant, active citizenry that understands and retells the stories that have inspired them. The ultimate desired result comes when visitors develop into well-informed stewards of their cultural and natural heritage. As discussed further in Chapter 3, interpretive activities contribute to the physical, mental, social, and spiritual health of park visitors.

Interpretation as Part of Recreation

In their leisure, people celebrate the exuberance and importance of life itself. Through outdoor recreation people exult in the joy of fresh contact with the natural and cultural richness that surrounds them. They can release and expand their minds in learning, fascination, and joy. In leisure people seek beautiful places. They search out inspirational history. They resonate with music, outdoor drama, games, and adventure. They try to engage the challenges of environments different from home.

Interpreters' first concern should be to enrich these recreational experiences, to make them more significant in some way. That means helping visitors to have more expansive learning, richer pleasure, and deeper joy. Surprisingly, that can be done with rather serious subjects, but not necessarily with a somber approach.

Interpreters offer the biggest and most important activity that a visitor may enjoy—not in competition, but in harmony with and enhancing the overall place. For example, if someone comes to an art museum to see the work of a painter, the interpreters have available signs, labels, references, apps, and their own presence to make information available so that the visit becomes more meaningful and enjoyable than just a glance at a picture.

Ideals of Interpretation

Interpretation serves as a *central visitor experience*—a key part of a visit to a cultural or natural heritage area. The interpreter serves as a property's official host, whether in person or represented through other media.

To increase interpretive reach, interpreters appeal to people in various ways. Some visitors will only read signs; others will seek out brochures, videos, or other entertaining but informative programs or technology. Others will want tours, hikes, laboratory study, or personal attention; still others may want only a few minutes in a visitor center to check the map or an exhibit.

Interpreters should make interpretation available where people gather. Interpretation opens minds to wonder and new ways of perceiving the world, beyond the mechanical, everyday modes of thinking. It promotes the power of perception among all clientele so they see the world in a more meaningful, complete way. This is especially important as more people become distracted by their technologies, immersed behind their screens (Beck & Dustin, 2016).

Many interpreters reach out *beyond the property*. They send out interpretive messages through newsletters, television, radio, newspapers, blogs, social media, and websites. In many cases, these mass media messages reach people the interpreter doesn't encounter on a hike or at an exhibit. The messages may help lead those people, eventually, to memorable and valuable *first-hand* learning experiences.

Interpreters strive to provide an authentic rendering of the places they interpret. This means that they need to practice their craft with integrity and a high regard for the truth. Ideally, interpreters reflect enthusiasm, knowledge, keen senses, ability to communicate, humility, a pleasant demeanor, a gentle sense of humor, strong group management skills, and adaptability (Beck, 2014).

The job: design rich, memorable experiences appropriate to the purposes of the place. Promote perception, enrich recreation, add meaning, and deepen understanding. Carefully place information and programs to offer opportunities to learn about the place or the artifacts and what is significant, allowing visitors to voluntarily participate, to learn, be inspired, and to enjoy (See Box 1.1).

Philosophy of Interpretation

Interpretation, properly carried out, serves as an indispensable tool to achieve successful cultural and natural resource stewardship. Interpretation takes people from passive appreciation to exciting understanding of the cultural and natural environments they experience.

Box 1.1
What Does An Interpreter Do? A Few Basic Guidelines

- Strives to embrace the wonder and beauty of life and share that with others.
- Shows enthusiasm for the interpretive site, and the visitors, and the work of interpretation itself.
- Reaches out to all potential clients with accurate, colorful, thoughtful interpretation and stimulates their imaginations.
- Remembers that interpretation focuses on what happens to the visitors and therefore offers experiences that involve people.
- Respects the moral worth of visitors and their potential for growth.
- Through words and deeds champions peace, beauty, truth, diversity, equity, health, freedom, sustainability…for a better world.

Interpretation also represents good business sense by public and private agencies. Effective interpretation improves the chances of success in their missions and in gaining public support. In effect, interpreters serve as the "sales force" for the values, missions, and policies of most museums, public land agencies, and many private enterprises. Careful reading of these missions reveals an explicit or implicit relationship to educational benefits of interpretation to help achieve a satisfied, informed, and supportive public clientele.

Interpretation can prevent destructive tendencies by building public interest and understanding about the significance of the place. Amateur interpreters rescued the Tippecanoe Battlefield from speculators who wanted to develop a housing tract on it. Interpretation of the Grand Canyon prevented its damming on several occasions. A lack of interpretation and awareness of Glen Canyon ("the place no one knew") allowed a major change in the Colorado River hydrological regime (Figure 1.6).

One of Abraham Lincoln's most quoted sentiments states that a nation with little regard for its past has little hope for its future. The heritage of any nation lies in its natural resources, its sense of historical connectedness, and its cultural achievements. Interpretation preserves and communicates this heritage. Moreover, the profession itself must advocate those "proven benefits of community health, environmental vigor, economic robustness, personal vitality, and heritage pride" (LaPage, 2014).

Figure 1.6. Interpretation might have saved Glen Canyon from becoming a reservoir. A row boat floats beneath the canyon walls ca. 1930. (CHSC-GWJ)

Summary

Interpretation is a large, diverse, and complex profession. Definitions vary among organizations and agencies. The history of the interpretive profession goes back more than a century. Museums, zoos, parks, forests, travel companies, resorts, camps, and even cathedrals and temples have employed interpreters. Interpreters, known by many different titles, seek to develop in their clients a sense of place, a set of skills for perceiving and experiencing, and an understanding of and involvement with natural and cultural resources. Interpreters serve their clientele by enriching recreational experiences. They connect people to the world around them. They serve their agencies and society by producing management benefits, inspiring resource stewardship, developing deep awareness of cultural and natural heritage, and perpetuating the deepest values and traditions of special places. In sum, interpretation makes for a better world.

Literature Cited

Beck, L. (2014). Authenticity of landscape and interpretation: A celebration. *Legacy, 25*(6), 24–28.

Beck, L., & Cable, T. (2011). *The gifts of interpretation: Fifteen guiding principles for interpreting nature and culture* (3rd ed.). Urbana, IL: Sagamore.

Beck, L., & Dustin, D. (2016). Technology on the trails. *Legacy, 27*(6), 20–22.

Edwards, Y. (1979). *The land speaks.* Toronto, ON: The National and Provincial Parks Association of Canada.

Ham, S. (2013). *Interpretation: Making a difference on purpose.* Golden, CO: Fulcrum Publishing.

Ham, S., Weiler, B., Hughes, M., Brown, T., Curtis, J., & Poll, M. (2008). *Asking visitors to help: Research to guide strategic communication for protected area management.* Final Technical Research Report (Project 80039). Gold Coast, Australia: Collaborative Research Centre for Sustainable Tourism.

Hartzog, G. (1974). Management considerations for optimum development and protection of national park resources. *Proceedings of the Second World Conference on National Parks.* Morges, Switzerland: IUCN.

Jarvis, J. (2014). Keynote Speech before Partners Outdoors 2014, in the U.S. Department of the Interior building, Washington, DC, June 9, 2014.

Knapp, D. (2007). *Applied interpretation.* Fort Collins, CO: InterpPress.

Kohl, J. (2017). Beyond the interpreter's words: Experiences erupt from the visitor's entire context. *Legacy, 28*(1), 6–9.

Lackey, B., & Ham, S. (2003). Assessment of communication focused on human-black bear conflict at Yosemite National Park. *Journal of Interpretation Research, 8*(1), 25–40.

LaPage, W. (2014). The interpreter as truth teller: Deep interpretation revisited. *Legacy, 25*(6), 34–35.

Maslow, A. (1962). Lessons from the peak experiences. *Journal of Humanistic Psychology, 2*(1), 9–18.

Nelson, K. (2005). Interpretation for good health. *Legacy, 16*(4), 28–31.

Mills, E. (1920). *Adventures of a nature guide and essays in interpretation.* Friendship, WI: New Past Press.

Sharpe, G., & Gensler, G. (1978). Interpretation as a management tool. *Journal of Interpretation, 3*(2), 3–9.

Stern, M., Powell, R., McLean, K., Martin, E., Thomsen, J., & Mutchler, B. (2013). The difference between good enough and great: Bringing interpretive best practices to life. *Journal of Interpretation Research, 18*(2), 79–100.

*Tilden, F. (1957, 1967, 1977). *Interpreting our heritage.* Chapel Hill, NC: The University of North Carolina Press.

Widner, C., & Roggenbuck, J. (2003). Understanding park visitors' responses to interventions to reduce petrified wood theft. *Journal of Interpretation Research, 8*(1), 67–82.

*Note that Freeman Tilden first published his classic Interpreting Our Heritage in 1957. The second edition of the book, in 1967, included a new chapter at the end of the book titled "Vistas of Beauty." The third edition of the book came out in 1977. No substantive changes were made to the book in the third edition. Then in 2007, a 50th Anniversary edition of the book was published, which included a new foreword by Russell Dickenson, a new introduction by R. Bruce Craig, and five essays from Tilden's later interpretive writings. The citation for the 50th Anniversary Edition follows:

Tilden, F. (2007). *Interpreting our heritage* (4th ed.). Chapel Hill, NC: The University of North Carolina Press.

CHAPTER 2
Who Offers Interpretation?

"Meet Up" Groups have become popular and allow people with similar interests to get together to watch movies, enjoy wine, ride bikes, and virtually any other activity you can imagine. The groups are organized online with descriptions of the events provided by the leader. One such group focuses on local history and hiking. At an event that featured hiking up and down hundreds of stairs on a hillside in La Mesa (a suburb of San Diego) the leader began with a 10-minute interpretive talk about the history and significance of the outdoor stairways. The leader brought forth meanings about the history of La Mesa, and the early founders, and how that related to the stairs about to be climbed. Therefore, participants could make a connection with the place and further understand how the past relates to the scene of the present. The leader had gone to the La Mesa Historical Society to find historic photographs and to gather information to be weaved into a riveting presentation. This was interpretation. Interpretation can be offered by just about anyone, just about anywhere. However, as we shall see, certain principles make for more effective interpretation.

Experts on traditional cultures throughout the world have noted that interpretation occurred around the campfire, in the home, and on the trail. Passing on traditions, ceremonies, and natural history lore made up the interpretation of long ago. Interpretation has long been conducted wherever people gather. Humans require interpretation to sustain a way of life, a culture, a set of skills.

Modern interpretation meets the needs of a specialized, urbanized society to make connections with culture and landscape. Its practitioners pass on the history and the understanding of nature in a purposeful manner. Those who specialize in this informal education find work in many organizations and institutions or as private businesses.

Study of the membership of the National Association for Interpretation (NAI) gives an idea of where professional interpreters are employed in North America. A majority of NAI interpreters work for a government agency—federal, state, or local. However, many work for private enterprises such as camps, tour companies, industries, nature centers, and environmental education facilities. Others work or volunteer as members of nonprofit associations that support zoos, museums, botanical gardens and historical sites. And more and more are coming to this Association from other countries around the world in various interpretive capacities.

> Professional interpreters work in many locations and interpretive work occurs at many levels of ownership.

The diversity of agencies and companies offering interpretation becomes evident in Box 2.1, by using the United States as an example. As can be seen, professional interpreters work in many locations and interpretive work occurs at many levels of ownership, from freelance, private, quasi-public, and industrial, to city, county, state, and federal.

Where Interpreters Work

Federal Agencies

In the United States, five federal land managing agencies have major interpretive responsibilities. In addition, the Smithsonian Institution, The National Aeronautics and Space Administration, and the military branches offer valuable museum interpretive services. The efforts and policies of the five land agencies described here demonstrate the long traditions of some and emerging growth of others.

Chapter 1 provided a brief history of interpretive work in the national parks of America and so we will begin here based upon the long tradition of interpretation in these places. Furthermore, much of the material presented about the national park system as a premier interpretive agency is instructional as we move forward to discuss other places where interpretation occurs.

National Parks

> "Not only do we save these lands, they save us. There is something about this wild continuity that gives us courage, that allows us to be the best of who we are as human beings. I think our national parks remind us that beauty is not optional, but at the very core of our being."
>
> –Terry Tempest Williams

Box 2.1
Organizations Providing Interpretive Services in the United States

Sector/Agency	Major Properties
Federal	
National Park Service	National Parks, Historic Sites, National Monuments
USDA Forest Service	National Forests, National Grasslands
U.S. Fish and Wildlife Service	National Wildlife Refuges
U.S. Bureau of Land Management	National Resource Areas
U.S. Army Corps of Engineers	Reservoir Recreation Areas
National Museums	Museums
Tribal/First Nation	
Tribal and Intertribal Councils	Centers, Parks, Museums
State	
State Park Agencies	State Parks
Special Districts	Parks, Conservation Areas, Nature Preserves
State Wildlife Agencies	Wildlife Refuges, Public Hunting Areas, Nature Preserves
State Forestry Agencies	State Forests
State Historical Agencies	State Museums
State Outdoor Recreation Agencies	Scenic Rivers and Trails
County/Township	
County Park/Conservation Districts	County Parks, Nature Centers, Trails
Multicounty Park Districts	Parks, Reserves, Trails
County Historical Boards/Museums	Museums, Historic Sites
City/Town/Municipality	
City Park Districts/Departments	Park and Trail Systems
Private Sector	
Industry	Company plant tours, industry museums, forest parks
Commercial Firms	Tourism/ecotourism package firms, resorts, caves, ships, trains, buses, museums and exhibitions, guiding services, flightseeing
Individuals and Groups	Freelance guides, speakers, writers, performing and graphic artists
Consulting Firms	Design and fabrication of exhibits, interpretive planning, training, coaching
Nonprofit Organizations	Art societies, zoos, botanical gardens, arboreta, historical societies, aquariums, nature center associations, camps, conservation organizations, educational centers, adventure and survival organizations, youth groups

Throughout the world, national parks and interpretation go hand in hand. The U.S. and Canadian models carry the tradition of a living museum. Here people can learn about their natural and cultural heritage from diverse interpretive media. Increasingly, countries such as Argentina, Ecuador, Costa Rica, South Africa, Kenya, Taiwan, Indonesia, and Russia provide well-trained interpreters in some or all of their parks. Chapter 20 of this book will focus in more detail on international interpretation.

The U.S. National Park Service (NPS) was established in 1916. The newly established agency would manage the existing parks such as Yellowstone, Mount Rainier, and Yosemite as a fledgling system (Figure 2.1). Over the past 100 years, many more were added, and the system now has more than 400 park units. The National Park Centennial was celebrated in 2016.

Figure 2.1. Early parks included Mount Rainier National Park described on a free NPS Centennial (2016) postcard as dramatic, epic, sacred, regal, mesmerizing, sublime, surreal, and unforgettable—among many other superlatives. (LB)

The national parks have been referred to by author Wallace Stegner as "America's best idea" (Duncan, 2009). Yellowstone National Park (established in 1872) is considered the first national park; not only in the U.S., but in the world. So the "national park idea" is indeed an American idea.

However, protecting lands for the future technically began with Abraham Lincoln in the midst of the Civil War. President Lincoln deeded federal land to the state of California through the Yosemite Park Act of 1864, which included Yosemite Valley and the Mariposa Grove of sequoias. The massive cliffs of Half Dome and El Capitan, and the giant trees, symbolized for our struggling nation stability, strength, continuity, and durability. Yosemite later became a national park in 1890, and therefore was not the first. Although President Lincoln would never personally see this remarkable landscape, he was aware of its grandeur from images by early photographers such as Carleton Watkins. Protecting Yosemite, in perpetuity, aligned with his belief that this land might serve as a source of national pride and heal the wounds of a fractured country. Protecting our natural heritage was an investment in the future and an act that symbolized strength and unity for a nation divided. Similarly, at this point in our history, our parks can inspire a point of unity, a sense of dignity, and a common pride in who we are (Beck, 2016).

One of the distinctions of the national parks when first established in America is that the lands were dedicated not for the nobility and the rich, but for everyone, for all time, in the spirit of the commonwealth. This idea, rooted in democracy, has now been embraced in countries around the globe.

The national parks represent stunning scenery, remarkable wildlife, and interesting chapters of the cultural history in America. These are places set aside for recreation, learning, and inspiration, as well as for protecting biodiversity.

The NPS has funded interpretation in its programming since the early 1920s. Previous to that, however, individual employees, private guides, and scientists provided visitors with information, the quality of which varied considerably.

The National Park Service conducts interpretive programs to orient people to their parks, with opportunities to form their own intellectual, emotional, and physical connections to the meanings and values found there.

An important outcome of the interpretive experience is that visitors can better retain information, grasp important meanings, and adopt new values and behaviors because they are *directly involved through authentic experiences* with our cultural and natural heritage. Facilitating such opportunities is intended to encourage the development of a personal stewardship ethic and broaden public support for protecting park resources.

In practice, each park develops an interpretive program around themes based on park resources, themes related to the park's legislative history and significance, and broader park and park service mission goals. Current complex issues that the Park Service is working on include the integrity of natural sounds and night skies in the parks, climate change, and the link between healthy parks and healthy people.

> "The national parks represent stunning scenery, remarkable wildlife, and interesting chapters of the cultural history in America."

The National Park Service has an outstanding website that offers detailed information about all of the units of the national park system (nps.gov). Through links on the website, there are online videos, virtual tours and distance learning with a ranger (such as the Channel Islands National Park Live Dive), webcams, a WebRangers program for children (an online extension of the Junior Ranger program), and connections to all major social media including Facebook, Twitter, YouTube, and iTunes. In addition, visitors to the parks may receive interpretation through mobile apps for specific parks. Furthermore, as a leader in the field, the National Park Service offers specialized training covered in more depth in Chapter 17.

Good interpretation of the cultural and natural resources in our national parks can result in something extraordinarily meaningful, joyous, and transformational. For example, in 1903, President Theodore Roosevelt requested that John Muir guide him in Yosemite on a camping trip (Runte, 1990). They bedded down one night on Glacier Point to wake up under a blanket of snow before descending to the Valley, where they spent the next night beneath the monumental granite massif of El Capitan on one side and the music of the great waterfall, Bridalveil Falls, on the other. "This," Roosevelt exclaimed, "has been the grandest day of my life" (Duncan, 2009).

In our lives we remember special moments, and these moments, for many Americans, are rooted in visits to our national parks. Furthermore, these moments may be enhanced through creative and inspired interpretation. President Theodore Roosevelt was sufficiently moved to claim a day in a national park with John Muir (a master interpreter before such a term was coined) as the grandest of his life. But such experiences may occur for more common folk and almost anywhere nature and culture are interpreted with passion and joy. And so, more than a century later, a Yosemite Conservancy donor explained, "My favorite memories—not only of Yosemite, but of my entire life—are right here at Tenaya Lake" (Bowman, 2014). These are indeed special moments of rapture through immersion in an authentic experience, one gained firsthand. Again, these may occur for just about anyone who ventures out to enjoy our cultural and natural heritage. We now turn to other special places administered by the federal government.

National Forests

"Only YOU can prevent wildfires."
–Smokey Bear

Virtually everyone has heard of Smokey Bear. The U.S. Forest Service has used Smokey in efforts to reduce wildfires since the 1940s in what has become the longest running PSA campaign in U.S. history. But what is the story behind the bear? Someday, someone may ask you. Or perhaps you will have the opportunity to initiate the story. For it captures a segment of our national history, our fascination and sentiments toward wildlife, while also exposing the power of creative communication strategies by a land-managing agency. Furthermore, such discussion may open opportunities to bring up the importance of and rationale behind controlled burns and the regenerative cycle of fire in natural systems (Connors, 2015).

In 1942, Walt Disney's motion picture, *Bambi*, was produced. Disney allowed the forest fire prevention campaign to use Bambi's image on a poster, which proved highly successful. However, the image was on loan for only one year, and the Forest Service had to find another animal to promote fire prevention thereafter. A decision was made that America's number one fire fighter would be a bear. On August 9, 1944, in the midst of WWII, a memo was signed authorizing the creation of Smokey Bear. Within a decade, Smokey Bear was so popular as to attract commercial interest. Therefore, an Act of Congress was passed to take Smokey out of the public domain. The Act placed Smokey under the jurisdiction of the Secretary of Agriculture.

Figure 2.2. "Little Hotfoot," renamed Smokey Bear, arrives in Washington, D.C. and is greeted by Forest Service Chief Lyle F. Watts (center) in the rain (left) and soon makes a new friend in Judy Bell as part of the publicity campaign (right). (both USFS)

Then, in the spring of 1950, in the Capitan Mountains of New Mexico, a small blaze became a raging fire. Several firefighters were caught in the path of the fire and barely escaped. Nearby, a black bear cub had also been caught in the fire's path. Although some controversy exists over who rescued the cub, ultimately the cub needed veterinary expertise and was flown in a small plane to Santa Fe where the burns were treated. The news of the little bear spread quickly and the story was picked up by national newslines. With so much attention, the New Mexico State Game Warden wrote an official letter to the Chief of the Forest Service. In the letter, an offer was made to give the Forest Service the bear with the understanding that it would be dedicated to a publicity program of fire prevention and conservation. With approval gained, the bear was sent to Washington, DC, where it found its home at the National Zoo, becoming the living icon of Smokey Bear (Figure 2.2).

Not long after, in 1952, Steve Nelson and Jack Rollins wrote a song about the popular bear. To keep the proper rhythm of the ballad it was necessary for them to insert "the" between "Smokey" and "Bear." The song became well known and set off a debate that has lasted ever since as to the correct name of the bear… which is Smokey Bear, since the name never really officially changed.

Lands of Many Uses. The United States has the fourth largest forest estate in the world behind Russia, Brazil, and Canada (Tidwell, 2015). As of 2017, more than 193 million acres of forests and grasslands are managed by the U.S. Forest Service (fs.fed.us). Many interpreters know that in the early 1890s, President Benjamin Harrison proclaimed the first *forest reserve* (now Shoshone and Teton National Forests, Wyoming) to assure habitat for wildlife. The second (White River National Forest, Colorado) had recreation and scenery as its primary values. Others were set aside because of Harrison's concern for watersheds (Pike, Mt. Hood and Angeles National Forests), fisheries (Chugach

National Forest), and marvelous scenery (Pacific and Grand Canyon forest reserves, parts of which are now designated as Mount Rainier and Grand Canyon National Parks).

The Forest Service has a multiple-use mandate from Congress, requiring it to manage its lands for grazing, recreation, wood, water, wildlife, and designated wilderness. At present, recreation leads other uses by almost any measure in the majority of the national forests. The agency provides more visitor days of outdoor recreation than any other single organization in the United States. However, the Forest Service has an up-and-down record of interpretive effort. Multiple unguarded entry points, immense acreages, and a public that visits the forest for highly diverse purposes create complexities for interpretive management. Problems also arise from the fickleness of Congressional funding for interpretation.

Nevertheless, the agency has an active interpretive policy (Figure 2.3). Forest Service goals emphasize that the visitor should (a) have an enjoyable experience and (b) develop awareness, understanding and responsibility toward the forests. With achievement of these goals, the public should gain a stronger sense of the agency's diverse roles, its science base, and its complex policies. Sophisticated and energetic interpretation at all levels seems indispensable to achieve these goals. For example, the Forest Service has embraced the vast potential of online resources to enhance the delivery of conservation education. Several advantages are noted that include cost effectiveness (as compared to print resources), efficiency (material can be changed or added immediately), physical access to the resource is not required (although desirable to visit forests firsthand, the learning doesn't mandate this and may foster more authentic experiences at a later time), low barriers of affluence (access to most online media has become ubiquitous), engaging different learning styles, and providing interaction (a variety of different instructional strategies meet individual learning preferences, and problem-solving and discussion activities allow for learner involvement).

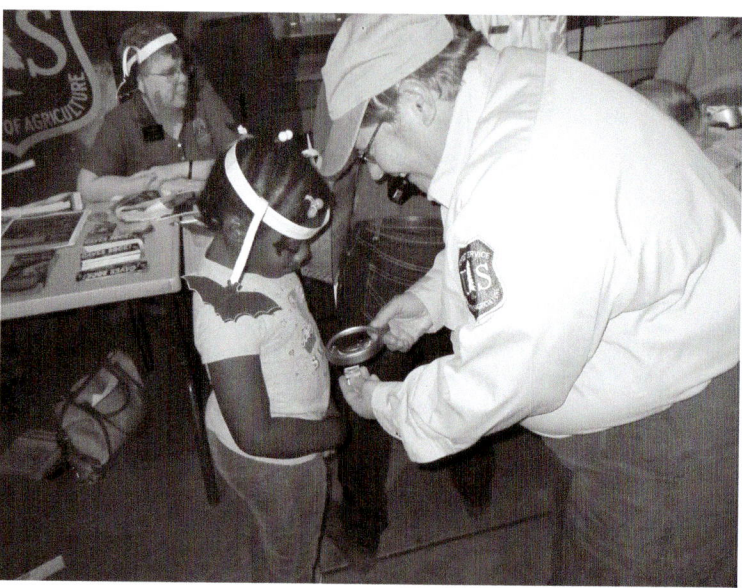

Figure 2.3. U.S. Forest Service interpreter shows a bat skull to a young person attending a special event to celebrate bats. (USFS-CMS)

Important areas of concern to the Forest Service now include such complex issues as pollinator protection such as the decline of honey bees and monarch butterflies in North America (Tidwell, 2013) and forests and climate change (Tidwell, 2015). In addition to providing for water supply and tremendous biodiversity, a critical ecosystem service from forests is carbon uptake and storage. Forests serve as a net carbon sink and take up about 12 percent of the carbon emitted in the U.S. each year.

The Forest Service built (usually with Congressional special funding) and maintains major interpretive centers in many national forests. Several interpretive innovations have developed within the Forest Service over the years which include travel interpretation, private sector partnerships, cooperating associations, special projects, and enterprise teams.

Travel interpretation. Since 1970, Forest Service interpreters have boarded various kinds of tour boats to explain the coastal Chugach and Tongass National Forests in Alaska. The interpreters operate a floating visitor center on board, and give a full array of talks, spot whales, count bald eagles, and offer cultural interpretation and children's programs.

Similarly, Forest Service interpreters staff a Gray Line tour boat and small commercial ferry on the waters of the Chugach National Forest, paid for by the boat companies as part of their use permit. Similar arrangements exist for trains and buses elsewhere in the United States.

Private sector partnerships. The Forest Service works with private outfitters, resorts, and other recreational businesses to blend interpretation into their amenity packages. In some cases, private interpretive/recreation companies help manage campgrounds and provide seasonal interpretive programs on contract. In Creede, Colorado, a miners association built a novel mining museum; the Forest Service paid for creating and installing the exhibits. In Seattle, agency interpreters offer presentations and training in a Recreational Equipment, Inc. (REI) store's meeting room, as well as helping with recreation logistics at interagency information centers in several other REI stores.

> The Forest Service works with private outfitters, resorts, and other recreational businesses.

Cooperating associations. Private organizations such as the Northwest Interpretive Association acquire and sell interpretive books, maps, and materials at or near Forest Service facilities. This bypasses the cumbersome federal Treasury accounting system. Some of these also provide interpretive programming assistance.

Special projects. Some of the best interpretation by the Forest Service has come in response to special situations. A prime case developed at the Mount St. Helens National Volcanic Monument in the Gifford Pinchot National Forest. After the 1980 eruption, the Forest Service faced a vigorous campaign by the National Park Service to take over the land and interpret it properly. In response, the Forest Service found the money and expertise to produce superb interpretive facilities, including visitor centers, wayside exhibits, films, environmental education, guided walks, and a plethora of contacts and collaborators throughout southwestern Washington.

After 9/11, the Forest Service became involved in the Living Memorials Project in which trees were planted in memory of those who died on that infamous day. The concept intertwined the universal concepts of life and death related to both human and forest communities. After a forest burns, the land shows its scars. But over time, new life takes over. There is a resiliency inherent in forest resources. Similarly, after 9/11, people showed their scars in sadness and mourning. But as time passes, there tends to be some element of recovery. There is a resiliency in the human condition as well. To assist in this period of recovery, trees were planted in the memory of loved ones lost on that fateful day and are now located in every state of the nation. Beyond planting commemorative trees, this project emphasizes living memorials as physical, social, emotional, and spiritual acts that are at the intersection of the hope found in human and natural systems.

TEAMS Enterprise Unit. The Forest Service allows teams of employees with special skills to operate rather independently. They can provide, for example, interpretive planning, design, writing, and special services to national forests and to other public agencies, for a fee. The income generated returns to the Forest Service to compensate their absence from regular duties. TEAMS stands for Talent, Expertise, Agility, Mobility and Simplicity. In 2015, one of these teams won a National Environmental Excellence Award. Interestingly, the concept began when a forest service manager read a book titled *The End of Bureaucracy and the Rise of the Intelligent Organization* and then invited the authors to join the team reinventing the Forest Service. The authors of the book were none other than Gifford Pinchot III, great grandson of the first Forest Service Chief, and his wife!

For years, our challenge has been to help people understand the importance of sustaining forests. We understand it ourselves, but we sometimes have trouble communicating outside our own echo chamber…As an agency, the Forest Service has started to shift our message from "why is what we do important for sustaining forests" to "why should people care about sustaining forests?" What's in it for them?
–Tom Tidwell, Chief, "Better Telling Our Story," 2015

National Wildlife Refuges

In 2017, the U.S. Fish and Wildlife Service (FWS) of the Department of the Interior managed 150 million acres of land and water. The FWS now has more than 560 National Wildlife Refuges that conserve habitat for migratory birds and other animals, provide for hunting and fishing, offer trail and auto routes, wildlife observation and photography, as well as environmental education and interpretation. The refuges host about 47 million visitors annually (fws.gov/refuges).

The National Wildlife Refuges (NWR) serve as outdoor classrooms, interpreting to recreational visitors and supplying educational assistance for schools. Increasingly, interpreters can make concepts such as habitat management and global environmental degradation mean something to the public by pointing out the migratory birds that live in the refuge part of the year and in another part of the world during the rest of the year. Other complex issues include invasive species, endangered species, and wildlife forensics.

> The National Wildlife Refuges (NWR) serve as outdoor classrooms.

Driving tours, publications, signs, exhibits, and visitor centers comprise the main interpretive tools with increasing reliance on new technologies as discussed above for our national parks and forests. A growing number of refuges also provide year-round personal interpretation and environmental education.

Many National Wildlife Refuges do not automatically attract visitors, except the traditional hunters, anglers, and birders. Few refuges offer spectacular scenery—most are flat and wet landscapes or desert areas. Without interpretation, a refuge seems to be just another swamp or parched landscape, attractive only to those in the know. It takes an able interpreter with skill and imagination to get the visitor personally involved in a memorable experience. Where interpreters operate, they offer programs to many visitors, schools, and community groups by providing interpretation that elucidates the special value of refuges. Interpretation and education now comprise an integral part of national FWS policy. In the mid 1970s, refuges moved from "sanctuaries" to "showcases for wildlife."

Several refuges, with strong backing from managers, offer outstanding interpretive services. One example, the Chincoteague NWR in Virginia uses a whole range of interpretive methods to help people understand its complex ecology, including a fine exhibit center. Another is the heavily visited Kenai NWR, where self-guiding trails, a remote roadside information cabin, and a rustic environmental education facility all complement a major interpretive center near Soldotna, Alaska. At the J.N. "Ding" Darling NWR, hikers can use a smartphone to link to videos while walking the iNature trail. Other refuges offer cell phone messages along an auto tour.

The FWS opened a National Conservation Training Center at Shepherdstown, West Virginia, in 1995. This provided a new dimension to the agency's growing dedication to interpretation and administration, providing time and resources for regular training of interpreters and managers. The 2014 FWS "Standards of Excellence for Urban National Wildlife Refuges" is consistent with quality interpretation as follows: 1) Know and relate to the community. 2) Connect urban people with nature via stepping stones of engagement. 3) Build partnerships. 4) Be a community asset. 5) Ensure adequate long-term resources. 6) Provide equitable access. 7) Ensure visitors feel safe and welcome. 8) Model sustainability (fws.gov).

The Canada Wildlife Act of 1973 authorized the Minister of Environment to promote and encourage interpretation, including establishing interpretive centers. Wildlife agencies in other countries have similar mandates and similar emphases on the interpretive dimensions of managing wildlife while serving the public.

Corps of Engineers

The Army Corps of Engineers (COE) got into the civil works business in 1936, altering the Mississippi River to enhance navigation and reduce most flooding hazards. Now, the COE manages 13 million acres of natural environment in and around its reservoirs. Its civilian interpretive personnel help to administer the recreation and conservation programs at more than 400 COE lakes (Figure 2.4). As the world's largest provider of water-based recreation access, the agency hosts approximately 370 million visits each year (usace.army).

Interpretive centers present information on COE areas and provide frequent outdoor and historical programs. The Corps' basic interpretive objectives include orienting the public to the project, enhancing visitor understanding and enjoyment of the project, aiding in achieving management objectives, and gaining public support by explaining Corps activities.

The COE also uses its interpreters to spread use to the various resources around the reservoirs by informing visitors about their various alternative opportunities. Water and boat safety messages in an interpretive manner also aids in recreation management.

Figure 2.4. At Tuttle Creek Reservoir in Kansas, the U.S. Army Corps of Engineers not only interprets the dam and lake but also the surrounding Flint Hills landscape. (TC)

As an indication to its commitment to natural resource sustainability, the COE Earth Day events in 2015 included the following: park cleanups, tree and garden planting, activity booths at Earth Day fairs, school presentations, Earth Day presentations on official websites, and a social media campaign that asked, "Now that we are celebrating 45 years of Earth Day, what does Earth Day mean to you?"

The Bonneville Lock and Dam Project in Washington and Oregon interprets through two visitor centers, an auditorium, three fish ladders, two historical sites, and display ponds in a fish hatchery. The interpreters are direct-hired COE career employees, considered as some of the best in the nation. This agency offers complete interpretive programs at hundreds of reservoirs throughout much of the nation.

Bureau of Land Management

The biggest federal landowner in the United States has approximately 250 million acres of desert, rangelands, tundra, and taiga. A 1976 law gave the Bureau of Land Management (BLM) a mandate to manage these lands permanently for multiple uses, including recreation. At the same time, growing use put pressures on fragile desert resources and particularly on artifacts from previous cultures. Interpretation came into play as a key to stronger management. Several visitor centers at key locations offer information to help people perceive the BLM properties as something besides wastelands. This agency's interpretive activities have since continued to grow.

One is at the BLM's Yaquina Head Outstanding Natural Area at Newport, Oregon. The center looms over the Pacific atop steep cliffs that support an 1872 lighthouse. Personal interpretation programs, roving naturalists, and exhibits enrich the visitor experience.

Another center lies in a colorful valley just outside Las Vegas, Nevada. The Red Rock Canyon Visitor Center offers spectacular desert and cliff views and wildlife exhibits. The BLM staff interpreters coordinate the work with a band of volunteers who lead hikes, conduct environmental education programs, and meet visitors at the information desk and auditorium.

An outstanding BLM museum sits above McPhee Reservoir in Southwestern Colorado. The Anasazi Cultural Heritage Center interprets the ancestral pueblo people who inhabited Mesa Verde and the Colorado Plateau. Coordination of information with several nearby archaeological projects keeps interpreters up to date and encourages people to visit the field sites. The facility invites participation with the exhibits' life size dioramas and models of the distant past, side by side with interactive computer quizzes that reinforce the key concepts, survival strategies, and principles that the exhibits describe. Located on the Dominguez-Escalante and Old Spanish Trail routes, the museum has small ruins just outside the southwestern style building.

Major resource issues the BLM faces include management of wild horses and burros, renewable energy on public lands, and sage grouse and sagebrush conservation. To help communicate various management messages the agency has compiled standards and policies for new media tools. The BLM website (blm.gov) indicates approvals of media sharing (YouTube and Flickr), blogging/microblogging (Tumblr and Twitter), social networking (Facebook, Instagram and Pinterest), Document/Data Sharing Repositories (Slideshare), widgets (Google maps), and video streaming (Livestream).

State and Provincial Governments

Historic Agencies

State historic agencies preserve and present homes, neighborhoods, battlefields, and other historic landmarks to the public. In addition, many states and provinces conserve their history through one or more museums. In some places, a nonprofit historical society manages the facilities in trust. In others, directly hired interpreters and curators work for an agency.

The Pennsylvania Historical and Museum Commission administers 27 historical and archaeological properties, from Washington Crossing to the Drake Well Museum and Old Economy Village. The private nonprofit Pennsylvania Heritage Society supports the Commission by funding the preservation and interpretation of Pennsylvania's history and publishing *Pennsylvania Heritage* magazine. The commission organizes various public programs and discussions. Each site has interpreters who develop exhibits, and conduct tours, workshops, classes and special events, such as the Lumber Museum's contests and demonstrations of lumberjack skills.

Parks and Forests

Virtually all Canadian provincial park systems and the 50 state park systems in the United States offer interpretive services to visitors. States and provinces started creating their park systems in the late 19th century and on through the 21st century. Their interpretive programs generally started with seasonal employees (often school science teachers). During the 1960s and 1970s, many states and provinces decided to hire a core of year-round interpreters for well-attended parks. Today some of the most professional and progressive interpretive organizations are state park agencies. They apply cutting-edge approaches and are fully committed to training their seasonal interpreters and to professional development of their permanent staff.

In some state forest systems, year-round interpreters play a useful role in describing the values of the properties for recreation and as demonstrations of various techniques of forest management. They also assist visitors to understand the many values of forest management on a sustained basis.

Tribal Interpretation

Many First Nation and American Indian tribal nations have developed strong interpretive programs and beautiful museum facilities. Interestingly, interpretation came late to tribal groups. Reticence about sharing cultural information and shyness about contact with tourists kept the opportunity for informative contacts to a minimum.

In recent years, major changes have occurred. New tribal and intertribal cultural centers and museums have welcomed public visits. Stimulated in part by healthy tribal pride, and a growing interest in tourism, and enabled in some places by gaming revenues, many tribes actively seek to interpret their heritage and preserve (or revive) their language, customs, and sense of identity. Navajo individuals work as interpreters in several National Park Service sites such as Glen Canyon National Recreation Area and guide visitors to the Monument Valley Navajo Park in Arizona. Several small enterprises and family businesses on the Navajo Nation offer professional interpretive guide services to individual tourists and groups.

> Many First Nation and American Indian tribal nations have developed strong interpretive programs and beautiful museum facilities.

The Makah Cultural and Research Center, at Neah Bay, Washington, recognized as one of the nation's finest tribal museums, features life of the pre-contact Makah people. The museum shows several large, cedar, dug-out canoes and an impressive exhibit on whaling and sealing as well as other traditional activities.

An elaborate, powerful experience awaits those who visit Tama'stslikt Cultural Institute, near Pendleton, Oregon. The Confederated Tribes of the Umatilla Indian Reservation interpret the history and cultures of the Walla Walla, Cayuse, and Umatilla peoples (*Tama'stslikt* means *interpret* in the Walla Walla language). The three major exhibit sections have simple subthemes supporting a gentle, assertive, thought-provoking major theme: *We Were, We Are, We Will Be.*

Local Governments

City, township, and county governments supply interpretation to a large clientele, many of who make return visits. Among the thousands of U.S. and Canadian local governments, designations include town, township, municipality, city, county, parish, and borough governments. In addition, interpretation is conducted in special park districts, historic districts, and school districts.

> City, township, and county governments supply interpretation to a large clientele.

Increasing development of urban interpretation and city park/museum/zoo education departments provides new opportunities in municipal governments. For example, Seattle City Parks in the state of Washington employ several year-round interpreters to run their Discovery Park interpretive center and trails, to offer environmental education at Camp Long, and to interpret animals at Woodland Park Zoo.

Most counties in the United States offer interpretation in one form or another. They support interpretation of their heritage through one or more museums, often with joint public-private funding. More than 1,000 of the 3,000 U.S. counties (parishes in Louisiana; municipalities and boroughs in Alaska) have park and recreation departments; most of these offer interpretive services, nature centers, or natural history museums. For example, Hennepin County Park District in Minnesota contains a system of nature centers and visitor centers in 26,000 acres of parks. The large interpretive staff offers programs in all of the parks.

Multicounty special park districts feature interpretation through large staffs and fine interpretive facilities. Three examples are California's East Bay Regional Park District, Michigan's Huron-Clinton Metropolitan Park District, and the Maryland National Capital Parks and Planning Commission. Their staffs of full-time interpreters consistently win top professional awards and provide leadership in the interpretive field.

Museums

One of the most remarkable facts about American museums is that they attract approximately 850 million visits each year which, to put it in perspective, is more than the attendance for all major league sporting events and theme parks *combined*. The American Alliance of Museums (aam-us.org) further notes that these popular places "tell important stories by collecting, preserving, researching and interpreting objects, living specimens and historical records" (Figure 2.5).

> American museums attract approximately 850 million visits each year.

Museums contribute greatly to the communities they serve by ensuring that people of all backgrounds have access to quality museum experiences. Most museums place a high priority on partnerships with schools with the typical museum spending three-quarters of its education budget on K-12 students. For example, students attending a field trip to an art museum experience an increase in critical thinking skills, historical empathy, and tolerance with even greater increases for students from rural or high-poverty regions (aam-us.org). In 2014, 2,200 museums offered free admission to military families through the Blue Star Museums initiative.

Figure 2.5. Museum interpretation takes many forms and includes outdoor airplane museums. (TC)

Overall, museums employ more than 400,000 Americans and directly contribute $21 billion to the U.S. economy each year (aam-us.org). Museums may feature art, history, local culture, science, industrial processes, military equipment and nature. The most common interpretive methods include exhibits, school education programs, docent-guided tours, guest lectures, festivals, and various applications of newer media that includes podcasts, apps, interactive websites, and virtual reality. A more detailed discussion of museums and visitor centers appears in Chapter 11.

Interpretive Villages and Farms

Many restored or recreated villages and farms interpret the past. At least a few suggest how people may live in the future. Living history farms range from a small operation with a garden, a few modern breeds of animals, and a farmstead tended by an interpreter or two in period dress, to a large facility re-creating many aspects of agricultural life as faithfully as possible, including the use of period crop varieties, historic livestock breeds, cultivation with historic methods and replica tools, and a large staff of interpreters representing the range of rural life of the period.

> "Historic villages and farms aim to portray the life of an historic period."

Historic villages and farms aim to portray the life of an historic period. Most of the farming activities are reduced in size to allow close observation and time for interpretation. Visitors spend time watching craft demonstrations, cooking, blacksmithing, school sessions, and children playing old-time games, plus studying the agricultural equipment, fields, and animals.

Most period farms and villages require high capital costs. Buildings that will host visitors must meet modern safety and access standards while appearing to be historically accurate. An interpretive farm true to its day will probably involve investments of several million dollars, plus costs of staff, maintenance, and animal care.

The Greenfield Village and Henry Ford Museum in Dearborn, Michigan, has 240 acres with 100 historic structures. A 14-acre indoor museum features vehicles and relics of the industrial revolution. Started in 1929 by Henry Ford and now run through the University of Michigan, the grounds feature buildings from the 17th to 19th centuries plus several trains. Some visitors spend an entire week at the facility.

At Pioneer, Arizona, near Phoenix, a private, nonprofit corporation operates a 550-acre ranch to bring history alive. The 1860s ranch house stands on the outskirts of a reconstructed settlement, with shops, a church, an opera house, a saloon, a miners' camp, a stagecoach stop, and a few homes. Visitors mingle in the shade of the barn to watch horseshoeing, leather tanning, and old-fashioned home economics.

Zoos, Wildlife Parks, and Aquariums

Zoological gardens rank among the most ancient of outdoor educational facilities. Before 1000 B.C., China's Empress Tanki built a marble house for deer and Wen Wang established a 1,500 acre *Garden of Intelligence (or Ling-Yu)* filled with animals. King Solomon, King Nebuchadnezzar, and Alexander the Great all kept zoos. A zoo established in Mexico in 1519 employed 300 keepers. European cities revived zoo keeping in the mid-1700s. One of the most innovative zoos emerged in 1828 under the auspices of the Zoological Society of London, which continues as a leader in caring for and interpreting animals and their habitats.

Zoo and aquarium objectives today feature study and research on animals, public education and interpretation, breeding endangered species, and conservation of natural habitats and populations. Virtually all zoos, wildlife parks, and aquariums offer interpretive tours, educational programs, and interpretive signs, as well as newer uses of technology such as smart phone apps.

In 2017 there were approximately 2,800 animal exhibitors licensed by the U.S. Department of Agriculture, of which fewer than 10% are accredited by the Association of Zoos and Aquariums (aza.org).

> "Virtually all zoos, wildlife parks, and aquariums offer interpretive tours."

Zoos in almost every nation of the world offer outstanding interpretive staffs. The Zoological Society of San Diego, famous for its large zoo and huge wild animal park, allows visitors to see animals without bars. At the Safari Park visitors travel by monorail through the habitat settings, which are really large paddocks. Pedestrians can also see in the paddocks from the perimeter walkways, where they benefit from the interpretive signs and brochure descriptions. "Night Time at the Zoo" bolsters visitation and allows exciting viewing of nocturnally active animals.

In contrast, the Alaska Zoo in Anchorage features only animal species native to that state, displaying most of them outdoors in natural conditions. Small nocturnal animals live in enclosed facilities darkened during the day and lit at night, so diurnal visitors see the animals in action.

Camps

Approximately 8,500 camps operate in the United States, offering outdoor opportunities to youth and adults. The owners include private business, religious groups, municipal governments, and quasi-public organizations (e.g., YMCAs, Scouts, Salvation Army). Some operate as resident camps and some as day camps. In 2017, the American Camp Association website (acacamps.org) listed more than 2,400 accredited camps.

Formal and informal environmental education programs operate in a majority of these camps, under names such as nature and environmental studies, outdoor living, and camping skills. In the United States many YMCA camps, some church camps, and a few Boy/Girl Scout camps also have adopted environmental education as a major activity year-round. The programs bring in groups that extend camp incomes and staff productivity. Private summer camps near urban areas also provide similar environmental programming for schools and youth groups.

Various camps make conservation their central focus. Among many sponsors, the National Wildlife Federation and the National Audubon Society provide adult and youth nature seminars in outdoor settings. The goals of conserva-

> "Various camps make conservation their central focus."

tion camps usually aim to instill understanding, respect, and value for natural resources; to train youth in recreational skills and ethics; to introduce resource management and safety; and to offer group recreation in outdoor settings.

Several state agencies sponsor educational camps to interpret nature and history. The Vermont Fish and Wildlife department offers sessions of the Green Mountain Conservation Camps throughout the summer season. Youth 12-14 years old learn outdoor skills, life sports, and resource management. Several states also sponsor state Youth Conservation Corps (YCC) camps. Youth 16-21 years old who qualify can work for pay and develop job skills. The YCC crews work on trails, environmental rehabilitation, signs, and rustic construction in national and state forests and parks. All participants receive training in conservation, first aid, leadership skills, communications, and working as a team. Furthermore, the Student Conservation Association (SCA) offers outstanding opportunities for students to work and learn at national parks and other land-managing agencies in a variety of jobs, some of which include interpretive duties.

Private Sector Interpretation

Luxury Cruising and Adventure Cruising

Many cruise ship companies now include interpreters (also referred to as lecturers) on their crews. In many locations, they take on collaborating interpreters from the territory they are visiting for specialized information and side trips. Lindblad Expeditions has long advertised their experienced naturalists as keys to their high quality adventure and nature cruises. The Seabourn Cruise Line features a "Dress Circle for Distinguished Lecturers" with expertise in fields ranging from environmental studies to space exploration. They provide "Land and Sea Knowledge" for the ship's passengers.

Adventure cruise firms seek guides who exhibit a high level of skill and experience in outdoor activities as well as in natural history, geography, ecology, and geology. These interpreters interact directly with clients who are generally highly educated, curious, and ready for action.

Private Commercial Interpreters

Resort naturalists go back to the origins of modern environmental interpretation. The U.S. Forest Service and Audubon Society collaborated to train naturalists for resorts in northern Minnesota and Arizona. The program, now nationwide, involves owners of small resorts who can provide well-planned seasonal naturalist services directly to their customers as value added, while the Forest Service can have confidence that users of the forests will be accurately informed.

> "Resort naturalists go back to the origins of modern environmental interpretation."

Whale watch ships in Baja, California; Cape Cod; Hawaii; Alaska; and many other places carry interpreters who describe the actions, physiology, ecology, and migration of whales. The commentaries may last two hours or more, including orientation, approach, sighting events, and follow-up summaries on the return trip.

Callaway Gardens in Pine Mountain, Georgia, supports an Education Department to operate a major interpretive enterprise. Its naturalists and horticulturalists offer tours, seminars, and educational publications at this huge botanical garden and forest resort.

Freelance interpreters offer services in many ways, some part-time and others as a main source of income. Several private "Native People" interpreters travel to talk with church, school, civic, and cultural groups, to interpret artifacts, symbols, and modern crafts. Many emphasize the old ways of living with a healthy environment and describe the relationship of their people with creation. On western Canadian islands, Haida people have long guided tourists toward understanding their fishing, culture, and arts. In Tucson, Arizona, a company called Sabino Canyon Tours provides narrated shuttle bus rides up a Forest Service canyon on a special use permit.

Richard N. Pawling has interpreted under the title *History Alive!* He conducts first-person living history performances, taking on the persona of a canal boat captain, a coal miner, a blacksmith, and other characters, including an early baseball player. He and his wife offer workshops for archaeologists, interpreters, teachers, historical societies, and industries.

Private interpretive guides demonstrate that the public puts a high value on their services. Guides and outfitters for wilderness travel, nature tours, and historical walks profitably provide interpretive services for small parties. In Alaska and Hawaii, particularly, interpreters collaborate with the travel-tourism industry, with resource management agencies, and with museums and cultural groups to provide excellent experiences for their clients.

Private Nonprofit

Numerous groups are private institutions that serve the public interest and therefore are tax exempt. YMCAs and their environmental camps, Scouts, Campfire, churches, historical societies, and many environmental groups offer diverse interpretive/educational programs and facilities (Figure 2.6). Two outstanding examples follow, one relatively small and the other quite large in influence and scope.

Figure 2.6. The private nonprofit Delaware Bay Schooner Project provides exciting interpretive experiences. (GS)

On the north side of Kalamazoo, Michigan, a private, nonprofit nature center offers a variety of interpretive events. The Kalamazoo Nature Center (KNC) covers a broad range of projects, the result of the fertile imagination of founder Dr. H. Lewis Batts, his professional staff, and active board members. The center's staff works in an unusual building full of exhibits, a sun-rain room, a gift and bookshop, and gathering places.

The National Audubon Society (NAS) has a long history with a number of Nature and Education Centers. Its publications in the 1960s aided many organizations in designing and operating interpretive centers and programs. The huge Audubon network of approximately a half million members in some 500+ local chapters holds diverse policy opinions but strongly advocates preservation, wilderness, and natural areas restoration. The ambitious program aims at developing a new, diverse constituency at Audubon Centers to make Audubon the most effective conservation group in the nation at influencing public policy decisions over the next century. Audubon membership leaflets announce a critical crossroads for our natural heritage and hypothesize that "victory in the public policy arena will belong to whomever strategically engages the most people." NAS volunteers are the key to several citizen-science efforts such as the Christmas and Great Backyard Bird Counts.

Industrial Interpretation

Many corporations and industries collect and display their own history, processes, and tools. The economic and technological impact of industries on communities and nations help to determine the fabric of the society. For example, the steel industry that made the character of Pittsburgh, Wheeling, Birmingham, and Pueblo has diminished or vanished in the last 50 years. All four cities now have different industrial mixes. The young residents today have little firsthand evidence of how and where their parents and grandparents made a living in these communities. Recent archival and museum organizations have started research and interpretation of this industrial history. Many successful contemporary corporations such as John Deere (Moline, IL), Caterpillar (Peoria, IL), and Walmart (Bentonville, AR) all have state-of-the-art museums with interactive exhibits, original artifacts, and educational activities.

The forest products industries may hold the lead in providing interpretation of their processes, products, and the natural environments in which they find their resources. The American Forest and Paper Association (AFPA) has offered interpretive and educational materials to the public for more than seven decades. Through the AFPA's American Forest Foundation, environmental education got a big boost with *Project Learning Tree*, starting in 1973. The sponsors and cosponsors insisted that the materials should not reflect an industry point of view, but rather teach children and adults how to make decisions based on facts about the environment and the economy. This book of learning activities and facilitation workshops has reached more than a half million teachers (plt.org). It has served as a model for *Project Wild* and *Project Wet*, and other successful curricula.

An industry consortium operates the Trees for Tomorrow Natural Resource Education Center in Eagle River, Wisconsin. The cozy residential campus has multiple nature trails, a river, forests, silvicultural samples, a library, classrooms, and dormitories. Clients include Road Scholars, schools groups, teacher workshops, gifted science students, and cross-country ski learning tours. The subjects include history of wood products supply, wildlife biology, water protection, recreation, and a sustainable forest resource that has supported the local economy for well over a century.

Other well-known interpretive tours and exhibits interpret power plants, factories, and many breweries and wineries.

Summary

Professional interpreters work in many locations and facilities. Interpretive work occurs at many levels of ownership, from freelance, private, quasi-public, and industrial, to city, county, state/provincial, and federal. Diversity characterizes the interpretive field. Cultural and natural heritage interpreters use the same techniques and principles, even though they may work in widely different environments. Many interpreters work with *both* cultural and natural themes.

The profession involves hundreds of thousands of interpreters and enjoys rapid expansion, particularly in the tourism sector. Interpretation seeks to engage all citizens, from beginners to experts, from children to adults, and everyone in between.

The importance of stewardship concerning our cultural and natural heritage—what we are as a nation, who we are as a society, who we are as individuals— is something that almost all Americans can agree on. This stewardship occurs in many different places. These special places that tell our story, remnants of wild America and our most important cultural icons, must be protected for this and future generations. The same reasoning holds true for all other nations. Therefore, protecting special places everywhere and interpreting them in meaningful ways makes for a better world. The next chapter looks more specifically at the values of interpretation to individuals and society.

Literature Cited*

*Official government and organizational websites cited in the text are listed by agency title followed by the website.

American Alliance of Museums: aam-us.org

American Camp Association: acacamps.org

Army Corps of Engineers: usace.army

Association of Zoos and Aquariums: aza.org

Beck, L. (2016). The national park centennial: What the parks mean to us today. *Legacy, 27*(5), 32–33.

Bowman, D. (2014). Tenaya's Sunrise Trail. *Yosemite Conservancy.* Spring/Summer 2014, 5(1), 6–7.

Bureau of Land Management: blm.gov

Connors, P. (2015). Beauty in the burn: Fire and rebirth in the forest. *Orion*, March/April 2015.

Duncan, D. (2009). *The national parks: America's best idea.* New York, NY: Knopf Borzoi Books.

National Park Service: nps.gov

Project Learning Tree: plt.org

Runte, A. (1990). *Yosemite: The embattled wilderness.* Lincoln, NE: University of Nebraska Press.

Tidwell, T. (2013). The role of pollinator protection in conservation. Speech to North American Pollinator Protection Campaign, 13th Annual International Conference, Washington, D.C. October 22, 2013.

Tidwell, T. (2015). Forests and climate change. Speech to NCSE 2015 Conference: Energy and Climate Change, Washington, D.C. January 15, 2015.

U.S. Fish and Wildlife Service. (2014). *Urban wildlife refuges: Standards of excellence.* October 2014.

U.S. Fish and Wildlife Service: fws.gov

U.S. Forest Service: fs.fed.us

SECTION II

Why Interpret?

CHAPTER 3
Values to Individuals and Society

Hiram Chittenden, U.S. Army Corps of Engineers, designed the roads in Yellowstone. He wrote in 1895 (1895, 1964) of local hostility to that great park:

> To most people it will seem impossible that there should be anyone who would seek the mutilation or destruction of this important reservation. Unfortunately there are many such. No session of Congress for twenty years has been free from attempted legislation hostile to the park. The schemes to convert it into an instrument of private greed have been many, and strange as it may seem, they are invariably put forward by those very communities to whom the park is, and must ever remain, the chief glory of their section. It is lamentable proof of the dearth of patriotic spirit that always betrays itself whenever the interests of individuals and of the public come into collision.
>
> It will not do, however, to assume that because these schemes have hitherto failed, they will always continue to fail. Since they have their origin in speculative ventures, they will be put forward so long as they offer the least pecuniary inducement.

As described more than 100 years ago, and still valid today, there will always be a few loud and selfish individuals who would be glad to destroy our magnificent heritage and make obscene profits for themselves at the expense of everyone else. First and foremost, interpretation can help protect against such shortsighted greed—for the sake of the commonwealth.

Beyond that, interpretation of our cultural and natural heritage lends toward significant benefits to individuals through providing educational, recreational, and inspirational experiences. Furthermore, interpretation benefits society in promoting healthy communities and the informed public a democracy requires.

> "Interpretation benefits society in promoting healthy communities and the informed public a democracy requires."

If you asked interpreters why they chose to work in their profession, you would probably get answers that reflect enthusiasm; a passion for the craft. Most interpreters find fascination in cultural and natural history. They find delight in continuing their quest for knowledge in these subject areas. Furthermore, most interpreters enjoy interacting with people and sharing their knowledge. They prefer interpreting to doing anything else; they receive pay for what they love to do.

So, interpretation may be more than a job or occupation. Rather it becomes a way of life marked by a long-term mission, depth of knowledge, a sense of wonder, and humility, serenity, and fulfillment. This is a high calling.

Despite their conviction that interpretation matters, few interpreters have clearly articulated precisely why their agency should allocate scarce resources to provide interpretive services. Yet, they often find it necessary to explain the purposes and benefits of their work to agency administrators, fund-appropriating bodies, and the visiting public. Failure to do so clearly and convincingly may result in limited support for interpretation. This chapter, and the next, should help in that task.

Benefits to Individuals

Why do people choose to spend their leisure time visiting nature centers and museums, attending interpretive events, and going on history tours or nature walks? They get benefits. They are inspired. They have fun. They value meaningful experiences.

People derive satisfaction from such outings, otherwise they would not attend voluntarily, incur travel costs and entrance fees, and spend valued time doing it. Moreover, society derives enough benefits to justify providing public and private funds to pay curators and interpreters and to support their places of work.

Many interpreters are public servants in the legal sense—their salaries come from local, state, or federal tax dollars. Many other interpreters work directly for paying clients. All interpreters should act as servants of the public in the broadest sense, in principle and in spirit (Tilden, 1967). Interpreters reach out to people and enrich their experiences. Interpreters dedicate themselves to serving others, offering their audiences *educational, recreational, and inspirational* experiences.

Educational Benefits

Traditional definitions of interpretation focus on the educational aspects of the interpretive experience. For example, Tilden's (1967) formal definition of interpretation begins with the statement that interpretation is "an educational activity…"

Many people attend interpretive programs or facilities because they find that acquiring knowledge is an enjoyable and enriching experience. By gaining more knowledge about the cultural or natural resources of an area, their visit (or their home territory) becomes more meaningful. For example, knowing the best places to see rare birds in a forest facilitates an enjoyable experience for a visiting bird watcher. Understanding unique geologic features could prompt a family to stop and look closely at what otherwise might have seemed to be "just rocks."

> "Acquiring knowledge is an enjoyable and enriching experience."

Commonly, interpreters at parks, zoos, and museums formally link their educational goals of interpretive programs with their local-and state-mandated public education competencies and learner outcomes. Teachers receive a list of the mandated competencies addressed in each interpretive program (Figure 3.1).

Some zoo educators have linked with schools by offering regular on-site classes and classroom facilities. The Minnesota Zoo offers teacher programs, teacher resources, zoo classes, zoo career days, homeschool family events, and exotic travel "EdVentures" for high school and college students to places, in 2017, such as Belize and Tanzania. Furthermore, "The School for Environmental Studies at the Minnesota Zoo," a local high school on the zoo site, provides opportunities to focus studies on environmental issues, practical science, communications, and social studies.

Figure 3.1. Interpreters visit classrooms and link content to mandated competencies. (AS)

Students can earn college credit through extended interpretation programs and workshops at many sites, such as Sea World of Florida. Several zoos and major museums also offer opportunities to earn college credit.

Linking interpretation programs with local school curricula produces mutual benefits for school administrators, teachers, and students. It also benefits interpreters by strengthening community support for interpretive services and increases participation in interpretive programs.

Recreational Benefits

Recreational experience cannot be taken lightly. Its results are neither frivolous nor merely entertaining. Aristotle linked the existence of the "state" with the purpose of securing happiness for its citizens 2,300 years ago in his book *Politics*. He stressed that leisure time is the resource of true citizenship, that individuals should be able to use leisure time well. Leisure is better than work and is its end, according to Aristotle.

In the Declaration of Independence of the United States, Thomas Jefferson included the "pursuit of happiness" as one of the three inalienable rights. True happiness produces more than temporary giddiness or some level of passing materialistic satisfaction.

Pleasant experiences seem necessary to maintain a high quality of life. They increase self-reliance and self-esteem (Dustin, McAvoy, & Beck, 1986), improve mental and physical health (Beck et al., 2015; Myers, 2008; Saxena et al., 2005; Schwab, Dustin, & Bricker, 2009), and alleviate anxiety (MacKinnon, 2015).

Most interpreters offer their programs at parks, zoos, and other recreational areas for people during their leisure time. Although people find learning to be a positive experience, most choose not to spend their limited and valued leisure time attending what they think could be a dry, technical lecture or a mundane march through the woods. Most people seek optimal experiences in recreational settings (Beck & Cable, 2011).

Tilden (1967) recognized that all interpretation should be recreational: "...we cannot forget that people are with us mainly seeking enjoyment, not instruction." Therefore, interpreters seek to produce interpretation that is fun—stimulating, pleasurable, compelling fun—that produces true happiness and satisfaction. Almost any recreational activity can have an interpretive element.

> Interpreters provide the opportunity and context for pleasurable recreational experiences.

Clever interpretive infusions include, in Manhattan, Kansas, a nine-mile bike and hike trail that has the relative distances between planets marked to scale, interpreting the solar system to recreationists along the way (Figure 3.2).

Interpreters provide the opportunity and context for pleasurable recreational experiences. They make a visit to a nature preserve, an historic home, or a seashore a richer, more memorable event because of something that they help the visitor do better or comprehend more readily. They make the special significance of the place more evident, thus deepening the experience.

Although researchers find it hard to quantify recreational benefits—even more difficult than educational benefits—participant surveys through several decades have revealed responses that consistently indicate pleasurable satisfaction from wolf howling expeditions, to eagle watches, to prairie days, to family nature classes.

Figure 3.2. Walkers and bicyclists can learn about the solar system on a trail that provides the relative distances of the planets from the sun. (TC)

Inspirational Benefits

Good interpretation is fun, but the best interpretation evokes an uplifting emotional response. Burroughs (1916) worried that nature study as pursued in schools was:

> Too cold, too special, too mechanical; it is likely to rub the bloom off Nature. It lacks soul and emotion. It misses the accessories of the open air and its exhilarations, the sky, the clouds, the landscape, and the currents of the life that pulse everywhere.

Enos Mills (1920) emphasized the inspirational component of interpretation as follows:

> A nature guide...is not a teacher. At all times, however, he has been rightfully associated with information and some form of education. But nature guiding, as we see it, is more inspirational than informational.

Interpreters hold a wonderful position to avail themselves of such exhilarating accessories and to touch the emotions of their audience. Tilden (1967) wrote:

> The finest uses of national parks, or indeed any of the preserves that come within the range of interpretation work, lie ultimately in spiritual uplift. This end ["spiritual uplift"] cannot be reached except through a walk with beauty of some aspect, in which the interpreter is not primarily a teacher, but a companion in the adventure.

Discovering the beauty in the workmanship of a piece of antique furniture, in a special adaptation of an insect, or in a majestic panoramic view is neither strictly educational nor merely "fun." It stretches the mind to something more (Figure 3.3). Such interpretive experiences can move a person profoundly, almost indescribably, making them difficult to measure. Such *optimal experiences* often elicit a sense of *ineffability*—that is, the inability to fully articulate the meaning of the experience (Maslow, 1962).

Interpreters can inspire by enhancing people's ability to sense quality in their surroundings (Beck & Cable, 2011). Aldo Leopold (1966) wrote, "Our ability to perceive quality in nature begins, as in art, with the pretty. It expands through successive stages of the beautiful to values as yet uncaptured by language." An interpreter assists people as they move through these stages so that eventually the individual will not only perceive beauty in spectacular mountain scenery, but also will find beauty and inspiration in tall-grass prairies and tidal flats as well. Quality interpretation can inspire people with spine-tingling experiences regardless of the setting.

Figure 3.3. Interpreters reveal beauty and inspire people by calling attention to the intricate beauty and symbolism of "Iron Crosses of the Great Plains." These grave markers made by blacksmiths to uniquely honor the deceased symbolize the resourcefulness and steadfastness of the people who settled in this harsh climate. (TC)

Striking a Balance

Balancing recreation and education in presentations and exhibits offers one of the most difficult challenges facing interpreters. At one extreme, interpretation could take the form of boring speeches or lectures, lacking a recreational or entertainment component. Likewise, a few exhibits and publications state little more than formal policy or treat topics academically. At the other extreme, some presentations might evoke laughter, involve games, or other fun activities, but contain little meaningful information to provide an educational or inspirational experience. The happy medium brings history, art, and science alive with exciting encounters that stimulate and satisfy people.

Tilden (1967) noted the difference between just informing and interpreting:

> Information, as such, is not interpretation. Interpretation is revelation based upon information. They are entirely different things. However, all interpretation includes information… Information is the raw material of interpretation.

The challenge lies in mixing and molding into the program just the right amount of the "raw material" to provoke and enrich the visitors with enough fun to make it enjoyable and enough depth to make it inspirational.

In 1916, John Burroughs wrote in *The Gospel of Nature*:

> To absorb a thing is better than to learn it, and we absorb what we enjoy. I am not merely contented, like Wordsworth's poetry, to enjoy what others understand. I must understand also; but above all things, I must enjoy. How much of my enjoyment springs from my knowledge I do not know. The joy of knowing is very great; the delight of picking up the threads of meaning here and there, and following them through the maze of confusing facts, I know well. To enjoy understandingly, that, I fancy, is the great thing to be desired.

Burroughs's succinct goal to "enjoy understandingly" presents a balanced approach to education and recreation, that ultimately inspires, that could serve as both a personal goal for interpreters and for their audiences, regardless of the media used (Cable, 1992).

Clearly, the interpreter's mission goes beyond just cajoling visitors into superficial awareness of key facts. The professional interpreter's function also goes beyond that of an actor or character reciting a memorized spiel to visitors passing by and offering little else. The strong interpretive program propels the participants along a path toward richer living through growing sensitivity and action favoring their past, present, and future cultural and natural heritage. It inspires people to see beauty in their surroundings, in themselves, and in others. It helps them to walk closer to and more lightly on their cultural and natural environments, with inspirational insight.

Interpreting for Individual Growth

Motivation theories help to explain why people seek out education and recreation, why they visit museums, forests, and attend interpretive events, and why they gain inspiration from them. Abraham Maslow (1954) developed a widely accepted theory that offers insights into these motivations. Although some have challenged this, and other theories mentioned in this book, our approach is to glean what may be useful to interpreters for meeting the needs of the public. His theory suggested that people have a hierarchy of needs or drives. He began with basic needs—physiological needs such as air, food, water, and sleep. Then, as people meet these *survival needs*, they move up to more sophisticated and socially oriented needs such as identifying with a group, being accepted and loved. After satisfying these needs of *social belonging*, a person may escalate to needs for *esteem* and *self-actualization*.

The basic physiological needs of survival tend to dominate a person's attention as long as they remain unmet, according to Maslow. If you are starving, your drive for food may override your need for social approval or intellectual satisfaction. That doesn't imply that a hungry person does not have other needs. It just suggests that satisfying acute hunger takes top priority.

The simplest characterization of Maslow's concept is to break the levels into two groups:

1. Basic needs
   - Physiological requirements such as air, food, water, and sleep
   - Safety needs
   - Security needs
2. Growth needs
   - Love and belonging
   - Esteem
   - Self-actualization

Although the desire for self-actualization is the pinnacle of growth motivations and is universal in people, Maslow thought it difficult to attain because it depends on the lower needs being met. He said only about one person in ten is *primarily* motivated by self-actualization needs. Most are lower on the hierarchy, being preoccupied by trying to satisfy esteem, love, or security drives. Box 3.1 presents ways interpreters can meet the needs of visitors regardless of their place in Maslow's theoretical framework.

Maslow (1962) referred to self-actualization experiences as "moments of highest happiness." Such optimal or "peak" experiences include feelings of exhilaration and deep enjoyment. They occur when our bodies and minds voluntarily stretch to their limits to accomplish something worthwhile (Csikszentmihalyi, 1990). Beck (1991) found that the characteristics of "peak" experiences attained by wilderness recreationists at Canyonlands National Park coincided with those reported by social scientists (e.g., Csikszentmihalyi, 1990; Maslow, 1962; Panzarella, 1980). Interpretation often facilitates the realization of these powerful and enriching experiences (Beck, 1993). According to Csikszentmihalyi (1990), any gain in promoting opportunities for optimal experiences will make life more enjoyable and more meaningful.

More recent research using a smartphone app that signals participants at random moments, and using GPS to determine geographical coordinates, indicated that participants were happiest in natural habitats (MacKerron & Mourato, 2013). These findings are consistent with research by Dacher Keltner and his associates who have studied the emotion of awe that most often occurs in nature (Green & Keltner, 2017; Keltner, 2016; Keltner & Haidt, 2003).

A great deal of work has been done with children and their relationship to natural environments (see Louv, 2005). For example, a park/school program developed by Urban Resources Initiative at Yale University's School of Forestry and Environmental Studies involved urban park rangers and teachers. It produced personal growth of inner-city fifth graders at several levels of Maslow's hierarchy (Milton, Cleveland, & Bennett-Gates, 1995). The children gained knowledge of forest ecology. Anxieties related to group participation diminished. Children seemed to gain self-esteem. They improved their social skills, showing increasing levels of respect to the adults, exhibiting more cooperation on their own, and increasing teamwork efficiency. Aspects of the program made the children feel "special" and more willing to take on new challenges. After completing the program, students felt more connected to the park, the park rangers, the project coordinator, and their teachers.

Box 3.1
Expanded Levels of Visitor Needs and How Interpreters Can Meet Them

Levels of Need	How Interpreters Can Meet Visitor Needs
Self-actualization	Help visitors to develop interpretive materials from their own perspectives. Provide resources for independent exploration and research.
Aesthetic	Offer seminars and training with experts related to visitor interests. Lead guided walks to places of special or unusual aesthetic interest. Hold art, photo, and writing exhibitions among visitors. Bring in artists, poets, and musicians to talk to and work with visitors.
Understanding	Provide for continued study in areas of visitor interest and ability. Provide access to reports, plans, and budgets; answer inquiries about policy, science, and regulations; post key questions and responses for all to see. Provide interpretive exercises, experiments, activities, and tasks for visitors to pursue on their own time.
Knowledge	Provide access to data and diverse library resources. Set up times for interpreters and managers to talk with visitors informally. Arrange for visitors to see practical applications of principles, concepts, and ideas.
Esteem	Recognize visitor achievements on bulletin boards, in park newsletters, on the park website, and at campfire programs. Give some visitors active roles on walks, at campfires, and during slide shows.
Love and belonging	Call the visitor by name—ask for it and use it. Make clear your pleasure in working with visitors and with each individual. Visit the campground and other gathering places to welcome visitors and invite their participation, prior to interpretive programs.
Safety and security	Publish and explain key security policies and follow them consistently. Provide consistent safety measures; project firmness and competence. Have trained first-aid personnel and equipment available.
Physiological needs	Check visitors for proper clothing, water, food, and protection at start of hikes or similar events. Provide for sanitation needs and a healthy environment. Announce times, locations, and strenuousness of program activities.

Where the interpreter has the luxury of repeat visitors, opportunities for a long-term visitor growth process exist. For example, a community nature center or historical museum often has life members who presumably seek interpretive benefits year after year. A progressive curriculum of reading, events, and skill lessons could enhance their pleasure and intrigue with their surroundings all through their membership. Within this framework, an interpreter can set long-term goals and then specify targets for each client. Thus, the interpreter serves as a professional guide and counselor to the longtime member, offering stepwise progression through a menu of scaled interpretive opportunities. The interpreter's job becomes more than a series of talks, exhibits, and newsletters. It helps clients become experts at subjects such as local history, pioneer gardening, astronomy, nature study, or practical skills and crafts. Clients may even become partners to the interpreter, leading workshops and demonstrations.

Benefits to Society

In addition to benefits accruing to individuals from quality interpretation, collective benefits also accrue to society. Besides providing broad individual benefits, interpretation serves the *public* welfare. Interpretation contributes values associated with improved family, community unity, and stability. Even decreased crime and higher rehabilitation rates seem to correlate with the availability of recreational opportunities.

There is a history of interest within public agencies to provide a service component to the populace that includes meaningful recreational opportunities and better understanding of our heritage. For example, the California Legislature recognized that interpretation serves to improve social values and further promotes awareness and understanding of California's rich multicultural heritage. More linkages are needed to relate today's cultural diversity to past events. Each group's unique contributions should be recognized.

Museums also encourage diverse segments of a local population to broaden their own sense of the community: our home, not just where we live for now. In this way, museums enrich lives with a deeper perspective of community value, continuity, and change. Leaders in the museum profession advocate more interaction with all peoples in a community. Museums may have their highest value as places of community construction.

> "Our parks and cultural landscapes contribute to positive health conditions."

Health Values

Our parks and cultural landscapes contribute to positive health conditions by providing places for physical exercise, relaxation and inspiration, and gathering places for families and friends. Yet the values of parks extend beyond the individual to a healthy *society*. The National Park Service launched the Healthy Parks, Healthy People initiative as "a holistic approach to promoting the health and wellbeing of all species and the planet we share" (NPS, 2013). Parks provide unique resources for practicing healthy lifestyles in the areas of programs, facilities, and environments (Figure 3.4). Programs may include interpretive offerings such as guided walks and hikes. Facilities may include places to purchase healthy food and drink, and perhaps bicycle or canoe rentals. Environments include lakes, rivers, and trails where activity can result in positive physical, mental, and social health benefits. Furthermore, human health is linked to the health of natural landscapes and all species. The NPS commitment to improving public health is also mirrored in internal programs for its workforce (NPS, 2013).

Dan Dustin has spent four decades teaching and writing in the broad areas of parks, environmental ethics, outdoor recreation planning and policy, and professional issues with 10 books that he has authored, co-authored, or edited on these subjects.

A professor at the University of Utah, he currently teaches a course titled "Healthy Parks, Healthy People." In addition to cultural and natural resources, our parks offer health resources as the medical profession shifts its orientation from treatment to prevention. Benefits accrue on an individual level, but also lend toward a healthier society and ultimately healthier ecosystems to include all species (Box 3.2).

Richard Louv coined the term "nature deficit disorder" to highlight the broken bond between people and the natural environment. The removal of people from nature—and especially with more time spent with various screen technologies—has physical, psychological, social, spiritual, and environmental implications. Louv's work focused first on children (2005), then adults (2011), and most recently on the community as a whole (2016). To avoid "nature deficit disorder" people can immerse themselves in natural environments such as parks.

Figure 3.4. Visitors are encouraged to get physical exercise and enjoy the beauty of Bryce Canyon National Park through the "I Hiked the Hoodoos" challenge. (LB)

In 2017, a landmark studied was published, titled "The Nature of Americans: Disconnection and Recommendations for Reconnection," headed by a research team including Stephen Kellert of Yale University. In this report, the researchers determined that the "vast majority of adult Americans surveyed reported that nature is highly important for their physical health and emotional outlook" (Kellert et al., 2017). The results further noted that being in nature brought adults among their happiest memories, a sense of peacefulness, and provided them with meaning and purpose. Similarly, contact with nature by children "made them happier and healthier and deepened their relationships" (Kellert et al., 2017).

For our society, a lack of activity is often associated with obesity, diabetes, heart disease, cancer, and other debilitating diseases. On April 24, 2016, the National Park Service launched its first National Park Rx Day Celebration to promote the growing movement of prescribing parks and nature to patients to improve their health. With health implications in mind, interpreters can promote activities that contribute to physical and mental health, and social well-being.

Even museums are sponsoring events that promote physical health. For example, in 2017, New York City's Metropolitan Museum of Art began holding morning workout sessions sending people in exercise gear chugging through 35 galleries. In between, participants engage in jumping jacks, squats, and other exercises, as well as yoga poses, all to a soundtrack of uplifting music. These events occur prior to opening hours to the public. The museum team noted that it worked "obsessively" in calculating how to keep a safe distance from the artworks. Although running against the culture of being in a museum, quiet and still and walking slowly, these events (known as "The Museum Workout") have been extraordinarily popular, selling out months in advance. Museums also can address mental health issues. In Great Britain, the House of Memories is a museums-led initiative launched by National Museums Liverpool that provides dementia care training and skills development for social workers and healthcare professionals.

Box 3.2
Greening Health

Dan Dustin, Professor, University of Utah

While the field of parks, recreation, and tourism has always been appreciated for its contributions to the aesthetic side of life, its contributions to health promotion are just now beginning to receive the attention they deserve. Given mounting social healthcare costs associated with a growing and longer living populace, the preventative and rehabilitative power nested in park, recreation, and touristic experiences is gradually being factored into the equation when assessing the field's overall role in contributing to the quality of life for humans and non-humans alike.

Rooted in humankind's long evolutionary history embedded in nature, the idea that we humans have an innate affinity for nature, that nature delivers health promoting benefits to our species, and that we are biologically "wired" to receive those benefits through encounters with nature, is rapidly gaining scientific credibility. Beginning with Roger Ulrich's (1984) now famous study of patients recovering from surgery quicker when afforded a room with a view unto nature as opposed to a view unto the built environment, scientists in a variety of fields, ranging from environmental psychology to architecture to various allied health professions, have begun to document nature's resiliency-building and restorative properties. From the physiological benefits of physical activity in natural settings (obesity reduction, lowered blood pressure, heart disease prevention) to the mental health benefits associated with immersion in outdoor settings (stress mediation, directed attention restoration, mood elevation, anxiety relief, depression reduction), to the social benefits stemming from family-based outings in nature (improved family cohesion and functioning), the message is increasingly clear—encounters with nature constitute a wellspring for the physical and mental health and well-being of individuals and groups, especially for a culture that is increasingly urban and detached from its biological moorings. We are also learning that while nature's health promoting properties benefit people in general, they have particular therapeutic value for people afflicted with various debilitating conditions, including physical, cognitive, and emotional maladies, such as combat-related posttraumatic stress disorder (Dustin et al., 2016). What we are beginning to acknowledge, then, is that parks, recreation, and tourism are not just about aesthetically pleasing leisure time engagements. They are also fundamentally about health promotion.

Underpinning this newly studied relationship between human health and nature-based experiences is an ecologic view of health that proceeds from the assumption that human beings are part of nature, are subject to nature's laws, and are obliged to conduct themselves in a way that benefits the larger community of life. From this perspective, humans are neither separate from nor superior to nature, and nature is not seen as having value only to the extent it serves human purposes. Rather, nature is viewed as a living library of evolutionary wisdom that can teach us how to live our lives in a socially and environmentally responsible manner. Moreover, health, from an ecological perspective, is a measure of the wellness of the individual and the community considered together. The individual cannot be healthy independent of the condition of the larger community, and the larger community cannot be healthy independent of the condition of the individuals constituting it. Healthy individuals require healthy families, healthy families require healthy communities, healthy communities require healthy nations, and healthy nations require a healthy planet. Health, at its core, is symbiotic in nature.

Box 3.2 continued

This ecological approach to health promotion frames the interconnectedness and interdependence of the natural and physical attributes of the world into a more coherent and systematic pattern of understanding. It illustrates the harmonious potential that should define humankind's relationship with the larger living world. As Figure A shows, there is a strong symbiotic relationship between ecosystem health and the health of the functional units that make up ecosystems, including humans. The model recognizes the role humans play in affecting ecosystems as well as ecosystem effects on humans. The emphasis is on sustaining the health of the planet as a whole as well as its interdependent parts.

Figure A
Ecological Model of Health Promotion

*Adapted from Dustin, D., Bricker, K., & Schwab, K. (2010). People and nature: Toward an ecological model of health promotion. *Leisure Science, 32*(1), 3–14.

Full citations for the references in this box are provided at the end of the chapter under Literature Cited.

Civics and Interpretation

Interpretation contributes several specific values in the civic operations of society. They include (a) information for democratic decision-making, (b) identity with our land and culture, and (c) an ethical sense of our place in history and our role in the world.

Democracy requires an informed public. Knowledge is vital in a democratic setting, where the people make the fundamental decisions, either on policy or on the choice of those who shall make the policy. The founding fathers of the United States recognized the needs for a well-informed public to sustain the governing principles of the new republic. They sponsored western exploration and interpretation of its results (e.g., Lewis and Clark) as well as many scientific inquiries. The detailed knowledge about animals and plants that came from these trips became the common legacy of the nation. Thomas Jefferson, in 1820, sought to spread the benefits of natural history work beyond the scientific world to include the civic education of the nation's citizens. He stated:

> **Democracy requires an informed public.**

> I know of no safe depository of the ultimate powers of the society but the people themselves, and if we think them not enlightened enough to exercise that control with a wholesome discretion, the remedy is not to take it from them, but to inform their discretion.

To this end, Jefferson sponsored public museums and libraries.

The same has happened in British society. The regents have sponsored museums and public libraries to encourage an informed populace. In the British case, the emphasis was often on educating about the entire globe-circling empire and its many varieties of people, plants, animals, and ecological conditions. These (British and other) museums and their learned societies were associated directly with much of the remarkable scientific discovery and discourse through the past two centuries.

Gilbert Grosvenor, in a brief talk before the 75th anniversary celebration of the U.S. National Park Service, recalled that we are all neighbors on planet Earth. We face many critical issues of public policy and action. Yet, the average American voter knows little about the issues. The public must see that parks are connected to the rest of the world. Parks are show places where people can see why and where things happen in this natural world that supports humankind.

Educating society does not happen only in schools. Parks, forests, refuges, zoos, camps, and museums also serve as classrooms. As one example, the U.S. National Park Service has more than 400 parks that can teach us about our present and our past through their Parks as Classrooms initiative. Thousands of other interpretive sites also play a role in educating people about our planet and past.

Former Secretary of Education Lamar Alexander (1991) noted that education will not change by recipe, program, or formula. He recalled visiting an African community where the people in the village trained each child. An elder commented that it takes an entire village to educate one child. It seems sensible that all "villages" should include outdoor classrooms, where naturalists and historians help with educating the children—and the adults.

Identifying with land and culture helps to sustain a society. Literary and artistic interpretation of the natural landscape played a major role in developing national identity in the United States. In the 1800s, hundreds of artists and writers expressed this land's natural beauty. The American landscape became a wellspring of nationalism. What America lacked in comparison with Europe's rich human culture was made up for in wild grandeur and scenery (Nash, 1982).

> **Identifying with land and culture helps to sustain a society.**

The features of the wild environment enriched the image of North America. The people accepted the notion that providence had specially blessed and endowed these nations and their peoples.

The citizens of any nation need to identify with the landscape and its natural and cultural resources. This helps them to feel part of the nation and thereby promotes unity and a sense of belonging. National identity and pride grow from a sense of place, the special qualities of the immediate surroundings and the people inhabiting them (Youngblood, 2004). This healthy pride may prevent foolish actions that could destroy the special resources of a nation. It may increase comprehension of the consequences of individual acts or community proposals. Urban children who grow up terrified of real and imagined things out in the unknown woods could someday destroy those unfamiliar haunts of perceived dangers. Likewise, if they never learn to enjoy the diversity of their fellow citizens' customs, styles, and attitudes, they may be intolerant of those who are different and therefore perceive them as dangerous. The same children, taught the secrets of the woods and the meanings of cultural variety by first hand interpretive experiences, often become the protectors of these resources and diversity, now internalized as part of *their* heritage.

> "National identity and pride grow from a sense of place."

A remarkable example exists in Indonesia's interpretation of its cultural identity as a unique blending of many traditions. The Mini-Indonesia park near Jakarta features the customs, clothing, environment, and architecture of the many different cultural components of the nation in a beautiful setting. This elegant folk museum unites the diversity in a most impressive, positive learning experience for Indonesians and visitors from abroad. Further, Indonesia's national parks and wildlife reserves conserve natural areas, even on densely populated Java and Bali. These reserves allow people to learn of their natural heritage through a vigorous interpretation program.

During times of national crises and trauma, interpretation of nature and culture becomes more than a positive diversion. It becomes an antidote to despair, providing solace and comfort that derives from finding understanding and meaning in the refrains of nature and history (Beck & Cable, 2011). Appreciation of their cultural and natural legacy inspires citizens to push ahead to seek personal fulfillment while contributing to the richness of their communities and nation. Attendance rose dramatically in many museums, state parks, and national parks after the terrorism of September 11, 2001, illustrating the powerful potential and responsibility that interpretation has in healing a society.

Interpreters help people to develop an ethical sense of their place and role in the world. Interpreters offer understanding and appreciation of our place and role in the world. They give people facts and experiences so they care enough to help make the story turn out right. James Gustave Speth (2012) wrote, "We need a compelling vision for a new future, a vision of a better country—America the Possible—that is still within our power to reach." Interpretation can help rouse people, with facts instead of propaganda, and point the way to constructive and intelligent action.

> "Interpreters help people to develop an ethical sense of their place and role in the world."

Interpreters already work in the front ranks to make society aware of the facts and opinions about the potential risks of global climate change, loss of biodiversity, and habitat alteration and destruction. At professional workshops, special sessions present methods of interpreting these issues objectively with discussions of the technical and political implications surrounding them (Covel, 2015).

Interpreters encourage people to see the world as interconnected and diverse. They show examples of our ability to alter the planet's life support systems. They encourage taking responsibility as stewards for the natural world. They clarify the debates that rage over these issues. They offer experience in the natural world to build the practical framework to better perceive the problems and study alternative solutions.

Perhaps the most fundamental need for interpretation arises from the "metaphysical and ethical need" of humans to know our place and role in the natural world and in the story of human history and culture (Marris, 2015). We need stories of where we are, of what *really* happened once upon a time. We need to learn the meanings of these events for the present and future. We need to study the natural history and ecology of the many species that co-habit the planet with us, and the natural processes that control our destiny as a species. We need to hear the stories and recognize the intrinsic worth of other people and species (Figure 3.5). We need to know the successes and failures of human history and a sense of how we might improve.

> Interpreters encourage people to see the world as interconnected and diverse.

Summary

Interpretation provides benefits to individuals that are educational, recreational, and inspirational. Especially when these all come together individuals may attain "peak" experiences. In addition, interpretation provides benefits to society. People practice healthy lifestyles at interpretive sites through available programs and facilities. Healthy individuals make up a healthy society. Furthermore, interpretation provides knowledge and experiences for democratic decision-making, helps people to identify with their land and culture, and provides an ethical sense of place.

Figure 3.5. Interpretation helps people develop an ethical sense of our place in the world and a respect for the plants and animals that share our planet. (TC)

Interpreters contribute to learning the art of life by offering rich, enjoyable, and informative experiences. Interpreters point out the handholds and footholds, the facts and frameworks, that help people to better perceive and make their way through this complex, dynamic home of ours. This historical perspective, the natural phenomena, and the ability to perceive them in context can touch the hearts and minds of people and change the story of our world.

Helping to guide the way we live in this world is a tall order and high calling. It is not only a worthy endeavor, but also a plausible and vital one that makes a difference. The interpreter's message spreads and multiplies from individuals to society at large. Ultimately, interpreters help people to identify with their land and culture, and develop a moral sense of their place in the larger scheme of things, making for a better world.

> "When we enter places of grandeur and sites of suffering, and inhabit landscapes of historical import and ecological splendor, we stand on the periphery of awe. How did this happen? Who were the witnesses? And what are we seeing now?"
>
> –Terry Tempest Williams

You Never Know

> You never know when someone
> may catch a dream from you…
> You never know when a little word
> or something you may do
> may open up the windows of a mind
> that seeks the light…
> The way you live may not matter at all
> but you never know, it might …
> and just in case it could be
> that another's life through you,
> might possibly change for the better
> with a broader and brighter view,
> it seems it might be worth a try
> at pointing the way to the light…
> Of course, it may not matter at all,
> but then again, it might!
>
> –Author unknown (Contributed by Susan Fowler)

Literature Cited

Alexander, L. (1991). *Address to 75th Anniversary Symposium of the National Park Service.* Vail, CO.

Beck, L. (1991). Promoting opportunities for optimal experiences in nature. *Journal of Recreation and Leisure, 11,* 76–83.

Beck, L. (1993). Optimal experiences in nature: Implications for interpreters. *Legacy, 4*(1), 27–30.

Beck, L., & Cable, T. (2010). *Interpretive perspectives: A collection of essays on interpreting nature and culture.* Fort Collins, CO: National Association for Interpretation.

Beck, L., & Cable, T. (2011). *The gifts of interpretation: Fifteen guiding principles for interpreting nature and culture* (3rd ed.). Urbana, IL: Sagamore.

Beck, L., Walkosz, B., Andersen, P., Abbott, A., Buller, D., Scott, M., & Eye, R. (2015). Communication strategies to promote health: Sun safety in outdoor recreation settings. *Journal of Interpretation Research, 20*(2), 41–50.

Burroughs, J. (1916). *Under the apple trees.* New York, NY: William H. Wise & Co.

Cable, T. (1992). To enjoy understandingly. *Legacy, 3*(2), 8–9.

Covel, J. (2015). Evaluating the effectiveness of certified interpretive guide training for climate change interpretation. *2015 Interpretive Sourcebook.* National Association for Interpretation Workshop, Virginia Beach, VA, November 10-14, 2015.

Csikszentmihalyi, M. (1990). *Flow: The psychology of optimal experience.* New York, NY: Harper & Row.

Dustin, D., Bricker, K., Negley, S., Brownlee, M., Schwab, K., & Lundberg, N. (Eds.). (2016). *This land is your land: Toward a better understanding of nature's resiliency-building and restorative power for armed forces personnel, veterans, and their families.* Urbana, IL: Sagamore.

Dustin, D., McAvoy, L., & Beck, L. (1986). Promoting recreationist self-sufficiency. *Journal of Park and Recreation Administration, 4*(4), 43–52.

Green, K., & Keltner, D. (2017). What happens when we reconnect with nature. *Greater Good: The Science of a Meaningful Life.* March 1, 2017.

Grosvenor, G. (1991). *Comments to 75th Anniversary Symposium of the National Park Service.* Vail, CO.

Kellert, S., Case, D., Escher, D., Witter, D., Mikels-Carrasco, J., & Seng, P. (2017). *The nature of Americans: Disconnection and recommendations for reconnection.* Retrieved from https://natureofamericans.org/

Keltner, D. (2016). Why do we feel awe? *Greater good: The science of a meaningful life.* May 10, 2016.

Keltner, D., & Haidt, J. (2003). Approaching awe, a moral, spiritual, and aesthetic emotion. *Cognition and Emotion, 17,* 297–314.

Leopold, A. (1966). *A Sand County almanac.* New York, NY: Oxford University Press.

Louv, R. (2005). *Last child in the woods: Saving our children from nature-deficit disorder.* Chapel Hill, NC: Algonquin Books of Chapel Hill.

Louv, R. (2011). *The nature principle: Human restoration and the end of nature-deficit disorder.* Chapel Hill, NC: Algonquin Books of Chapel Hill.

Louv, R. (2016). *Vitamin N: The essential guide to a nature-rich life.* Chapel Hill, NC: Algonquin Books of Chapel Hill.

MacKinnon, J. B. (2015). Facing fear: How nature cured one man's anxious mind. *Orion,* May/June, 52–55.

MacKerron, G., & Mourato, S. (2013). Happiness is greater in natural environments. *Global Environmental Change,* 23(5), 992–1000.

Marris, E. (2015). Handle with care: The case for doing all we can to save threatened species. *Orion,* May/June, 22–26.

Maslow, A. (1954). *Motivation and personality.* New York, NY: Harper & Row.

Maslow, A. (1962). Lessons from the peak experiences. *Journal of Humanistic Psychology,* 2(1), 9–18.

Mills, E. (1920). *Adventures of a nature guide.* Garden City, NY: Doubleday, Page & Co.

Milton, B., Cleveland, E., & Bennett-Gates, D. (1995). Changing perceptions of nature, self, and others: A report on a park/school program. *Journal of Environmental Education,* 26(3), 32–39.

Myers, J. (2008). The health benefits and economics of physical activity. *Current Sports Medicine Reports,* 7(6), 314–316.

Nash, R. (1982). *Wilderness and the American mind* (3rd ed.). New Haven, CT: Yale University Press.

National Park Service. (2013). *The national parks and public health: A NPS healthy park, healthy people science plan.* U.S. Department of the Interior. July 2013.

Panzarella, R. (1980). The phenomenology of aesthetic peak experiences. *Journal of Humanistic Psychology,* 20(1), 69–85.

Saxena, S., van Ommeren, M., Tang, K., & Armstrong, T. (2005). Mental health benefits of physical activity. *Journal of Mental Health,* 14(5), 445–451.

Schwab, K., Dustin, D., & Bricker, K. (2009). Parks, recreation and tourism's contributions to Utah's health: An ecologic perspective. *Leisure Insights,* 29(1),12–14.

Speth, J. G. (2012). America the possible: A manifesto, Part II. *Orion,* May/June, 62–69.

Tilden, F. (1967). *Interpreting our heritage* (Rev. ed.). Chapel Hill, NC: University of North Carolina Press.

Ulrich, R. (1984). View through a window may influence recovery from surgery. *Science,* 224, 420–421.

Youngblood, L. (2004). A sense of place. *Legacy,* 15(4), 8–9.

CHAPTER 4
Values of Interpretation for Management

We have all heard the excuse, "With everything we have to do, we don't have time for education and interpretation!" According to Patrick Barry, retired Corps of Engineers ranger, people who say this do not realize that doing interpretation now may save time and more importantly, people. As an interpreter involved in outdoor recreation, among the worst tasks one may have to assist with is a "search and rescue" effort. These events can be dangerous and take considerable time. They can be emotionally taxing for rescuers as well as family members and friends of the person being rescued. Could effective interpretation make a difference? Barry provides the following four examples of how the Corps has used safety campaigns to achieve its management goal of visitor protection.

- During an evening program, Jonathan Friedman, a Corps park ranger at Lake Kaweah in California, described what people look like while drowning. The next day, a woman who had attended the program saw two girls drowning. With help from another person, she saved the girls. She said she knew they were drowning only because she attended Jonathan's interpretive program.
- Using tips she learned in a water safety class, a 10-year-old saved her 8-year-old cousin after he fell off a fishing dock into Lake Leon in Texas. She remembered what she learned from Tim Horn, when the Corps park ranger visited her school. He taught the children to "reach or throw, but don't go."
- For many years, one or two anglers drowned each year because of improper anchoring in the deep, cold, and fast-moving currents of the Columbia River downstream of Bonneville Lock and Dam. Brian McCavitt and other Corps park rangers started a multi-faceted safe anchoring campaign, using flyers, posters, a video, and even bumper stickers. There have been no anchoring-related fatalities for more than 15 years since these interpretive efforts have been in place.
- At Berlin Lake in Ohio, one visitor drowned and another became paralyzed after hitting rocks below a popular rope swing near a campground. For years, the Corps cut down the swings, only to find them replaced again by visitors. Rangers verbally informed people that were using the swings of the dangers and issued written warnings, but accidents still occurred. People stopped using the rope swing after park ranger Julie Stone created a compelling interpretive sign warning of the dangers at that location.

Spending time planning and implementing interpretive efforts is a more efficient use of time, money, and energy than writing violation notices, filling out incident reports, or searching for drowning victims. So, Barry advises that if you hear the excuse, "We don't have time to do interpretation," suggest that they think about the alternative.

As noted in Chapter 1, the definition of interpretation as adopted by the National Association for Interpretation begins with the words "A *mission-based* communication process." Over many decades, interpretation has proven to be a powerful tool in helping managers achieve their missions and increase public support for that mission. Long before NAI adopted that definition, Freeman Tilden stumbled upon a statement in a National Park Service Manual that articulates the link between interpretation and the manager's concern about protecting the resource. Tilden (1957) wrote the following:

> I find in the Park Service Administrative Manual a concise and profound statement, and my heartiest thanks go to whoever it was that phrased it: "Through interpretation, understanding; through understanding, appreciation; through appreciation, protection."

As this slogan implies, interpretation plays a vital role in the mission of protecting natural and cultural resources. Interpretation provokes people to know, understand, and appreciate a place, a historic event, or a culture. Eventually, through interpretation, individuals may come to love a place or people. With love comes a desire to nurture and maintain. People must care *about*, before they care *for*.

When we speak of using interpretation as a management tool, we refer to shifting people's behavior to support stewardship of cultural or natural resources. Interpreters may discourage vandalism and littering, encourage financial support of a museum, or enhance political support of park-related policies or legislation by providing the scientific evidence and reasoning that went into the decision-making processes. Also, as seen in the introductory story, interpretation can keep people safe as they enjoy the outdoors.

> People must care *about*, before they care *for*.

A Tool with a History

"The evolution of the field suggests the primary emphasis of interpretation is that it is designed to 'make a difference on purpose.'"

—Sam Ham

> Stephen Mather perhaps was the earliest to recognize agency benefits from interpretation.

National Park Service Director Stephen Mather perhaps was the earliest to recognize agency benefits from interpretation. When Mather decided in 1919 to hire interpreters into the national parks, he explained the action in terms of resource protection: to "counteract those persons who would selfishly destroy park values" (Weaver, 1982). Similarly, the U.S. Forest Service initial impetus for the Visitor Information Service came from a need to generate support for forest management policy.

Chief of Interpretation for the National Park Service, William Dunmire (1976) wrote, "Interpretation should be employed by management as the primary means of achieving all management objectives directly affecting the public." He further remarked that he had little difficulty persuading managers in the field to place interpretation high in their priorities. Rather, he found it most difficult to persuade the budget examiner and others far removed from the resources (Dunmire, 1976). Managers at state and county parks and federal wildlife refuges also overwhelmingly supported interpretation as a management tool (Cable & Knudson, 1983) as did practicing interpreters (Hooper & Weiss, 1990).

In the 1990s, the Authority of the Resource Technique (ART) became a widely used approach to improve compliance with regulations in wilderness and other protected areas. In applying ART, park rangers combine law enforcement with interpretation. Rather than merely citing the authority of the agency in giving out citations, fines, or warnings, ART educates the offender about ethical behavior in natural areas. The interpretation of the reason for the regulation and the natural authority of the resource is specific, interactive, and personal. The reasons behind regulations or ethical behaviors can be interpreted in ways that are interesting, enlightening, and persuasive (Wallace & Gaudry, 2002).

Historical, cultural, and natural resource agencies still look to interpretation for help with management problems. The U.S. Fish & Wildlife Service website (fws.gov) notes:

> "Historical, cultural, and natural resource agencies still look to interpretation for help with management problems."

> Well-designed interpretive programs can be effective resource management tools. For many visitors, taking part in an interpretive program may be their primary contact with a refuge, the Refuge System, and the Service.… Through these contacts, we have the opportunity to influence visitor attitudes about natural resources, refuges, the Refuge System, and the Service and to influence visitor behavior when visiting units of the Refuge System.

Success Stories

Sharpe and Gensler (1978) were among the first to present an overview of interpretation as a management tool. They gave examples of interpretation having been used to decrease vandalism, poaching, and other depreciative behaviors such as souvenir collecting and unauthorized motor bike use. They also noted that interpretation could increase the social carrying capacity of a site by redistributing and softening use, increase visitor safety, and increase public support for policies and management practices. Their collection of success stories illustrated that interpretation could indeed effectively address specific management problems. The following is a sample of success stories found in the research literature arranged by the benefit provided to managers. These examples demonstrate the breadth of benefits from interpretation.

Resource Protection

Roggenbuck and Berrier (1982) documented successful dispersal of wilderness campers using brochures and personal contact. In a Corps of Engineers study, distributing an interpretive brochure about low-impact camping reduced tree damage and littering in campsites by 50%. When this brochure was distributed through personal contact, a reduction of about 80% was achieved (Oliver, Roggenbuck, & Watson, 1985). At Shiloh National Military Park, Vander Stoep and Gramann (1987) documented a decrease in depreciative behavior along trails as a result of interpretive messages personally delivered to youth groups. Wagstaff and Wilson (1988) found that verbal appeals and role modeling reduced litter from river recreationists.

Interpretation increased awareness and protection of endangered species such as the red-cockaded woodpecker (Kulhavy & Costa, 1990). In Hawaii, interpretation lessened impacts of recreational use on coral reefs and improved visitor safety in Hanauma Bay (King & Tabata, 1992). Establishment of a visitor information center offering posters, displays, and videos resulted in a reduction of deliberate touching of dolphins and other inappropriate behaviors during dolphin feeding sessions at the Tangalooma Moreon Island Resort in Australia (Orams & Hill, 1998). Trailhead signs and a brochure reduced theft of pumice at Mt. St. Helens (Martin, 1992), and three interventions (a sign, a pledge card, and presence of a uniformed volunteer) each significantly reduced the theft of petrified wood from Petrified Forest National Park (Widner & Roggenbuck, 2000; Widner & Roggenbuck, 2003).

Twenty-first century examples of interpretation being used to protect the resource include reducing off-trail hiking at Canada's St. Lawrence Islands National Park (Bradford & McIntyre, 2007) and Sequoia and Kings Canyon National Parks (Winter, 2006). One study showed reductions in deer feeding at Shenandoah National Park (Hockett & Hall, 2007) in which researchers found that both fear appeals (deer could cause harm to people) and moral appeals (feeding harms the deer) reduced self-reported frequencies of deer feeding.

At Algonquin Provincial Park in Ontario, Canada, interpreters offer Public Wolf Howls. Interpreters give a talk about wolves and then take visitors, in their cars, to a location where staff have heard a wild wolf pack the previous night. The Park has had a major impact on changing the public's attitudes towards wolves and for the importance of protected spaces (Stronks, 2010).

Another creative use of interpretation to protect the resource invites hikers to carry rocks up to the alpine tundra in New York's Adirondack Mountains. Alpine tundra is the rarest ecosystem in New York and also one of the most heavily used by recreationists. Rocks are scarce at high elevations and moving them would disturb the fragile soils. Yet, they are necessary to create rock walkways, cairns to mark the trails, and scree walls to protect fragile areas. Through the Summit Stewards program, every year hikers carry several tons of rocks to the summit with a sense of pride and stewardship (Goren, 2009).

Safety

As shown in the introductory story, the U.S. Army Corps of Engineers has been a leader in using safety campaigns to enhance water safety. The Corps use designated water safety rangers and various media including posters, decals, signs, radio broadcasts, and newspaper articles to increase compliance with boating safety rules (Figure 4.1).

> "Interpretation enhances visitor safety in many ways and can be life-saving."

Since the beginning, National Park Service interpreters have warned of such threats as dangerous plants, extreme weather conditions, chemical hazards, and risks of climbing and hiking (Cunningham, 1985). Interpretation has been used to protect people from wildlife ranging from bees (Cantrell, 1987), to bears (Lackey & Ham, 2003; Stalder & Cahill, 1992), to bison (Figure 4.2).

Public Support

In the aftermath of the 1988 Yellowstone fires, interpreters famously mitigated the bad publicity and eventually won much public understanding by explaining fire cycles and showing recuperative powers of the vegetation and soil. Similarly, a study conducted by Wiles and Hall (2005) at Mesa Verde National Park found that interpretation messages embedded in a 90-minute tour had a positive impact on visitor knowledge and attitudes about the ecological role of wildland fire in that park. The National Park Service uses interpretation at many parks throughout the U.S. to generate support for the controversial practice of prescribed burning (Evenson et al., 2010) (Figure 4.3).

A decision at Channel Island National Park to remove wild hogs from the park received public support after interpretation of the reasons and methods (Spears, 1992). Likewise, interpretation has been used to increase public acceptance of controversial urban deer herd management strategies (Broder, Fish, & McDonald, 1994).

Interpretation has been used to convince tourists to voluntarily donate money to conservation efforts. A theme-based communication campaign designed by Sam Ham for Lindblad Expeditions targeted cruise passengers in the Galapagos Islands and significantly increased donations by the passengers to the Galapagos Conservation Fund (Powell & Ham, 2008). These efforts involved interpretive panels, personal interpretation by tour guides, and pre-trip information sent to passengers.

Another management benefit is realized when interpreters acquaint folks with resources and recreational opportunities at seldom-visited historic sites, parks, or refuges. Interpreters can motivate the public to explore these sites by providing enticing information in brochures, and on television, radio, and websites about experiences offered.

Figure 4.1. U.S. Army Corps of Engineers interpreter demonstrating how to wear a personal floatation device. Interpreters can save lives by teaching important safety techniques. (USCOE).

Figure 4.2. Interpreters at Yellowstone National Park designed this effective warning about the dangers of approaching bison. (TC)

Chapter 4: Values of Interpretation for Management

Interpretation as a Management Tool: In Theory

Figure 4.3. Interpretation garners public support for prescribed burning by calling fire "a healthy prescription" at a wildlife refuge in Louisiana. (TC)

When Tilden adopted the aforementioned NPS motto linking interpretation to appreciation and protection he did not know that it had a strong theoretical basis. However, Ham (2009) evaluated the statement and found it to be supported by two popular theories of persuasion and behavior; the Elaboration Likelihood Model of Persuasion and the Theory of Planned Behavior. These theories help us understand when, how, and why interpretation succeeds as a management tool.

Overviews of these two helpful theories are presented below, along with a third theory, The Self-Perception Theory, that takes a different approach in explaining relationships between attitudes and behavior.

Elaboration Likelihood Model

Tilden's bold principle that "the chief aim of interpretation is not instruction, but provocation" clearly implies that interpreters often want to persuade people to think or act differently. This certainly is the case when interpretation is being used as a management tool. The Elaboration Likelihood Model (ELM) proposes two routes to persuasion. The "central route" involves mindful thinking whereby the person "draws upon prior experience and knowledge to scrutinize and evaluate the issue-relevant arguments presented in the communication" (Petty, McMichael & Brannon, 1992). This "elaboration" or additional thinking on the persuasive interpretive message requires a visitor to do the following:

- Pay attention to the message (receive it attentively).
- Call upon memory to *relate* the message to experiences and to make associations.
- Make inferences from the message.
- Personally evaluate the merits of the message to accept or reject it.

Visitors must have both the motivation and ability to process the merits of the message and accept or reject it (Petty, McMichael, & Brannon, 1992). This is the interpretive goal associated with Tilden's first and second principles calling for interpreters to motivate audience members to contemplate the interpretive message by relating it to their past experiences and by making it understandable, relevant, and personally meaningful. The result of this central route of persuasion is an attitude that is integrated into the person's belief system. Interpreters can expect such visitor attitudes to be long-lasting, predictive of behavior, and resistant to change.

The second route of persuasion in the ELM model is the "peripheral route," whereby cues peripheral to the core message affect attitudes. For example, audience members may be persuaded based on feelings of happiness associated with reading/hearing the message, rather than a thorough, thoughtful evaluation of its merits. If visitors associate a good feeling with a particular presentation, they may adopt the desired attitude. This is the classical conditioning approach, whereby pleasing stimuli result in positive responses toward the message. People who are unable or unmotivated to *analyze* the persuasive interpretive message may take this route. For interpreters the implications of the peripheral route are as follows:

- A celebrity or charismatic interpreter who presents a particular point of view may evoke agreement (attitude change) in visitors merely because they associate the advocated position with the admired person.
- An expert interpreter will often gain adherents to an idea out of deference to the interpreter's expertise, without thinking about the merits of the message.
- If audience members perceive that a consensus exists, they often adopt the desired attitude based solely on the consensus, rather than personal analysis of the argument. If something is popular, many people will accept it as good.

Interpreters can use each of these peripheral routes to effectively change attitudes; however, these passively formed attitudes are weaker (like a plant with shallow roots). These attitudes tend to be short-lived and easily changed by contradictory messages.

For example, if interpreters want to stimulate widespread change in attitudes for a short-term campaign (e.g., to save a local historic building or wetland) they might use a celebrity spokesperson or "feel-good" special programs. Or, if a consensus exists about saving the historic building, call attention to it, encouraging people to join the crowd and lend their support. However, if interpreters want to permanently change how people value all such historic buildings or wetlands, then attempt the central route of persuasion with facts and reasoning clearly presented in a memorable way.

The ELM can guide interpretation research. For example, Manfredo and Bright (1991) used the ELM model in a study of the impact of brochures on recreationists' behavior at the Boundary Waters Canoe Area Wilderness. This study found information packets did indeed affect behavior of some canoeists through the central route of persuasion by generating thought and analyses and by introducing new beliefs.

The Theory of Planned Behavior

Interpreters have long recognized that factual knowledge alone about a policy or conservation issues does not lead to public support or stewardship. The Theory of Planned Behavior (TPB) helps interpreters understand behavior change and how they might promote it.

TPB indicates behaviors are based upon intentions to perform the behavior, and these intentions are based upon three factors (Ajzen, 1992): the person's attitude about the behavior, subjective norms (i.e., what other people think about the behavior), and the person's belief that they have control over the behavior (i.e., the ability to perform it). Interpreters can influence each of these three aspects of the theory.

- **Attitudes** are a function of personal beliefs and evaluation of the outcome of the behavior. Effective interpreters routinely change beliefs or judgments about certain behaviors, thereby potentially affecting behavior.
- **Subjective norms** are determined by beliefs about what significant others think the person should or should not do and by motivations to comply with those other people. Social or group norms and their degree of motivation on the individual to comply thus have great importance in determining behavior. Interpreters can have a powerful normative impact on behaviors. The perceived wishes of significant others may be affected by interpretive presentations and their implied or explicit normative content. Moreover, interpreters can highlight the performance of good normative behaviors to increase compliance with rules.
- **Behavioral control** is another factor in achieving behavior change. People need to believe that they control the desired behavior. Some people may believe they lack the ability to carry out the action or they believe barriers exist that prevent them from carrying out the behavior. Interpreters teach skills, encourage confidence and self-efficacy, and remove barriers to participating in the desired behavior.

It is interesting to consider that TPB applies to all reasoned behaviors, not just those related to interpretation. It might help explain your dietary behaviors or recreational pursuits. Also, the relative importance of attitudes and social norms varies with the intention; for some intentions, attitudinal considerations may be more important, while in other cases normative considerations determine the intention. Moreover, some people are generally more concerned with fitting in and being accepted or pleasing others, whereas others are driven by their own attitudes and care little about social or group norms (e.g., think of outrageous Hollywood celebrities who are constantly in the entertainment news for their non-normative appearance, clothing, or behavior). Audiences will have individuals from all along this continuum and possibly even some at the extremes. So affecting changes in attitudes *and* norms increases the likelihood of impacting more visitors.

In summary, this theory specifies that interpretive messages can and should target beliefs—*beliefs* that shape attitudes, *beliefs* regarding perceived norms, and *beliefs* regarding ability to control and change behaviors. By changing the beliefs that influence norms, attitudes, and abilities, interpreters can affect the behavior of those in their audiences. One caution in applying this theory concerns the level of specificity of attitudes and behaviors. Specific behavior changes rarely arise from general attitudes. People sometimes fail to distinguish between single actions and behavioral categories (e.g., turning down a candy bar versus going on a diet). Interpreters must be precise in their messages when targeting specific behaviors.

TPB has been used to model and provide a framework in studies evaluating the impacts of interpretation. For example, Reigner and Lawson (2009) used TPB at the Pools of 'Ohe'o in Haleakalā National Park to examine relationships among visitors' attitudes, subjective norms, and perceived control regarding exploration of tidepools, their intentions to explore, and their actual behaviors at tidepools. They also evaluated the effect of persuasive messages on visitor behavior. The successful application of TPB in this study allowed researchers to make specific recommendations to the National

Park Service about signage and specific interpretive themes to reduce visitor impacts on the tidepools.

Self-Perception Theory

An alternative theory offers a completely different perspective of the attitude-behavior linkage. "Self-perception theory" states that behavior causes attitudes—just the opposite of the relationship between attitudes and behavior proposed in the TPB.

Self-perception theory proposes that as individuals participate in a particular behavior, they develop an explanation for their behavior from observing and evaluating themselves, their beliefs, and their feelings. Freedom and choice are important to most individuals, so one tends to attribute behavior to one's own internal motivation (perceiving the choice of action was voluntary, rather than to avoid penalties or to follow the crowd unthinkingly). Over time, the individual forms beliefs and attitudes that reinforce the behavior.

In applying this theory, if park managers wanted to reduce an undesirable behavior, rather than using interpretation to educate the public about the ramifications of the behavior, they would post and enforce regulations about the behavior. Initially, some people would adopt the desired behavior out of fear of being penalized for breaking park rules. However, in time, the individual will attribute it to personal choice; eventually the person would develop attitudes and beliefs to justify that behavior.

McAvoy and Dustin (1983) made a strong case for using this approach of direct, coercive management to ensure the appropriate behavior. Direct regulation is most appropriate when vigorous enforcement of behavior is necessary due to safety or urgent resource protection concerns. In the context of Self-Perception Theory, interpretation's role as a management tool promotes the development of desired attitudes and behaviors by encouraging the internalization of existing behaviors generated by direct regulation.

Why Behavior Does Not Always Change

Traditional views of persuasion hold that six steps occur when persuasive communication results in behavior change: exposure, attention, reception, interpretation, integration, and action (Petty, McMichael, & Brannon, 1992). The persuasion process (interpretation) can break down at any of these levels. People may not see a written message and therefore not be *exposed* to it; or they may not pay *attention* to the interpretive message. Or, the message may be attended to, but not make more than a fleeting impression. If it is not committed to memory, it is not *received* and therefore it is unlikely to affect beliefs or actions. Some interpretive messages may not make sense to people as they try to personalize them. At this stage, in the context of the ELM, a person will reject the message if they do not understand it. In the context of TPB, at the *integration* stage, strong subjective norms or conflicting attitudes may exist that prevent changes, intentions, and actions. This means even if audience members are attentive and learning occurs, attitudes will not necessarily change as the new knowledge may not be integrated into existing beliefs. Moreover, when interpreters successfully change a belief, the related attitude might not change, because an attitude may be the result of several different beliefs. Finally, in terms of the TPB people must believe they have control over and ability to perform the *action*. If this belief does not exist, then the desired behavior will not be adopted. Interpreters play a key role in teaching people how to perform certain behaviors and giving them confidence that they can do it on their own. Failure at any of the six steps may prevent interpretation from changing behavior (Figure 4.4).

The inability to demonstrate a change in behavior does not necessarily indicate an unsuccessful interpretive effort. An individual can accumulate knowledge gradually. Every interpretive event won't produce radical change of mind; several beliefs may have to change before an attitude changes. Also, the audience receiving the interpretive messages may already possess the desired attitudes. In this case, interpretation reinforces these existing appropriate attitudes and behaviors.

Sometimes misguided interpretation efforts can make a visitor behavior problem worse. Robert Cialdini (1996) researched the role of norms in persuasive communications and found "descriptive norms" describing what people do actually can increase the undesirable behavior. So interpreters who make an appeal for better behavior by pointing

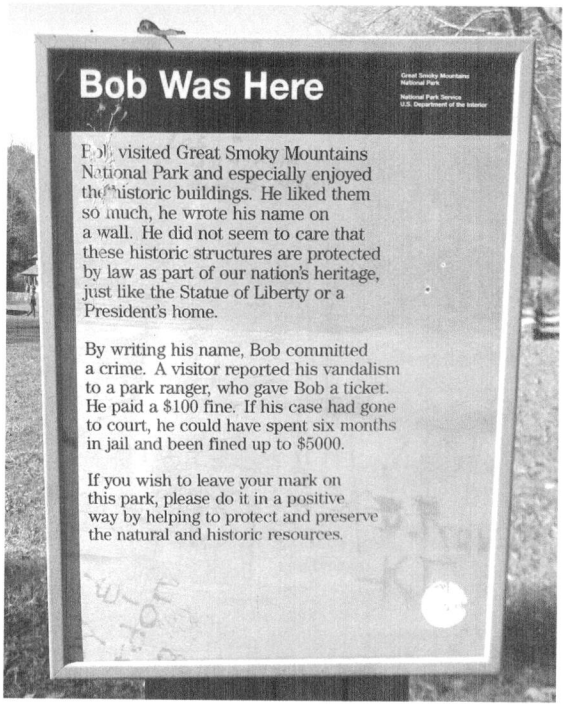

Figure 4.4. A creative approach to interpreting vandalism is itself vandalized in Cades Cove, Great Smoky Mountain National Park. (TC)

out a widespread problem and a high frequency of unwanted behavior, actually tend to increase the unwanted behavior by making it appear normative. For example, in one study, people whose attention was drawn to the widespread littering of others, littered more, not less, as a consequence of hearing this message (Cialdini, 1996). Cialdini's practical advice to interpreters is to use "injunctive norms" in their messages—meaning that by describing what most people disapprove of, interpreters can suppress undesirable actions. Rather than complaining about the violators, wise site managers now include messages making the desired behavior appear normative by communicating that the vast majority of visitors act appropriately (e.g., obey the park speed limit, stay on designated trails).

As indicated in the TPB, barriers may prevent or discourage people from adopting desired behaviors even after well-done interpretive efforts and each will require a different intervention strategy (Burn, 1996) (Figure 4.5). The emerging field of conservation psychology will continue to provide new insights into how interpreters can more effectively foster conservation behaviors in audiences.

Interpretation as a Management Tool: In Practice

As noted previously, not every application of interpretation as a management tool will produce success. Like any tool, for it to work, it must be used skillfully and prudently. Interpretation used as a management tool takes the form of persuasive communication as interpreters attempt to foster support for agency policy and stewardship of the natural or cultural resource base. The principles of effective interpretation coincide with many principles of persuasive communication. Box 4.1 borrows from practical persuasive theory to provide 13 specific tips for enhancing the effectiveness of persuasive messages.

Box 4.1
Tips for More Powerful Persuasive Messages

The following are 13 practical tips for enhancing the effectiveness of persuasive messages (from Burn, 1996).

1. The source of the message should be trustworthy.
2. The source of the message should have expertise or authority.
3. The source of the message should be likable.
4. Choose personnel with the above qualities to deliver persuasive messages at the highest use entry points.
5. Vivid dramatic information is more persuasive than factual data.
6. Emphasize the negative consequences of the behavior but point out that behavior change will be effective.
7. Emphasizing negative personal consequences (such as fines) will be ineffective unless the individual perceives a high likelihood of receiving these consequences.
8. Include information suggesting that behavior change is socially desirable.
9. Include reasons for asking that recreationists do or not do something.
10. Individuals must be told exactly how to perform desired behaviors.
11. Face-to-face communications are most persuasive
12. Make written communications direct.
13. Tailor your message to your audience.

In addition to using persuasive messages, interpreters use other strategies to influence behavior. The U.S. Forest Service published a manual offering a four-step process to curb undesirable behaviors and to provoke positive behaviors (Burn, 1996).

Step 1: Specify the problem behavior. What exactly is the problem behavior? When and where does it occur? What do you want the people to be doing instead of the bad behavior?

Step 2: Identify barriers to the performance of desired behaviors. Six categories of barriers discourage or prevent desired behaviors, each requiring a different intervention strategy to overcome the barrier (See Box 4.2).

Step 3: Design interventions based on the specific barriers operating in the setting. A variety of problem-specific interventions should be applied because one single intervention may not be effective with everyone.

Figure 4.5. Providing binoculars and field guides removes the barrier of not having the equipment to observe and identify wildlife. (TC)

Step 4: Implement interventions. List chronologically the tasks necessary to implement the intervention and set target dates for completion of those tasks. Then begin applying interventions.

This U.S. Forest Service approach to changing undesirable behavior can function well in circumstances that interpreters face in historic sites, zoos, museums, refuges, or other sites.

Box 4.2
Six Barriers to Appropriate Visitor Behavior and Suggested Interventions

People have reasons for failing to behave appropriately. Based on the theories presented in the text, interpreters can counter those reasons to encourage better behavior (from Burn, 1996).

1. **Social norms may specify competing behaviors. Visitors may get their ideas about what is acceptable or socially correct from other visitors.**
   - Construct signs that prompt "good" norms and override "bad" ones.
   - Clean up and rehabilitate degraded areas as quickly as possible.
   - Use live role models.
   - Enlist the help of respected and influential group members in cases where the undesired behavior is performed by a group who regularly visits the site.
   - Use role models in social and mass media campaigns.
   - Remind visitors that environmentally responsible behavior is socially agreed-upon.
   - Emphasize that only a few people cause a lot of the damage by undesirable behavior.

2. **Competing attitudes, values, or motives may specify contrary behaviors. For example, visitors may care about the environment, but attitudes toward saving money may be stronger and lead to environmentally unsound practices.**
   - Make the desirable attitude dominate by obtaining a voluntary public commitment to perform the desired behavior. For example, ask individuals to sign pledge cards in front of others promising to act appropriately or have children wear stickers promoting the desired behavior. People are less likely to perform behaviors incompatible with their publicly stated promise to behave responsibly. Written commitments have more effect than verbal commitments.
   - Use focus groups, surveys, or informal interviews to identify and eliminate competing attitudes, values, or motives.
   - Link the desired environmentally responsible behavior to attitudes and values important to the particular user group.

3. **The design of the physical environment makes performance of desirable behaviors difficult and/or undesirable ones easy.**
   - Determine which site features interfere with performance of desired behavior; remove these barriers if possible.
   - Determine what setting features could be added to create a barrier to the undesired behavior.
   - Compare your site design with other places used for similar purposes, but that do not have the same problem. Are there design differences that can be applied?

4. **Individuals may want to behave responsibly but do not know how to do the desired behavior.**
   - Identify information gaps and educate visitors.
   - Maximize the impact of educational interventions by using additional behavior change strategies.
   - Remember that education is unlikely to translate into new behaviors if other barriers remain.

5. **Lack of knowledge may lead to irresponsible behavior. People may perform environmentally degrading behaviors out of ignorance.** (These are the same interventions that are listed under Number 4.)
   - Identify information gaps and educate visitors.
   - Maximize the impact of your educational interventions by using additional behavior change strategies.
   - Remember that education is unlikely to result in new behavior if other barriers remain.

6. **An undesirable behavior might be a habit, performed without thinking.**
   - Make setting changes that will trigger the desired behavior.
   - Use incentives for behavior change in verbal or written communications.
   - Obtain a public commitment to perform the desired behavior.
   - Use negative consequences (e.g., citations, fines, social disapproval) to motivate behavior change.

Applying the Tool Appropriately

As with any management tool, interpretation can be misused. As managers become aware of the powerful role of interpretation in shaping attitudes and behaviors some may be tempted to modify or eliminate interpreters' messages to serve their own agenda. Interpretation can deteriorate into propaganda or proselytizing sometimes called "*interpreganda*." Exaggeration, embellishments, and what Tilden called "florid Chamber of Commerce descriptions" of a place can make interpretive presentations into nothing more than infomercials. Likewise, sometimes what interpreters don't say is also self-serving. At one county park, interpreters weren't allowed to discuss water quality problems in a river where the park department operated lucrative canoe trips even though the river was in violation of public health standards. Likewise, an innocent question by a student on a field trip about a controversial national park policy went unanswered, as the interpreter indicated that, by answering the question, he would put his job at risk.

Interpreters may find these situations surprising and uncomfortable. Is this a form of censorship? How does loyalty to the agency and being a good team player affect the choice to deliver the agency message? Certainly, in the private sector, employees are not free to discuss specific information. Should the organization's motives be considered? Misinformation may enhance park visitation and hence revenues. At other times, misinformation may be given to protect a scarce resource. For example, interpreters may deny the presence of a rare raptor nest to reduce the chance of unscrupulous falconers disturbing the birds. This important issue should be a matter of introspection by every interpreter. Are there *any* circumstances when you would knowingly disseminate misinformation or fail to answer a visitor's question? Interpreters must decide whether the situation and long-term consequences balance out in consonance with their sense of ethics. Some will choose to leave the agency in protest. Others will persevere despite disagreements because they can do more good for the citizens, the resources, and the long-term support of the interpretive program by staying on rather than by resigning.

Another concern is that as interpreters promote management applications of their work to administrators, pressure could arise to use it *only* as a management tool, thus losing the essence and inspirational spirit of interpretation in enriching visitor experiences (Dustin & McAvoy, 1985). Interpreters fear the art of interpretation could be reduced to public relation tasks or agency "press secretaries." The challenge for interpreters is to assist in meeting management goals without compromising the traditional values and philosophy of interpretation.

> "Interpreters see themselves as people who try to make a difference."

Should Interpreters Change Attitudes?

Interpreters see themselves as people who try to make a difference. Either explicitly or implicitly they often strive to inspire stronger civic and environmental ethics. Historical interpreters often seek to heighten civic pride, increase cultural sensitivity, and reduce tensions among racial or ethnic groups (Hall & James, 1992). Yet, some interpreters are uncomfortable with the topic of persuasive interpretation. They are concerned the goals of affecting attitudes and behavior may not be appropriate. They ask, should public servants do things "*for* people" or "*to* people?" When a government agency talks about changing attitudes, it opens itself up to charges of elitism or arrogance. Critics sense that the government is telling people what they must think and that the values and attitudes of the "unconverted" public are inferior or misguided.

However, persuasion does not have to be confrontational or unpleasant. Persuasion can be gentle, friendly, and factual. The persuasive communication of interpretation almost invariably works on a positive, constructive, uplifting level, whereas being argumentative or unpleasant normally has the effect opposite of persuasion. Rather than regarding their public as ignorant or inferior, most interpreters see their job as one of helping elevate consciousness of a place or event with which most visitors have limited familiarity. According to Dabney (1988), Freeman Tilden considered interpreters as "…engaged in a field essentially of morality—the aim of man to rise above himself and to choose the option of quality rather than material superfluity." However, Tilden defines how the teaching of morals need not be elitist nor narrowly arrogant (Dabney, 1988):

> "Persuasion does not have to be confrontational or unpleasant."

> We shall not teach morals as such. We use our vast natural and historic resources to show what true morals are. We do not tell people what they must do, but what they can do; not what they must be, but what they can be…

Do park agencies want interpreters to persuade people that the environment is worth protecting, that good reasons exist for management decisions, that a museum's historical message and collection offer useful clues to past and present culture? Does the nature interpreter seek to guide people to respect the miracle of the humblest of species and to assure protection of plants and animals in danger of extinction? Does the interpreter at national memorials seek to impart a sense of inspiration in the national heritage? If so, they are in the business of uplifting, pleasant, gentle, and civilized persuasion. If interpreters do not seek to change people, then they become nothing more than a butler and court jester providing superficial courtesy and light amusement.

A final concern about interpretation's use as a management tool is that interpreters are "preaching to the choir." That is to say people who come to interpretive sites and programs are already "converted" in that they already share the interests and values of the interpreter. This phenomenon can be mitigated through using social media and traditional media outlets to reach out to new and different audiences. However, as we will see in the next section, "preaching to the choir" has great value in that it *reinforces* the existing appropriate values and behaviors.

Long-term Management Benefits

"Don't judge each day by the harvest you reap but by the seeds you have planted."
–Robert Louis Stevenson

Many famous environmentalists began their love of nature through direct experience of it and through exploration and adventure (Curtin & Kragh, 2014). This seems to be generally true of current conservationists. Interviews of 18 West African conservationists of different cultures (Cable, 2002) and life histories of 51 natural-history oriented professionals (Bixler, James, & Vadala, 2011) reveal extensive nature experiences through early adulthood. Interpreters play a key role in providing experiences that shape the lives and careers of future generations of cultural and natural resource stewards (Figure 4.6).

Figure 4.6. Second graders who learn about Snowy Plovers from U.S. Forest Service interpreters may become future stewards of the dunes because of these early childhood experiences. (USFS)

Bixler and his colleagues (2011) noted that natural history has all but disappeared from formal education in the United States. Universities focus on theoretical concepts, modeling, and other sophisticated approaches to biological conservation rather than "old-fashioned" natural history courses such as those teaching field identification of plants and animals. They conclude that "this places the responsibility of introducing people to natural history within nonformal educational settings with interpretive naturalists taking a leading role." Although a single program can serve as an introduction or expansion of a park visitor's interests in natural history, socialization theories indicate that to have a lasting impact it is of utmost importance to have frequent and repeated experiences with nature within a supportive social world.

Bixler states, "In light of constructivist notions of learning, no one program or experience is enough. We are constructing our identities and understanding along with building emotional ties to parks and other special places. No matter how good an interpretive program appears to be, it fails unless it somehow motivates future engagement" (Bixler, pers. com., 2015).

To compensate for the lack of formal natural history education, Bixler and his colleagues (2011) recommend that interpreters do the following:

- Use the time before and after programs and other casual contacts to foster or reaffirm interest in natural history.
- Be aware of the range of other regional opportunities for visitors to have additional natural history related experiences.
- Add a formal "Program-to-Program Transition" component to interpretive program plans to help audiences extend the experience after the program and to help them transition from program to program.
- Work with their own families and in their own neighborhoods by referring teachers, parents, and children to summer camps with nature study programs, excellent local scout leaders, and schools with opportunities for outdoor study.

Interpreters plant intellectual and emotional seeds in the lives of young people and adults today that will bear fruit many years later in the form of a new generation of stewards, scientists, and conservation-minded citizens.

Summary

Virtually all interpreters and many citizens believe interpretation's contribution to enhancing visitor enjoyment and inspiration is sufficient justification for interpretive programs and facilities. Pragmatically, however, to ensure the survival of interpretive programs, interpreters must help resolve management problems. Interpreters need to work closely with agency personnel to assure that their messages support management objectives. Theories and empirical studies complement the scores of anecdotal success stories. Armed with this evidence, interpreters can persuade taxpayers, donors, park managers, and government officials of the values of interpretation.

Interpretation brings managers and the public together for the benefit of both. Ultimately, interpretation helps protect the very resources being interpreted. Furthermore, through factual persuasive messaging, interpretation can assist people to act in ways that recognize, protect, and celebrate the diversity of different peoples and cultures, and ecosystems and species, all toward the pursuit of a better world.

"Good interpretation will contribute more than anything else to park management success."

–William Penn Mott
former director of California State Parks
and the National Park Service

Literature Cited

Ajzen, I. (1992). Persuasive communication theory in social psychology: A historical perspective. In M. Manfredo (Ed.), *Influencing human behavior: Theory and applications in recreation, tourism, and natural resources management* (pp. 1–27). Urbana, IL: Sagamore.

Barry, J. P. (2008). Interpretation saves lives! In *2008 Interpretive Sourcebook*, Fort Collins, CO: National Association for Interpretation.

Bixler, R. (2015). Personal communication to Ted Cable.

Bixler, R., James, J., & Vadala, C. (2011). Environmental socialization incidents with implications for the expanded role of interpretive naturalists in providing natural history experiences. *Journal of Interpretation Research, 16*(1), 35–64.

Bradford, L. E. A., & McIntyre, N. (2007). Off the beaten track: Messages as a means of reducing social trail use at St. Lawrence Islands National Park. *Journal of Park and Recreation Administration, 25*(1), 1–21.

Broder, P., Fish, V., & McDonald, B. (1994). Interpreting deer management: Before, during, after. In *1994 Interpretive Sourcebook*. Fort Collins, CO: National Association for Interpretation.

Burn, S. M. (1996). *Environmental intervention handbook for resource managers*. USDA Forest Service, Pacific Southwest Research Station, Riverside, CA. PSW-96-0024

Cable, T. (2002). *Commitments of the heart: Odysseys in West African conservation*. Urbana, IL: Sagamore.

Cable, T., & Knudson, D. (1983). Interpretation as a management tool: The manager's view. In *Proceedings, National Interpreters Workshop*, Association of Interpretive Naturalists, West Lafayette, IN: Purdue University.

Cantrell, J. C. (1987). Interpretation helps solve problems at DeGray. In *RecNotes*, U.S. Army Corps of Engineers. Vicksburg, MS. Vol. R-87-2.

Cialdini, R. B. (1996). Activating and aligning two kinds of norms in persuasive communications. *Journal of Interpretation Research*, 1(1):3-10.

Cunningham, R. L. (1985). Visitor safety interpretive survey. *Trends, 22*(4), 37–39.

Curtin, S., & Kragh, G. (2014). Wildlife tourism: Reconnecting people with nature. *Human Dimensions in Wildlife, 19*(4), 545–554.

Dabney, W. D. (1988). Travels with Freeman. *Journal of Interpretation, 12*(1), T7–T8.

Dunmire, W. (1976). Stretching recreation dollars through interpretation. In D. M. Knudson (Ed.), *Managing recreation resources for century III* (pp. 92–100). West Lafayette, IN: Purdue University.

Dustin, D., & McAvoy, L. (1985). Interpretation as a management tool: A dissenting opinion. *The Interpreter, 16*(Spring), 18–20.

Evenson, R., Maxfield, K., Adams, M., Isaacson, S., Steichen, K., Baldwin, A. & Schweizer, D. (2010). Fire Interpretation in the National Park Service. In *2010 interpretive sourcebook*. Fort Collins, CO. National Association for Interpretation.

Goren, J. (2009). Heavy rocks and sexy flowers: Enlisting citizens as stewards and scientists. In *2009 interpretive sourcebook*. Fort Collins, CO. National Association for Interpretation.

Hall, E., & James, D. (1992). The education program at Jefferson Expansion National Memorial celebrates the 75th. *Interpretation* (fall/winter), 20–24.

Ham, S. H. (2009). From interpretation to protection: Is there a theoretical basis? *Journal of Interpretation Research, 14*(2), 49–57.

Hockett, K. S., & Hall, T. E. (2007). The effect of moral and fear appeals on park visitors' beliefs about feeding wildlife. *Journal of Interpretation Research, 12*, 5–27.

Hooper, J. K., & Weiss, K. S. (1990). Interpretation as a management tool: A national study of interpretive professional's views. In *Proceedings, National Interpreters Workshop*, NAI, Charleston, SC.

King, L. M., & Tabata, R. S. (1992). Hanauma Bay educational programs: Interpretation as a park management tool. In *Proceedings, National Interpreters Workshop*, NAI, San Francisco Bay Area, CA.

Kulhavy, D., & Costa, R. (1990). Interpretation of an endangered species. In *Proceedings National Interpreters Workshop*, NAI, Charleston, SC.

Lackey, B. K., & Ham, S. H. (2003). Assessment of communication focused on human-black bear conflict at Yosemite National Park. *Journal of Interpretation Research, 8*(1), 25–40.

Manfredo, M. J. (Ed.). (1992). *Influencing human behavior: Theory and applications in recreation, tourism, and natural resources management.* Urbana, IL: Sagamore.

Manfredo, M. J., & Bright, A. D. (1991). A model for assessing the effects of communication on recreationists. *Journal of Leisure Research, 23*(1), 1–20.

Martin, D. C. (1992). The effects of three signs and a brochure on visitors' removal of pumice from Mount St. Helens. In H. H. Christensen, D. R. Johnson, & M. H. Brookes (Eds.), *Vandalism: Research, prevention, and social policy* (pp. 121–131). Portland, OR: USDA Forest Service, Pacific Northwest Research Station, Gen. Tech. Rept. PNW-GTR-293.

McAvoy, L. H., & Dustin, D. (1983). Indirect versus direct regulation of recreation behavior. *Journal of Park and Recreation Administration, 1*(4), 12–17.

Oliver, S. S., Roggenbuck, J. W., & Watson, A. E. (1985). Education to reduce impacts in forest campgrounds. *Journal of Forestry, 83*(4), 234–236.

Orams, M. B., & Hill, G. J. E. (1998). Controlling the ecotourist in a wild dolphin feeding program: Is education the answer? *Journal of Environmental Education, 29*(3), 33–38.

Petty, R., McMichael, S., & Brannon, L. (1992). The Elaboration Likelihood Model of Persuasion: Applications in recreation and tourism. In M. Manfredo (Ed.), *Influencing human behavior: Theory and applications in recreation, tourism, and natural resources management* (pp. 77–101). Urbana, IL: Sagamore.

Powell, R. B., & Ham, S. H. (2008). Can ecotourism interpretation really lead to pro-conservation knowledge, attitudes and behaviour? Evidence from the Galapagos Islands. *Journal of Sustainable Tourism, 16*(4), 467–489.

Reigner, N., & Lawson, S. (2009). Improving the efficacy of visitor education in Haleakalā National Park Using the Theory of Planned Behavior. *Journal of Interpretation Research, 14*(2), 21–45.

Roggenbuck, J., & Berrier, D. L. (1982). A comparison of the effectiveness of two communication strategies in dispersing wilderness campers. *Journal of Leisure Research, 14*(1), 77–89.

Sharpe, G. W., & Gensler, G. L. (1978). Interpretation as a management tool. *Journal of Interpretation, 3*(2), 3–9.

Spears, C. J. (1992). Using the press in controversial issues. In *Proceedings of National Interpreters Workshop*. National Association for Interpretation. San Francisco, CA.

Stalder, M., & Cahill, B. (1992). Bears, bears, and more bears—Interpretation as a resource management tool. A success story! In *Proceedings of National Interpreters Workshop*. National Association for Interpretation. San Francisco, CA.

Stronks, R. (2010). Algonquin's public wolf howls: Connecting the masses. In *2010 Interpretive Sourcebook*. Fort Collins, CO. National Association for Interpretation.

Tilden, F. (1957). *Interpreting our heritage*. Chapel Hill: The University of North Carolina Press.

U.S. Fish and Wildlife Service. (2015): fws.gov

Vander Stoep, G. A., & Gramann, J. H. (1987). The effect of verbal appeals and incentives on depreciative behavior among youthful park visitors. *Journal of Leisure Research, 9*(2), 69–83.

Wagstaff, M. C., & Wilson, B. E. (1988). The evaluation of litter behavior modification in a river environment. *Journal of Environmental Education, 20*(1), 39–44.

Wallace, G. N., & Gaudry, C. J. (2002). An evaluation of the "Authority of the Resource" interpretive technique by rangers in eight wilderness/backcountry areas. *Journal of Interpretation Research, 7*(1), 43–68.

Weaver, H. (1982). Origins of interpretation. In G. W. Sharpe (Ed.), *Interpreting the environment* (2nd ed., pp. 28–51). New York, NY: John Wiley & Sons, Inc.

Widner, C. J., & Roggenbuck, J. (2000). Reducing theft of petrified wood at Petrified Forest National Park. *Journal of Interpretation Research, 5*(1), 1–18.

Widner, C. J., & Roggenbuck, J. (2003). Understanding park visitors' response to interventions to reduce petrified wood theft. *Journal of Interpretation Research, 8*(1), 67–82.

Wiles, R., & Hall, T. E. (2005). Can interpretive messages change park visitor's views on wildland fire? *Journal of Interpretation Research, 10*(2), 18–37.

Winter, P. L. (2006). The impact of normative message types on off-trail hiking. *Journal of Interpretation Research, 11*(1), 34–52.

SECTION III

What Guides Us?

CHAPTER 5
Guiding Principles of Interpretation

As a student-trainee in the Old Faithful area of Yellowstone National Park for the summer, about to return to complete his last semester of college, Walt Dabney received a letter with the prospect of a special assignment upon graduation (Dabney, 1988). In sum, the proposed job was to serve as an aide to Freeman Tilden in an excursion throughout the national park system. Walt was 23 at the time, and Freeman was 87 years old. They traveled tens of thousands of miles together, all over the country, visiting national parks and observing programs. Walt carried Freeman's typewriter and suitcase, drove the car, and provided interpretation program observations to Harper's Ferry Center. Freeman spent his time writing and teaching park staff. They also met with people from other agencies and the private sector to determine the proper role of NPS interpretation for meeting the environmental crises of the day. With so much time together they talked about almost everything and became good friends. Can you imagine getting *this* as your first job out of college? Now retired after his own 30-year career with the National Park Service, Walt Dabney was chosen as the keynote speaker for the 2016 National Association for Interpretation conference in Corpus Christi, Texas to share insights into Freeman Tilden who is, to many, the father of interpretation. Dabney noted in his speech that one of the things Tilden inspired in him and others was the importance of "continuing to learn and broaden yourself."

Figure 5.1. Enos Mills, kneeling, was among the founders of the interpretive profession. Above him are Horace Albright, second director of the National Park Service, and Mr. and Mrs. Sherman, early benefactors and supporters of what was to become Rocky Mountain National Park. (NPS, 1915)

Figure 5.2. Freeman Tilden's principles of interpretation still form the basis of good interpretation. Tilden took interest in interpretation at the age of 58 as a long and distinguished second career. (NPS- MWW)

This chapter presents a history of traditions and principles of interpretation. The traditions demonstrate the permanency of interpretation's underlying purpose, despite the vicissitudes of time, and the changing of public policies. The principles of interpretation have evolved over time as a philosophy for interpretation continues to be written, following in the footsteps of Enos Mills (Figure 5.1) and Freeman Tilden (Figure 5.2).

As described in Chapter 1, interpretation is an old parks tradition. In the early years national and state parks provided an intellectual accommodation for the natural curiosity of the visitor. The idea was to make the visit interesting, informative, and enjoyable. Parks people learned quickly that their visitors wanted and needed guidance.

These visitors not only had little outdoor experience or equipment, but also possessed limited familiarity with natural (or historical) phenomena. They sought and paid for guide service, often tipping informative guides handsomely. In the absence of organized professional interpretation, some of the wranglers, hotel employees, and drivers eagerly posed as interpreters, often improvising interesting tales and fascinating explanations that had little to do with reality.

Long before the National Park Service took over in 1916, Army park guards enlightened tourists at Yellowstone. Their commanders sought enlisted men familiar with ornithology and zoology. With time, they developed further knowledge about the curiosities and history of the park.

Principles: An Evolution

As noted in Chapter 1, Enos Mills—writer, resort owner, and self-taught nature guide—led people through what is now Rocky Mountain National Park from 1889 through the early 1920s. He also travelled the nation as a lecturer, friend of presidents, and lobbyist for stronger interest in nature by the public and the congress.

> "Enos Miller led people through what is now Rocky Mountain National Park."

Mills distinguished the "nature guide" from the horse wrangler or hunter type of guide. "Natural history has been incidental to all previous types of guides, while to the nature guide it is the essential feature of every trip" (Mills, 1920). He claimed that a nature guide is neither an ordinary type of guide nor a teacher. The methods of formal education in those days were not seen favorably by Mills. He thought they were too rigid and structured to stimulate interest among the students. He insisted that nature guiding should be more inspirational than informational. "People are out for recreation and need restful, intellectual visions, and not dull, dry facts, rules, and manuals" (Mills, 1920).

Mills' "formula" for the best nature guiding seems to apply equally well to historical and cultural topics:

- Appeal to the imagination and the reason.
- Give flesh and blood to cold facts.
- Make stories to breathe life into inanimate objects.
- Deal with principles rather than isolated information.
- Give biographies rather than classifications.

In the late 1950s, Freeman Tilden wrote down some intertwined, poetic, and inspiring "principles of interpretation" that resemble the earlier observations of Mills. Tilden's (1957) principles have guided interpreters since. They have stood the test of time, perhaps because of their turgidity and lucidity, perhaps because of their slight inscrutability that rings with a sense of truth. These principles serve as guidelines for performance, for evaluation, and for training. Box 5.1 presents Tilden's six principles.

Tilden also taught that love of the place and love for the visitors constituted the key or priceless ingredient—the overriding principle of interpretation (Tilden, 1957).

> If you love the thing you interpret, and love the people who come to enjoy it… you not only have taken the pains to understand it to the limit of your capacity but you also feel its special beauty in the general richness of life's beauty.

Both Mills and Tilden noted that interpretation sometimes uses judicious silence. Some scenes need no words; "reporting" the beauty of a scene might reduce the opportunity for inspiration. Often the scene interprets itself, so interpreters need not impose. Harold Ickes (1938), Secretary of the Interior from 1933–1945, also took a dim view of eager interpreters who do not allow beauty to speak for itself:

> We have too much of a disposition not to allow people freely to enjoy the parks for what they can get out of them for the refreshment of their spirits and the

good of their souls. Our guides insist on describing the beauties and the wonders of nature in trite and uninspired words. Nothing makes me want to commit murder so much as to have someone break in on a reverential contemplation of nature in which I may be indulging by giving me a lot of statistical or descriptive information relating to what I am looking at.

Box 5.1
Tilden's Principles of Interpretation

I. Any interpretation that does not somehow relate what is being displayed or described to something within the personality or experience of the visitor will be sterile (Figure 5.3).
II. Information, as such, is not interpretation. Interpretation is revelation based upon information. But they are entirely different things. However, all interpretation includes information.
III. Interpretation is an art, which combines many arts, whether the materials presented are scientific, historical, or architectural. Any art is to some degree teachable.
IV. The chief aim of interpretation is not instruction, but provocation.
V. Interpretation should aim to present a whole rather than a part and must address itself to the whole person rather than any phase.
VI. Interpretation addressed to children should not be a dilution of the presentation to adults, but should follow a fundamentally different approach. To be at its best it will require a separate program.

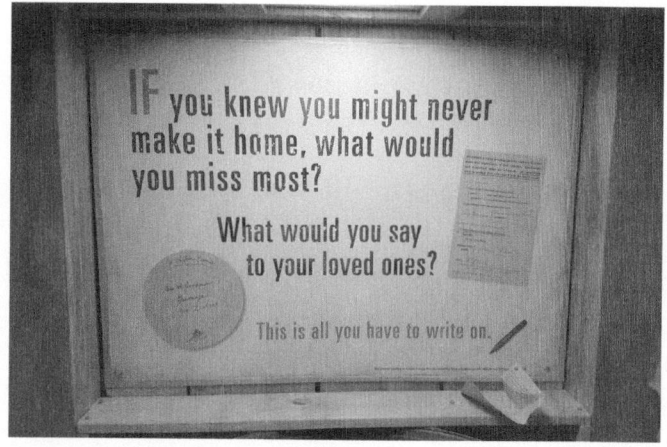

Figure 5.3. A WW I exhibit relates to every visitor and adds personal meaning to the experience of war. (TC)

Based on Tilden (1957)

Building on the work of Mills and Tilden an expanded set of interpretive principles has been offered (Beck & Cable, 2011). Furthermore, each of the 15 principles has been associated with a gift. The first six principles are consistent with Tilden's since these principles are so well known among interpreters, although they have been updated. (Box 5.2)

In addition to these 15 gifts, each associated with one of the principles listed, the conclusion of *The Gifts of Interpretation* notes one last gift, the gift of hope. As Beck and Cable (2011) noted, "The beauty of human integrity commemorated in events of the past and the beauty of the intricacies of nature give rise to hope, and these are the tools of the interpreter."

Box 5.2
A Further Developed Set of Principles and Associated Gifts

Principle	Gift
To spark an interest, interpreters must relate the subject to the lives of the people in the audience.	The Gift of a Spark
The purpose of interpretation goes beyond providing information to reveal deeper meaning and truth.	The Gift of Revelation
The interpretive presentation—as a work of art—should be designed as a story that informs, entertains, and enlightens.	The Gift of Story
The purpose of the interpretive story is to inspire and provoke people to broaden their horizons.	The Gift of Provocation
Interpretation should present a complete theme or thesis and address the whole person.	The Gift of Wholeness
Interpretation for children, teenagers, and seniors—when these comprise uniform groups—should follow fundamentally different approaches.	The Gift of Targeted Programs
Every place has a history. Interpreters can bring the past alive to make the present more enjoyable and the future more meaningful.	The Gift of Personalizing the Past
Technology can reveal the world in exciting new ways. However, incorporating this technology into the interpretive program must be done with foresight and thoughtful care.	The Gift of Illumination through Technology
Interpreters must concern themselves with the quantity and quality (selection and accuracy) of the information presented. Focused, well-researched interpretation will be more powerful than a longer discourse.	The Gift of Precision
Before applying the arts in interpretation, the interpreter must be familiar with basic communication techniques. Quality interpretation depends on the interpreter's knowledge and skills, which must be continually developed over time.	The Gift of Professionalism
Interpretive writing should address what readers would like to know, with the authority of wisdom and its accompanying humility and care.	The Gift of Interpretive Writing
The overall interpretive program must be capable of attracting support—financial, volunteer, political, administrative—whatever support is needed for the program to flourish.	The Gift of Relationship
Interpretation should instill in people the ability, and the desire, to sense the beauty in their surroundings—to provide spiritual uplift and to encourage resource preservation.	The Gift of Beauty
Interpreters can promote optimal experiences through intentional and thoughtful program and facility design.	The Gift of Joy
Passion is the essential ingredient for powerful and effective interpretation—passion for the resource and for those people who come to be inspired by it.	The Gift of Passion

Based on Beck & Cable (2011)

Thematic Interpretation

Sam Ham has guided the interpretive profession over the past four decades through his extensive research and writing. Of his many contributions to the field, he has authored two landmark books: *Environmental Interpretation* and *Interpretation: Making a Difference on Purpose* (Ham 1992; 2013). He is best known for his refinements and advancement of thematic interpretation. The theme of an interpretive program is the overarching idea that the interpreter develops which may also be referred to as the main message or moral to the story (Figure 5.4). The theme provides focus, purpose, and strategy for the interpretive message.

> "Sam Ham has guided the interpretive profession over the past four decades."

The use of themes in interpretive work was initially promoted by Bill Lewis (1980) in a thin book titled *Interpreting for Park Visitors*. Ham has elaborated on the concept over the years and his work in the area of thematic interpretation is recognized and used by the interpretive profession all around the world.

Ham (2013) provides the following cornerstones of the interpretive approach to communication:

T (thematic with a focus on the main message conveyed)
O (organized to provide structure and meaning)
R (relevant to the audience)
E (enjoyable for the audience)

Initially presented as the EROT framework (Ham, 1992), the same four qualities of thematic communication are now listed in reverse (Ham, 2013) noting that the **T** (theme) at the front represents focus and direction for the qualities that follow. Ultimately, using the TORE model of thematic communication can enhance a person's experience, create or reinforce a positive attitude about something, and can influence a person's behavior (Ham, 2013; Box 5.3).

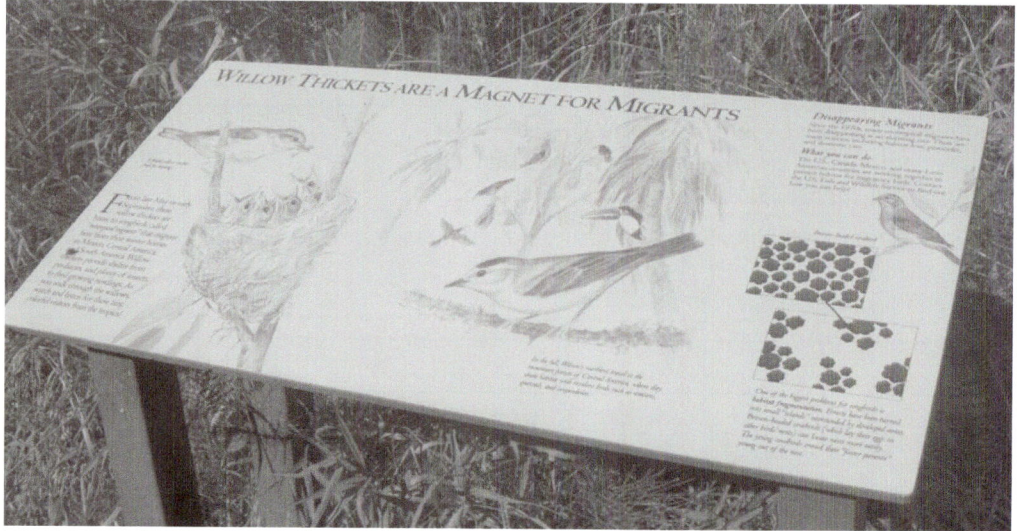

Figure 5.4. This interpretive sign clearly states the theme in the title addressing the question, *Why should I care about willows?* (TC)

Box 5.3
TORE Starts with the T for a Reason

Sam H. Ham, Author and Professor Emeritus, University of Idaho

Those four letters, T (Thematic), O (Organized), R (Relevant) and E (Enjoyable), result from about a century of research on how communication affects human beings. They just remind us that when holding attention and making a thought-provoking point are outcomes of interest to an interpreter, the likelihood of success is significantly enhanced when the interpreter's presentation is guided by a strongly relevant theme which s/he develops in an easy-to-follow and enjoyable way (TORE). No rocket science there.

But the key to it all is the T, which must matter to the audience. By definition, a strong theme is one that provokes thought, and dozens of studies have shown that to accomplish this basic goal the theme must be relevant, not just to the interpreter, but to the audience. Too often interpreters struggle to provoke thinking because their themes matter only to them. According to a vast body of contemporary research, failure is practically guaranteed when an interpreter's theme is weak. Indeed, excellence in thematic interpretation is predicated on themes being strong—which means each is relevant to the audience it's chosen for.

Like all forms of interpretation, thematic interpretation can be done well or poorly. TORE describes excellent interpretation. And when thematic interpretation falls short of excellence it's usually because the interpreter's theme was weak. It makes little sense to assume that an idea that is unimportant to an audience is going to engage them or provoke much thinking. That also is not rocket science.

It's important for interpreters to understand that the purpose of thematic communication isn't to "teach" a theme to an audience, as some current analysts seem to think. Indeed, most interpreters shouldn't care if even one person in an audience can say or paraphrase the theme after an interpretive exchange. Likewise, whether an audience agrees with the theme, or accepts it as fact, could be completely unimportant depending on the interpreter's objective. Likewise, a theme's purpose isn't to be remembered or parroted back by an audience, and its purpose isn't to tell an audience what meanings matter most. Its singular purpose is to stimulate thinking about the theme and around the theme. When interpreters don't understand these basic cornerstones of the thematic approach, misguided practice and poor performance usually result.

In this sense, a theme is simply the moral of the story an interpreter wants an audience to consider. You see, it's a platform for their own thinking. Elsewhere (Ham, 2013) I've described it as a "focal point for provocation," an overarching idea an interpreter develops so that people in the audience will think their own thoughts about it and make their own meanings with respect to it. The meanings they make may or may not be consistent with the theme itself, and whether that even matters will depend on the interpreter's purpose for doing interpretation at all. So when certain critics proclaim that thematic interpretation necessarily dictates to audiences what things mean and which meanings matter most, they are just plain wrong. But when they condemn approaching interpretation in any form with this "one-meaning-only" mind-set as poor practice, I think they're making a valid point.

In *Interpretation—Making a Difference on Purpose*, I attempted an understanding of this issue by offering the "zone of tolerance" concept (ZOT). An interpreter's (or organization's) ZOT is simply the amount of deviation they're happy to accept between the theme that was developed and the thoughts it stimulates an audience to think. Depending on their purpose, a ZOT might be ultra-wide and unlimited wherein any and all thoughts—even those that are counter to the theme, morally opposed to the theme, or factually inaccurate—are completely acceptable. In this unrestricted ZOT, the idea is to stimulate audiences to think their own thoughts regardless of what they might be. I personally believe this is the most common ZOT and the one that many interpreters value most.

Box 5.3 (continued)

But I also describe two other possibilities. One is a very wide ZOT that is only subtly restricted by a value orientation of some kind (e.g., national parks are good or heritage preservation is important to society). Audience thoughts that conflict in some way with these values are considered less desirable than those that are consistent with them. And finally, I describe circumstances in which a narrow ZOT might prevail (for example when an interpretive activity is expected to support a mandated school curriculum or when promoting a specific behavior is warranted). Which of these ZOTs will prevail in a given situation can only be decided subjectively by the interpreter or her/his organization. But whichever it is will most certainly for them determine whether the interpretation they planned and delivered succeeded or fell short.

So thematic interpretation is successful when it provokes audiences to think thoughts that lie within a ZOT—whether it is narrow, wide or completely unrestricted. And according to an impressive empirical record, to accomplish this lofty goal will require interpretation that is TORE quality.

Other writers in the field of interpretation have expanded on the acronym to include other letters to represent other qualities, but always with TORE as part of the core. For example, in *Personal Interpretation,* Lisa Brochu and Tim Merriman (2008) use the POETRY framework developed by interpreter Wren Smith, adding a P to stand for purposeful and a Y at the end for you, the interpreter.

Tangibles and Intangibles

The effective interpreter will use the tangible elements of the place—plants, rocks, streams, wildlife—to advance intangible meanings associated with them. David Larsen promoted linking tangible things (those things you can touch and see) with intangible meanings. For years he presented his thoughts on these issues at workshops and conferences, followed by a book titled *Meaningful Interpretation.* Larsen (2003) noted that various interpretive resources are made up of tangible objects, places, people, and events and that these are linked to various ideas, feelings and meanings such as love, courage, beauty, freedom. Ham (2013) suggested "intangible meanings are about symbolism—what something represents to an audience." Through making a connection between a tangible thing and an intangible meaning the full spirit of a place or an event may emerge. Because many of the intangibles reflect on feelings that everyone can relate to (suffering, triumph, love, generosity) these may be referred to as universal concepts.

> Use the tangible elements of the place to advance intangible meanings associated with them.

To provide a vivid example, John Burdee (2007) recounts a visit with his family to Wilson's Creek National Battlefield, Missouri. There remains one structure on the battlefield that is original, that was used as a field hospital, and it is known as the Ray House.

> The on-site interpreter was presenting a program on the importance of the house in the course of battle. He used the universal concept of pain to describe the day's events. Civil war injuries frequently involved amputation; the sight of the scalpel and bone saw created a knot in the stomach. Removed human limbs

were tossed through an open window and collected in a large pile beside the house. Medicines, especially anesthetics, were scarce. The sights, sounds, and smells in the Ray House must have been horrific; the cries of the wounded chilling. One visitor fainted.

The power of the resources comes from their capacity to reveal meanings, those things that we have felt ourselves and can move our souls. The charge of the interpreter, then, is to help make the connection between the tangible elements of the resource and intangible meanings they are associated with in the hearts and minds of visitors. Ham (2013) elaborated, "When you successfully make a tangible-intangible connection, provocation usually follows." So, by making a tangible-intangible connection, the interpreter is relating to the background of the audience, revealing meanings, telling a story, provoking members of the audience, and relaying the message as part of a larger whole of understanding. These are all principles of interpretation that were touched on earlier in this chapter.

Genius loci

Each park, forest, museum, camp, historic building, and cave has its own characteristic values and uniqueness. A site may represent an ecological, geographic, artistic, or architectural phenomenon. A visitor should have the central experience of understanding these special or representative values: *Why was this place set aside? How is it distinct from other places? How does it fit into a pattern of similar places (such as Civil War battlefields)? What "don't miss" features should I see and understand?*

> The distinctive nature (*genius*) defines the significance of the place (*loci*).

Interpreters explain and translate the central values to visitors, thus enriching the experience by presenting the essence of the place. *Genius loci* refers to the particular character of the site. The place (*locus*) may refer to an historic building (e.g., Windsor Castle) or a large ecosystem (e.g., the tundra of Gates of the Arctic National Park and Preserve, in Alaska). The distinctive nature (*genius*) defines the significance of the place (*loci*) (Figure 5.5).

Interpreters find and study this special character of place so they can define it for visitors, and tell its stories. To apply the concept of *genius loci* interpreters may explore such things as the name of the place and its significance. For example, in 2015 the name of Mt. McKinley, the highest mountain on the North American continent, was changed to Denali. Visitors to Denali National Park and Preserve will wonder why. ("Denali" is the native Koyukon Athabascan name which means "the

Figure 5.5. Interpreters reveal the subtle beauty of the prairie landscape and help visitors experience its genius loci. (NPS)

high one."). As a further guide, interpreters can determine the most frequently asked questions of their visitors and construct interpretation of the *genius loci* accordingly.

Promoting Perception

Aldo Leopold (1966) wrote, "To promote perception is the only truly creative part of recreational engineering." The key job of the interpreter boils down to one of helping people to perceive more acutely the world around them, the cultures that preceded and coexist with their own, and how they can affect the future ways in which humans will live in this world harmoniously.

On the one hand, the interpreter helps people to gain some understanding of the unusual and curious places of the land and the people that inhabit[ed] it, trying to impart a sense of wonder in the mind of the perceiver. On the other hand, the interpreter helps people to gain new perspectives on the commonplace and new understandings of the world around them. One way is to seek patterns in nature. Many visitors want help in perceiving patterns that they may not recognize without assistance such as those that characterize tree species or architectural styles. Here, the artistic and scientific mind can blend together nicely, finding patterns within apparent chaos.

The identification of patterns in a complex, variable world has become known as the "science of chaos." From it, Benoit Mandelbrot, a mathematician, invented fractal geometry and fractal relationships. This mathematical inquiry seeks uncanny, subtle, intricate structures in places that some see as disorderly or without significant pattern.

Examples of structure appear in slopes, in grasses strewn in a meadow, in cracks of a dry mud bed, in ice, in lichen blotches on a tree trunk, in the trees themselves, and in the clustering of galaxies. These apparently random phenomena have long intrigued artists and photographers. Mandelbrot saw rhythms in the shapes of rocks and plants, in the life of a river, in cloud dynamics, and in the interfaces between two fluids.

Many interpretive naturalists explain these often overlooked patterns since few people can see the patterns without assistance. Some chaotic patterns that naturalists have found worthy of study include the following:

- Clouds—weather forecasters have known their patterns for millennia, but few study them for order or meaning now.
- Rivers—drawing the basic shape of a river not as a line but as a tree; this dendritic pattern repeats itself wherever nature drains land of water.

An interesting photography tour or illustrated talk may examine images of the unconventional beauty of untamed, undomesticated, unregulated wildness (Figure 5.6). One of the finest photographers of this genre, Eliot Porter, observed that we usually notice flowers, autumn foliage, mountain landscapes, and other summits of nature's displays. Underlying them, patterns and slow, quiet processes pass almost unnoticed. "Yet, how much is missed if we have eyes only for the bright colors…The essence of the earth's beauty lies in disorder, a peculiarly patterned disorder, from the fierce tumult of rushing water to the tangled filigrees of unbridled vegetation" (Porter & Gleick, 1990).

Interpreters gladly accept the thesis that beauty is in the hard-to-perceive order of the universe. Visitors may share similar preferences if given a chance to better understand.

Total Programming

Interpretive programming extends beyond walks, talks, and evening campfire programs. It seeks to involve visitors in a variety of activities to offer them a complete experience. This does not mean that the visitor surrenders the entire visit to the interpreter, but rather that choices are made available.

Total programming covers all the bases. The interpreter provides the visitor with a full menu of personal, self-guiding, and open-ended opportunities that offer the chance to partake fully from a rich array of interpretive facilities and events. Programming includes exhibits, demonstrations, and printed material designed to meet the needs of general audiences while also providing specific opportunities for children, older adults, teenagers, foreign visitors, and families. Total programming goes beyond the visitor center. It includes mass media, tours, and one-on-one interactions. Quality interpretation seeks to reach the whole of the clientele—on site and at home (through an innovative website, apps, or blogs).

Figure 5.6. Intricate details in a geyser basin at Yellowstone National Park. (LB)

The visitor to a fully interpreted park or museum or camp will encounter many levels of learning and skill development. As indicated earlier, a key to progressive interpretation comes from helping visitors to grow in skill and perception. A total program offers gradations of intellectual challenge. It can include some information that excites beginners as well as some that challenges and equips experienced people to continuously expand their knowledge.

The diversity of activities, programs, and ever-ready self-guiding facilities allows the person to completely immerse in interpretive recreation. With the ubiquitous nature of technology come abundant opportunities for visitors to engage in podcasts, or learn from various apps, or dial a cell phone for specific details on a particular location within a park. However, personal interpretation is still an important part of the mix. Furthermore, there should be opportunities for visitors to simply go out and enjoy the wonders of the resource on their own, taking in all aspects of the beauty of the resource through their senses.

Applying Education and Communication Theory to Interpretation

Much of what we understand to contribute to effective interpretation comes from other fields of study such as education and communication. Education theory includes an approach called "constructivist." Put simply, it involves building new knowledge, values, and beliefs on each individual's earlier constructs of knowledge and values. It recognizes that people learn in different ways, so that each person's new "construction" may differ from those of other people. The principles of Mills and Tilden suggest that interpreters have long used this philosophy. This approach is also consistent with the notion that visitors to a park are sovereign; they will come up with their own conclusions and create their own experiences.

Mills, Tilden, and modern constructivist educators apparently have roots that go far back, perhaps with some different emphases. One who seemed to embody the principles was Dr. Maria Montessori, whose last name still appears on many preschools. This Italian educator developed a philosophy that focused on individual learning.

Montessori believed that no person is educated by another, but must do it individually or it will never be done. A truly educated person continues learning long after the hours and years spent in the classroom because motivation comes from within by a natural curiosity and love for knowledge.

Modern constructivists often suggest keeping classroom lecturing to a minimum and individual interaction with problems and real objects to a maximum. Most interpreters apply this to adults as well as children, using the outdoors or museum objects to do much of the teaching. The approach requires that the interpreter focus on ways that visitors may learn instead of concentrating solely on what to say or do. The interpreter plans with less thinking about being the deliverer of information and more about the clients as the learners and the doers. Of course, circumstances will dictate to what extent this approach can be fully used and time is often a limiting variable. Frequently, interpreters are called upon to give an interpretive talk that will provide a broad overview of the wonders of a site and the most logical way to proceed is to depend on the interpreter's knowledge to concisely present and interpret to the audience.

Similarly, communication theory can be adapted for use by interpreters. Communication is the essence of interpretation. Interpreters use communication principles in public contact, campfire presentations, guided activities, signs, exhibits, audiovisual programs, publications, and other means of presenting interpretive information, such as websites, apps, podcasts, and blogs.

A person's reaction to word selection, tone of voice, actions, attitudes, mood, personality, and appearance determines much about the learning process. A negative reaction to any one of these reduces acceptance and message effectiveness.

Interpreters must be conscious of their own image and presence, but not distractingly self-conscious. They should focus on the visitors' reception of the messages. Attention to feedback from the visitors—their body language, questions, and interest—helps an interpreter to adjust the presentation to achieve its objectives.

People's responses to and understanding of interpretive messages depend on their reactions to the person who interprets, the location, and their own physical or emotional conditions, prejudices, and experiences.

Interpreters often have great motivating power over visitors by their position of relative authority, force of personality, and intimate knowledge of the local environment. Simply put, they are authority figures and that makes them credible.

However, they can erode their credibility by presenting invented or erroneous information or by actions that communicate insecurity or hostility. Persuasion theory suggests that several factors affect credibility: rate of speaking, diversity of vocabulary, physical appearance (e.g., uniform, posture), plus verbal and nonverbal expressions of confidence. Interpreters can use all of these factors to enhance their effectiveness and persuasiveness. Simple courtesy and consideration of others affects response positively. In sum, be professional, make eye contact, smile, and "exhibit warm body language" (Buchholz, Lackey, Gross, & Zimmerman, 2015).

The location may also affect reception and acceptance. The place establishes a mood and this can be used to advantage as visitors look out upon a beautiful scene. Similarly, the interpreter who seats the audience so they face the historic buildings being discussed provides an excellent backdrop for a talk.

> "Interpreters often have great motivating power."

Some visitor characteristics and attitudes make communications tough. Most of these barriers lie beyond the control of the interpreter. Some visitors suffer personal distractions. Others may come with strong preconceptions about the topics or the agency. A few play psychological games by trying to figure out the interpreters, suspecting motives, or assuming that what they say and what they mean are two different things. Still other people have real challenges in reading, hearing, or perceiving. Many foreign visitors will have trouble with colloquial English.

Although Marshall McLuhan (1964) persuaded North Americans that "the medium is the message," the content and characteristics of messages also persuade, thereby affecting changes in attitudes and behavior. If the messages conflict with the visitor's previous beliefs, they must be stated with strong supporting evidence to produce a shift. If the beliefs of the interpreter and the listener are in concert, the visitor will more likely accept the suggested actions.

The interpreter's job of communicating vital concepts and provoking new levels of seeing and enjoying the environment is no simple task. It requires theory, considerable practice, and evaluation. The key is to engage the mind of the audience member in a lively process of idea exchange. That process can take several forms and follow any of several techniques. More coverage of education and communication theories will be provided in the following chapters.

The Interpreters' Clients = Everyone!

"Everyone" means "everyone," including those who may not even be present at the site. To gain constituents, interpreters must vigorously make resources available, presenting alternatives so people can choose the interpretive services that are most appealing to them. These may include an interpretive talk, guided tour, evening program, demonstration, exhibit, self-guided trail, podcast, or park website. Convenient, well-identified, self-guiding facilities will get the message across to many more people than an interpreter can ever hope to reach personally. For example, at Grand Canyon National Park you can "discover the canyon with your phone." The 2015 park newsletter suggests that visitors enjoy two-minute park ranger talks about the park's cultural and natural history at 30 different locations. Hosted by the Grand Canyon Association, visitors look for cell phone tour signs, dial the number, and enter the stop they are at. Visitors can also discover EarthCaches™ specifically tailored to geology and other educational experiences by checking in with the visitor center or park website. Then they can start their adventure using their own GPS device.

For maximum effectiveness, personally conducted interpretive programs should start at places and times convenient for visitors; this may stimulate impulse participation. In many zoos and historic sites or historic villages, interpreters station themselves at key sites, encountering virtually every visitor who strolls through, offering explanations and demonstrations.

When timed well and done right, visitors will respond. Obviously, interpreters should advertise and inform people about the programs. Personal contact, in particular, tends to increase participation. Interpretive staff should devise programs that offer continuing interest. In other words, defeat the "been there, done that" response. For example, the junior ranger/naturalist programs bring in repeat visitors and ensure progressively deeper experiences. An evening program at Mount Rainier National Park was based on a familiar TV game show by featuring park *Jeopardy*.

A more detailed analysis of serving diverse audiences will appear in Chapter 7.

Difficult Issues

Many museums, parks, forests, wildlife refuges, historic areas, and other interpretive sites deal with one or more critical issues. These issues may relate to the past, the present, or the future. They may involve either or both natural and cultural resources. They may be local, regional, or global in scale.

Interpreters may address many kinds of difficult issues. For example, they interpret racial tensions and civil rights at Martin Luther King, Jr., National Historic Site. They demonstrate how heavy metals accumulate in the food chain at Everglades National Park and Indiana Dunes National Lakeshore. They speculate about overpopulation and agricultural practices at Mesa Verde National Park.

In its early years, interpretation focused on ecology or history lessons in the field or around the campfire. The emphasis was on the site's grandeur and special features. This approach remains important. But in addition, today's visitors seek more. The United States has set aside many parks that address native Americans, civil rights, the women's movement, and, more recently, the LGBT community. Issues also arise in relation to natural resources to include carbon dioxide in the atmosphere. Interpreters—and the interpretive centers and museums they work at—have the opportunity, indeed the duty, to become a source of accurate information. What are the facts of the matter? What does science tell us? In this way, challenging issues can be addressed as a community and public service.

> What are the facts of the matter? What does science tell us?

Religion and Politics

Don't talk religion or politics (unless everyone agrees). This old adage, with our own parenthetical addition, urges keeping social peace in families, at company picnics, and at social dinners. Although good advice, it is not always possible, and interpreters may find themselves touching on these issues. The key point here is to be aware of many different points of view and to avoid arguing with others to the detriment of your program's message. The history of religious groups in a community can make one of the most fascinating interpretive topics. Consider the absurdity of avoiding religion at places like Martin Luther King, Jr. National Historic Site or his church in Birmingham; the Women's Rights National Historical Park; the Mormon Pioneer National Historic Trail; or almost any Native American context.

Similarly, religion is hard to avoid when talking about geology, the development of species, glaciers, dinosaurs, the universe or anything else that involves estimates of past time periods. The roots of such issues go back in human history for many centuries. In modern times, arguments still rage, leading to challenges for interpreters of the natural scene.

Likewise, anything political may offend someone at some time, so there is no sense in compromising a good interpretive message with irrelevant or divisive talk. If and when political issues come up, you should be courteous. If a visitor asks questions about your personal preferences in these areas one-on-one, perhaps after your program, that is different from advocating a personal political view in front of an audience of 500. Basically, discernment is necessary and how far you go in the realm of politics and religion will often depend on your particular circumstances. As Snyder and Ash (1999) point out, quality interpretation at these sites requires staff openness to different points of view, training to deal with issues, and management support. Diplomacy and tactfulness remain essential.

Nonetheless, this discussion does not suggest that interpretation should be "safe," avoiding all aspects of controversy. As noted, courtesy and respect are paramount, not only with politics and religion, but also race, national origin, gender, and so on. However, interpreters have important messages to share, based on facts and science, and interpretation of such should not be made ineffective for fear of stepping on someone's toes.

Wildlife Rehabilitation

With animal rights advocates and sport hunters butting heads, any talk or exhibit about wildlife carries explosive potential, as well as being a top attention-getter. Wildlife rehabilitation centers, often attached to interpretive facilities, also provoke controversy. They require high expenditures for cages, flight pens, feeding, veterinarian services, and routine care and cleaning, as well as specialized permanent personnel. To be effective, they require an interpreter. Live animals provide interpreters the best visual aids available and can help emphasize important messages about environmental stewardship.

Some suggest that wild animals should take care of themselves and there should be no interference in their welfare. On the other hand, rehabilitation centers create public enthusiasm, a mostly positive image of the agency, increased opportunities to interact sincerely with citizens at a serious level, and invitations to visit camps, clubs, and schools. Having live animals can open the discussion for wildlife management, the critical importance of habitat, and factors that threaten various species.

A thoughtful, knowledgeable, and tactful interpreter seems vital to making wildlife rehabilitation a positive and beneficial interpretive experience. Without a high level of interpreter/visitor interaction, there may be negative educational effects (Baker, 1988). Manes (1990), while warning against exploiting live wild animals for interpretation declared:

Rehabilitation efforts are valid if they provide unreleasable specimens that are properly employed to foster public understanding and appreciation of wildlife resources and issues…A park interpreter…can guarantee program participation by carrying a live owl through campgrounds when promoting a program about raptors…Rehabilitation programs put to use animals that would otherwise be lost from human benefit—perhaps a vital form of conservation.

Controversial issues such as religion, politics, and using live animals for education constitute only a portion of what may stir interest and controversy. Resource management also comes up in local and national debates. Visitors expect interpreters to explain the facts about how resources may be best managed (e.g., controversial timber harvest methods, prescribed burning, hunting restrictions). Interpretation serves as an active, influential part of the agency. Interpreters need to conduct careful research and read widely on all sides of the issue. Inviting subject matter authorities to discuss the issue can be helpful for staff and can be opened up to park visitors as well.

Climate Change

Returning full circle to the introductory story for this chapter, we add at this juncture that the joint assignment Walt Dabney and Freeman Tilden embarked on included identifying "the proper role for the NPS to play through its interpretive programs to address the growing awareness of the 'environmental crisis.'" One of the key features of interpretation is to promote stewardship of our cultural and natural resources. Although interpreting difficult issues will come up again in other chapters, we will focus on just one other overriding issue that requires special attention here.

The science of climate change goes back several decades and culminated in a statement by international scientists (Intergovernmental Panel on Climate Change, 2007) as follows:

> Warming of the climate system is unequivocal, as is now evident from observations of increases in global average air and ocean temperatures, widespread melting of snow and ice, and rising global sea level.

However, acceptance of the science has been slower. Nonetheless, as scientific evidence has become clearer in what people can see and experience personally, there has been a progressive shift in public opinion.

Many organizations have made interpreting climate change and its implications an important component of their interpretive services (Box 5.4). The National Park Service Climate Change Response Program, initiated in 2010, focuses on four areas of emphasis: using science to help parks manage climate change, adapting to an uncertain future, mitigating or reducing our carbon footprint, and communicating to the public (and employees) about climate change. The NPS seeks to be a model of responsible stewardship.

Box 5.4
Interpreting Climate Change

Jess Reese, Interpretive Programs Supervisor at the Brookfield Zoo

The public has been divided on the issue of global climate change, from their opinions of causality, to their feelings of empowerment, to their personal level of responsibility. The biggest challenge in interpreting climate change lies in creating messages that induce unity and empowerment, rather than contributing to the divisiveness and despair that surrounds this issue for many people.

Interpretation has the potential to inspire hope and feelings of optimism in addressing the challenges that climate change presents, as well as fill in the cognitive holes that prevent the public from turning toward solutions. By forging intellectual and emotional connections, interpreters have the potential to move audiences from complacency to compassion as well as address gaps in audience knowledge and assist in connecting the dots between causes, effects, and solutions.

The Association of Zoos and Aquarium Institutions in the United States reach 181 million visitors a year, which is more than the total of all visitors to major U.S. sporting events. Interpreters in these and other institutions have the potential to be a force to unify and create "multipliers" who become messengers that can build public support for solutions that match the challenges of the problem.

In 2010, interpreters across the nation began learning how to change the public conversation about climate change, by incorporating strategic framing tools in their informal learning centers. The five month-long study circles were run by The National Network for Ocean and Climate Change Interpretation (NNOCCI). Under National Science Foundation grant funding and the leadership of the New England Aquarium, these intensive training sessions trained interpreters to communicate the complex scientific issues that relate to oceans and climate change. The study circles were run by New England Aquarium staff, as well as staff from the Frameworks Institute, who conducted the social science research that the strategic framing recommendations are based on. By the end of 2016, the five year program trained approximately 300 interpreters in such varied informal education centers such as zoos, aquaria, national parks, museums of science and industry, marine sanctuaries, national estuarine research reserves, NOAA staff, Woods Hole Oceanographic Institution post docs, and many more.

Strategic framing is a communication process that uses the research of social science scholars to carefully craft a message with an awareness of how that information might be filtered and interpreted by an audience. With regard to strategically framing climate change, NNOCCI's goal was to increase understanding and impacting behavior. NNOCCI's interpretive recommendations are based on five core strategic framing elements that are designed to move the conversation away from blame and toward solutions that are systemic, community-based, and empowering. They are as follows:

- **Neutral Tone** encourages healthy, solutions-oriented discussions.
- **Value statements** explain why this issue matters and include shared, cherished ideals that every American can relate to, such as Responsible Management and Stewardship.
- **Explanatory Metaphors** are like linguistic spackle to fill the cognitive holes which prevent people from understanding the mechanisms of climate change, which impedes thinking that leads to productive solutions.
- **Explanatory Chains** connects the cause of the issue to the effect by explaining how "A" leads to "B," which leads to "C," and so on.
- **Community Level Solutions** that appeal to guests as citizens rather than consumers and facilitates a "we," rather than "me" mindset (frameworksacademy.org).

Interpreters can create opportunities for authentic dialogue, inspire hope, fill the cognitive gaps and find the common ground that we all share. Interpreting climate change using strategic framing tools can help you tailor messages to reach every American's heart and mind, crafting a country that is united in sustainable actions.

In conjunction with the National Park Centennial, several books came out each of which considered the challenges of climate change in the parks: *The Hour of Land: A Personal Topography of America's National Parks* (i.e., Glacier National Park and glacial melting) by Terry Tempest Williams (2016), *Lassoing the Sun: A Year in America's National Parks* (i.e., Dry Tortugas National Park and rising sea level) by Mark Woods (2016), and National Geographic's *The National Parks, An Illustrated History, 100 Years of American Splendor* by Kim Heacox (2016). In the latter of these books, Jon Jarvis, NPS Director, writes in the foreword that the park service has taken on the complex issue of climate change: "We asserted that the climate is changing, that it is caused by human activities, and that our national parks are natural solutions."

The national parks are being impacted *now*. Warmer temperatures have increased the rate of glacial retreat in Alaska's Glacier Bay and Kenai Fjords National Parks. In the 1800s, there were 150 glaciers within the boundaries of Glacier National Park. Today there are 25 glaciers and USGS scientists estimate that by 2030 much of what remains will be gone. Joshua Tree National Park may also suffer the fate of the namesake of the park disappearing. Joshua trees require cool winters and freezing temperatures in order to flower and set their seeds. Scientists have documented considerable mortality of Joshua trees and predict that due to climate change the trees will be unable to persist much longer within the park (Figure 5.7). At Yellowstone, the warmer winters have enabled bark beetles to significantly increase mortality of whitebark pines, the seeds of which are a critical food source for grizzly bears and which threaten their survival rates. Indeed, rising temperatures at Yellowstone (and other parks) will result in entire plant communities shifting upward to cooler climes with less forest-dominated vegetation and more desert scrub vegetation (Abrahamson, 2016).

A three-part series on interpreting climate change appeared in *Legacy*, the magazine of the National Association for Interpretation. In this series, Patricia Walsh summarized current training strategies such as the NPS Interpreting Climate Change Self-study Modules, the National Network of Ocean and Climate Change Interpretation, and NASA Earth Ambassador Program. Walsh (2016a) noted that the more facts you offer a climate skeptic, the less they are likely to hear. Therefore, avoid arguments that will be counterproductive. For example, an NPS training handout is titled, "Embrace Controversy—Avoid Conflict."

Without going into the depths of the science of climate change, interpretive trainers recommend the "heat-trapping blanket metaphor." This is a simple overview that notes that the burning of fossil fuels such as coal and oil emits excess carbon dioxide that acts like a heat-trapping blanket and disrupts the climate (Walsh, 2016b). Local examples are encouraged. For example, interpreters on the Washington D.C. Mall can point out that the peak bloom of cherry trees is now harder to predict, proving a challenge to local hotels and restaurants that count on this seasonal display for tourist revenue. Here we see real impact on those who serve in the hospitality industry.

An innovative project by staff-volunteer teams at Capulin Volcano National Monument bands and releases hummingbirds in studying the impacts of climate change on these remarkable migratory birds. Members of the public assist by cradling each banded hummer before it flies away. The project aims to create a lasting impact and, ideally, visitors who are more sensitive to the issue (Walsh, 2016b).

Figure 5.7. The stunningly beautiful Joshua Tree is one of many plants threatened by climate change. (LB)

Interpreters are encouraged to have a sense of humor. In addition, it is important not to despair, but rather to find solace in nature, the very thing interpreters hope to protect (Walsh, 2016c). By staying positive, interpreters can share hope in such a way that people will ask what they can do to help solve the problem or will want to learn more. Government actions toward clean energy development and use will be essential (McKibben, 2016).

The discussion now is on how to cope with the reality of what is happening. Hardin-Nieri (2016) indicates that climate change is "not a liberal, conservative, rich, or poor issue; it is everybody's issue."

> "Climate change is everybody's issue."

Provoking Thoughtful Analysis and Solutions

Interpreters serve as agents of change. Not all change involves difficult issues, but much of it does. And controversy can get people's attention. The interpreter presenting facts and artifacts in a rational way can encourage visitors to reason with evidence. Many years ago, Freeman Tilden (1957) wrote about relating the interpretive message to people's lives back home and provoking new ways of looking at things. To relate to people and to provoke public involvement and action, the interpreter can use three strategies:

1. Use the story line approach to describe the physical environment and social processes. Demonstrate the relevance of the site to involve the public. The interpreter serves as the expert and guide, getting the people started with historical and scientific information presented in understandable ways.
2. Facilitate use of the museum or interpretive center as a clearinghouse that encourages exchange of information. Offer programs by invited speakers, conduct research, and maintain a reference service (books, journals, accurate websites, maps, data bases, and so on).
3. Host public forums that may lead to community involvement. Allow the citizens to talk to each other, while the interpreter provides a setting for the forum.

Archibald (2001) advocated that:

Museums can become the places of dialogue, the new town squares. We can be collaborators, conveners, facilitators, places where community is constructed and the future incubated.

Therefore, this three-stage structure can stimulate the public to do its own exploring, thinking, and concluding, using the cultural or natural resource base (e.g., museum, park, science center) as a community setting and catalyst.

Essence of Interpretation

True love, deep love, abiding love sustains us as a people in a complex society and ecosystem. Producing this kind of love can come only from direct acquaintance.

Direct involvement with objects and people and real places produces a key component of interpretation (Beck, 1986). Colin Turnbull (1981) identified the frustrations of many "tourists that are carefully kept at a distance from…the animals, the land, the people. They are denied the opportunity many of them sought." Of course, in some instances, concern for visitor safety or the integrity of the resources require restrictions. But this is the exception. Interpretation's essence involves visitors directly in a participatory experience. They learn "through the use of original objects, by firsthand experience" (Tilden, 1957). Members of an interpretive audience may actively examine a nugget of gold, an owl pellet, an arrowhead, or a caribou antler. Or they may learn Native American or frontier skills—the "primitive skills in pioneering travel and subsistence" (Leopold, 1966).

An important characteristic of interpretation is that it implies interaction. It calls for participation by all present—more than reading labels, listening to podcasts, referring to apps, or tagging along. It means actively taking in information and experiences, and creating meanings for oneself. The interpreter structures the program so people may feel, smell, taste, see, hear, walk, talk, think, experiment, and perceive. Thus interpretation becomes an experience. The full impact of interpretation may come in the aftermath, as the experience revives and grows into a continuing process of reading the landscape, reliving the story, seeking more answers, and carefully applying the lessons through a life of stewardship of natural and cultural heritage.

Summary

The interpretive profession has grown in the fertile ground of museums and outdoor resources through many decades of careful cultivation. Enos Mills and Freeman Tilden described principles that help to get messages across to people. Much of their emphasis has roots in education and communications theory. More recent work has expanded on their interpretive principles. Furthermore, there has been professional interest in the use of thematic communication and making connections between tangibles and intangibles that further express basic interpretive principles.

Quality interpretation calls for emphasis on the special character of a place. Through total programming, interpretation aims to serve as a central experience for visitors as well as to extend the major messages to all citizens. Interpreters craft their themes and then offer total programming for diversity of experience and, over the long run, growth in skills. The interpreter seeks to bring people into more intimate contact with their natural and cultural surroundings so they can develop respect and love for them and come to their own conclusions.

Ultimately, interpretation is a *visitor* experience. Although interpreters often speak of interpreting *for* the visitor, in reality the visitor's mind does the perceiving and interpreting of artifacts and nature. The professional interpreter facilitates these perceptions by providing information, activities, trails, exhibits, blogs, websites, and many other methods to develop the perceptive skills of each visitor. The interpreter clearly has a role, a very important role, in laying a foundation for quality visitor experiences. By following the guiding principles of interpretation the recipients of the interpretation are more likely to be moved by their experiences and will recognize, more deeply, both their privileges and obligations toward the planet, therefore making it a better place.

Literature Cited

Abrahamson, J. (2016). Yellowstone 2.0. *Sierra*, July/August, 36–41.

Archibald, R. (2001). Reaching in: The community and the museum. *History News*, 56(3), 6–9.

Baker, R. (1988).Wildlife rehabilitation as an interpretive tool. In *Proceedings, 1988 National Interpreter's Workshop*. Fort Collins, CO: National Association for Interpretation.

Beck, L. (1986). A hierarchy of interpretive programs. *The Interpreter*, Winter, 18–20.

Beck, L., & Cable, T. (2011). *The gifts of interpretation: Fifteen guiding principles for interpreting nature and culture* (3rd ed.). Urbana, IL: Sagamore.

Brochu, L., & Merriman, T. (2008). *Personal interpretation* (2nd ed.). Fort Collins, CO: Interpress, National Association for Interpretation.

Buchholz, J., Lackey, B., Gross, M., & Zimerman, R. (2015). *The interpreter's guidebook.* (4th ed.). Stevens Point, WI: UWSP Foundation Press.

Burdee, J. (2007). War west of the Mississippi. *Legacy*, 18(6), 40.

Dabney, W. (1988). Travels with Freeman. *Journal of Interpretation*, 12(1):T7–8.

Ham, S. (1992). *Environmental interpretation*. Golden, CO: Fulcrum Publishing.

Ham, S. (2013). *Interpretation: Making a difference on purpose*. Golden, CO: Fulcrum Publishing.

Hardin-Nieri, S. (2016). An ecological conversion. *Legacy*, 27(3), 20–21.

Heacox, K. (2016). *The national parks, an illustrated history, 100 years of American splendor*. Washington, D.C.: National Geographic.

Ickes, H. (1938). Letter to Jens Jensen (Container 222, Ickes Papers, Library of Congress). In B. Mackintosh (1985), Harold L. Ickes and the National Park Service. *Journal of Forest History*, (2), 78–84.

Intergovernmental Panel on Climate Change. (2007). *Climate Change 2007*. Sweden: Published by the Intergovernmental Panel on Climate Change.

Larsen, D. (2003). *Meaningful interpretation*. Fort Washington, PA: Eastern National.

Leopold, A. (1966). *A Sand County almanac*. New York, NY: Oxford University Press.

Lewis, B. (1980). *Interpreting for park visitors*. Philadelphia, PA: Eastern Acorn Press.

Manes, R. (1990). Creating public misconceptions. *Human dimensions in wildlife newsletter*, 9(1), 12–14.

McKibben, B. (2016). A world at war. *The New Republic*, August 15, 2016.

McLuhan, M. (1964). *Understanding media: The extensions of man*. Toronto, ON: McGraw-Hill.

Mills, E. (1920). *The adventures of a nature guide*. Garden City, NY: Doubleday & Co.

Porter, E., & Gleick, J. (1990). *Nature's chaos*. New York, NY: The Viking Press.

Snyder, M., & Ash, C. (1999). Interpreting historic religious sites. *In 1999 interpretive sourcebook*. Ft. Collins, CO: National Association for Interpretation.

Tilden, F. (1957). *Interpreting our heritage*. Chapel Hill, NC: University of North Carolina Press.

Turnbull, C. (1981). Tourism as pilgrim. *Natural History*, 90(7), 76–81.

Walsh, P. (2016a). The more facts you give, the less they hear. *Legacy*, 27(1), 36–39.

Walsh, P. (2016b). Strategies for interpreting climate change. *Legacy*, 27(2), 36–39.

Walsh, P. (2016c). Keeping calm and carrying on. *Legacy, 27*(3), 36–39.

Williams, T. T. (2016). *The hour of land: A personal topography of America's national parks*. New York, NY: Sarah Crichton Books.

Woods, M. (2016). *Lassoing the sun: A year in America's national parks*. New York, NY: Thomas Dunne Books.

CHAPTER 6
How People Learn

In an episode of *60 Minutes*, Charlie Rose visited the office of Bill Gates to get a sense of how the billionaire philanthropist draws intellectual inspiration. In this episode, Gates leads Rose to a bookcase filled with DVDs from the Great Courses, approximately 200 volumes. The Great Courses rely on outstanding professors who lecture on everything from science to religion, and from mathematics to music. Among partners of the Great Courses are National Geographic, the Smithsonian, and the Culinary Institute of America. The courses can be enjoyed on apps for iPad, iPhone, Android, Kindle, or on a laptop or desktop computer.

A noteworthy trend is that more people seek to learn for the sole purpose of… learning. This trend is accelerating due to live-streaming of TED talks, Lynda.com, the Great Courses, learning through travel such as Road Scholars, Osher Lifelong Learning Institutes, and brain-training games. People are seeking to learn and they are seeking to learn in ways that may permanently change them. Interpreters, of course, may offer just such learning experiences. And one doesn't have to be a billionaire to learn and be engaged by our vast reservoirs of cultural and natural resources.

In this chapter, we explore how people learn and we make application to the interpretive arena. Understanding the different ways people learn helps interpreters to organize experiences people will remember and find meaningful. Educational theories give interpreters *guidelines* for communicating more relevantly. However, the reader is cautioned that the volume of literature in the field of education is immense and there is widespread controversy regarding some theories. Extensive work has been done in the area of learning styles, for example, with many *different* theories that have been advanced. Therefore, we present theories in this chapter with the intent that readers will gain a *broad* idea of how researchers suggest people learn and that these ideas can *apply* to the field of interpretation through developing and delivering programs and exhibits.

Good interpretation, just as good teaching, enriches and alters individuals' information bases, skills, attitudes, and subsequent behaviors. But unlike traditional classroom education, interpreters integrate a spirit of recreation and offer numerous first-hand experiences with real objects in natural and cultural environments. Interpretation differs from schooling, yet people learn much from it.

Interpretation of natural and cultural resources involves and uses many education principles. This chapter provides an overview of educational theories that are significant foundations of the professional practice of interpretation. Several of these are "classic" theories that have been practiced for decades and may be useful to the interpreter. In addition, more recent literature continues to shed light on how people learn (i.e., Brown, Roediger, & McDaniel, 2014; Duhigg, 2012; Foer, 2011; Gardner, 2011; Kahneman, 2011; Mayer, 2010).

Receiving and Processing Information and Ideas

Traditionally, we observe that people operate within three general learning domains. The *cognitive domain* involves using the rational mind to process information. This "intellectual knowledge" helps make sense of the environment through facts and by developing concepts and classifications. Interpreters reach this domain with talks, written materials, charts, and exhibits. However, weak cognitive skills in reading and calculating may preclude some people from receiving the full message. With about 20% of the U.S. population being relatively illiterate or having reading difficulties, exhibits or brochures with emphasis on written material alone may be problematic for one in five visitors. Exhibit planners and brochure writers can help overcome this by telling the story, as much as possible, through the sequence and display of objects and graphics as well as with podcasts and various apps.

The *affective domain* relates to one's feelings. The individual learns at the emotional level, responding by expressing attitudes or sentiments. Common interpretive approaches that reach this domain include discussion, photography, paintings, music, and drama, although powerful talks, stories, written materials, and exhibits may also elicit learning responses from the affective domain (Figure 6.1).

The *kinesthetic domain* involves motor skills. Learning occurs through physical movement and skill development. The interpreter may use participatory activities, hiking through the swamps, crossing glaciers, and shucking corn to promote this learning domain.

Throughout this chapter we will advocate using several different learning theories in order to best facilitate learning for a wide diversity of learners. For example, interpreters can expand the knowledge, attitudes, and skills of people through appropriately mixing the domains just presented. Furthermore, we advocate multisensory learning (Figure 6.2). People take in information through their senses. Therefore, the more we can employ the use of *all* senses the more likely we will enhance learning. Roger Riolo (2014) sums up the value of a multisensory approach as follows: "Stated simply, multiple senses employed in the delivery of information create multiple areas for retention and multiple areas for recall" (see also Sousa, 2011) (Figure 6.3).

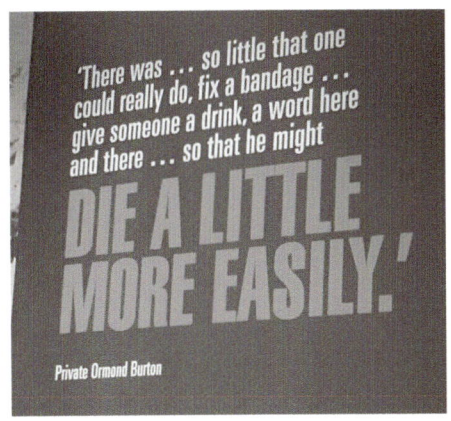

Figure 6.1. An exhibit about the horrors of World War I in the Te Papa Museum in New Zealand uses a quote from a medic to evoke a powerful response in the affective domain. (TC)

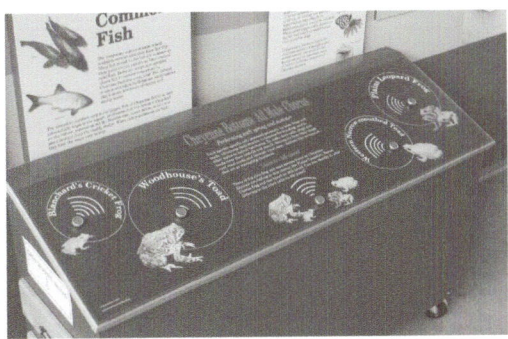

Figure 6.2. This multisensory exhibit allows the guest to both see the frogs and toads and hear their "all male chorus." (PM)

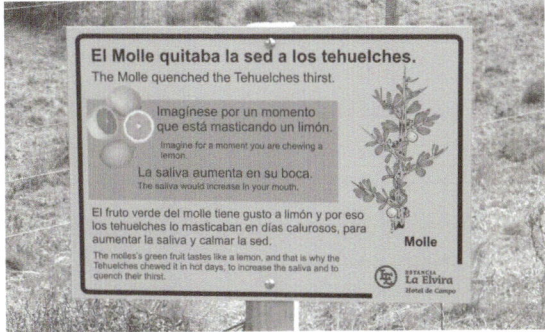

Figure 6.3 This interpretive sign in Argentina appeals to both the sense of smell and taste along the trail. (VF)

Major Learning Theories and Useful Strategies

> The more we can employ the use of *all* senses the more likely we will enhance learning.

This section describes several different models or theories of how people learn. Some theorists describe how learning abilities are age related. Others describe learning strategies of individuals of all ages. The popular theory of constructivism states that humans build on what they know and have experienced. The end of the chapter includes commentary about the importance of life-long learning.

Cognitive Development Theory

According to cognitive development theory, people learn according to their own level of cognitive maturity. Piaget (1952, 1955), a Swiss psychologist, described learning at four stages of childhood: from birth to 2 years, 2-7 years, 7-11 years, and more than 11 years (Box 6.1). Of course, *individuals* develop at different rates. Still, Piaget's model gives a broad overview of learning patterns as children mature. Simply put, this hierarchy specifies that concepts develop from simple to complex and from concrete to abstract. Application of this theory will be especially useful for interpreters who work with children.

Stage 1: Sensorimotor

The first stage in Piaget's model includes infants and toddlers. From birth to 2 years, learning occurs primarily through sensory and motor activities. Even at this early age, infants and toddlers have surprising capacities for learning. Toddlers can learn bird names and flowers quickly. Parents and interpreters can introduce them to experiences in nature, help them to feel comfortable in an outdoor setting, and allow them to explore using all of their senses.

> People learn according to their own level of cognitive maturity.

The questions that these children commonly ask relate to place and name. These very young learners ask *where*, *what*, and *who*, questions.

Stage 2: Preoperational

In the second stage, 2- to 7-year-olds master symbols and words. The child can focus attention on only one characteristic at a time, so interpretive programs designed for children in this age range should concentrate on one central idea. As Ralph Waldo Emerson observed, "To the young mind, everything is individual, stands by itself... Later remote things cohere and flower out from one stem" (Tilden, 1967).

After age 2, *when* and *why* questions emerge, sometimes with irksome frequency. These are questions of cause and time.

Box 6.1
Piaget's Stages of Cognitive Development

Age	Stage	Development Abilities
0-2 years	Sensorimotor	Develops organized patterns of behavior and thought (schemes). Uses sensory and motor activities, primarily.
2-7 years	Preoperational	Masters symbols (words). Centers attention on one characteristic at a time. Cannot mentally reverse actions.
7-11 years	Concrete operations	Generalizes from concrete experiences. Unable to mentally manipulate conditions not yet experienced.
> 11 years	Formal operations	Able to form hypotheses. Deals with abstractions. Solves problems systematically. Engages in mental manipulations.
Adapted from Pomerantz (1990)		

Stage 3: Concrete operations

Piaget's concrete operational stage includes children from 7-11 years of age. Preadolescents tend to limit their thinking to those things they have experienced concretely and directly. Therefore, interpretive programs for this age group focus on those aspects of cultural and natural history that they can directly experience. For example, a multisensory approach that allows for personal examination of various qualities of an interpretive site is appropriate for this age range.

Stage 4: Formal Operations

The formal operational stage covers people beyond age 11 years. At this stage of cognitive development, youths can solve problems systematically and deal with abstractions. Adolescents engage in mental manipulations and form hypotheses. As a consequence, interpretation can challenge youth in more cognitive, abstract ways.

These stages of cognitive development can help in designing effective interpretive materials and methods for various age groups. Practical application of these concepts starts with Mills' (1920) recognition that children and adults learn differently and have distinct capabilities. Tilden (1967) reiterated that interpretation addressed to children "should not be a dilution of the presentation to adults, but should follow a fundamentally different approach."

Interpreters apply Piaget's theory by (a) offering information consistent with how the children in the audience can process it, and (b) using different interpretive techniques that fit the different levels of cognitive development represented in the audience.

Piaget's contribution was to identify stages of "readiness" for different kinds of learning. He contended that readiness is advanced by active experience. For example, abstractions and talk of cause-and-effect may get responses from adults, while children will not comprehend the discussion. A nature hike or museum tour should progress in some orderly, story-like fashion so as not to surpass the abilities of young children (Grinder & McCoy, 1985). This does not mean that interpretation for mixed age groups should aim at the lowest common denominator. With mixed audiences, the interpreter can offer concrete experiences and a variety of age-appropriate activities to meet the needs of all the members of the group. Interpreters and other educators therefore can organize programs to anticipate the next stage in development.

Bettelheim (1989) built on Piaget's scale of development to focus on how children perceive their world. "To the child, there is no clear line of separating objects from living things…" A child's thinking remains animistic until early adolescence. They think rocks, tress, and animals can tell us things if we tune into them. It seems reasonable to expect answers from those objects that arouse our curiosity. As many interpreters know, some adults can also think this way (LaPage, 2001; Roads, 1987). For example, gifted Australian and Native American elders have somehow retained and refined this communication with the environment into a highly sensitive, almost mysterious, kind of intelligence. It allows them to make amazingly accurate diagnoses of natural phenomena and of the past as they walk on certain lands. It seems clear that for them, "the land speaks" (Edwards, 1979).

Learning Styles

Various learning style theories suggest that different individuals learn in different ways and that students can succeed if they learn according to their own styles. In practice, learning style theory serves as a framework for teachers who seek to accommodate different types of learners. Likewise, interpreters can benefit from an understanding of how different people most effectively take in and process information. However, as noted previously, there are many *different* theories on learning styles and some question their validity at all (Reiner & Willingham, 2010).

Our primary message about learning styles is that variety in the presentation is key. Orchestrating interpretive programs to meet the needs of diverse visitors results in innovative and stimulating events. People who learn best by different styles can be equally intelligent (Brandt, 1990). The interpreter can introduce information through a person's particular learning style and help the individual to "stretch" by learning through other styles as well (O'Neil, 1990). Furthermore, recent research indicates that people have multiple forms of intelligence and that "you learn better when you 'go wide,' drawing on all of your aptitudes and resourcefulness, than when you limit instruction or experience to the style you find most amenable" (Brown, Roediger, & McDaniel, 2014). Again, variety in presentation proves to be the most useful and meaningful for learning to occur, and will be most interesting to participants.

Multiple Intelligences

In addition to work on learning styles the similar theory of multiple intelligences has been advanced. Howard Gardner (2011) wrote *Frames of Mind: The Theory of Multiple Intelligences* that categorized relatively independent intelligences with individuals showing varying degrees of ability in each. Since his initial work in 1983, he has included other intelligences and updated his text. His notion of multiple intelligences has been adopted at schools, museums, and businesses around the world.

> Applying the various intelligences provide many possibilities for engaging visitors in interpretive programs.

Following is a brief description of each of these intelligences (Gardner 2011), as well as a listing of five activities for each that we believe may be relevant. That is, applying the various intelligences provide many possibilities for engaging visitors in interpretive programs. Circumstances, of course, will determine the applicability of many of our recommendations.

Bodily-Kinesthetic: The capacity to use the body or certain parts of the body (such as the hands) to solve problems or create products. To be potentially included in interpretation:

- Crafts
- Creative movement
- Using manipulatives
- Dramatizing
- Going on field trips

Spatial: The ability to conceptualize and manipulate large- or small-scale spatial arrays. For interpretive purposes:

- Graphing
- Photographing
- Mapping stories
- Using or making 3D projects
- Creating charts

Logical-Mathematical: The ability to conceptualize the logical relations among actions or symbols. To be used in interpretive programs:
- Collecting data
- Solving puzzles
- Sequencing
- Playing logic games
- Problem solving

Musical: The capacity to play musical instruments, sing, or compose music based on sensitivity to rhythm, pitch, meter, tone, melody and timbre. For use in interpretation:
- Playing background music
- Playing instruments
- Tapping out poetic rhythms
- Singing
- Rapping

Linguistic: Sometimes referred to as language intelligence this relates to sensitivity toward the meaning, order, sound, and rhythms of words. For the purposes of interpretation:
- Reading aloud
- Process writing
- Listening
- Debating
- Storytelling

Interpersonal: This is sometimes called social intelligence and refers to the capacity to interact effectively with others. Potential uses in interpretation may include the following:
- Brainstorming
- Sharing
- Discussing
- Cooperative learning through group work
- Social awareness

Intrapersonal: Also referred to as self-intelligence, this is awareness of one's own feelings and goals. For interpretation various application may include the following:
- Personal response
- Individual projects
- Independent reading
- Journaling
- Personal goal setting

Naturalistic: This is the last of the multiple intelligences that Gardner has most recently added, although he suspects there could be even one or two more showing that this, and educational theory in general, continues to evolve. This particular intelligence is especially pertinent in regards to nature interpretation. It involves the ability to make distinctions in the world of nature and is sometimes referred to as nature intelligence. Applications in interpretation include the following:
- Going on a nature walk
- Planting a garden
- Observing the stars
- Collecting rocks
- Identifying plants, insects, reptiles, amphibians, birds, and mammals

Having an understanding of multiple intelligences may assist interpreters in better knowing their own preferences toward learning and the 40 examples we provided across the spectrum of intelligences should be helpful in determining a variety of elements that may be incorporated into interpretive programs.

Cognitive Map Theory

Cognitive map theory provides a foundation for understanding how people assimilate information, code it into simplified units, and store it in relation to other information. Cognitive maps, then, resemble mental structures that contain information about how the environment is organized. As a result of these organizing functions, cognitive maps serve to facilitate the absorption and comprehension of details (Neisser, 1976). These "mind maps" provide the mental scaffolding for organizing otherwise fragmentary pieces of information into a meaningful structure.

As it relates to interpretation, cognitive map theory matches external stimuli with an individual's internal model for meaning to occur. Hammitt (1981) observed that cognitive map theory correlates to Tilden's (1967) first principle of interpretation.

> Any interpretation that does not somehow relate to what is being displayed or described to something within the personality or experience of the visitor will be sterile…The visitor ultimately is seeing things through his own eyes, not those of the interpreter.

To best relate to and serve visitors, the interpreter must strive to recognize the mental models that visitors possess and to present information in those terms. This will often require the use of comparisons, contrasts, analogies, and metaphors (Hammitt, 1981).

In addition to relating to existing cognitive models that each visitor holds, the interpreter can also try to create a basic cognitive map for first-time museum or forest visitors. Richard Knopf (1981) conducted research at Gettysburg National Military Park and suggested that cognitive map formation early in an interpretive experience can aid in assimilating more information. To apply this, prior to immersing visitors into a novel cultural or natural environment, an interpreter could present an overview orientation of the entire setting. An effective cognitive map defines the bounds of the environment to be explored and gives the visitor a sense of clarity. According to Knopf (1981):

> It allows details of the interpretive message to become more relevant, it yields the capacity to see where the interpretive message is heading, and, most signifi-

cantly, it gives one the ability to predict—to guess and fill in pieces of the picture that have not been made explicit.

In large and complex interpretive settings, different activities and programs can be designed to build on one another. Interpretive managers should determine which order of visitation should be promoted to provide for optimal interpretive experiences.

Proster Theory

Advances in understanding the human brain led to the "proster" theory, developed by Leslie Hart (1983, 1991). This approach and its derivatives build on findings from a number of disciplines, including the neural sciences, ethology, brain evolution, and computer science. Hart synthesized this work into a theory of learning with educational applications. He applied the proster theory to create brain compatible learning situations.

According to Hart (1991), the human brain acts aggressively, not passively, as was long believed. Through intensely aggressive action, the brain steadily makes sense of the world by extracting patterns from huge amounts of input (making order of chaos). Several principles of proster theory applied to interpretive situations follow:

1. Create effective learning environments with an absence of threat. The neocortex does not function well under pressure. Processing in this portion of the brain is cut short and the limbic system exerts more influence when a person feels threatened. Learners need to feel secure and at ease for effective learning to take place.
2. Encourage the basic skills of communication (oral or written) by their purposeful use.
3. Give learners freedom to manipulate materials in hands-on situations that provide large amounts of input to the brain.
4. Emphasize exposure to reality, not to contrived situations.
5. Address learning through performance.

Consistent with learning style theory, proster theory advocates applying the smorgasbord principle, which permits broad recognition of and allowance for individual differences. In interpretive programming, a variety of strategies should be used to meet the wide range of needs of those participating in the event.

Constructivist Learning or Meaning-Making

The constructivist approach to education seems to dominate American education in recent decades. It attempts to define how people *make meanings* of new information (Silverman, 1997). Something like it has dominated interpretive theory and practice for even longer (Saunders & Deyette, 1999). In many ways, Enos Mills practiced constructivist approaches. Freeman Tilden's principles borrowed components of Mills' lessons. Virtually every interpreter attempts to help people to make meanings in their own ways (e.g., incorporating participatory methods, drama, real objects in exhibits, discussions of natural phenomenon, historical presentations, and cultural interpretation).

Constructivist theory asserts that everyone has a *construct* (e.g., cognitive map) of information and attitudes that they bring to any learning process. Then any new information absorbed attaches to that mental structure, is affected by it, and affects it as the construct adjusts in a way unique to the individual. This echoes the 19th century concept of the *mechanism of apperception*, whereby new ideas associate with existing ideas to form a matrix of ideas called the apperception mass. New ideas assimilate with the old, altering the matrix.

Educators used this concept to define five steps for a lesson: preparation, presentation of new material, association, generalization, and application. Early versions of this emphasized the teacher's role. Constructivist revisions aim at promoting pupil (interpretive participant) activity. A few extreme constructivists limit the role of the teacher to convening the group, suggesting a topic, and then letting each pupil work on his or her individual constructs. The idea of recognizing different mind-sets and accommodating different stages of learning makes good common sense and enriches interpretive activities.

The differences in constructs become sharply evident when people (e.g., news reporters and politicians and forest ecologists) react publicly to quick environmental changes such as big forest fires in national parks. Often the reporters and politicians see a fire (and the forest) in the short run, using terms such as *disaster, devastation, scorched earth,* and *gone forever.* Forest ecologists often react with *long overdue, stimulates new growth, natural cycle,* and *better wildlife habitat.* The construct of the short-term emotional values provides a different way to process the perception of a fire than does the long-term, holistic, experienced view.

The key to using constructivist approaches in interpretive practice comes in recognizing that (a) visitors bring different constructs to interpretive sites and (b) they will process the message theme(s) differently. For example, if interpreting fire ecology, recognize that divergent preconceptions arrive in the heads of different people. By interpreting so that different learning processes, stages, and styles can operate, the message may come across to all. The interpreter offers direct encounters with the real thing, such as forest floor fuel buildup and demonstrations of natural reseeding. The interpreter also uses abstract symbols (e.g. fire triangles, ignition points), similes, weather charts, experiments, and models to show changes over many years. Then, different constructs get expanded and the messages about fire get reinforced in various ways.

This happens every day in history and nature interpretation. Interpreters can and do use many media and visitor participation methods to build understanding and perception into the constructs of human minds. Not all will come out with exactly the same ideas, but allowing for the variations will help the key messages to become part of the constructs of each individual.

Compassionate Intelligence

If he is indeed wise, he does not bid you to enter the house of his wisdom but rather, leads you to the threshold of your own mind.

–Kahlil Gibran

Research has confirmed what has been intuitively suspected all along: Children who are removed from opportunities to bond with nature are also denied the opportunity to establish a more balanced moral compass (Louv, 2005). For example, Gordon (2001) noted the importance of building a foundation for *compassionate intelligence.* Up until age 7, the child will bond with his or her primary nurturers. The role for parents or other caring adults at this stage is to provide opportunities—trips to the beach, the local nature center, the forest—and to ensure that the child feels safe and confident. Silvovsky (2001) noted that "early and middle childhood is the time to lay the foundation for future caring by providing kids lots of positive, meaningful joyful experiences." From experience as an interpreter, she warned against messages of doom and gloom.

The child who received a positive introduction to nature will usually develop a positive world-view. This approach includes opportunities for unstructured play so children may develop a sense of delight and wonder in nature. Many children in this day and age lead such structured lives that they have little time for free play. Many kids, captured by their various electronic devices, further isolate themselves from nature and culture. Getting them to pursue opportunities in nature and the wider cultural world at their doorstep becomes a challenge for parents and the community (Louv, 2005).

From 7 to 14 years, a growing sense of discovery and excitement helps to extend ties beyond the family to parts of the society and the earth's community of life. However, our urbanized culture has increasingly isolated people from the natural world. Therefore, when the child is ready to bond with something beyond the family, the prevailing "culture" stands more readily available. This produces bonding to a materialistic and consumer-oriented society, expanding technology, and the most aggressive or receptive peer group. Often the gang, the drug culture, or the street (rather than the woods) draw them in. Gordon (2001) summarized: "In this environment, children gradually forget their earlier instincts that drew them to the Earth and lose their sense of belonging to something wild and wonderful."

There are reasons for hope. Many schools, youth groups, and interpretive centers now provide opportunities for children to reawaken that sense of wonder in the natural environment. But parents and society need to continue to make efforts in that direction (Louv, 2005; 2011; 2016).

Gordon (2001) concluded that, if a child's experiences through the formative years have been grounded in the natural world, then a growing sense of autonomy will also incorporate a "profound reverence for all life and a desire to give back to the world." The child will have forged a foundation for a compassionate intelligence—a way of relating to the world that is healthy for the individual and for society at large.

Moral Development Theory

Educational theorists have also defined various stages of moral development, an understanding of which may assist interpreters. Kohlberg (1971) devised six stages of moral development, which provide an overview of how people arrive at the moral choices they make (Box 6.2).

Preconventional morality or the morality of the child includes the first two stages. Fear of punishment characterizes Stage One morality. An appropriate decision (e.g., not stealing a piece of petrified wood) arises out of a concern for the consequences of getting caught and the ensuing punishment. Fear of punishment still motivates Stage Two morality, but here the person makes a conscious evaluation of whether a certain behavior is worth the price of getting caught.

The next two stages make up *conventional morality* or the morality of the parent. They represent the moral level of most people. Concern for being an upstanding member of the family and the community dominates. Stage Three represents an evolution of behavior beyond selfish considerations that define preconventional morality. This stage of moral reasoning extends beyond the individual to include the well-being of family and friends. Stage Four extends concern to even broader applications—moral decisions expand to encompass the general welfare of society as a whole.

Postconventional morality or the morality of the adult includes the final two stages. Stage Five represents a shift back to the individual, but not in the same sense as ego-centered preconventional morality. Rather than passive acceptance of societal norms, this stage depends on individual evaluation of the appropriateness of conventional morality. Stage Six produces a way of life that fosters self-respect with the individual taking complete responsibility for his or her actions. It represents conviction of purpose and a commitment to ethical principles.

Kohlberg (1971) believed that people cannot skip stages in their moral development, but rather they advance in their morality one step at a time. Interpreters can use this to steer visitors toward environmentally responsible conduct. For example, an interpretive message often carries the "why" of keeping a reasonable distance from (and not feeding) the wildlife or from not touching the paintings. To meet the various moral stages of the visitors, interpreters can design informational messages that target different moral stages of development and expose visitors to the next higher stage of moral reasoning. Box 6.3 shows an example of a multistage message to safeguard fragile Anasazi cliff dwellings and granaries.

> Interpreters can design informational messages that target different moral stages of development.

Of course, a person can make the same choice after starting from any of the six stages. If the behavior is the same, does the motivation behind it really matter? Dustin (1985) suggested that it does, for three reasons:

1. Making moral choices based on reason and understanding is better than making them based on fear and ignorance.
2. Feeling responsible for one's actions is better than feeling irresponsible for them.
3. Answering to oneself is better than answering to others.

Kohlberg found that as people advance through the six stages their decisions become more consistent. This implies that a child (or adult) who behaved one way in the presence of an interpreter and the opposite way in the absence of the interpreter may evolve into someone who behaves consistently and responsibly regardless of the interpreter's whereabouts. Furthermore, if interpretive messages are well thought out and justifiable to the public, the advanced moral thinker can be expected to support them.

Although Kohlberg's conceptualization received wide support in the literature, two criticisms of his work deserve mention. First his theory is based largely on hypothetical situations. Second, he based his stages of moral development on studies of men. Carol Gilligan (1982) offered a different developmental scheme for women who behave with reference to their care and concern for others. Still, the two developmental models do not differ much and the overall perspective provided by moral development theory has much to offer the designers of interpretive messages (Christensen & Dustin, 1989). Gordon Sanders (2001) concluded that good teaching is inspirational, "in particular when it deals with moral realities."

Box 6.2
Kohlberg's Six Stages of Moral Development

Stage	Principal Concern
Preconventional morality	Fear of punishment Maximizing pleasure/minimizing pain
Conventional morality	What significant others think What society thinks
Postconventional morality	Justice and fairness Self-respect

Box 6.3
This Message Appeals to Several Moral Levels (Dustin, 1985)

Do Not Go Beyond This Sign

Violators Will Be Prosecuted

You are standing before a gift from the ages.

It is a priceless reminder of our human heritage, of our link to the past.

This pueblo is fragile and irreplaceable.

Enjoy it from a distance so that your children and your children's

children can enjoy this gift as well.

They, and your ancestors, the Anasazi, will be forever grateful for your concern

for the future and your respect for the past.

Outdoor Programs and Interpretive Applications

All of the theories discussed so far have practical relevance. Most of these theories get heavy use in preparing and presenting environmental education and interpretation programs. Dozens of programs have published materials, curricula, and philosophical approaches that interpreters use throughout the world based on educational theory. Most focus on youth, but the adult population gets increasing attention.

Project Learning Tree and Project Wild have among the widest and most popular acceptance. Many other useful materials from Canadian and U.S. agencies and organizations are available upon request to assist teachers, historians, naturalists, and art directors to deliver *developmentally appropriate* interpretive messages and experiences. Likewise, exhibit planning and design should consider the developmental characteristics of children (Oltman, 2000). By providing quality learning experience aimed at young children and their families, museums and visitor centers will play a more influential role in the 21st century (Semlak & Beck, 1999). Descriptions of three programs with direct ties to nature education follow.

Flow Learning

Joseph Cornell (1989) developed an interdisciplinary approach to nature education, based on his years of experience as a nature educator and established educational principles. Flow learning consists of a four-step sequence of games and activities that harmonize with human nature and flow from one to another in a logical manner (Box 6.4). Cornell (1998) suggested that a sense of joy should permeate all experience in nature.

Flow learning aims to provide all participants with a deep and uplifting experience. An activity's first step *awakens enthusiasm*. This stage is meant to be playful and fun (Figure 6.4). Although teens and adults tend to be more skeptical than children, appropriate games and activities can generate interest and enthusiasm without bending the dignity of the participants.

> "Flow learning aims to provide all participants with a deep and uplifting experience."

Figure **6.4**. A playground slide simulating the colors and shape of a Milk Snake (a) and an eagle's nest perch (b) outside of Milford Nature Center (KS) provide joyful experiences, connect children to nature, and appeal to their love of play. (TC)

The second step *focuses attention*. Based on the enthusiasm of Stage 1, this step concentrates attention so that people become more alert and observant. Cornell suggested that the key is to isolate one of the senses and devise a way for participants to concentrate on it. This helps to settle the group down after the playful first stage while also enhancing their awareness of the environment.

Focused attention inspires an inner calm that promotes the third step of the sequence, *direct experience*. During this step people become directly involved with the natural setting, focusing intensely to become absorbed and to "flow with" the experience. A sense of wonder and reflection is awakened through personal discovery.

The fourth stage of the experience *shares inspiration* to strengthen and clarify individual experiences. In this "debriefing" step, people not only talk about their own experiences but also hear of the insights, adventures, and ideas of great naturalists such as Aldo Leopold, Rachel Carson, and John Muir. This tends to draw the group together and sets the stage for future enriching experiences in nature. Cornell (1998) provided representative activities appropriate for all ages that correspond to each of the four stages.

Box 6.4
Stages of Flow Learning (Cornell, 1998)

Stage	Purpose	Quality	Benefits
1.	Awaken enthusiasm	Playfulness and alertness	Builds on children's love of play Creates an atmosphere of enthusiasm Dynamic beginning gets everyone saying "Yes!" Develops full alertness, overcomes passivity Creates involvement Gets attention and minimizes discipline problems Develops rapport with the leader Creates good group dynamics Provides direction and structure Prepares for later, more sensitive activities
2.	Focus attention	Receptivity	Increases attention span Deepens awareness by focusing attention Positively channels enthusiasm from Stage 1 Develops observational skills Calms the mind Develops receptivity for more sensitive nature experiences
3.	Direct experience	Absorption	People learn best by personal discovery Gives direct, experiential, intuitive understanding Fosters wonder, empathy, and love Develops personal commitment to ecological ideals
4.	Share inspiration	Idealism	Clarifies personal experiences Builds on uplifted mood Introduces inspiring models Gives peer reinforcement Creates group bonding Provides feedback for the leader Leader shares with a receptive audience

From *Sharing Nature with Children* (Cornell, 1988), Sharing Nature Foundation

"Nature Literacy" and the Orion Society

The Orion Society promotes nature literacy to expand powers of observation and creativity. This approach has also developed independently in many nature centers and schools around the United States and Canada. The program promotes the ability to *learn from* and *respond to* direct experience of nature (Beck, 2000). The approach gives children the opportunity to bond with nature—to learn to love it before being asked to heal its wounds (Sobel, 1996). In other words, teaching about the plight of the Amazon rain forest or the Arctic National Wildlife Refuge gains relevance only as children mature and develop a connection to the natural world. The Orion Society *Nature Literacy Series* emphasizes *place-based* or *locally focused* learning. Inspired teaching integrates all the arts from literature to drama and storytelling. It also incorporates science and history as pathways to ecological learning. Experiences in local landscapes serve as the bases for community awareness, self-discovery, and respect for the land (Orion Society, 1998).

This approach to learning also promotes expanding observation skills and creative expression through nature journaling and drawing. According to Leslie, Tallmadge, and Wessels (1999):

> Nature journaling is hands-on learning at its best…In addition to offering students a one-on-one connection with their own immediate environment, the nature journal is a wonderfully flexible teaching tool. It integrates many disciplines and allows opportunities for various styles of learning.

The Orion Society also advocates the importance of "stillness" in our lives as a vehicle to help us deepen our connection with the natural world as a source of personal enrichment and inner renewal (S. Sanders, 2001).

Vitamin N

Work by several researchers and authors has indicated the importance of nature in our lives and especially for children. However, it was Richard Louv (2005), in his landmark book, *Last Child in the Woods*, who brought widespread attention to the alienation of children from the natural world, coining the term "nature-deficit disorder." A subsequent work titled *The Nature Principle* expanded on the importance of nature in our lives to include adults as well (Louv, 2011).

Most recently, Louv (2016) has written *Vitamin N: The Essential Guide to a Nature-Rich Life*. In this newest work, Louv expands on the importance of Vitamin N (Nature) to enrich the well-being and joy of the family and local community. He begins the book by referring to a keynote speech by Janet Ady of the U.S. Fish and Wildlife Service. At this gathering organized by the Children & Nature Network, she displayed an outsized pharmacy bottle with a physician's prescription as follows:

> DIRECTIONS: Use daily, outdoors in nature. Go on a nature walk, watch birds, and observe trees. Practice respectful outdoor behavior in solitude or take with friends and family. REFILLS: *Unlimited*. Expires: *Never*.

The contents of the prescription bottle included a listing of National Wildlife Refuges, a guide to animal tracks, ways to experience nature with minimum impact, information on planting native vegetation to help restore butterfly and bird migration routes, and other items. In *Vitamin N*, Louv provides further contents for the prescription including "500 ways to enrich the health and happiness of your family and community and combat nature-deficit disorder." Some of the activities have been borrowed (from Joseph Cornell, for example), but many are original and provide impetus to get outside, be active, explore your local bioregion, and connect with others who share similar values (Figure 6.5).

Recent Contributions to How We Learn

A 10-year research grant titled "Applying Cognitive Psychology to Enhance Educational Practice" culminated in the book *Make It Stick: The Science of Successful Learning*. The authors emphasize that learning is an acquired skill and it is "deeper and more durable when it's effortful" (Brown, Roediger, & McDaniel, 2014). In other words, learning, to be effective, is not an easy endeavor…it requires effort. The authors note that many effective learning strategies are not intuitive. For example, people tend to be poor judges of when they are learning well and when they're not, and the popular exercise of rereading text may be among the least productive strategies for learning. The more effective strategy for learning is "retrieval practice" which means recalling facts or concepts or events from memory. Furthermore, "elaboration" is the process of explaining new material by expressing it in one's own words. Again, this takes effort. But this is where the most effective learning takes place. Ideally, learners should be able to explain how their new learning relates to their prior knowledge and how they might make application of it. In regards to applying this research to the field of interpretation it may be useful in exhibits, or after interpretive programs, to encourage visitors to review in their own minds, or to journal, those things that they found most interesting and would most like to remember.

Figure 6.5. Kenyan school children and their teacher escape the bustling city of Nairobi and arrive at Nairobi National Park to get essential doses of Vitamin N. (TC)

Future Directions

Learning: For Fun, Health, and a Longer Lifespan

The inaugural celebration of "Lifelong Learning Day" occurred on October 15, 2015. Although "lifelong learning" in the broadest sense can mean that anyone can pursue learning as long as they live, the term is also used in a more specific sense for those who are in the older stages of their lives. Either way, you arrive at the same conclusion: Lifelong learning is good for you. And, like Earth Day, we believe that although it is meritorious to acknowledge lifelong learning on this one day, it is something that should be observed and practiced *every* day.

As stated by James Moses, President and CEO of Road Scholar, "Most of all, we hope the occasion of Lifelong Learning Day inspires all Americans to learn and to make a habit of lifelong learning. I promise you: It will make you feel good, it may help you live longer and, most importantly, you'll meet interesting people and have fun along the way" (Moses, 2015). Indeed, research in the fields of gerontology, psychology, and neuro-science has established that mental stimulation and social engagement correlate highly and lead to better cognitive health, higher degrees of personal well-being, a more positive outlook on life, and longer life spans (Perls,

2015). The implications for interpreters, especially those who offer personal contact to individuals and groups, are obvious.

Information Technologies

The growth in information technology has skyrocketed and seems destined to continue expanding and changing. Interpreters face challenges and opportunities to use information technology to get valid conservation and preservation messages to the public through new technologies. O'Meara (2000) noted that "information technologies not only shape our world view, they also give us greater power to change our world. We have a responsibility to harness these tools to build a healthier, greener, and more equitable future."

Millennials are considered "digital natives" with parks and museums striving to find ways to attract them to their sites. One approach is to attempt to engage them by sharing personal stories on social media as the National Park Service did during its Centennial campaign. According to James and Ginder (2017), "As interpreters, we cannot think of digital technology as a distractor, but [rather should] begin to see it as a facilitator." One approach for doing that, they suggest, is to have people use their devices during programs by encouraging certain apps that correspond to the interpretive topic. Museums are also devising creative strategies to engage millennials as discussed further in Chapter 11.

However, we need balance in this arena. Although information technologies can help us to better understand cultural and natural heritage and how we affect it, digital technologies cannot replace the direct contact and appreciation that first-hand experience with the world around us provides (Birkerts, 2015; Carr, 2014). Important to our overall well-being are those moments when we slow down and aren't distracted (Sunim, 2017). In these instances, especially in nature, people tend to be more creative and more alive (Williams, 2017).

Summary

The educational theories presented in this chapter summarize some of the best-known work that relates directly to interpretive applications. For practical purposes, the interpreter needs to study these ideas, develop programs and methods that respond to the most sensible ideas, try them out, adjust them, and use them to the clients' advantage.

A summary list of learning concepts from educational theory brings together much of the information covered in this chapter. These take-aways serve interpreters as common sense reminders of theoretical understanding:

1. Learning is an act of structuring and relating information and experiences. Learning takes effort.
2. People process information differently, at different ages, and among different individuals.
3. A sense of comfort and security affects a person's readiness to learn.
4. When people feel good about the person facilitating the experience, they more likely care about and remember the information presented.
5. People learn more effectively when they use many of their senses.

6. Many people tend to remember most what they *do*, less of what they *see or read*, and least of what they *hear*.
7. A variety of approaches to a subject enhances the learning process by making it more interesting and challenging for all learners.
8. Self-discovery is a powerful motivator and learning tool.
9. An organized presentation of information and activities helps people learn.
10. Repetition can effectively facilitate learning.

Continual attention to developments in the educational literature should prove fruitful for interpreters who make the effort to stay abreast of techniques and strategies that could improve their professional efforts. Interpreters can use many of these models to plan strategic learning approaches for their audiences.

Much current learning theory points to an inclusive smorgasbord approach in programming. This serves up a variety of activities and approaches that match different learning styles and stages of development. Evaluation of these approaches over the long run may well result in refinements. Nevertheless, interpreters who follow these principles move the profession far beyond a simple "walk and talk" approach. They serve as true educators for all people and throughout the lifespan.

Therefore, with more interpreters adopting strategies gleaned from educational theory, visitors to interpretive sites will learn more effectively and have more powerful experiences. This in turn lends itself to better informed individuals, a more educated and enlightened citizenry, and a better world.

"The ultimate purpose of the national parks is the education and inspiration of the people...that idea infuses our entire cause from top to bottom. One of the destinies of our national parks, then, is to become the great school houses for nature and science of this American people."
–R.S. Yard (1917)

Literature Cited

Beck, L. (2000). Resources for the twenty-first century. *Legacy, 11*(6), 26–36.

Bettelheim, B. (1989). *The uses of enchantment*. New York, NY: Vintage Press.

Birkerts, S. (2015). *Changing the subject: Art and attention in the Internet age*. Minneapolis, MN: Graywolf Press.

Brandt, R. (1990). On learning styles: A conversation with Pat Guild. *Educational Leadership, 48*(2), 10–13.

Brochu, L., & Merriman, T. (2008). *Personal interpretation: Connecting your audience to heritage resources* (2nd ed.). Fort Collins, CO: InterpPress.

Brown, P., Roediger, H., & McDaniel, M. (2014). *Make it stick: The science of successful learning*. Cambridge, MA: The Belknap Press of Harvard University Press.

Carr, N. (2014). *The glass cage: How our computers are changing us*. New York, NY: W. W. Norton & Company.

Christensen, H., & Dustin, D. (1989). Reaching recreationists at different levels of moral development. *Journal of Park and Recreation Administration, 7*(4), 72–80.

Cornell, J. B. (1989). *Sharing the joy of nature*. Nevada City, CA: Dawn Publications.

Cornell, J. B. (1998). *Sharing nature with children* (Anniv. ed.). Nevada City, CA: Dawn Publications.

Duhigg, C. (2012). *The power of habit: Why we do what we do in life and business*. New York, NY: Random House.

Dustin, D. (1985). To feed or not feed the bears. *Parks & Recreation, 20*(10), 54–57, 72.

Edwards, Y. (1979). *The land speaks*. Toronto, ON: National and Provincial Parks Association of Canada.

Foer, J. (2011). *Moonwalking with Einstein: The art and science of remembering everything*. New York, NY: Penguin.

Gabler, I., & Schroeder, M. (2003). *Constructivist methods for the secondary classroom: Engaged minds*. Boston, MA: Allyn & Bacon.

Gardner, H. (2011). *Frames of mind: The theory of multiple intelligences*. New York, NY: Basic Books.

Gilligan, C. (1982). *In a different voice*. Cambridge, MA: Harvard University Press.

Gordon, D. (2001). Building a foundation for compassionate intelligence. *Timeline, 56*, 1–7.

Grinder, A. L., & McCoy, E. S. (1985). *The good guide: A source-book for interpreters, docents, and tour guides*. Scottsdale, AZ: Ironwood Press.

Ham, S. (1992). *Environmental interpretation: A practical guide for people with big ideas and small budgets*. Golden, CO: Fulcrum Publishing.

Ham, S. (2013). *Interpretation: Making a difference on purpose*. Golden, CO: Fulcrum Publishing.

Hammitt, W. (1981). A theoretical foundation for Tilden's interpretive principles. *Journal of Environmental Education, 12*(3), 13–16.

Hart, L. (1983). *Human brain and human learning*. New York, NY: Longman Publishing Group.

Hart, L. (1991). The "brain" concept of learning. *The Brain Based Education Networker, 3*(2), 1–3.

James, J., & Ginder, J. (2017). Puzzled about your audience? *Legacy, 28*(2), 30–33.

Kahneman, D. (2011). *Thinking fast and slow*. New York, NY: Farrar, Straus and Giroux.

Knopf, R. (1981). Cognitive map formation as a tool for facilitating information transfer in interpretive programming. *Journal of Leisure Research, 13*(3), 232–242.

Kohlberg, L. (1971). Stages of moral development as a basis for moral education. In C. M. Beck (Ed.), *Moral education: Interdisciplinary approaches*. Toronto, ON: University of Toronto Press.

LaPage, W. (2001). Nature "speaks": Exploring the inspiration of public parklands. *Legacy, 12*(5), 8–23.

Leslie, C., Tallmadge, J., & Wessels, T. (1999). *Into the field: A guide to locally focused teaching*. Great Barrington, MA: Orion Society, Nature Literacy Series, No. 3.

Louv, R. (2005). *Last child in the woods: Saving our children from nature-deficit disorder*. Chapel Hill, NC: Algonquin Books of Chapel Hill.

Louv, R. (2011). *The nature principle: Human restoration and the end of nature-deficit disorder*. Chapel Hill, NC: Algonquin Books of Chapel Hill.

Louv, R. (2016). *Vitamin N: The essential guide to a nature-rich life*. Chapel Hill, NC: Algonquin Books of Chapel Hill.

Mayer, R. (2010). *Applying the science of learning*. Upper Saddle River, NJ: Pearson.

Mills, E. (1920). *The adventures of a nature guide*. Garden City, NY: Doubleday, Page & Co.

Moses, J. (2015). Learn something new today. In *Lifelong learning: A national resource for well-being in retirement*. Elderhostel, Inc.

Neisser, U. (1976). *Cognition and reality*. San Francisco, CA: W.H. Freeman & Co.

Oltman, M. (2000). Creating exhibits for the very young. *Legacy, 11*(6), 15–19.

O'Meara, M. (2000). Harnessing information technologies for the environment. In *State of the World 2000*. New York, NY: Norton.

O'Neil, J. (1990). Making sense of style. *Educational Leadership, 48*(2): 4–9.

Orion Society. (1998). *Stories in the land: A place-based environmental education anthology*. Great Barrington, MA: Orion Society, Nature Literacy Series, No. 2.

Perls, T. (2015). Mental stimulation, social engagement, and longevity. In *Lifelong learning: A national resource for well-being in retirement*. Elderhostel, Inc.

Piaget, J. (1952). *The origins of intelligence in children*. New York, NY: International Universities Press, Inc.

Piaget, J. (1955). *The language and thought of the child*. New York, NY: World Publishing, Inc.

Pomerantz, G. (1990). Understanding children's perceptions of nature through developmental theory: Implications for interpretation. *Legacy, 1*(3), 12–19.

Riener, C., & Willingham, D. (2010). The myth of learning styles. *Change: The magazine of higher learning, 45*(5), 32–35

Riolo, R. (2014). Let's talk senses. *Legacy, 25*(4), 24–26.

Roads, M. J. (1987). *Talking with nature*. Tiburon, CA: HJ Krammer, Inc.

Sanders, G. (2001). Teaching twelve years in: How to inspire students. *Thought & Action, 42*(1), 31–40.

Sanders, S. (2001, Spring). Stillness. *Orion*, 64–71.

Saunders, D., & Deyette, D. (1999). Interpretation meets science education. In *1999 interpretive sourcebook* (pp. 200–201). Ft. Collins, CO: National Association for Interpretation.

Semlak, S., & Beck, L. (1999). Visitor centers and museums as learning environments for young children. *Legacy, 10*(5), 28–34.

Silverman, L. H. (1997). Personalizing the past. *Journal of Interpretation Research, 2*(1), 1–12.

Slivovsky, K. (2001). Confessions of a passionate interpreter. *Legacy, 12*(5), 38–39.

Sobel, D. (1996). *Beyond ecophobia: Reclaiming the heart in nature education.* Great Barrington, MA: Orion Society, Nature Literacy Series, No. 1.

Sousa, D. (2011). *How the brain learns* (4th ed.). Thousand Oaks, CA. Corwin: A SAGE Company.

Sunim, H. (2017). *The things you can see only when you slow down.* New York, NY: Penguin Books.

Tilden, F. (1967). *Interpreting our heritage* (Rev. ed.). Chapel Hill, NC: University of North Carolina Press.

Walsh, J., & Sattes, B. (2005). *Quality questioning: Research-based practice to engage every learner.* Thousand Oaks, CA: Corwin Press.

Walsh, J., & Sattes, B. (2011). *Thinking through quality questioning: Deepening student engagement.* Thousand Oaks, CA: Corwin Press.

Ward, C., & Wilkerson, A. (2006). *Conducting meaningful interpretation: A field guide for success.* Golden, CO: Fulcrum Publishing.

Williams, F. (2017). *The nature fix: Why nature makes us happier, healthier, and more creative.* New York, NY: W.W. Norton & Company.

Yard, R. S. (1917). Educational day (Introduction). In *Proceedings, [U.S.] National Parks Conference, January 2-6.*

CHAPTER 7
Serving Diverse Audiences

"My audience was my life. What I did and how I did it, was all for my audience."
—Cab Calloway

In 2014, the Mountains Recreation and Conservation Authority (MRCA) partnered with the Boys & Girls Club of Mar Vista Gardens, located within a low-income housing project in Los Angeles to provide a Junior Naturalist program for youth, aged 12-16. The Junior Naturalist program met twice weekly during the summer and took the youth to parks and beaches for lessons about watersheds, ocean ecology, and native plants and animals. The Boys & Girls Club provided vans for the daily field trips. Despite living only a couple miles inland, lessons at the beach were the first time many of the youth saw the ocean. Lack of transportation and parents who were unable to take them had been barriers to accessing nature. MRCA naturalists started each lesson connecting the kids with natural wonders near their homes. After two months, the kids better understood the importance of nature. The program culminated in an overnight camping trip. When the Junior Naturalist program started youth and parents thought only homeless people slept outside. Parents had worked hard to put a roof over their children, why would they want to sleep in a tent? Because parents were skeptical, MRCA hosted a pre-camping trip family pizza night within the housing projects for the parents to ask questions, learn more about the staff, and ease their worries. In the end, not only did the youth have their eyes opened to the excitement of camping, but the parents did, too. As they heard exciting stories from their children about Junior Naturalist experiences, the adults began viewing camping and nature in a new light.

Interpreters are guided by the understanding that if audience members have not learned, seen, or felt something, then interpreters have been talking to themselves. Thoughtful preparation, good organization, enthusiasm, and professionalism can be discerned and appreciated by all audiences. Fun or emotionally engaging programs attract audiences and hold their attention. Applying the principles presented in Chapter 5 and elsewhere in this book will help interpreters serve audiences more effectively and impact them more powerfully. This chapter further focuses on those receiving the messages. It also encourages interpreters to reach out to specific, often underserved, audiences such as the youth in the projects of Los Angeles in the story above. This chapter offers ideas on how to effectively provide all audiences with enjoyable and relevant experiences. Along with the great entertainer Cab Calloway, interpreters should say, "our audiences are our life."

Getting to Know Audiences

Interpretation and presentation programmes should identify and assess their audiences demographically and culturally. Every effort should be made to communicate the site's values and significance to its varied audiences. Article 1.3 ICOMOS Ename Charter

Figure 7.1. Getting to know your audiences is the key to serving them effectively. (RS)

To effectively serve and relate to audiences, you must know them. Knowing whether visitors are local or transient, young or old, and other demographic characteristics will guide interpreters as they plan activities, message content, and delivery. Moreover, knowing audience member's motives for attending as well as their attitudes and values allows interpreters to target messages and experiences more precisely and effectively (Figure 7.1).

How to Know Audiences

Studies have shown that interpreters often don't know their audiences well and have misguided beliefs about audience values, beliefs and motivations (e.g., Morgan, 2000; Stern, Powell & Hockett, 2011). Getting to know your audience can be as simple as showing up early for a program or hike and speaking with people as they arrive. Simple conversation starters such as, "Where are you from?" "Is this the first time you have visited here?" "What brings you to the park?" can tell astute interpreters useful information about their audience members that can help relate the interpretation to their interests and

> "Interpreters often don't know their audiences well."

experiences. Or it can be as easy as reviewing comments on your site's website, Facebook page, or monitoring other social media. These informal conversational approaches to knowing your audience should be routine when encountering and communicating with guests. Being able to apply this knowledge quickly to an existing program is the mark of a creative and experienced interpreter.

More formal methods of evaluation are presented in Chapter 19. These methods may include systematic observation of visitors as they move through your site. Several approaches can provide useful results and serve as important tools used by professionals to better know an audience. The scope of these data collection efforts depends on the questions you wish to answer. It is important to have evaluation expertise or to seek the help of professionals in survey design, sample selection, and data analyses. Such help may be available within a large agency or organization. Help can often be found at local colleges or universities. Marketing firms can be hired to do this work. Finally, some interpretive sites have found it useful to establish Citizen Advisory Boards or similar bodies to regularly provide input on how to better connect with current and potential audiences.

What To Know About Audiences

One important thing to know about audiences is *why they come to programs*. If interpreters aspire to meet audiences' needs and expectations, then it is imperative that they understand their motivations in attending. For example, a study of why park visitors to the Great Smoky Mountains National Park attended interpretive programs found that the top three motivators were: 1) the desire to be entertained, 2) to have a better chance to actually see the park's unique attractions (that otherwise might be missed), and 3) to have a good group experience, including providing a good experience for other members of the group (Stern, Powell, & Hockett, 2011).

To attract a wider audience, interpreters should strive to know why people do not come to programs and facilities. At most sites, a relatively small percentage of visitors attend the interpretive programs. For example, U.S. National Park Service statistics showed that in parks primarily focused on the interpretation of natural resources, only about 12% of visitors attend an interpretive program during a visit; and in national parks focused primarily on cultural resource preservation, not including living history sites, only about 30% of park visitors attend live interpretive programs (Stern, Powell, & Hockett, 2011). These attendance statistics probably are similar at other interpretive venues worldwide. Therefore, it behooves interpreters to understand why the majority of visitors choose not to attend programs.

In general, nonparticipants either (1) do not know about the interpretive opportunities, (2) do not perceive value in participating, or 3) want to participate, but encounter real or perceived barriers. Such barriers may include physical impediments that limit access by the elderly and those with physical disabilities. Or, social or psychological barriers may exist from feeling unwelcome or irrelevant. These barriers as they affect specific groups will be discussed in more detail below. If interpreters understand the reasons for nonparticipation, they can strive to make everyone aware of the opportunities, link programming to the interests and values of the nonparticipants, and eliminate physical, psychological, and social barriers.

Studies that address why people don't come to interpretive programs include the following. Attendance at interpretive programs in Smoky Mountain National Park found that the main barriers resulting in nonattendance were a lack of awareness, visitors' perceptions of insufficient or inconvenient timing, and a preference for a more solitary experience (Stern, Powell, & Hockett, 2011). Similarly, Goodrich and Bixler (2012) studied campers at three state parks in the southeastern U.S. and found the major constraints to attending interpretive programs were 1) a lack of awareness about programs; 2) life stage barriers, particularly as it related to the timing or scheduling of the programs; 3) a desire to experience unstructured time; and 4) the relative attractiveness of competing activities in the park (e.g., swimming or boating). Knowing these reasons for nonattendance can direct efforts to increase participation in interpretive programs.

Once visitors come to a site, it is important to know their preferences about facilities and program delivery to keep them coming back. The literature abounds with studies of visitor preferences. The following four examples illustrate how sites have attempted to understand the preferences of their visitors. 1) Clark, Legg, Williams, and Darville (2011) studied visitors to the historic Kingsley Plantation and found that their favorite activity was walking around the plantation and that they were most interested in the personal stories about the daily life of the people that had lived there, whereas they were less interested in scheduled ranger led programs. 2) Davis and Thompson (2011) found that visitors to local community natural areas preferred signs that show a three-dimensional object, a picture of local wildlife, a large title, and show something that otherwise cannot be seen such as an underground dwelling. 3) Fraser, Bicknell, Sickler, and Taylor (2009) evaluated the preferences of guests at three zoos and two aquariums regarding what they would like to see on animal identification labels. Across all five sites they found that their guests preferred information about odd facts/behaviors, endangered status of the animal, where they live in the world, and the number of years they live. Visitors were least interested in the animal's scientific name, length of pregnancy, and phylogeny. 4) Yamada and Knapp (2009) conducted a preference study at Okutama-Kohan Park in Japan and found that adults viewing the exhibits accompanied by an interpreter was the most preferred activity.

Information such as that gained in the above studies is useful to interpreters who wish to provide satisfying experiences for their audiences.

Connecting to Sovereign Audiences

"Think like a wise man but communicate in the language of the people."
—William Butler Yeats

Audiences at interpretive sites typically participate in what Falk and Dierking (2000) refer to as free-choice learning, which is self-directed, voluntary, and guided by an individual's needs and interests. U.S. National Park Service interpretation training manager and author David Larsen (2003) called attention to these free-choice behaviors by noting, "The visitor is sovereign." By this he meant that visitors have complete control over what they believe, think, and feel. Larsen wrote, "No matter how much confidence we may have in our science and our professional procedures, no matter how enthusiastic and polished our presentations, the audience ultimately decides if the resource has value. The audience determines if they will care enough about the resource in order to support the care for the resource."

Freeman Tilden referenced this sovereignty when he stated, "The visitor ultimately is seeing things through his own eyes" (Tilden, 1977). This perspective requires interpreters to understand audiences and engage them in the context of their own understanding and values. It does not mean that visitors can do whatever they want at our sites. Resource protection responsibilities and organizational mission take precedence over accommodating all the wishes of visitors. However, it does mean that interpreters cannot impose their truth on them. Acceptance or rejection of messages ultimately lie with the visitor.

In light of the visitors' "sovereignty" or power over their own thoughts and feelings, audience members also have rights. National Park Service interpreter and administrator Robert Fudge developed what he called, "The Visitor's Bill of Rights." It states visitors have the right:

- To have their privacy and independence respected (Interpretation should not be *inflicted* on visitors.)
- To retain and express their own values
- To be treated with courtesy and consideration
- To receive accurate and balanced information

How, then, do interpreters approach diverse and "sovereign" audiences? One way is to approach the task not as one of indoctrination, coercion, or conversion, but rather to provide emotionally and intellectually meaningful experiences that lead the audience member to care about the resources in the context of their own values and understandings. Focus should be on providing opportunities for guests to personally experience a resource in a new way—an enriching way that is meaningful to them. Much of the best work of interpreters is merely the work of a matchmaker to design and offer opportunities for people to come into contact with the resources while setting a positive, receptive and uplifting mood for them. This "matchmaking" may result in people falling in love with a place, resource, or historical story.

As mentioned in Chapter 5, using universal concepts is another way of reaching a wide variety of audience members. Universals are concepts or ideas that mean something significant to almost everyone. Examples of universals include such concepts as fear, freedom, family, courage, survival, beauty, integrity, friendship, and power. Building universal themes and concepts into interpretation increases the likelihood of relating to diverse and "sovereign" visitors. These universals can be applied to interpreting both history and nature. For example, interpreters can encourage audiences to care about a nondescript plant or animal by revealing hidden beauty or function. Interpreters can increase connections to a historic event by telling compelling stories of heroism, sacrifice or integrity.

Connecting to Diverse Audiences

This book refers generically to visitors, guests, and audiences. Any implication of the existence of groups of identical average visitors oversimplifies reality. Each visitor brings along a personal set of experiences, interests, knowledge, ability, and personality. At its best, interpretation is an intensely personal service. It involves engaging *individuals* in finding personal meanings and relevancy in the resources being interpreted. It involves the *individual* seeing the beauty or understanding the significance of the resource.

> Formulate group-specific messages.

Because the "average visitor" does not exist, it is dangerous to generalize about groups of people. Yet, it has long been accepted that when given the chance to interpret to relatively homogenous audiences (again recognizing that no group is purely homogenous in every aspect), it is an opportunity to formulate group-specific messages and deliver them effectively at the target audience. Advertisers with millions of dollars at stake have turned targeting identifiable audiences into a science. Compare, for example, the commercials on the Cartoon Network, MTV, and Arts and Entertainment Network to see this.

The following sections offer insights into approaches to minimize barriers and increase participation by relatively homogeneous groups. Interpreters can expand their sphere of influence by reaching out proactively to segments of society that typically feel barred from many interpretive experiences or those that benefit from specific approaches. Cultural minorities, children, teenagers, older adults, and individuals with disabilities participate more readily when interpreters make special efforts to welcome and better serve them (Figure 7.2).

Figure 7.2. Everyone is welcome at this national park in Thailand. (TC)

Underserved Populations

"On the social front, the parks provide one of the few truly democratic facilities for enjoyment and inspiration of all of the people. To the extent that we become inclusive in our welcome, understanding, accommodation, and interpretation of all constituent populations, we reduce fragmentation and strife."

–William Brown, 1971

In the broadest sense, an underserved audience is any group that interpreters don't communicate with or serve. An underserved audience could be people afraid of bugs or bears or a group defined by some demographic characteristic such as age, race, or ethnicity. Moreover, underserved audiences differ among different countries and regions within countries. They might be Vietnamese families in rural Kansas, Aboriginal communities in Australia, or children in poor neighborhoods in Los Angeles (Figure 7.3).

Although these differences are important on a broad scale, interpreters must recognize that much diversity exists within these groups. People labeled as Hispanic may represent more than 30 different countries and cultures. Stereotypes such as minorities being poor or not interested in nature do not apply to all members of these groups which are merely sociological constructs.

In the United States, "underserved populations" often refers to African-Americans and Hispanics (composed of people from a variety of nations, races, and reflecting ancestral ties to Spain), the two largest minorities in this country. These groups typically are underrepresented among park visitors. For example, Taylor, Grandjean, and Gramann (2011) studied attendance at national parks and found U.S. residents who could name a unit of the National Park System they had visited in the two years before the survey were disproportionately White non-Hispanic, and that Hispanic respondents (of any race) and African-Americans each comprised a smaller share of recent visitors.

Figure 7.3. Visitors from all ethnicities can learn about the role of hunting at the Cheyenne Bottoms Wetlands Education Center in Kansas. (TC)

Why Don't More Minorities Come?

Pease (2015) provided a thorough review of the literature about interpretation and underserved audiences. Based upon this literature review, the following barriers have been found to discourage park attendance and participation in interpretive programs by minority populations.

> Barriers have been found to discourage park attendance and participation in interpretive programs by minority populations.

- **Economic barriers.** The lack of a personal vehicle or public transportation is a huge barrier for large segments of populations. Other costs associated with accessing interpretive sites such as entrance fees, lodging, or food may also limit visitation. The focus on differences in participation due to a lower socioeconomic position in society is referred to as the Marginality Theory.
- **Cultural barriers.** Ethnicity Theory suggests that differences in participation is based on cultural preferences related to such factors as their history, family structure, and values. For example, as noted in the introductory story interpreters might think of camping as an iconic park activity but many urban minorities see camping as something only rich white people do for fun. For them, sleeping in a tent is associated with being homeless.
- **Communication barriers.** Language barriers may prevent interpreters from serving some audiences. For example, Thapa, Graefe, and Absher (2002) studied visitors to National Forests in southern California and found that whereas

Whites generally used all information sources (brochures, maps, bulletin boards, guidebooks, personal contact with rangers), Hispanics were unlikely to approach rangers or use other personal information sources. Roberts (2007) also listed the absence of Spanish-speaking interpreters and Spanish printed materials and signs as a limiting factor in visitation to sites in Golden Gate National Recreation Area. The lack of brochures, exhibits, trail guides, and signs in anything other than English and the lack of bilingual interpreters limited communications and the opportunity to interpret to Hispanic visitors at a Minnesota nature center (Hong & Anderson, 2006).

- **Lack of knowledge.** Roberts (2007) identified a lack of awareness of where to go, what to do, and how to prepare for a visit as key barriers to minority visitation. Likewise, in Taylor et al.'s aforementioned study among respondents who had not visited in the past two years, the primary reason for not visiting more often was that they "just don't know that much about National Park System units." Hispanic and African Americans were more likely to agree with that statement than were Whites, both among recent visitors and among nonvisitors.
- **Fear.** Fears of wildlife encounters, getting lost, not being able to read signage, general safety concerns, and fears of discrimination or poor service limit many from participation. Rideout and Legg (2000) found that African Americans, in particular, were fearful about some of the wildlife in natural areas. They also found that fear of racial discrimination was a significant barrier. Taylor et al. (2011) found that few Whites saw NPS units as unsafe, unpleasant, or providing poor service, whereas up to a quarter of those in minority groups agreed with these reasons for not visiting. In fact, among both visitors and nonvisitors, only a small percentage of Whites said that NPS employees give poor service, whereas three times as many of those in every other race/ethnic group felt that way.

Recommendations for Inclusive Interpretation

The following recommendations are aimed at increasing interpretation's sphere of influence and service to nontraditional audiences by addressing the barriers mentioned above.

1. **Reduce economic barriers by providing transportation to interpretive facilities or by taking the interpretation to the people.** In urban areas interpreters can coordinate the scheduling of museum or park programs with the availability of public transportation or, better yet, provide vans or buses to bring underserved audiences directly to the site. Nature Mobiles and History Mobiles, vehicles with portable exhibits and activities, extend many interpretive centers and museums into the streets, schools, churches, and community centers close to the target population.
2. **Reduce cultural barriers by personally "inviting, including, involving" minority populations** (Chavez, 2000). Building trust and credibility with minority groups can best happen through personal contact, rather than through websites or publications. Personal *invitations* through churches, schools, social clubs, youth groups, and neighborhood organizations can be effective. Attracting

families to nature centers and programs may start with attracting their children who will bring parents and other adult family members. James and Ginder (2017) suggested interpreters consider "the concept of *pester power*, a marketing concept that describes the ability of a child to influence their parents' purchasing decisions" and extend this concept by having children encourage their parents to take them to interpretive sites.

Roberts (2001) studied minorities at Rocky Mountain National Park and recommended having a park ranger or staff person serve as a liaison for ethnic communities and assigning minority rangers to attend career fairs at local schools to talk about opportunities with the National Park Service. *Including* minorities in the planning of facilities and programming can make them feel welcome and safe thereby reducing social barriers to visitation (Figure 7.4). Such involvement can teach us much about their preferences.

Figure 7.4. Minority interpreters may make minority visitors feel more comfortable in some park settings. Here a member of the Houston-based Buffalo Soldiers National Museum answers audience questions during an event at the Historical Museum at Fort Missoula, MT. (USFS)

For example, many studies have shown that Hispanics and people from some Asian cultures prefer to visit parks in large groups of extended families and friends (Pease, 2015). This lesson has been learned by park managers who find their solitary scattered picnic tables moved into clusters of tables after each weekend of use by these groups of visitors. Providing programs and well-developed sites that accommodate large groups and families with children would accommodate these preferences. This strong family orientation also has implications for reaching these audiences through programs designed for the whole family. The Latino Outdoors organization reflects this desire to be *involved* stating, "Beyond just being "recipients of programming," we want to see ourselves reflected in leadership and decision-making capacities of the conservation movement" (see latinooutdoors.org). This organization aims to promote opportunities for Hispanics to tell their stories as they relate to heritage interpretation and through their stories contribute to conservation and heritage interpretation.

3. **Reduce communication barriers and enhance knowledge through strategic communications using multiple languages and varied media.** The most

obvious communication barrier is when guests do not speak the language. At sites in Europe or at international tourism destinations it may be necessary to have signs and publications in five or six languages. Shenandoah National Park receives diplomats and other internationals from the Washington, DC area, so they offer their park brochures in 10 languages including Farsi, Hindi, Arabic, Japanese, and Korean. Often in the U.S., the greatest need will be for materials in Spanish, but some communities have large Vietnamese, Hong, or Somali populations (Figure 7.5). In Canada, for example, French and English are required for government agencies, whereas in Europe interpretive sites typically have signs and publications in German, French, Spanish, and English.

In addition to using foreign languages, communication with underserved ethnic groups can be enhanced by using advertising to inform audiences about special accommodations for large groups and opportunities for celebrating cultural holidays or participating in other culture-specific activities. Taylor et al. (2011) found differences in the use of various interpretive media by minority groups. Hispanics were less likely than Whites or African Americans to talk informally with a park ranger and to view indoor exhibits, whereas Asians were the most likely to view indoor exhibits and go to a visitor center. Of the minority groups studied, African American visitors were the most likely to view outdoor exhibits and to participate in cultural demonstrations and ranger-led tours. Using photographs of minorities in promotional and educational materials also is recommended to communicate visually with minorities (Roberts, 2001).

Figure 7.5. Interpretive panels in Spanish and English are commonplace and required in many regions of the United States. (TC)

Organizations such as the aforementioned Latino Outdoors and Outdoor Afro (outdoorafro.com) use their websites to communicate directly with these historically underserved minorities and encourage them to get outside. The tagline for Outdoor Afro is "Where Black People and Nature Meet." When this meeting occurs, it is the interpreter's responsibility and privilege to make the experience relevant, rewarding, and hopefully repeated.

4. **Reduce fears by increasing staff diversity by hiring more minority interpreters.** A lack of diversity has been identified as one of the key challenges for the National Park Service. Roberts (2007) considered lack of diversity on staff as a significant barrier to minority visitation at Golden Gate National Recreation Area. Role models are important in generating interest in any field. Having minority or bilingual staff members present may alleviate fears associated with visiting an interpretive site and may make minority visitors feel more welcome.

> "Role models are important in generating interest in any field."

An example of a program that successfully applies these four recommendations to serve inner-city audiences is another initiative of the aforementioned Mountains Recreation and Conservation Authority (MRCA) in southern California. The Transit to Trails program provides free bus trips to the mountains and beaches from communities that lack access to public transportation. However, even with free transportation, interpreters noticed that participants were uncomfortable exploring a park on their own, unsure of park rules, and fearful about potential wildlife encounters. To address these fears, each trip is staffed by a Naturalist to explain the day's schedule, lead an interpretive nature hike, and alleviate any participant concerns. The Transit to Trails goal is to have a bilingual staff for those programs and at a minimum, have non-Spanish speaking staff carry a translated list of common local nature terms so they can share the natural world with the Spanish-speaking participants. Naturalist Carolyn shared the rewards of working with these underserved audiences:

> An unforgettable experience I had while on a Transit to Trails trip was during our lunch break, after hiking for the morning. An older woman who spoke Spanish with a little bit of broken English waved me over. It had been a while since I have taken a Spanish class, so I only remembered some basic phrases and words. What proceeded was a wonderful conversation about local wildlife with my broken Spanish, her broken English, and with some occasional help from others to translate certain words or phrases. She asked mostly about osos (bears) and I allayed some of her fears about the dangers of wildlife. Despite our language barrier, we shared a mutual moment of understanding, her about nature and me about how it is perceived.

Why it Matters

Throughout Europe, Australia, and North America countries are becoming more culturally and ethnically diverse through immigration from undeveloped or war-torn countries and through the population dynamics of certain cultures. In the U.S., by 2060, just 36% of all children (people under age 18) will be non-Hispanic white. The minority population (all groups other than non-Hispanic white) is projected to rise to 56% of the total in 2060 (U.S. Census Bureau, 2015). Responding to these changes is both an opportunity and challenge for interpreters. Knowing and celebrating cultural differences can help interpreters serve everybody more effectively. Although interpreters may never overcome all of the cultural and social barriers that limit participation, the more interpreters understand their constituents, the better they can serve them. All groups are made up of individuals whose lives can be enriched through interpretation. Moreover, this future minority-majority has the potential of being new stewards of our cultural and natural resources and of providing critical public support to ensure the preservation of these resources. Box 7.1 presents stories about how programs reaching out to minorities have changed the lives of two young people. These stories demonstrate why interpretation to the underserved matters!

> "Knowing and celebrating cultural differences can help interpreters serve everybody more effectively."

Box 7.1
Changed Lives: From the Projects to a Profession
Andy Bleckinger, Interpretive Naturalist, Mountains Recreation and Conservation Authority

Jessica, a high school student from Compton, California comes from an environment that she describes as "a world surrounded by walls and a closed door. Sunlight never comes in. Everything I needed was in my room." She was afraid to try new things and stayed locked in her comfort zone. Then one day she was introduced to the Mountains Recreation and Conservation Authority Naturalist Explorer program. Naturalist Explorers create a meaningful and relevant project from start to finish, including assessment, planning, and implementation. These skills help in the transition from teenager to responsible adult citizen. As part of this program, Jessica learned teamwork and began to experience new adventures and challenges. She wrote about what the program meant to her:

> I met new people I now see as family and discovered things about myself I never knew. My new friends motivated me to keep moving forward and to never give up. Helping each other and working as a team helped me get through the days. Although I'm one of the quiet ones, they never gave up on me; they taught me that no matter how difficult the obstacle no one ever gets left behind. One of my favorite experiences during the program was the time the naturalist took us hiking for the first time at the Santa Monica Mountains. It was one of the hardest things I had to face, especially because I'm not an exercise type of person. At one point, I felt like I couldn't take it anymore; however, one of the Outdoor Leaders, Antwan, pushed me and motivated me to keep going and told me that all the hard work was going to pay off. I didn't understand what he meant, but the instant we reached the top of the mountain, feeling the breeze and staring at the amazing view took my breath away. I felt as if I was on top of the world. I realized then that life was like climbing to the top of a mountain, at first it's hard and every step you take seems never ending, but once you reach the top and look at how much you've accomplished, it's a feeling that no word can describe. My experience in the MRCA program has opened a different world in my life. It has given me a different perspective to admire the beauty life has to offer. Being outdoors in nature, learning about wildlife, admiring my surroundings gave me a feeling I never encountered in my room.

Jessica currently works for MRCA as an Outdoor Leader leading free public campfire programs and assists on Transit to Trails programs in her neighborhood.

Jonathan grew up the oldest of six children living with their hardworking single mother. He worked at McDonald's, and the $300 every two weeks was more than enough to buy himself a pair of shoes, clean clothes, and most importantly allowed him to help his mom. But Jonathan made bad choices that led to incarceration. "Losing my freedom and being around others who had lost their path with no vision, no hope, no nothing, but sorrow and guilt was my worst nightmare."

Box 7.1 continued

Fortunately a nonprofit, The LA Conservation Corporation, gave Jonathan the opportunity to get his high school diploma and job skills. He started with planting trees and specialized in urban forestry. Jonathan said, "Every time I planted a tree along the sidewalk, in a park, or gave it away to residents in the Los Angeles area, I claimed a new life in the world, almost like a baby. I connected with the tree. I treated the tree like my '*camarada*'; in other words, my friend."

Jonathan joined The Bridge to Parks Career program. He learned about ecosystems, plants, animals, and that "interpretation can bring a voice to living organisms that cannot speak for themselves, but only express themselves through form and adaptation. I never realized interpretation even existed." Now Jonathan is a NAI Certified Guide and naturalist for the Mountains Recreation and Conservation Authority and a role model for his younger siblings. He concluded:

Before this program, I had low self-confidence. I didn't have access to the mountains and instead I was isolated in my own small, concrete world. Now I have been recharged with curiosity about life. I learned that when you reach the top of a mountain, the view is much clearer than from down below. Now I'm hungry not only for knowledge, but for success to make a change in peoples' lives nationwide.

Serving Guests with Disabilities

"Interpretation and presentation activities should also be physically accessible to the public, in all its variety."
–Article 1.5 ICOMOS Ename Charter

One of the great joys of being an interpreter is having the opportunity to serve people with disabilities. It is also an important responsibility. In the United States, this responsibility is mandated by the Americans with Disabilities Act (ADA) of 1990. This law extends federal protection and specifies standards for the elimination of discrimination against people with disabilities.

The ADA states that everyone, regardless of disability, should have full enjoyment and equal opportunity of public services, facilities, employment, and goods. The law mandates that policies and practices accommodate everyone. The law applies to all facilities except private clubs and religious organizations. In the decades that followed the passage of the ADA, virtually all interpretive sites have removed or circumvented physical barriers limiting participation. Such accommodations as curb cuts, ramps, accessible labeled bathrooms, and wider hallways are now the norm at most interpretive sites.

ADA also requires equal access in terms of programming. This means that registration for events must be available online or by phone. It also means that an equal number of interpretive programs must be offered that are available to people with disabilities and these programs must be scheduled with the same frequency as those that might have safety or other accessibility limitations. Likewise, any fees associated with interpretive programs must be the same for everybody regardless of abilities. Most public agencies and organizations offering interpretation have an ADA coordinator to ensure that interpretive facilities and programs are accessible and that the requirements of the law are being met.

The ADA also specifies that government agencies receiving federal funds (including local and state park agencies) must make their websites accessible (Bahram, 2016). Of course this should be the goal of all organizations offering interpretation. For the blind or those with impaired vision, two commonly used technologies are screen readers and refreshable Braille displays. Screen readers are computer programs that speak the text that appears on the computer display, beginning in the top-left corner. A refreshable Braille display is an electronic device that translates text into Braille characters that can be read by touch. Although these technologies read text, they cannot translate images or video into speech or Braille. Interpreters should add a text equivalent to every image. Not merely a label, the tag should include the same meaningful information that other users obtain by looking at the image or video. Moreover, not every person sees colors in the same way. Instead of dictating colors and font sizes, websites should be designed so they can be viewed with the color and font sizes set in users' web browsers and operating systems so that they can specify the text and background colors as well as the font sizes needed to see webpage content.

Other suggestions for making websites more inclusive include making sure that all audio is also available in text as captions to aid the people with hearing impairments, and minimizing or eliminating blinking, flashing, or other distracting features.

Other countries have similar laws as serving people with disabilities is clearly a global obligation and privilege. In meeting the requirements of any law addressing equal access, it is important to remember two things:

1. Making interpretation more accessible for people with disabilities also allows those without disabilities to more easily enjoy an interpretive site. For example, families with young children in strollers also prefer curb cuts, gentle trail slopes, and ramps. Designing sites that serve all people with or without disabilities has come to be known as Universal Design. Similarly, providing better access to everyone for engagement in learning is known as Universal Design for Learning (Rappolt-Schlichtmann & Daley, 2013). Many people, including older adults, benefit from larger fonts, sound enhancement, or closed captions. People for whom English is not their native language will find alternative message formats helpful. In these ways, ADA and similar laws can enhance *everybody's* experience and increase the effectiveness of the interpretation.

2. Most people are likely to be disabled at some point in their lives. This is part of the human condition. As noted in the *World Report on Disability,* "Almost everyone will be temporarily or permanently impaired at some point in life, and those who survive to old age will experience increasing difficulties in functioning" (World Health Organization, 2011). This report suggested treating disability as a continuum rather than categorizing people with disabilities as a separate group (i.e., disabled is a matter of more or less, not yes or no). Indeed, Universal Design for Learning (UDL) provides a model regarding design of programs and exhibit spaces that is aligned to progressive concepts of disability. According to Rappolt-Schlichtmann and Daley (2013), "Under UDL, disability is understood as an artifact of limitations of the designed environment. Disability is not situated within the person, but rather in the interaction between the person and the environment."

Integrating Disabled Individuals into Interpretive Programs

The ADA broke tradition by mandating integrating individuals with disabilities with the nondisabled rather than on providing expensive and seldom-used special facilities such as Braille Trails that were once a popular idea. Such integration is cost-effective and appropriate. Separate tours, hikes, programs or facilities are expensive, often unattractive, and they may offend individuals with disabilities because they focus on their inabilities, rather than on similarities with other people. Integration serves all audiences by providing opportunities for building social skills and self-esteem for those with and without disabilities as they interact with one another.

> "Integration is cost-effective and appropriate."

Box 7.2 gives specific tips and approaches for serving people with physical disabilities, impaired vision and impaired hearing. However, application of these recommendations help everybody if individuals with disabilities are integrated with people without disabilities.

**Box 7.2
Disability Etiquette**

Tips and Advice for Working with People with Disabilities
- Don't mention the person's disability unless it is relevant to the conversation or unless the person mentions it first. Remember, it is also okay for the individual to choose not to talk about it.
- Don't be afraid to ask questions when you're unsure of what to do or what words to use.
- When introduced to a person with a disability, it is appropriate to offer to shake hands. People with limited hand use or who wear an artificial limb can usually shake hands. (Shaking hands with the left hand is an acceptable greeting.)
- Speak directly to the person you are addressing, not to a companion or interpreter.
- If you offer assistance, wait until the offer is accepted. Then ask for instructions.
- Don't "talk down" to a person with a disability. Treat adults as adults and children as children.
- If visitors are using wheelchairs, consider line of sight from the lower height so that they can see the speaker or objects of interest.
- Be equally courteous to everybody in a group. For example, if you are shaking everyone's hand, make sure not to exclude anyone with a disability. Likewise, only address people who have disabilities by their first names when extending the same familiarity to all others.
- If you feel like you forgot some courtesy or made a mistake offer a sincere apology, but keep a sense of humor, and be willing to communicate so that you learn how to better handle that situation in the future.

Tips for Communicating with Individuals Who are Blind or Visually Impaired
- Speak to the individual and state clearly who you are when you approach him or her.
- Speak in a normal tone of voice. Don't raise your voice.
- Remember to identify yourself and the others when conversing in a group with a person who is blind.
- Tell the individual when you are leaving.
- Resist the urge to pet or distract a service dog without first asking the owner. Remember, they are always working.

Box 7.2 Continued

- Do not attempt to lead the individual without first asking permission.
- Be descriptive and specific when giving directions. Verbally give the person information that is visually obvious to individuals who can see. For example, if you are approaching steps, mention how many steps. Point out any upcoming obstacles.
- If you are offering a seat, gently place the individual's hand on the back or arm of the chair so that the person can locate the seat.
- When helping to guide someone, allow the person to take your arm so that you are not pushing or pulling the person.
- For objects that can be touched, ask what the person can see and then identify additional features. For artifacts or objects that cannot be touched, provide a touchable replica.
- Offer written material in large print, braille, or in audio form.

Tips for Communicating with Individuals Who are Hearing Impaired
- Gain the person's attention before starting a conversation (i.e., tap the person gently on the shoulder or arm).
- Look directly at the person and speak slowly and clearly in a normal tone of voice. If you experience difficulties, do not shout, but look for other ways to communicate, like writing notes. Come prepared with pen and pad for writing.
- If the person can read lips, make sure you are in a well-lit place or face a light source. Avoid eating or chewing gum. If you are in a group, make sure the person can see who is talking. Not every deaf person can read lips, so use facial expressions and body language to help communicate.
- If the individual uses a sign language interpreter, speak directly to the person, not the interpreter.

Tips for Communicating with Individuals with Mobility Impairments
- If possible, put yourself at the wheelchair user's eye level. Find a chair and sit down. It will save you both from a neck cramp.
- Do not lean on a wheelchair or any other assistive device. Holding on to or leaning on someone's wheelchair is the same as leaning or holding onto a person. Assistive devices are an extension of their personal space.
- Consider the extra time it might take for someone to complete a task. Let the person set the pace.
- Never patronize people who use wheelchairs by patting them on the head or shoulder.
- Do not assume the individual wants to be pushed—ask first.
- Offer assistance if the individual appears to be having difficulty opening a door.

Tips for Communicating with Individuals with Speech Impairments
- If you do not understand something the person says, don't pretend that you do. Ask the individual to repeat what he or she said and then repeat it back.
- Be patient and encouraging. Take as much time as necessary with your full attention.
- Try to ask questions that require only short answers or a nod of the head.
- Concentrate on what the individual is saying.
- Do not speak for the individual or attempt to finish her or his sentences.
- If you are having difficulty understanding the individual, consider writing as an alternative means of communicating, but first ask the individual if this is acceptable.

Tips for Communicating with Individuals with Cognitive Disabilities
- If you are in a public area with many distractions, consider moving to a quiet or private location.
- Be prepared to repeat what you say, orally or in writing.
- Offer assistance completing forms or understanding written instructions and provide extra time for decision-making. Wait for the individual to accept the offer of assistance; do not "over-assist" or be patronizing.
- Be patient, flexible, and supportive. Take time to understand the individual and make sure the individual understands you.

As previously suggested, a hard-packed trail surface benefits visitors with visual impairments, those who use wheelchairs, older adults, small children, families with strollers, and any visitors with difficulty in walking. Ramps are easier than stairs for everybody and lower water fountains serving those in wheelchairs also makes fountains available to children. Audio headsets benefit those with hearing problems, but also to children and those who have difficulty reading. Having a printed version of the text or closed captioning could serve those with hearing impairments or those who want to learn at a slower pace.

Interpreting Appropriately

How do you treat a person with a disability? You treat him or her as a *person*. Many interpreters are fearful or nervous when interpreting to people with physical or mental disabilities (Mayorga & Cable, 2015). To these interpreters the best advice is to "Just relax!" Be yourself and let feelings of friendship guide you through any awkwardness. People with disabilities are as fun and engaging as anyone else. Treat them the way you would want to be treated and the way you treat other guests at your site. Like interpreting to any other audience, with practice these strategies will become second nature to the experienced interpreter (Figure 7.6).

Figure 7.6. People with mental disabilities enjoy learning about prairies at the Flint Hills Prairie Discovery Center in Kansas. (JK)

When interpreting to mixed groups of people with and without disabilities, involve individuals in cooperative rather than competitive tasks and reward effort and nonphysical accomplishments. Creating group challenges that allows for everyone's participation to achieve group success works better than focusing on and rewarding individual tasks and accomplishments. Activities that involve all of the senses allows for participation of those with hearing or vision limitations. Also, it is important when assigning leadership positions in group activities that leadership is spread evenly among people with differing abilities. Finally, try to anticipate accessibility issues when planning events. If you cannot avoid all barriers, talk with any attendees it might affect and work to make it possible for them to participate.

When speaking or writing, use words that offer dignity by focusing on the person rather than on their limitations. Emphasize abilities rather than disabilities One easy way of doing this is always using person-first language; putting the person first, then the disability. For example, say "child with a disability" rather than "disabled or handicapped child." Or refer to a "person who is blind" rather than "blind person" which seems to make the limitation the defining characteristic of the person and making it more important than the individual. Sensitive interpreters will avoid labels that are inappropriate such as crippled, slow, or handicapped.

In summary, interpreting to people with disabilities involves getting people to participate and learn by building on their knowledge, interests, and skills, just as with any group of visitors. Offer pride; don't take it away by doing for them what they can do and have done for themselves. Let them say when they need help. Don't be offensive either by excessive kindness or by avoiding them. Most of all, just relax and enjoy their company!

Serving Different Age Groups

Tilden (1977) recommended taking advantage of a specific homogenous group opportunity when he stated, "Interpretation addressed to children (say, up to the age of 12) should not be a dilution of the presentation to adults, but should follow a fundamentally different approach. To be at its best it will require a separate program." Beck and Cable (2011) expanded this principle to state that, "Interpretation for children, teenagers, and seniors— when these comprise uniform groups—should follow fundamentally different approaches."

Children

> "What nobler employment, or more valuable to the state, than that of the man who instructs the rising generation?"
>
> –Cicero

Our most important audiences might be our smallest and youngest ones. These groups are the future stewards of our natural resources and cultural heritage. They are our hope for the future. At these young ages, they are most impressionable, as they form beliefs, attitudes, and emotional responses to their environments that may last a lifetime. Interpreters can play a role in shaping the personalities and interests of young people. Negative experiences can result in a lifetime of fear or apathy, whereas a positive childhood experience may spark a lifelong passion (Place, 2000). Interpreters impact the future by interpreting to children today.

Children are important for a second reason. Middle-age adults are the missing age group at many interpretive sites. Kammen (2000) challenged professionals to develop strategies to attract this missing group. One way to reach them is through their children. Children, in a sense, bring their parents and grandparents to the park, zoo, or museum— not the other way around. Ottman (1998) reports that preschool programs are among the Houston Zoo's most successful and well-attended programs. Adults receive the interpretive messages along with their children.

> "Our most important audiences might be our smallest and youngest ones."

Even when the adult does not attend, children interpret to adults at home as they share the interpretive messages they learned. Children may teach their parents about such things as recycling or energy use around the house. Environmentally responsible children can result in environmentally responsible adults. Moreover, in the critical realm of emotional attachments to places and programs, if you capture a child's interest, you will capture the hearts of the parents. Beyond the goodness of building family unity and camaraderie, this phenomenon has been used strategically by park agencies, zoos and museums to generate political support by winning over the youth to reach the adults. As the Danish proverb says, "If you take the child by the hand, you take the mother by the heart." If the children love the site or programs, parents will often become volunteers, donate materials, transportation or money, assist with fund-raising efforts, and promote the site by spreading "word-of-mouth" publicity through the community.

Some sites whose messages are specifically targeted for adults, use creative ways to engage the children in meaningful, but separate, activities. This lessens the demands on parents so that they can pursue their interests and concentrate without interruption on the interpretive experiences aimed at them. For example, a "Public Awareness" area at the Canadian Forestry Service's Petawawa National Forestry Institute had a tree house for children to play in while their caregivers were exposed to exhibits dealing with adult themes such as forest management practices, forestry research, and the economic importance of Canada's forest industry.

Spennemann and Taffe (1998) recommend that when interpreting to children at cultural heritage sites it is important to provide "controlled environments in which children can satisfy their needs of examining artifacts and sensitive items on their terms through touch tables and other interactive displays." To reduce undesirable impacts to the site and artifacts, they recommend outdoor "adventure playgrounds" linked to the interpretive themes. Such playgrounds address both learning and "energy dissipation" needs and are particularly useful for remote parks and heritage sites where an outlet is needed to "let off steam" after a long ride in a car or bus. In other words, managers should satisfy the children's need for physical activities by giving them something fun and productive to do in a reinforced area. This reduces site management problems, and enhances the interpretive experiences of both children and adults.

Sobel (2008) noted that regardless of social status, ethnicity, or ecosystem children exhibit seven play motifs when they have free time in nature. He expressed these as seven design principles for connecting children to nature. Interpreters can apply these principles when designing experiences for children. They are as follows:

- Adventure—provide opportunities for exploration of the unknown.
- Fantasy and Imagination—Create worlds for children's imaginations to run wild.
- Animal Allies—Animals play an important role in the emotional development of children and their care about the environment. Introduce children to animals and allow children to pretend to be animals and experience life as that animal.
- Maps and Paths—Children love to explore, find short-cuts, and use maps to find magical places and treasures.
- Special Places—Children like to create their own special places (e.g., "forts" with couch cushions, hide-outs in closets or attics or out in the woods). Take advantage of and encourage these special places they create outdoors.
- Small Worlds—Children love to create miniature worlds. Miniature worlds allow them to see the bigger picture of a community or natural area. It encourages them to notice and care for small things.

- Hunting and Gathering—Humans have this natural tendency to collect things. Encourage children as they search for and collect shells, leaves, rocks, feathers and other such items from nature. They will enjoy the quest and discover new things along the way. Collections allow children to learn to classify and sort artifacts. [In some park reserves, of course, this may be prohibited.]

Preschool Programs

"Every child should have mud pies, grasshoppers, waterbugs, tadpoles, frogs, mud turtles, elderberries, wild strawberries, acorns, chestnuts, trees to climb, brooks to wade in, water lilies, woodchucks, bats, bees, butterflies, various animals to pet, hayfields, pine cones, rocks to roll, sand, snakes, huckleberries, and hornets; and any child who has been deprived of these has been deprived of the best part of his education."

–Luther Burbank (1907)

Interpreters can provide the things in Burbank's list to children regardless of their age. If given opportunities, young children can bond with nature purely and intensely on their own. They have an active curiosity and keen sensory abilities. Flowing water, piles of dirt, flowers, and frogs can fascinate a child without any adult intervention. Many organizations offer programs for preschoolers. For example, The Missouri Department of Conservation has a "Babes in the Woods" program for children from birth up to 3 years old (for 3- to 5-year-olds they have a separate "Little Acorns" program). Parents or other caregivers push strollers along paved trails on naturalist-led hikes lasting 45 minutes. Babies and adults use all of their senses to find out that nature is not scary or dreary, but fun and fascinating. They also have indoor programs for preschoolers that involve sitting on carpet squares, playing games, telling stories, interacting with puppets, or doing simple crafts (Baumer & Crabtree, 2000). Tips for working with preschool children are provided in Box 7.3. These practical tips and those dealing with older children and teens are provided by experienced frontline interpreters, but many of them are supported by empirical research (e.g., Kahn & Kellert, 2002).

Exhibits can also be used to reach preschool audiences. At the Houston Zoo exhibits in the Children's Zoo are no higher than 28 inches and signs communicate only with pictures for pre-readers. Oltman (2001) stated, "Durable, educational, hands-on exhibits are possible for preschoolers, toddlers, and yes, even infants!" This author recommends that because infants are developing depth perception and learning to remember location of objects, exhibits for them should have changes in levels, steps, slides, hide and seek drawers, doors, and hiding holes. Older preschoolers are developing social skills. Exhibits with costumes and props allow them to play a variety of roles and experience different social perspectives. "Book nooks" within exhibits can promote literacy in beginning readers.

Having preschool interpretive programs is important because many young people associate fear and/or disgust with nature and natural objects. Such anxiety presents a barrier to enjoying and learning about nature. Early firsthand experiences with nature may "inoculate" babies and young children against these fears and anxieties (Bixler, Carlisle, Hammitt, & Floyd, 1994). Also early childhood experiences may counteract the misinformation these children will be receiving about big bad wolves, bloodsucking bats, and mythical cartoon creatures.

Box 7.3.
Tips for Working with Very Young

Preschoolers

Carpet squares/area rugs. These define an area for children to gather. Each child has a specific spot (instead of chairs). Telling 2-year-olds to sit in a circle won't work, but they can find a square or area rug to sit on. This establishes some control at the beginning of the program.

Low tables. Use low tables for crafts. Children live in an adult world. It helps the interpreter in the long-run if you make the world as comfortable as possible for them.

Big books. Use the readily available oversized books to introduce topics with a story. Big books have large photos so the whole group can see. Or scan small books and use PowerPoint to project them on a screen.

Ink stamps. Stamp each child's hand as you say good-bye to them at the door. Kids love it and it helps them remember what they learned about. Then they can go home and tell the family what they learned about at your program.

Puppets. They are popular, but treat puppets with the same respect as a living animal, especially if names are given to them. It can be upsetting to small children to see the puppet thrown into a box.

Snacks. Supply snacks for programs longer than one hour, although treats are a nice touch for any program. Make sure they are safe and thematic for the age of the group. Kids can choke on small hard candies.

Surprises. Children and adults love surprise. Work several into your program.

Name tags. This allows you to call each child by name.

Big words. It is okay to use big words. Just explain them and have the children say them and go on without a lot of elaboration. For example, say opossums are *nocturnal* animals. This means they are awake at night. Now can everybody say "nocturnal?" Say nocturnal just for fun and then go on with the program.

Parents. Don't be intimidated by other adults in the room. Tell them what you expect of them at the beginning of the program. Have them sit on the floor and play along with the activities. In this way they can model appropriate behaviors, guide the child, and support the interpreter as necessary, and share in the fun. Otherwise they will become disengaged and stand in the back of the room or chat among themselves. Sometimes they are less well behaved than their children. Experience has shown that it works best if there is only one adult for each child. With more than one they can distract from the interaction between the interpreter and child by talking between themselves. This gives parents the freedom and opportunity to play too. Provide fun outdoor games and learning activities so parents can be comfortable playing with their kids in the future.

Be flexible. No two groups are alike.

Focus on the process, not the product for craft projects. Do not focus on end result. Let them be creative and make the craft to be their own.

Appeal to all the senses, allow children to see, touch, hear and smell things.

Use several short activities in quick succession. Children have short attention spans.

Encourage movement. Involve physical movements such as crawling through a tunnel as a burrow like a woodchuck or coming out of a cocoon like a butterfly.

Use noncompetitive games. Games have been shown to be more popular than even live animal experiences.

Box 7.3 Continued

Encourage vocalizations. Kids like to make noise. Keep them singing, repeating important words, rhymes, or animal noises.

Listen to questions and don't stifle them as you might with older children. It's okay to get sidetracked with this age group. Let them talk. You will get lots of questions! Expect them and plan for them. They will be repetitive. Repetition is not a bad thing at this age as it reinforces the answer. They are curious about everything and that is why they ask questions.

Emphasize positive feelings, instead of merely teaching facts.

Emphasize concrete and relevant topics. Children only understand topics that relate to their own lives (e.g., what animals eat, where they live, how they move). Programs should be appropriate for a variety of learning styles and the children's emotional and cognitive levels.

Schedule in mid-morning naps after breakfast and before lunch. Temperatures may be more moderate and afternoon times may conflict with naps.

Offer self-directed activities for children as they arrive so they do not get bored or distracted while waiting for the program to begin.

Get down to their level. Interpreters should be down near eye level with the children to help connect with them. Have the teaching tools and props close by so you do not have to get up and down repeatedly. This can be disruptive to the children (and tiring for the interpreter).

Personally interact with each child if possible.

Minimize directions. Give only one command at a time. Telling the children to put on their coats, pick up a butterfly net, and line up at the door, does not work. They will pick up the nets and start running all over. Give one command at a time. Also commands that work with second graders will not work for preschoolers (e.g., preschoolers cannot just be told to line up or sit in a circle).

Be safe. Make sure any "give away" item is big enough so that children cannot put it into their mouths and potentially choke. Make sure you have enough adults on hikes, and count the kids when conducting outside programs. Make sure the area is childproof (e.g., beware of electrical outlets, sharp edges, etc.).

Adapted from Ottman (1998) and Baumer & Crabtree (2000).

Preschool programs bring the same rewards for the interpreter as other interpretive programs, but also some special joys. They might be best conveyed in the following passage from an unsolicited, spontaneous email to one of the authors from Robin Grumm, a seasoned interpreter, who has been doing Babes in the Woods programs for years. She felt compelled to share her joy after coming back into her office after a "Babes" program.

> It is a glorious day outside! The breeze is cool, fresh, and full of life. It is a day for laughing, for playing, for running, and for jumping. I did just that with a group of parents and their children in a 'Babes in the Woods' program. It was invigorating. I can easily lose myself in a program like that. Surround me with children, the youngest among us, and I am happy. They crawl through the mulch without giving a thought to dirty pant legs. They make wonderfully joyful noises as they celebrate the sunshine and the wind on their faces. The moment is what is important and no more than that!

Older Children

"It is more important to pave the way for the child to want to know than to put him on a diet of facts he is not ready to assimilate."

–Rachel Carson (1965)

Older children benefit from interpretation in many ways. The personal benefits of interpretation as outlined in Chapter 3 apply to school-age children as well as adults. But benefits associated with learning important life skills are especially critical to the development of young people. One such skill is team building and the associated skill of teamwork. More and more teachers, camp counselors, and other youth leaders are using interpretive programs and venues to teach team-building skills to young people.

The Park/School Program developed by the Yale School of Forestry and Environmental Studies links park rangers with urban fifth graders in neighborhood parks. It results not only in learning about nature, but in building the students' social skills (Milton, Cleveland, & Bennett-Gates, 1995). Teamwork in particular was one of the skills enhanced by this program.

Another interpretive program focused on helping youths achieve broader self-improvement goals is the Delaware Bay Schooner Project with the A.J. Meerwald, New Jersey's official tall ship. It takes teamwork to sail any vessel and this is no exception. On board, interpreters lead special team building programs. Young people learn communication skills, and the importance of collaboration and cooperation as well as problem solving and decision-making processes as a result of fun and thought-provoking activities on this sailing ship. They also learn about the history and culture of the Delaware Bay watershed and the environmental issues affecting the bay.

The challenge for interpreters in working with older children, as with any audience, is holding their interest. As with the preschoolers, because of limited attention spans interpreters must keep it active, hands-on, short, fun, and relevant. Using approaches that allow for multiple learning styles is important for children as is applying age appropriate approaches that recognize the different stages of childhood cognitive and emotional development (as presented in more detail in Chapter 6).

Another key concern of interpreters when working with children is the concept of ecophobia. In his book, *Beyond Ecophobia: Reclaiming the Heart in Nature Education*, David Sobel writes, "If we prematurely ask children to deal with problems beyond their understanding and control, prematurely recruit them to solve mammoth problems of an adult world, then I think we cut them off from the possible sources of their strength." (Sobel, 1996).

Sobel identified three stages of childhood that define appropriate approaches to interpreting to children about nature and conservation. Between the ages of four and seven, interpreters should focus on creating empathy with nature. The objective should be to foster positive feelings about common animals and plants through stories, songs, moving like animals, celebrating seasons and nurturing what Rachel Carson called "the sense of wonder." It is not appropriate to present dilemmas of endangered species, habitat loss, or other such negative issues. Between the ages of seven and 11 interpreters should emphasize exploration of the surrounding landscape, beginning with the home and school and then expanding out to the neighborhood, community and region. Activities such as scavenger hunts, fort building, following streams or trails are recommended. Caring for gardens and animals is also appropriate for this age group. It is only about the age of 12 that social action should be included in interpretive programs.

As adolescents begin to feel a part of society, issues like saving endangered species or habitats becomes important to them. Sobel identifies the problem of too much education aimed at children as "premature abstraction" (i.e., presenting young people with information that they are not prepared to process). His recommendation is "no tragedies before fourth grade," meaning no talk of oil spills, genocide, or rainforest destruction, and similar distressing topics. Children need to learn to love their own local natural history before asking them to solve global problems and care for far-away places.

This approach to interpreting to children was eloquently captured by environmental educator Michael Weilbacher (quoted in Leinbach, 2008), who said, "Eight-year-olds should not be asked to become warriors or worriers. Children have much more important work to do: Watch ants. Grow flowers. Dance between the raindrops. This is sacred work, and childhood needs to be preserved just as much as rain forests and wetlands."

Knapp (1997) extends this caution to avoid doom and gloom messages to all audiences regardless of age. Emphasizing the beauty, power, and intricacies of nature lays the foundations for stewardship in young and old alike. Acting on this same conviction, in 2016, IUCN Commission on Education and Communication adopted an educational campaign called "*Love. Not Loss*" based on the belief that the best way to rekindle a caring relationship with nature is not to talk about what went wrong –extinction, habitat loss or resource scarcity, but rather to remember what we loved in the first place. The premise of this program is that if you want a happy ending for nature and for people, it has to be a love story. Short videos and other educational materials give positive case studies, teach participants how to tell a nature love story, and challenge interpreters to create messages inspired by awe and wonder, not loss and extinction.

Serving Teens

Teens may be the most overlooked audience at most interpretive sites. Yet, they are an important audience. As noted above, it is in the teen years that young people can become active in addressing community and global challenges. According to Bradley, Waliczek, and Zajicek (1999), 8th to 11th grade students are the ideal age for gaining an ethical and ecological appreciation of our world. Moreover, they report that secondary school students who are engaged with environmental programs or activities often show increased environmentally responsible behavior.

> Interpretation can be fun and engaging for teenagers.

Interpretation can be fun and engaging for teenagers. The physical challenges of the environment stir many youths to adventure, risk recreation, and a sense of oneness with the world. For earlier generations, the lessons of hunting, fishing, and working the woods with dad were rites of passage. Stories passed down from grandparents were history lessons. Today, the interpretive naturalist may be the only person that a youth meets who can provide the deep-woods knowledge to inspire deeper probing for revelation and self-actualization. The historical interpreter may be their only window to the past. The contemporary challenge in reaching teenagers is to entice them away from smartphones, iPods, ear buds, video games, social media and other distractions that compete for their attention.

Or, rather than trying to get young people to cut their ties to technology interpreters can use those technologies in ways to gain attention and interest (James & Ginder, 2017). For example, students near the Harpers Ferry National Historic Park analyze primary resources dealing with the Civil War and then create a documentary presenting their own interpretation of historical events (Mast, 2011). Students film their peers acting out the story and post the video podcast on the internet or download the video to their smart phones. The program known as "Of the Student, By the Student, For the Student" causes students to look at history through their own eyes and completely immerses them in the historical events. Students do the writing, acting, editing, set designing, and all other aspects of the production. Young people are more likely to watch documentaries made by their peers than those made by historians, and for those directly involved in creating the video, the historical events they recreated come to life. In this way, technology becomes the friend, rather than the foe, of interpreters.

Teens are eager to gain independence from their parents, be given responsibility, and to take on leadership roles. Being with their friends is an important motivation for many teenagers who participate in interpretive programs. Whether interpreting nature or history, attracting teenagers lies in appealing to what they enjoy—fun, adventure, physical challenges, and socializing with peers (especially mixed with eating!). To hold their attention, be sure to interpret topics that teens relate to and find important.

For example, at the Old Spanish Missions in Texas, a program attracts teens by drawing parallels between native adolescent hunters and themselves (McGahee, 2008). Teens are exposed to tattoos, masks, body piercings and music of native adolescents. Then they paint in groups, creating their own mask. Teens learn that piercings, tattoos, and music played a major role in early North American cultures. Today's teens connect closely with tattoos, piercings, music, and drumbeat, and the wearing of masks. They recognize that most teens "wear a mask" to some degree of a persona they wish to project as they mature into adulthood.

Teenagers make wonderful volunteers. Many zoos, nature centers, and museums rely heavily on teenage docents or volunteer naturalists to not only use their energies doing physical labor, but also helping with special events and conducting interpretive programs. Teens want to volunteer to gain valuable experience that will prepare them for college or careers. Volunteering gives them confidence, leadership skills, and the feeling of being needed and valued. Often their youthful enthusiasm and energy result in lively, engaging, and effective programs. Teens are particularly successful when working with children as they can match their energy and are willing to get dirty and play with their young audiences. Through word of mouth, teens can recruit their friends and make volunteering at the interpretive site "cool." Morgan, Absher, Loudon, and Sutherland (1997) studied youth naturalists in a U.S. national forest and found they can be effective in changing audience attitudes and achieving other interpretive objectives.

One successful program that brings together teens to do good work is the Teens for Planet Earth initiative of the Bronx Zoo's Education Department. This program guides teams of young people through service-learning projects focused on helping the environment in their own community. Since its inception Teens for Planet Earth has organized more than 100 teams in 33 countries.

The Missouri Department of Conservation (MDC) sponsors Teen Clubs at their Nature Centers (Figure 7.7). Activities include canoeing, muzzleloader and shotgun shooting sports, birdhouse building, and fly-fishing. Michele Baumer worked with teenagers for many years at MDC's Runge Nature Center. She notes that interpreters must understand working with teenagers is not only a professional task but also a personal one. Teenagers are trying to find out who they are and what they stand for and they will seek your opinion on everything from drugs and sex to music. Then they compare your answers to the answers of their peers and parents. Teenagers question everything, including themselves. Many seek praise and acceptance, because although they may appear confident on the outside, they often are less so on the inside.

Figure 7.7. Teens, along with a teen volunteer, participate in a fun survival activity at Runge Nature Center in Missouri. (KC)

With teenagers, an interpretive supervisor may spend as much time talking about personal relationships as ecological ones. Because the social aspect of participation is so important to teenagers, interpreters must be keenly aware of group dynamics. "Cliques are a cancer to teenage groups," says Baumer. She recommends having regular field trips, overnight "lock-ins" at the nature center, and using team challenge courses to enhance team work and to eliminate cliques. These challenge courses bring out surprising strengths in individual teens and the group.

Baumer tells interpreters not to be discouraged if teens drop out when they turn 16 years old. At this age they have new freedom and mobility since they can drive. They also may have their own money as they get their first paying jobs. These may compete successfully with your program initially, but by the time they turn 18 years old, many will return more motivated than ever, as they think of gaining experience for college and preparing for careers.

Finally, Baumer notes that working with teenagers not only requires a lot of time and physical energy, but that because the relationships are so personal, much emotional energy is needed. Teenagers will sense if you seem to be "too busy" or "too tired" to deal with them. This will cause them to drift away from the program. In short, to successfully work with teenagers the most important requirement is that you must genuinely care about them as individuals and enjoy their company.

Serving Seniors

This section discusses serving people at the other end of the age spectrum—seniors. The average and median ages of Americans have been increasing since the mid-1800s. All population projections indicate that median and average age of U.S. citizens will increase along with life expectancy. The 65-and-over age group will continue to grow in numbers and mobility. By the year 2033, the population of people 65 and older will outnumber people younger than 18 years old. (U.S Census, 2015) Therefore, older adults make up an increasingly important audience for interpreters.

At some times of the year, seniors make up the majority of visitors in parks and historic sites. Not restricted by school schedules, they avoid summer crowds by traveling in the fall, winter, and spring. During these off-season periods, interpreters can focus their attention on serving the sophisticated needs and abilities of this age group.

Although seniors experience physical changes that affect how they recreate, they don't all act frail and feeble. Many are active athletes and have great endurance and enthusiasm. However, over time, humans slow considerably as muscles lose tone, bones lose calcium, and sight and hearing become impaired. Application of the tips previously mentioned in Box 7.2 will enhance service to seniors who have some of the same limitations.

> Older adults make up an increasingly important audience for interpreters.

On trails, gentle slopes, smooth surfaces, and frequent benches make walking more appealing to those with limited stamina or mobility. Regarding age-related hearing loss, some seniors are too embarrassed to ask you to speak louder, so watch for visual clues such as lack of eye contact and failure to respond readily to questions. The simplest remedy is to speak louder. Captioning on films helps the hard of hearing, the foreign visitor, and it reinforces or clarifies the message for all visitors. Because many people won't ask for captioning, use the captioned version all the time to maximize its benefits. As adults age, the pupil size decreases, making it necessary to have more lights to see well. Exhibits and pathways need to be well-lighted for older visitors. The ability to read small print often decreases with age as does distinguishing colors. Those who wear bifocals (not necessarily the older adult) prefer signs placed on exhibits at 3.5 to 5.5 feet in height to avoid cricks in their neck from having to look up at the text. Large-print publications and large fonts on exhibits will make reading the text easier.

Programming for Seniors

Many senior retirees are able to be generous with their time and money. Many organizations have experienced tremendous rewards associated with scheduling programs specifically for seniors. For example, interpreters in Iowa are reaping these benefits from a program especially for seniors. They developed a program called OWLS (Older, Wiser, Livelier Seniors). This program offers a monthly luncheon/conservation program. It has awakened seniors' curiosity and led them to get involved in local conservation activities and issues as volunteers and benefactors (Zaletel, 2001).

Based upon a study of seniors using three national parks by Bultena, Field, and Renninger (1984) the following are recommended approaches to serving seniors.

1. **Schedule daytime and early evening programs.** Night programs often conflict with the "early to bed, early to rise" schedules of many seniors.
2. **Offer age-specific programs.** Special age-defined programs for seniors provide social interaction with peers and allows appropriate level of discourse and topics. For example, seniors can relate to long-term concepts such as succession,

eutrophication, and life cycle processes in ecosystems, social systems, and human life. Age-specific programs also eliminates distractions from noisy or active children. Although seniors don't like disruptions from other people's children, they enjoyed taking their own grandchildren to evening programs.

3. **Offer a variety of in-depth presentations or publications.** Many seniors are knowledgeable and seek more sophisticated information than an introductory interpretive talk or a nature video can provide. They often find the interpretation to be superficial, uninformative, and unchallenging. Many older campers can find evening interpretive programs uninformative and redundant. Because they stay in one place longer than younger people, they can quickly exhaust the interpretive offerings in the area, unless allowed to choose progressively deeper programming. Interpreters who limit themselves to two or three talks per season, repeated on a cycle, won't remain interesting to long-term visitors.

4. **Involve seniors.** Seniors tend to exhibit strong commitment to local heritage and environments. They are tremendous sources of historical information and typically are anxious to share their knowledge. Many have scrapbooks, data, or stories to share. They have hobbies, talents (e.g., photography, storytelling, crafts skills) that can contribute to the site's programming. When interpreters serve older adults it may lead to volunteering, where they often do outstanding jobs. It may also lead to philanthropy and other forms of support.

Programs aimed at seniors almost always are popular if you approach them like any other audience and offer them fun and meaningful interpretation. Fontenelle Nature Association, a nature center in Nebraska, provides 150 programs that have attracted as many as 3,500 seniors annually (Kuper, 2007). Fontenelle staff offer the Traveling SUN (Seniors Understanding Nature) program designed for seniors unable to come to Fontenelle Forest Nature Center. Interpreters travel to facilities where seniors live or gather to give one of 14 interactive programs. Thus, seniors living in an assisted living site or a senior church group can learn about "butterflies and wildflowers" or play "nature bingo."

Another successful program has been Senior Wednesdays in Wichita, KS. Ten organizations, including The Wichita Art Museum, Sedgwick County Zoo, Sedgwick County Historical Museum, Great Plains Nature Center, and Old Cowtown Museum partnered to offer classes as varied as the venues themselves: anything from Quilt History, The Titanic, Dissecting Owl Pellets, Sculptures, or Native Wildflowers. Each venue provides refreshments and light snacks as well as a bit of social time prior to the event. The program rotated among the sites and fostered lifelong learning and encouraged active healthy lifestyles and engaging social opportunities for seniors (Hay, Albers, & Geist, 2007).

Approaching Audiences

Shenandoah National Park has about 1.3 million visitors annually. Of these, 400,000 go into the visitor center and 30,000 attend scheduled ranger-led interpretive programs. This means that more than 800,000 visitors each year visit the park but do not talk to a ranger. Even fewer talk to an interpreter (Graves, 2015). Such statistics are similar to what many parks experience. Only a small percentage of visitors avail themselves of interpretive services and programs. What can be done about those many thousands of visitors who don't talk to an interpreter? One strategy is to go find visitors where they're at and take interpretation to them, rather than expecting them to come to you. To this end, Shenandoah has converted a new van into a "mobile visitor center" that takes exhibits, artifacts and, of course, an interpreter out on the road to find visitors who might not come into the traditional visitor centers (Figure 7.8).

This approach, called "roving interpretation," has been widely promoted and adopted by many agencies as a strategy to reduce barriers and increase contact with guests. Knapp (2007) defines roving interpretation as "personalized, face-to-face communication where the audience has chosen the venue, the resource is the stage, and the interpreter is the catalyst for knowledge." Roving interpretation happens when the interpreter goes out to find guests, welcomes them and then engages them (if they are willing) in a friendly and casual conversation about the resource. The conversation is customized to the people encountered. Visitors ask questions related to their personal interests, rather than a predetermined topic. Roving not only personalizes the interpretation, but eliminates the constraints and barriers associated with requiring visitors to show up for a formal program at a specific time and location.

> Only a small percentage of visitors avail themselves of interpretive services and programs.

Figure 7.8. Shenandoah Mobile Visitor Center. (NPS-NL)

Roving interpretation works anywhere visitors congregate: campgrounds, trails, picnic areas, scenic overlooks, museum galleries, zoo grounds, and even parking lots. Interpreters can even rove in the gift shop to visit with guests.

Roving interpretation is sometimes referred to as "informal interpretation" or "spontaneous interpretation" and indeed it is spontaneous interaction with guests. However, that should not imply that it is unplanned or unorganized. In fact, roving is a challenging activity requiring many skills. Agencies and professional organizations now offer formal training in the art of roving interpretation. It requires interpreters to have a plan to engage individuals, families or groups of friends, a plan to gracefully disengage from these folks, a broad knowledge of the resource, and a creative and quick wit to respond to the personalities, interests, and unpredictability of the audience. It may appear that roving interpreters are adlibbing or giving an impromptu presentation, and in some respects they are, but it is only through preparation and practice that interpreters can rove effectively. With experience interpreters will be able to better predict what visitors will be most interested in at particular locations. One part of preparation is packing a traveling box of props, artifacts, maps, photos, or other tools to share with interested visitors.

> Agencies and professional organizations now offer formal training in the art of roving interpretation.

Roving interpretation allows for a constructivist approach to learning. Knapp and Forist (2014) advocate the use of a constructivist framework as a new interpretive pedagogy. This approach focuses on learning as an active process in which learners select information and construct new ideas or concepts based upon their own existing knowledge. Here, the interpreter becomes more of a facilitator, leading a discussion or dialogue with visitors that links directly to the visitor's current knowledge and values. In this approach the visitor and interpreter engage in two-way conversation rather than the interpreter merely lecturing or performing. Even in Tilden's day, he recognized that a visitor "does not so much wish to be talked *at* as to be talked *with*" (Tilden, 1977). Roving allows interpreters to talk *with* visitors. The interpreter probes with thoughtful questions and receives and responds to feedback from the visitor. The starting point is identifying what the visitor is curious about and what Tilden called the visitors' "first interests." Using a roving constructivist approach meets guests' needs for understanding and enriches their visits in a most personal way.

Other Reasons to Rove

Besides the opportunity to reach visitors who do not come into visitor centers or attend programs, roving has other benefits. Mingling with visitors where they are allows interpreters to learn more about the visitors; what they like and what doesn't interest them. It can make people feel more at ease and more welcome and ultimately build public support by presenting a friendly face to the guests. An initial personal encounter with a smiling friendly person in uniform reduces tension and fears of visitors, particularly if the interpreter can speak the first language of the guest. Guests also benefit from roving interpretation by having the opportunity to experience the resource directly, first-hand, and perhaps even be immersed in it.

By being out in the field or "on the floor" interpreters are positioned to encourage resource protection and enhance visitor safety. Resource protection is seen as one of the most significant benefits of roving by those who have adopted this approach. Roving interpreters may encounter visitors violating a rule. Instead of issuing a citation, roving interpreters can offer an explanation for the rule and interpret the resource or safety concern being protected by the rule. To mingle these roles of protection and interpretation, agencies have turned their ranger and security staffs into roving interpreters. For example, Monterrey Bay Aquarium security officers receive interpretation training and become Certified Hosts or Certified Guides by completing NAI's certification programs. Now instead of ordering guests to stop feeding the gulls, they interpret why it is important not to feed the gulls (Wright, 2015). At Jefferson County (CO) Open Space parks, 14 park rangers make 10,000 resource protection contacts annually while roving (Bonnell, 2015). At Lake Mead National Recreation Area the presence of roving interpreters not only protects sensitive natural areas and archeological sites, but it also enhances visitor safety. Roving interpreters monitor lake conditions, visitor use patterns, and adapt and target safety messages accordingly (Riter & Oakleaf, 2003).

Finally, roving interpretation allows interpreters to take a break from the sometimes monotonous information desk or entrance gate duty and get outside and reconnect with people more intimately and enjoy the resource they are interpreting (Figure 7.9). Roving is clearly an excellent approach to serving and growing our varied audiences. It means interpreters can reach as many people as possible who visit interpretive sites.

Figure 7.9. An interpreter in Germany's Black Forest connects with people and enjoys the resource by using a modified bicycle to take artifacts and fun activities to people who do not visit the nature center.

Summary

The interpreter has many audiences to serve, diverse in nature, and yet all share some commonalities. This chapter offered suggestions on how best to relate to many different groups.

The challenge is clear. Although many people have traditionally enjoyed opportunities to experience nature and culture firsthand at parks, zoos, museums, and other interpretive sites, only a fraction of these visitors attended interpretive programs or other special events. So there is plenty of room to expand participation in programs by gaining more of the existing visitation to the interpretive site, so these people too can enjoy the benefits of interpretation. In addition, there are those who don't visit interpretive sites at all.

When interpreters successfully attract new audiences and they mix with traditional visitors, a logical approach is to select subject matter that appeals to commonalities and interests of all members of the community (e.g., using universal concepts), rather than focusing on the differences between people. However, in some cases, interpreters may identify and address distinct preferences of certain groups, whether teens or underserved ethnic groups.

As interpreters seek to cast interpretive nets more widely—in addition to removing social, psychological and physical barriers—the key to serving new audiences is to know them. Seek relevancy by learning what matters most to them, their values and interests. Take time to build an active relationship of trust and involvement. Then make the interpretive site familiar and comfortable for all.

Getting closer to your audience may involve changing from being a "sage on the stage" to serving them as a "guide on the side," from being the expert and authority to being a facilitator and co-learner, from being leader to friend. When programs are relevant and people feel welcomed, respected and valued they will come, join in, and give you the joy of working with them.

As audiences become more diverse, with a welcoming and meaningful approach, more and more people will become involved in learning about and supporting interpretive sites. These increased numbers of people, and therefore increased levels of knowledge and stewardship, will most certainly contribute to a better world.

Literature Cited

Bahram, S. (2016). Make your website accessible before you are forced to. *Museum*, July/August 2016, 17–18.

Baumer, M., & Crabtree. R. (2000). Children and Nature. Presentation materials distributed at *NAI Region VI Workshop*., Manhattan, KS.

Beck, L., & Cable, T. (2011). *The gifts of interpretation: Fifteen guiding principles for interpreting nature and culture* (3rd ed.). Urbana, IL: Sagamore.

Bixler, R., Carlisle, C., Hammitt, W., & Floyd, M. (1994). Observed fears and discomforts among urban students on field trips to wildland areas. *Journal of Environmental Education, 26*(1), 24–33.

Bonnell, M. A. (2015). Resource protection through roving. *Legacy, 26*(1), 26–28.

Bradley, J. C., Waliczek, T. M., & Zajicek, J. M. (1999). Relationship between environmental knowledge and environmental attitude of high school students. *Journal of Environmental Education, 30*(3), 17–21.

Brown, W. E. (1971). *Islands of hope*. Arlington, VA: National Recreation and Park Association.

Bultena, G., Field, D. R., & Renninger, R. (1984). Interpretation for the elderly. In G. E. Machlis & D. R. Field (Eds.), *On interpretation* (rev. ed., pp 69–76). Corvallis, OR: Oregon State University Press.

Chavez, D. J. (2000). Invite, include, and involve! Racial groups, ethnic groups, and leisure. In M. T. Allison & I. E. Schneider (Eds.), *Diversity and the recreation profession: Organizational perspectives* (pp. 179–191). State College, PA: Venture.

Clark, C., Williams, P. S., Legg, M., & Darville, R. (2011). Visitor responses to interpretation at historic Kingsley Plantation. *Journal of Interpretation Research, 16*(2), 23–33.

Davis, S. K., & Thompson, J. L. (2011). Investigating the impact of interpretive signs at neighborhood natural areas. *Journal of Interpretation Research, 16*(2), 55–66.

Falk, J. H., & Dierking, L. D. (2000). *Learning from museums: Visitor experiences and the making of meaning*. Walnut Creek, CA: Altamira Press.

Fraser, J., Bicknell, J., Sickler J., & Taylor, A. (2009). What information do zoo and aquarium visitors want on animal identification labels? *Journal of Interpretation Research, 14*(2), 7–19.

Goodrich, J. L., & Bixler, R. D. (2012). Getting campers to interpretive programs: Understanding constraints to participation. *Journal of Interpretation Research, 17*(1), 59–70.

Graves, M. (2015). Personal communication with Matt Graves (NPS Ranger).

Hay, C., Albers, L., & Geist, A. (2007). Senior wednesdays: A collaborative informal education community engages Wichita senior citizens. *Proc. NAI National Workshop*. Wichita, KS.

Hong, A., & Anderson, D. H. (2006). Barriers to participation for Latino people at Dodge Nature Center. *Environmental Education Research, 37*(4), 33–44.

James, J., & Ginder, J. (2017). Puzzled about your audience? *Legacy, 28*(2), 30–33.

Kahn, P. H., & Kellert, S. R. (2002). *Children and nature: Psychological, sociocultural, and evolutionary investigations*. Cambridge, MA: The MIT Press.

Kammen, C. (2000). Educating our other audiences. *History News, 44*(4), 3–4.

Knapp, D.H. (1997). Back to basics: Interpreting to the lowest common denominator. *Trends,* 34(4), 17–21.

Knapp, D. H. (2007). *Applied interpretation: Putting research into practice.* Ft. Collins, CO: Interpress.

Knapp, D. H., & Forist, B. (2014). A new interpretive pedagogy. *Journal of Interpretation Research, 19*(1), 33–38.

Kuper, C. M. (2007). Senior citizens: An eager audience for nature programs. Proc. NAI Workshop, Wichita, KS.

Larsen, D. (Ed.). (2003). *Meaningful interpretation: How to connect hearts and minds to places, objects, and other resources.* Ft. Washington, PA: Eastern National.

Leinbach, K. (2008). It's kind of fun to do the impossible: The story of Milwaukee's urban ecology center. *Children, Youth and Environments,* 18(2), 180–196.

Mast, B. (2011). The Civil War through the lens of an adolescent. *Legacy,* 22(3, 12–15.

Mayorga, M., & Cable, T. (2015). Just relax! Interpreting for people with disabilities. *Legacy,* 26(6), 9–11.

McGahee, D. D. (2008). Encounters and exchanges: Tattoos, piercings, masks, and rhythm. *Proceedings NAI National Workshop.* Portland, OR.

Milton, B., Cleveland, E., & Bennett-Gates, D. (1995). Changing perceptions of nature, self, and others: A report on a park/school program. *Journal of Environmental Education,* 26(3), 32–39.

Morgan, J. M. (2000). Perceptions of a zoological park: A comparative study of educators and visitors. *Journal of Interpretation Research,* 5(1), 19–33.

Morgan, J. M., Absher, J., Loudon, B., & Sutherland, D. (1997). The relative effectiveness of interpretive programs directed by youth and adult naturalists in a national forest. *Journal of Interpretation Research,* 2(1), 13–26.

Oltman, M. (2001). Early childhood EE: Exhibits for young children. *Proceedings NAI National Workshop.* Des Moines, IA.

Ottman, L. (1998). Why teach toddlers and preschoolers? "It is not educational and is a waste of time!" In *Proceedings 1998 American Zoo and Aquarium Association Annual Conference,* Tulsa, OK.

Pease, J. L. (2015). Parks and underserved audiences: An annotated literature review. *Journal of Interpretation Research,* 20(1),11–56.

Place, G. S. (2000). *Impact of early-life outdoor experiences on an individual's environmental attitudes.* Unpublished doctoral dissertation, Indiana University, Bloomington, IN.

Rappolt-Schlichtmann, G., & Daley, S. (2013). *Curator: The museum journal,* 56(3), 307–321.

Rideout, S., & Legg, M. H. (2000). Factors limiting minority participation in interpretive programming: A case study. *Journal of Interpretation Research,* 5(1), 53–58.

Riter, M., & Oakleaf, G. (2003). Raving about roving. In *Proceedings National Interpreters Workshop,* NAI. Sparks, NV.

Roberts, N. S. (2001). Attitudes, perceptions, experiences across cultures: Case study of Rocky Mountain National Park. In *Proceedings National Interpreters Workshop,* NAI, Des Moines, IA.

Roberts, N. S. (2007). *Visitor/nonvisitor use constraints: Exploring ethnic minority experiences and perspectives.* General Technical Report submitted to Golden Gate National Recreation Area and Golden Gate National Parks Conservancy, San Francisco, CA: San Francisco State University.

Sobel, D. (1996). *Beyond ecophobia: Reclaiming the heart in nature education.* Great Barrington, MA: Orion Society.

Sobel, D. (2008). *Childhood and nature: Design principles for educators.* Portland, ME: Stenhouse Publishers.

Spennemann, D. H. K., & Taffe, R. (1998). Managing children's interactions with cultural heritage places. *Journal of Park and Recreation Administration, 16*(2), 73–87.

Stern, M. J., Powell, R., & Hockett, K. S. (2011). Why do they come? Understanding attendance at ranger-led programs in Great Smoky Mountains National Park. *Journal of Interpretation Research, 16*(2), 35–54.

Taylor, P. A., Grandjean, B. D., & Gramann, J. H. (2011). *National Park Service comprehensive survey of the American public 2008-2009: Racial and ethnic diversity of national park system visitors and nonvisitors.* U.S. Dept. of Interior, National Park Service. Ft. Collins, CO.

Thapa, B., Graefe, A., & Absher, J. (2002). Information needs and search behaviors: A comparative study of ethnic groups in the Angeles and San Bernardino National Forests, California. *Leisure Sciences, 24*(1), 87–107.

Tilden, F. (1977). *Interpreting our heritage* (3rd ed.). Chapel Hill, NC: The University of North Carolina Press.

United States Census Bureau. (2015). https://www.census.gov/content/dam/Census/library/publications/2015/demo/p25-1143.pdf

World Health Organization. (2011). *World Report on Disability.* WHO/NMH/VIP/11.01. Geneva, Switzerland.

Wright, K. (2015). Interpretive security. *Legacy, 26*(1), 20–22.

Yamada, N. & Knapp, D. H. (2009). Adult participants' preferences for interpretation at a Japanese nature park. *Journal of Interpretation Research, 14*(2), 59-63.

Zaletel, L. R. F. (2001). Who gives a HOOT? OWLS (Older, Wiser, Livelier Seniors) Do! In *Proceedings National Interpreters Workshop*, NAI. Des Moines, IA.

SECTION IV

How to Interpret

CHAPTER 8

Interpreting to the Masses

Can wildlife interpretation happen in cyberspace and is it as good as when it is done in the field? Interpreters at Katmai National Park and Preserve (King Salmon, Alaska) are exploring these issues through the innovative use of webcams. Katmai receives approximately 25,000 visitors annually. While this may seem relatively small compared to approximately five million annual visitors to Grand Canyon or Yellowstone, those 25,000 are rewarded with some of the most stunning and unique wildlife viewing in America—real-life bears, the size of a Volkswagen, romping and chasing fish through flowing rivers.

Katmai is home to more than 2,000 brown bears. During the summer and fall, many of these bears descend to the riverbanks to feed on one of the largest sockeye salmon runs in the world. The bears' activities are so predictable that several viewing platforms have been constructed, and many visitors often point out they can identify individual bears after only a few days. This distinctive and personalized experience with the bears led managers to explore other ways of sharing this phenomenal opportunity with a wider audience. Enter webcams, or more precisely, "bear cams."

For the past few years, Katmai has been broadcasting the daily activity of the bears on live feeds over webcams. Additionally, park interpreters present interactive Ranger Chats online. The results have been nothing short of spectacular. During the four months the bears are most active, the webcams draw more than two million views from every continent. Furthermore, bear cam viewers are forming online communities and chat rooms focused on bear management and conservation. By expanding the media toolbox to include webcams, Katmai has created virtual visitation rates nearly 100 times their onsite rates.

Researchers Drs. Jeff Skibins and Ryan Sharp at Kansas State University are working with Katmai managers to understand the impact of the online viewing experience and how it compares to seeing the bears in the wild. News of the research spread and was covered by local and national news outlets, online newsfeeds, and daily updates. Skibins reported that stories about bear cam research appeared on National Public Radio, *Newsweek* magazine, all three major television networks (ABC, CBS, NBC), among others. Impact metrics indicate several million people were made aware of the bear cams and bear conservation.

The ability to reach beyond park boundaries is an enormously powerful application of media and technology. Imagine the urban commuter on the train streaming live feeds of your interpretive site to their tablet, or Google alerts sent to millions of phones around the world highlighting news of the day for your nature center or historic site. Such applications have the ability to create a groundswell of support for your site and agency. Jeff Skibins noted, "It would be foolish for interpreters to not to take advantage of it!"

> *"Put it before them briefly so they will read it, clearly so they will appreciate it, picturesquely so they will remember it and, above all, accurately so they will be guided by its light."*
>
> —Joseph Pulitzer

Figure 8.1. Competing for attention of park visitors is more challenging when Wi-Fi towers sprout in the woods. (TC)

Today more than ever before, people are inundated with information, personal messages, and short blasts of entertainment, ranging from silly to serious. The interpreter's first challenge is to capture people's attention amidst all of the competing messages and digital distractions (Figure 8.1). Then the next challenge is to entice people to expend the effort to get intellectually and emotionally involved with the message. To accomplish these goals, as Pulitzer noted in the pre-digital age, interpreters still need to communicate briefly, clearly, picturesquely, and accurately. This chapter presents ideas to help interpreters break through the noise and use mass media to reach large and diverse audiences beyond their borders.

Digital Media

Websites

Most advice on developing a great website is a restatement of the interpretive principles presented throughout this book. Being relevant, provocative, and thematic all play a role in successful websites. However, the application of the third principle of interpretation—the principle of story—is especially important when designing websites. Most interpreters begin their story with the *what*: what programs they offer, what experiences they produce, what facilities they have, what artifacts or animals are on display. However, successful companies like Apple, Nike, and Disney claim the key to their success is that they start first by articulating *why* they do what they do. Starting with *why* is a powerful phenomenon (Sinek, 2009). The following three steps apply to both interpretive organizations and individual interpreters when they present themselves to others:

> "The interpreter's first challenge is to capture people's attention amidst all of the competing messages."

1. **Why?** This is the core belief of the organization/interpreter. It's *why* the organization exists. State your purpose and *why* people should care.
2. **How?** This is *how* the organization/interpreter fulfills that core belief.
3. **What?** This is *what* the organization/interpreter does to fulfill that core belief.

Sinek (2009) added, "People don't buy *what* you do; people buy *why* you do it." Interpreters can learn from successful companies when designing their websites by communicating *why* they offer interpretive services. Tell audiences your purpose and your passions before telling them what interpretive programs you offer.

A website is an essential tool for connecting both with the nontraditional audiences who would not normally visit a site and loyal friends and visitors. For the vast majority of potential visitors the site's website will shape their first impressions of the place. Often websites offer virtual tours or hikes, links to live webcams, a schedule of events, a mission statement, downloadable publications or videos, and a contact page for connecting with the staff. Even in this digital age include the physical address and telephone number of the organization.

> "Websites keep people up to date on interpretive opportunities."

Websites keep people up to date on interpretive opportunities and allow potential visitors to plan their visits before leaving home. Websites easily can be updated. To celebrate its centennial in 2016, the National Park Service along with the National Park Foundation and corporate sponsors developed a Find Your Park website (findyourpark.org) along with a Twitter link at #findyourpark to connect people with parks in their area and interpret them (Figure 8.2). This endeavor also allowed visitors to post their own stories and photos of their park visits.

Figure 8.2. Websites and social media allow the public to learn about Petrified Forest National Park and find their own park. (TC)

Another advantage of websites is that interpretive programs can be given live or recorded as webcasts to audiences around the world. For example, during an annual "Bat Week" celebration, Bat Conservation International's website annually hosts a series of 15-minute inspirational webcasts featuring children around the world involved in bat conservation.

Websites rely on people finding them and clicking on them. This means linking your site to other credible sites, and actively promoting your website during in-person programs, in agency publications, and on social media. These are important factors in driving traffic to the site. Make sure your site is "responsive" (meaning it adjusts to phones and tablets as well as to desktop computers) and registered with the common search engines. Website managers strive for a "high ranking in search" so the site appears early in search results. If a website does not show up early in a search, people are unlikely to take the time to look further. One way to achieve a high search ranking is to generate a lot of traffic to the site.

Fundamentally, the most important factor in attracting viewers is to have quality content (i.e., good images, easy navigation, relevant and interesting information). Also, drive traffic to your site by promoting it on Twitter, Facebook, Instagram, and Snapchat and other social media. Another strategy to drive traffic to your site is through a provocative and entertaining blog. Many interpreters enjoy writing and this gives them an outlet where they can develop a loyal following. Publish new blogs on a regular schedule so readers know when to expect new content at the site.

Once people find the site, like all good interpretive media and programs, the first impression is critical in holding their attention. Traditional graphic design concepts such as typography, layout, and color theory are just as important here as with other traditional graphics. A standard rule of web design is: Repetition. Repetition. Repetition. The use of the same colors, styles, shapes, and other design elements can work together to provide balance, harmony, and mood. The more attractive the site is, the longer users will want to look at it.

Most interpretive organizations will have a webmaster on staff or under contract who is responsible for designing and updating the site. It often is up to the interpreter to provide interesting information and photographs and to *interpret* the material.

Overall, what is it that you want people to do once they have visited your website? How do you want them to feel as they interact with the various elements presented? And what should be the *lasting* experience for the users?

Web designers seek to create sites that load quickly with the most important information visible without requiring the user to scroll down. They make the website's appearance neat and attractive, and use compelling images and fun graphics to capture attention. As with all interpretive efforts, make it simple to understand and navigate, and easy for visitors to provide feedback. To keep people coming back, update the content often. If websites are simple, interesting, constantly updated, and responsive to user feedback, people will return regularly.

Social Media

Whereas websites are passive in that people must find and go to them as noted above, Facebook, Instagram, Twitter, and other social media push interpretation out beyond the borders of historic sites, museums, and parks. Social media allows for personal communications to reach friends and followers. It gives a voice to the public as people can chat with a ranger or docent, respond to a blog post, or participate in an online forum or online community. Because social media allows posting pictures and videos, and because users repeatedly visit the sites throughout the day, it is a powerful tool to reach visually oriented people in exciting and compelling images. Social media expands its reach as users share the images or information with their friends. Interpretive messages or images may even go viral without any additional effort. Of course, negative comments and messages about programs or facilities may also spread widely and do significant damage to reputations.

Many agencies and interpreters use Twitter. Interpreters are specialists when it comes to using short messages to convey important ideas, and so Twitter, with its 280-character limit, lends itself well to accomplished interpreters who are skilled at saying a lot in a few words.

Instagram is particularly popular with young adults and teens, two demographic groups that are difficult to reach through traditional media (Smith, 2015). Instagram can deliver exciting visual content from your site to audiences through still images and 15-second videos. The key to successfully using Instagram is posting compelling photos that capture attention and tell a fun or exciting story on their own. To maximize its power, post images that evoke emotional responses so that people will want to share them with their network of followers.

The key value of social media is the immediacy of interaction. An interpretive site must have someone with a fresh and patient voice monitoring and moderating the communications. Nothing kills social media more quickly than someone asking a legitimate question, then getting no response for several days, if at all. Most organizations will have a tech-savvy person who serves as a social media specialist. This person coordinates the messages going out over various social media. These communications and conversations become the online voice of the organization. Social networking sites have evaluation tools built in, so the media specialist can learn almost immediately what resonates with people and what does not. This helps interpreters with the critical challenge of knowing their audience.

> "Most large organizations will have a tech-savvy person who serves as a social media specialist."

Social media are constantly evolving and undoubtedly new ones will appear. Paul Caputo, Deputy Director of NAI in charge of the organization's visual and digital identity, says regardless what the future holds and which specific social networks are used, the most important thing is to not be boring (See Box 8.1).

Box 8.1
Social Media for Interpreters: Don't Be Boring

Paul Caputo, Deputy Director, National Association for Interpretation

Implementing a social media plan can be overwhelming. Questions abound about choosing the best platform, the best moderator, and the best content to share. The technological landscape shifts like sand under our feet, the data we use to analyze the reach and impact of our social media presence are ephemeral in a really infuriating way, and even the goals we set as content providers are difficult to measure. So how can we set hard and fast rules about best practices for a field that can be so difficult to quantify?

Sometimes we measure social media success with actual numbers. We know how many Twitter followers we have. We know how many likes, comments, and shares we get on Facebook. And we can track how many people like our Valencia-filtered photos versus our Kelvin-filtered photos on Instagram. But those numbers are more circumstantial evidence in the larger question of whether we are achieving our social media goals.

As with all things interpretation, our goals should answer this question: *Are we getting our message out?* Many interpretive sites err on the side of merely providing information or promotions ("Come visit our new exhibit." "Buy this sweatshirt." "Donate to our cause.") Instead of actual interpretation. This is a missed opportunity, like a museum using exhibits to direct visitors to the gift shop.

Box 8.1 continued

As we struggle to measure and quantify our social media success, I propose this one-and-only, hard-and-fast, unmeasurable rule of social media: *Don't be boring.*

It sounds obvious, but the most important thing an interpreter can do on social media is *be interpretive*. Not only does interesting, interpretive online content get your important messages out into the world, it's more likely to help you achieve your social media goals. Interpretive content, which by its very nature is meant to provoke, is more likely to be shared around by your followers, and is therefore more likely to gain you more followers who are interested in the content you're providing. As you build your social media audience through interesting, interpretive content, you'll have more eyes to see the (occasional) boring program announcement that you need to share.

Interpreters online are forced to compete in a landscape of cat videos and short attention spans and need to exhibit creativity when generating content—the same sort of creativity they use in creating programs, exhibits, publications, or any other interpretive content. So before you hit that "post" button with your next social media update, the first question you need to ask yourself might seem obvious, but it's the only one that matters: *Is it boring?*

Taking Photos/Videos for Social Media

With almost everybody carrying a camera in their phone, opportunities abound for posting photos on websites or social media. Interpreters can capture spontaneous and surprising events or scenes. These images often communicate better than words. However, not all photos are equally as effective in gaining and holding attention.

> "Images often communicate better than words."

Whether using a standard camera or a phone camera, several simple principles of photographic composition will immediately make your photographs more professional looking. Professionals don't merely *take* a picture; they *make* a picture. Just as good sentences only communicate one idea, good photos have one strong center of attention. The subject of the photo should be obvious. Generally adding people in action adds interest. Framing a photo with an object (e.g., leaves, branches) along the edge in the foreground adds depth. As with most things, this should be done in moderation as it should not detract from the subject of the photo. A well-known and important composition principle is the "rule of thirds." The rule states that rather than putting the subject in the middle of the photograph as if you were shooting it as target practice, offset the subject to the left or right or above or below the center. For example, in landscape photos rather than having an equal amount of sky and land decide whether the land or sky is most interesting and then move the horizon to make the most interesting feature to be two-thirds of the photo rather than half. If people and wildlife are in the photo, have them offset from center and facing or moving into the center of the frame from their "rule of thirds" position. Box 8.2 gives tips for taking good photographs and videos with a phone camera. Of course, the tips also apply to standard cameras. For short, prerecorded videos interpreters can use YouTube to reach audiences. YouTube is particularly effective because it is available on phones.

Box 8.2
Tips for Taking Better Photos and Videos with Your Phone
Gerry Snyder, Instructional Technologies, Kansas State University

Photos

People take more photos with their smartphones than with digital cameras. Here are a few ideas to improve your ability to capture high quality images using your smartphone.

- Choose a high image quality setting for your pictures. Many smartphones exceed 16 megapixels in resolution quality. The more megapixels, the better the quality. Use at a minimum, six megapixels.
- Use a phone that has plenty of digital storage. Many smartphones have the ability to record to external storage cards. If that's the case, purchase a 32GB card or larger for recording your pictures.
- Use a smartphone with an optical 4x zoom or higher. This is especially important for wildlife shots. Avoid using the digital zoom as the image will deteriorate.
- Capture the moment. Timing is everything. Being in the right place at the right time makes all the difference from a good to great photo. Anticipate when an event might happen. Keep your smartphone close by for those sudden and surprising pictures.
- Know your phone camera features. Your smartphone is essentially a small computer packed full of extra camera functions. Many have low-light detection, face detection, metering modes, selective focus, exposure controls, grid lines, white balance, and HDR (High Dynamic Range, one of my favorite options for rich colors) options. Check to see which ones are turned on or off by default.
- Try using different photo modes. By default, most smartphone cameras have controls set to Automatic. Look for modes that match the subject. Various modes include panorama (great for landscapes), portrait (for close-ups of people), night time (for low light photos), action (to reduce blur on moving images), snow-sand (for pictures in bright environments) and many more.
- Turn off the flash. This will prevent draining your phone battery and often leads to better pictures. The tiny flash on a smartphone is only good up to 10 feet. Use it only when the subject needs it within that close distance.
- Keep your lens clean and scratch free. Many people keep smartphones in pockets where they are prone to smudging and scratching. Protect the smartphone camera lens and periodically clean the lens with a soft cloth.
- Be creative and unique. Take lots of photos of the same subject. Try moving around the subject. Use different high and low angles. Use light on the subject emphasizing highlights and shadows. Take advantage of different times of day and seasons.

Videos

Anyone with a smartphone and a little know-how can make a fun and informative video. Smartphones can shoot and even edit a good quality video. Here are a few tips for creating your masterpiece. Once you are finished with your video, you can upload it to many free online websites for others to enjoy.

Start by planning. Who is your audience? What is the main message that you want people to learn from viewing your video? What do I need to create the video?

- Most information today is delivered in short chunks of information. Make your video between two and five minutes long. If you have more information, then make another video.
- Think of video making as recording a story. Shoot lots of video. This includes recording the audio as well as any and all supporting video that represents your story (this is known as B-roll or background video).
- Keep your video camera/smartphone steady. Nothing worse than a shaky image. If you have access to a tripod, use one. If not, try setting your camera on a stable surface while recording.
- Make sure your subject has good lighting. Avoid harsh shadows especially on a person's face.
- If you are interviewing someone, keep your smartphone at eye-level with them. It's a good technique to compose using just the head and shoulders of a person. Check for background clutter and unwanted lines such a tree branches that appear to be going through the person's head.
- Record good clean audio by being close to your smartphone microphone. Optional external microphones can plug into your phone for better audio quality.
- If you are outdoors, be careful of wind and other external sounds. Once again, move in closer to your microphone. Try recording in early morning when wind is at a minimum.
- It looks more professional to add a title screen to your video.
- Use instrumental music to create a mood for your video.
- Look online for additional still and video images to support your video subject, but be careful not to violate any copyright laws.

Will Technology Replace Authentic Experiences?

"When technology has nothing more for man, then nature will go on showing him her wonders."

–Eduardo Arango

This quote was found on a sign at Isle of Salamanca National Park in Colombia in the early 1980s (Sutton, 1982). The technology that exists today was not imaginable back then, but that same belief is still held tightly by 21st century interpreters in spite of our new technologies. Virtual hikes on trails all over the world are available on YouTube and on park apps. For example, NPS has the iHike program allowing virtual hikes on selected trails in national parks. With the advent of augmented and virtual reality, live webcams (Figure 8.3), and virtual tours and hikes, some are concerned technology-based experiences may replace actual visitation to interpretive sites, particularly with millennials who hold tightly to their technology. Julia Hartz, co-founder of Eventbrite, is not worried technology will detract from live experiences. She notes technology increases the desire for live events because it takes advantage of the need for belonging (Hartz, 2016). Technology makes connecting to others and following up *at* live events easier. Hertz calls millennials the "experience generation," as they are characterized by an overwhelming desire to purchase experiences rather than material goods. This trend called Hedonic Adaptation recognizes that manufactured goods lose value over time, whereas memories and experiences gain value over time. Technology may aid in enhancing live experiences as participants gain personal ownership of the experience by taking selfies to document their participation, but also in digitally connecting with other participants and the site itself in myriad personal ways.

Figure 8.3. Webcams provide visitors a close-up look at a Bald Eagle feeding her young without going into the field and disturbing the birds. (TC)

Media Relations

The first step toward successful media relations involves getting to know the right people and developing a friendly relationship with them. When the time comes to send a message, better results can be obtained by talking to a person with a name, not just a "station" or a "newspaper." For radio or television, contacts include the program director, news director, assignment editor, and the person responsible for public service announcements. At the local newspapers, identify the relevant editors (e.g., managing editor, city editor, outdoor editor, feature editor). Make sure editors know who you represent and provide them with phone numbers and email addresses so they can call you for clarifications or when an unexpected news story occurs.

When something happens that is newsworthy, either negative or positive, managing the message can be critical. Before making any public statements, decide on the content and tenor of the message that you want conveyed to the public. Identify a spokesperson to deliver the message and respond to questions consistently. If it is advantageous to schedule a news briefing, be aware of other coverage opportunities at the same time (e.g., the mayor is giving an important speech at that time) and reschedule to avoid competing with other hard news events for coverage. As always, be honest, open, clear, confident, and forthcoming with the media unless the new information would threaten someone or the resource. If questions go off-topic, answer the questions that should have been asked. It is a good idea to role play briefly before taking an issue to media to anticipate any confusion or challenges.

> "The first step toward successful media relations involves getting to know the right people."

Treat all the stations and papers in the area equally by providing them with the same information, unless they specifically state they do not use such material. To keep all the media outlets informed develop a contact list and send them newsletters, program schedules, and other routine mailings. Keep a file of media's email address, and day and night phone numbers, for reporting news stories quickly. When they air or print the story express appreciation by sending a thank-you to the responsible parties and their superiors.

If editors or broadcasters rewrite or condense a story, accept it as normal. If they never use the material, or if they call frequently to fill in gaps in the information, ask how their needs for information can be better met.

Print Media

Newspapers, books, and magazines get wide use for interpretation. Many national and state parks and museums produce their own quarterly or monthly publications to provide schedules and feature articles describing their attractions. However, most interpretive sites have now shifted to e-newsletters.

From the traditional print media, city daily newspapers provide more in-depth coverage of news than radio or television, and sometimes stories about interpretive sites are included. To reach broader audiences, daily papers may allow an interpreter space for a regular column, if they are consistently well written and faithfully submitted on time. Other outlets include weekly "shopper" papers. Interpreters write regular columns that add local color, information, and even fun or inspiration to a paper filled with advertisements.

Magazines provide an excellent outlet for in-depth interpretive writing and photography. A good place to start is with local or regional publications. Most states have a magazine published by the Department of Natural Resources or an equivalent agency that might welcome a contribution from an interpreter. Likewise, tourist regions have commercially-produced, high-quality magazines featuring regional attractions and history. Specialized magazines maintain relatively small staffs, relying on contributing editors and freelance writers. This provides an opportunity for interpreters to access this medium.

Park Newspapers: A Case Study

The following case study provides both specific and general lessons about how to best serve park visitors. As with many national parks and other interpretive sites, Grand Canyon National Park published and distributed a park newspaper, *The Guide*, for more than 40 years. The newspaper was comprehensive and grew larger and larger in an effort not to leave out anything and to be all things to all people. Johanna Lombard (2016), the publications program manager at Grand Canyon, shared the two major mistakes that were made in continuing this publication for so long. The *first mistake* was not knowing the audience. Lombard explained, "They differ in age, race, ethnicity, education, income, family size, values, life goals, and goals for their visit. How could you possibly meet every need with a newspaper?" And yet that is exactly what the park tried to do over the course of four decades with a paper that grew to 24 pages.

Then in 2015, the park discontinued printing *The Guide*. It was replaced with a program to meet the needs of more specific groups of visitors and included the following:

1. Pocket map for the half-day visitors who make up 75% of visitation, provided at the entrance station for every visitor (as was *The Guide*).
2. Hiking brochure for the relatively small percentage of visitors who actually need it.
3. Seasonal rack card produced quarterly to update changing information.
4. Interpretive magazine focused on the park's research and projects.

At many interpretive sites, much of this could be offered in digital media, but print media was chosen at Grand Canyon due to unreliable phone service and network connectivity throughout much of the park.

The *second mistake*, according to Lombard (2016), was calling facts interpretation. A critical point made throughout this book is that information is not interpretation. Lombard pointed out, "Interpretive writing is challenging. It takes time and it's often easier to write an informative, factual article, so we do that." Going through the history of the *The Guide* newspapers, Lombard found almost nothing that could be described as interpretive, nothing that would "engage the readers, lead them to form intellectual and emotional connections with the resource, nor prompt them into any action of stewardship." So, after identifying the needs of the half-day visitor the focus became meeting the interpretive needs of the visitors. As listed above, the interpretive magazine is designed to connect with visitors in meaningful ways on topics such as recent designation as an International Dark Skies Park, studies on rare plants, effects of climate change, and other areas of interest. The interpretive magazine is intended to celebrate the many research projects and to protect Grand Canyon's heritage in the future. Details of interpretive writing are presented in Chapter 14.

Broadcast Media

Radio

According to the U.S. Federal Communications Commission in 2016, over 15,000 radio stations were broadcasting in the U.S. In cities, the abundance and diversity of stations allows interpreters to target stations with specific types of audiences.

Radio's greatest advantages come from its potential to reach many people, its high local interest, and its inherent flexibility in targeting specific audiences. Radio still serves as the first source of news each day for most people. In the U.S., adults listen on the average about 13 hours per week.

Interpreters should listen to prospective stations and adapt their messages to the format and target audience. Stations featuring expanded news coverage or talk shows have audiences geared toward discussion and conversation rather than music. Such audiences may be especially receptive to interpretive messages.

Figure 8.4. Ozark Highlands Radio brings the stories and music of Arkansas' Ozark Folk Center State Park to the world. (TC)

When talking to the producer about appearing on a talk show, present a brief overview of the feature story and ideas for the show. If they accept the offer, prepare a suggested opening statement for the host and a list of questions the host can use. Hosts may not stick to those questions, but it improves the chances that appropriate information goes out over the air waves.

Some interpreters have their own radio programs. These broadcasts range from one-minute fishing or stargazing reports to half-hour call-in shows dealing with complex natural resource issues. To build an audience, the show must air on the same days and at the same time so listeners learn when and where to find it. Usually stations use these types of broadcasts as a public service, but sometimes sponsors will support them.

> "Radio's greatest advantages come from its potential to reach many people."

Some agencies produce short radio features. Sound carries the whole message so background music and sound effects help. Timing with a radio feature must be more precise than when preparing an interpretive talk. On the radio you have a strict time budget. The radio personality might merely present the interpretive information as a monologue. This format fits best for brief programs (1-5 minutes). Or, professional narrators can record the program before it is distributed. For example, the Missouri Department of Conservation produces Nature Notes consisting of 52 episodes for a once-a-week series. These prerecorded programs go, at no cost, to any radio stations that will broadcast them. Arkansas State Parks goes beyond its borders by broadcasting music and stories from Ozark Folk Center State Park online. This "radio" broadcast called Ozark Highlands Radio (ozarkhighlandsradio.com) has listeners on every continent (Figure 8.4).

Finally, remote local radio broadcasts from a special event at an interpretive site can form a beneficial collaboration between the radio station and the site by generating station sponsorships as well as visitation to the event.

Low Wattage Radio: TIS

Travelers' Information Stations (TIS), low-wattage radio transmitters, broadcast local information at AM 530 or 1610 on the dial. Interpreters tape short messages that play continuously. These stations deliver orientation information to people in their cars. TISs explain fees, accommodations, weather conditions, interpretive program schedules, or safety warnings as visitors approach a park or scenic byway. They also call attention to and interpret specific roadside features or views. Messages should be five minutes or less, depending on the travel speed. The signal may range from a quarter mile in hilly terrain to five miles or more in flat areas.

Like all interpretive efforts, successful implementation depends on planning. Place signs to allow lead time for people to locate the designated station. Typical signs say "Park Information—Tune AM 1610." More specific signs such as "Wildlife Viewing Information" or "Campground Information" may entice more listeners.

TIS units deliver information at a low cost per visitor contact and messages can be changed easily. Visitors find TIS a convenient, efficient way to receive information.

Television

With almost a billion television sets in the world, interpreters have a colorful way to reach most people. And the world is indeed watching. According to the National Association of Broadcasters, American adults spend on the average 36 hours a week watching television, almost as much time as they spend working.

Television shows action and emotion well and it can condense time in telling stories. The disadvantage of television is that it requires special equipment, facilities, and trained personnel, so interpreters have fewer production opportunities than with other media. Large agencies that produce television shows will have specialized professionals, so interpreters focus on content and presentation rather than production.

Many cable companies dedicate a channel for community service programming. Using this channel may be as simple as a Community Calendar text that scrolls across the screen announcing interpretive programs or it may provide time for a regular feature about nature or historic living skills. Some local television stations produce similar shows as a public service. Although they are taped during regular business hours to take advantage of the production personnel's schedules, unless these have sponsors, they typically appear at odd hours.

When preparing to be on a television show keep props simple for this visual medium. Wear something appropriate to the theme or activity (e.g., a suit and tie would not be appropriate for a story on hiking trails), but get advice on clothing colors to avoid disappearing into the backdrop. As always, never wear anything that will compete with or detract from your message. Plan for eye contact; avoid hats or sunglasses. Learn to properly use the microphone in the studio and the field.

Begin the program with something unusual or provocative to get the audience's attention. Remember the visual nature of the medium requires that you *show* things. Avoid long monologues. Talk casually yet alertly. Look at the guest or look directly at the camera as if it were a single person.

The producer keeps track of time, sets the pace, and makes the transitions and adjustments to have the program end at the right time. Both guest and host should have some extra material to use if the show proceeds faster than anticipated.

As with other interpretive media, focus on a particular theme in each program, or in the case of longer programs, a theme for each segment, rather than producing a show that superficially covers many topics. Interpreters often prepare the script outline, questions, visuals, and props. Although the interpreters may plan the show's content, they should defer to experts about other matters on the set. The professional technicians, directors, and producers determine the best way to create and deliver a program.

A few large agencies make their own videos for television. For example, over more than 70 years the Missouri Department of Conservation (MDC) has produced interpretive films and videos which they distribute on a free-loan basis throughout the state or for sale outside the state. The diverse titles include *Blooming Secrets, The Snake's Tale, Creating an Urban Oasis*, and *Streams: The Force of Life*.

News Releases

When a news story breaks at your site, alert your contacts at the news desk at local newspapers, radio, and television stations. They may send out a reporter, film crew, or ask you questions over the phone. For less urgent communications, such as information about an upcoming event or something newsworthy that has already occurred, submit news releases (also called press releases). Some news releases, if picked up by a national newspaper or network, may reach millions of people as was the case for the bear webcam story that introduced this chapter.

Most news directors or editors will receive many more news releases than they can use. The following will improve the chances of a news release being used (Fazio & Gilbert, 2000):

- **Timeliness**. An event should have just happened or be about to happen. Or it may relate to other events of current interest. An example of the latter: an item on Christmas tree cutting in early December.
- **Human Interest**. As noted in previous chapters, certain universal story characteristics hold special interest to people. In addition to these universals, keep in mind that most media outlets focus on telling stories about people, not merely things or events. Stories about a person who is hiking an entire trail end to end or a person who used a park as the place for an Eagle Scout project will garner more interest than a story about an event or specific natural resource. The easier it is to personalize the story, the better the chance for coverage.
- **Proximity**. The information you send should relate to the *community served* by the publication.
- **Prominence**. Well-known people or places attract attention. For example, the visit of a well-known dignitary to a park or museum may make a newsworthy story.
- **Consequence**. To be newsworthy, the information must be important to the audience. For example, hazardous water conditions in a park may affect local readers.

To write a news release, collect and verify all the facts, including the traditional five Ws and H. Specifically, these elements upon which reporters and editors focus are: *What* happened, *Who* did it, *Why* it happened, *Where* it happened, *When* it happened, and *How* it happened.

Journalists present the information in the inverted pyramid style (Figure 8.5). This means the key facts appear in the first paragraph within the first three or four lines. This is called the "lead." Make sure the headline and lead grab the reader's attention so it stands out from all of the other press releases. Clearly state why people should care about the story. The next paragraph should present the next most important facts. More detailed explanation of the first two paragraphs follows. Newspaper editors typically start cutting at the end of a story to trim it to fit in the space available, working their way up. The release should be written so it will make sense regardless of where the editor cuts it. This inverted pyramid is becoming less important in web-based news reporting with a reduced emphasis on strict word count limits. However, regardless whether writing for traditional or web news the key is to make sure your message is refined and not too broad. Hit the major points in a way the reporters will easily understand. They will take those points and tell the story in the way they see fit.

> Clearly state why people should care about the story.

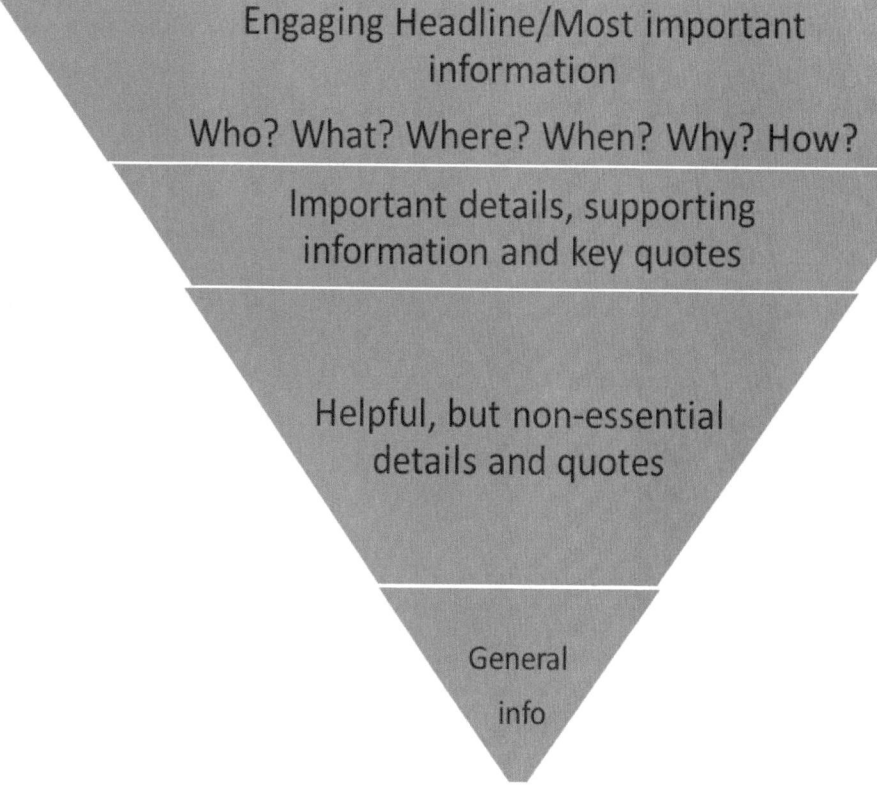

Figure 8.5. Diagram structure of a news story.

Keep words, sentences, and paragraphs short. An easy-to-read release reduces the chance of errors creeping into the story. Since releases often do not reach the editor the day they are written, answer the "when" question precisely with days and dates. Terms such as today, tomorrow, this weekend, and next week lose their meaning over time.

Include the following information at the top left corner of the release: your name, agency, address, phone number, and a short headline. Specify a release time or date. Indicate "For Immediate Release" unless there is a specific reason to delay the announcement. Indicate if photographs accompany a story. Releases often go out in packets containing several news stories. Agencies send such packets on a regular basis, so news directors can plan ahead on receiving and using them.

Almost all media outlets, even small ones, require material to be submitted electronically so they can easily cut, edit, and post the content on websites and other platforms. Check with the editor for details of format and filing procedures. Formatting recommendations include the following:

- Strive for a professional appearance (e.g., letterhead, no typos). A press release will end up in the garbage if dates, names, or numbers are wrong.
- Use double spacing.
- Leave wide margins.
- If more than one page, type (more) at the bottom. Better yet, try to condense it to one page. Information on the second page may not be read.
- At the top left corner of following pages type an abbreviated identification (e.g., last name) and the page number.
- Type end marks (###) after your last sentence.

Writing news releases for *radio or television* is trickier than for print. For broadcast media, one writes for the announcer's tongue and the listener's ear. A clear text, spoken well, helps the audience understand it. The following advice helps both the announcer and the listener:

> "For broadcast media, one writes for the announcer's tongue and the listener's ear."

- Use contractions and nontechnical words to make the speaking sound more natural.
- To make reading easier for the announcer avoid abbreviations by spelling out names of states, months, and days. Abbreviations are acceptable when commonly known and pronounced as a word (e.g., NEPA). When they should be read as individual letters, separate them in the copy with hyphens (e.g., C-C-C).
- Construct sentences so the announcer can breathe and speak naturally. Sentences should sound conversational. Read the text aloud to see if it works.
- For a difficult name include the actual spelling along with the phonetic pronunciation in parentheses (e.g., Kenai [keen-eye], Yosemite [yo-sem-it-tee]).
- Minimize the use of quotes. They can confuse and slow down the announcer. Furthermore, unless it is an extremely controversial topic and there is no other way of presenting it, a station will never use quotes on the air without that person saying it on camera.
- Time the script carefully to assure it fits within the allotted time frame.
- Write out words rather than using symbols (e.g., dollars, cents, percent) to make it easier for the announcer to read.
- Spell out numbers from one to ten. Use numerals for 11 to 999. Write out the words hundreds, thousands, millions, billions. Use numerals for all times and dates.
- As with all professional writing, proofread the copy more than once and if possible have another person check it over.

Public Service Announcements

A way of accessing free radio and television air time is through public service announcements (PSAs). Familiar images and phrases like Smokey Bear and his famous "Only You Can Prevent Forest Fires" and "Friends Don't Let Friends Drive Drunk" first entered our culture as PSAs. In the United States, radio and television stations licensed by the Federal Communications Commission must devote a percentage of their air time to nonprofit public service organizations. Similar regulations exist in other developed countries. Competition for free PSA air time gets fierce at times. Radio stations receive many poor quality PSAs. If an interpreter can submit an exciting, colorful, and professional quality PSA, it has a better chance of being broadcast. The following are the steps required to produce a successful PSA:

1. Identify and prioritize stations that will reach your target audience (e.g., oldies music, all-news, hip-hop). Then call the station and find out who handles public service programming; learn deadlines or special requirements for submission of PSAs.
2. Identify and limit the subject to one specific idea for the PSA. However, having different versions of the same PSA will reduce the chances of listeners getting tired of your message.
3. Begin with a "hook"—something clever, shocking, funny, or even a catchy tune to capture the listener's attention. Then write a short, simple, factual statement, to answer the traditional questions of who, what, when, where, why, and how. Make the PSA's length 15 seconds (30-35 words), 20 seconds (40-50 words), or 30 seconds (60-75 words). Most stations prefer 30-second PSAs, although at some stations, the shorter the statement, the more likely it will receive air time.
4. If you know somebody who has radio/television experience, ask the person to review your PSA and offer suggestions. Likewise, find people who are members of your target audience, show them the PSA script, and ask them for critical feedback.
5. PSAs look like press releases in layout. However, add the name and contact information of the person preparing the copy and the length of the PSA (e.g., 15-second announcement).
6. Most organizations submit their script "live copy"—a simple script ready to be read by a live, on-air announcer. Live copy is inexpensive and used extensively in radio. However, television stations rarely use live copy scripts. Television stations require a prerecorded version. Some organizations have the specialists and equipment to record their own PSAs, whereas others contract with a studio or a radio station to produce their PSAs. Sound effects improve the effectiveness as they make mental images more vivid and memorable in the "theater of the mind."

Interviewing and Being Interviewed

Interpreters who write regular columns for newspapers or who have a regular radio or television spot often interview local experts, policymakers, agency personnel, or active community members. Box 8.3 presents tips for how interpreters can conduct an effective and professional interview.

Box 8.3
Tips for Conducting a Successful Interview

- Prior to the interview, "do your homework" and get background information about the guest and the topic.
- Welcome your guest well before air time. Before beginning, identify the key points the guest wants brought out in the interview. Remind your guest about the nature of the audience.
- Begin by quickly introducing your guest. Explain his or her relationship to the program and provide background information that will make the guest seem more personable.
- The first question should serve as an "ice breaker" and should establish the guest's credibility. Allow the guest to talk about himself or herself briefly (e.g., "How did you get interested in this topic?").
- Arrange the questions in a logical order (e.g., chronological, geographical, simple to complex, by species).
- Keep the questions short. The audience should hear the guest more than the host.
- Do not ask questions that will bring a simple "yes" or "no" answer and avoid "how many" questions that may produce only a number for an answer.
- Make short transitions from question to question by using the preceding answer as a springboard into the next question.
- Avoid double-barreled questions. Ask only one question at a time.
- Do not routinely restate interviewee's answers by saying "in other words." Clarify ambiguous answers, however.
- Keep it conversational and friendly. Avoid asking surprise questions about unrelated topics and avoid potentially embarrassing questions.
- Seize control of the interview near the end so you do not have to interrupt the interviewee to end the show.
- End with a summary of the main points you want the audience to remember or the specific actions you desire them to take.
- Always conclude by thanking the guest and by repeating the name, title, and affiliation.

Adapted from Fazio & Gilbert (2000).

Because interpreters are the communication link between resources and the public, interpreters often have the opportunity *to be* interviewed. Prior to the interview, ask the reporter for his or her name. Also ask what the story angle is and specifically how you can help. Refer the reporter to someone else if you are not the best person to be interviewed. If you are called unexpectedly, ask the reporter if you can call back in 15 minutes. This allows time to collect thoughts and solidify your message. Try to anticipate the tough questions and consider how to turn a negative question into a positive response.

In terms of the interview, Jacobson, McDuff, and Monroe (2006) give the following advice. First, relax. Think of the reporter as a neighbor or park visitor that you are conversing with about the subject. Be friendly, even if the interviewer isn't. If you are on camera, keep your eyes focused on the reporter. Try not to fidget or make other distracting movements with your hands. It is best to wear neutral colors and avoid busy fabrics. If the reporter fails to ask the most important question related to what you want to communicate you can volunteer the information the audience needs to hear. Confirm that the reporter understood what you have said, if any doubt exists. Reporters have to know a little about almost everything, so they will probably only have a cursory knowledge of your subject and may have gained that knowledge in the hour prior to the interview. It is okay to correct the reporter if they have wrong information, but do so in a kind and nurturing way. Again, focus on your message and answering the question the reporter should have asked. Also, be prepared to be asked for your opinions, including opinions about situations for which you have no direct knowledge (e.g., happenings in other parks or museums, or impacts of national or regional governmental actions). When asked about such things it is okay to say "I don't know." Never just make stuff up. If you have an opinion be sure it is fact-based, but that you do not present the opinion as fact. Finally, there is no such thing as "off the record." It implies that you know something others should not know and it can damage your career to engage in such discourse.

Summary

Print media, radio, and television, along with the Internet and social media provide interpreters with powerful tools for reaching enormous numbers of people, including people who do not ever visit natural and cultural heritage sites. In doing so, interpretive messages are carried to people with different values and beliefs, allowing interpreters to do more than "preach to the choir."

Mass media interpretation is its own form of programming requiring special approaches and targeting new audiences. As this chapter suggests, interpreting through mass media involves much more than just advertising programs and facilities, but rather using interpretive principles to advance deeper and more meaningful messages.

Mass media, when used effectively, produces greater awareness of and support for historical and natural resources and the agencies that manage them. This may lead to greater attendance at onsite interpretive programs and meaningful connections by those who may never arrive such as those people who watch bears on live webcams without leaving their home. By using mass media, interpreters truly can broaden understanding and support of the masses; to create a better world.

Literature Cited

Fazio, J. R., & Gilbert, D. L. (2000). *Public relations and communications for natural resource managers.* Dubuque, IA: Kendall/Hunt.

Hartz, J. (2016). Where millennials spend their time and money. Retrieved from julia-hartz/why-millennials-spend-money-on-live-experiences.

Jacobson, S. K., McDuff, M. D., & Monroe, M. C. (2006). *Conservation education and outreach techniques.* Oxford, UK. Oxford University Press.

Lombard, J. (2016). Why your park newspaper might be the biggest publication mistake you are making. *Legacy, 27*(4), 10–13.

Sinek, S. (2009). *Start with why: How great leaders inspire everyone to take action.* New York, NY: Penguin Group.

Sutton, M. D. (1982). Interpretation around the world. In G. Sharpe (Ed.), *Interpreting the environment* (pp. 645–663). New York, NY: John Wiley & Sons.

Smith, C. (2015). Interp-stagram. *2015 interpretive sourcebook.* Ft. Collins, CO: National Association for Interpretation.

CHAPTER 9

Personal Interpretation

Imagine being immersed in the subalpine grandeur of Yosemite National Park with an interpretive naturalist who brings forth the hidden meanings and compelling stories of the place; an interpreter who knows the place intimately and shares her knowledge with humility and passion; a companion who helps you forge intellectual and emotional connections to the spectacles of Yosemite's high country.

Yosemite National Park, in cooperation with the park concessionaire, offers five-day and seven-day interpretive loop trips among the High Sierra Camps that surround Tuolumne Meadows. This is among the premier interpretive events offered by the National Park Service and was initially envisioned by its first director, Stephen Mather.

Leading such trips is considered the ultimate work assignment and requires some seniority. Ranger Adrianna, although she has been at Yosemite much longer, has been guiding these loop trips for seven seasons. One author had the pleasure of completing the seven-day interpretive loop trip. These trips encompass hiking approximately 8-10 miles per day and staying in the backcountry camps each night. Throughout the day, Adrianna provided interpretation of the surroundings such as the colorful wildflowers, majestic trees, forest birds, deep canyons, granite domes, insects, skittish deer and other mammals, cascades and waterfalls, and sunrises, sunsets, and stars.

Each day was concluded with a sunset talk and later a traditional campfire program. Sunset talks offered incredible views overlooking the Grand Canyon of the Tuolumne, or a sweeping view of Tenaya Canyon with Half Dome off in the distance, or looking out upon a huge alpine meadow or granite monoliths. One included a poetry reading next to Merced Lake.

For most sunset talks, Adrianna had visuals and inspiring quotes that she took from her special bag of tricks that held endless surprises during the day. During the last sunset talk, Adrianna read excerpts from the National Park Service Act and Wilderness Act and commented on their mandates fostering the very experience we were having.

One of the most beautiful and emotional moments on the trip was when Adrianna sang a song, a familiar song in which she changed the words to be about Yosemite, to conclude that last evening's sunset talk. She asked us to look out at the stunning landscape before us and not at her, since she said she was embarrassed and didn't have a great voice. But she did it anyway. After the song, when we turned around to face her again, she was wiping away tears.

Over the course of the week, Adrianna exhibited confidence, enthusiasm, intimate knowledge, a strong ability to communicate, vivid stories, a pleasant demeanor always, and a gentle spirit. Ranger Adrianna had strong group management skills. She kept a pulse on the mood of the group and was adaptable. Furthermore,

Adrianna displayed her own love for this incredible landscape and spoke passionately about it as she weaved her interpretation with a spirit of kindness and joy (Beck, 2014). She fully embodied Freeman Tilden's (1977) statement: "To go on a walking trip with a naturalist guide…is to have an enthusiast for a companion."

This chapter concentrates on personal delivery of interpretive messages and provides the nuts and bolts of preparing and delivering meaningful and powerful interpretive programs. In personal interpretation, the interpreter works with knowledge and skill in direct contact with visitors (individually or collectively) in a number of ways. Often these encounters begin at the entrance gate or information counter and they may last until the interpreter says goodnight at the end of an evening program.

Information Duty

Many interpreters begin their careers as seasonal employees with a primary duty of fee collection or information desk duty. Fee collection involves making monetary transactions with visitors as they enter the park and answering basic questions about the area. Information desk duty often occurs at ranger stations, visitor centers, or museum entry halls. It provides orientation and information to visitors. The interpreter at these places gets the visitors started on their interpretive experiences.

Although information duty sometimes gets tedious, it plays an essential role in an interpretive setting. It offers information that visitors need for a safe, enjoyable, and life-enhancing experience. Furthermore, visitors' first contact with information personnel can strongly influence their impressions of an area. With the proper perspective, information duty can reap satisfaction—after all, interpreters get paid to stimulate and to guide people who come to them in a spirit of leisure and seeking personal enrichment (Figure 9.1).

> "Information duty plays an essential role in an interpretive setting."

Figure 9.1. Information desk duty serves a vital function in facilitating a positive experience for visitors at the multi-agency Northwest New Mexico Visitor Center. (TC)

Basic initial questions may address where one may find food, drink, or the rest room. According to Maslow's hierarchy, people have to satisfy their basic needs prior to higher order needs. Understanding this will help interpreters to remain patient and friendly. Likewise, at the start of a hike, such things as comfort, security, and time planning concerns take temporary precedence over curiosity about the subject matter.

Whether visitors ask more penetrating questions depends a great deal on whether or not they feel secure, comfortable, and welcome. Interpreters can meet their basic needs and then help people to switch on their curiosity about the essence of the place. Quality interpretation moves the participants along the scale until the visitors themselves make their own connections with the place (Beck, 2001).

Information staff should be readily available as visitors enter the facility and should greet them with a genuine welcome. In some settings, interpreters approach visitors to indicate their availability to answer questions. Emerging from behind a desk or counter removes both a physical and psychological barrier and allows for more personal communication.

An interpreter should attempt to treat each visitor contact as a new situation, even though he or she has just heard a popular question several times. Interpreters should try to actively learn about each individual so that they can structure their responses to that person's interest and experience. An interpreter needs to discover the visitors' purposes and expectations. Determining if the visitor has been to the facility before can provide some background for suggesting experiences and activities. When appropriate (time and visitor interest permitting), the front desk staff introduces major points to indicate the significance of the place.

> Treat each visitor contact as a new situation.

The information interpreter often serves as an advocate or agent for the visitor's background and perspective. For example, some visitors to a botanical garden come with deep botanical knowledge. Most, however, like plants and flowers but don't remember much about pollination strategies, ecology, or Latin names. The interpreter at the front desk can set up a system to direct these different people to the appropriate programs, exhibits, books, Internet sources, apps, blogs or other resource materials, thereby optimizing experiences.

Although the purpose of information duty is to meet, greet, and talk to people, interpreters have to prevent any one visitor from dominating their time. Out of respect for other visitors, interpreters must firmly and courteously control those who want to "shoot the breeze."

When confronted by a difficult or angry visitor, remain calm. The most important thing is to have a restrained, calm presence in the midst of emotional anger (Friedman, 2007). Do not take the problem or behavior personally. Listen carefully to the person and try to understand the situation. Attempt to correct the problem and fill out a complaint form if necessary. If appropriate, refer the person to another staff member. The situation may present an opportunity to improve customer service in the future. An important aspect of resonant leadership that takes into account emotional intelligence requires displaying a calm, empathetic demeanor (Goleman, Boyatzis, & McKee, 2013).

Information Personnel Should...

Know the Resource

By definition, information duty staff must know about the park, museum, or other resource being interpreted, as well as the surrounding area (Box 9.1). For seasonal or volunteer staff, the permanent interpreters should take them on regular visits to the exhibits and facilities to make sure they comprehend the meanings and significance of the place. Volunteers and seasonals should also attend presentations by different interpreters to better understand the resource and so they can promote these programs.

Box 9.1
Local Service Information List

Many information centers keep notebooks as a quick reference for visitors, arranged by category. This same information may also be provided on computers for visitor use. Major headings and items include those listed below:

Automotive Services
- Gas stations
- Motor home supplies, services
- Repair shops
- Towing

Emergency Service
- Ambulance
- Fire Station
- Hospitals (with maps)
- Police or Sheriff

Food and Lodging
- Bed-and-breakfasts
- Grocery stores
- Restaurants
- Camping and RV parks
- Hotels, lodges, motels
- Youth hostels

General Services
- Banks
- Souvenir shops
- Ice vendors
- Sewage disposal
- Camera stores
- Churches
- Veterinarians

Natural and Cultural Features
- Cultural and historic information
- Natural history information (e.g., geology, plants, animals)

On-Site Interpretive Opportunities
- Interpretive guidebooks (e.g., reference and sale items)
- Programs (e.g., schedules, topics, and locations)
- Self-guided opportunities (e.g., trails, wayside exhibits, audio tours, apps)

Outfitters, Guides, and Other Recreation
- Climbing instruction
- Golf courses
- River trips
- Diving
- Horse rentals
- Swimming

Regional Attractions (with travel distances and times)
- Art galleries
- Wine tasting
- Children's attractions
- Theatres, outdoor dramas
- Museums
- Monuments
- Scenic drives
- Other parks (local, state, federal)

Safety Hazards
- Dangerous wildlife
- Poisonous plants
- Site-specific hazards (e.g., cliffs, flash floods, thermal pools)

Transportation Services
- Airlines
- Car rentals
- Taxis
- Bus schedules
- Sightseeing tours
- Travel agencies

The information duty staff should prepare answers to common questions and know how to quickly find the answers to more unusual questions. Strive to relate the answers to the experience of the visitor. For example, while answering a simple inquiry about a campsite, call attention to an interesting plant, animal, or geological feature that can be seen at that location. Furthermore, as residents in a certain setting, interpreters should constantly renew their own observations of the complexity and wonder of the place. This helps the interpretation remain fresh and visitors will sense enthusiasm. Good interpretive supervisors allocate sufficient time for continued learning about the resource, for the sake of both the interpreters and the visitors.

> "Interpreters should constantly renew their own observations of the complexity and wonder of the place."

Admit When They Don't Know the Answer to a Question

The interpreters' training and personal study will prepare them to answer most questions. Still, occasional stumper questions come up. In these instances, refer the question to a more seasoned employee or supervisor, look up the information, search the Internet, or make a phone call. If all this produces no answer, the question was a tough one and perhaps the visitor would appreciate a future response by e-mail if an answer can later be found.

Provide Handouts and Maps

Brochures and other handout materials give the visitor something to take for further reference. These inexpensive materials generally list interpretive programs, natural history (e.g., bird lists), safety concerns (often half-page flyers), and nearby attractions. Keep all handout materials up to date. When visitors seek detailed information, reference to these items will prove useful. In addition, be familiar with information on your website, pertinent apps, podcasts, blogs, and other technology that can offer more information. Furthermore, because many visitors are new to the area, make reference to maps when giving directions. For backcountry hikers, refer to detailed maps for sale in the bookstore.

Know How to Respond to Emergencies

Information personnel should know basic first aid and CPR. They also need quick, handy reference to emergency contacts next to the telephone and/or radio. Supervisors should cover site-specific emergency procedures early in training, with regular all-staff refreshers. In addition, post a sequence of actions for emergencies at the information desk and outside.

Provide After-Hours Information

On a well-lit outdoor bulletin board, provide updated weather information, safety precautions, important park regulations, emergency phone numbers, and visitor procedures for times that the information center is closed. Some parks use computer screens to provide this and similar information. In case of power outage, post paper duplicates. Also, since many visitors arrive at odd hours, post current interpretive activity schedules prominently.

Be Friendly and Respectful

Interactions with visitors should be enjoyable. Some interpreters become brash, jaded, or just plain dull over time. The visitors that walk in the visitor center door include special people of great skill, education, and/or accomplishment. Knowing them can enrich the interpreter's life. They will appreciate and respond to a vibrant, alert, helpful interpreter. Whatever their backgrounds, the visitors deserve courtesy and respect, even when they act temporarily disoriented, nervous, or upset.

Go the Extra Mile

Barry (1998) suggested reviving the meaning of civil servant to describe a "courteous public servant." This means "plus it up" and exceeding the expectations of visitors. According to Barry, at the U.S. Army Corps of Engineers Bonneville Lock and Dam Visitor Center, comments frequently seen in the guest register include "We are glad that our tax dollars are being used for this facility." Among other extras, the staff places fresh-cut flowers in the restrooms.

Roving Interpretation

As introduced in Chapter 7, roving interpretation is an important component of the program mix to reduce barriers and increase contact with park guests who may otherwise not gain from the presence of a park interpreter.

Roving interpretation generally refers to the stationing of interpreters in high use areas for informal contacts with visitors. In contrast, station interpreters work at particular spots, often in a museum, in the front of a visitor center, or along a walking route. Often, they demonstrate a craft or special skill related to the theme of the interpretive program. Sometimes they teach the skills to visitors as they come by. In other cases, they present a short talk or activity.

Roving interpreters roam about interpreting to people about the site or about nearby exhibits. This approach works well near a major museum exhibit or at an outdoor overlook, where people concentrate to see a certain feature. For example, at Cabrillo National Monument in California, interpreters go to the whale overlook where they help visitors to spot gray whales migrating south during the winter months. They discuss natural history of the gray whales and answer other questions about the park. Similarly, at Yosemite, long-time volunteers Jeff and Chris Lashmet spend much of the day at Olmsted Point to answer common questions about the iconic landscape.

A common practice among roving interpreters is to carry a small pack with items that may be useful to help visitors interpret the area: binoculars, field guides, a few rock samples, first-aid supplies, and maps. A small box with exhibit materials, identification charts, and free brochures help interested visitors get involved. Furthermore, the interpreter may carry a tablet, or smartphone, with apps for identifying insects, bird songs, mammal tracks, wildflowers, or other interesting features of the site. (See Box 9.2)

Box 9.2
Things To Take During Roving Interpretation

- Pad of paper and pencil for notes or sketching
- Tablet or smartphone with photos of resources and useful apps
- Magnifying glass
- Binoculars or a spotting scope
- Camera
- Field guides and/or plant keys
- Small plastic bag for samples
- Small mirror or laser pointer to point out objects
- Site brochures (in multiple languages if possible)
- Maps of area
- First-aid kit and latex gloves
- Radio and/or cell phone
- Water to share with visitors (small paper cups)
- Sunscreen and/or insect repellant to share

Adapted from Sexton (2015)

Visitors may not realize that the roving interpreter came to the site to talk with people and answer their questions. Many visitors assume that interpreters came for other business, so they may hesitate to approach them. Therefore, behavior as a host should make evident the availability to talk and to demonstrate the resource values. This may include a friendly greeting and an offer to assist with any questions the visitor may have.

Because roving interpreters locate themselves where many people congregate, they often see violations of regulations, such as collecting shells in a tide pool area, picking wildflowers, or feeding wildlife. As also introduced in Chapter 4, Wallace (1990) recommended a three-point nonthreatening sequence when contacting visitors who have committed minor infractions:

1. Provide a descriptive account of the observed situation. Talk about the infraction in the context of the resource without reference to agency regulations.
2. Explain the impact of the action on the resource as well as how the action impinges on the enjoyment of the resource by other visitors.
3. Provide the visitors with an assessment of how the situation can be remedied.

This three-point interaction emphasizes the values of the site and the consequences of the actions rather than castigating an individual for violating regulations. The focus centers not on the enforcer or getting caught, but on the resource and what happens to it. Thus the interpreter seeks to change behavior by "revealing the authority of the resource" (Wallace, 1990; see also Wallace & Gaudry, 2002).

Most interpreters enjoy roving duty because they interpret features first-hand, spontaneously, and to individuals. It requires considerable knowledge and flexibility, so experienced personnel do the job best. From the perspective of resource managers, it provides good public relations with people who otherwise might not come in contact with an interpreter. Roving interpreters often give visitors current information about hazards such as inclement weather or dangerous wildlife. They can also feature special ephemeral interpretive opportunities, such as a mayfly hatch, a shad run, a historical reenactment, or a nearby tribal celebration.

> "Roving duty requires considerable knowledge and flexibility."

Lewis (1980) suggested that roving interpreters provide "mini walks" to groups of people interested in a short, guided tour of the area or a section of the museum. These informal and impromptu mini walks use many of the principles listed in the following sections.

Interpretive Talks

Interpretive talks may take place almost anywhere. Most commonly, talks occur in relatively formal settings such as auditoriums, outdoor amphitheaters, museums, and on visitor center porches. Talks are also given on-site in aquariums, gardens, zoos, historical, archaeological, and natural areas.

Talks can vary in length from short 10 minute "porch talks" on the patio of the interpretive center; "theater talks" of variable length, usually not more than 45 minutes in an indoor or outdoor theater; or "evening campfire talks" of approximately 45 minutes. Some "talks" last for a weekend or even more than a week, well-mixed with activities, such as the interpretive loop trips in Yosemite National Park mentioned in the opening story, Rocky Mountain Field Seminars, and Road Scholar courses. Talks also occur on ships, buses, trams, trains, and other modes of transportation.

A visitor chooses to attend a talk and can decide to leave any time (except on a small boat). A "noncaptive" audience expects an informal, nonacademic, and enjoyable presentation. An effective interpretive talk will fill the audience with interest and excitement about the place they came to visit. It may encourage them to attend other programs. On the other hand, a poorly executed talk can discourage visitors from experiencing any more interpretation.

People typically retain only a small fraction of what a speaker offers, assuming an attempt to absorb the message. Therefore, a speaker does well to choose a few key ideas on which to concentrate so that the audience does not become overloaded with information. Citing a history of studies on this subject, Sam Ham (2013) indicates that the number of main ideas in an interpretive program should be limited to four or fewer.

> "The "A, B, Cs, (and D and E)" of good public speaking."

Basic Qualities for Effective Speaking

An effective interpreter shares many of the same characteristics and uses many of the same techniques of any competent public speaker. Books on how to speak in public to an audience generally include standard qualities of good speakers. We have arranged several characteristics alphabetically and refer to them as the "A, B, Cs, (and D and E)" of good public speaking.

Amiability

Effective communication begins with an open, friendly, and good-natured demeanor on the part of the speaker. Because interpretation takes place in recreational settings, aloofness and grim solemnity do not fit. This does not suggest that interpreters, who offer important messages, should act like comedians, but rather that they exhibit genuine friendliness, good humor, authentic emotion, patience, and concern for the wellbeing of visitors. Interpreters have the good fortune of being "lifelong students as well as teachers" who joyfully share their insights with and for visitors (Rutherford, 2000).

Belief

Meaningful and convincing communication also requires belief in the importance of the subject matter. If the interpreter isn't enthused and truly enthralled by the subject matter then the audience won't be either. As Ham (2013) duly noted, "No topic is inherently boring or interesting. There are only people who make them that way."

There is a correlation between passion and activism—interpreters often have passion for achieving a purpose (activism). LaPage (1998) opined that heroes of interpretation (e.g., Enos Mills, John Muir, Edward Abbey, Terry Tempest Williams, Rick Bass) were (or are) activists, just as we should be. We can learn and grow by emulating the enthusiasm of such role models (Cable, 1999).

Confidence

Good speakers radiate self-assurance and poise. They know their stuff and have prepared sufficiently to shine. Interpreters have the advantage of initial credibility because of the agencies they represent and the uniforms or identification they may wear (Figure 9.2).

Virtually every interpreter builds up a normal sense of anxiety just prior to a talk. They join most actors in their stage fright. An elevated adrenaline level can benefit the talk because the interpreter becomes more alert and focused on the task at hand. As Steve Jobs said, if you pretend that you are completely in control, people will assume you are (Isaacson, 2011). Confidence and good delivery skills depend on a strong grasp of the subject matter. Furthermore, a well-prepared program produces increased self-assurance.

With experience, interpreters learn to control various outward signs of nervousness, such as fidgeting, slouching, using a

Figure 9.2. Excellent interpreters such as these historical interpreters appear both confident and amiable when in front of an audience. (MSP)

podium as a crutch, saying "uh" in excess, avoiding eye contact with the audience, and crossing both arms across the chest. Colleagues and supervisors can act as coaches to alert less experienced speakers to how they portray a lack of confidence and help convert those habits into more inspiring behavior.

Delivery

For good delivery, speak conversationally. Interpreters strive to speak *with* (not at or down to) the audience, personally and informally. Informality does not preclude rigorous preparation. Using simple, vivid words helps to make a point.

Several delivery faults turn off listeners. Some speakers tend to talk in a monotone. Speech that consistently goes too fast or too slow, too loud or too soft, too insistent or too docile, can frustrate and irritate members of an audience. Varying the rate, volume, and force of speech, within reasonable limits, will increase the attentiveness of the listeners. So will a natural use of appropriate gestures. Slang or profanity have no place. Neither do potentially insulting references about people or places. Even "cute" jibes at states, universities, or towns sorely offend some people.

To improve speaking habits, study and emulate speakers you admire. Compare them to video or audiotapes of your recent efforts, then adopt their best qualities to enhance your interpretation. However, avoid direct mimicking; adapt rather than impersonate.

Ideally give interpretive talks without using notes. Reading from paper or cards may distract and interrupt eye contact with members of the audience. Some interpreters want to write out and memorize their talks. Unless the speaker has a special talent, this can cause the talk to lose its spontaneous and conversational tone. It can also be a disaster if the interpreter forgets any segment of the presentation and fails to get back on track. An effective approach is to organize an outline, memorize the major headings, and then talk about each of the sections in order. It also provides a degree of flexibility depending upon the specific needs of any particular audience.

Enthusiasm

As the old adage goes, enthusiasm is contagious. The interpreters who seem truly excited about what they discuss create an atmosphere of inspiration. This affinity both for the subject being interpreted and the people who have gathered to hear the message can capture and hold the attention of the audience. Of course, the reverse is also true. An interpreter's lack of energy can put an immediate damper on the spirit of an audience.

> A good presentation entails a great deal of research, thought, care, and rehearsal.

A good presentation entails a great deal of research, thought, care, and rehearsal, as well as flexibility to handle different audience situations. An audience senses when a speaker has committed substantial effort to the work (Beck & Cable, 2010). Amiability, belief in the product, confidence, strong delivery, and an impassioned interpreter can engender true enthusiasm and attention in the audience.

Components of an Interpretive Talk

The components of an interpretive talk include an overriding theme, introduction, body, and conclusion. The interpretive talk should flow in an orderly sequence with logical transitions. Use a few appropriate cues that tell the listener that the talk is moving forward in an orderly way. This helps the audience follow the presentation without confusion. Specific objectives or learning outcomes are sometimes used to define what visitors may gain from the program.

Theme

Each presentation focuses on a certain topic (e.g. geology, wildlife, desert ecology, human history). Out of this comes the theme or the message to be conveyed about the topic. The theme, in a sentence or two, presents the central idea that the full presentation reveals in more detail (as previously introduced in Chapter 5).

Bill Lewis (1980) brought the word *theme* into the interpreter's vocabulary. Since then, Sam Ham (1992, 2013) has greatly elaborated on the concept. Based on this work, the following are key elements of theme development.

1. State the theme concisely, simply, and clearly in a sentence or two.
2. Convey the one central idea, or overall message of the presentation in the theme.
3. Word the theme in an interesting, provocative manner (use engaging action verbs).

Ham (2013) noted that for the interpreter the theme is the main point, the moral of the story, the big picture. This is what the interpreter will focus on. And for the audience the theme is the key idea taken, lessons learned, and thoughts stimulated. Through the use of themes the interpreter helps answer questions the audience may arrive with such as "Why is this important?" and "Why should I listen?"

The theme dictates the kind of information needed to construct the program and is therefore essential to the interpreter in program development. Because the audience may hear the theme early in the presentation, it aids in providing organizational structure and clarity. Therefore the theme should clearly express the key concept that visitors may take from the presentation. It serves as the take-home message, the unifying idea of the presentation. Themes usually directly relate to key features of a particular park, forest, wildlife refuge, museum, or other interpretive site.

One of the tips Ham (2013) offers is this: "Start by stating your theme using words and sentence structure that inspire and motivate *you*. Then play with it and edit it until you transform it into an expression that you think will have the same effect on your audience." He also noted that a strong theme has "high provocation likelihood." In other words, the presentation is more likely to provoke thought or action. The following theme is an example from Ham's book (2013) *Interpretation: Making a Difference on Purpose*:

> Because we rarely see them, nocturnal birds around here are the subject of local superstitions and potentially threatening misconceptions. Fortunately, there's something all of us can do to correct the situation.

Considerable professional discussion revolves around when (and even if) the theme should be revealed to an audience. Although several models exist, perhaps the most useful for most interpreters is what Ham (2013) refers to as the "sandwich theme model" in which the theme is expressed both in the introduction and in the conclusion of the program. In this way, the theme is presented up front to provide scaffolding for the presentation and again at the end for reinforcement of the main point. Some interpreters are now referring to this approach as the "Ham Sandwich Model."

Introduction to the Talk

The introduction defines the purpose of the presentation, creates a cognitive map to help visitors follow the talk, and creates a favorable atmosphere for discovery and learning as a group.

The introduction of a talk provides the audience with key information, often including the theme, that will help them to understand the balance of the presentation. Many effective communicators make use of a "grabber" in the introduction to catch the interest of the audience. This strategy employs the use of a quotation, an anecdote, humor, or conundrum related to the theme.

> Effective communicators make use of a "grabber" in the introduction.

In practice, begin the talk by welcoming the group and introducing yourself clearly. Generally, include the theme of the program, give a quick preview of what's about to happen, and suggest how long it will take. If after-the-talk activity is available for learning (e.g., inspection of samples) or social interaction (e.g., cocoa and cookies), let the people know at this point and remind them again later.

Body of the Talk

The introduction should flow smoothly to the body of the talk. The theme develops within the body through four or fewer main points (Ham, 2013). The body consists of a logical sequence of information cued by transitions from one of these key ideas to the next. List and enumerate major ideas to help the audience perceive the organization. Then develop the key points in detail. Public speakers use several strategies to convey a message (Box 9.3). The body of a talk should have these characteristics:

1. **Narrative quality**—a story approach that pulls people along.
2. **Cohesiveness**—a sequential outline and effectively connected by transitions.
3. **Cues**—verbal and visual signals that identify progress through the key points.
4. **Suspense and climax**—posing a question and gradually revealing the answer, or otherwise moving toward a powerful conclusion.
5. **Completeness**—relating the specific subject to the larger whole of the place.

Conclusion of the Talk

In the introduction the audience learns what the speaker aims to do. In the body of the talk, speakers do what they said they would. In the conclusion they tell the audience what they did. Interpreters strive to make the presentation more memorable to the audience in the conclusion. "*Well, that's about it,*" or "*Okay, any questions?*" are poor excuses for vivid and inspiring conclusions. The good conclusion summarizes the talk's key points and restates the theme. It may circle back to a statement or question that is posed in the introduction.

> Have a final tactic that brings the subject to a dramatic close.

Make the conclusion direct and unambiguous. If possible, have a final tactic that brings the subject to a dramatic close—a quote, a story, a poem, a song (such as that by the interpreter at Yosemite to conclude her sunset talk). An interpreter at Denali National Park and Preserve, for example, concluded his evening auditorium programs by reciting Robert Service poetry about the wonders of the Far North. Dr. Martin Luther King, Jr. ended the most famous speech of recent times with a quote that summarized his theme and carried its own dramatic impact: "Free at last! Free at last! Lord, God Almighty, we are free at last!"

End the talk definitely and clearly, with a bang, then stop. Let go of the limelight. Do not add new material or linger with add-ons. If a "conclusion" runs on after an impressive statement, the magic vanishes. Leave people inspired, wanting to learn and experience more.

Box 9.3
Strategies for "Spicing the Program"

Stories	Illustrate your message with stories to captivate the interest of your group. Make the whole interpretive message a story.
Anecdotes	Concise and pertinent biographical stories should somehow relate to the theme of the presentation. The audience will be interested in how you are "moved" by your place of work and your experiences over time.
Quotations	Quoting others briefly, particularly those who are associated with the cultural or natural history of the area, can add interest and color to a talk.
Examples	Examples give the audience detail and specifics to help understand the broad points or context of the message.
Analogies	Explain something by making a comparison to something similar that is more familiar to the audience.
Metaphors	Give a name or quality to something when it literally does not fit, but figuratively describes it.
Similes	Similes use the words "like" or "as" to relate characteristics of two items.
Current News Events	Use current news events at the local, state, national, or international level to relate to site history or as an example of a key point.
Repetition	Repeat key phrases to create powerful, memorable messages. In Martin Luther King, Jr.'s most famous speech, he started eight sequential paragraphs with the statement "I have a dream."
Humor	Humor, used appropriately, can loosen up the audiences and the speaker and drive home some key points.

Adapted from Kawasaki (1991)

Avoid asking for questions as part of the conclusion of the talk. Allow a clear break of one or two minutes so those who wish can depart. However, the interpreter who also serves as host should remain available after the *end* of the program to answer individual questions. This one-on-one contact can provide the more interested visitors with recommendations for gaining even deeper perspective on the subject and gives them an opportunity to share their stories, insights, and appreciation with the interpreter. Wise interpreters gain much from interacting with audience members after a presentation.

Illustrated Talks

Illustrated talks employ all of the previous principles. In addition to spoken words, illustrated talks have the added dimension of visual aids. Although excellent interpretive talks can be conducted without visual aids, their addition can make presentations more understandable to the audience. Interpreters may present illustrated talks indoors, such as in a visitor center auditorium, and outdoors as part of the evening program, as discussed in the following section.

> "Illustrated talks employ all of the previous principles."

In developing an illustrated talk, build the outline and narrative before selecting images. Inexperienced interpreters commonly choose a set of images, then attempt to develop a talk. Therefore, the first step is to develop an effective narrative that stands on its own. Words alone can create vivid pictures. After developing the talk, determine if visuals will enhance the prepared materials. If visuals will make the talk more comprehensible and entertaining then use them. If visuals will distract the audience or result in a more complex message then avoid them. Complex drawings or illustrations may only confuse the audience members.

When using visual aids, several guidelines will help the presentation. Most important, make sure that everyone in the audience can see the visuals. The object, picture, chart, or image displayed should be sufficiently large so the people in the back row can see it clearly. Use large, simple, straightforward visuals.

Use a visual only for the length of time that the commentary corresponds to it. Once the visual no longer offers relevant information, remove or replace it. Otherwise, it serves only as a distraction. Furthermore, to hold attention and prevent boredom it is important to not project the same image on a screen for more than a few seconds (some experts say no more than 6 seconds!). Multiple different images of the same subject will be required if you will be spending considerable time discussing a particular object. Although some find it a difficult habit to break, *avoid talking to the visual.* Face the audience, from the front, even in the dark. See tips in Box 9.4.

As with all programs, the speaker must arrive early. Illustrated presentations require set up and equipment checks. Know the equipment well before trying to use it in the dark under pressure. Ideally, a speaker will set up prior to the arrival of visitors and well before starting time. This allows the speaker to mingle with visitors before the program begins. After conducting any warm-up activities, introduce the program and turn down the lights. Generally, start (and end) with a dark screen. Use a remote device to advance the visuals.

Know the narrative and image order well. Remember that the visuals do not drive the talk. The images *illustrate* the narrative. That thought should help reduce the use of the phrases "This picture shows…" or "Here is a picture of…" These weak transitions strongly suggest to the audience that the visuals run the interpreter's reactive mind and preparation was poor.

> "The images *illustrate* the narrative."

Presentation software has allowed for quick and easy construction of an illustrated program in which it is a simple process to add text, pictures, video, and various effects. To avoid a bad PowerPoint (or other) program, the interpreter should limit text to the essentials (often none at all is best), avoid reading off the screen if there is text, refrain from putting multiple images on a slide which can become confusing and reduces the full visual impact of full-screen images, avoid clip art clichés and standard templates that are overused, and avoid too many "bells and whistles" that will most likely only lead to distraction (Buchholz, Lackey, Gross, & Zimmerman, 2015).

> **Box 9.4**
> **Simple Tips for Quality Illustrated Talks**
>
> These simple guidelines for an illustrated talk follow common sense. The suggestions apply to any kind of image—drawn, painted, film, or digital.
> - Use the best images available—focused and properly exposed.
> - Use images with good composition.
> - Use pictures that do not confuse the audience.
> - Use images that illustrate the point being discussed.
> - Use a title or theme slide and an end image that assists concluding the program when appropriate.
> - If available, use a series of images, progressing from overview shots to close-ups.
> - Avoid showing any one image for too long. The audience will lose focus on the flow of your talk.
> - Avoid playing music while speaking at the same time. Generally, use music with images at the introduction or conclusion of the program for an inspirational beginning or end.
> - Arrange images so they convey the theme of the talk (e.g., a seasonal progression of images for a presentation of seasons).
> - Avoid all but the simplest of maps, graphs, and charts.
> - Pause during the talk at important points to let the words sink in a bit.
> - Use moments of pause to strengthen the speech. The narrative may lead up to a photograph or a series of images that do not require words. This technique, when well-orchestrated, can have a powerful effect.
> - Start an outdoor evening program only when the sky is dark enough so the illustrations can be clearly seen.

Evening Programs

The interpreter will incorporate much of what has been discussed above for evening programs. For example, the evening program should follow a theme and include a strong introduction, body and conclusion. It should be site-specific. It should connect the audience to the tangible and intangible dimensions of the place (as also discussed in Chapter 5).

The evening program provides a contact point for inviting overnight visitors to explore and to use other interpretive services. It helps them get acquainted with other visitors and the staff. Evening "campfire" programs need not include flames and wood, although that adds to the color and character. If campfires are used keep dry wood available (to keep smoke to a minimum) and keep an extinguishing device at hand. Avoid putting the fire in the center, where it will reflect on the projection screen; likewise, do not put the fire ring upwind of the audience, the projection screen, or the speaker.

The evening program, to a certain degree, can become a social event and helps visitors to feel comfortable in their temporary surroundings. Just with any social occasion, it requires planning, careful preparation, and friendly, positive delivery.

> The evening program, to a certain degree, can become a social event.

In the half hour preceding the program, while welcoming early arrivals, interpreters can assess the immediate audience composition. Try to answer the following questions about the audience:

- To whom am I speaking?
- Where do they come from?
- Have they been here before?
- How long have they been here and what have they seen?
- What special experiences have they had here?
- What do they want to understand and experience?
- What common characteristics and differences do they possess?

Then, during the program, be sure to integrate what was learned about the audience.

Early Arrivals

In addition to learning about the audience, interpreters can provide activities for early arrivals. These ideas for evening programs may also be appropriate for other types of programs. The key to success in working with early arrivals is a calm, friendly interpreter who initiates contact and includes others as they arrive. Interpreters often use these specific techniques.

- Play music appropriate to the theme of the program. Make it loud enough to remind campers that something will start soon. Keep the aural intrusion short, however, to prevent irritation.
- To prepare for any group singing, get the early birds to practice helping with the fun parts (e.g., motions, rounds, percussion, sound effects). Their early involvement attracts other people and gives a signal that the program will soon be underway.
- Create demonstration packs that relate to the interpretive site and allow early arrivals to examine them and carry them around. These can include a Civil War soldier's pack, a miner's grubstake pack, a modern backpack equipped for five days in the wilderness, a firefighter's pack, a horse or mule pack, or a bicycle pack for a three-day ride. Other display items related to the topic of the program could pique interest.

Icebreakers

Similarly, icebreakers can be used across many different interpretive programs, but most often are associated with the traditional evening program. Every interpreter has strategies to get interaction among audience members. Some are done too often and come off as artificial stimulants to sociability. The most common device is asking people where they are from. This approach, although perhaps trite to some, may lead to discussions with visitors from foreign countries or from common states. Enrich this practice with questions about what they have seen or want to do.

Another icebreaker activity requests visitors to introduce themselves to people seated nearby. This appropriate courtesy can have obvious benefits. It gets people acquainted who may be spending several days together in the same area.

> Icebreakers can be used across many different interpretive programs.

Group singing can help relax and unite people without coercion. Ideally, choose thematic songs to fit the main message of the event. Lead with vigor and enthusiasm, but keep the singing session brief and light. A serious visitor coming to a program about geological strata could be put off by a 20-minute song fest. Select two or three well-known selections that relate to the area or the topic of the evening, even if in a humorous way. Provide words on the screen. Another popular strategy lets the audience repeat the key lines sung by the leader. Sometimes, a guitar-playing interpreter may do a little singing to wind up a program.

Many visitors will be perfectly contented without any social interaction. Specific circumstances often define their use or lack thereof. Singing and similar activities, however, if conducted thoughtfully and in moderation, can develop a sense of community and fun.

Interpretive Walks

Walks, hikes, and tours represent "typical" interpretation to many people. Interpretive walks employ the same principles as talks, but with two advantages: (a) the audience gets to hike and therefore can't sleep and (b) the topics show up as real things during the walk. In national parks, historic homes, archaeological sites, factories, and environmental education centers, guided tours or hikes often make up the central visitor experience. Descriptive and clever names help to attract people to history tours and nature walks such as this program title at Arches National Park in Utah: "The Greatest Earth on Show."

> Guided tours or hikes often make up the central visitor experience.

Interpreters can plan each walk as they might plan a theatrical play. Research the subject and the setting, and develop the theme just as with an interpretive talk. Locate or collect props. Check out the scenic backdrops and use them with good timing (Figure 9.3). In some instances, it may be possible to identify tensions that provide dramatic struggle as the activity progresses. Build toward a climax that resolves the tensions. Bring down the curtain at the appropriate time.

From this type of conceptual plan, the interpreter can specify group activities, sequences, and equipment needed based on the specific site. This approach takes the event beyond theory and stimulates visitors' powers of inquiry and observation.

Note that guided hikes and tours may face logistical problems in some areas. These issues can be dealt with according to the site. Also, visitation to these programs, generally open to all comers, can fluctuate greatly. Therefore, some interpretive agencies set limits on the number of people that participate to maintain a level of quality that is associated with the interpretive experience. For example, guides limit number of participants to the Betatakin cliff dwellings at Navajo National Monument in Arizona. Larger groups may diminish the quality of the experience or damage the resource. Small groups allow more personal attention from the interpreter. Concerns for safety and resource protection also come into play.

Effective hikes differ from ineffective ones in the details of courtesy to the visitors, as much as in the information and learning theory used. Most interpretive manuals have lists of dos and don'ts for guiding people. They all focus on common-sense courtesy. To better relate to visitors, interpreters can put themselves in the visitors' place by attending walks led by others, then adapting the best features to their own events.

Figure 9.3. Dramatic scenic backdrops supplemented with explanatory visual aids are characteristics of a good interpretive hike. (TC)

Going all the way back to Paul Risk (1982), and Knudson, Cable, and Beck (1995), and others more recently, authors have provided a number of timeless leadership techniques for the mechanics of interpretive walks, condensed and adapted as follows (see also Buchholz, Lackey, Gross, & Zimmerman, 2015).

Inventory the Area

Interpreters should become thoroughly familiar with the trail or tour route and each of the stops planned along the way. An outline that lists the stops and the key ideas for each will guide hike development. Get to know specific places along the way that should be highlighted or may produce questions from visitors.

Keep Stops Brief

Stops should average between three and seven minutes. Several may take only one to two minutes. A few stops may take longer, to conduct an activity, to tell a story with meaningful implications, or to give the group a sense of peace, solitude, and immersion. Heat, cold, weather, terrain, and physical condition of the audience will affect stop length and frequency. For example, at mountainous Big Bend and Zion National Parks, interpreters beat the summer heat and steep grades by walking slowly and talking in shady spots for five or ten minutes per stop. On winter walks, vigorous, longer stretches between shorter stops help keep people warm.

Stay in Front

Here, the leader can control the pace of the walk to keep the group together. Approaching a stop, slow down gradually and bring everyone together before starting an explanation.

Face the Group

Talk to the group, not to the object being interpreted. Look around and talk to everyone, not just to those who are nearest (Figure 9.4). Position yourself so group members have their backs to the sun.

Figure 9.4. Interpreters should take care to face the group and gather the group to ensure that everybody can see and hear. (TC)

Be Sure that Everyone Can See

Arrange each stop so that everyone in the group has the opportunity to study the object being interpreted. Invite children to get closer so adults can see over them.

Speak with Enough Volume

Consider the size of the group and environmental conditions (such as wind) and speak loudly enough so that everyone in the back of the group can hear.

Know When to be Quiet

While observing wildlife, a spectacular overview, a sunset or moonrise, or a dramatic piece of art, silence is appropriate. Let the visitors enjoy the moment in peace.

Be Flexible

If an interpreter sees something of interest that is not in the plan, adapt so that visitors have the opportunity to witness the event of the moment.

At any time during the walk it may be possible to introduce a "teachable moment," depending on what occurs along the way. The possibility of the unpredictable can make such walks exciting. The interpreter should remain alert to the possibilities and allow for flexibility in the planned program in the face of something unusual or exciting that occurs.

Other Guided Travel

Moving around a museum, a zoo, a camp, a forest, a refuge, a factory, or even a wilderness with a guide can shed light on the site in unique ways. The interpreter shows the visitor the artifacts or environment, weaving a walk or ride into a whole story. The abstractions stop at the beginning of the tour. The interpreter leads visitors to art works; exhibits full of artifacts; or the trees, plants and waterfalls of the forest, explaining them in ways that provoke the visitor to investigate them in detail.

Visitors seek and expect rewarding experiences. Guided travel made relevant and enjoyable becomes more than sightseeing. Interpretation thus enriches the experience. For example, bus tours in Denali National Park and Preserve, Alaska, provide low-impact ways of presenting the resources to many people. Monorails at the San Diego Safari Park carry visitors and interpreters over and around paddocks of animals, where automobiles and pedestrians cannot go.

Since the year 2000, free canyon shuttles at Zion National Park have proven useful to interpretation and extended the patience of the visitors and rangers. No more do traffic jams and parking confusion on the narrow valley road cause distress and haze. Instead, informative drivers tell the visitors about the features and trails, letting them on and off at viewpoints and trailheads. The drivers also let the riders in on recent observations of wildlife and the best times and places for pictures.

In preparing any guided travel program, the interpreter follows a similar organization pattern to that for interpretive talks: develop a theme, introduction, body, and conclusion. Within this structure, fold in ways that may involve visitors directly in connecting with the site through activities that reveal meanings and produce interest. Any written announcement of the trip, as well as the introduction, should include the theme, length of program, distance covered, beginning and ending point, difficulty of terrain, supplies needed, and other pertinent information.

Other types of guided travel may include Segway® tours, auto tours, horseback rides, snowmobiles, canoes, trains and buses, boats, dogsled, plane and helicopter, and big recreational vehicle caravan tours, among others (Figure 9.5). Specific procedures will factor in the mode of travel, equipment used, the rate of travel, and the space and facility of stopping. Normally, the faster and bigger the conveyances, the farther apart come the stops. And, the speed of group movement and attention spans of individuals both decrease as group size increases.

Figure 9.5. Interpretive guided travel may include a cross-country ski hike led by a U.S. Forest Service ranger at a ski resort. (USFS)

Demonstrations and Activities

Demonstrations and activities can (a) stand on their own at a specific place on a property, (b) integrate into a program or coordinated *set* of demonstrations, or (c) travel to off-site events such as fairs, schools, and festivals. A demonstration or participant activity offers a unique way to get a point across, directly involving, and interesting the visitors.

Most *demonstrations* show visitors how to do something (Figure 9.6). At an historic site, visitors learn to churn butter, make soap, dip candles, grind acorns the Native American way, weave wool, or "smith" iron objects. However, Luzader (2001) cautioned that these have become so common and routine that "we need to move away from the 'candles, butter, and soap' syndrome of demonstrations." His criticism arises from demonstrations that come with no telling of the context, the why, the rest of the story. In other words, the demonstration should serve as an opening for interpretation, not as an end in itself.

> "A demonstration or participant activity offers a unique way to get a point across."

A natural history demonstration might include live animal species and pelt displays. To make it interpretive, the 10-20 people gathered round need to hear something about life in the wild of these animals, how they use their feet, teeth and tails to survive, the problems they overcome, the economic role of the pelts in history (Brochu & Merriman, 2008).

A related approach uses *activities* that involve several members or all of an audience. Group members may act out or pantomime natural processes. Using well-known environmental education activities (e.g., Cornell [1989, 1998]), usually creates camaraderie as well as helping people better sense natural processes. For example, individuals form a model of a tree, each taking a different role of the taproot, lateral roots, heartwood, sapwood, cambium, phloem, bark, twigs, and leaves. Then they act out natural processes such as roots absorbing water that goes up the tree to transpire from the leaves.

Activities often involve improvised role playing. At Denali National Park and Preserve, some interpreters who present sled dog demonstrations line up visitors to represent the lead dog, swing dogs, team dogs, and wheel dogs according to their positions. Role players both demonstrate the procedure and entertain the entire group. Then the real dogs get into harness and show how eagerly and vigorously they pull this important mode of transport over the snow. At several other Northwood locations, visitors get an interpretive demonstration followed by first-hand experience with a ride in a sled.

Figure 9.6. A Missouri interpreter offers a demonstration to urban youth about how Native Americans used flint to start their campfires. (MDC)

Demonstration and activities involve visitors, offer group interaction, provide hands-on learning possibilities, and show things that otherwise might be mere abstractions. The interpreter relates the demonstration or activity to the theme, providing a holistic picture.

Questioning Strategies

Many interpreters provoke thought with questioning strategies. This approach can serve as an icebreaker in the introduction of any program or can be used throughout the program, generally if the group is relatively small. Questioning strategies can generate a quick audience analysis to draw on later in the presentation (Brochu & Merriman, 2008). Questions also work to direct attention to discovery activities and to provoke deeper thought. When used excessively, however, they can seem like an examination. So, generally, questions are used to complement the overall program.

Roger Riolo is a National Association for Interpretation Master Trainer. His work takes into account the notion that questions from the audience and questions interpreters pose to an audience may play a vital role within any visitor contact or learning experience. Riolo (pers. comm., 2016) suggested interpreters should look at what types of questions are best suited to connect with the audience, hold their attention, and increase their participation. Interpreters may use questions for several purposes. Educators use the term *scaffolding* for questions tiered by design. Riolo suggested that interpreters can scaffold their questions by considering those who are "dragged along" or uninterested, *and* include a series of questions to account for visitors who are curious or interested in the topic, while *also* providing something to provoke further thought or help formulate opinions for yet others who may be highly invested and fascinated by the topic.

Riolo noted that different interpretive and educational texts use their own terminology for types of questions (Brochu & Merriman, 2008; Gabler & Schroeder, 2003; Ham, 1992; Knudson, Cable & Beck, 1995; Walsh & Sattes, 2005; Walsh & Sattes, 2011; Ward & Wilkerson, 2006). For the purposes of this discussion we provide a mixed set of question types based on NAI certification materials and input from Riolo (pers. comm., 2017) of which the most common follow:

1. **Directed or Undirected Questions:** All questions are either directed or undirected. Most questions are directed toward an audience or an individual. Undirected questions (often called rhetorical questions) may be used as a teaser for things that will follow, something to provoke further thought, or to trigger mental images (e.g., What image comes to mind of Glacier National Park without glaciers?).
2. **Open Questions:** Open questions generally have no right or wrong answer. Response can take place with little or no risk. Open questions can open conversations, create dialogue, and engage audiences. They are also a good technique for gaining specific knowledge about the audience (e.g., What is your favorite wildflower?).
3. **Content Questions:** Sometimes called memory, data recall, or concept questions. These can be used to gauge audience prior knowledge and can be an effective tool for reviewing your topic (e.g., What animal is the keystone species for this ecosystem?).

4. **Process Questions:** These are "thinking" questions. They invite the visitor to formulate an opinion, show a relationship, make a projection, consider impacts, or offer an evaluation. These are good questions for stimulating discussion and provoking further action (e.g., What do you think would happen if all of the predators were removed from this habitat?).

Riolo suggested that prior to formulating any question, the interpreter should be able to answer, "What is the purpose for asking this question at this time?" Interpreters should focus on the content of their questions and decide what type of question will best engage the particular audience. Questions can fail to engage the audience if they are not connected to the audience's past experience or do not challenge them at the appropriate level. Interpreters should determine what is critical to know and formulate questions based on those points. After the question comes a response.

Riolo concluded that a good questioning strategy and appropriate response technique invites participation, creates engagement, stimulates interest, facilitates learning, provokes thought, and helps change attitudes (Box 9.5). Scaffolding questions, good listening skills, wait time, and encouraging the answering process with positive feedback facilitates effective interpretation. It is an essential skill in developing a formula for effective interpretive and training programs.

Box 9.5
Quality Question and Response Habits

Roger Riolo, Master Trainer, National Association for Interpretation

Wait Time:

Prior to responding to any visitor question, answer, or comment, a process of assimilation should take place. Too often interpreters are too eager to answer the question we think we are hearing. Or, we might believe we are hearing the same question for the hundredth time. In either case, we could be wrong in our assumptions. A moment's hesitation prior to responding can allow us to absorb what was actually said. Educators use the term wait time for this short period of silence. Most experts recommend three to five seconds wait time. It is an important element in developing good response habits. Much can take place within a few seconds of wait time. It allows for one to listen to the question, understand what is being asked, formulate an answer, and have time to rethink and revise.

Encouraging the Answering Process:

Wait time is not only important to the interpreter, it is equally important to use wait time after posing a question and before directing it to someone for response. Processing the question is important for the audience as well and will make for more complete or better answers. Although it may seem like an eternity, if answers are not offered immediately by the audience, allow 15 to 20 seconds to elapse before restating the question. Giving the audience time to think about the question will result in better responses. Furthermore, interpreters who cannot tolerate the 15 seconds of silence and rush in to answer their own questions reduces the likelihood of the audience members answering future questions.

Visitor participation is facilitated through several other response techniques. Primary among those is feedback. Feedback is necessary for maintaining an open exchange and continued audience engagement. A simple nod of the head signifies passive acceptance and goes a long way toward creating a risk free atmosphere. Prompts, cues, clues, and probes can also be used as feedback and to reinforce new concepts. These are good techniques for creating more complete answers and stimulating further discussion. Redirecting or rephrasing questions can encourage the answering process. Furthermore, a follow-up question, or piggybacking questions, encourages visitor elaboration. Overall, courtesy and respect create an environment for acceptance. Interpreters can create a healthy environment for exchange with active listening and by demonstrating an interest in each visitor.

Facilitated Dialogue

A deliberate approach to questioning strategies is used by the National Park Service to encourage dialogue among program participants, especially regarding sensitive topics. (See Box 9.6) Lisa Nagurny is a park ranger at Great Smoky Mountains National Park who has been involved with NPS Facilitated Dialogue trainings in Harper's Ferry. Nagurny (pers. comm., 2016, 2017) noted that in a facilitated dialogue program, participants do not simply watch the interpreter speaking to the group. Rather, the interpreter is the facilitator. In this role, the facilitator strives to provide a space where people feel comfortable talking with each other. To do this, the facilitator should describe to the group what the program will look like and the importance of participation.

Box 9.6
Facilitated Dialogue? What's That?

Lisa Nagurny, Park Ranger, Great Smoky Mountains National Park

The quick description of facilitated dialogue is that it is interpretation *with* visitors instead of *to* them. In today's social climate, we need to get people talking to each other. Our cultural and natural sites are great places for many of these discussions to take place and facilitated dialogue provides visitors an opportunity to have a meaningful conversation.

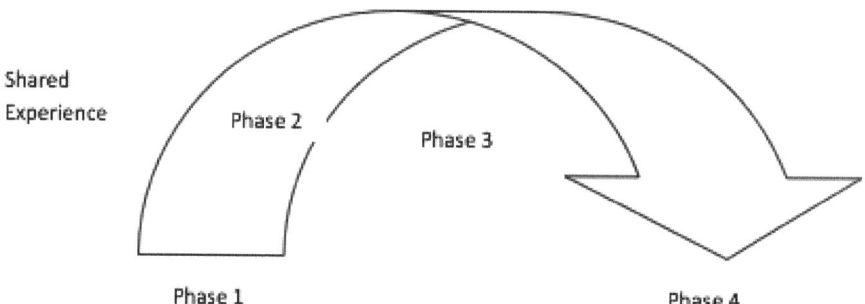

Facilitated dialogue programs sometimes follow what is known as the "Arc of Dialogue." The facilitator (interpreter) asks questions in each phase that move participants through their discussion, similar to how a book moves readers through a story. The Shared Experience (a photo, ranger talk, nature hike, etc.) focuses the conversation around an aspect of the site's resource. Phase 1 establishes community building by introducing the visitors to each other, enabling all voices to be heard. In Phase 2, participants share their own experiences. Like a story, Phase 3 in a facilitated dialogue is the climax. In this phase, participants explore each other's perspectives through dialogue. Lastly, Phase 4 synthesizes and brings closure to the dialogue by encouraging visitors to take action.

The Arc is not the only way to do dialogue! Many techniques can be included in programs to encourage dialogue. Even existing programs can be adapted to include dialogic elements. The important thing is that people are talking to each other!

Keys to success: Ask open-ended, experience-based questions—it encourages dialogue. Collaborate—you are writing questions for several people, so it is fitting to have multiple people working together to develop the questions. Limit your contributions—when the facilitator lets his/her opinions show, it can make participants hesitant to share conflicting opinions. Be flexible—participants might take the conversation in a way you did not expect, and that's okay! Remember, you are there facilitating a program for the participants, not for you!

Source: Model adapted from International Coalition of Sites of Conscience.

In addition, the interpreter explains the importance of being open to hearing new perspectives and reacting respectfully to differences. Throughout the program, the facilitator asks questions to encourage dialogue. These questions should be open-ended (have no "right" answer) and experience-based. Experience-based questions (*each* person has something to say based upon their personal experiences) allow everyone in the group to be able to respond and break down hierarchies in the group so the "experts" are not the only ones who can participate.

The NPS Interpretive Development Program (2014) provides a rationale and sample questions for each of the four phases of the Arc of Dialogue. These are presented, adapted, and summarized as follows (from NPS, 2014).

Phase 1: Building Community

This phase opens the dialogue by introducing the topic and noting that the purpose is to learn from one another's experiences and beliefs. The questioning begins with a welcoming and non-threatening question that everyone is able to respond to.

Sample questions: "When people ask you where you're from, what do you say? What do you like most about where you live?"

Phase 2: Sharing Experiences

In this phase, audience members share their experiences related to the topic and further get to know about one another. The facilitator keeps the dialogue on track so that discussion is focused on the topic at hand, sees that everyone contributes, and keeps things moving. The facilitator also helps participants to recognize how their personal experiences are different or alike.

Sample questions for the topic of immigration: "What impact, if any, does immigration have on your daily life? What images come to mind when you hear the word immigrant?"

Sample questions for the topic of civil rights: "Describe a situation where you witnessed someone being treated unfairly; how did it make you feel; what did you do?"

Sample questions for the topic of climate change: "What first shaped your relationship with the natural environment? What do you most value about nature?"

Follow-up questions on any of these topics: "What does this issue *mean* to you? What differences in the responses from others did you notice?"

Phase 3: Exploring Perspectives Beyond Our Own Experiences

At this point, the questions are designed to move beyond the participants' personal experience with it. Here is where the audience members learn from one another. Facilitators should place minimal value judgment on responses and there should be no indication of preferred responses. All participants should be able to contribute with a sense of respect and openness.

Sample questions for the topic of immigration: "How should our nation decide who is able to immigrate and who is unable to do so? What are the values that should drive our immigration policy?"

Sample questions for the topic of civil rights: "What impact does cultural identity have on our perspectives of civil rights? How do you suppose people feel when they are excluded based upon their appearance?"

Sample questions for the topic of climate change: "What is most troubling about our collective relationship to nature? What is most reassuring?"

Follow-up questions on any of these topics: "Why do you think our interpretations of this topic are different? What might be the source or the cause of these differences?"

Phase 4: Synthesizing and Bringing Closure to the Dialogue

In this last phase, the facilitator helps participants synthesize the experience. At this stage, participants identify common threads from the discussion. The facilitator also brings closure to the experience by offering final observations. Of course, this doesn't mean that everyone agrees on the topic, but that rather everyone has had a chance to be heard and that perhaps everyone has also gleaned new insights into the topic.

Sample question for synthesis: "What if anything did you hear that challenged your assumptions or provided another way of looking at things?"

Sample question for closure: "What is one insight that you will take away from today's experiences?"

Specific circumstances will dictate the potential benefits of a facilitated dialogue program. Under the proper conditions, it can be a powerful approach to programming.

Facilitated dialogue is just one specific approach in the broader movement within the NPS and other interpretive organizations to emphasize Audience-Centered Interpretation. Audience-Centered Interpretation involves engaging audiences in shared experiences and then creatively reflecting on those experiences as a group. This movement's overarching goal is to replace programs that feature one-way communication with the interpreter as the presenter with programs that allow participants to contribute to a meaningful exploration of a topic. Audience-Centered Interpretation encourages collaboration among audience members and promotes the use of their problem-solving and critical thinking skills.

Promoting Participation—A Combined Approach

Various techniques encourage participation by visitors. Getting people to handle objects, to make observations, to discuss findings, to express opinions, and to develop skills can foster powerful visitor experiences. Preparing for demonstrations and participatory exercises calls for special planning, however. Attracting audience participation takes planning, practice, continual evaluation, and adjustment.

Although first-hand experience and observation characterizes interpretation, a few interpreters talk so much that the visitor has little or no chance to participate. Talking is relatively easy—and necessary—but promoting participation is tougher. Structuring and promoting participation requires more planning, but can produce rewards in visitor response. Strang (1999) successfully used participatory methods of enhancing sensory capabilities through several group exercises (e.g., wide-angle vision, focused hearing).

He suggested that these exercises apply to directing the senses, helping people become more alert to the landscape. This enhanced awareness may be valuable to many kinds of natural and historical interpretation.

To make a program as interesting as possible, and to touch on as many diverse learning styles as possible, an interpreter can offer a variety of approaches. Overall, interpreters who strive to orchestrate well-balanced and diverse programs using many different interpretive approaches often enjoy success.

Research on Interpretation's Best Practices

In 2012, a seminal article on best practices in the interpretive field, identified from key interpretive training texts, included the importance of theme development, a multisensory approach, linking tangible dimensions of the interpretive setting to universal concepts, active engagement of the audience, and messages focused on the relationship between the visitor and the site (Skibins, Powell, & Stern, 2012).

More recently, a "Special Issue" of the *Journal of Interpretation Research* (2013) focused on visitor outcomes from live interpretive programs in the areas of satisfaction, visitor experience and appreciation, and behavioral intentions. The articles in this issue consisted of an empirical analysis of hundreds of live interpretive programs conducted by the U.S. National Park Service at 24 cultural and natural settings that included Bryce Canyon, Grand Canyon, Mesa Verde, Gettysburg National Military Park, and the National Mall. In the "Introduction to the Special Issue" Sam Ham describes this project as "perhaps the most comprehensive examination of interpretation ever attempted" (Ham, 2013). In sum, shedding light on potential "best practices," researchers Marc Stern and Robert Powell (2013) noted the importance of characteristics such as interpreter confidence, authentic emotion and charisma, appropriateness for the audience, organization, connection, humor quality, consistency, a clear message, responsiveness, verbal engagement, audibility, and appropriate logistics and pace. Furthermore, in conjunction with some of these same attributes, they found "Interpreters who explicitly aimed to increase their audience members' levels of concern or change their behavior were more likely to achieve more positive post-program behavioral intentions than others" (Stern & Powell, 2013).

In the final article of this special issue, Stern and his associates (Stern, Powell, McLean, Martin, Thomsen, & Mutchier, 2013) distinguished between "good" interpretive programs that may be defined as adequate and "great" interpretive programs that touch personal values and/or provoke deeper thoughts and leave long-lasting impressions. They use the analogy of one's response to a powerful movie by quoting Oliver and Bartsch (2010) as follows: "An experiential state that is characterized by the perception of deeper meaning, the feeling of being moved, and the motivation to elaborate on thoughts and feelings inspired by the experience." Outstanding musical theater may also induce such deep responses in audiences and has also been compared to great interpretation (Beck & Cable, 2010). In other words, several authors are now linking powerful human responses to great art (film and theater) with the same types of responses that interpreters are capable of achieving.

Summary

The interpreter conducting personal interpretation serves as the key image of the interpretive site and may be the only professional person visitors encounter. Therefore, as the person in charge, representing the organization, the interpreter should look and act professionally at all times portraying a confident, friendly demeanor.

This chapter emphasized the vital personal services work of the interpreter. Whether providing information via desk duty, roving interpretation—or any of a variety of tours, demonstrations, and talks—the interpreter strives to serve visitors in an organized yet informal manner. Although specific principles apply to each of these functions, quality interpretation starts with attitude, including qualities such as amiability, belief in what one has to say, confidence, delivery that is conversational, and enthusiasm that is contagious. These combine with content coordinated by a holistic theme, involving first-hand experiences that reveal and relate things to individuals and the world around them.

> "Several authors are now linking powerful human responses to great art (film and theater) with the same types of responses that interpreters are capable of achieving."

The interpreter aims to enrich and to excite people regarding the magic of the place they have come to visit and to provoke them to reflect and perhaps do something more based on what they have learned. Such personal services offer important tools for fulfilling that responsibility and give real life to the place. Personal service interpreters are the hosts and living symbols of the agency and the facility. They are capable of providing deep, powerful, and moving experiences for the visitors to their interpretive sites. These programs inform and inspire, enhance visitor experiences, and potentially change lives. This personal dimension of the work of the interpreter certainly makes for a better world.

Literature Cited

Barry, P. (1998). Promoting excellence in interpretation by keeping the customer satisfied. In *1998 interpretive sourcebook*. Ft. Collins, CO: National Association for Interpretation.

Beck, L. (2001). What is the essence of our professional responsibility? *Legacy, 12*(4), 29–32.

Beck, L. (2014). Authenticity of landscape and interpretation: A celebration. *Legacy, 25*(6), 24–28.

Beck, L., & Cable, T. (2010). *Interpretive perspectives: A collection of essays on interpreting nature and culture.* Ft. Collins, CO: National Association for Interpretation.

Brochu, L., & Merriman, T. (2008). *Personal interpretation* (2nd ed.). Ft. Collins, CO: InterpPress.

Buchholz, J., Lackey, B., Gross, M., & Zimmerman, R. (2015). *The interpreter's guidebook: Techniques for programs and presentations* (4th ed.). Interpreter's Handbook Series. Stevens Point, WI: UWSP Foundation Press, Inc.

Cable, T. (1999). Becoming better interpreters. *Legacy, 10*(6), 14–16.

Cornell, J. (1989). *Sharing the joy of nature.* Nevada City, CA: Dawn Publications.

Cornell, J. (1998). *Sharing nature with children* (rev. ed.). Nevada City, CA: Dawn Publications.

Friedman, E. (2007). *A failure of nerve: Leadership in the age of the quick fix.* New York, NY: Seabury Books.

Gabler, I., & Schroeder, M. (2003). *Constructivist methods for the secondary classroom: Engaged minds.* Boston, MA: Allyn & Bacon.

Goleman, D., Boyatzis, R., & McKee, A. (2013). *Primal leadership: Unleashing the power of emotional intelligence.* Boston, MA: Harvard Business Review Press.

Ham, S. (1992). *Environmental interpretation: A practical guide.* Golden, CO: North American Press.

Ham, S. (2013). *Interpretation: Making a difference on purpose.* Golden, CO: Fulcrum.

Ham, S. (2013). Introduction to Special Issue. *Journal of Interpretation Research, 18*(2), 3–5.

Isaacson, W. (2011). *Steve Jobs.* New York, NY: Simon and Schuster.

Kawasaki, G. (1991). *Selling the dream.* New York, NY: Harper Business.

Knudson, D., Cable, T., & Beck, L. (1995). *Interpretation of cultural and natural resources.* State College, PA: Venture.

LaPage, W. (1998). The activist interpreter—The unspoken principle. *Legacy, 9*(4), 12–15.

Lewis, W. (1980). *Interpreting for park visitors.* Philadelphia, PA: Eastern Acorn Press.

Luzader, J. (2001). Rungs from the chair. Kinship with the past. *NAI Section Newsletter, 5*(4):1–2.

Nagurny, L. (2016, 2017). Personal communication with Ted Cable and Larry Beck.

National Park Service Interpretive Development Program. (2014). The Arc of Dialogue. *Professional Standards for Learning and Performance*, 03/2014.

Oliver, M., & Bartsch, A. (2010). Appreciation as audience response: Exploring entertainment gratifications beyond hedonism. *Human Communication Research, 36,* 53–81.

Riolo, R. (2017). Personal communication with Larry Beck.

Risk, P. (1982). Conducted activities. In G. W. Sharpe (Ed.), *Interpreting the environment* (2nd ed.). New York, NY: John Wiley & Sons, Inc.

Rutherford, J. (2000). Reflections of a first-time interpreter. *Legacy, 11*(6), 10–11.

Sexton, P. (2015). Structured randomness. *Legacy, 26*(1), 23–25.

Skibins, J., Powell, R., & Stern, M. (2012). Exploring empirical support for interpretation's best practices. *Journal of Interpretation Research, 17*(1), 25–44.

Stern, M., & Powell, R. (2013). What leads to better visitor outcomes in live interpretation? *Journal of Interpretation Research, 18*(2), 9–43.

Stern, M., Powell, R., McClean, K., Martin, E., Thomsen, J., & Mutchier, B. (2013). The difference between good enough and great: Bringing interpretive best practices to life. *Journal of Interpretation Research, 18*(2), 79–100.

Strang, C. (1999). *Interpretive undercurrents.* Ft. Collins, CO: National Association for Interpretation.

Tilden, F. (1977). *Interpreting our heritage* (3rd ed.). Chapel Hill, NC: The University of North Carolina Press.

Wallace, G. (1990). Law enforcement and the authority of the resource. *Legacy, 1*(2), 4–8.

Wallace, G., & Gaudry, C. (2002). An evaluation of the "Authority of the Resource" interpretive technique by rangers in eight wilderness/backcountry areas. *Journal of Interpretation Research, 7*(1), 43–68.

Walsh, J., & Sattes, B. (2005). *Quality questioning: Research-based practice to engage every learner.* Thousand Oaks, CA: Corwin Press.

Walsh, J., & Sattes, B. (2011). *Thinking through quality questioning: Deepening student engagement.* Thousand Oaks, CA: Corwin Press.

Ward, C., & Wilkerson, A. (2006). *Conducting meaningful interpretation: A field guide for success.* Golden, CO: Fulcrum.

CHAPTER 10
Arts in Interpretation

The La Jolla Playhouse is known for world premiere theater events with a history of many reaching Broadway and ultimately winning Tony Awards. In the summer of 2015, the Playhouse launched a fact-based musical, "Come From Away," rooted in the events of 9/11, which indeed hit Broadway in 2017. When all U.S.-bound air traffic was ordered to land on September 11, 2001, 38 jetliners descended on Gander, Newfoundland, population 11,000. With all the unexpected passengers, the population jumped to almost 18,000. The universal concepts of good and evil are explored in this emotional portrayal as theater patrons witness warmth and humanity on a day otherwise known for darkness and despair. Because on that day the people of this Canadian town responded to the "plane people" as if they were native sons and daughters—taking the displaced travelers to their homes, feeding them, housing them, letting them shower, sharing their phones for long-distance calls. When the world was witnessing the worst of mankind, this tiny little town was witnessing the best of it. The book, music, and lyrics are by the husband-and-wife team of Irene Sankoff and David Hein. On the 10th anniversary commemoration of 9/11, the writers talked to townspeople and passengers who returned to Gander for the event in countless interviews, each lasting up to four hours that the writers noted "came with a level of responsibility to get their stories right." All of this was transcribed and condensed into a 90-minute show without intermission. The score is performed by an eight-person, on-stage band that stays true to the sound of Newfoundland. And the overall result is an uplifting experience that runs the gamut of emotions from laughter to tears. This combination of song, dance, instrumentation, costuming, acting, and set design may be the epitome of using the arts in interpretation. But, as we shall see, there are many possibilities.

The Use of the Arts in Interpretation

"The interpretive arts bring to many a temporary vitality and a sharing of one another's truth. I am passionately convinced that art can serve to enhance our moral sensibilities and to promote in many a sense of environmental integrity."

–Lee Stetson

Artists of the 19th century created paintings that convinced Congress to set aside wilderness landscapes and protect them for future generations. For many modern-day artists, the quest is the same (Stern, McGarry, & Dunn, 2013). Through the arrangement of colors and forms, vibrant images resonate in the viewer's mind in ways that celebrate the world we live in. Viewers, moved by what they see, want to protect our natural blessings. For example, artists and scientists have joined forces to offer a creative view on the issue of climate change. An exhibit at the La Jolla Historical Society, "Weather on Steroids: The Art of Climate Change Science," offers unique perspectives on the issue with visual portrayals of the effects of climate change (Schimitschek, 2017). The artwork includes sculpture, mosaic, and photography with each piece associated with two panels of text—one from the artist and one from a climate scientist working at Scripps Institution of Oceanography. A long history of visual art celebrates the wonders of, and our relationship with, nature.

Performing and visual arts have long been counted among the tools of interpretation, and especially within the last two decades there has been considerable growth in this realm. Professional interpreters increasingly use the arts as platforms for the interpretive messages they convey. There is a natural connection between the arts and interpretation of our culture and landscape.

> "Performing and visual arts have long been counted among the tools of interpretation."

Furthermore, interpretive professionals *interpret the arts*. Appropriate interpretation enriches art museums, folk music festivals, sculpture, photography, dance, and drama. While museums once expressed disdain for "explaining" the arts, now they have found ways to interpret while enhancing visitors' experiences. From YouTube, to television, to museums, we now find many outlets that tell the stories of art and the artists, helping people to enjoy artistic performance with enhanced perception.

People perceive natural resource, historic, and artistic values emotionally as well as intellectually. Professional interpreters use a mix of emotional and intellectual approaches to communicate. Using the arts judiciously helps to convey the messages and to create richer experiences, making good programs great (Wheeler, 2016) (Figure 10.1).

> "People perceive natural resource, historic, and artistic values emotionally as well as intellectually."

As noted by Jay Griffiths (2013), "Art elicits sympathy, conjures empathy, and these emotions are requisites for a kind, kinned sense of society...For the greatest artists do not make their best works of art in clay or paint or sound or words; they make them right inside us, within the heart of the reader or audience." Similarly, the greatest interpreters make their best works within the hearts and minds of those they interpret to. The use of the arts has gained sophistication in efforts to ultimately entertain, educate, convey culture, and to make emotional impacts. (Box 10.1)

Interpretive Theater

Figure 10.1. Erica Wheeler presents musical keynote addresses and "Soulful Stewardship" and "Sense of Place" workshops throughout North America. (JN)

Barry Edelstein (2015), artistic director of the Old Globe, notes that *beauty* is a word he associates with theater, one of its greatest effects: "Alive and in front of us, happening in the here and now, beauty on stage has a visceral strength, a physical manifestation. It impacts us with an unusual force that stays with us…a beauty that transports us, moves us, and delights us."

In many ways, those in the profession of heritage interpretation are in a similar business as those who perform on Broadway (Beck & Cable, 2010). The interpretive mission is to convey deep meaning that members of the audience may connect with. Interpreters use tools of voice, movement, music, props, and storytelling to reveal universal concepts. Just as Broadway musicals may be awe-inspiring and transformational in their portrayal of universal concepts, so are the places that interpreters work and the stories they tell.

Interpretive theater refers to dramatic performances in the popular sense, with or without a theater stage. Such presentations range from the elaborate and costly to the basic and inexpensive. They may include puppet shows, short tableaux, long dramas, and reenactments of historical events. Their approaches can include everything from farce to tragic history to allegories to nature portrayals to purely aural theater. The players may come from the audience on the spur of the moment or from professional troupes that have spent months in preparation, and everything in between.

Productions may include specialized equipment, props, costumes, and in-house or professional salaries. Equipment, like funding and talent, will vary according to the needs. Auditoriums with a stage and elaborate light and sound systems can enhance a performance, but are not necessary. Indeed, most living history drama occurs outdoors on porches and lawns of historic sites.

Specialized skills, including script writing, directing, and acting may vary according to the professionalism of the program. These skills require either staff time (assuming the talent exists) or contractors. Interpreters may develop a script with current staff, advertise for script submissions, commission a writer, or purchase an existing script. A director and actors, if not on the staff, may come from a local high school or college drama department, or a community theater group. A suggested production checklist for planning effective interpretive theater appears in Box 10.2.

Box 10.1
The Arts Provide Another Dimension to Interpretation
By Rita Cantu, Singer/Songwriter

An American Indian saying asserts: If the songs are not sung and the stories are not told, the land will die. An interpretive corollary can affirm: If the songs are not sung and the stories are not told, danced, painted, or acted, our spirits will die as well.

Imagine our work and play when we believe that. Our myths, symbols, and rituals give meaning to the world around us. The arts give expression to that meaning. The connection of the heart as well as the head—of the intuition as well as the intellect—springs to life through using the arts in interpretation.

The arts in themselves are not the only keys, but they can spark the "Oh! I got it!" discovery of something newly understood. That's what we're after as interpreters. Our main work aims to make connections. We are all storytellers, fisherfolk, casting a line through the air with an "Ah-ha" on the hook. We try to reel in wonder, understanding, mystery, a sense of the sacred. We are catalysts, sparking relationships between Something Without and Something Within.

The arts move our minds from the ordered and sequential logic into the deeper, more cyclical world of imagery, values, metaphor, and symbolism. Logic's straight lines attach at each end, becoming interconnected circles and systems. If people's responses are indicators, this approach wins hand down.

In interpretation, the arts are a means, but rarely the ends. Living history presenters use their art to dramatize the timeless messages of the time and people they represent. Music draws and focuses attention, to increase receptivity to a message. Storytelling uses allegory and metaphor to broaden the scope and deepen the message of a theme. The visual arts and traditional crafts illustrate life styles and values of a people and a period, visually presenting concepts and connections.

Performing arts help a group focus on connecting points and values of a theme. They help create cohesiveness of the story. Arts unify and connect the group. They provide moments for direct experience of values, perceptions, feelings, allegory, imagery, archetypes, and hero stories unique to a particular setting. An artistically designed setting creates an interpretive experience around a sign, exhibit, or trail.

Resource managers and museum curators have long used good science to communicate issues and actions. Their messages, usually 99% logic and science, too often are met with critical reaction. The public is accustomed to image-based messages that appeal to the emotions and to "What's in it for me?" We need to balance our messages to at least 70% left brain and 30% right brain. We need an integrative, whole-brain approach for communicating complex concepts in clear and compelling ways. The arts provide tools for crafting holistic messages that integrate biological and social sciences, emotion and intuition, for effective communication.

In an essay titled "The Farmer as a Conservationist" Aldo Leopold wrote, "There is drama in every bush, if you can see it. When enough men know this, we need fear no indifference to the welfare of bushes, or birds, or soils, or trees." A Lakota phrase, mitakuye oyasin ("all things connected"), points to the role of interpreters to reveal those connections on as many levels as possible. Arts provide a vital tool for that revelation.

In our roles as interpreters and stewards of the land and culture, we both reveal and discover the songs and tales and visions of the people and place—even while dealing with the complexities of politics, science, and the cycles of change. As interpreters we face the generalist tasks of integrating biological, political, societal and historic perspectives in an artistic whole, creating rich experiences for all.

Box 10.2
A General Production Overview

- Audience needs and expectations
- Program outline (events and characters)
- Facilities and equipment
- Costumes and props
- Budget preparation and fundraising (if appropriate)
- Staff assignments
- Contracts (if appropriate)
- Research materials and writing script
- Auditioning
- Planning rehearsals and preparing actors
- Rehearsals
- Production schedule
- Publicity
- Evaluation

Many interpreters who are not professional actors don costumes to get across their messages. As Peoples (2001) noted, "there is just something about seeing interpreters in costume that the visitors love." Sometimes they present a whole program. Other times, they present a skit or brief segment of their programs in a persona other than their own. These modest dramas may have convincing, humorous, and highly motivating moments. They can stimulate all the senses. They can involve the audience in the action. The drama can produce memorable experiences. For example, interpretive actors portray characters who have messages about weather, the water cycle, wildlife, recycling, insects, and many historic or mythological characters.

Recognizing the value of using theater in interpretation, a training session was developed for the Missouri State Parks and Historic Sites. *Lessons from the World of Theater* was designed to teach interpreters how to develop the skills to "look natural in front of an audience" (Blank, 2010). The training was broken into three major sections: Relaxation and Pre-Program Preparations, Acting and Theater Techniques, and Improvisational Techniques and Games. Theatrical techniques are taught so that the program comes across as effortless as possible, in order for the audience to get fully immersed in the drama.

Drawing others who are willing into a program can have positive effects, especially with children. For example, researchers found that incorporating improvisational theater games into interpretive programs at Banff National Park contributed to enjoyment and perceived learning of children (Macklin, Hvenegaard, & Johnson, 2010). Incorporating sensory awareness, physical involvement, collaboration, creativity, and guided interaction involved children in ways that promote critical social, cognitive, and emotional development.

Interpretive theater has also been used to attract more diverse audiences. The Monterey Bay Aquarium sought to diversify their audiences to better reflect the make up of the community and therefore created a number of special event weekends to target Hispanics (Mortan, 2008). For the Fiesta del Mar, the Aquarium commissioned El Teatro Campesino to develop a 15-minute "acto" that is bilingual and focuses on concerns over plastic debris in oceans. This show proved successful, for both Spanish and English speaking audiences. Subsequently, another show was added that addressed the need to conserve energy. Surveys showed that a strong majority of the audience "learned something new about ocean conservation and would also consider doing something different based on the program" (Mortan, 2008). Furthermore, the Hispanic audience at the Aquarium continued to grow.

Other methods to increase interest and attendance include the use of magic. Steve Craig is an excellent interpreter/magician who conducts programs for schools and NAI events. As a professional magician, he uses his skills to teach about nature. His magic shows include topics such as butterfly conservation and water quality.

Lee Stetson on Interpretive Theater

Figure 10.2. Professional actor Lee Stetson portrays John Muir in interpretive theater.

Lee Stetson is a professional actor who has written and performed several portrayals of the life of John Muir, presented at Yosemite National Park and throughout the country (Figure 10.2). By 2015 he had performed before more than a quarter million visitors to Yosemite eliciting emotions from wonder to laughter to tears. As an actor who has performed more than 50 major roles, Stetson has much to offer in way of advice and insight regarding interpretive theater and related the following counsel for developing an effective dramatic presentation (see also Beck & Cable, 2010).

A show that works requires the most rounded characters possible. In addition to reading all of John Muir's books and articles, Stetson read every source he could find written *about* Muir to learn more about his lifestyle. He looked for aspects of the character's life that show the faults, foibles, and funny moments that all of us experience. Incorporating these aspects of the character enriches the show enormously.

To provide another element of authenticity, Stetson concerned himself with what a 75-year-old man is all about, to match the age that he chose to portray. Likewise, he insisted on attention to detail in the development of costuming and props. These accessories often make a big difference and allow the character to shine.

Stetson believes in limiting complex lighting and sound effects as much as possible. He noted, "In most parks, people are trying to get away from the kaleidoscope of images that assail them in the city. I think there is a visceral connection between a live performer and the audience" (Beck & Cable, 2010).

Stetson believes that interpreters doing basic theater need not have extensive dramatic training. The quality of acting derives from the depth of connection the actor has with the character. To convey a message the actor shows the character, rather than telling about the character. The actor commits to delivering the joy, the anger, and the overall passion of the character. Using the full gamut of emotions, from laughter to sorrow, elicits reactions from the audience. Stetson advised, "The character must be moved to expect the audience to be moved also" (Beck & Cable, 2010). Working hard on the acting techniques will allow one to become fully engaged in each and every moment. However, amateur actors may find it difficult to sustain a show over a long period of time.

It isn't necessary for interpreters to develop a full-length production from scratch. They can develop smaller projects that lie within the capabilities of most interpreters. These demand less in terms of research, script writing, and dramatic endurance. This approach allows interpreters to hone their skills over time and continue adding segments in the development of a larger production over a couple of years. Large park operations might also consider bringing in dramatic coaches to help rehearse interpreters in the skills necessary for theatrical interpretive programs.

The other approach, of course, brings professional actors into the parks on some type of contract. Based on his association with Yosemite, Stetson advocated more arts in the parks—from theater to storytelling to music. At Yosemite, the Muir shows pay Stetson's salary, a technician, promotion, and other costs. The shows' ticket receipts bring an infusion of surplus funds into the park for various conservation efforts. The arrangement has proved successful from a financial standpoint and an interpretive standpoint, through the enhancement of the park experience by thousands of visitors.

Kaiulani Lee as Rachel Carson

Kaiulani Lee performs as Rachel Carson in a one-woman show. Lee found theater by accident when she went to New York City and soon became a Broadway actress. She found that theater touched people like other things didn't. With her practice and training she learned that an honest actor must be able to zero in on what is important.

Lee read Paul Brook's biography of Rachel Carson. Although people have heard quite a bit about the environment from many different angles, Carson's personal story, with a human, small-scale approach has incredible impact. Her portrayal of Rachel Carson interprets a great woman's life in an educational, enriching, emotional, and inspirational way.

Outdoor Dramas

Outdoor dramas offer among the ultimate of interpretive experiences. These are stories on or near the historic sites, performed in the elements, presenting the character of the place and the people who made history there in a holistic way. Outdoor theater dates back to the Classical Greeks, where people came to learn more about their heritage.

Modern outdoor dramas may be as elaborate as the Greeks offered, with dozens of actors, outrageous props, and plenty of action. Among the most venerable interpretive dramas is *Shepherd of the Hills,* which operated as a commercial business long before country singers found Branson, Missouri. The drama recounts a 1900s novel that portrayed isolated rural life in southern Missouri. The huge theater operates all summer. The stage is the size of a football field with close to a hundred actors and actresses, more than 20 horses, donkeys, and mules, a flock of sheep, gunfights, and a real cabin that is burned every night. The year 2014 marked the 55th season of this historic drama that includes a love story and an incredible moral message that rings just as true today as when the original book was published in 1907.

Theater and Difficult Topics

Theater is increasingly being used to tackle difficult topics in history and science. For example, 19th century American abolitionist John Brown is often a footnote in the teaching of American history. But was he a hero or a traitor? The History Alive! Theater Program at the National Museum of American History, Smithsonian Institution, developed a theater program titled *The Time Trial of John Brown*. The theater performance allowed audience members to be involved. The museum became "a space to engage in difficult conversations about personal issues that shape national identity" (Evans, 2013). This interactive theater program challenged visitors to arrive at their own conclusions about John Brown's legacy by providing a format through which audiences were able to better understand history as a series of acts and decisions, "while learning firsthand about their role in creating a shared knowledge of American history" (Evans, 2013).

> "Theater is increasingly being used to tackle difficult topics in history and science."

Theater is also being used to engage the public with scientific issues such as climate change. A New York-based theater company, the Civilians, received a three-year grant from the National Science Foundation to create a play that focuses on the complexity of climate change (Wasserman & Young, 2013). The production, titled *The Great Immensity*, provides a balance of scientific content and public engagement. Scientists were included during the artistic development process.

Similarly, the National Park Service launched its Climate Change Response Program in 2010 to educate general audiences about climate change. To reach a broader public, the NPS encouraged interpreters to use creative techniques and engagement strategies. Glacier National Park can be considered the "Poster Park for Climate Change" since the impacts of global warming are directly evident. An artistic place-based interpretive program was presented at the Logan Pass Visitor Center titled *Goodbye to Glaciers*. The program related Glacier's tangible resources affected by climate change (mountains, glaciers, mountain goats, pikas, ptarmigans, and alpine vegetation) to intangibles such as change, loss, renewal, hope, personal responsibility, and passage of time (Barrett & Mowen, 2014). The program theme was, "Through their power and their persistence, the glaciers of Glacier National Park have shaped the world around them, but now our changing world is changing them." The "resolution" portion of the program entailed singing the lyrics of, or reciting a poem titled "I am a Glacier." Researchers determined that the "nonconfrontational" program was "associated with favorable short-term emotional, intellectual, and stewardship responses among program attendees" (Barrett & Mowen, 2014).

Furthermore, a longer and more elaborate program was commissioned by the Glacier National Park Conservancy titled *Changing Balance/Balancing Change*. This program featured dance, original music, choreographed narration, video projection, and live interactions with the audience members.

Storytelling and Poetry

Storytelling can powerfully convey information about cultural and natural history. Stories have the potential to hold the attention of large, mixed-age audiences. Because the images of stories are vivid in the minds of listeners, and help them to grow in mind and spirit, they retain what they have heard (Bruchac, 2005). Storytelling is a relatively straightforward and inexpensive interpretive technique (Box 10.3).

Box 10.3
The Story and the Interpreter—Sometimes One and the Same

For most of us a simple object can hold stories and memories that reveal something of us. Wilson Hunter (1990) told of one case in which a sensitive interpreter revealed details of a culture through personal narrative.

An interpreter at Canyon de Chelly developed such a story around the prosaic cradle board. Her purpose was to take her audience beyond the obvious, that the board is made of certain materials and is used in such-and-such a way.

She tells how the person who makes a cradle board does not just find a well-shaped branch or bush and simply cut it down. Certain things must be said and done before removing these things from nature. Prayers are involved, and the necessary proprieties are observed. A child will start his or her life and begin the process of learning personal identity on this cradle board; it must be a good board.

And after it has served its purpose, it must not be discarded as if it had no value. It is something lent by nature, and must be returned to nature in the appropriate way.

In the taking and the returning, one must be cognizant of the importance to maintain a harmony with nature. In other words, a perceptive and understanding interpreter tells not only what a cradle board is, but what it means. In so doing, one brings out of that simple and common object something of the Indian's worldview, what things are important, and why.

Whole cultures have persisted through centuries by oral tradition, passing their rituals, beliefs, skills, and perceptions from generation to generation through stories. Indeed, stories in many forms comprise the core of interpretive speech, writing, and audiovisual materials.

> "Whole cultures have persisted through centuries by oral tradition."

Most interpreters faithfully subscribe to Tilden's dictum that "the story's the thing." Interpretation is an art, using artistic forms and methods while drawing on all of science. Emphasis on the story line approach recognizes it as a key to effective interpretation.

Susan Strauss (1996) contributed to the field with her instructions on how to approach storytelling. She makes a living working with interpretive stories. She revives (and sometimes revises and invents) stories based on characters of Native American and rural folk societies.

In *The Passionate Fact*, Strauss (1996) shares a wealth of philosophy and practices to guide any storyteller. A few of her how-to tips are summarized here.

- Start simply—tell anecdotes of your own experiences and observations.
- Use legends, folk tales, fables, parables, myths, and fairy tales as they fit.
- Use details—create images and depict simple actions to add life, feeling, and meaning.
- Translate information into imagery—broaden the ways something may be shown.
- Show relationships and context—create a sense of journey.

- Engage all the senses.
- Frame any interpretive talk with a story related to the theme.
- Use a flexible voice, gestures, and movement.
- Practice, practice, revise, and practice again—tell your good stories often.

Other helpful tips include creating a mood in which to tell the stories and to carefully orchestrate expressions and gestures as an essential component of the storytelling. Finally, if original stories are not available or appropriate, then it is possible to diligently research a subject to create your own (as revealed in the introductory story of this chapter). Sources may include people who lived through an event, local newspapers, and journals.

In America, a wealth of folklore includes American Indian myths, plantation slave folk tales, sea chanteys, and legendary stories of folk heroes. For the settlers in this country, survival took much of their energy. Yet they created legends and ballads to describe the vast frontier and its wildlife. Some of these are educational, while others (e.g., Paul Bunyan and Pecos Bill tales) amuse and entertain listeners who yearn for simpler and more innocent times.

The earliest folk tradition in this country developed from the Native Americans. Among the common themes of native legends are explanations of how things came to be. A version of how the earth was formed offers an interesting interpretive possibility (Robinson, 1985).

> "The earliest folk tradition in this country developed from the Native Americans."

The Great Spirit searched through all the animals of the sea to find the right one to carry the mud to form the earth. Finally, He found Grandmother Turtle, piled mud high on her back, and the first piece of the earth was formed. Because of her help, the turtle is the only animal today who is at home beneath the water, within the earth, or above the ground. But for all times, the Grandmother Turtle and her ancestors must move very slowly, for they carry the weight of the world on their backs.

Although storytelling is an ancient craft, there is a revival that is occurring now as evidenced by the popularity of Story Collider. Ben Lillie is the co-founder and host of Story Collider, a live storytelling series, podcast, and online magazine devoted to presenting true, personal stories about the effect of science on people's lives (Linett, 2013). Scientists and amateurs tell stories at bars and other casual venues in New York and other cities, which are also available on the Story Collider podcast.

Overall, storytelling, in its myriad forms, can serve as the basis for an entire program or just one small segment. Stories can be incorporated into a traditional campfire program or nature walk. According to storyteller Susan Strauss (1988), "in the world of interpretation, the job of the storyteller is to bridge the gap between human beings and the natural world."

Storytelling through poetry read during interpretive programs can evoke a special feeling or give a little spice to the presentation. Native Americans often used poetry to teach about ethics and religion. Furthermore, African, European, Japanese, Chinese, and other cultures, too, use poems to express deep feelings, react to the landscape, express their joy, lament their misery.

Interpreters who encourage people to write poems provide a creative program element that provokes close observation of nature or exhibits. In environmental education groups, the follow-up reading of haiku or cinquain or diamante poems also provide great fun and fine openings for reviewing ecological concepts.

Poetry can be used in exhibits or on signs along trails. For example, the North Olympic Library System worked with the National Park Service to offer "Poetry Walks," including a trail in the Hoh Rainforest in Olympic National Park, Washington (Figure 10.3). The Poetry Walk features signs along a short trail with site-appropriate poetry by masters such as Mary Oliver. The poetry draws visitors into deeper emotional engagement with the magnificent rainforest setting.

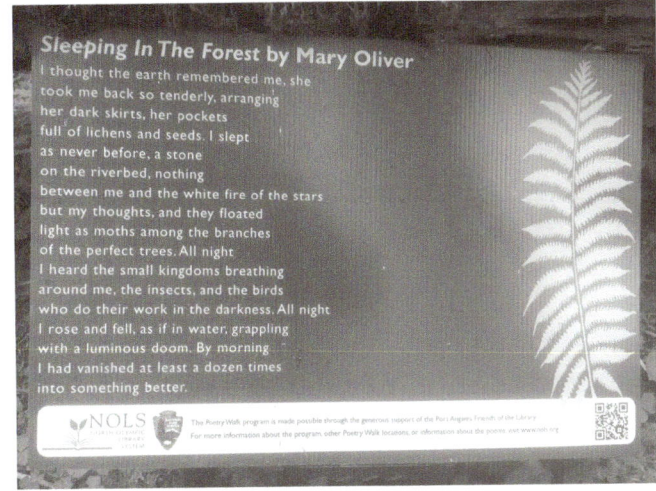

Figure 10.3. Poems are displayed along the Poetry Walk in Olympic National Park. (LB)

Music

That music can help people to remember messages comes as no surprise to anyone who has listened to advertisements on radio and television, where companies put big money on public attention and response. Interpreters use many types of music, from background music during a presentation to authentic music played or sung by the people of the period. Often there is some element of audience participation. Traditional music brings the audience in direct contact with different lifestyles and portrays how people saw themselves and their times.

Music as part of interpretation goes way back in history. In the early days of Yellowstone, Wylie Camps used songs and performance as an integral part of every evening campfire. Interpreters often play guitars, banjos, and accordions to enrich campfire programs in national and state parks.

"Singing for ecology" livens up interpretive events and often includes audience participation. A West Coast group called The Banana Slug String Band performs zany music, with costumes and choreography, and compelling environmental messages. They continue to perform in many K-12 school venues and offer teacher workshops for mixing music, theater, puppetry, and audience participation to convey ecological principles.

Similarly, Emmy Award-winning educators and entertainers, Jan and George Syrigos, make up the musical group known as WildHeart. They entertain young audiences with a strong science message that explores wildlife, habitats, and natural history (Figure 10.4). They, too, have a full schedule performing for school groups. Jan

Syrigos created a songbook that offers teachers a variety of children's songs that are fun and active, with behavioral and learning objectives associated with each song. Many interpreters have followed suit and sing from scientific and emotional bases to promote environmentally sensitive behavior.

Songs can work in several ways: first, to get words and facts to stick in the minds of listeners; second, to paint a picture in the imagination; and third, to reach the emotions of the listener. Some songs evoke strong emotions, which makes them memorable. Others have catchy tunes that people remember long after a performance. Songs can also work effectively with children as noted above. Earth tunes (songs about science and nature) include "Dirt Made My Lunch" by the Banana Slug String Band, which shows how almost everything that people eat is connected through the food chain and depends on soil.

Figure 10.4. Jan Syrigos leads children in a song and dance about caves and bats as part of the Critter Rock DVD and songbook program produced by the Missouri Department of Conservation. (MDC-CW)

Another dimension of music is use from a particular time period, which helps to set the mood as a component of the history of the place. At Cades Cove in Great Smoky Mountains National Park, an Old Timers' Day incorporates music of the Cable Mill Settlement era. The music makes the outdoor exhibit come alive. Musicians drive long distances to participate, gathering in groups to play old-time music on fiddles and banjos. In sum, a guitarist, fiddler, or Native American flautist adds "a whole new dimension to the experience of visiting a historic exhibit" (Golden, 2001).

Dance

Dance, like music, touches the emotions. It can take visitors back to another time and enrich their experiences. In some instances dance may be offered as a complement to a program for the audience as spectators, and in other instances the audience may be invited to participate. Often people enjoy moving to the music of a historical period, even when the steps get intricate. This adds another dimension to the history of the place.

> "Dance, like music, touches the emotions."

Postlewait (2001) has described the use of dance as an interpretive tool. At Ernie Miller Nature Center in Kansas, interpreters have added simple dance and movement patterns to both living history and nature awareness programs. "Prairie Dog Dave," a living history character, tells classroom students that settlers came together for weddings, barn raisings, and other social events. The kids get involved in clapping and stomping to establish a beat, since there were few musical instruments out on the prairie. Dance movements satisfy the need for kids to move about and expend physical energy.

Similarly, at the same nature center, a preschool program about insects has children doing the "bug dance" with hopping, skipping, and crawling motions.

Several other possibilities exist for including dance in interpretive programs such as these recommended by Postlewait (2001):

> How about teaching a jig step after a Brer Rabbit story or an African tribal dance during the telling of an African folk tale? Add the 'Boogie Woogie Bugle Boy' and a jitterbug demonstration to a World War II historical presentation.

Interpreters, limited only by their imagination, can explore many possibilities for including dance in their programs that will enrich and extend the experiences for their audiences. Postlewait (2001) concluded, "Throughout time people have always danced. For entertainment and social experience, dance is part of most cultures' heritage."

Visual Arts

Art museums thrive on interpretation. Most art museums now do enlightened interpretation of their collections. This requires care and sensitivity. Many local art museums actively train their public in art skills. Most offer lectures, short courses, and tours to bring people and art together. Many interpretive sites involve the artists themselves in helping the public to interpret the beauty and complexity of the place. The visual arts, in the broadest sense, help us manage the tensions and confusions of modern life and provide tools "to extend the range and impact of what we admire in works of art across our whole lives" (de Botton & Armstrong, 2013). In some instances art can be used in innovative ways to beautify the park grounds (Figure 10.5).

Figure 10.5. Art by local artists is used creatively to camouflage a maintenance building in a national park in Thailand. (TC)

Teaching Art Skills

Most local museums conduct classes to develop art skills, from photography, painting, and sculpture to art appreciation. The teachers, often local artists of some renown, charge modest fees to help aspiring artists. The classroom interaction strengthens the local community of artists and often leads to festivals and projects in particularly scenic locations. Interpreters in parks, historic sites, and museums often encourage group efforts that help them to interpret the site (Figure 10.6).

Interpreting Art

For centuries, artists have resisted having anyone "explain the meaning" of a painting or sculpture; they insist that each person should have an individual response and interpretation of the significance of the work. Artists become testy when someone seeks to explain the artist's purposes or intentions or feelings when they created the work.

Figure 10.6. The U.S. Army Corps of Engineers uses a chalk art competition to enhance artistic skills and more importantly to promote water safety. (USCOE)

The tension that exists about this subject has often inhibited museum curators in their presentation of information in art exhibits. This view pervaded the curator profession and the elite patrons of the arts. Though perhaps unintentionally, art became an exclusive thing—if one lacked the "proper background" to appreciate art, then one need not expect answers to uncouth questions.

Traditionally, art labels contained only the title of the piece, the artist, and the year or period. Further information appears in an arcane catalog, but little of it helps the visitor to relate to the picture personally. Theoretically, the visitor should get all of that by studying the art itself and responding in a personal way.

Nevertheless, the human impulse to seek meaning in works of art involves social discourse and probably always shall. Owners of art enjoy talking about their own responses to their purchases with visitors to their homes. Viewers of art like to share their impressions with other people. At seemingly every art exhibition, the questions come up: *What does this signify? What was the artist trying to express here?*

Recently, art museum curators have taken a greater interest in interpretation. They have accepted a broader view of what interpretation does. Rather than just "interpreting a painting" or "speculating on the painter's intentions," the art interpreters seek to communicate a broader range of relationships of time, place, character, and relevance of the subjects (or abstract patterns) to the modern viewer. They organize exhibits in a manner that reveals a theme. They offer an artist's retrospective and give it some perspective, rather than just hanging a series of pictures on the wall. They seek to make labels or catalogs in a way that relate to the experience and interests of the viewers. They use a story approach, weaving together the pieces into a holistic view.

Various Uses of Art at Interpretive Sites

Museums have long brought painters into their galleries to teach by example and demonstrate their skills (Figure 10.7). "Art in the Parks" programs have also brought artists and photographers into the parks. Some of the work may stay to symbolize park themes.

LaPage (2001) described the inspirational process and aesthetic experiences that artists to Maine landscapes have shared. The paintings and the recorded inspirations prove useful to both interpreters and resource managers.

Figure 10.7. "The Solitary Artist (A Study on Monet)" at the National Gallery of Art, Washington, D.C. Artist replicating Claude Monet's *Rouen Cathedral, West Façade.* (SB)

National and state/provincial parks in the United States and Canada have maintained cooperative arrangements of mutual benefit to the park (publicity), the artist (sales), and the public (learning from artists). One multifaceted event is the popular "Art along the Trail" event at the Great Plains Nature Center where artists set up their easels along the trails and paint while the public looks on (Figure 10.8). One winner is chosen by an expert panel and another is selected by voting of the general public. Winners then have their works reproduced on postcards for sale in the gift shop.

The Omaha Zoo uses art as a fund-raising device. They auction prints donated or sold at bargain prices from well-known wildlife artists and usually raise considerable sums for the Friends of the Zoo. The Sunset Zoo in Manhattan, Kansas, presents its school and public programs with theater, puppet shows, crafts, and music. A large poster contest focuses on illustrating the contestants' messages about animals.

At Parson's Lodge in the Tuolumne Meadows region of Yosemite National Park there is an annual "poetry festival" orchestrated by a supervisory interpreter. These events have attracted various poets who provide public readings at the "lodge," including Joseph Stroud and Norman Schaefer. Limited collector's edition broadsides are printed and available for sale and for framing. Authors who have attended the event to provide lectures and readings include luminaries such as Scott Russell Sanders, Roderick Nash, Terry Tempest Williams, Jack Turner, David Abram, and Bill McKibben. Carefully designed programs that bring artists to the parks produce many powerful benefits for the visitor experience.

Putting It All Together

An effective blend of music, drama, art, and stories occurs at Harpers Ferry National Historical Park on the Fourth of July. A group of volunteers from Frederick, Maryland, comes in period dress to put on an old-fashioned Fourth of July stump-speaking event as if it were 1860. Park interpreters in period dress join the crowd. As "residents" of a town with loyalties divided between the North and the about-to-secede South, the speakers stand on a porch and vigorously present both sides in a civilized debate; the organist plays music; the performers and audience sing songs appropriate to the day; the event closes with the national anthem; and the day-long picnic continues. Tourists in modern garb drift right in to the listening area and generally become engrossed in the event, just as they would have in 1860.

Figure 10.8. A family paints together at the Art Along the Trail special event at Great Plains Nature Center in Wichita, Kansas. (GPNC-RS)

Summary

The use of the arts in interpretation has proven to be extremely effective in attracting and serving visitors. Indeed, many have recognized that this style of programming strongly attracts the "unconverted"—those people who are not necessarily passionate about the environment or history. Drawing a larger and broader segment of the population to interpretive programs may well stimulate more widespread concern about cultural and environmental issues.

Art has the power and transforming qualities to move people in extraordinary ways. The greatest insight Lee Stetson gained from the study and character enactment of John Muir is the great hunger on the part of the public to hear a simple truth eloquently told. He emphasized, "The arts are a medium for the gentle awakening of the unconscious good people and we desperately need more unconscious good people becoming conscious" (Beck & Cable, 2010). This most certainly lends itself to a better world.

Literature Cited

Barrett, A., & Mowen, A. (2014). Assessing the effectiveness of artistic place-based climate change interpretation. *Journal of Interpretation Research, 19*(2), 7–24.

Beck, L., & Cable, T. (2010). *Interpretive perspectives: A collection of essays on interpreting nature and culture.* Fort Collins, CO: National Association for Interpretation.

Blank, M. (2010). Lessons from the world of theater. *2010 Interpretive Sourcebook*, NAI National Workshop, Las Vegas, Nevada, 81.

Bruchac, J. (2005). Storytelling. *The Interpreter, 1*(4), 12–13.

de Botton, A., & Armstrong, J. (2013). *Art as therapy.* New York, NY: Phaidon Press.

Edelstein, B. (2015). From the artistic director. *Performances: The Old Globe.* October 2015:7.

Evans, S. (2013). Personal beliefs and national stories: Theater in museums as a tool for exploring historical memory. *Curator: The Museum Journal, 56*(2), 189–197.

Golden, J. (2001). Listen up, interpreters. *Legacy, 12*(4), 33–34.

Goodrich, J., & Bixler, R. (2010). From hilarity to despair: A left brain look at programming emotional content. *2010 Interpretive Sourcebook*, NAI National Workshop, Las Vegas, Nevada, 25.

Griffiths, J. (2013). The exile of the arts. *Orion, 30*(5), 10–11.

LaPage, W. (2001). Nature "speaks"-Exploring the inspiration of public parklands. *Legacy, 12*(6), 28-32.

Linett, P. (2013). Ben Lillie on science and the storytelling revival. *Curator: The Museum Journal, 56*(1), 15–19.

Macklin, E., Hvenegaard, G., & Johnson, P. (2010). Improvisational theater games for children in park interpretation. *Journal of Interpretation Research, 15*(1), 7–13.

Mortan, S. (2008). Using museum theater to attract diverse audiences. In *2008 Interpretive Sourcebook*, NAI National Workshop, Portland, Oregon, 109-110.

Peoples, S. (2001). What I learned over my summer vacation. *Legacy, 12*(2), 29–32.

Postlewait, M. (2001). Dance as an interpretive tool. *Legacy.* 12(3), 9-12, 36.

Robinson, L. (1985). As legend has it—The use of folklore in environmental interpretation. *Trends, 22*(4), 46–47.

Schimitschek, M. (2017). Artists, scientists join forces. *Night + Day.* February 16, 2017:21.

Stern, J., McGarry, S., & Dunn, T. (2013). *Art of the national parks: Historic connections, Contemporary interpretations.* Santa Fe, NM: Fresco Fine Arts Publications.

Strauss, S. (1988). Storytelling and the natural world. *Journal of Interpretation, 12*(1), 4–7.

Strauss, S. (1996). *The passionate fact: Storytelling in natural history and cultural interpretation.* Golden, CO: North American Press.

Wasserman, S., & Young, M. (2013). The Great Immensity: A theatrical approach to climate change. *Curator: The Museum Journal, 56*(1), 79–86.

Wheeler, E. (2016). The craft of engagement. *Legacy, 27*(6), 29–31.

CHAPTER 11
Museums and Visitor Centers

In 2015, the "7 billion Others" exhibit, on a world tour, opened in the United States at the Museum of Photographic Arts in San Diego's Balboa Park. This global multimedia exhibition provides an immersive, technology-driven experience that reveals the collective image of the voices, perspectives, and faces of the "7 billion" human beings living on this planet.

The project was the idea of Yann Arthus-Bertrand who had been constructing a portrait of the earth through his aerial photographs. Although his travels provided a global vision of the world as seen from above, without borders, he felt something was missing from his universal testimony: the voices of the humans who live on the planet. He and his associates began collecting interviews now numbering more than 6,000, in 84 countries, in more than 50 languages.

The exhibition begins with an enormous video art display, "Mosaic," projected on a wall 46 feet in length that can be seen from the lobby. The mosaic provides seemingly countless faces as a sampling of different cultures and perspectives that make up our common humanity. Individual interviews (with subtitles) are highlighted on the screen. The exhibition then continues in small, intimate screening spaces which highlight thematic films in which people all over the globe answer questions about such universals as love, progress, war, education, health, home, and the meaning of life.

Visitors next move on to discover how the project came to be in film footage that looks at what went on from the other side of the camera. "Making-Of" is a key element of the exhibition and answers such questions as: *How did the reporters meet the people interviewed? How did the interviews unfold? What did the reporters feel after thousands of hours listening to the stories of people from all over the world?* Here visitors see yet another perspective from the other side of the lens.

The exhibition ends with a second art installation, "Messages," which highlights the final question posed by reporters, "We are 7 billion human beings on Earth; what message would you like to address to the inhabitants of the planet?" The replies are often cries from the heart of hope or despair, frustration or gratitude, anger or love, that resonate with each and every one of us.

In this exhibition it is clear, as Yann Arthus-Bertrand insists, that we *must* learn to live together. He notes, "For in struggles to come, whether it is the struggle against poverty or climate change, we cannot act on our own. The times in which one could think only of oneself or of one's own small community are over. From now on, we cannot ignore what it is that links us and the responsibilities that this implies." He concludes that this exhibition encourages us to take action through learning more about "those Others who are so far away, yet so close to us."

As you look into the eyes of people from all over the world, confiding their deepest fears and dreams, the wisdom of this project is revealed. There are no "Others."

As noted above, museums and visitor centers provide experiences that illuminate and inspire our lives. Museums are places that encourage deeper learning through first-hand exposure to objects both local and from around the world. Museums offer restoration, for many visitors, from day-to-day routines and obligations. And museums can prompt us to action as we learn more about natural history, social justice, science, culture and other issues that have a bearing on the lives of us all (Figure 11.1).

What a Museum Does

"In everything museums do, they must remember the cornerstone on which the whole enterprise rests: to make a positive difference in the quality of people's lives. Museums that do that matter—
they matter a great deal."

–Stephen Weil (2002)

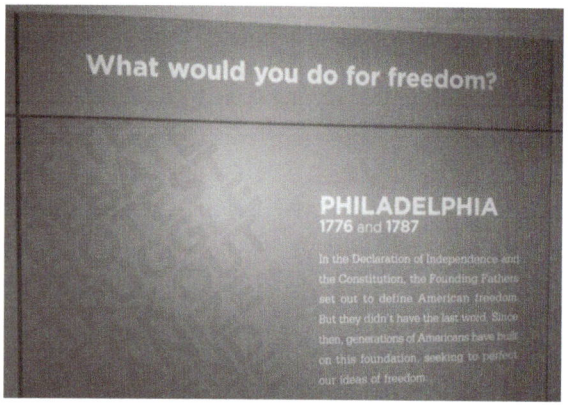

Figure 11.1. Modern museums are places of reflection and self-examination and they tackle universal concepts such as the meaning of freedom. (TC)

What does a museum do? Museums function primarily as places for people, not just places for storing artifacts and collections. At the turn of the 21st century, museum directors and curators examined their roles in communities through professional journals, conferences, and intense internal analysis. Archibald (2001) described a growing consensus of greater interest in the community (outreach—delivering services) and in bringing the community in (inreach—allowing the public into the institution for *their* own purposes). He urged trustees, curators, and directors to embrace the notion that "the public makes its own meanings in museums." The museum facilitates that meaning making. This implies that the public and the museum join as partners. Archibald (2001) further noted that "museums are vital to the future of our communities and our nation." As "a place to build the future," a museum serves special roles, including the following:

> Museums function primarily as places for people.

- To reflect what humans have and value
- To examine the ways people describe the universe, existence, and themselves
- To evaluate the consequences of choices past, current, and future
- To engender exploration of values, common and disparate, such as the value of clean water, biodiversity, beauty, art, stories, a wild animal, a forest, the community's future

Graffagnio (2001) echoed the desirability of museums becoming more community centered and community responsive. He called on historical groups to emphasize how history can link the past to help shape the future.

Defining the Clientele

"The museums of the future in this democratic land should be adapted to the needs of the mechanic, the factory operator, the day laborer, the salesman, and the clerk, as much as to those of the professional man and the man of leisure....The public museum is, first of all, for the benefit of the public."

–George Brown Goode (1888)

Most societies have opened museums to everyone. The free or low-cost museum offers visitors the option of seeing and studying the works, the stories, the science of the past, along with facts about the present and future. Thus, scientific and artistic knowledge was opened to all, and no longer confined to aristocratic classes.

How museums relate to those who visit them continues to be a topic of importance. Zahava Doering (2010) presented three ways in which museums consider their visitors as either strangers, guests, or clients. The view of visitors as *strangers* occurs when museums contend that their primary responsibility is to the collection and not to the public. Visitors are viewed as *guests* to the extent that they are provided for, primarily by means of "educational" activities. Finally, visitors may be considered *clients* when the museum believes that its primary responsibility is to be accountable to the visitor. Doering (2010) concludes, "social trends will force museums to treat visitors as clients."

A great deal of introspection by the museum profession is evident in the various journals and books about museums. Current concerns include uneasiness about the museum's relationship to the general public and methods of outreach to attract those who don't currently visit museums including disenfranchised ethnic and socioeconomic groups. Outreach is also focusing on persons with disabilities, youth, and elders.

Museum Philosophy

Museums have changed dramatically in the past few decades to increasingly focus on the people who visit. The American Alliance of Museums 2016-2020 Strategic Plan states, We Believe:

- Museums educate and inspire, nourish minds and spirits, enrich lives, and create healthy communities.
- Museum experiences are characterized by encounters with objects and living populations, stories, experts, and primary learning experiences in welcoming places, supported by scholarship and knowledge.
- In the integrity of research, the preservation of cultural heritage and the celebration of human achievement.
- Our strengths lie in both the diversity of the people we represent and the breadth of museums we engage.
- In active participation in the global community and embracing international perspectives. (American Alliance of Museums *2016-2020 Strategic Plan*, 2016)

> "Both museums and visitor centers interpret to the public."

Interpreting in Museums and Visitor Centers

Both museums and visitor centers interpret to the public. The basic interpretive concepts do not differ much, so they are treated together throughout this book. Similarly, museum researchers John Falk and Lynn Dierking (2013) use the term *museum* to refer to a wide range of free-choice/informal educational institutions including traditional art and natural history museums, "zoos, arboretums, botanical gardens, science centers, historic homes, interpretive sites like national parks, visitor centers," and so on. However, some distinctions separate museums from centers that relate to the approach toward the subject matter.

The *museum* contains original objects, brought for display and study in a convenient place, close to where people live or travel. The objects often come from afar. The museum generally displays the artifacts and messages indoors. The museum itself serves as the destination for the visitor.

The *visitor center* or *interpretive center* may also present original objects, but they come from just outside the door as representative of the immediate place (Figure 11.2). The center, located at or near the resource, serves as a portal to the "living museum" just beyond, which is often the visitor's principal destination. Visitor centers and nature centers may be found in forests, wildlife refuges, state and national parks, and Corps of Engineers rivers and lakes (Figure 11.3). Many hundreds of counties and cities also have their own nature centers, interpretive centers, and visitor centers. Likewise, private, nonprofit, industrial, and other organizations maintain interpretive centers at their facilities.

Yet another facility is the *tourist information center* that may offer local or regional attraction information, as well as orienting visitors to recreational opportunities. In this instance, locations relate to travel pat-

Figure 11.2. Visitor centers, unlike museums, focus on what is just outside the window. (TC)

Figure 11.3. The U.S. Army Corps of Engineers' Grand Ecore Visitor Center serves as a portal to the historic Red River in Louisiana. After passing through the exhibit hall, visitors exit the building to experience the magnificent river below. (TC)

terns—at the portals of a state or province, or at major road junctions. These information centers often have impressive exhibitions and bookstore/gift shops.

Overall, museums and visitor centers connect people with special places that enrich their lives and interpretation is an important part of the equation. Although museums and various centers may be different in some ways, all benefit from quality interpretation to generate optimal visitor experiences. Both museums and visitor centers serve as interpretive institutions to the greater world around them.

Michael Gross and Ron Zimmerman (2002) state, "Even the most humble center provides shelter, comfort, and an escape from the mundane. The best centers expand our vision and offer insights into our deep connections with the earth and each other." Indeed, "despite the wide variety of museums, all are *essentially* institutions of public education" (Falk & Dierking, 2013).

> Museums and visitor centers connect people with special places that enrich their lives.

Figure 11.4. Balboa Park is the home of 17 museums including natural history, art, science, anthropology, a sports hall of fame, a botanic garden, and the San Diego Zoo. (LB)

This *wide variety* of facilities includes the following (Figure 11.4):

- Botanical gardens
- Zoos
- Anthropology museums
- Art museums
- Galleries
- Children's museums
- History museums
- Park museums
- Living history villages/farms
- Historic trail centers
- Natural history museums
- Industry museums
- Sports halls of fame
- Park interpretive and nature centers
- Tribal cultural centers
- Military museums
- Aquariums
- Science/technology museums
- Paleontology museums

Falk and Dierking (2013) state, "Museums have become a growth industry and have emerged as one of the most important leisure-time venues in the developed and, increasingly, the developing world." The museum tradition thrives on all continents, with vigorous, long-term efforts throughout Latin America, Southeast Asia, Japan, China, Australia, and New Zealand. Africa has some of the oldest and some of the newest museums. Due to the current rapid growth of tourism in equatorial Africa, many new visitor centers and museums now focus on tourists. The former USSR and eastern Europe created museums out of churches and castles, opening up the treasures of Czars and kings to public view.

Historically, museums have placed their collections and research over that of education in terms of institutional priorities. Within the past few decades most museums have shifted to serving as centers for public learning. Furthermore, museums are placing more emphasis on understanding their audiences and finding connections with the local community. The American Alliance of Museums has formally put education and interpretation into the forefront of its criteria for accreditation, thus officially headlining it as one of the key activities of museum work as follows:

- The museum clearly states its overall educational goals, philosophy, and messages, and demonstrates that its activities are in alignment with them.
- The museum understands the characteristics and needs of its existing and potential audiences and uses this understanding to inform its interpretation.
- The museum's interpretive content is based on appropriate research.
- Museums conducting primary research do so according to scholarly standards.
- The museum uses techniques, technologies, and methods appropriate to its educational goals, content, audiences, and resources.
- The museum presents accurate and appropriate content for each of its audiences.
- The museum demonstrates consistent high quality in its interpretive activities.
- The museum assesses the effectiveness of its interpretive activities and uses those results to plan and improve its activities. (aam-us.org, 2016)

History of Museums

The background of the word museum (a Greek word meaning *temple of the Muses*) suggests some of the diversity of themes found there. The Muses of Greek mythology were the nine daughters of Zeus and Mnemosyne. Each presided over one of the arts to inspire mankind: Clio, muse of history; Calliope of epic poetry; Erato of love poetry; Polyhymnia of sacred song; Euterpe of music; Thalia of comedy; Melpomene of tragedy; Terpsichore of dance; and Urania of astronomy. Obviously, the range of subjects has expanded beyond the special domains of the nine muses.

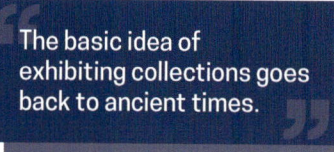
" The basic idea of exhibiting collections goes back to ancient times. "

To collect, conserve, and exhibit precious and beautiful things seems to be human nature. The basic idea of exhibiting collections goes back to ancient times. The Greeks who went to the Delphi Oracle carried statues and other gifts that were kept in treasuries, or temple-like warehouses. Today, many of these treasures can be seen in modern museums near the ruins of the treasury buildings at Delphi and other points throughout Greece (and in other European museums).

The same is true of Egypt and China and other ancient civilizations that have not been totally ravaged. Chinese, Japanese, Muslim, and Christian tombs, temples, mosques, and cathedrals served as repositories for precious relics and art work.

In medieval Europe, princes, dukes, kings, and bishops collected avidly. Most European royal private collections featured works of art. The objects served as a form of prestige and accumulated wealth that could be used to raise funds for military campaigns and other state expenses. One result of the Crusades was the transfer of pillaged Middle Eastern art works to western European collections.

European colonization of Africa likewise produced numerous natural, mineral, and cultural specimens for the growing number of show places in Europe. Back in the seats of political and economic power, people could see the wonders of the far-flung empires. The collections and their study did much to advance science and to broaden knowledge of the diversity of the world. Only much later did the colonies themselves enjoy these benefits. Indeed, the now independent African nations have advanced their own museum traditions. They proceed with enthusiasm, despite weak funding in most cases. They recognize the values to citizens and from foreign tourists. International agencies help with some of the financial and technological assistance.

Most early museums had little or no educational function. When wealthy individuals collected and stored precious metals, art, or artifacts in castles or churches, few people saw these treasures. Later, display took precedence, and then education became important. The educational value of many museums became evident in the Victorian period. Victorians were the great museum builders. "They sought to collect and assemble materials, to categorize and organize them to try to comprehend the technological, cultural, and natural information explosion" (Vogel, 1991).

Interpretive or educational museums in the United States trace back to painter/collector/public educator Charles Wilson Peale in Philadelphia (Vogel, 1991). Peale opened his Museum of Natural History in the mid-1780s with the patronage of Thomas Jefferson. His rather eclectic collection included scientific curiosities, mounted animals and birds, patriotic symbols, and paintings of the heroes of the American Revolution. The museum attracted many who became influential in their own right including painters George Catlin and John James Audubon.

Peale's museum started in his home, then moved to the American Philosophical Society and subsequently to the State House (now known as Independence Hall). Many decades later, P. T. Barnum bought the collections (Vogel, 1991). Peale's museum helped to create an informed public which the new nation needed for success. The key was that it served not just the elite nor one man's private collection. Peale (and Barnum) reached out to educate the public, and to offer knowledge—a chance to see the real things, beyond what one could see with personal resources. They "let the rabble in" and the "rabble" went out as better informed, stronger citizens.

National museums now represent part of most nations' cultural identities. For example, Mexico's world-famous anthropology museum helps to create pride in the artistry and intelligence of its many native peoples. British policy extends support to local and regional museums in the national interest. Local museums throughout England receive support through national subsidies with Parliament's authorization to collect and display local historic, artistic, industrial, and natural features.

Some nations have used museums as political and social tools. In Russia, the revolution of 1917 crushed out the "royalty" of the Czars and ushered in an egalitarian philosophy. The new government opened many royal collections for at least two reasons: to demonstrate the opulence of the oppressive Czars and to encourage education and culture for all the people. The artifacts of history and culture helped to engender national pride even while displaying the marked discrepancies in wealth between the rulers and the ruled. Any pre-1990 visitor to Moscow and Leningrad could not help but be impressed at the long lines of museum attendees, even in cold weather. Likewise, the numbers of palaces, churches, and other buildings used as museums is impressive.

U.S. Government Museum Development

Many early government interpretive museums and visitor centers started with private impetus and funding, often with individual benefactors, curators, or rangers taking the initiative. The 1846 bequest to the United States from Englishman James Smithson, who had never seen the United States, came with a philosophy. He saw the museum as an interpretive medium "for the increase and diffusion of knowledge among men." Today's 15 Smithsonian museums plus the National Zoo support a large research component as well as many diverse educational/interpretive programs (Figure 11.5).

Another key example is the National Park Service. Ranger Frank Pinkley started a collection and display of artifacts and structural diagrams at Casa Grande National Monument in Arizona in 1901, long before there was a park service or any official effort to set up museums. National Park Service exhibits and museums officially began in Yosemite National Park, where forester Ansel Hall's collection of natural materials and cultural artifacts opened to the public in the summer of 1920 in a ranger office.

Figure 11.5. "The Castle" of the Smithsonian Institution represents the beginnings of the U.S. national museum. (DK)

Congress acted slowly to fund the National Park Service's early efforts (1918-1924), although agency officials believed in the idea of park interpretive museums. NPS Director Stephen Mather wrote in his 1920 annual report to the Secretary of the Interior: "One of the most important matters to receive earnest consideration is the early establishment of adequate museums in every one of our parks" (Burns, 1941). Nevertheless, it took financial support from private groups for public park museums to begin. Their success finally convinced the U.S. Congress that interpretive museums were popular and important.

An earlier perspective of museums being primarily about collections, in the United States, has shifted toward museums as places that promote social inclusivity (Schultz,

2011). This came about in part during the 1960s and 1970s with significant uprisings against injustices that included civil rights issues. As a result, many cultural groups questioned how their cultures were being represented in museums.

> "An earlier perspective of museums has shifted toward museums as places that promote social inclusivity."

For example, the American Indian Movement was born out of these upheavals and argued that museums represented colonial attitudes. Other criticisms focused on the display and collection of human remains and sacred objects. The Native American Graves Protection and Repatriation Act of 1990 required that federal agencies or other institutions receiving federal funds return Native American cultural items to descendant communities. Therefore, the display of skeletal remains, funerary objects, and other sacred objects in museum collections has been significantly reduced. Nonetheless, in 2016 the National Park Service was "astonished" to find out that a superintendent at Effigy Mounds National Monument stole the museum's collection of ancient human remains that he stored in his garage for two decades (to avoid returning them to affiliated tribes) and a subsequent superintendent oversaw construction of boardwalks through the monument's burial and ceremonial mounds (Foley, 2016; Williams, 2016).

The U.S. Government continues to promote social inclusivity. In 2016 then-President Barack Obama declared the Stonewall Inn and its surrounding area as the Stonewall National Monument. Located in New York City's Greenwich Village, the Stonewall Inn was the site of a 1969 uprising when patrons of the bar fought back against police harassment. This was a major turning point in the modern-day LGBT rights movement and the bar continues to be an important place of meeting and celebration such as when the Supreme Court legalized same-sex marriage. In establishing the monument, Obama said:

> I believe our national parks should reflect the full story of our country—the richness and diversity and uniquely American spirit that has always defined us. (June 24, 2016)

Similarly, the National Museum of African American History and Culture, opened on the National Mall, in 2016. Obama said that the institution, which was decades in the making, was a powerful place because "it tells the story of all of us." As the nation's first black president wiped away a tear he spoke of how slaves were "bought and sold, and bid like cattle." He continued:

> This national museum helps to tell a richer and fuller story of who we are. It helps us better understand the lives, yes, of the president, but also the slave. The industrialist, but also the porter; the keeper of the status quo, but also of the activist seeking to overthrow that status quo; the teacher or the cook, alongside the statesman. And by knowing this other story we better understand ourselves and each other. (September 24, 2016)

Different Museums for Different Purposes

The simplest classification of museum collections divides them into four types: art, historical, science, and general. The diversity of museums and collections defy such neat and simple classification, however. Museums cover art, science, natural history, human history, industry, religious groups, trades, professions, and transportation. Specialized museums exist for children, and others may focus on farms or military equipment. Others feature automobiles, glass, native peoples, cowboys, police, sports heroes, and loggers. They include planetaria, aquaria, herbaria, botanical, and zoological gardens. The following discussion is an overview of several different types of museums.

History Museums

Almost every city and county maintains some kind of historical artifact collection. It may be exhibited in the most modest circumstances—a room in the courthouse basement or an old store on Main Street. Or it could be a neighborhood of stores and houses and factories staffed by costumed interpreters, such as Richmondtown on Staten Island, New York.

Preserving facts and giving perspective to memory constitutes a key function of the historical museum. The several Holocaust museums in the world guard a negative set of memories—the extermination of six million Jews during World War II by the Nazis. The aim is to remind people of their potential for inhumanity, highlighted by the slogan, "Never again." General Dwight D. Eisenhower, Allied Commander for the European theater of war, visited the labor and death camps as the liberation proceeded. His summary of the horrors appears in several of the Holocaust Museums and dramatizes this role of museums in protecting factual reality. Eisenhower correctly foresaw the tendency to deny the reality of the Holocaust. Less than 50 years after World War II, some members of a new generation of Germans claimed vehemently that the stories told by survivors could not be true. Eisenhower's words and the ample material and photographic proof in several museums preserve the grim reality for all to ponder:

> "Preserving facts and giving perspective to memory constitutes a key function of the historical museum."

> The things I saw beggar description…The visual evidence and the verbal testimony of starvation, cruelty, and bestiality were…overpowering…I made the visit deliberately in order to be in a position to give *first-hand* evidence of these things if ever, in the future, there develops a tendency to charge these allegations merely to "propaganda." (April 15, 1945)

David Fleming (2016) notes that the role of museums goes far beyond the custody and care of collections as an end in itself, but rather is a process of public enlightenment and improvement. He argues that the "modern, socially relevant museum" should not be *neutral* when it comes to issues of human rights and social justice.

Historic Buildings

In some cases, the museum is the resource itself. "A historic building authentically furnished and exhibited becomes a museum" (Lewis, 1976). This occurs in most historic homes (e.g., James Whitcomb Riley House) as well as in ruins of earlier cultures (e.g., Mesa Verde National Park).

Conservation and restoration require accuracy and authenticity. The building's doors, stairways, windows, and carpeting must remain in or get restored to historic condition. On the other hand, modern laws and ethics require a system of access for visitors with limited mobility. Reinforcement for durability and interpretation to handle hundreds of visitors per day will also modify the historic conditions somewhat. The need for balance of appropriate preservation and interpretation often produces ingenious solutions and compromises.

Rural and Agricultural Museums

In 1891, Artur Hazelius founded the Skånsen Folk Museum near Stockholm, reputedly the first open-air museum. Hazelius felt that exhibiting old structures and farm implements alone presented only a dry shell of the past, so he added appropriately dressed people to demonstrate and tell the story of rural traditional Swedish life. Hazelius described the aim:

> We shall rebuild the old farmsteads…People shall behave in those houses as they did before, the cat shall lie and purr by the stove, the dog shall sun itself in front of its kennel, the animals shall graze on the meadow (Edenheim, 1995).

This outdoor, first-person, living history museum shows old farmsteads and tells the story of each. It seeks to depict a whole of the array of Swedish life and culture. Today, the portrayal of living history has spread throughout most of the world.

In the 1920s, the Rockefeller family funded Colonial Williamsburg, using many of the same concepts. Every year, several hundred thousand visitors delve into a bygone era so they can better understand the present by looking at the past. Adjoining the College of William and Mary, this site recreates the time of the founding fathers of the United States when Thomas Jefferson walked the same streets. Colonial Williamsburg operates to the great benefit of the visiting public as well as offering technical and inspirational support to others who seek to put on this type of programming.

Museums such as this lift us above the lament that history is boring. They show what happened to the commoner; they strengthen a sense of heritage. These museums contain people who relive the past, every day. In this type of museum, staff emerge from behind the glass into a human environment, sweeping visitors into their time and lives. The physical evidence of the rural way of life in some past era surrounds the visitor. A small village has buildings devoted to various trades and professions important to survival and comfort. The typical rural village or farm museum includes at least one farmhouse, tool shed, garden, and small field. A barn, several farm animals, a corral, and pasture show the vital role of livestock. The fields and pastures are usually smaller than the originals, serving as interpretive fields and gardens. Here visitors see animals and crops as close-up demonstrations.

> "Museums such as this lift us above the lament that history is boring."

Near Plymouth Rock, a private village recreates the past. Plimoth Plantation takes the visitor into the 1620s with its architecture, clothing, and economy. First-person portrayals include the unsung pilgrims of Plymouth—the roofer, the milkmaid, the indentured servants. Someone may explain that Governor Bradford is busy governing and that Miles Standish went out on a surveying job, but should come home this evening, if you care to wait. Meanwhile, there's work to do, such as gardening, milking, preparing the stew, weaving, blacksmithing, and keeping more than 30 buildings in repair, if you care to watch.

Morwellham Quay, Devon, England, a commercial outdoor living history museum, revives an old mining and shipping town, with costumed interpreters and sales persons of the past century. It offers various experiences such as horse-drawn wagon rides, a tram tour into a tin mine, and a photo opportunity complete with Victorian clothing for everyone.

In Kentucky, Daniel Boone's village of Boonsboro lives again in a state park. Massachusetts' venerable Old Sturbridge Village, South Carolina's Middleton Plantation, and Iowa's Living History Farms represent the many outstanding efforts—mostly self-supporting or foundation supported—to bring history alive.

Art Museums

Hundreds of art museums and galleries present all types of artistic accomplishments, from the great masters to the work of amateurs. National museums and galleries collect and display representative work of their own citizens, as well as world classics. Local museums usually have great flexibility to present a range of local artists as well as many traveling exhibitions from the famous to new finds. These local museums also foster the arts through classes, workshops, and local festivals.

Art museums sometimes lead and sometimes follow in interpretive philosophy. On the one hand, there has been a long tradition of letting art interpret itself. Most artists insist that individual reactions should remain purely individual. No one should presume to "explain what the artist wanted to depict." On the other hand, many visitors and museum members wish art museums would help them to do more than mutter approval as they gaze at puzzling paintings or pottery. Furthermore, many visitors want to know more about the fundamentals—to develop their own skills to learn painting, photography, or sculpture at the museum from skilled people.

Interpretation surely will play a growing role in art museums in the future. Alain de Botton and John Armstrong (2013) suggested, "The agenda for art in a liberal society would be to assist the individual soul in its search for consolation, self-understanding, and fulfillment." These authors continued, "Artworks would look to commemorate, give hope, echo and dignify suffering, rebalance and guide, assist self-knowledge and communication, expand horizons, and inspire appreciation."

Specialized Museums

A great number of museums focus on specialized topics from children's museums to technology museums. Many of these are owned and operated by a family or small enterprise. Others grew out of a group of hobbyists (e.g., model railroaders, hunter/conservationists). Some record the history of a prominent individual (e.g., John Deere, President Benjamin Harrison, John Wayne, Frank Lloyd Wright, Elvis Presley). Some archive and display the history of a business or industry. Other specialized museums include the International Surfing Museum in Huntington Beach, California.

> "A great number of museums focus on specialized topics."

Tribal cultural centers and museums often unite the art, history, traditions, and aspirations of one group of people. Many of the 574 federally recognized tribal nations and dozens of other groups of native peoples have recently exerted strong efforts to revive and share their cultural heritage through museums and cultural centers. Tribal gaming laws of the 1990s provided wherewithal to some of the tribes to build elaborate, state-of-the-art exhibits in beautiful buildings. Others maintain more modest facilities but do excellent cultural work.

A museum with a unique twist specializes in Women of the West. It operated without an exhibit building until its merger with the Autry Museum of Western Heritage. Its exhibits appear online (wowmuseum.org). Just as any other museum, local programs and lectures support the mission—to inspire women of the present by introducing them to women of the past. Monthly book reviews, profiles of women writers, traveling exhibits, lesson plans for teachers, and community event participation keep its staff busy. The virtual museum has a virtual store offering tangible books, mugs, a T-shirt, and prints. It has a distinguished board of trustees, organized in 1992, and buoyed since 1996 by the endorsement of five honorary trustees: Lady Bird Johnson, Betty Ford, Rosalynn Carter, Nancy Reagan, and Barbara Bush.

Many museums are specialized as science or art museums. However, some museums have experimented with how science can inspire art. Now there is also interest in how art can inspire interest and learning about science. For example, Alan Friedman (2013) discussed three different types of artworks as tools for communicating science in museums. *Particle Fever* is a film about particle physicists and the mysterious Higgs Boson, *The Great Immensity* is a musical about climate change, and *Guardians* is a ballet co-produced by and performed in an aquarium. Indeed, interest in promoting science through the arts has led to a STEAM (Science, Technology, Engineering, Art, Math) movement to teach art among the STEM disciplines.

The goal of some specialized museums is to use exhibits to provoke particular feelings in visitors. In England, which has long been a leader in museum studies and innovations, the Museum of Emotions provided opportunities and space for visitors to scream, sigh, and experience love, lust, and to work through the seven stages of grieving (Patey, 2016). Similarly, London's Museum of Empathy was developed with the belief that empathy is one of the most important skills we can develop, and that the world needs an empathy revolution as an antidote to consumerism, narcissism, and homogenization of culture (Patey, 2016). At the Empathy Museum, in an exhibit titled Walk a Mile in My Shoes, visitors enter a shoe shop, try on shoes with the only information being the person's name who wore the shoes. They then walk a mile in those shoes while wearing headphones to listen to an MP-3 story about the person who wore those shoes. Visitors step into life of a Vietnam vet, refugee, neurosurgeon, ex-prisoner, lifeboat operator, sex worker, or myriad other personal stories. Experiencing another person's life by wearing and literally walking in their shoes, creates a physical, emotional, and imaginative journey leading to empathy—the trait that makes us most human (Patey, 2016).

Museum Programming (With a Look to the Future)

People seek museums for a special kind of education. The key to getting messages across seems to come from visitors getting involved in the interpretive activities of the institution. Many ways exist to get visitors involved. For example, the timber company train at Laona, Wisconsin, doesn't just sit on a siding for people to see the machine once used in railroad logging. It loads people into train cars (at a few dollars per ride), cranks up the steam, and takes them through a bit of the company's managed forest. Then visitors get out to wander around an old farmstead and feed the livestock. They may also take a short pontoon boat ride through the company's wetlands or a wagon ride through the big trees before they climb aboard for the short train ride back. These visitors get directly involved in the subject—an actively managed forest.

> "Many ways exist to get visitors involved."

These kinds of museums encourage the involvement of all the senses where possible. Facilities can provide for touching, smelling, hearing, and tasting, as well as seeing. If an artifact is too delicate, use replicas that people can handle. Interpreters have often allowed visitors to use replicas to grind and taste cornmeal with a mano and metate, or to write with a quill pen, or to don articles of period clothing. They have added to static visual exhibits with audio devices and the sounds of specimens, such as a rattlesnake, songbird, or blacksmith's hammer. Appropriate odors enhance interest in a period kitchen, a granary, and even a medieval street scene. The two learning principles these examples present are that (a) people remember what they do more easily than what they just see, and (b) people learn through reinforcement by using several senses.

The use of citizen science has become increasingly prominent (Figure 11.6), as has crowdsourcing, by attracting input from a large number of interested people to work on natural history and cultural projects. In the cultural arena, crowdsourcing projects ask the public to help transcribe, describe, locate, or categorize cultural heritage resources. Mia Ridge (2013) suggested that crowdsourcing projects "can also be a powerful platform for audience engagement with museums, offering truly deep and valuable connection with cultural heritage through online collaboration around shared goals or resources."

Consistent with a different approach to programming, after-hours functions have become common throughout the country and may include everything from drinks, to live music, to staged readings, to food trucks at museums.

An outside-the-box style of museum programming has received considerable attention through its attempts to spice up the museum experience. Museum Hack is among the forerunners in creating new museum experiences. Their tours offer a fun and unconventional way (referred to as "renegade") of exploring renowned museums such as the Metropolitan Museum of Art, the American Museum of Natural History, and the National Gallery of Art. Guides customize tours based on their own favorite exhibits and specific galleries the group wants to learn more about.

Museum Hack offers seven reasons their tours are different (museumhack.com):

- **We curate by passion.** We talk about pieces we are excited about. Furthermore, the excitement of being reverently irreverent is infectious and people can feel that sort of energy.

Figure 11.6. The Hobbs State Park Visitor Center, Arkansas, devotes space for a Citizen Science Corner, which is a nexus for data collection about the park's butterflies and other wildlife. (TC)

- **We make content accessible.** One of our mantras is that people have been people since they've been people. The artists and scientists behind the objects are people, the people depicted in the art are people, the people in the museum's history are people, and people have been doing people stuff forever. We reframe the artworks and artifacts using storytelling and pop-culture references—because a lot of the characters in history have modern counterparts.
- **We are low tech/high touch.** We like to get to know our guests, which is why we have a nine person-per-guide limit. (Note that although Museum Hack advocates a high-touch approach, they find creative ways to incorporate technology that people commonly use, such as their smartphone cameras.)
- **We know how to fight museum fatigue.** We address the perils of the condition and fight to prevent it. We try to balance content delivery with active participation. This may include games and activities, personalizing the experience through taking photos, incorporating short "physical and brain breaks," which might mean a water break, a minute of just walking around without guided content, some quick stretching or yoga, five minutes to write a postcard about the experience, or on evening tours a glass of wine. (Note that museum fatigue was first described by Benjamin Gilman (1916), and its precise meaning is somewhat controversial. Although the concept has changed over time, it generally refers to the decline of energy that occurs as a museum visit continues. This condition often results in observing fewer exhibits and spending less time at them as the museum visit wears on. Museum fatigue is generally considered to be a combination of physical and mental tiredness.)
- **We have the Outsider/Insider scoop.** With Museum Hack you get the insider scoop from an outsider. We're not affiliated with the museum, so we'll tell you

things you'd never hear from an official guide including conversations that may be a little irreverent, sometimes revealing scandals, or too "low brow" for your average tour.

- **We mix it up and keep it fast paced.** We think of our tours as a tasting menu of the museum, showing off some of the choice pieces. Some will be thought provoking, some will have a great history lesson built in, some will spark debate, and some will be funny. We won't spend forever at each piece; we keep it moving.
- **We break down traditional museum behavior conventions.** You don't have to be rigid and silent. You should be respectful of the artifacts and other museum visitors. But there's no reason for people to be intimidated, or feel they're not worthy or educated enough to pass judgment or have an opinion about something.

Museum Hack especially tries to appeal to millennials. Although baby boomers have supported museums, they are gradually aging out, and museums across the country are wondering who will take their place. So museums are looking to become more personalized and engaging, without compromising their core mission. Part of the strategy is to simply get people over the threshold of reluctance to visit a museum. Yet, upon crossing the threshold once, and having a good experience, they are more likely to do it again. Herein builds a new generation of museum visitors. More visitors translates into stronger museums.

The popularity of Museum Hack suggests that people are actively seeking an alternative museum experience, and perhaps the traditional way is not the only way. Indeed, their Renegade Museum Tours are consistently ranked among the top things to do in New York City, Washington, D.C., and San Francisco.

This irreverent approach to experiencing a museum may not be for everyone. Yet much of what Museum Hack advocates, and is doing, is interpretive in nature. They want to make a difference. They want people to have fun. They want people to come back. Their intent is that you have "an experience you will remember for the rest of your life." And they back that with their 110% guarantee—if you don't have a good time they will refund all of your money, plus a little extra (and they will even "eat the museum admission fees").

> "People are actively seeking an alternative museum experience."

Museum/Visitor Center Design

The architectural design of many older museums reflects the treasury influence of ancient times. Only in the 20th century did the architecture begin to show the new emphasis on public education. The use of natural materials and architecture that blended into the landscape of national parks led the way toward museums that focused on visitor use and relevance to the environment being interpreted.

Visitor center/museum design itself can convey part of the message and express the theme. Gross and Zimmerman (2002) indicate that interpretive centers are "contemporary temples in sacred places" and that ultimately they may serve to "illuminate the spirit of the site." Various elements can be woven together to create a "harmonious design" (Gross, Zimmerman, & Buchholz, 2006).

For most agencies, the center must be accessible by all, energy efficient (many seeking LEED certifications), constructible at a low cost, and have a low visual and physical impact on the site. First and foremost, however, comes the experience offered to visitors—welcome, comfort, orient, inform, and invite participation with an easy flow. The prime interpretive aim allows the visitor to orient and focus on the resource.

Entry and Theme

The importance of the museum (and visitor center) lobby is absent from much of the museum community research and yet the entry is the first encounter visitors have and the last impression they take home and share with others (Mortensen, Rudloff, & Vestergaard, 2014). Of course, there is no perfect model for the entrance hall/lobby/community space of a museum or visitor center; this will vary according to the site. General guidelines are presented that focus on the theme of the site. Upon entering, give visitors a perception of where they are and why they came (Figure 11.7). Provide answers that respond to such visitor questions as: *What is this place? Why is it here? What are the main attractions? What can we do here? Where do we start?* Even the informed person will enjoy a brief statement of the theme and the special character of the place. Therefore, the entry theme should do the following:

- Intrigue without perplexing the visitor
- Offer a clear message that illuminates even the repeat visitor
- Provoke but not be too cute or contentious
- Be profound but not obscure

Figure 11.7. Visitor centers provide visitors with an initial orientation and an opportunity for them to get their bearings. (TC)

The simple theme at the Wright Brothers' Memorial near Kitty Hawk, North Carolina, lets everyone know the significance of the place: *Here Man First Flew*.

Overall, it has been said that good design is invisible and immerses users in an experience. This is also true for a well-designed exhibition that may represent a transformative experience for visitors. A thoughtfully designed exhibition creates a powerful experience for visitors that engages the senses, stimulates the intellect, and frees the imagination (Beghetto, 2014).

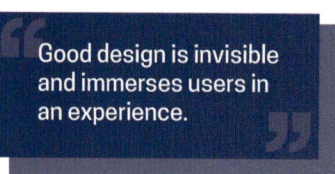
"Good design is invisible and immerses users in an experience."

Exhibitions

The exhibits are considered the "heart" of the museum experience and should be well planned and organized for ease of navigation, ready comprehension, and convenience.

Besides regular "permanent" exhibits, most museums and visitor centers offer short-term exhibits as well. Many visitors to local and state parks, museums, and nature centers make repeat visits. By knowing their visitation patterns, one can plan the exhibit rotation accordingly. Highlight seasonal changes or mark an anniversary to emphasize timely aspects of the interpretive theme. When some exhibits stay up too long, they lose much of their value. To counteract this, the Pratt Museum in Homer, Alaska, regularly changes one of its four major exhibit areas by featuring recent paintings or photographs by local artists. This keeps local interest alive and helps to spur on local artistic productivity. Further discussion of exhibits will be covered in Chapter 12.

Auditoriums

For auditoriums that orient visitors, the simpler and more flexible the design, the greater the net economic benefit in most cases. Only when a room will be heavily and almost constantly used for a single purpose (e.g., a daily dose of 8–20 showings of an orientation video) should it be outfitted exclusively as a theater. Then the facility would require another room for *flexible* use. A big room that has only one possible use will be hard to rent, expensive to alter, and may sit empty much of the time. Professional contractors can provide recommendations on design from an experienced perspective.

Fixating on recent technology may build in obsolescence. Sensible design will allow for using reliable, durable, excellent materials and provide flexibility for new equipment that will soon arise. Simplicity and flexibility in design seems prudent. Sometimes, simpler technologies produce more effective interpretation.

Other Museum Facilities and Services

- **Parking**. Museum administrators should strive to provide parking that is reasonably close to the museum and offers ways for visitors to easily remember where they parked their cars. Convenient and available parking means less stress for visitors (as they begin their experience) and helps prevent later fatigue. When possible, the walk to the museum should be a thematic introduction (with advance organizers) to what the museum offers. Keep in mind the museum visit actually begins in the parking lot.
- **Information desk**. Entry personnel should greet visitors as they arrive and ideally provide a brief orientation and answer any questions. In large museums, a map is often provided. Some centers have opted for an open plan where

interpreters are exposed to the public at all times to increase ready visitor contact. But the interpreters and docents also need space that is not interrupted, for work on program preparation, scheduling, correspondence, and projects.

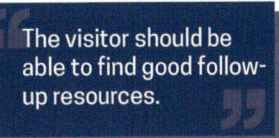
> The visitor should be able to find good follow-up resources.

- **Bookstore/gift shop**. The visitor should be able to find good follow-up resources here that relate to the museum, as well as quality, thematic mementos that will bring back positive memories of the experience. Larger museums may have many smaller gift shops scattered throughout that relate to nearby exhibitions. The "job" of the gift shop is to "ensure that the lessons of the museum, which concern beauty, meaning, and the enlargement of the spirit, can endure in the visitor far beyond the actual tour of the premises and be put into use in daily life" (de Botton & Armstrong, 2013). The role of gift shops is discussed in more detail in Chapter 16.
- **Picnic area/restaurant**. Many museums now serve food. Strive to provide healthy, tasty menu items that are locally produced and/or relate to the theme of the museum. Note that visitors deem the quality of the gift shop and food services as a very important component of the *overall* museum experience.
- **Restrooms**. The rest rooms should be easily located and clean. Some museums have related exhibit content in the restroom; others may provide fresh flowers, and the Arizona-Sonora Desert Museum, in Tucson, provides sunscreen dispensers in all restrooms.
- **Guided tours of center/museum and grounds**. Many visitors appreciate a guided tour by a friendly and knowledgeable guide.
- **Roving interpretive services**. Many museums, parks, zoos, botanic gardens, and other interpretive sites offer "station" interpretation at popular exhibits or roving interpretation. This has become increasingly popular.
- **Library, meeting areas, and other facilities**. The library often houses books; research reports printed by the museum; computerized reference and information retrieval service; and audiovisual collections and equipment. Meeting areas are important for staff meetings and to provide meeting places for community groups. Other common facilities include a bird observation room with natural sounds from a secluded outside feeding area (Figure 11.8).

Museum Administration

Museum and visitor center administrators face many policy and management decisions, including structure and organization, governing mandate, governing body, monetary support and problems, membership organizations, space requirements, and security of collections and exhibits.

Marketing and development comprise another major area of responsibility, including publicity of the museum's programs and development of funding resources. One of the keys to success in running museums comes from developing "buy-in" by the public and community leaders. The balancing act between public interest and professional control over programming, exhibitions, and operations requires skill and good sense.

Figure 11.8. Bird observation rooms provide orientation to the local avifauna. (TC)

A mix of private donors and public agencies supports most museums, zoos, botanical gardens, and visitor centers. Most of these public centers operate cooperatively with private associations. Virtually all seek donations. That adds up to the staff serving several masters. The mix requires sensitivity, nimbleness, and adroit leadership.

Most private museums in the United States operate as nonprofit organizations. This gives them and their donors important tax breaks. Many museums benefit from benefactors whose financial gifts and labor keep the site open. The influence of these people arises from their social, political, financial, or philosophical interest as well as their active participation on museum boards and committees. In many communities, work on the art association board or as a governor of the historical society is expected of "leading citizens" and representatives of local industries. These people put their money and time where their hearts are.

Research conducted by Elyssa Figari (2016) revealed several strategic methods to meet modern cultural and economic challenges in museums. Her study included literature research and interviews with top consultants and museum professionals. Paraphrased summaries of recommendations for museum administrators are as follows:

- **Engaging the community**. This was cited as the primal method because it clearly addresses cultural challenges. To begin, "the most important step is to develop a true sense of the community's interests and values; all other steps depend on this initial information." Local communities want to be involved, want to feel like they are making a difference, want to be activists for their cultures, and want to be connected to their own social circles. Museums can reach out to related organizations, work with the community on common interest programs and

exhibits, bring in local artists and other experts, and offer museum space for community gatherings.
- **Clear mission statement**. The mission statement should focus the staff efforts around a core set of principles. The statement should include the service the museum provides to the community and should be reviewed frequently.
- **Strong leader and board of directors**. Characteristics of a strong leader (executive director or CEO) include someone who inspires others, has a unified vision, is flexible and aware of changing circumstances, and promotes the organization rather than himself or herself. The strong leader needs the support of a strong board of directors. Board members should be supportive with strengths in finances, fundraising, community connections, and marketing.
- **Better business model**. A strong grasp and application of business principles is essential including effective fundraising and marketing strategies (see Chapter 16).
- **Volunteers**. Volunteers have become essential to the wellbeing of museums. Depending on their background and expertise, volunteers can be used to perform many critical services.

A success story that encompasses many of the above methods is that of the San Diego Natural History Museum, which had struggled financially and had nine directors in 13 years. Then Michael Hager was hired in 1991 as CEO, and the museum experienced an amazing turnaround in the following 25 years. The budget increased six-fold, staff grew from 60 to more than 150 employees, there are now 700 volunteers, a long list of donors, and nearly half million visitors per year. Hager attributes the turnaround to several factors but believes the most important is the focus of the museum on the *immediate geographic region* of southern California and Baja California. This strategy not only resonated with the local community but with visitors from all around the world (Figari, 2016).

Focus on the Museum Experience

Ronald Beghetto (2014) observed that "different people visit museums for different reasons." John Falk and his associates have reported considerable research on the visitor experience. They note that the museum experience is generally a leisure experience and is designed to meet identity-related leisure-time needs. For example, Falk, Heimlich, and Bronnenkant (2008) found it possible to cluster museum visitors into five categories of visit motivation and these categories appeared to be related to visitors' desires to use the museum for fulfilling their own personal identity-related needs as follows:

- **Explorers** are curiosity-driven with a general interest in the museum's content. They expect to find something that will grab their attention and fuel their learning.
- **Facilitators** are socially motivated. Their visit is focused primarily on enabling the experience for others in their accompanying social group (e.g., leading youth group on a museum field trip).

- **Professional/hobbyists** feel a close tie between the museum content and their professional or hobbyist passions. Their visits are typically motivated by a desire to satisfy a specific content-related objective.
- **Experience seekers** perceive the museum as an important destination, so their satisfaction derives mainly from having "been there and done that."
- **Rechargers** are primarily seeking to have a contemplative, spiritual and/or restorative experience. They see the museum as a refuge from the work-a-day world.

More recently, two additional categories were added to reflect the growth of exhibitions devoted to specific national, ethnic/racial, or affinity groups (Falk & Dierking, 2013).

- **Respectful pilgrims** are people who visit museums arising from a sense of duty to honor the memory of those represented at the memorial.
- **Affinity seekers** are motivated to visit a museum or specific exhibition because it resonates with their sense of heritage or personhood (Figure 11.9).

Figure 11.9. Affinity seekers at the Chicago Historical Society Museum may enjoy seeing toys from their childhood that evoke pleasant memories. (TC)

Application of such knowledge about visitors allows interpreters to provide satisfying experiences for audiences with those varied motivations and successfully meet visitor expectations. Of course, a number of variables may impact the overall experience including ease of parking, appearance and attitudes of front-line staff, gift shops, food service, restrooms, as well as the exhibits.

Due to the fast-paced nature of the lives many now lead, there has been considerable interest in the importance of "restoration" as an outcome of a museum visit in which visitors can relax and recover from the stresses of their lives (Packer, 2008). Packer and Bond (2010) studied visitors to a history museum, an art museum, an aquarium, and a botanic garden and found restorative qualities that facilitate recovery from mental fatigue. Indeed, "for some people, museums are at least as restorative as natural environments."

> "Visitors can relax and recover from the stresses of their lives."

The relationship between museums and the field of interpretation continues to advance. In 2017 the National Association for Interpretation (NAI) joined the American Alliance of Museums (AAM) Council of Affiliates. This council brings together national museum service organizations representing various segments of the broader museum network. The Executive Director of NAI, Margo Carlock, was formerly Executive Director of the Virginia Association of Museums.

Summary

Museums and visitor centers have the role of maintaining and communicating a place's heritage. Interpretive/visitor centers bring people into a building to discover the significance and character of the place, as well as guide them to opportunities for first-hand experiences with the historical or natural resources that they find outside. Museums, homes, farms, and villages offer much more than nostalgia. They tie people to their roots, allow them to understand how their forebears lived, and give them perspective on their own scale of living. Some historical and anthropological museums give a time perspective to the modern world, dramatizing that only the past few generations of *Homo sapiens* have "needed" modern conveniences. Some technology museums and theme parks predict how humans may live in the future.

This chapter showed the complexity of museum and visitor center purposes, philosophy, policy, and administration. The growing focus on the visitor and the community will make these institutions more effective in their roles as guardians, expositors, and forums for the value of our cultural and natural heritage. In doing so, they will build a society of greater cohesiveness and understanding where people might live better in the present, and learn how they may more completely and intelligently enjoy and tend to our natural and cultural environment for a better world.

Literature Cited

American Alliance of Museums: aam-us.org

American Alliance of Museums. (2016). 2016-2020 Strategic Plan. Approved by AAM Board of Directors February 24, 2016.

Archibald, R. (2001). Reaching in: The community and the museum. *History News. 56*(3), 6–9.

Beghetto, R. (2014). The exhibit as planned versus the exhibit as experienced. *Curator: The Museum Journal, 57*(1), 1–4.

Burns, N. (1941). *Field manual for museums.* Washington, DC: National Park Service.

de Botton, A., & Armstrong, J. (2013). *Art as therapy.* London, UK: Phaidon Press Limited.

Doering, Z. (2010). Strangers, guests, or clients? Visitor experiences in museums. *Curator: The Museum Journal*, Version of Record online: 24 May 2010.

Edenheim, R. (1995). *Skånsen: Traditional Swedish style.* London, UK: ScalaPublications.

Falk, J., & Dierking, L. (2013). *The museum experience revisited.* Walnut Creek, CA: Left Coast Press, Inc.

Falk, J., Heimlich, J., & Bronnenkant, K. (2008). Using identity-related visit motivations as a tool for understanding adult zoo and aquarium visitor's meaning making. *Curator: The Museum Journal, 51*(1), 55–79.

Figari, E. (2016). *Survival methods: Anthropological approaches for successful museums.* Thesis: Master of Arts in Anthropology, San Diego State University.

Fleming, D. (2016). Do museums change lives? Ninth Stephen Weil Memorial Lecture. *Curator: The Museum Journal, 59*(2), 73–79.

Foley, R. (2016). Park service 'astonished' by scandals in Iowa. *San Diego Union-Tribune.* A25. Sunday, August 14, 2016.

Friedman, A. (2013). Reflections on communicating science through art. *Curator: The Museum Journal, 56*(1), 3–9.

Gilman, B. (1916). Museum fatigue. *Science Monthly*, 12, 62–74.

Graffagnio, J. (2001). Using the past to change the future: A strategy for historical organizations. *History News, 56*(3), 1–15.

Gross, M., & Zimmerman, R. (2002). *Interpretive centers: The history, design, and development of nature and visitor centers.* Interpreter's Handbook Series. Stephens Point, WI: UW-SP Foundation Press.

Gross, M., Zimmerman, R., & Buchholz, J. (2006). *Signs, trails, and wayside exhibits: Connecting people and places* (3rd ed.). Interpreter's Handbook Series. Stephens Point, WI: UW-SP Foundation Press.

Lewis, R. (1976). *Manual for museums.* Washington, DC: National Park Service.

Mortensen, C., Rudloff, M., & Vestergaard, V. (2014). Communicative functions of the museum lobby. *Curator: The Museum Journal, 57*(3), 329–346.

Packer, J. (2008). Beyond learning: Exploring visitors' perceptions of the value and benefits of museum experiences. *Curator: The Museum Journal, 51*(1), 33–54.

Packer, J., & Bond, N. (2010). Museums as restorative environments. *Curator: The Museum Journal, 53*(4), 421–436.

Patey, C. (2016). One step at a time. *Journal of the Association for Heritage Interpretation, 21*(1), 27-31.

Ridge, M. (2013). From tagging to theorizing: Deepening engagement with cultural heritage through crowdsourcing. *Curator: The Museum Journal, 56*(4), 435–450.

Schultz, L. (2011). Collaborative museology and the visitor. *Museum Anthropology, 34*(1), 1–12.

Vogel, M. (1991). *Cultural connections: Museums and libraries of Philadelphia and the Delaware Valley*. Philadelphia, PA: Temple University Press.

Williams, T. T. (2016). *The hour of land*. New York, NY: Sarah Crichton Books.

CHAPTER 12
Exhibits

We strive to highlight in this book that interpretation can happen anywhere. This would include interpretation through meaningful exhibits. Among the most unique exhibits are the lampshades of Paradise Inn at Mount Rainier National Park.

Suspended above the guests in the lobby, dining room, and balcony are 64 cylindrical lampshades of varying sizes, some more than four feet in height. The original lampshades were made decades ago by the wives of park employees. Focus of the paintings adorning each shade was on the abundant colorful wildflowers found in the alpine meadows outside of the Inn (Figure 12.1).

Figure 12.1. Lampshades at Paradise Inn at Mount Rainer National Park interpret plants and animals found in the park. (LB)

These original artworks graced the Inn for more than 50 years. But over time the lampshades became brittle and began to fall apart. When examined by conservators the shades were determined to be beyond restoration.

So in the late 1980s, Dale Thompson was commissioned to paint and assemble new lampshades for the Inn. He was the retired former Chief Park Naturalist for Mount Rainier National Park. The new paintings showcase the native flowering plants, shrubs, and trees, including some butterflies and birds.

Next, the Washington's National Park Fund (WNPF) improved an out-of-date publication to provide interpretation of the plants depicted on the shades, titled *Guide to the Lampshades of Paradise Inn*, published in 2013. The following are a few examples:

Lewis' Monkeyflower, *Mimulus lewisii*. This perennial herb is found near small streams in alpine meadows. It is named for Meriwether Lewis, of the 1804-1806 Lewis and Clark Expedition—the first U.S. transcontinental expedition to the Pacific Northwest.

Red Columbine, *Aquilegia formosa*, was used by Plateau Indians as perfume and used medicinally by several Native American tribes.

- **Green False Hellebore**, *Veratrum viride eschscholzianum*, is commonly called Corn Lily for its corn-stalk tassels. It is often mistaken for Skunk Cabbage, which is marginally edible. False Hellebore, however, contains POISONOUS steroidal alkaloids that can be fatal. The roots, rhizomes, and young shoots are particularly toxic.
- **Subalpine Fir**, *Abies lasiocarpa*, provides a perch for the Clark's Nutcracker, or "Camp Robber." This tree is well suited to our area because its short, stiff branches leave little area exposed and easily supports the winter snow load. In such harsh conditions, growth is very slow. A five- or six-inch-diameter tree may be over 100 years old.

As indicated in this brief sample, the lampshade paintings assist in identification of park wildflowers that abound in the summer and interpretation brings together the interconnectedness of climate, plants, wildlife, explorers, and Native Americans.

The guide is available for a nominal charge to all visitors. It offers a map to 15 different viewing points throughout the Inn along with the descriptions. Those associated with WNPF note that it could be especially meaningful for people with disabilities who may not be able to walk the trails to see the wildflowers personally. Furthermore, proceeds from sales of the guide help to fund park projects in science, visitor experience, volunteer service, and connecting youth to the park.

"Exhibition design is both an art and a science. The best exhibitions incorporate healthy doses of both."
—Stephen Bitgood, 2013

What Exhibits Do

Factors for exhibit designers to consider involve what people seek, how they move through museums, what they see in exhibits, and what they miss. Many interpreters design and/or use exhibits, some simple, others highly complex. They show objects such as artwork, models, reproductions, ancient artifacts, tree seeds, and "gadgetry" to make an interpretive message vivid. Exhibits help tell the story of a place and contribute to the experiences of visitors.

Exhibits may be tiny or large. Small objects include gems, bird eggs, or microscopic creatures under magnification. On the large side, the Bronx Zoo opened a $43 million African rain forest exhibit. The special admission fees go to habitat protection, scientific research, or environmental education in central Africa. While in the exhibit, the visitor uses a touch-screen vote to choose the species and type of action they want their admission fee to support (Ebersole, 2001).

When writing a label, designing a display, choosing an object, creating an app, making an interactive exhibit, or commissioning a video or a computer game, the curator/interpreter communicates as one human being reaching another, since pictures and artifacts do not always provide full context to speak for themselves. Furthermore, the best exhibits will immediately convey the theme, the genius loci, the compelling story, the big idea (Ham 2013; Serrell, 2015).

Any set of exhibits exists to communicate. For success, the curator must give effective interpretation a top priority.

Exhibits Use Things

Objects or artifacts have great importance in museums and visitor centers. People stood in line for as much as an hour to see the Hope Diamond at the Smithsonian. That one object has enough "celebrity value" or intrinsic interest to make it such a popular feature (Figure 12.2). Museums use objects in at least three different ways.

In a decorative arts museum, a chair goes in a case or on a pedestal. The curators feature the chair so visitors may admire its grace, workmanship, wood, style, and age, or perhaps the significance associated with its owner or fabricator.

In an interpretive exhibit, the same chair goes behind a table to create the sense of a room. The essence of this historic room experience consists of context. People relate easily to spaces; they understand a room. The room becomes a springboard to developing a stronger sense of the central interpretive theme. Objects have importance in an interpretive exhibit; putting them in context enriches their meaning.

In a participatory exhibit, the visitor might sit in the chair and enjoy rocking while listening to its story, sensing how the owner might have felt.

Figure 12.2. Some objects such as this piece from the King Tut exhibit may have celebrity value. Long lines of people will stand and wait to see popular exhibits. (LB)

Exhibits Present Messages

As in any interpretation, themes and compelling stories make up the key part of the museum or visitor center experience. The first consideration in exhibit planning involves identification of the key messages (Serrell, 2015). From these, planning focuses on how best to communicate the messages and to whom. No longer is a museum or a visitor center just a collection of random things. Instead, the treasured objects are presented in an organized, informative, intriguing, and meaningful way.

Exhibits Provide Knowledge and Interest

Exhibits are educational. Visitors should leave with a deeper understanding of the topic and how it relates to their own lives. Some will leave with motivation to learn more (perhaps a book picked up at the gift shop) or visit a related place with eyes open wide.

Exhibits Enhance Experiences

The visitors come for more than looking at a series of cases or panels. The interpretive exhibit involves them, excites their imaginations, challenges them, and gets them talking, exploring, and discovering.

Exhibits Affect Emotions and Attitudes

Tears, joy, or the thrill of discovering a vision may come from instant reactions to an exhibit. Other emotions include curiosity and heightened sensitivity to other people or creatures or places. Tying an exhibit to the web of human experience and knowledge helps to develop a holistic sense and may touch on many universal themes.

Exhibits Influence Behavior

While people are in the visitor center or museum some exhibits may cause them to pause and marvel. Furthermore, the content may influence their actions after they leave. Inspiration from an exhibition may lead to commitment to a stronger stewardship of the place and of the planet.

How People Visit Exhibits

Edward Stevens Robinson (1928) noted, "The behavior of the museum visitor offers an inexhaustible stock of problems." Researchers have found that people have different approaches to viewing exhibits. Nonetheless, researchers and consultants have discovered many patterns of visitor behavior (Falk & Dierking, 2013; Packer, 2006).

Interpreting to Different Visitors

Visitors seem to approach an exhibit in different ways by the following:

- Ignoring it altogether
- Glancing at it briefly
- Looking at the graphics and artifacts
- Reading the messages (all or in part)
- Starting in the beginning or the middle or near the end
- Grasping hold of an interactive device

How can an exhibit designer attract and interpret to these different people with different levels of attention and interests? From long experience, Serrell (2015) suggested interpreting to visitor similarities, rather than segregating them by their perceived differences and interpreting differently to each stereotype class. Rather, prepare information and materials that will attract and inform all. Involve various senses to reinforce the message. Offer some detail for the person with enough interest and/or time to pursue it.

The recommended procedure is to select the messages, choose the media that best transmit them, and prepare the messages and media in the way that will enable the most people to find something of value.

The Viewers at Three Speeds

Identity-related motivations (e.g., Falk & Dierking, 2013) for why people visit museums, in general, was covered in the last chapter. However, the speed at which people move through exhibits, although simplistic, can still offer lessons for interpreters.

For example, interpreters can consider visitor behavior and accommodation based on different rates of viewing and duration of attention. The exhibit planner may seek to get the major message across even to those who stop by for a quick look, while also providing enough opportunity for learning for those who get captured by the compelling presentation of the subject matter. This simple division of exhibit viewers recognizes three levels of viewing speed: the skaters, the strollers, and the studiers.

The **skaters** pass by the exhibit with little apparent attention or interest in anything except perhaps the theme and the big objects. Some use the skating approach to get the lay of the land, and to reconnoiter for topics of interest for later study. Others scan, getting the "table of contents" in a short time.

The **strollers** get the big picture in more detail, because they pick up the major points and more of the details. The museum text writer keeps some of the key ideas in large print for them. They may stop and look at details of some exhibits, but generally they will skim through the museum selectively, seeing most of the exhibits but getting only the key ideas and most compelling facts.

The **studiers** read the smaller print and examine every object—at least in areas of special interest to them. If the exhibit is laid out without them in mind, they may also become barriers to traffic as they park in front of a panel full of interesting details.

People who visit museums may act in each of these roles at different times. In some high-volume visitor centers where managers have to get visitors in and out the door with basic orientation, the exhibits may not include the details. In other visitor centers and museums where visitors can stay longer without impeding service or traffic, the exhibits may be quite thorough, while still informing those who come in for a quick look around.

For example, the Wisconsin State Museum, Madison, in the Native American exhibits, accommodates each of the three levels of viewing speed. A quick look at the large type and the big graphics gives a clear picture of the key message. The second level provides additional details in a few lines of type and further attention to artifacts. Within the same exhibit, however, someone who becomes intrigued can spend more than an hour in an exhibit room, studying more detailed information and artifacts. Thus, the museum meets its educational aims in the exhibit hall; even the viewer who has time to study finds satisfactory detail. Furthermore, the museum has excellent reference material—maps, journals, books, and articles—as well as a series of lectures and well-informed curators for deeper exploration of the subject.

> "For visitors to learn from exhibits, to enjoy exhibits, be entertained by exhibits, and to potentially be transformed in their thinking and actions by exhibits…they must pay attention to exhibits."

Further Observations: The Importance of Attention

For visitors to learn from exhibits, to enjoy exhibits, be entertained by exhibits, and to potentially be transformed in their thinking and actions by exhibits…they must pay attention to exhibits. Stephen Bitgood and his associates have conducted dozens of studies over the course of several decades that focus on visitors who view exhibits in museum settings. Much of this work is summarized in his landmark book titled *Attention and Value*.

Bitgood (2013a) defines visitor attention as a group of psychological processes that involve three stages: capture, focus, and engagement. These three stages make up a continuum (overlap from one to the other) and are summarized below.

The capture stage is when interest first occurs and the visitor is attracted to an exhibit (looking at and approaching it). This stage is important in attracting the visitor in the first place and may reflect the visitor's interest in the subject. Furthermore, elements of an exhibit that may gain attention include large items, movement, lighting of the exhibit, isolation from other exhibits, and multisensory elements such as sound, touch, and smell (Figure 12.3). The focus stage represents a commitment to the exhibit to the exclusion of other exhibits or competing stimuli. In this stage, the visitor has narrowed his or her attention to a single element of the exhibit. The engagement stage is determined by a high degree of focus on the exhibit content that may include close observation of objects, reading the label text, conversing with group members about exhibit content, thinking about the implications of the exhibit in one's own life, and perhaps taking notes or photos for later reference (Figure 12.4).

Figure 12.3. Large items such as this bat head capture the visitor's attention. (TC)

With an understanding of visitor attention, Bitgood (2013a) then presents an attention-value model that asserts that depth of attention to an exhibit is determined by the ratio of benefits to costs. In other words, the benefits that may accrue by engaging with an exhibit are weighed against the costs. Individual computation of the benefit divided by the cost is more of a reaction to many variables and not necessarily associated with conscious awareness of such a calculation (Bitgood, 2013a).

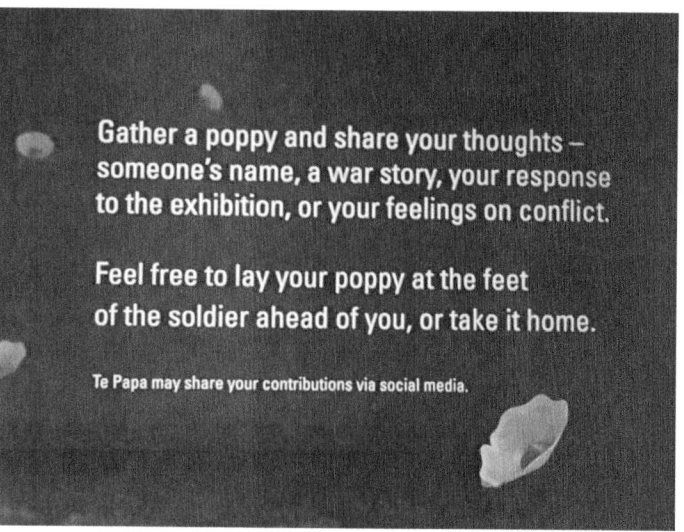

Figure 12.4. This exhibit promotes the "engagement stage" as it invites visitors to write their own thoughts on a paper poppy and leave it at the feet of a life-like replica WW I soldier. (TC)

Benefits to the visitor may by predicted by his or her interest level in finding out more, prior knowledge about the topic, reasons for visiting the exhibition in the first place, and various elements of the exhibit itself. Costs of engaging with an exhibit take into account the time and effort to do so, such as reading labels or watching videos embedded in the exhibit. The monetary cost of entering the museum may also factor into whether the visit even occurs in the first place.

> The benefits that may accrue by engaging with an exhibit are weighed against the costs.

But once the visitor is inside the museum, the benefit-cost analysis determines which exhibits are seen and for how long. Bitgood (2013a) summarizes, "The value ratio combines personal and psychological factors (e.g., interest level in exhibit content, agenda for a particular museum visit, decision-making processes, perceptual processes, state of energy level) with environmental or setting variables (e.g., exhibit, social influence, architectural design) to predict what and how much attention will be given to exhibit elements."

In regard to the costs, Bitgood (2013b) advocates the small chunk theorem that suggests visitors will make small investments of time-effort (repeatedly), and this can add up, resulting in increased overall attention to an exhibit. For example, one study showed that reading increased from 11% to 28% of visitors when a label with 150 words was divided into three labels of 50 words each (Bitgood, 2013b). Indeed, Bitgood (2013b) has indicated that "reducing the cost may be more important than increasing the interest according to a number of studies we have conducted."

Reducing the Cost

"We label writers are really lucky people because we get to craft less text with more focus on real things in real spaces for visitors in meaningful places with shared boundaries, unlike the virtual, unbounded, unlimited Internet."

–Beverly Serrell, 2015

Serrell (2015) noted various guidelines for text in her book, *Exhibit Labels*, that should produce an integrated flow of messages that will attract readers as follows:

- Use bullets so lists are easier to read.
- Keep paragraphs short.
- Vocabulary should be appropriate.
- Labels should not all be the same length. Mix it up some. Labels describing the most interesting objects should be longer than others.
- The labels should be short enough so that people are inclined to read the whole thing.
- Labels should be visible to children and those in wheelchairs.
- Labels should be well-lighted (avoid shadows).

Additionally, to reduce the "cost" of reading an exhibit, present the most important idea up front, on top, and in larger type (Figure 12.5), and make the message simple and straightforward (Youngentob & Hostetler, 2012).

Other Visitor Behaviors

A long history of observations of visitor behaviors in museums and nature centers has guided interpreters for many years (Yalowits & Bronnenkant, 2009). DiMaggio, Useem, and Brown (1978) reviewed 250 studies, mostly in the 1970s, offering data on

Figure 12.5. This simple sign illustrates many of the tips on exhibit design including a clear thematic title, use of bullet items, small amount of text, most important idea presented at the top and in large type, and relevance to the reader. (TC)

audiences at cultural institutions and events. In general, the public that "consumes" culture is more educated than the norm, and they have higher incomes and higher status jobs. This continues to be the case, but as detailed in the last chapter, museums are striving to reach out to broader audiences.

A series of Studies in Museum Education published by the American Association of Museums (now American Alliance of Museums) in the 1920s and 1930s produced a base for how exhibit design has been measured for decades. Guidelines included observing more and speculating less; watching the visitors more and talking about them less; using measurable and useful questions. These guidelines were behind the studies by Robinson (1928) and others. The questions included the following:

- What do people do when they come to this exhibit?
- How long do they stay?
- Is there an easy and natural manner for prolonging their stay?
- What do they look at?
- What do they pass by?
- How can the visitor's behaviors be influenced through the location, size, or color of exhibits?

The data came from discrete observation of visitors with a stopwatch and small notebook in hand, noting what they looked at and for how long. This kind of study continues, at many museums, nature centers, and even on interpretive trails (MacRae & Serrell, 2000).

Masberg and Silverman (2004) have also defined the value of measuring visitor experiences in World Heritage sites and similar cultural locations. Their studies documented a need for more careful site management, including changes in marketing, advertising, programming, and site missions.

Several general observations based on visitor behavior studies describe how visitors view and interact with exhibits. Some of the earlier studies led the way in visitor studies and continue to be consistent with visitor behavior now.

> "Several general observations based on visitor behavior studies describe how visitors view and interact with exhibits."

Visitors enter a display area and tend to turn right, then go around the room counterclockwise. Museum (and supermarket) designers have known for a long time that about 65% to 75% of people go right, then curve leftward, given the choice (Falk & Dierking, 2013; Melton, 1935). Ice skaters and roller skaters circle their rinks the same way, as do dancers in a ballroom and runners on a track. Reversing the direction requires special mental and physical effort.

Visitors pay more attention to exhibits first encountered and those on the first floor of a museum. Research has shown that the exhibits that are first encountered are more heavily viewed than those deeper in the museum and (independent of content or quality of design) exhibits on the main floor receive more attention than those on upper or lower floors (Falk & Dierking, 2013).

Exhibit position affects the number of views. Paintings in an art gallery "... immediately to the left of the entrance received less attention than any other group of paintings in the gallery, and the paintings immediately to the right of the entrance received more attention than any other group..." (Melton, 1935). In some cases, the difference between the two positions was three-fold. A similar pattern exists for natural history exhibits.

Viewers do not study all the pictures in an art show or all the exhibits in an interpretive center. Robinson (1928) studied visitors and the number of paintings they looked at in four art museums. On average, in a large museum with about 1,000 paintings, visitors stopped to look at about 10% of the paintings they passed. These proportions generally continue to hold.

Variations in display methods can lengthen interest in specific exhibits. Wells (2000) found that interactive exhibits had greater holding power than static exhibits. However, if interactives require too much time-effort they generally fail (Bitgood, 2013b). Also, exhibit observation time increased for large, moving, close, and easily visible objects or animals (Parsons, 1965). Furthermore, working with architects and engineers on an exhibit can help maximize visitor experience and knowledge retention (Brunswick & Ryan, 2015).

Unaccompanied visitors will view signs less. A study conducted by Hall, Ham, and Lackey (2010) found through their test of message modification of park signs at Yosemite National Park that visitors were more likely to ignore signs and messages if they were alone, in contrast to accompanied people ignoring park signage.

Attentiveness fades with time in the exhibit area. Researchers found that most exhibit label reading occurs in the first 20-30 minutes of a museum visit (Falk & Dierking, 2013).

People can be involved through interpretive play. Some zoos and aquariums involve children (and uninhibited adults) at exhibits that encourage actions related to animals' physical skills. Providing opportunities to imitate animal actions with a jump, a safe climb, investigating and discovering, swinging on rings, and building beaver dams, for example, offers imitative learning that will stick long after the experience is over (Bassett, 2014).

John Veverka has served as an interpretive consultant for several decades in many countries and has summarized some basic principles on how exhibits communicate with the audience. (Box 12.1).

Box 12.1
The Visitors and Exhibits

- Visitors will be drawn to exhibits that have information or artifacts of intrinsic interest to them.
- Provocative headlines and graphics draw attention.
- Before you write an exhibit headline ask, "Why would a visitor want to know this?" The answer to that question might end up as your exhibit header.
- If you can't get the main point across in about 15-20 seconds, you probably won't get it across at all.
- Visitors do not really like to read labels. If a label is more than 50 words long it probably will not be read. If the label uses small type (less than 30-point type) there is even less chance of it being read. If the label is on glass, even less chance of it being read.
- The average viewing time for a visual program embedded within an exhibit is about three minutes before the visitor loses interest and walks away. It will be less if the visitor doesn't know how long the video will take. Be sure to have a label that states "Push for a two-minute video" or whatever the time length is. The average viewing time for sit-down AV programs in small theaters is about seven minutes before the visitors begin to lose interest.
- Note that Bitgood (2013a; 2013b) also confirms that visitors spend limited viewing time to watch videos. The point here is that if videos are to be used they must be integral to the exhibition and should almost always be shorter rather than longer.

Sources: Veverka (2001); Bitgood (2013a; 2013b).

Exhibiting Controversies

Controversial subjects can make fascinating exhibits. Sometimes, the more controversial a topic, the more public attention it garners. Even exhibits about carefully documented phenomena can produce some type of controversy.

Population Impact

Almost all environmental problems are associated with the extraordinary growth in human population over the past century including such issues as air and water quality, climate change, water shortages, deforestation, endangered and extinct species, and depletion of ocean resources. Beth Redmond-Jones was the exhibit developer and project manager for "Population Impact," an exhibition at the Carnegie Museum of Natural History. In a case study, she describes the three key messages of the permanent exhibition concerning the results of human populations on the environment (Redmond-Jones, 2011):

> Sometimes, the more controversial a topic, the more public attention it garners.

- Earth's resources sustain life.
- Populations do not grow without consequences.
- Our human choices (decisions) affect the world that we live in, now and in the future.

More specific topics focused on the rate at which human population is growing, how human population growth impacts the overall environment and specifically where we live, and the factors that effect population change such as war, famine, natural disasters, birth control, and healthcare (Redmond-Jones, 2011). Interestingly, a display that showed in real time the number of humans on the planet was not initially understood. A label explaining to visitors what the number referred to was determined to be necessary.

Climate Change

"Changing California" in the Oakland Museum of California (OMCA) Gallery of California Natural Sciences is a 25,000-square-foot natural history gallery completed in 2014. Referring to California's threatened biodiversity the entrance label reads:

> It's one of the world's most biologically diverse places—and one of the most threatened. Profoundly changed by humans in less than 200 years, California faces even more change as the planet warms.

From a case study by Nadja Lazansky (2014), project coordinator and exhibit developer, natural history museums are determining the role they should play in "one of the most pressing and dire issues of our time—climate change—and how to balance serving" in a trusted traditional role "while taking on a very active position as advocates and actors" in the areas of policy and political action. Visitors to the gallery can reminisce about their own experiences in nature, gain new perspectives about the dramatic changes that have occurred within the state, and feel a call to more deeply experience nature on their own and/or take direct conservation action.

> Visitors feel a call to more deeply experience nature on their own and/or take direct conservation action.

The Makah and the Whale

The Makah Museum in Neah Bay, Washington, recognized as one of the nation's finest tribal museums, welcomes visitors to experience the life of pre-contact Makah people. The permanent exhibits include artifacts from the Ozette collection, uncovered from a Makah village partially buried by a mudslide nearly 500 years ago.

A nationally publicized controversy erupted when gray whales came off the endangered species list in 1994. The Makah Tribe on a remote, tiny reservation in northwestern Washington exercised one of its treaty guarantees and rowed out in two large canoes carrying harpoons to revive its whaling culture (successfully).

Makah community members had carefully studied exhibits and archival materials to gather information on the whaling tradition. The tribally owned Makah Cultural and Research Center (MCRC) held most of these archives and had exhibited whaling boats and weapons for several years.

Whaling had become a highly emotional issue in North America due to the severe decline in populations of the mammals. When the gray whales recovered from near extinction to 23,000, the Makah Nation decided to hunt again, as an exercise of spiritual and physical strength, preparedness, and communication. "Whaling defines Makah identity…" said Janine Bowechop (2001), executive director of MCRC.

Opponents to whaling took a strong stance against the tribal action. For months, they stood at the entry to the reservation with signs (and broadcasters) proclaiming that the Makah had no real whaling tradition. When visitors to the museum came away understanding the depth and history of the tradition, the opponents called for a boycott of the museum. They charged the MCRC with confusing people. Nonetheless, attendance statistics proved no impact on visitation.

A personal visit to the museum by one of the authors revealed powerful exhibits with straightforward evidence and explanation of the whaling tradition and virtually no reference that could be called propagandistic. As Bowechop (2001) reported, "The MCRC has made no organized effort to convert each visitor into a pro-Makah whaling camp, but the MCRC is making every effort to discourage misrepresentation of Makah history and culture."

The issue is complex and continues to be held up in the courts. In 2002 the 9th U.S. Circuit Court of Appeals required the Makah to obtain a waiver of the Marine Mammal Protection Act to legally whale again. After terminating a draft study in 2012, in March 2015 a new draft study was released by NOAA Fisheries that outlines six alternatives from no hunting to taking up to 24 whales over a six-year period (Bernton, 2015).

Darkened Waters: Profile of an Oil Spill

Kathleen McLean (2011) provided a case study of the "Darkened Waters: Profile of an Oil Spill" exhibition, which launched at the humble Pratt Museum in Homer, Alaska. The project was about the enormous oil spill (11 million gallons) that occurred in Prince William Sound when the oil tanker Exxon Valdez ran aground. In reflecting on the challenges of such an exhibition, McClean noted a contagious paranoia, saying, "We were dealing with a contentious and troubling event, and from the beginning came warnings from colleagues, funders, and politicians." In addition to the politics and forthcoming litigation against the oil industry's Exxon, came the concern that visitors don't attend "downer exhibits."

But, indeed, visitors began arriving in droves and the relevance of the exhibition was not lost on them. They needed an outlet. A "Darkened Waters" visitor comment book was provided. The first entry in the first comment book read simply, "This exhibit should travel throughout the state of Alaska and the rest of the U.S. to show the devastating story of how we treat our environment." And so a full commitment was launched to turn "Darkened Waters" into a traveling exhibit. The exhibit consisted of basic plywood, latex paint, oil barrels, spill response gear, and the like. This was a very basic exhibition, and due to the influence of the oil industry, other museums wouldn't touch it.

> The human psyche responds vibrantly in the presence of originals.

The outlook was not bright until another museum finally did agree to take the exhibition next: the National Museum of Natural History at the Smithsonian. Although there were concerns by the Smithsonian regarding the low production costs, the Pratt Museum insisted on keeping to the spirit of the exhibition's origin. Included, too, were photographs that were donated by world-class photographers.

Overall, "Darkened Waters" was organized around seven major communication goals:

- Alaska is a national treasure that must be protected.
- It [the oil spill] was a huge disaster.
- It changed people's lives.
- We couldn't clean it all up.
- It's not over.
- We learned (and are continuing to learn) lessons we shouldn't forget.
- I've got to do something. What can I do?

> Many visitors wept quietly as they moved through the exhibits.

What began in a small natural history museum in Homer, Alaska, ultimately traveled to the Smithsonian and a total of 17 venues over 11 years. The exhibition made a difference in our understanding of the vast wildness of Alaska and the horror of what happened there. A unique exhibition fueled by a storytelling approach from a variety of those who experienced the disaster, and powerful images, resulted in many visitors who wept quietly as they moved through the exhibits.

Originals or Reproductions?

Historic interpreters and museum curators often share intense concern with authenticity. That concern extends to all exhibits including textiles and papers. Even the authenticity in methods of manufacturing and invisible details capture the attention.

Original artifacts provide a certain inspirational value that affects the intensity of an interpretive exhibit (Figure 12.6). Facsimiles and reproductions may look the same, but somehow the human psyche responds vibrantly in the presence of originals of some things. The real Declaration of Independence at the National Archives draws hundreds of thousands of viewers per year. Original uniforms of the Royal Canadian Mounted Police featured in several Canadian museums clearly have much greater value than the many facsimiles available. So do original jewelry, stone weapons, and weavings of Native Americans, the ancient Celts, the Romans, and the ancient Benin Kingdom of West Africa. Their value incites collectors to expend much time, energy, and even moral capital in their pursuit.

Exhibiting or using original artifacts is not always prudent or practical, however. When educational activities allow people to touch artifacts, they must be abundant and replaceable, or reproductions. Some materials obviously do better than others. Most silk deteriorates within 30 years, regardless of how well it is kept. Reproductions of, rather than original, silk clothing are essential for historical collections. On the other hand, stone survives for millennia. When stone implements abound, originals may be used for both exhibits and participatory activities.

When using reproductions of artifacts, "museum ethics require that visitors be told in an effective manner the true nature of reproductions" (Lewis, 1976). Clear, permanent marking on the bottom or other inconspicuous place prevents mistaking them for originals. That may prompt a story in itself; where the reproductions came from.

Figure 12.6. Original authentic objects attract and hold attention. This book began by saying interpretation was worth a million bucks. This exhibit at the U.S. Federal Reserve money museum in Chicago displays one million dollars in real $20 bills illustrating in a tangible way interpretation's value. (TC)

Sometimes, authenticity conflicts with fiercely held modern attitudes, creating a practical dilemma for interpretive administrators. In the mid-1800s, the only women to enter a men's clothing store were seamstresses who quickly and discreetly delivered clothing they had sewn at home. Women did not work behind the counters nor did they appear in the stores with their husbands. Such indecorousness surely would have embarrassed the male customers; it simply was not done.

Spittoons were part of all stores where men gathered, yet, in one historic store, interpreters put them away, out of sight. On the other hand, chamber pots appear in virtually every pre-plumbing bedroom on display in museums and historic homes. Some interpreters take pains to bring the pot out from under the bed, as if to emphasize the beauty of the porcelain or to make it clear that not everyone ran out into the nighttime snow.

Animals: Dead or Alive?

Zoos and aquariums, of course, feature live animals. Animals bring in the crowds, as proven by the waiting lines at the San Diego Zoo and the National Aquarium of Baltimore. Copeland, Randall, Gill, and Wright (2015) recommend interpretive strategies for zoo and aquarium planners when it comes to visitors with strong emotional connections to the environment and animal rights. They suggest planners should understand as society changes so do the perceptions of zoos and aquariums, and with the changes comes misinformation about the purpose of their institutions. Transparency with visitors and environmental organizations about the "true meaning and the importance of zoos and aquariums" can address controversy and resolve misguided information.

John Falk and his associates addressed "Why Zoos and Aquariums Matter." To determine if they successfully promote conservation, the Association of Zoos and Aquariums (AZA) undertook a three-year, nationwide study of the impacts of zoo or aquarium visits (Falk et al., 2007). The researchers found that going to AZA-accredited facilities in North America does have a measurable impact on conservation attitudes and understanding of visitors. Key results, derived directly from the study, included the following:

- Visits to zoos and aquariums prompt individuals to reconsider their role in environmental problems and conservation action, and to see themselves as part of the solution.
- Visitors believe they experience a stronger connection to nature.
- Zoos and aquariums support and reinforce the values and attitudes of the visitor.
- Visitors arrive with specific identity-related motivations and these motivations directly impact how they conduct their visit and what meaning they derive from the experience. (Falk et al., 2007)

Should smaller interpretive centers and museums also exhibit live animals? This controversy has seen sharp swings in the past few decades. At present, few nature centers have caged animals. Live displays have few advocates among interpreters and park administrators due to the effort and cost required, as well as ethical considerations.

If a park visitor center serves as the portal to the natural features and wildlife of the park, some argue that it seems inconsistent that the local animals should be featured in cages. On the other hand, stuffed and mounted road-kill in the museum allows visitors to identify a well-lighted specimen, with a chance for careful study and questions to the resident naturalists (Figure 12.7).

Figure 12.7. A mounted specimen allows careful study not possible with a live animal. (TC)

Exhibit Planning and Design

Good displays and exhibits orient the visitor to a site. Exhibits may also serve in preparation for a forest, factory, or park tour, or enrich a visit as a post-tour extension. In museums, where the exhibits comprise the destination, their composition and quality make or break the whole experience. Criteria for a good exhibit should include 1) a good concept (a clear theme message that's novel); 2) careful research to get the facts straight; 3) contents—artifacts, graphics, writing—that convey a message clearly; 4) design and layout of the exhibit for optimal presentation; and 5) providing a visitor experience that makes the message memorable.

Planning for exhibits requires many talents. The planner must think about the following:

- The interpretive messages, facts, and their sequences
- The media for presenting the messages—print, audio, digital, interactive methods
- Writing style and organization that focuses on the artifacts
- The visitors, their behavior, their interests, their comforts, their interactions with others
- Visitor vision and line of sight
- Lighting and sound design
- The use of touch, sound, odors, kinetics, maybe even taste to communicate
- Visitor traffic flow accounting for variable rates of movement and volume
- The aesthetics of interior design and color
- The harmony of exhibits working as a cohesive group—size, colors, typography, content
- Costs and benefits
- Evaluation throughout the process (this is covered in Chapter 19)

One current line of thinking suggests that visitors also gain knowledge through movement of their bodies as they travel from exhibit to exhibit. Emerging research has indicated connections between physical posture and cognition. Overhill (2015) suggested that exhibit planning could encourage body awareness through reference to or practice of such things as sports, dance, and yoga.

Common Elements

Some things will be common to many exhibit centers. Samples of common elements include the following:

- **Anything alive:** Today, most interpreters prefer to build observation blinds or offer walks to see special wildlife habitats.
- **Rugged instruments:** Binoculars, magnifying glasses, telescopes, and other equipment to aid perception of the environment by enhancing visual powers.
- **Fireplace:** A cool-season fireplace or a wood-burning stove promotes comfort and creates a sense of memorable hominess (Figure 12.8).
- **The story of land use in the area:** Economics and ecology of former occupants along with current stories of land restoration add human interest to an area.
- **Models:** A working mill, a still, a bird in flight, tools that visitors can handle, or archaeologists at work all interpret how things operate.
- **Life cycle of an animal:** An in-depth description of one species of animal can be effective and individualized.

- **Furs and mounted animals:** Children are fascinated with the opportunity to stroke the fur of common animals. Road kills and local taxidermist assistance can add meaningful, replaceable displays.

Types of Exhibits

Traditional Exhibits

Exhibits behind glass, flatwork diagrams, and mounted artifacts or specimens will continue to have a dominant place in most museums. Other traditional types of exhibits include those described next.

Relief models/maps receive heavy use for orientation purposes in most visitor centers and many museums. In some instances, these become the most popular exhibit.

Figure 12.8. Many exhibit spaces offer a place to relax complete with fireplace, water feature, large windows, and plenty of reading material. (TC)

Dioramas or habitat groups are miniature or life-sized scenes featuring three-dimensional figures and objects in front of a painted background. A diorama may be as simple as a stuffed bird on a twig placed in a corner case with the background painted as a forest scene. Popular large wildlife dioramas have attracted people to the American Museum of Natural History, Field Museum of Natural History, Denver Museum of Nature and Science, and Texas Museum of Natural History. Dioramas require thorough and accurate scholarship and craftsmanship. Even given the expense, a diorama serves as a unique teaching instrument. It attains even more teaching power when accompanied by a taped or written explanation.

Cycloramas were popular attractions before movies and television. Very large paintings of complex scenes such as Civil War battles (e.g., Gettysburg), wrap 100-300 feet around the inside of a circular building. Viewers stand in the middle of a mostly darkened room following the action of an event by a narrated sequence of selective spotlighting of key features on the painting. They sometimes take dioramas to a grandiose, circular scale by placing scaled figures of people, horses, houses, vegetation, rocks, and fences on a sculptured foreground that represents the land's formation; this blends artfully with the perspective of a painting in the background. Only a few of the several hundred cycloramas that once existed remain in operation.

Hands-on exhibits allow the visitor to touch, feel, and manipulate something. Kinetic participation, puzzle-solving, and actually feeling textures or how something works should increase the interest and learning experience more than mere observation. The manipulation may be as simple as lifting a flap or pushing a button to find an answer to a written question about the exhibit. Discovery rooms in museums and nature centers draw thousands of children to the boxes full of puzzles and games.

Holography creates three-dimensional models by visual and artistic effects. Holography uses continuous wave laser beams to make a moving 3-D image on a nearly flat surface.

Planetariums, aquariums, beehives, and wildlife windows bring the outdoors inside to provide excellent visibility for processes and phenomena that otherwise can't be seen easily.

Simulated immersion attempts to immerse the visitor in a feeling of being transported to another time and place (mentally discounting the reality of the museum location) so the exhibit becomes more meaningful (Figure 12.9).

Figure 12.9. A wide-screen immersive theater at the Flint Hills Prairie Discovery Center allows visitors to feel the vibrations of stampeding bison and the heat of wildfires. (JK)

Formerly, the kinds of exhibits that produced a feeling of immersion included realistic looking animal mounts or casts; vegetation; thematic backgrounds; recorded or real sounds; and other aspects of the actual environment (Bitgood, Ellingsen, & Patterson, 1990). Now museums are experimenting with virtual reality (Gamerman, 2015) and telepresence robots to "beam" tour guides to exhibit halls (Kanno-Youngs, 2015). For example, at the American Museum of Natural History a BeamPro SPS robot conveys information from a native Haida Gwaii curator in Canada, live to visitors in the Hall of Northwest Coast Indians.

Incorporating Newer Technologies

Freeman Tilden (1977) predicted that the future would hold "more automatic projection equipment, more sound installations, more recorders and tapes, more gadgets to be self-operated by visitors and so on." The world has changed dramatically since then and new technologies are accelerating. Any discussion about current technology and any projections about the future may be obsolete in a matter of years.

Museums are experimenting with current technologies in efforts to assist visitors to have more meaningful experiences. However, Beverly Serrell (2015) suggests that traditional labeling and exhibitions will continue to function as the "first option" form of interpretation. Similarly, Wayne LaBar (2014) notes that visitors don't come to museums for technology. Rather, visitors come to museums for experiences they can't get at home or from other places. However, he suggests, new technologies are helping to raise the experience bar.

Perhaps most promising, and at least presently most likely to endure, are our personal mobile devices. Smartphones have become ubiquitous and are used to manage our calendars, leave ourselves notes, get news, listen to music, take photos, make videos, email, text, play games, manage finances, check social media sites, monitor fitness and health, and make phone calls. The use of mobile devices in museums began with audio tour technology that now seems quaint. Museums increasingly provide visitors with opportunities to learn more and engage with exhibits through use of bar codes, audio codes, QR codes, and other digital tags (LaBar, 2014). Smartphones can be used in museum environments by making application of audio features, links to the Internet, video features, apps, multimedia, and interactive games (Serrell, 2015).

Gaming can be a powerful mode of engagement and often relies on the visitor's mobile device. A recently launched company is called Capture the Museum. Usually during a special event, or after hours, people are divided into teams and then use their phones to work together to complete challenges. This requires the visitors to explore the museum. But unlike the old scavenger hunts using paper and pencil that had little to do with the exhibition theme, the digital interfaces can be designed to correspond with the intended storyline of the exhibition for a more educational, meaningful, personal, and memorable experience (LaBar, 2014).

Apple's iPad can be mounted on walls or carried by visitors to offer more information including introductory written or spoken labels, thematic or representative music, images and maps, graphs and diagrams, interactive games, and seemingly limitless content. These have been adopted at many museums including the American Museum of Natural History. Furthermore, Apple's iPad can be used to explore New York City as an electronic guide to the big city. The 2015 opening of the One World Trade Center Observatory (100 floors up) relied heavily on the Apple iPad as both a virtual tour guide and payment terminal.

The use of physical/digital interfaces is a blending of the physical and digital worlds so that visitors can interact with physical objects located at museums. For example, at the ECHO Lake Aquarium and Science Center in Burlington, Vermont, visitors can "play" in a real sandbox to create mountain ranges and other topographical features. Projection and 3D visualization technology is used to explain how watersheds work. That is, the technology shows how water, projected on the surface of the sand, behaves and flows (LaBar, 2014).

Jason Jay Stevens (2013) describes a "multiple system integrated deployment of cutting-edge interpretive technology" in his critique of Gallery One at the Cleveland Museum of Art. Gallery One opened to much fanfare in 2013. It has six large multi-touch displays called "Lenses"; the huge Collection Wall that features gesture-based interaction; and a family area known as Studio Play. The "Lenses" are found throughout the gallery in the midst of a grouping of thematic artworks with various opportunities for engagement. For example, visitors can draw lines across the screen and the system can find an item in the museum collection that is similar. Likewise, they can make facial expressions and the system will find something that matches. Visitors may also imitate different sculptures by striking similar poses and are rated on how closely their attempts match the artwork. However, Stevens (2013) personally observed that although visitors were certainly engaged in the games, most were not bothering to even read the name of the sculpture they were imitating and no visitors clicked for additional information. He noted, "Sometimes what is popular is also the most superficial." On the other hand, he felt that having the opportunity to rearrange the elements of a Picasso while in the presence of the original artwork rated as one of his "favorite-ever art class exercises."

> Sometimes what is popular is also the most superficial.

The tech museum offers exhibits that explain how technology works. For example, the San Jose Tech Museum of Innovation (appropriately in the Silicon Valley of California) shows how technology affects who we are and how we live. The museum launched in 1978 and has grown to house permanent, themed galleries on innovation, green technology, exploration, and how technology influences our lives. Of course, the museum offers plenty of interactive exhibits and virtual technology. It also offers signature programs such as the Tech Awards, which presents honors to international laureates who are using technology to solve the world's biggest problems and the Tech Challenge, which is for Grades 4-12 to use engineering design to solve real-world problems. The Geektoberfest is the Tech's annual celebration of "science and suds" with tastings from local craft breweries. In 2015, the Tech was awarded the National Medal for Museum and Library Service.

The museum of the future will offer even more application of current and evolving technologies. Gelt (2015) suggests it "functions as seamlessly as an Apple store, makes recommendations like Amazon, speaks in hashtags, loves Tumblr, and is ready for its selfie". It may send a push notification to the visitor's phone suggesting a visit to a particular exhibit based on what was observed on the website's online collection. For example, the Los Angeles County Museum of Art provides push notifications to alert visitors when the bulbs on Chris Burden's landmark "Urban Light" sculpture turn on. But all of this, again, comes with a warning. Although many visitors are thriving on the new technologies, others are seeking a more contemplative experience without distraction and with the serendipity of making discoveries on their own (Gelt, 2015).

> Although many visitors are thriving on the new technologies, others are seeking a more contemplative experience.

In planning for use of the newer technologies, the following should be kept in mind:

- The technology should be engaging and should focus the visitor on the theme of the exhibit.
- The technology should be intuitive and dependable.
- Staff should be available for ready assistance for those who need it.

- In efforts to embrace younger visitors, smartphone features such as taking and sending photos or updating on social media should be encouraged (Serrell, 2015).

As Wayne LaBar (2014) admonished, "But remember: Use technology when it is appropriate to the design and the story, not technology for technology's sake."

Exhibit Plan

Generally, three components of an exhibit convey messages and provide the context: (a) object, (b) text, and (c) design. These three components make up the interpretive language of exhibits. An exhibit plan focuses on objects, text, and design and combines them to relate to the future exhibit viewers. When an exhibit involves multiple stations or displays, four planning documents guide the work.

One document inventories the likely objects to be included with notes about their interrelationships—in the case of loans, the sources of these loans are listed as well. A second document becomes the exhibit script. It states the theme and character of the exhibition; lists every exhibit panel or case; details of each item; and the text to be printed as signs, labels, and guides. The third document includes information and a map plus sketches of the layout of the exhibit. The fourth planning document presents studies, comments, and analyses of audiences and the conditions or events related to the proposed exhibit. This may also have references to key literature used, local experts or groups who can act as sources, interested viewers, plus logistics and plans for openings.

Exhibit Layout and Lighting

Every exhibit presents many basic options that affect display arrangement. For example, how should objects be displayed (e.g., chronologically, in related groups, as species)? How many objects should appear? Should objects be isolated to give immediate impact and elegance? Or should groups of related objects be used to provide more coherence and comprehension? Can object touching and manipulation work, or must objects be protected against theft, dust, and humidity?

Studies of visitor behaviors show that people select exhibits and objects that dominate by size, movement, and visibility. In a museum space, this can be aided by lighting and arrangement that add depth and vividness to the scene. Spotlights, floods, and general lighting, as well as care with shadows, help to make exhibits visible. Polarized, ultraviolet black lighting and colored lights give dramatic special effects. Lighting experts should help guide decisions in placement, venting, and installation. They can add much more value than what they cost.

Exhibit Accessibility

Knowing the location ahead of time for interactive exhibits can help with accessibility planning for visitors with disabilities. For example, when planning for an exhibit from a visitor center, proper layout can insure clear space for a person to maneuver a wheel chair in front of the exhibit (Brunswick & Ryan, 2015) (Figure 12.10). Other aspects of providing accessibility and full experiences for diverse visitors were covered in Chapter 7.

Summary

When people come into museums, zoos, aquariums, or visitor centers, they spend part of their time interacting with exhibits. (They also spend time at the café and gift shop, which also makes up part of the experience). Interpreters invest much energy, thought, and finances into designing and placing exhibits to provide meaningful experiences for visitors.

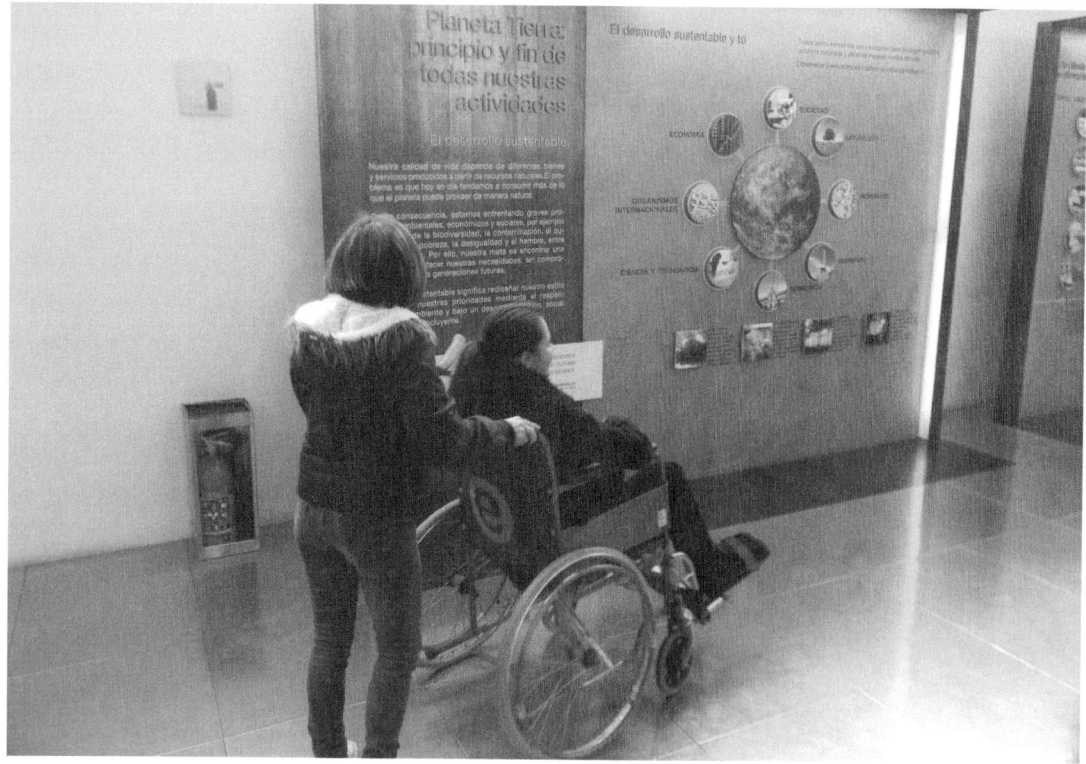

Figure 12.10. This museum in Mexico City leaves plenty of space for wheelchairs. Having ample floor space also allows multiple groups of people to view the same exhibit at the same time. (TC)

This chapter encompassed many practical suggestions of how to make exhibits communicate messages, values, connections, and inspiration. To do that requires recognition of the complexity of the audience. Different degrees of attentiveness and backgrounds affect what people see and absorb. A continuum of studies of visitor use patterns from the 1920s confirms the challenges to designers and suggests strategies that aid in effective design.

The exhibit planner/interpreter brings everything together with the numerous tools of the trade. He or she combines them with thematic goals, the physical facilities, the lighting and labeling options, and the intellectual content to create a house of truly interpretive exhibits. Evaluations before, during, and after installation guide the efforts to produce exciting interpretive experiences.

Meaningful exhibitions can enlighten, entertain, and educate. They may provide a lens for deeper understanding and may influence beliefs and actions. Such exhibitions truly lend themselves to making the world a better place.

Literature Cited

Bassett, L. (2014). More than monkey bars: The power of play in zoos. *Legacy, 25*(3), 18–20.

Bernton, H. (2015). NOAA study could set the stage for Makah whaling to resume. *The Seattle Times*. Originally published March 6, 2015. Environment/Local News/Northwest.

Bitgood, S. (2013a). *Attention and value: Keys to understanding museum visitors*. Walnut Creek, CA: West Coast Press.

Bitgood, S. (2013b). Lessons learned from a visitor research perspective. Session handout from the Annual Meeting & MuseumExpo, Baltimore, MD.

Bitgood, S., Ellingsen, E., & Patterson, D. (1990). Toward an objective description of the visitor immersion experience. *Visitor Behavior, 5*(2), 11–14.

Brunswick, N., & Ryan, C. (2015). Teamwork: Tips for working with landscape architects, architects and engineers for a quality interpretive experience. In *2015 interpretive sourcebook* (pp. 32–33). Virginia Beach, VA: National Association for Interpretation.

Copeland, A., Randall Gill, S., & Wright, K. (2015). The value of interpretation at zoos and aquariums. In *2015 interpretive sourcebook* (pp. 25–26). Virginia Beach, VA: National Association for Interpretation.

DiMaggio, P., Useem, M., & Brown, P. (1978). *Audience studies of the performing arts and museums: A critical review*. New York, NY: National Endowment for the Arts, Research Division, Report 9.

Ebersole, R. S. (2001). The new zoo. *Audubon, 103*(6), 64–72.

Falk, J., & Dierking, L. (2013). *The museum experience revisited*. Walnut Creek, CA: Left Coast Press.

Falk, J., Reinhard, E., Vernon, C., Bronnenkant, K., Deans, N., & Heimlich, J. (2007). *Why zoos and aquariums matter: Assessing the impact of a visit*. Silver Spring, MD: Association of Zoos and Aquariums.

Gamerman, E. (2015). A look at the museum of the future. *The Wall Street Journal*. October 15, 2015.

Gelt, J. (2015). How museums are adapting to 'selfie culture'. *Los Angeles Times*, October 23, 2015.

Hall, T., Ham, S., & Lackey, B. (2010). Comparative evaluation of the attention capture and holding power of novel signs aimed at park visitors. *Journal of Interpretation Research, 15*, 15–36.

Ham, S. (2013). *Interpretation: Making a difference on purpose*. Golden, CO: Fulcrum Publishing.

Kanno-Youngs, Z. (2015). Robo tour guides are ready to roll at museums. *The Wall Street Journal*, October 16, 2015.

LaBar, W. (2014). Tools of engagement. *eg magazine, 9*, 52–56.

Lazansky, N. (2014). "Changing California"—Gallery of California Natural Sciences. (Case study of an exhibition.) Published on October 2, 2014 and modified October 14, 2014. Exhibit Files: A Community site for exhibit designers and developers (exhibitfiles.org).

Lewis, J. (1976). Reconstructing a Maine lumber camp of 1900: The diorama as a historical medium. *Journal of Forest History, 20*(4), 191–202.

MacRae, J., & Serrell, B. (2000). Paying attention: Visitors' time in exhibitions. In *2000 interpretive sourcebook* (pp. 213–214). Ft. Collins, CO: National Association for Interpretation.

Masberg, B., & Silverman, L. (2004). Visitor experiences at heritage sites: A phenomenological approach. *Journal of Travel Research, 34*(4), 20–25.

McLean, K. (2011). Darkened waters: Profile of an oil spill. (Case study of an exhibition.) Published on January 9, 2008 and modified August 8, 2011. Exhibit Files: A Community site for exhibit designers and developers (exhibitfiles.org).

Melton, A. (1935). *Problems of installation in museums of art*. Washington, DC: American Association of Museums, New Series, No. 14.

Overhill, H. (2015). Design as choreography: Information in action. *Curator: The Museum Journal, 58*(1), 5–15.

Packer, J. (2006). The visitor motivation scale: An instrument for measuring the relative importance of reasons for visiting education leisure sites and activities. Paper presentation, Visitor Studies Association Conference, Grand Rapids, Michigan: July 27.

Parsons, L. (1965). System testing of display techniques for an anthropological exhibit. *The Museum Visitor, 8*(2), 167–196.

Redmond-Jones, B. (2011). Population impact. (Case study of an exhibition.) Published on August 24, 2010 and modified October 10, 2011. Exhibit Files: A Community site for exhibit designers and developers (exhibitfiles.org).

Robinson, E. (1928). *The behavior of the museum visitor*. Washington, DC: American Association of Museums, New Series, No. 5.

Serrell, B. (2015). *Exhibit labels: An interpretive approach* (2nd ed.). Lanham, MD: Rowman & Littlefield.

Stevens, J. (2013). Critique of Gallery One and the ArtLens, Cleveland Museum of Art. *Exhibitionist, 32*(2), 97–100.

Tilden, F. (1977). *Interpreting our heritage*. Chapel Hill, NC: The University of North Carolina Press.

Veverka, J. (2001). *Where is the interpretation in interpretive exhibits?* (Rev. ed.). Retrieved from heritageinterp.com.

Wells, M. (2000). Summative evaluation of Golden Gate State Park visitor center. In *2000 interpretive sourcebook* (pp. 184–185). Ft. Collins, CO: National Association of Interpretation.

Yalowits, S., & Bronnenkant, K. (2009). Timing and tracking: Unlocking visitor behavior. *Visitor Studies, 12*(1), 47–64.

Youngentob, K., & Hostetler, M. (2012). *Environmental interpretation: How to communicate persuasively*. Gainesville, Florida, Department of Wildlife Ecology and Conservation, Florida Cooperative Extension Services: WEC 169.

CHAPTER 13
Trails and Byways

*"The trail is the thing, not the end of the trail.
Travel too fast and you miss all that you are traveling for."*
–Louis L'Amour

During Runge Nature Center's annual Holiday Happenings event, Robin Grumm offered a self-guided trail experience called Nature Boxing. Visitors could pick up a brochure that gave clues that led to stations where they found a box. Inside the box were activity ideas and props to do them. The box contained a stamp so visitors could stamp their brochure upon completion of the activity. The brochure told them to share the completed brochure with a staff person and tell them about something they did or saw while on the trail. Then they would receive a prize. This was not a short walk. Visitors were told to plan at least an hour for this activity. This weeded out some families, but for the adventuresome, it was great. The folks who participated absolutely loved it and made it a point to say as much. Several families thanked Robin because the trail forced them to slow down and notice things they had not seen before. One in particular thanked Robin for slowing them down because they never realized the sound of the water in the creek was so relaxing. Other families reported that this trail was "just what they needed." They actually played together, outdoors. One enthusiastic family came in off the trail and grabbed Robin right away. The son said, "It said to share what we saw, so I want to tell you we saw a deer and we found a feather, and we discovered a cemetery!" Self-guided trail experiences are most rewarding when people make discoveries along the trail, discoveries about the resource and about themselves.

Interpretive trails and byways allow individuals to connect directly with heritage, landscapes, and ecosystems. The best ones promote in people a sense of wonder as they wander. As seen in the above example, like a progressive dinner, building a sense of mystery, competitiveness, and fun entices visitors to move eagerly along the route.

This chapter presents interpreters with options for using trails and roadways to touch people with stories found in the landscape. It will encourage interpreters to use trails and automobile tours to create enjoyable, educational, and memorable experiences.

More specifically, this chapter focuses on *self-guiding* interpretive trails and byways. It is important to note that although interpreters can lead a *guided walk* or tour on virtually any trail or road, not every trail or road is suitable for a *self-guided* interpretive experience. Designing interpretive trails and road tours involves application of all of the previously presented interpretive principles. Like all interpretive efforts, to reach their full potential, self-guided paths, walking tours, and driving routes must be designed with effective communication of compelling content in mind. However, trails and byways present special challenges and opportunities because the audience is moving along a defined route either on foot or in a vehicle. The best self-guided interpretive media mimic a pleasant and informed traveling companion who tells the right stories at the right time without detracting from the travel experience.

> Designing interpretive trails and road tours involves application of all of the previously presented interpretive principles.

Although some people categorize self-guiding approaches as "non-personal interpretation," they must never be "impersonal." Even when an interpreter is not present, audience members should believe the interpretive messages along their journey were designed with their personal interests in mind.

Trails that Teach, Trails that Touch

"Methinks that the moment my legs begin to move, my thoughts begin to flow."
–Henry David Thoreau

Perhaps the first thing you think of when you read about an interpretive trail is the generic "Nature Trail" found in many parks and refuges. Although these footpaths provide a leisurely stroll, they can offer much more than merely a walk in the woods. It is a guide *into* the resource, not a pathway through it. The best interpretive trails create experiences that *teach* and *touch* the visitor. With those goals in mind, some design considerations become evident.

Self-guided trails allow people to move at their own pace. As noted in the introductory story, they can encourage people to slow down and use all of their senses to notice new sounds and sights (Figure 13.1). They provide groups or individuals contact with and sometimes even immersion *in* the resource. Self-guided trails are accessible even when staff members are not available, thereby being an efficient approach to interpreting to large numbers of visitors.

> The best interpretive trails create experiences that *teach* and *touch* the visitor.

284   Interpreting Cultural and Natural Heritage

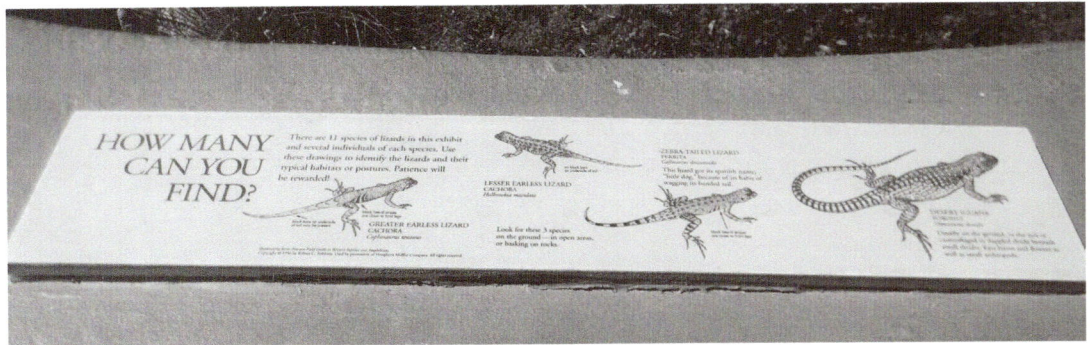

Figure 13.1. Self-guided trails encourage people to slow down and notice more along the way. (TC)

In spite of the advantages of being multisensory and self-paced, trails are not always the best approach, particularly if they are poorly planned. They can be expensive to build and maintain, and trails may have adverse impacts on local wildlife and plants.

Planning a Trail

One approach to planning a trail is to answer the following questions before building the trail.

Why do we need a trail? The first step in planning a trail is to determine whether it is necessary. What will its purpose be? Is the trail necessary to communicate an important theme? Will it enrich the visitor experience? Is it consistent with the sites' Interpretive Plan or Master Plan? Will it support the agency's mission? Too often park staff build a generic nature trail merely because other parks have them or because an Eagle Scout needs a project. These trails are almost inevitably under-used and ineffective.

Where to locate it? The answer to the "*why*" question along with an inventory of the site's resources and facilities will often make the decision about *where* to establish the trail obvious.

Who will use it? As with any interpretive media, it is essential to understand the audience. Will it be school groups, families, people with disabilities, or busloads of tourists? These factors will inform design considerations including the width, length, and tread of the trail as well as the interpretive messages presented.

Trail Design

After answering those questions of why, where, and who, interpreters can address trail design. The following discussion presents considerations about designing self-guided interpretive trails.

Location. The trail's theme will dictate the general location of the trail as it brings people in contact with features associated with the theme. However, planners should avoid sensitive cultural features or plants that might be prone to collecting or vandalism unless barriers or other protection strategies are used. To avoid disturbing breeding birds, trails should not pass too close to permanent locations of heron colonies or eagle nests. Responsibility to protect resources trumps the interpretation of them along a self-guided trail (Figure 13.2).

Ideally, the trailhead would be near a visitor center providing orientation and a larger context for the trail. A visitor center can serve as a portal to set visitor expectations and provide a transition from the outside world to the natural world or a historic time experienced along the trail. If not near a visitor center, then trailheads should at least be near facilities where people congregate such as campgrounds, playgrounds, and parking lots. However, remember that the visitors at each of these locations may have different interest levels and motivations in walking the trail. Trails at these locations should keep the likely users in mind.

Use of existing trails, abandoned roads, and animal paths will decrease the impact on the environment. However, avoid a view of a parking lot, campground, or visitor center that might entice a person to short cut back rather than finishing the trail.

Whereas excellent hiking trails provide physical challenges, strenuous activities are not appropriate for interpretive trails. Interpretive trails are not meant to be obstacle courses or exercise trails, so locate them in areas with minimal physical barriers including fallen trees, low hanging branches, and boulders. These things distract from the message and experience. In short, as people walk the trail make them feel comfortable and eliminate distractions, just as you would indoors.

Figure 13.2. When planning a trail, locate it to minimize impacts on the soil and vegetation. (LB)

Figure 13.3. Trails with severe slopes may put certain visitors at risk, particularly at higher elevations. Although the sign advises caution, it doesn't specifically state why. (TC)

Avoid hilly terrain if possible. It is tiring for people and fatigue or concern about it being too physically demanding detracts from attention to the messages (Figure 13.3). Mitigating this fatigue issue can be problematic. Steps on slopes are helpful to walkers, but they present a barrier to wheelchairs and strollers. Switchbacks reduce the rate of climb for walkers by creating a gentler slope, but they lengthen trails and can promote off-trail shortcutting. If switchbacks are required, create physical barriers to shortcutting by building brush piles or planting dense thorny shrubs. Some agencies discourage shortcutting across switchbacks by warning about venomous snakes or poison ivy. If the trail begins with a steep incline at the entrance it will discourage people from walking it as they will think it will not be worth the effort.

Water issues are another reason for avoiding slopes. Rainwater running down steep trails can cause severe erosion on the trails and puddles of standing water in low areas.

Water bar structures, culverts, boardwalks, and other trail improvements can mitigate the water problems, but they require additional expense and maintenance (Figure 13.4). Minimizing slopes and choosing areas with well-drained soils reduces maintenance expenses. It also allows users to focus on the messages, rather than on keeping their feet dry.

Layout. If possible, make the trail a one-way loop. Loop trails are preferred because of the following reasons:

- Loops decrease the monotony and boredom of retracing steps.
- Having foot traffic moving in one direction decreases congestion and enhances flow.
- One-way traffic means fewer encounters with other people and therefore results in more solitude and fewer distractions.
- Fewer encounters with others also means increased potential for mystery as visitors have less of an opportunity to hear comments about what lies ahead.
- People find comfort, security, and convenience in ending up where they started.
- One-way loops are necessary to have an introduction, body, and conclusion sequence to the interpretation.

Figure 13.4. When designing a new interpretive trail, planners should try to avoid including long straight stretches. (TC)

Loop trails should have only one access point. This reduces confusion and allows managers to more easily monitor and control trail use. As noted in Chapter 11, people tend to move to the right when given a choice. Therefore, interpreters should arrange the interpretive content along the loop to align with a counter-clockwise traffic flow. Make clear which is the proper direction to follow by using a sign or directional arrow.

Trail planners should avoid long straight stretches. Straight lines seldom exist in nature. Gentle curves promote interest and a sense of mystery about what lies ahead since curves limit the view. Curves enhance a sense of solitude as the vegetation hides other walkers. However, too many sharp curves cause frustration and a sense of not making progress, which may lead to off-trail shortcutting. Side loops add flexibility for people without time constraints by increasing trail length. They give people options to learn about and experience additional features.

Length. Because self-guided trails aim to communicate information, planners consider attention span and stamina. For this reason, interpretive trails are usually short.

Generally, they are less than a mile long. The time necessary to walk an interpretive trail is usually 30-60 minutes, much like the typical length of an interpretive program. Length will vary with topography. The hillier the terrain, the shorter the trail, as fatigue reduces attention span. Likewise, for special audiences such as young children or people with disabilities, shorter trails would accommodate their needs.

Tread. For high-volume trails near a visitor center the trail surface should be at least 6 to 8 feet wide; enough for two people walking side by side or use with a wheelchair. Trim back vegetation three feet on the sides of the trail and eight feet above the trail to account for branches drooping with rain or snow or users walking atop snow pack. This width allows use of a garden tractor or ATV for maintenance.

Ideally, the surface is smooth, firm and free of obstacles. Trampling by walkers will help maintain the tread, but putting material down can improve drainage, reduce erosion, and identify the trail route when other informal trails intersect, thereby reducing the need for directional signage. Gravel, cinders, and pea gravel provide drainage and a firm footing, but they are noisy when groups are walking on them. This crunching sound detracts from tranquil experiences and makes observing birds and other wildlife difficult. Wood chips have the advantage of being cheap or free as parks and utility companies use chippers in their vegetation management programs. They also appear more natural and provide a soft and quiet walking experience. Woodchips do deteriorate, however, and can wash away so such trails need to be rechipped regularly. Asphalt trails provide the best surface for wheelchairs and people with limited mobility. However, asphalt trails are expensive to build and can become hot and tacky on warm days. They are clearly not natural and therefore may not be aesthetically pleasing.

Vandalism concerns. Most vandalism occurs near trailheads, so trailheads and the first stretch of trail should be easily visible to park rangers and law enforcement. Place benches and other facilities farther along the trail. Putting numbered guideposts or signs at least three feet away from the edge of the trail reduces damage caused by people leaning on them or easily touching them. Smooth-barked trees such as aspen and beech are prone to people carving initials or other messages. If possible, leave vegetation screening between the trail and such tempting trees. Likewise, rather than using spray-paint or blazes to mark trees along the trail use temporary flagging. Paint and cuts into the trees send the wrong message to visitors.

Interpretive Considerations

All of the principles of interpretation presented in earlier chapters apply to self-guided trails. Trails should tell stories and provoke thoughts and actions. They should elucidate a powerful theme that makes the resource relevant to the visitor. The following tips will make self-guided trails meaningful and memorable. Most importantly, the content should motivate people to move eagerly along the trail. Building in games such as eye-spy, a continuing story, or other activities involving trailside discoveries (as noted in this chapter's introductory story) will keep young and old enthusiastically engaged in the trail.

Arrange interpretive stops along the trail like an interpretive talk with an introduction, body, and conclusion. Present the theme in the introduction and restate it at the conclusion of the trail. Typically, interpretive trails have between 10 and 20 stops. This, of course, will vary with the theme and resource. Too few stops may cause people to lose interest between stops and may render useless any transitions or efforts to build upon previous messages. Too many stops, like a guide who is never quiet, may frustrate visitors who will eventually ignore the messages. On busy trails, too many stops too close to one another can cause congestion. Crowding around a trailside panel can discourage the use of that panel by approaching walkers (Koenen, Legg, & Darville, 2007). Placing stops in high traffic flow areas may increase the number of people seeing the interpretation, but due to crowding it might decrease the *percentage* of visitors stopping at the wayside. When fewer trail users are present, a higher percentage of walkers will stop at waysides (Koenen et al., 2007).

Relevancy seemed to be the most important factor in whether people stopped to read a wayside exhibit (Koenen et al., 2007), so choose locations where people can clearly see the subject being interpreted and then, of course, apply Tilden's first principle and relate that subject to their lives. In the end, the important stories along the trail will dictate the placement and number of stops.

Provide benches or seats fashioned from rocks or stumps at the top of hills or in tranquil shady spots. These inviting features allow visitors to catch their breath and refocus their attention on the trail's theme.

> Trailheads should attract potential users with a catchy thematic title.

Interpretive trails should not be multipurpose trails. By prohibiting horseback riding, mountain biking, or other competing uses, distractions will be reduced and communication of the interpretive messages will be enhanced. People can focus on the interpretation rather than dodging bikes, joggers, or horses. Limiting trail use to walking also reduces maintenance problems.

Trailheads should attract potential users with a catchy thematic title, rather than the oft-used Nature Trail name. To inform audiences about what they will experience, the trailhead should include information about the trail length, time necessary to walk it, and the terrain or difficulty of walking. A map is a nice touch as it decreases uncertainty about the trail's route and reassures users about where they will end up (Figure 13.5). To entice folks to walk the trail, a short theme statement provides another reason for walking and heightens anticipation about what people will see and learn along the trail.

Trail Media

Even in this digital age, many self-guided trails still use either signs or brochures associated with numbers along the trail (Figure 13.6). This is changing as phone apps or downloaded information increasingly provide

Figure 13.5. Trailheads with maps orient visitors and give them confidence that they will not get lost. (LC)

interpretation along trails, although the old ways have a rustic charm.

Each medium has advantages and disadvantages. Signs, if well done, may be more impressive and therefore more powerful than merely a number on a post. Signs eliminate the need to deal with brochure distribution issues such as keeping a brochure box filled or having distribution limited by office or visitor center hours. Compared to numbered posts, signs can better orient the user to the exact location of the interpreted feature and because they are more conspicuous, people are less likely to miss them. Disadvantages of signs versus brochures/numbered posts are that signs are more expensive to install and maintain, they may be prone to vandalism, and if all the readers must stand in one spot to read the sign they may interfere with each other and compact the soil. People are less inclined to read large amounts of text on signs than in brochures or other printed matter.

Brochures linked to numbers along the trail have the advantages of being cheaper than signs, less prone to vandalism, less visually obtrusive, and if the number is removed, the users could still read the story along that stretch of trail. Brochures can serve as souvenirs to reinforce messages and memories later. Generally, brochures can offer more detail and text than a series of signs. Disadvantages of trail brochures include the aforementioned distribution issues and the fact that if one feature changes along the trail the whole brochure will need to be reprinted.

Figure 13.6. Numbered posts offer a minimal amount of information, but are linked to a brochure or other medium to provide additional interpretation. (LC)

Some managers are concerned about brochures contributing to litter. However, providing a box at the end of the trail to allow for reuse or recycling of the brochures and making the brochures so attractive that people want to keep them rather than throw them on the ground will limit littering. People will be less likely to litter if they have paid even a small price for the publication, so that might be a reasonable approach, although most agencies do not want to create financial barriers to receiving interpretation.

Regardless, for signs or numbered posts, create them using the same size and style to produce unity and decrease costs. In addition, inexpensive temporary signs can supplement the interpretation and interpret fleeting things such as bird nests, blooming wildflowers, or animal signs.

A powerful aspect of using digital media such as apps or QR codes along trails is that audio features can supplement or replace interpretive text. In the past, interpreters could only provide audio to trail users carrying a tape or CD player or by installing expensive audio stations that would require pressing a button or lifting a receiver to listen. Having visitors use their personal devises saves the costs of investing in expensive handheld or stationary equipment.

Audio enhances the interpretation by allowing visitors to hear special voices, including the voices of historic characters telling the stories. This makes the interpretive effort more personal. Audio allows for sound effects such as birdcalls or the sounds of human activities. It serves people with limited sight and those with full sight can concentrate on looking at the resource instead of having to read. People are better listeners than readers so messages can be a bit longer if presented as audio. As is often the case, using more than one strategy along the trail can reach people with different preferences.

Of course, digital approaches require a smartphone and Wi-Fi service along the trail, which can limit their use in remote natural areas. Because of this reliance on good Wi-Fi, the most widespread application of interpretive apps has been to guide visitors on walking tours through museums, historic sites, cemeteries, public gardens, and zoos.

People are coming to expect to receive interpretation through their personal devices. Visitors find it routine to have a personal interpreter in their pocket. The best digital approaches are interactive, allowing the visitor to make choices and respond to questions. Some allow for real time online chatting or texting with docents or other staff as the guest strolls through the site. Upon completion of the visit with digital connections, interpreters can easily gather feedback from the guest, collect data from the phone interactions to evaluate their exhibits, and find ways to stay in touch with the guest electronically.

John Muir said, "In every walk with nature, one receives far more than he seeks." The best self-guided trails, regardless of the interpretive medium or venue, amplify the rewards received by walkers.

Water Trails

Not all interpretive trails are on dry land. Boardwalks provide access into mangrove and cypress swamps, cattail marshes, wet meadows, and bogs. Canoe trails, boat trails, and underwater trails interpret rivers, lakes, estuaries, bays, and coral reefs. The approaches used in planning and interpretive media are similar to those found on terrestrial trails. One difference is that water trails are often shorter due to the physical exertion required.

Along lake or river shorelines, wayside signs or numbers indicate interpretive stops. In open water, buoys (some as simple as painted milk jugs) with numbers identify the location of the next story. At some sites, the interpretive messages are printed on buoys. Paddlers or boaters pick up the buoy to read the message. This creates mystery and anticipation like opening a fortune cookie. Often these stories will pertain to something along the shoreline, but sometimes they reveal what lies beneath the surface. At Straits of Mackinac Underwater Preserve in Michigan, boaters experience shipwrecks by reading interpretive information attached to the shipwreck mooring buoys. People encounter exciting, and sometimes heroic, sometimes tragic, stories of the shipwreck that lies directly below them.

Along underwater trails, snorkelers or scuba divers read signs through their masks. These trails only work well in shallow (well-lit) areas with clear water for good visibility. Such trails typically use anchored signs made out of non-corrosive materials such as porcelain. Or, just as on land, numbered posts along the underwater route correspond to stories on printed materials. Waterproof brochures, booklets or plastic cards with text on them link to the submerged numbered stops. Popular underwater interpretive trails can be found at John Pennekamp Reef State Park in Florida, Virgin Islands National Park, and at many other coastal resorts and parks. The underwater trail at Trunk Bay in the Virgin Islands is particularly popular as it accommodates even beginners. Snorkelers read underwater plaques and enjoy coral and colorful fish along the trail, which goes for about 300 feet before making a U-turn and returning to the beach.

Byways that Beckon

"The world is a book, and those who do not travel read only a page."
–Saint Augustine

Sometimes the only practical way to experience a park, region, or landscape fully is from a vehicle. Most large national parks and battlefields and many national forests and grasslands have road tours to allow visitors to move between widely spaced sites that are important to the interpretive themes of the site (Figure 13.7).

Figure 13.7. Road tours and byways provide an overview of expansive landscapes such as this stop on the Cimarron National Grasslands Road Tour. (TC)

The most important advantage of interpretive road tours is that they allow visitors to see the big picture by providing a holistic overview of the site. For some visitors this broad exposure will be sufficient to complete a satisfying visit. To many others, an interpretive road tour is just the beginning. After getting a general introduction to the landscape, resources, activities, and facilities, they then decide how to experience the special place.

Road tours can serve large numbers of people in groups ranging from individual drivers to families on vacation to busloads of tourists. They are easily accessible to people with disabilities.

Planning a road tour is much like planning a self-guided interpretive trail. Planners link the route to the key features and stories to meet interpretive goals. Like interpretive trails, one-way loops are optimal but often not possible, since existing public roadways are used. In choosing the roads, it is important to avoid distractions like heavy truck traffic, steep slopes, tight curves, stretches prone to lots of dust, mud, and water-crossings because they compete for the attention of the travelers. Moreover, like trails, the length of the interpretive auto tour should be limited to the audience's interest level. Typically, road tours in national parks or forests are less than 100 miles in length.

> "Interpretive road tours allow visitors to see the big picture by providing a holistic overview of the site."

The single most important consideration in designing road tours is safety. Traffic congestion can occur at popular stopping points or roadside attractions. Using wayside exhibits will require people to be pulling off and back on to the road. This increases the opportunity for accidents. If interpreters provide interpretation through audio recordings or printed materials to be read as the vehicle is moving along the highway, they create a distraction for the driver. All of these concerns are inherent in this interpretive approach. Interpreters should acknowledge and mitigate them as much as possible. For example, encourage listeners to turn off the audio as they pass over railroad tracks or through potentially dangerous stretches of road.

Beyond the Park or Historic Site

Many countries have designated scenic byways. In the U.S., the Department of Transportation has designated more than 150 National Scenic Byways or All-American Roads based on archaeological, cultural, historic, natural, recreational, and scenic qualities. To be designated a National Scenic Byway, the route must have at least one of these six intrinsic qualities, whereas an All-American Road must have at least two of those qualities that do not exist elsewhere and are important enough to be considered tourist destinations. Both of these designations require a Corridor Management Plan that includes signage to enhance the experience of the traveler. The All-American Road Plans must specifically address interpretation along the route and the needs of non-English speaking travelers.

> "All-American Road Plans must specifically address interpretation along the route."

In addition to these roads, most states have their own scenic byway systems. They provide exceptional opportunities for interpretation to millions of travelers. Because federal and state byways are managed mostly through local grassroots efforts, the roadside interpretation is often rich in local color and culture as residents eagerly share stories of their heritage and landscape. Often agencies hire professional interpretive planners to oversee the identification and development of the interpretive elements along the route. Interpretive plans for byways identify an overarching theme and a few broad storylines. A storyline, like the plot in a novel, organizes the individual stories and relates them to the theme in a linear fashion geographically or chronologically (Eubanks, 2014).

Land management agencies also administer and provide interpretation along byway systems. The Bureau of Land Management (BLM) has developed National Back Country Byways, many of them unpaved. BLM offers four types of motorized byways ranging from paved roads to trails for snowmobiles and ATVs, and each features self-guided interpretation along the route. Similarly, the U.S. Forest Service established a system of more than 100 byways to interpret the history and scenic features of national forests.

The U.S. National Trail System includes 11 national scenic trails, 19 national historic trails, and over 1,000 national recreation trails. The 30 scenic and historic trails total nearly 60,000 miles in combined length—more than the entire interstate highway system. These National Trails are managed by federal agencies, including the National Park Service, Bureau of Land Management, USDA Forest Service, U.S. Fish & Wildlife Service, and U.S. Army Corps of Engineers. Although the Federal Highway Administration provides the bulk of the funding, the National Trail System relies heavily on local volunteers to take the lead in nearly all aspects of trail planning and management, including developing the interpretation along the route.

Private commercial interests, particularly in areas with high levels of tourism, often create and sell interpretive DVDs that interpret roadside scenes and attractions. One such example is the Hana Road audio tour on the Hawaiian Island of Maui. This audio CD comes with a map and poster of wildflowers seen along the route. The stories range from the history of sugar cane production to the sport of surfing. Similarly, guidebooks interpret sites and landscapes along interstate highways that carry millions of travelers annually (e.g., Cable & Maley, 2017; Cadden & Cable, 2013). Interstate guidebooks interpret routes many people think of as notoriously boring stretches of highway and attempt to transform them into fun and engaging drives.

Special Interest Road Tours

Road tours devoted to special topics, products, or hobbies are popular. These are sometimes called "affinity trails" or "experiential trails." They connect people to their personal interests in everything from country churches to craft beers, ghost towns to gastronomy, and wildflowers to wineries. In the Auvergne region of France, one auto tour is devoted to showing off medieval dovecots while another, the *Route du Fromage*, is dedicated to connecting visitors with cheese caves, cheese-making hamlets, dairy farms, and interpreting local cheeses (Cable & Morgan-Proux, 2006). Perhaps the most popular and widespread auto tours are Birding Trails. They exist in more than 40 states and several foreign countries in Africa and Latin America. Box 13.1 presents guidelines for planning interpretation along birding trails and other special interest byways.

> "A well-planned interpretive experiential trail meanders along a continuum, intermittently punctuated with moments of discovery, epiphany, poignancy, and bliss."

According to Eubanks (2014), experiential trails are interpreted itineraries. They offer the interpreter a well-defined interpretive opportunity, since the interpreter establishes a theme (or at least thematic boundaries) at the outset and then orchestrates an array of supporting interpretive experiences along a linear path. Ideally, a well-planned interpretive experiential trail meanders along a continuum, intermittently punctuated with moments of discovery, epiphany, poignancy, and bliss.

Some byways have lofty educational goals. For example, the goal of the Roadside Heritage Program is to teach informal science education along rural scenic highways on the Eastern Sierra region. A consortium of universities, community-based groups, and interpreters received National Science Foundation Informal Science Education funding to teach science heritage by telling the stories "hidden in the sand and sagebrush" along byways that pass through the Great Basin Desert, Mojave Desert, and steep Sierra Escarpment (Williams, Robertson, & Bard, 2008).

Box 13.1
Steps to Designing Experiential Trails
Ted Eubanks, President/CEO of Fermata, Inc.

The theory behind experiential trails is simple. A trail is an interpretive platform, a foundation upon which interpreters can construct a set of interpretive experiences. Here are five simple steps for organizing an experiential trail such as a birding trail.

1. **Define an interpretive Zone of Influence (ZOI).**

   On a map, draw a circle around the area where your new trail will be located. Geographical boundaries or sideboards are critical for keeping the trail within a manageable scope of work.

2. **Inventory specific locations or sites within the ZOI.**

   Inventory the sites within the ZOI where visitors can be directed to experience the focus of the trail (e.g., birds). This inventory should look at constraints that may limit interpretive opportunities at specific sites.

3. **Develop an interpretive plan.**

   Using the inventory, the interpreter should be able to construct a simple interpretive strategy with an overarching theme and a set of storylines derived from this theme.

4. **Select sites.**

   Using the interpretive strategy, select sites that most effectively embody the theme and storylines of the interpretive plan. Sites may differ. For example, one site may be the best for illustrating one (but not all) of the storylines in the interpretive strategy.

5. **Develop a trail plan.**

   With this information in hand, you are ready to develop a plan for organizing an experiential trail. This development plan should include not only the physical arrangement of the trail (usually shown on a map), but should also provide a media strategy for how the interpretive messages will be communicated to the public.

Media Options

As with walking trails, media options for auto tours include printed materials (brochures or books), wayside signs or exhibits, and apps for phones or tablets. QR codes on printed materials or waysides sometimes link to additional information or graphics. Using apps with GPS to trigger audio and video at specific locations along the route is particularly effective. This approach ensures that the travelers receive the interpretive story at precisely the correct location. Moreover, audio presenting human voices (from the past or present) is more personal. Apps with video content are more dynamic than merely reading text from a brochure or exhibit. When creating audio or video segments for hand-held devices keep them at about two minutes or less to maintain interest. Using this digital approach for trails and byways has the additional advantage of being able to use these recorded segments on associated websites. In this way, more potential visitors can hear them.

An excellent example of this approach is the Creole Nature Trail in Louisiana. A professional interpreter worked with local tourism officials to identify key stories and then wrote the script. Videographers then shot the stories at each location along the route and a narrator delivered the script. The result is a free app that people can download to hear stories about marshlands teeming with alligators and birdlife, four National Wildlife Refuges, Gulf of Mexico beaches, fishing, crabbing, Cajun culture, oil and gas production, rice and crayfish harvests, and more. As people drive the 180-mile long loop, built-in GPS markers trigger the stories at the appropriate locations giving a thorough overview of southwest Louisiana.

As noted in Chapter 8, Traveler's Information Stations are low-powered AM radio stations used along byways. Travelers tune their car radios, usually to 530 or 1610 on the dial, to hear a message about the site or byway. These messages can be easily updated and reach large numbers of potential visitors.

Wayside Design

Although the use of GPS-linked content on phones and tablets is growing, the standard approach to interpretation along most auto tours is still the wayside exhibit. Waysides take two forms, either low profile or upright. Low profile exhibits interpret features that travelers can readily see from that specific location, whereas upright exhibits inform visitors about the general area or amenities such as trails. Low profile exhibits are aligned to draw attention to the object being interpreted. Upright exhibits often are clustered into a kiosk that matches surrounding architecture and provide unity to the other signs and structures along the route. These kiosks typically include rules and safety information, bulletin boards, and brochure boxes. Some have roofs to protect the exhibits and the people from the elements and some have lighting to make them useful after dark. They serve an important purpose of being available when visitor centers and other facilities are closed.

Whereas the function of most upright wayside exhibits is providing information, the function of low-profile exhibits is interpretation. They occur where there is a significant observable feature and a compelling story to go along with it. The wayside's low angle and position should align with the subject and direct traveler's attention in a specific direction toward the landscape or object. The traveler should be able to look directly over the top of the wayside to see the intended feature. The typical angle of a low-profile wayside is 45 degrees (Figure 13.8).

Regular maintenance is an important factor when planning and managing road tours. Check waysides frequently for vandalism and cleaning. Clear brush away to maintain the view and ensure visitor safety. Panel materials will weather in the outdoors. Life spans vary greatly depending on climate and the material, but a rough average for NPS wayside signs is about five years (NPS, 2009). Box 13.2 presents a comparison of the pros and cons of various sign materials as provided by a leading interpretive sign manufacturer.

The National Park Service advises the following considerations when planning interpretive waysides along an auto tour (NPS, 2009):

Safety first. Locate wayside pull-offs in areas where traffic congestion is unlikely and with good visibility of on-coming traffic. Straight and flat stretches allow for drivers to see cars entering or exiting the wayside pull-off and those pulling back on to the roadway can see on-coming vehicles. Adequate space allows multiple vehicles to pull well off the roadway.

Figure 13.8. Low-profile exhibits are used where there is an observable feature and a compelling story to go along with it. The traveler should be able to look directly over the top of the wayside to see the intended feature. (TC)

Use waysides judiciously. Too many waysides will fatigue or overwhelm travelers causing them to skip some of them. Too few waysides may leave important stories untold and beauty unrevealed. This cheats the unwitting traveler. In choosing locations, make sure that there is a compelling story to tell at that location and then stick with only that story. The location should foster opportunities for visitors to connect personally with the resource. Ask yourself, *"What is important about this spot and why should a person care about what they see here?"*

Do not use waysides when they create an intrusion on the aesthetics of a natural landscape or historic site. Likewise, do not use them to direct attention to fragile resources such as archeological remains or nest sites. Resource protection takes precedent over putting the resource at risk through directing people to it.

Use site-specific graphics. Site-specific photographs or artwork are the key to successfully telling the story of a site. The main image should convey much of the story. If such an illustration is unavailable, use a bold attention-grabbing illustration. Historic photos taken from the exact location are particularly powerful.

Box 13.2
A Comparison of Materials Used for Interpretive Signs and Waysides
Compiled by Interpretive Graphics, Inc., Salt Lake City

Exterior Sign Materials

	Sign Material	Graphic Capability	Thickness	Requires Backing or Frame	Ability to Cut to Shape	Ability to Print Double-sided	Scratch Resistance	Graffiti Resistance	Warranty	24"x36" Single-sign Cost; not incl. setup, proofs, shipping	Notes
A.	Porcelain Enamel	4-color process, 2400 dpi, vivid colors	16-gauge steel (approx 1/8")	Yes (can flange edges w/ plywood backer)	Yes	No	High	Clean with solvent	25 years	$2,000.00	
B.	Chemically Etched Anodized Aluminum	150 dpi, 65-line screen, halftones, line art	Up to 3/8"	No, 1/4" thick or thicker	Yes	Yes	High	Clean with solvent	Lifetime	$1,700.00	
C.	Gel-coat Laminate	Full-color, 1200 dpi	Up to 1/8"	Yes	Yes	Yes	Medium	Clean with solvent	10 years	$350.00	Unit cost decreases as additional signs are purchased.
D.	Fiberglass Embedment	Full-color, 1200 dpi	Up to 1/4"	Yes	Yes	Yes	Medium	Clean with solvent	10 years	$350.00	Unit cost decreases as additional signs are purchased.
E.	High-pressure Laminate	Full-color, 1200 dpi	Up to 1"	No, 1/2" thick or thicker	Yes	Yes (2 panels bonded back-to-back)	Medium	Clean with solvent	10 years	$300.00	
F.	Fused Poly-carbonate	Full-color, 1200 dpi	Up to 1/2"	No, 1/2" thick	Yes	No	Medium	Clean with solvent	10 years	$250.00	1/2" thick panels cost more.
G.	Composite	Full-color, 1200 dpi	Up to 1/8"	Yes	Yes	Yes	Low	Low	None	$220.00	Expect life of 3 years.
H.	Fused Graphics	Full-color, 1200 dpi	Up to 1/4"	No	Yes	Yes	High	Clean with solvent	10 years	$175.00	$225.00 for double-sided.

This chart compares the merits and relative fabrication costs of various exterior sign materials. Additional selection factors include: need for color, likelihood of vandalism, type of vandalism, need for replacement, mounting system, and replacement cost.

Apply Exhibit Design Principles

Chapter 12 presented tips on how to design effective exhibits for visitor centers, zoos, museums, and other indoor spaces. All of those tips as well as the previously discussed principles of interpretation apply for outside wayside exhibits. These tips include the following:

- Have a compelling thematic title to capture attention and communicate something concrete rather than merely a subject or topical title.
- Limit text by communicating graphically instead of with words. Try using fewer than 100 words in the main body of the wayside.
- Use of colorful or insightful quotations about the place or event can personalize the subject and site. Quotes add another voice to the interpretation.
- Write in a style that is active rather than passive, non-technical (avoiding jargon), and concise.
- Avoid having too many colors, styles, and decorative elements. Keep it neat and simple.
- Avoid having several small photos on a wayside. Instead, have fewer large photos.
- Likewise, avoid having many logos on the wayside. Find other ways of recognizing partners.

- Use large point sizes, appropriate fonts, and short lines of text for easy reading. Make sure the text contrasts sharply with the background.
- Assist the traveler in finding personal meanings by answering the question, *"So what?"* Present the significance and relevance of the subject gently without telling people what to think or pontificating about a subject.

Box 13.3 gives additional suggestions from Jeremy Shellhorn, a graphic design professional who has designed waysides for national parks.

QR codes and Augmented Reality can supplement waysides if Wi-Fi is available. QR codes allow the visitor to link to and receive detailed information about the subject of the wayside. Typically, a smartphone acts as a QR code scanner. Augmented reality (AR) is a technology with huge implications for interpretation. AR blurs the line between what is real and what is computer-generated by enhancing what is seen and heard. AR uses image recognition software so that if a person points their phone or tablet at a sign or roadside symbol, it can come alive on the screen. Portraits of historic characters can speak, images of rivers can flow, and wildlife and historic figures and structures can appear. The applications for interpreting both history and nature are seemingly endless and they overcome many of the limitations of static images and text on waysides.

Using a variety of media is generally a good approach to reach a diverse audience of different learning preferences. However, a word of caution is prudent. People do not like to read and listen at the same time, and when they try, they do neither very well.

Box 13.3
Tips on Designing Waysides

Jeremy Shellhorn, Professor of Graphic Design, University of Kansas

A good wayside design can engage and connect visitors to things seen and unseen. It can help them understand, reflect upon and/or question a place and the event(s) that have shaped those places. Here are a few prompts that my students, park rangers, collaborators and I use during the wayside design process:

Design the Process
As any designer will tell you, the design process is as important as the solution. We really learn our way to a successful wayside design by making multiple iterations and testing them along the way. Forming a collaborative team, clearly stating goals, and understanding the audience and context in which this wayside will live in is vital. It is also vital to test visual concepts with the audience along the way to make sure your design choices are working.

Start with a Visual Concept
As designer, Petrula Vrontikis says, "Practice Safe Design: Use a concept." The visual concept is the idea behind a design. It is how you plan on solving the wayside design problem that you and your team are working on. It is the underlying thinking and rationale for how you will make choices in graphics, photography, color and typography. Every visual design decision you make will use your visual concept as a framework for direction.

Write Titles that Engage, Provoke, or Question
If a good wayside is like a caption in space then the title has to do a lot of the work. Caption literally means, "to capture" and that is what you should expect out of your title. Draw viewers in, but more importantly, if they give it a quick look they can get the big idea.

Box 13.3 continued

Stay on Site, Stay on Message
The power of waysides are that they are posters in a specific context. They have a reason for being in the spot they are in. Make everything directly relate to what the viewer is seeing at that site and do not make them remember something they will see down the trail or saw a minute ago. The connection to the exact place they are standing gives the viewer a context and privileges them to learn something they cannot somewhere else.

Hone your Typographic Voice
Good typographic design is in the details from the spacing between letters, to the spaces between lines, to the spacing between paragraphs. Everything has a reason for being there and each typeface or "font" is chosen for its visual voice. Typography is language made visible, so do not treat all text the same just like you do not treat all the words you say the same. Use scale, color, layout, and typeface choice to put emphasis and create different voices on your wayside. Title, main text, bullet points, captions…these do not all need to look the same, but still need to feel connected. Stick with one-two typefaces and do not be afraid to use the different weights included in the typeface (thin, regular, bold etc.) when you need something to "stand-out" or have contrast.

Keep it Clear: Use a Grid
The main use of a grid is to keep your elements (imagery, text, and graphics) sequenced, ordered, and organized, so the hierarchy is clear. A grid is a made up of a series of intersecting straight lines that are used to structure content. Remember those ruled lined notebooks you used in school? Grid lines help you lay out your design elements into a unified whole, because grids encourage alignment, variety, and consistency. Establishing a grid system will set a structure for you to align elements against, keeping your layout clean and speeding up the design process by helping you decide where content should be placed rather than wondering arbitrarily where everything should go.

Be Visual: Show Don't Tell
What is unique about waysides is that they are essentially posters designed for a specific place. Being in that place is important to the communication so a good reminder is to "Show, Don't Tell." This technique enables the viewer to experience the interpretive content through the senses, through imagery, graphics, diagrams, photography, and feelings rather than through descriptive text alone. Make it visual as much as possible.

Call to Action
So you have engaged your viewers and your interpretive wayside has resonated with people…what is next? How can they act on this new information? Tilden's fourth principle states that interpretation should provoke a thought or action. A Call to Action is an objective you want to provoke your viewers to complete, whether it is reflecting on their own resource use, signing up for an e-newsletter or volunteering. Creating an effective call to action is an essential part of any wayside. It focuses their attention, directs them to next steps, and provides a way for you to measure success.

Railroads and Bike Paths

Although walking and driving are the two most common forms of trail travel, self-guided interpretation is sometimes offered to those traveling by train and bicycle. Cross-country Amtrak train routes offer detailed interpretive publications, called Route Guides, in addition to their on-board interpretive programing. Armchair travelers can use these downloadable guides as well. Many private scenic or historic railroads offer printed guides to the features seen along the route.

Likewise, bike trails often have wayside exhibits particularly at overlooks and features where bikers would be likely to dismount and linger. For example, the KATY Trail in Missouri, the longest rail-to-trail project in the U.S. at 238 miles, has wayside exhibits along the route for bikers and walkers. KATY Trail waysides interpret the travels of Lewis and Clark, geology, agriculture, and railroad history.

Summary

Self-guided trails and byways by definition do not involve interpreters accompanying the guests, yet the best trails and byways present interpretation in an amiable and personal manner. With wise planning, the media function like a knowledgeable traveling companion as they answer questions, meet specific visitor needs, and enhance experiences.

Trails and byways allow folks to travel at their own pace and linger at locations that speak to them. They put audiences in direct contact with the resources and they are always on duty. Typically, they will reach many more people than can be reached through interpretive programs.

Applying the principles and design tips in this chapter will reduce the costs and management problems of trails and byways. It will minimize impacts on the resource and increase their interpretive effectiveness. Self-guided byways and trails provide excellent opportunities to connect people to significant sites and inspiring landscapes which will lead to a better world.

"Not all who wander are lost."
–J.R.R. Tolkien

Literature Cited

Cable, T., & Maley, W. (2017). *Driving across Kansas* (Revised and updated edition). Lawrence, KS: University Press of Kansas.

Cable, T., & Morgan-Proux, C. (2006). Interpreting Auvergne. *Legacy, 17*(3), 12–17.

Cadden, L., & Cable, T. (2013). *Traveling through Illinois: Stories of landmarks and landscapes between Chicago and St. Louis.* Charleston, SC: Acadia Press.

Eubanks, T. (2014). *Kansas byways: An interpretive plan.* Austin, TX: Fermata, Inc.

Koenen, S., Legg, M., & Darville, R. (2007). Monitoring visitor behavior at interpretive waysides at Muir Woods National Monument. In *2007 interpretive sourcebook* (pp. 104–105). Ft, Collins, CO: National Association for Interpretation.

National Park Service. (2009). Wayside exhibits: A guide to developing outdoor interpretive exhibits. USDI National Park Service, Harpers Ferry, WV.

Williams, P., Robertson, T., & Bard, L. (2008). Audio engagement: Putting a new spin on science. In *2008 interpretive sourcebook* (pp. 113–114). Ft, Collins, CO: National Association for Interpretation.

CHAPTER 14
Interpretation and the Written Word

"The two most engaging powers of an author are to make new things familiar, and familiar things new."

–Samuel Johnson

Naturalist LuAnn Cadden asks young writers to imagine themselves as a character in a natural habitat. What if they had to survive in this setting? What do they see around them that they could eat? What do they see that they could use for a home, for tools? Young writers seem to like the "survival story" in the wilderness as their character must find food and shelter. It's a great way for them to notice the smallest details and connections in nature—blossoms that will eventually form fruit, thorns that can be used as tools, animal tracks that could lead to a meal. When guiding individuals in nature journaling, LuAnn tries to encourage their own style and let that writer's style guide their discoveries and revelations. She asks if they keep diaries or journals, enjoy science or literature, and what they like to read and write. Then she gets to know them through informal conversation and gently inspires them with just a soft nudge. Their writing, then, prompts them to ask more questions about the resource. They come to understand connections and see that it isn't "the big bad woods." Their curiosities encourage them to want to know more. Through their pens, they make the woods whatever they want. Through their pens, the woods become theirs. This ownership inspires appreciation. Journaling prompts protection for the new world they discover. The following quotes from one of her journaling programs illustrates the power and joy of journaling:

> I had a great time with you, but mostly you inspired me to not just think about myself but to explore the world and help other people. I hope I can come again. –Alana

> You've inspired me to care for animals and forests. When I grow up, I want to be a nature journalist. –Zoey

> You really changed how I look at nature and bugs and stuff. I hope someday since you inspired me that I can inspire somebody else. You answered some questions I've had for two years! –Macy

Writing is a powerful interpretive tool. It can educate, entertain, and persuade. The adage about "the pen being mightier than the sword" is based on historical precedent. The written word can indeed change history. Written accounts of the western United States by explorers generated interest in what would become our first national parks. Writers garnered support for our first state parks, our first wilderness areas, and national forests. Rachel Carson's book *Silent Spring* energized the environmental movement as she called attention to the use of pesticides and their devastating effects on birds. Ultimately her efforts led to important changes in policy and laws protecting endangered species. This chapter presents ideas about how interpreters can write effectively so they can enrich the lives of readers and encourage them to think and act in new ways.

Interpretive Writing

Alan Leftridge has been involved with interpretive writing for more than 40 years. He served as editor of *The Interpreter* magazine, the *Journal of Interpretation*, and *Legacy* magazine. He is the author of several books on natural history and the leader of dozens of "Art of Interpretive Writing" workshops. Indeed, Leftridge (2006) wrote the book on interpretive writing titled *Interpretive Writing*. In this book he asserts that interpretive writing is more than good writing; it is an art form.

> "Interpretive writing is more than good writing; it is an art form."

Leftridge (2006) explains that interpretive writing is a genre, a definable style of writing. It is "intended to make intellectual and emotional connections between the reader and the resource, and it is goal-directed, with the intent of eliciting a pro-social response from readers." These foundational ideas, that help define interpretation, have been covered in previous chapters. In sum, Leftridge (2006) suggested that interpretive writing takes into account the following:

- The writing relates to the life of the reader and addresses a complete storyline. It encourages the reader to care about the subject.
- It relates to something tangible that may include a historic artifact, an entire cultural site, an object from a place, a wildlife species, or any other tangible element of the resource.
- The writing encourages the reader to make an intellectual and emotional connection with those tangible attributes. That is, the writing uncovers universal concepts (love, war, peace, friendship, courage, faith) that readers can relate to in their own lives.
- It is goal directed and therefore challenges the reader to think, do, or feel something beyond what was the case prior to the reading.

With these guidelines fulfilled, Leftridge (2006) noted, then interpretive messages will also be "enjoyable, personable, creative, light-hearted, and informative." With his expertise in writing, editing, publishing, teaching, and leading workshops, Leftridge provides the following counsel regarding the importance of a strong title and lead to capture the reader's attention. (Box 14.1) The title and lead may be crafted early in the writing process, or late in the process, or somewhere in between. We will now turn to the process itself.

Box 14.1
Two Essentials of Every Written Message: Interpretive Titles and Leads
Alan Leftridge, Author, Editor, Writing Workshop Leader

Titles are meant to attract. They are the first words readers see. Titles contain the keywords of your message that focus on your concept, topic, or theme. Keep your titles short, familiar, and easy to read. Favor titles that use an action verb to describe, such as this label from the Art Gallery of Ontario:

How to Spot a Maharaja

On the other hand, you may wish to use a single word or phrase to attract attention as with this example from the Cincinnati Zoo & Botanical Garden:

Fishing Cat

There is a single criterion for assessing a title: Does it get the reader to read further?

Effective titles draw readers into your lead, which in turn convinces them to continue. If the lead does not keep your reader's interest, your efforts are in vain. Short leads are more likely to hold interest. Even in a feature article, if your lead is over 65 words, it probably is too long.

Here are the names and examples of nine leads that I use.

Summary

The following is the lead for the 231-word article announcing the assassination of President Lincoln from the *New York Herald*, April 15, 1865. The article has the most important information at the top and the least important at the bottom. This strategy is the mainstay of the journalistic approach.

This evening at about 9:30 p.m. at Ford's Theatre, the President, while sitting in his private box with Mrs. Lincoln, Mrs. Harris and Major Rathburn, was shot by an assassin, who suddenly entered the box and approached behind the President.

Question

Is yawning contagious?

This straightforward question speaks to any audience. People are attracted to questions. Anticipate and use the most important question your readers might have about your theme.

Announcement

Declarations heighten people's attention. Begin with a leading statement about the theme that will follow. Refrain from starting with… "I'm going to tell you about…" Allow your readers to determine what the interpretation is about. Example:

This is Arnold – a chimp whose favorite drink is Pepsi Cola!

Figurative Language

Symbolic language provides abstractions that adults find mentally challenging and entertaining. There are many forms of figurative language; I prefer metaphors, similes, and personifications. They are fun to craft and connect with readers.

Metaphor: Spring: A Leap into Life.

Simile: Spring is *Like* a Leap into Life.

Personification: Spring awaits us with a youthful smile.

Box 14.1 continued

Factual Statement

Every agency, site, or organization has a fundamental premise on which it is established. Start your message with the agency's position about the principle. These are usually bold, challenging statements, and the reader will know the agency's position right away. A brochure for The Negro Leagues Baseball Museum begins with:

Discover Greatness!

Within the story of baseball lies one of the most shameful chapters in American history.

Quotation

Some famous people have been overcited. Use special care when selecting quotations from Muir, Leopold, Twain, Emerson, and Thoreau. Make sure the excerpt relates to your theme and not just a quotation to establish an emotion in an obtrusive manner. Select short quotations.

Writing is refined thinking.
-Stephen King

Curious Statement

A fun way to attract your readers' attention is to get them "off balance" with a discordant claim. Make an assertion that does not make sense. Here's a site bulletin from Joshua Tree National Park:

Cheaters Sometimes Prosper:

Exotic Grasses in Joshua Tree National Park

Sensory Visualization

Challenge the senses with colorful imagery. Larry Watson uses Freeman Tilden's "light touch" in his novella, Montana 1948:

The house always had a strange smell, as though Daisy had found some vegetable to boil that no one else knew about.

Narrative

We are storytellers. Begin your message with a narrative. The wayside panel that interprets the Smith Mine Disaster illustrates this style:

Smoke pouring from the mine entrance about 10 o'clock the morning of

February 27, 1943, was the first indication of trouble.

"There's something wrong down here. I'm getting out," the hoist operator called up.

He and two nearby miners were the last men to leave the mine alive.

Titles capture the attention of readers; leads draw them into your interpretive message. Become an observer of how other writers use titles and leads on the internet, in magazines, newspapers, brochures, and signs. Play with progressions of ideas and words. Rewrite titles and leads until you feel that they work. Evaluate them by asking your colleagues and friends if your words provoke their interests.

The Process

"In a good piece of nonfiction, there has to be a story."
—Terry Tempest Williams

Preparing to Write

The process of writing is much like processes associated with any interpretive effort. The first decision is to identify the *story* that needs to be told. The story should serve a specific purpose. Furthermore, interpretive writers must consider their *audience*. Will this story be relevant and interesting to them? What does the audience already know? What will they need or want to read?

One of the best preparations for good writing is good reading. Popular writer Stephen King (2010) wrote, "If you want to be a writer, you must do two things above all others: read a lot and write a lot. There's no way around these two things that I'm aware of, no shortcut." The best writers are the best readers. In fact, many accomplished writers believe it is so essential they set aside time during the week specifically for reading. Reading provides new ideas and fresh perspectives to contemplate. Reading other authors and noticing their use of words may expand the interpreter's vocabulary and may shape a personal style. King (2010) noted that every book has its lessons to convey, and that the bad books often have more to teach than the good ones. He concluded, "So we read to experience the mediocre and the outright rotten; such experience helps us to recognize those things when they begin to creep into our own work, and to steer clear of them. We also read to measure ourselves against the good and the great, to get a sense of all that can be done."

> The best writers are the best readers.

Many interpretive sites have book clubs wherein the public and the interpreters read and discuss important books together. This provides the double benefit of preparing the interpreter for good writing as well as providing an opportunity to interact with folks who might not be attracted to other types of programs. Furthermore, the National Association for Interpretation offers a book club in which recommended books are posted on their website. More recent books feature podcasts of the authors holding question and answer periods with those who have read the book, such as Nina Simon's (2016) *The Art of Relevance*.

Getting Words on the Page and First Drafts

"Writing is the hardest work in the world not involving heavy lifting."
—Pete Hamill

Perhaps the greatest impediment to writing is actually getting words on the page. This malady is known as writer's block. Award-winning writer John McPhee (2013) published an essay in the *New Yorker* about this near-universal barrier for writers. McPhee's solution to writer's block? He writes a letter to his mother. He tells her how miserable he is feeling and how he can't seem to get started on the subject he is writing about (a bear). He continues bemoaning the fact he can't get started, that perhaps he wasn't meant to be a writer after all, that he'd really like to engage readers with the sheer size of a bear, and that it can be a lazy creature, often sleeping 15 hours a day, and on and on about what he really hoped he could write. "And then you go back and delete the 'Dear Mother' and all the whimpering and whining, and just keep the bear" (McPhee, 2013).

Writers approach the hard work of writing differently, but many find it useful to first create an outline laying out the theme and subthemes in logical order. They then plunge right in and write quickly filling out the outline from start to finish. These writers do not stop to deliberate over particular words or to check precise punctuation. When the right word or concept eludes these writers, they type in a series of question marks or asterisks in the space and move on. If more than one idea or word seems appropriate, they write both and make the choice later. Because the outline metaphorically resembles a skeleton, writing the quick rough draft is sometimes called "fleshing out" the outline or adding meat to the bones. After the rough draft, go back and reorder the outline.

Writing quickly captures fleeting thoughts and creates a momentum that makes it easier to keep going or to get started again if the writer must stop for a period. This strategy allows one to write enthusiastically, which leads to enthusiastic reading. Writing enthusiastically becomes difficult if the writer is struggling over word choices, punctuation, or sentence structure. Those important things should be dealt with in the revising and polishing stage.

The importance of that first draft cannot be overstated. Because once something tangible exists, the writer will continue to think about it and think about ways to add to it and improve it. As McPhee (2013) further advised, "In short, you may actually be writing only two or three hours a day, but your mind, in one way or another, is working on it 24 hours a day—yes, while you sleep—but only if some sort of draft or earlier version exists. Until it exists, writing has not really begun."

The grasp of something new, for anyone, is often clumsy. But once the mind is engaged in trying to make sense of something new, "the mind begins to 'knit' at the problem on its own" (Brown, Roediger, & McDaniel, 2014).

Finally, although distraction may be the writer's worst enemy, the deadline may be the writer's best friend. Deadlines move writers to action, a reality that every student knows well (Clark, 2016).

Structure

As noted in Box 14.1, the written product starts with a lead designed to capture the reader's attention. It can be a quote, a catchy anecdote, or an introduction of an intriguing character. Editors often accept or reject freelance pieces based primarily on the captivating power of the lead.

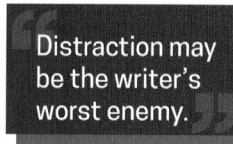
"Distraction may be the writer's worst enemy."

After the lead, the writer will want to transition into the key points of the body of the article. This transition is sometimes called a bridge or nut paragraph. It introduces the subject and its relevance to the reader. It articulates the theme of the article and answers the question "so what?" Why should the reader continue to read the piece?

The body of the article presents the key story or discusses the issues associated with the theme in a logical order. Chronological order works well for how-to stories, stories showing cause and effect, or reports of historical events. Deductive order takes the reader from familiar information to unfamiliar concepts. It works well for scientific subjects that introduce difficult concepts.

Finally, a well-written piece will have a strong ending. Save a powerful quote or surprise the reader with a colorful and memorable anecdote. Sometimes it is possible to come full circle back to the beginning of the piece. The ending often reminds the reader of the theme and then invites the reader to think or act differently.

Revising

"I have rewritten—often several times—every word I have ever published. My pencils outlast my erasers."

–Vladimir Nabokov

Professional writers revise their manuscripts multiple times with the delete key often taking the place of the eraser. The story of Abraham Lincoln writing the Gettysburg Address on the back of an envelope while riding the train to Gettysburg is a myth. He worked on the speech for more than two weeks and revised it at least five times. He probably revised it again on the train.

After completing a first draft, go back and fix the big issues of typos, inaccurate or awkward passages, or misplaced punctuation. Built-in tools often help in this regard such as those found in Microsoft Word. Be sure to double check any questionable statements or data to make sure they are accurate. As noted above, this may involve several drafts as well as the following recommendations:

- **Read the manuscript aloud.** This helps identify punctuation problems and ease of reading. Trust your ear to judge what sounds correct.
- **Lay the manuscript aside for several days or even weeks, if possible, between revisions.** Rest gives a fresh perspective on the writing. Our eyes play tricks on us as they "see" what they expect to find, especially when being read by the writer of the text (Box 14.2).
- **Ask someone else to review the manuscript.** A thorough and honest review by another person will undoubtedly find minor errors or give different perspectives that could save much embarrassment later.

Writing expert William Zinsser (2006) wrote that, "The essence of writing is rewriting." Interpreters should consider that before rushing their work off to the printer or posting the work on a website or a blog.

Box 14.2
The Proofreading Problem

Your ability to read the following paragraph demonstrates the challenge of proofreading. Our eyes gloss over mistakes to see the expected words instead of what is actually there. It is even more difficult to catch mistakes if the proofreader is also the author of the writing.

Aoccdring to a rescheearch porejct at Cmabrigde Uinervtisy, it deosn't mttaer in what oredr the ltteers in a word are, the olny imprmoetnt thing is that the frist and lsat ltteer be at the rghit pclae. The rset can be a total mses and you can still raed it wouthit a porbelm. This is bcuseae the human mind deos not raed ervey lteter by istlef, but the word as a wlohe. Amzanig, huh?

Polishing

Polishing the manuscript consists of making more subtle improvements to the text. One type of improvement is going through the piece and attempting to pick the best words to communicate with decisiveness, precision, and power. Writing well is a matter of choosing the best words and putting them in the right order. Use the convenient thesaurus found in word processing programs or more thorough published ones to find the best word. Other polishing revisions can focus on applying the tips mentioned in the next section of this chapter such as replacing all passive verbs with active verbs.

Techniques and Tips for Effective Writing

Interpretive writing depends on tried and true writing techniques, and we offer the following "baker's dozen" tips on effective writing. Whether the interpreter is writing for print media, such as a booklet or brochure, or for digital media, such as a blog or website, correct writing enhances credibility and readability. Writing riddled with errors in grammar, punctuation, or spelling distracts and discourages the reader. It implies that the writer was either ignorant or apathetic. That will reflect poorly on the writer and/or the organization the writer works for. Likewise, the content must be correct. Interpreters must never deal loosely with the facts to simplify the subject or make it more interesting. *Concise* and *clear* writing improves readability and makes meanings lucid (Figure 14.1).

> Interpreters can use the "baker's dozen" tips for effective writing.

The following are 13 ways to enhance the quality of interpretive writing:

1. Generally, keep sentences short. Sentences with fewer than 20 words make reading easier. Sentences longer than 30 words may confuse a reader. Vary the length of sentences for variety, but limit a sentence to one idea. If the sentence contains more than one idea, break it into two shorter sentences. Condense wordy phrases by eliminating needless words. Box 14.3 gives examples of reducing needless words.

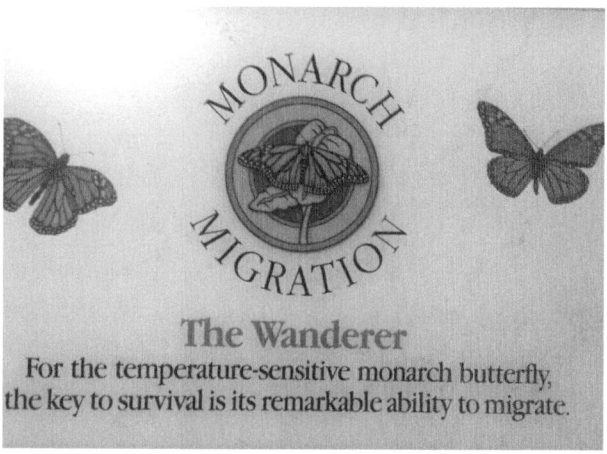

Figure 14.1. A concise and clear message about monarchs is communicated with just a few words. (LB)

2. Vary the length of paragraphs, but keep them short. Paragraphs of 50-60 words or fewer should be the goal. Paragraphs of 100 words look intimidating in narrow brochure columns. An often-used rule of thumb is to limit paragraphs to fewer than 15 typewritten lines. Many good writers occasionally use a one-sentence paragraph for emphasis.

3. Replace hard words with easy words. Hard words generally have three or more syllables. But some short words are considered hard (e.g., aerial), and some long words are easy (e.g., beekeeper). Read the text aloud to identify hard words. Box 14.4 gives examples of simple words to replace hard words. The hard words in the following sentence can be replaced with easy words to make the same point as a familiar saying. "It has been posited that a high degree of inquisitiveness proved lethal to a feline." Or as the writer's joke goes, "never use a big word when a diminutive one would do."

Box 14.3
Cutting Wordy Expressions and Phrases

Instead of	**Use**	**Diluted Verbs**	**Stronger**
a number of	some	give consideration to	consider
at the present time	now, at present	make preparations for	prepare
due to the fact that	because	make use of	use
for the purpose of	for, to	is applicable to	applies to
in the amount of	for	is indicative of	shows
in the near future	soon	undertake an analysis	analyze
on a quarterly basis	quarterly		
the month of June	June		

Redundancies to Avoid

pleased and delighted	subject matter
stimulating and interesting	future plans
review and comment on	period of time
most unique	circular (oval, square) in shape
alternative choices	heavy in weight
absolutely complete	past history
join together	at an earlier time
past memories	very special
reduce down	very urgent
help and support	

Note: the word "very" is seldom necessary. Pick a stronger, more intense descriptor.

Box 14.4
Everyday Words to Replace More Difficult Words

For this	**Use**	**For this**	**Use**
appreciable number	many	methodology	method, way
assistance	help	preclude	prevent
has capability to	can	terminate	end
consequently	so	timely	prompt, on time
endeavor	try	utilize	use
equitable	fair	nevertheless	still
expedite	hurry, speed up	aforementioned	the, that, those
indicate	show	heretofore	until now
magnitude	size	notwithstanding	in spite of

4. Use verbs rather than nouns or adjectives made from them. For example, say "increased" rather than "experienced an increase," or "I recommend" rather than "I make a recommendation," or "we intend" rather than "our intention is."

5. Use active voice rather than passive voice. "The fox ate the rabbit," has more action and fewer words than "The rabbit was eaten by the fox." People usually prefer reading sentences structured as subject-verb-object. Passive voice reverses the order to object-verb-subject. This makes sentences longer, less clear, and less lively.

6. Use positive words rather than negative words. Say what things are rather than what they are not. Rather than "The exhibit won't be ready until Monday," say "The exhibit will be ready Monday." Double negatives require unnecessary mental gymnastics. Replace double negatives with positive statements (e.g., replace "not unimportant" with "important").

7. Try to avoid sentences that begin with "It is" or "There is." Make these sentences more active and concise. Unless "it" refers to something mentioned earlier, "it is" tangles sentences, encourages passive voice, and delays meaning. One can often eliminate "There are" or "there is" without losing meaning. For example, rather than "There are some trails that are closed," write "Some trails are closed." During revisions use your word processor's search functions to find all uses of "there is" or "it is" and try to eliminate them.

8. Keep related words together and unrelated words apart. This improves clarity. For example, "A small bird in the tree" is clearer than "A bird in the tree that was small." In this example the reader would not know if the tree or the bird was small.

9. Beware of dangling modifiers. These words or phrases have nothing to logically modify or they seem to modify something in a word that they cannot possibly modify. Examples: "Tacked to the bulletin board the interpreter read the activities schedule." "Having been run through the computer, the interpreter used the statistics in the exhibit."

10. Be definite and specific. This approach will stimulate the reader's interest. Write "Rain fell every day for a week," instead of "A period of inclement weather set in." Use concrete examples to illustrate a point: "Spinach, carrots, and squash contain Vitamin A," is more concrete than "You get Vitamin A in dark green leafy or deep orange vegetables." Instead of "The rabbit ran through the grass," be more specific and dramatic by replacing "ran" with words like "leaped," "darted," or "sprinted." Use a thesaurus to help select picturesque and powerful words.

11. Avoid clichés and jargon. Try to eliminate clichés and jargon that may distract the reader. If a technical word must be used, explain the word with a simple definition or example. Repeat new or unfamiliar words several times to make them more familiar to the reader.

12. Be gender inclusive. Avoid pronouns that identify one sex (e.g., he, his, she, her) when referring to both sexes. Avoid exclusive pronouns by using the plural form. For example, "The interpreter must make sure she welcomes visitors" can become "Interpreters must make sure they welcome visitors." Also names of occupations contain some gender-free alternatives (e.g., reporters rather than newsmen; anglers rather than fishermen). Failure to write inclusively may offend and alienate readers, distract from the message, and reduce credibility.

13. Write in order to think deeply about things. This is the bonus in our "baker's dozen." The process of writing forces the writer to delve more deeply into the issues and become creative in expressing them concisely, with force and logic. As writers become immersed in the subject they learn more about it and they learn more about themselves. Ultimately, this inspiration transfers to others to learn and grow as well.

Style

"I love writing. I love the swirl and swing of words as they tangle with human emotions."
–James Michener

Unlike technical scientific writing, interpretive writing is colorful and personal. Metaphors and similes help readers relate to the subject, a key principle of all interpretation (Figure 14.2). Metaphors can enhance understanding and help readers see familiar things in a new way. A touch of humor, when appropriate to the subject matter, grabs and holds the reader's attention and may set the tone for the rest of the story (Figure 14.3). Questions posed to readers cause them to ponder what was written and may help them find personal meaning in the words (Figure 14.4). As noted in the introductory quote, interpretive writing can and should be personal. Interpreters see nature and culture through their own eyes. They can share those perspectives through evocative and provocative writing. All of this "color" leads to what is referred to as writing style (Figure 14.5).

Figure 14.2. An interesting metaphor in the title increases interest in the subject. (TC)

Figure 14.3. Using a pun in a title captures the attention of the museum visitor. (TC)

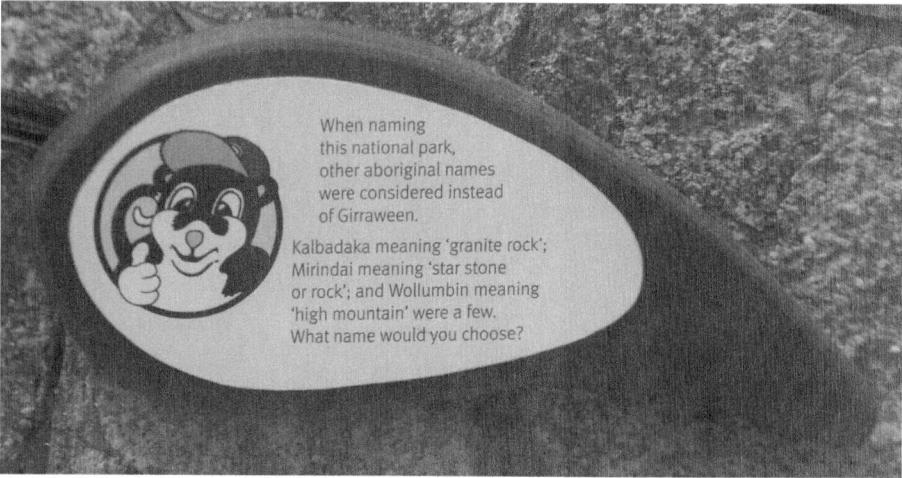

Figure 14.4. The use of questions draws readers in and makes them think about personal meanings. Girraween, incidentally, means "place of flowers" for the incredible spring blooms in this national park in Queensland, Australia. (TC)

Figure 14.5. This sign is the work of a writer whose style communicates an important regulation in a fun and unusual way. (DK)

Style is the way chosen words are put together to form sentences and sentences strung together to make paragraphs. Therefore, style affects the sound of the words on paper and in the mind. Everybody chooses and arranges words differently. Each writer is unique. Each has his or her own stories, voice, and passions. Style is being yourself in print.

Zinsser (2006) stated, "Readers want the person who is talking to them to sound genuine. Therefore, a fundamental rule is: be yourself." It takes courage and confidence to be yourself in print. But the rewards are great. Strunk and White (1999) recommended that "to achieve style, begin by affecting none. . . . Style will emerge from careful, honest writing." Readers want to believe that what they are reading is being told by a real, recognizable, and trustworthy person—a person like you.

Rating Readability

Several quantitative formulas allow one to assess readability. The two most popular that have withstood the test of time have been the Flesch Index (Flesch, 1974) and Gunning's Fog Index (Gunning, 1962). Government agencies and corporations have used these techniques to ensure their clientele will find their publications readable. Consistent with many of the tips given above, these tests use sentence length and word length to estimate the ease of reading.

Newspapers and popular publications seek to write at the fifth to eighth grade level. Most bestselling books and much of the Bible are seventh or eighth grade level. The average reading level for adults in the United States is about seventh grade (Bixler, 2016). However, Leftridge (2006) cautioned that the "general public" is actually made up of many different publics and that effective messages should be composed to meet the interests and needs of specific audiences.

Flesch's readability formula helps writers to score their drafts for *ease of reading* from very easy to very difficult. It derives from two counts: average sentence length and number of syllables per 100 words. Flesch (1974) also developed a *Human-Interest Index* based on personal words and personal sentences. The more personal words used, the more "dramatic" (vs. "dull") human interest the writing may carry. Personal words include specific individual pronouns (e.g., I, you), gender-specific words (e.g., she, hers), and group words (e.g., our, their). Personal sentences include dialogue type "spoken" sentences, questions, commands, exclamations, and incomplete sentences whose full meaning is inferred (e.g., Oops!).

Another venerable method to calculate readability is the Fog Index (Gunning, 1962). To make the calculations, select a sample of writing at least 100 words long:

1. Count the words, then divide the total number of words by the number of sentences to determine the average number of words per sentence.
2. Count the number of words of three or more syllables in your sample. Do not count capitalized words, easy compound words such as beekeeper, or verbs that gained their third syllable by adding -ed or –es such as "created." Add this number to that from the first step.
3. Multiply the total by 0.4. This number gives you the Fog Index roughly corresponding to the number of years of schooling a person would need to read and understand the passage easily.

Fazio and Gilbert (2000) reported that using Flesch tests and the Fog Index over several decades showed that federal publications related to outdoor recreation rated as "fairly difficult" as per difficulty, and "dull" to "mildly interesting" as to human interest.

Readability indices appear in many computer software packages that evaluate grammar and style. The Spelling and Grammar Tools in Microsoft Word provide a readability measure based upon an adaptation of the Flesch test (Flesch-Kincaid). Such tools can be useful and provide general guidelines to interpretive writers. However, writers should be cautious about rewriting their text, if analysis shows it to be too difficult, merely to "please" the software program. Evaluations of this strategy "strongly suggest that rewriting text by breaking long sentences into shorter sentences and replacing polysyllabic words with short words produces ineffective prose" (Bixler, 2016). The real test is how real people respond, rather than how software reacts to the writing. Although readablity indices may suggest that the writing might be too technical or wordy, they do not take into account organization, content, and layout.

For example, a nonsensical or erroneous piece of writing could score well on readability. Ease of reading does not imply desirability or benefit of reading. Writing guru Roy Peter Clark (2016) admonished, "The good writer must believe that a good sentence, short or long, will not be lost on the reader."

Written Media

Considerable changes have occurred through advancing technologies over the past decades regarding the use of written words to inform and influence people. Printed media was traditionally read in the form of newspapers and books. Now much of the news and books that people read are consumed electronically. Similarly, more interpretive written material is available to people through blogs, tweets, websites, social media, and so on, as discussed elsewhere throughout this book such as Chapter 8. Nonetheless, some use of printed material still has its place at interpretive facilities, as well as making use of electronic media.

Labels

Even as technology continues to advance, labels will be an important component of exhibits. Beverly Serrell (2015) wrote the definitive book on labels, *Exhibit Labels*, which pointed out many of the common mistakes made in the writing and design of labels. Although she indicated that label *writing* has improved over the years, problems continue with *graphic design* such as type that is too small, not enough contrast to the background, and unintelligible icons. As for the *writing* portion of labels, Serrell (2015) compiled a summary of "Ten Commandments" intended to remind the label writer of what to do (and therefore what to avoid). These commandments follow many of the interpretive principles provided in general throughout this book. Here is a summary:

1. Labels should make visual reference to the objects they interpret.
2. Labels should focus on the big idea (theme).
3. Labels should be interpretive (offering provocation over information).
4. Labels should take into account the audiences they are intended for.
5. Labels should focus on questions that are the questions of the visitors.

6. Label design should be organized and consistent.
7. Labels should be written with an accessible vocabulary.
8. Labels should be concise, "more like a tweet than a tome."
9. Labels for interactives should provide useful explanations.
10. Label typography should be legible and attractive. (Serrell, 2015)

Among Serrell's conclusions in her work over many years is that when visitors find labels to be interesting they will read them aloud more than others. This increases intragroup social behavior and learning. Similarly, a greater likelihood of reading aloud to children exists if labels are easier to read without need to paraphrase (Serrell, 2015).

> "When visitors find labels to be interesting they will read them aloud."

Brochures and Park Newspapers

Brochures (leaflets, pamphlets) and park newspapers are the most commonly used form of printed written interpretation. Government agencies and private organizations produce many written publications each year. However, this is changing as agencies turn to other strategies as detailed in the discussion in Chapter 8 about the discontinuation of park newspapers at Grand Canyon National Park. Websites and social media will be increasingly used to inform the public. The advent of electronic media should challenge interpreters to produce attractive, useful, and popular brochures and to distribute them wisely. As with all interpretive media, using brochures has advantages and disadvantages. Many of the advantages can be carried over to digital distribution of the materials.

Advantages:

- Can be distributed offsite, at libraries, schools, restaurants, motels, gas stations, rest stops, at offsite programs, and other parks or museums.
- Can be mailed to inform members and potential visitors about the programs/facilities. Such mailings not only entice people to come, but also prepare them for a rewarding visit. Educational brochures can go to people who cannot visit.
- Can be read later or kept as a memento of the visit. This "souvenir value" may recall the value of the visit and aid information retention
- Are available to the public continuously. As long as people can access a brochure rack or box, they can enjoy interpretation, even when no staff members are present.
- Can reduce the burden on information desk staff by providing answers to the most often asked questions.
- Are self-paced. People can slow down, speed up, go back to the beginning or stop reading at their own choosing.

Disadvantages:

- A surprising number of people cannot read easily. Others dislike making the effort to read while doing something else such as walking.
- Are an impersonal medium. Readers cannot ask questions or discuss and interpreters get little feedback on the effectiveness of the brochure.
- Do not present dynamic topics well.

- Concern about littering may limit use. Reduce litter potential by keeping a clean, well-maintained area. Also, a high-quality, useful brochure seldom appears on the ground. Collection boxes at the end of trails encourage return of unwanted trail brochures for reuse. Finally, a small charge imputes some value to the publication and reduces the chance that it will end up as litter.

Newsletters

Most interpretive organizations produce a newsletter. More and more these are sent out electronically. Because newsletters often provide an organization's most regular and tangible contact with people, they will create, maintain, and reinforce the organization's image. Because they represent the organization, they should look professional (in printed or electronic form) and consistent in appearance. Over time they become immediately recognizable.

Newsletters can be used to educate and to entertain their public, to solicit volunteers and specific donations to meet needs, and to call attention to staff, volunteers, and others deserving recognition. They announce schedules, special events, and new developments. Newsletters make a convenient item to send to other agencies, politicians, mass media reporters, and others whom the organization wishes to inform.

Newsletter content typically includes a column written by the editor and director, some form of feedback items, feature articles, a calendar of events and exhibits, short news items, and membership information.

Box 14.5 gives tips for designing brochures and newsletters. The National Association for Interpretation published *Interpretation by Design* (Caputo, Lewis, & Brochu, 2008), which is an excellent reference for an in-depth treatment of the design process.

Box 14.5
Design Tips for Brochures and Newsletters (Printed or Digital)

Tips for Brochures

Title. Catchy titles improve the chances that a brochure will be picked up. Provocative or humorous statements and questions in titles make them more interesting.

Color. Bright colors command more attention. Primary colors speak to action. Pastels evoke a relaxing mood. Choose the logical colors that fit the content (e.g., orange for fall colors or hunting, red for warning or danger, blue for water themes).

Layout. An attractive cover design strongly influences whether a person will pick up the brochure or stay on the website. Leave enough white space to achieve a clean uncluttered appearance. Break up the text with short paragraphs, subheadings, photos, or other graphics. People look at photos first and then if provoked seek an explanation.

Margins. Make the margins wide and left justified rather than full justified. Having both margins justified wastes space and appears too stiff and formal. Short lines of only two or three words will be too choppy. If they are too long readers will have a hard time moving from line to line. One standard is to use fewer than 65 characters per line.

Box 14.5 continued

Font. Select fonts with care. Each font conveys a mood and some are easier to read than others. Word processing software provides dozens of choices. Fonts are categorized into two families: serif and sans serif. Serif fonts helps the eye flow from word to word. It presents a warmer or friendlier feeling. Sans serif fonts are less personal. They often are used for warning signs or road signs meant to be read quickly. Stick with one font throughout your publication, although you can deviate for titles, headlines, tables, or captions. Avoid fancy fonts. They are more difficult to read.

Tips for Newsletters and eNewsletters

Format. Stick with a consistent design and sequence of sections. This will help readers to easily follow the logic and key points of the publication.

Length. Keep it short, usually no more than eight pages. If it gets much longer, people are less likely to read it.

Nameplate and masthead. The nameplate should be catchy and distinctive. It should immediately connect the reader to the organization's identity. The masthead contains the organization's name, volume number, issue, and often the name of the editor, board members, contact information, and a list of contents.

Columns. One column across the entire page is easiest to format and gives a business-like appearance. Two columns work well for newsletters with long stories. They appear simple and uncluttered. Three column newsletters require more hyphenation and eye movement, but they work for short stories and brief news items. They also allow flexibility for placing illustrations or photos.

Headings and subheadings. Use these liberally to tell the reader what comes next and to break up long columns.

Writing in the Digital Age

Many of the traditional advantages of brochures and newsletters can be accomplished more effectively through websites, blogs, apps, or social media. These digital media eliminate printing and distribution costs, avoid potential litter, and can be more personal in providing opportunities for feedback. They can include audio and video along with the text. Because of these many advantages, digital approaches are replacing paper publications. Writing for digital media uses the previously mentioned rules and tips regarding correct, clear, and concise writing. However, when writing for the internet keep in mind the strategic use of keywords in titles and text, and active links to other sites and publications. Keywords and links are essential to help readers find your writing.

> Digital approaches are replacing paper publications.

Journaling and Poetry

"The discipline of the writer is to learn to be still and listen…"
–Rachel Carson

The Joy of Journaling

As noted in the introductory story, journaling is a fun and effective way to directly and intimately connect people to an interpretive site. It fosters creativity and is multisensory. Journaling is not only multisensory, but it is also multidisciplinary. It blends science, art and language. Participants go beyond merely seeing to making deeper, more detailed observations. Journaling causes people to *notice* things. And it appeals to natural curiosity, love of drawing, and joy of discovery (Figure 14.6).

> "Journaling is a fun and effective way to directly and intimately connect people to an interpretive site."

Interpretive journaling activities invite visitors to sketch and write about a place. Typically an interpreter will lead the group to a destination and then direct their attention to a particular subject. The interpreter may prescribe writing or drawing tasks or it might be more freeform with participants writing and drawing whatever catches their eye. The interpreter gives encouraging words to inspire the group to look closely, to use all of their senses, and to find personal meanings in the resource. Typically participants are asked to describe something in detail as if they have never seen it before. Drawing the object—even if only a rough sketch—forces the participants to focus more closely on it. Even comically-bad drawings serve their true purpose of careful observation. With practice, sketches will improve. Reluctant or embarrassed participants can be encouraged by the words of the famous bird painter John James Audubon, who said, "The worse my drawings were, the more beautiful did the originals appear."

Interpreters often ask participants to note any connections that occur to them and write down questions that arise from their observations. Most importantly, participants are encouraged to record their feelings about the place or object. A key to journaling programs is to provide sufficient quiet time for such observation and contemplation.

Besides hosting journaling activities, interpreters can promote personal journaling by members of their audiences. For centuries, explorers and scientists kept journals to record their observations. Today the public can participate as citizen scientists by recording their observations in field journals. Interpreters can teach journaling techniques such as the importance of recording date, location, time, and weather conditions for each entry. They can provide tips on field guides and other helpful resources. And, they can communicate the importance of making careful and consistent observations to add to the journal's scientific value.

Figure 14.6. Journaling helps visitors see the Kansas prairie with new eyes. (TC)

Interpreters can guide people in buying the appropriate tools aligned with their specific needs. Colored pencils and waterproof notebooks are typical tools. But many choices exist. For example, some may prefer the convenience of a pocket-sized notebook, whereas others would want a notebook suitable for large drawings. Lined paper interferes with drawings, but lines facilitate neater note-taking. Some folks prefer notebooks or binders with pockets to hold leaves or other objects. Still others have adopted various software programs that may be used to create verse or drawings on laptops or tablets.

Furthermore, social media allows field notes and journal pages to be read by people worldwide. One 21st century extension of journaling is a social media site linked to Facebook, Instagram and Twitter called Field Notes Friday that is administered by a Texas interpreter with the *nom de plume* "The Happy Naturalist" (happynaturalist.com). Individuals can digitally share their sketches and observations to instruct and inspire others.

In journaling programs, participants not only learn about nature or history, but they also learn about themselves. Journaling can become a lifelong process that documents an increasingly intimate personal relationship with one's cultural and natural heritage.

> "In journaling programs, participants not only learn about nature or history, but they also learn about themselves."

Poetry

Poets love to play with words and focus on choosing the correct ones. Interpreters also focus on choosing the best words. Interpreters, like poets, use words to reveal beauty and awaken personal meanings (Figure 14.7).

Poetry is an underused tool by interpreters. Interpreters and their audiences are all poets and every poem is an act of interpretation (LaPage, 2009). Interpreters can help people find their inner poet while connecting them to history or nature. Poet Robert Frost's oft-quoted statement, "I am not a teacher, but an awakener" sounds much like Tilden (1977), who wrote, "The interpreter is not primarily a teacher, but a companion in the adventure."

Figure 14.7. A poetic quote creates a sympathetic mood to enrich the experience. (LB)

Poetry can be read aloud during programs or hikes to powerfully illuminate interpretive themes. Enos Mills wrote that poetry sustains and develops people's imagination and that "the nature guide should know Shakespeare and many of the great poems" (Mills, 1920). In fact, Mills in several places referred to his ground-breaking work as "poetic interpretation of the facts of nature" (e.g., Mills, 1920). Reading these great works will feed your own imagination and nourish your interpretive writing.

Having children or adults writing their own poems during interpretive programs can be fun and deeply rewarding. However, often audiences are reluctant to write poems. Some feel it is too personal or they feel inadequate to the task. Using formulaic poetic forms such as Haiku and Cinquain make writing a poem easy. They can even be used to have timid people write a poem without them knowing it, thereby avoiding any fears or doubts.

For example, in using Cinquain, ask people to write the following about the subject (e.g., decaying log, cattail marsh, piece of historic furniture, or antique tool):

- Line 1 – two descriptive words
- Line 2 – three action words
- Line 3 – four to five words about the subject
- Line 4 – one-word summary
- Ask participants to go back to the top and add a title because they have written a poem!

These step-by-step poetry-writing exercises are fun, instructive, and often inspirational. The results can be insightful and profound.

Summary

"Eloquence is the painting of thoughts."
–Blaise Pascal

The art of interpretive writing involves using artful language. Creative writing employs language that paints word pictures and tells stories. It makes connections that allow readers to turn abstract words into pictures in their minds. It builds bridges over which ideas travel smoothly, making the journey from a page or label into the mind. Effective writing creates images that focus the readers' attention and interest, excite the imagination, provoke the deepest curiosity, and incite the true joy of greater perception.

The pen can be more powerful than the sword, but only if you know how to use it. The process of learning to write never ends. Hemingway once said about writers, "We are all apprentices in a craft where no one ever becomes a master." As with other skills, writing will improve with practice. The tips and principles in this chapter should speed the improvement of anyone's writing. Merely using short words, short sentences, short paragraphs, and action verbs to produce lively enthusiastic writing can make a difference. Follow up with ruthless revising to polish the piece. By following these simple practices and developing a personal, engaging style, people will want to read what you write.

Interpreters face the challenge to design publications that people find easy to pick up and hard to put down. In the digital realm the challenge is to provide content online that attracts readers and holds attention so they don't click off to another site. Interpretive writing provides extraordinary opportunities to inform, entertain, and influence visitors and non-visitors alike in ways that will help them grow in their passion for and desire to protect their cultural and natural heritage; therefore making the world a better place.

"Good writing is supposed to evoke sensation in the reader—not the fact that it is raining, but the feel of being rained upon."
–E.L. Doctorow

Literature Cited

Bixler, R. (2016). Reading ease isn't so easy. *Legacy, 27*(6), 38–39.

Brown, P., Roediger, H., & McDaniel, M. (2014). *Make it stick: The science of successful learning.* Cambridge, MA: The Belknap Press of Harvard University Press.

Caputo, P., Lewis, S., & Brochu, L. (2008). *Interpretation by design: Graphic design basics for heritage interpreters.* Ft. Collins, CO: InterpPress.

Clark, R. P. (2016). *Writing tools, 10th anniversary ed.* New York, NY: Little, Brown and Company.

Fazio, J. R., & Gilbert, D. L. (2000). *Public relations and communications for natural resource managers* (3rd ed.). Dubuque, IA: Kendall/Hunt.

Flesch, R. (1974). *The art of readable writing.* New York, NY: Harper & Row.

Gunning, R. (1962). *New guide to more effective writing in business and industry.* Boston, MA: Industrial Education Institute.

King, S. (2010). *On writing: 10th anniversary edition.* New York, NY: Pocket Books.

LaPage, W. (2009). In the beginning was the word: Demystifying poets and poetry. *Legacy, 20*(3), 24–26.

Leftridge, A. (2006). *Interpretive writing.* Ft. Collins, CO: InterpPress.

McPhee, J. (2013). Draft no. 4. *New Yorker.* April 29, 2013, 32–38.

Mills, E. (1920). *Adventures of a nature guide and essays in interpretation.* Friendship, WI: New Past Press.

Serrell, B. (2015). *Exhibit labels: An interpretive approach* (2nd ed.). Lanham, MD: Rowman & Littlefield.

Simon, N. (2016). *The art of relevance.* Santa Cruz, CA: Museum 2.0

Strunk, W. Jr., & White, E. B. (1999). *The elements of style* (4th ed.). Upper Saddle River, NJ: Prentice Hall.

Tilden, F. (1977). *Interpreting our heritage* (3rd ed.). Chapel Hill, NC: The University of North Carolina Press.

Zinsser, W. (2006). *On writing well: 30th anniversary edition.* New York, NY: Harper Collins.

CHAPTER 15
Interpreting History

Most students from the Cabot Yerxa Elementary School in Desert Hot Springs, California, come from poor families, many of which are relatively recent immigrants into the United States. It may be the poverty or maybe the proximity to the glamour and affluence of nearby Palm Springs that causes these children to feel inferior, ashamed of their school and poor community. However, according to volunteer guide Susan Forgrave, their outlook changes when the children visit the Cabot's Pueblo Museum. The museum is located in what was Cabot Yerxa's Hopi-inspired homestead. Cabot built the 5,000-square-foot, 35-room pueblo out of repurposed materials collected throughout the desert. With 150 different-sized windows and 65 doors, weird corners and nooks, the three-story home can be best described as imaginative or even poetic.

The students learn that their school is named after a bright and ambitious man, who followed his heart, traveled the world, and accomplished countless things. Cabot was an artist, writer, builder, architect, adventurer, explorer, collector, visionary, and entrepreneur. Before settling in the California desert, Cabot Yerxa traveled to Mexico, Alaska, Cuba, and Europe. He studied art in Paris. In 1913 at age 30, Cabot homesteaded 160 acres in what is now Desert Hot Springs. Pressed for water, he dug a well with pick and shovel, discovering the hot mineral waters of Desert Hot Springs. Nearby, he dug a second well and discovered the pure cold water of the Mission Springs Aquifer.

Even in their poverty, it is hard for modern-day students to imagine that Cabot lacked modern conveniences. They learn he was strong, resilient and resourceful, all requirements to live in the desert. For the art portion of the visit, the children sit under an old Palo Verde tree and draw and color postcards just as Mr. Yerza had done. As they draw with watercolor crayons they sense the beauty in the building, gardens, surrounding hillside, and the mountains in the distance. When Susan leads tours, the excitement of the parents and children bring her great joy. They can't believe Cabot made his own house and created all of those paintings and gardens. The most rewarding thing for Susan is watching the young ones look at photos of Cabot and see the man who gave his name to their school. The change that comes over the children is in Susan's words "priceless!" After visiting Cabot's Pueblo Museum, the children and their parents have something for which they can be proud—their school and town are uniquely associated with an amazing man.

Why Interpret History

"History serves us in many ways. It can delight and enrich us, inspire and caution us, inform and educate us, help us make thoughtful decisions, enlarge and intensify the experience of being alive."

—American Association for State and Local History (AASLH)

This quote from the AASLH summarizes nicely the value of knowing about history. Without interpretation, artifacts are merely old things, historic buildings are just old buildings, and ceremonies and festivals are merely entertainment. Interpretation breathes life and meaning into past events, architecture, and artifacts. In doing so, it nurtures the development of a personal identity as individuals hear inspiring or thought-provoking stories of the past, and it forms values to guide living in the present. Interpreting history contributes to vibrant and unified communities as a commitment to community is enhanced through the collective memories, stories, and shared traditions. Local history contributes to economic development and quality of life as it makes communities more meaningful places to live and work.

Perhaps the most compelling and obvious benefits of interpreting history are educational benefits. Interpreters help people see how history relates to their own lives by telling exciting, enriching, entertaining, and educational stories in contemporary interpretive programs. As illustrated by the introductory story, this can result in new life changing perspectives in citizens (both young and old) about themselves and their community (Figure 15.1).

Figure 15.1. The story of Cabot Yerxa, as told by interpreters at Cabot's Pueblo Museum, builds self-esteem and civic pride in those who visit. (SF)

Preserving and Interpreting Memories

"We need the past for our sense of who we are. We need the past for a sense of our civic responsibility, how all these benefits and freedoms came to us, and what it is our duty to protect."

—David McCullough

Another reason to interpret history is to remember. To remember not only the happy stories of our past, but also the tragic ones. Stories of atrocities, discrimination, and ethnic conflicts may be lost with the passing of those who experienced those events. Keeping memories alive may be the most significant role of history interpreters. In fact, the term "place of memory" is now being used in international heritage protection and management. ICOMOS explains a place of memory as "a property or site vested with historical significance due to the nature of the historic events that occurred there. What differentiates places of memory from other categories of heritage is the relation between the material and non-material components of the site. In 'places of memory' the nonmaterial component is of far greater importance than the material one."

> Interpreters help people see how history "corresponds" with their own lives.

The global leader in efforts to preserve and interpret places of memory is the International Coalition of Sites of Conscience (ICSC). ICSC's goal is "to use places of memory to engage the public in connecting past and present in order to envision and shape a more just and humane future" (sitesofconscience.org).

Why is it important to interpret the stories such as the struggle for equal rights for women, civil rights for minorities, the atrocities of dictatorships, or the pain associated with war? It is because we can find inspiration in the stories of survivors and those who became agents for change. It is critical to preserve and interpret memories so those memories can inspire action today. The approximately 200 Sites of Conscience include U.S. National Park sites like *Brown v. Board of Education* National Historic Site in Topeka, Kansas and the Little Rock Central High School National Historic Site in Arkansas that celebrate the efforts to desegregate schools in the U.S. They also include the Minidoka Internment National Monument in Idaho and Manzanar National Historic Site in California where Japanese–Americans were held during WW II. Sites outside the U.S. include WWII Holocaust Museums and concentration camps in Europe (Figure 15.2), museums interpreting Siberian gulags, and the slave trade in West Africa and the Caribbean, and sites preserving the memories of genocide in Cambodia and Apartheid in South Africa. The profoundly named "Museum of Memory" in Paraguay is the very building where clandestine tortures and executions took place under the Stroessner dictatorship. The museum's mission is instructive and reminds again why interpreting history is important: "This is a space for reflection and dialogue on the past so that the visitor may learn and comprehend the factors that make state terrorism possible so as to prevent it from being repeated in the future, and to cultivate a culture of peace."

> We can find inspiration in the stories of survivors and those who became agents for change.

History delights, informs, and inspires us with joyful stories of success, innovation, integrity, resourcefulness, and times of prosperity. But we also interpret history and preserve memories so that by looking at the past, people will be called to seek a better future through civil discourse, civic action, and by cultivating a culture of peace.

Approaches to Interpreting History

When history is taught to the general public outside classrooms and universities, it is called Public History. Public historians, unlike academic historians, work for and with the general public at museums, historic sites, parks, and libraries (Figure 15.3). Interpreters work in this realm of Public History.

"EVERY PERSON HAS A NAME"

The six million Jews who were murdered in the Holocaust have no graves and no tombstones. The physical extermination was accompanied by the deliberate, sweeping erasure of the memory of each individual. With the assistance of partners around the world, Yad Vashem, Israel's national authority for the remembrance of the Holocaust and its victims, has undertaken the vast and complex task of collecting and documenting the names of the murdered. These names are collected through Pages of Testimony submitted by family members and by researching lists from archival sources. As of 2013 more than four million names have been collected and our collective efforts continue. Because entire communities were wiped out, it will never be possible to compile a full list.

The names of the countries in which Jews were murdered have been cited according to the European borders of 1938. Lists of Holocaust victims have been collected from different sources in the course of the last 60 years. In certain cases, these sources did not state the name of the country in which the murder site was situated.

Figure 15.2. Exhibits at the Auschwitz Concentration Camp in Poland use photos, personal belongings, and the names of those murdered to help personalize the past. (TC)

Figure 15.3. Larger-than-life-size soldiers, created with exacting detail by the same studios that produced *Lord of the Rings* films, bring the history and horrors of WW I to the public. The words of the men portrayed appear as handwriting on the wall of the exhibit to further increase the power of this public history effort. (TC)

Museum exhibits, trails, byways, campfire talks, walking tours, websites, and printed materials all are used to interpret history to the public. The advice given in earlier chapters about using these media applies to history interpretation. In most ways, interpreting history is similar to interpreting nature or anything else. Like all interpretation, it requires telling a compelling story, relating to the audience, focusing on a theme, provoking thought or action, and applying all the other principles of good interpretation. Interpreting history, like all interpretation, is about making the subject engaging, inspiring, and personally meaningful.

Similarly, history interpretation and nature interpretation can, and often should, be offered at the same site or facility. Every natural site contains a history, and every historical site has natural resources. Often the natural resources and history stories are closely linked. (Figure 15.4). However, history interpretation has specialized approaches and history interpreters face distinct challenges. These approaches and challenges are discussed next.

Figure 15.4. Stories of nature and culture are closely linked in places like Cades Cove in Smoky Mountain National Park. (TC)

Living History

"A good costumed interpreter (whether in first or third person) has to combine the skills of a host, a storyteller, an entertainer, an expert, a psychologist, a guardian (of the site and its artifacts), a tour guide, a stand-up comedian (when and if appropriate), a therapist and a counsellor."

–Marc Wallis, Director of Past Pleasures (UK)

A specialized approach dealing with historical themes is called Living History. NAI defines living history as "An attempt to accurately replicate the past through the use of a physical environment and the sights, sounds, and smells of the period being represented." This form of personal interpretation portrays life in the past to tell a story. Living history when done well is a powerful blend of entertainment and enlightenment. (Figure 15.5).

Figure 15.5. Children get to meet a pioneer woman at Prairie State Park in Missouri. (MSP)

Professional living history in North America may have begun with Isaac Rice, a veteran of the U.S. Revolutionary War who gave guided tours and gun demonstrations at Fort Ticonderoga at the turn of the 18th century. Living history in open area museum settings began in 1891 when as described in Chapter 11, Arthur Hazelius opened Skansen in Stockholm, Sweden. Living history in museum settings spread to the U.S. in the 1920s with notable sites being Henry Ford's Greenfield Village in Michigan and the beginning of restoration of Colonial Williamsburg in Virginia. Greenfield Village had a particularly auspicious opening. The dedication of Greenfield Village was held on the 50th anniversary of Edison's successful creation of the incandescent lamp and was billed as "Light's Golden Jubilee." In what would be the first historic reenactment at the site, 82-year old Thomas Edison himself reenacted the successful first lighting of his lamp in front of President Hoover, Henry Ford, a cheering crowd, and a national radio audience. Henry Ford expressed the spirit and mission of many current living history sites when he said, "When we are through, we shall have reproduced American life as lived; and that, I think, is the best way of preserving at least a part of our history and tradition."

Living history has grown into an honorable profession, and a popular and enriching hobby for thousands of serious and knowledgeable amateurs. It is accepted professionally and has achieved such status that some of these amateurs serve as consultants for films or plays depicting the past. Millions of people are entertained and educated by living history programs each year ranging from Renaissance Fairs, to battle reenactments, to visits to such well-known sites as Old Sturbridge Village, Plimoth Plantation and the aforementioned Colonial Williamsburg. Today living history programs present events and people from the 1960s and Vietnam War era and as time passes eventually current events of the 21st century will be the subject of living history interpretation.

Living history interprets the lives of people, and therefore focuses on human emotions, challenges, courage, resourcefulness and resiliency. Like a Broadway play or Hollywood movie, living history, when well done, can be fun, educational, emotionally moving, thought provoking, or all of those things at once. Living history also has the advantage of being hands on. Living history allows for maximum involvement with the audience as all of their senses can be engaged with the presentation as also discussed in Chapter 10 regarding interpretive theater.

> Living history has grown into an honorable profession, and a popular and enriching hobby.

On the other hand, living history is not easy to do well. It takes considerable investment, research, planning, and practice. This in turn can make it an expensive proposition as agencies pay for time spent in research and preparation as well as in acquiring and maintaining artifacts, props, and costumes. Equally important is that living history requires a commitment of time and energy on the part of the audience. Shy visitors may be intimidated or confused if they are personally engaged by a living history performer in costume. Visitors with limited time may want to keep moving. Another challenge that presents itself to living history interpreters as they try to create a historical context are the ubiquitous modern distractions which must be minimized or ignored (e.g., planes overhead, trains or traffic passing by, and the sounds of phones or sirens). Finally, interpreters can be challenged by audiences with a distorted, oversimplified or romanticized image of complex historical events or eras. Of course all interpreters, regardless of the subject matter, need to concern themselves with these same issues of context, competing views, and complexity associated with their themes. But history themes, because they focus on *human* history, can also be painful. In spite of these challenges living history is often meaningful, memorable, and even life-changing.

As noted in Chapter 9, to reach this full potential, living history should be more than what Luzader and Spellman (2003) call "CBS interpretation," meaning candles, butter, and soap. The overuse of cliché demonstrations of making these three products in history presentations is particularly misguided when it is not appropriate to the site, time period, or season. Moreover, Luzader and Spellman (2003) warn that if you ever hear any of the following statements from living history interpreters you can be sure that increased professionalism is needed:

- "We are just having fun."
- "The public won't know any better."
- "It looks old-timey." (i.e., any old costume or artifact will do if it looks old)
- "But the public loves or expects it" (i.e., keep the customers happy regardless of accuracy).
- "It's how they do it at the other sites" (even if those sites are thousands of miles away and represent a different time period).
- "We can just pretend" (i.e., we can't let go of an idea just because it can't be presented accurately).

To promote professionalism Luzader (2016) provided ethical and practical principles in carrying out living history programs (Box 15.1).

Box 15.1
Costumed Interpretation: Thoughts From a Living History Professional
John C.F. Luzader, Principal, Living Museums of the West

Seldom do I hear folks mention our responsibility to the public, the site, and to other interpreters in our costumed interpretive programs. It is the ethical responsibility of any interpreter and educator to provide the most accurate, professional materials available and to allow the public to ask questions and make their own conclusions from the material provided.

When we—the organizers, managers, staff, and volunteers—deliberately and knowingly provide misinformation to our audiences how can we call ourselves professionals? We become enablers of poor and inaccurate interpretation and information that will live long past our lifetimes. When we fail to provide better guidelines, increase our own knowledge, and better train interpreters who are to be on our sites, we become the problem.

When we in the name of entertainment enable poor historic representations, or allow individual preferences or needs to supplant the site or agency's mission or allow ourselves to be frightened of the pressures of political correctness and feared lawsuits, we have failed.

The following basic principles might improve the field of living history.

- Look beyond just the entertainment value. Quality living history will provide entertainment on its own.
- Ensure that the chosen interpreters whether volunteers or a visiting group practice the basic standards of quality interpretation.
- Assess whether a uniformed presentation will be more effective than just having costumed living history presenters on site. If you do not have enough men or women to accurately represent a job or activity in a costumed historic portrayal, get rid of the costumes and go to a uniformed representation. It is better to have good interpretation than inaccurate portrayals.
- If representing a specific event and period, be able to document and confirm any activity being displayed.
- Make use of senior interpreters by having older soldiers reflecting back on their experiences of war 10, 20, 30 years after the war, without wearing uniforms, and telling how those events changed them.
- Mixed ages of interpreters can represent families worrying about loved ones who moved to the West or went to war.
- Script your event for specific characters and for specific ages and body types. A Confederate soldier representing a long march culminating at Appomattox Court House should not be well-fed, overweight, or 75 years old!
- Illustrate all aspects of the theme when possible, good and bad. Our heritage is both the good and the bad. No one can fully understand how and why our ancestors behaved in the manner they did and why they made the choices that directed their lives without understanding all viewpoints of the time.

We have great opportunities in allowing living history to augment written and static presentations with the ability to see, hear, and experience a bit of the past first hand. However, whenever we portray the past, it should be ethically and honestly.

One popular approach is first-person living history. First-person living history involves an interpreter portraying a particular person from the past. They become this person as if it is a ghost from the grave. The interpreter uses the first-person tense (I or

We) hence the name first-person interpretation. First-person requires interpreters to do considerable research on the person they are portraying. Sometimes this is a famous person, whereas other times first-person interpreters present the life of a lesser known individual. In either case, it requires knowing everything from who their relatives were to knowing their political and religious views. When performing, interpreters are totally immersed in being this person in every way possible. They wear their clothes, use their tools or weapons, eat their food, and use their speech. When in character they are not only portraying the specific person, but they are presenting the person in a specific historical context and period. Sometimes interpreters create composite characters that are representative of people who lived at a particular time and place. The best first-person interpreters cannot be drawn out of character by a modern distraction or question about current events. However, if interpreters know their subject's values and opinions well enough they can answer a modern question as the person being portrayed likely would have answered it. Box 15.2 presents an outline of the research and preparations needed when planning a first-person program.

> First-person living history involves an interpreter portraying a particular person from the past.

Box 15.2
Steps to Development of a Living History Program

Adapted from Johnson County Parks and Recreation (KS) training materials

- Decide what theme you want to present
- Conduct research (identify primary and secondary sources)
- What character will best teach the information?
- Choose which style you want to use to deliver your living history program (First-person or Third-person)
- Select costuming and props
- Determine site location and historical year
- Identify a reason for character's presence at the site
- Identify a reason for visitor's presence at the site
- Plan presentation (greeting, activities, humor, stories, songs, demonstrations, closing)
- Develop the specific "character profile" including the following:
    - Character name
    - Parents' names
    - Birth/death dates
    - Place of birth
    - Other areas of residence
    - Spouse
        - Date of marriage
    - Biographical highlights: education, social class, trade/skills, talents, interests
    - Character's relationship with the historical site/event
    - Significant events occurring at the site and nationally during that period and the character's likely opinions about them
- Determine an appropriate evaluation method

Another approach to living history is third-person living history. As the name suggests, interpreters engaged in this method use the third-person tense, saying such things as "they wore this" or "a woman would do this." Often, third-person interpretation is called costumed interpretation. However, others use the term to describe either first or third-person living history whenever interpreters are wearing period clothing or historic uniforms.

The relative merits of first and third-person interpretation have been the subject of much discussion among history interpreters. Before deciding first or third-person, the first decision to make is whether the costume is even necessary. As Freeman Tilden said, "The story is the thing." If a costume adds to the telling of the story, then it is a desirable addition. Certainly if the costume is not accurate or in some way distracts from the story then the interpreter is better off in the standard uniform. A competent presentation in an agency uniform is always superior to a poor presentation in costume, no matter how elaborate or interesting the costume appears.

The second choice is to decide whether a first-person or third-person presentation would be more effective. Both have their advantages. A convincing first-person portrayal has a powerful "time-machine" effect where you can talk to and interact with a former president, general, or common person who seemingly has returned from the grave. First-person effectively shows the lifestyle of the period and gives the historical experience of a particular individual. Many interpreters find it rewarding to delve into a past person's life and learn not only the details of how they lived, but also their joys, heartaches, challenges, losses, successes, beliefs, values and legacy. The public gets to know a real person from the past. The power of personality may enhance the perceived credibility and impact of the information. Clearly, if it is important that the public meet a specific person from history then first-person would be the way to go. On the other hand, first-person living history is demanding on both the interpreter and the visitor, and it is limited by being locked into a specific period.

Third-person interpretation has the benefits of allowing the interpreter more freedom since he or she is not tied to representing a specific person. Likewise, since they are "in the present" they can respond to modern issues and are not bothered by modern distractions. To illustrate some of the benefits of third-person interpretation, Magee (2009) reported on a case where Historic Fort Snelling in Minnesota made a controversial change from first-person to third-person interpretation. Box 15.3 tells the story of this switch. Magee concluded, "Third-person interpretation has proven to be more flexible, more visitor friendly, and more intellectually honest."

Reenactment is another living history activity. Typically, the term *reenactments* refers to living history events (most often battles) carried out by serious amateurs or hobbyists who are motivated primarily to satisfy their own desires to experience history (Figure 15.6). As with many hobbies, they may also be motivated by a desire for camaraderie, fun, intellectual curiosity, and travel. Reenactments began after the U.S. Civil War in the late 1800s. They grew both in popularity and sophistication throughout the 20th century. The 100th anniversary of the Civil War was a catalyst for much of this growth. Although it is carried out by amateurs, reenactors strive for

> Reenactment is another living history activity.

authenticity in their uniforms, firearms, and other equipment. However, at times they are less concerned with telling the authentic story of an event. Reenactors seldom focus on targeting the audience's needs, yet watching reenactors can be a dramatic experience, both educational and entertaining. Living history interpreters can make good use of reenactors to supplement their own programs, but interpreters must be alert to quality control in terms of accuracy and authenticity as will be discussed below.

Box 15.3
Switching from First-person to Third-person Interpretation at Historic Fort Snelling
Adapted from Magee (2009)

First-person interpretation had always been practiced at Historic Fort Snelling and the staff was fully committed to that approach. However, managers began noticing problems. The success of the first-person encounters with the public depended greatly on the talent of the interpreter and the willingness of the public to suspend reality and play along. Moreover, conflicts would arise as modern visitors took offense to historic views and practices presented by the character being portrayed. This would lead to visitors trying to draw the interpreter out of character. Finally, management realized it required considerable resources to do the necessary research on the individual being portrayed, acquire the necessary props or original objects, and to train modern interpreters to do first-person living history effectively. Management was also concerned with declining visitation, a story stuck in 1827 needed to be opened to other periods and stories, and what they perceived as a stagnant interpretation program at the site. For all of these reasons, they switched most (not all) of their efforts to costumed third-person interpretation. Because first-person was the heart and soul of the site, about 10% of the interpreters did not return, and remaining staff found it difficult to leave their characters behind when talking to the public. However, the switch to third-person has been a success. Now interpreters answer visitors' questions directly and can admit when they do not know the answer to questions about life in 1827. Now interpreters can talk about slavery, the U.S.-Dakota War, and the World Wars rather than being trapped in 1827. Apparently, the public approves as attendance has rebounded and continues to grow.

Many organizations provide guidance, supplies, encouragement, and education to living history interpreters. Besides general interpretation organizations (e.g., Interpret Europe, Interpretation Australia, National Association for Interpretation) living history interpreters have many specialized organizations that offer support and training. One of the largest is the Association for Living History, Farm and Agricultural Museums (ALHFAM), an international organization of living history professionals founded at Old Sturbridge Village in Massachusetts. ALHFAM serves as an umbrella organization for several other smaller organizations. For example, The

Figure 15.6. Reenacting is not just about the fighting. It also is about the food. (MSP)

Midwest Open Air Coordinating Council (MOACC) is a popular and well-respected group in North America that is linked to ALHFAM.

In recognition that first-person living history and reenacting involves acting and other aspects of the theatre, ALHFAM spun off an organization called the International Museum Theatre Alliance (IMTAL). Sister organizations IMTAL Europe and IMTAL Asia-Pacific serve living history interpreters at museums in those regions. These IMTAL organizations are grounded in the belief that museum theatre is a powerful tool for entertaining and educating audiences in cultural institutions. Indeed, many living history interpreters have backgrounds and training in theatre arts.

Other professional organizations and publications focus on specific wars or periods of history. Historynet.com serves as a portal to magazines related to specific topics such as Women's History, Aviation History, or the Vietnam War. This site also has interactive activities, photo galleries, and other resources for the historical interpreter.

Challenges of Interpreting History: Accuracy and Authenticity

Accuracy

After visiting New Orleans and listening to guides tell conflicting and often fanciful stories about the French Quarter, veteran interpreter and NAI officer Cem Basman was moved to propose the following additional principle of interpretation (Basman, 2016).

> Any interpretation must be presented with the utmost attention to personal and professional integrity to assure that the recipients (clients and customers) of the interpretive effort are presented with the truth.

Beck and Cable (2011) proposed a similar principle among their 15 principles of interpretation: "Interpreters must concern themselves with the quality and quantity (selection and accuracy) of the information presented. Focused, well-researched interpretation is more powerful than a longer discourse." Similarly, their Interpreter's Creed (See Appendix A) directs interpreters to "Seek to convey only well-documented, accurate information."

Although interpreting the truth is critical in all interpretation, the truth often seems to be more difficult to arrive at in history than when interpreting typical nature-related themes. Perhaps this is because history interpreters are faced with interpreting interpretations of history and these interpretations are dynamic and evolving. On their website (alhfam.org) the ALHFAM notes interpretation of the past is always changing and living history interpreters actually "produce history" just as teachers, authors, and film directors do.

Moreover, the meanings associated with past events change both with time as values change, and with geography as local cultures interpret the same events differently from people in other locations. Nevertheless, interpreters should strive for the truth through thorough and unbiased research. Another reason why truth might be more difficult to come by in historical settings is the perceived need to entertain in the tourism sector. At a recent international tourism conference one of the authors was asked during the Q&A following a keynote address his opinion about "always having to tell the truth to clients." It was not self-evident to tour guides in that audience that they should always tell the truth to their audiences. The goal should be to make the truth more entertaining than the myth.

Then there is the question, *What is truth?* In this "information age," it is challenging to sort through the deluge of information to find truth. Media outlets act as gatekeepers and filter the news based upon their own organizational values and the messages they feel are important to project to the public. However, the lines between editorials and commentary and journalistic reporting often get blurred. Internet sources are generally less reliable than other media making it critical that the researcher understands the identity and potential biases of the source (Figure 15.7). Many find it difficult to distinguish between news and "fake" news.

When conducting research, generally primary sources are the most reliable way to get at truth. These sources are directly linked to the event or person being interpreted. Primary sources include personal journals or diaries, legal documents or government records, transcripts of speeches, interviews with people who witnessed the event, and original artifacts. Secondary sources are sources written about an event based on primary sources or photographs, drawings or replicas of artifacts. Secondary sources might be textbooks, biographies, or encyclopedia entries. Tertiary sources would be sources which relied on secondary levels of sources. With each level removed from the primary source more unintentional errors may creep into the accounts.

Figure 15.7. Interpreters must use care when doing historical research on the Internet. (www.likecaptions.com)

Although primary sources are preferred, they are not perfect. Primary sources themselves can be biased or inaccurate in reporting events. Artifacts and documents can be forgeries. So even with primary sources interpreters must be prudent in their selection and interpretation of them.

Another method of gathering and documenting historical information is through oral histories. If done correctly, they can provide interesting and useable information. Williams and Floress (2003) stress three key principles of ethics, respect, and flexibility when conducting oral histories. First, because the interviewees have their own feelings, lives, and living relatives, interviewers must handle their stories *ethically* with integrity and honesty. Likewise, the researcher must *respect* the people being interviewed regardless of their culture or lifestyles, and show appreciation for them sharing their memories. Finally, one must be *flexible* when scheduling and conducting interviews. Researchers may have to change the direction of questioning as discoveries are made about the person being interviewed. Williams and Floress note that in addition to gaining important historical data and perspectives, conducting oral histories may create connections to special communities and thereby attract their visitation and support. Box 15.4 gives other tips about conducting oral histories.

Box 15.4
Recommendations for Conducting Effective Oral History Interviews
Adapted from Williams & Floress (2003)

- Assemble all of your equipment into one bag and have backup batteries or a charger.
- Test the equipment before the interview and practice on friends or relatives.
- Prepare a standard set of questions before conducting the interviews, but be flexible if unexpected recollections arise. Capture them and then get back on track.
- Contact the person to be interviewed by phone prior to the interview so they get accustomed to hearing your voice and get to know you. Ask them where they would like to be interviewed. Some prefer home but others prefer a neutral site like a church or coffee shop.
- Limit the interview to about an hour. Attention spans wander and the interviewee may get fatigued.
- Do your homework and learn background about the location, time period, and as much as possible about the person being interviewed.
- Before leaving, have the source complete release forms for material and photographs. Then offer to provide copies of the recording and a transcription to the family for their archives.
- Send a thank you note to personally thank them for their time and cooperation.

Authenticity

The word "authentic" commonly is used to describe something real or true, rather than imaginary, false, or imitative. In this sense, every heritage interpreter would agree it is important to be authentic rather than fake. This interest in authenticity is mirrored in many other organizations. For example, World Heritage Sites include authenticity as a criterion for their designation, and in 2016 they convened a task force to work on enhancing authenticity at heritage sites. However, authenticity is a concept that includes more than merely being factually accurate. Rather, the term has evolved to include broader issues of context and visitor experience. Originally in the tourism literature authenticity was seen as a quality judged by experts (e.g., archeologists, ecologists, museum curators), not perceived by visitors. Today interpreters understand that visitors may or may not perceive objects, places, and experiences as authentic regardless of how experts label them. Perceptions of authenticity should affect interpretation planning and delivery because these perceptions influence visitors' willingness to engage in the interpretation, enjoy it, and find it credible.

Hill and Cable (2006) called attention to a framework showing three key types of authenticity–the objective, the constructed, and the personal–that can be applied to interpretive sites, and an experience might include all three types of authenticity for visitors.

Objective authenticity is tied strongly to original artifacts, historic buildings, places where well-known events occurred, and other tangible aspects of authenticity. In some views it requires the site to be noncommercial. An obvious but important implication is that because the past is gone, even tangible features of a site can no longer be "experienced" in an absolutely genuine way (Figure 15.8).

Constructed authenticity occurs in constructed or reconstructed space. This view means traditional symbols, products, or art created in newer ways can be authentic in a constructed sense. An important point is that various stakeholders may have differing views of authenticity, which does not mean an object, event, or perspective is inauthentic.

Competing authenticities exist, as becomes even clearer when considering the third type of authenticity.

Personal authenticity takes place when the visitor transcends time and space. Even if a historic moment never again can occur or place be visited as it was in the exact particulars, the visitor is "there." Objectively authentic artifacts and constructed-yet-authentic views of docents may lead to a personally authentic experience for visitors who feel they actually have experienced the historical event in a meaningful way. Likewise, others may perceive the same interpretation as inauthentic because, for instance, they do not understand or react sympathetically to views of docents.

Figure 15.8. A slave collar that prevented slaves from escaping through dense vegetation lends a powerful dose of objective authenticity to the interpretation of slavery. (TC)

Gilmore and Pine (2007) studied how consumers value authenticity. They found that consumers want the real thing, not products or experiences they consider fake. Consumers subconsciously base their perceptions of authenticity on five genres of authenticity. These genres of perceived authenticity can be connected to offerings found at interpretive sites:

- **Commodities**–Natural authenticity. People tend to perceive as authentic that which exists in its natural state in or of the earth, remaining untouched by human hands; not artificial or synthetic.
- **Goods**–Original authenticity. People tend to perceive as authentic that which possesses originality in design, being the first of its kind, never before seen by human eyes; not a copy or imitation.
- **Services**–Exceptional authenticity. People tend to perceive as authentic that which is done exceptionally well, executed individually and extraordinarily by someone demonstrating care; not unfeelingly or disingenuously performed.
- **Experiences**–Referential authenticity. People tend to perceive as authentic that which draws inspiration from human history, and tapping into our shared memories and longings; not derivative or trivial.
- **Transformations**–Influential authenticity. People tend to perceive as authentic that which exerts influence on other entities, calling humans to a higher goal and providing a foretaste of a better way; not inconsequential or without meaning.

Kohl (2014) applied Gilmore and Pine's work to interpretation. He noted that applying all five genres is not always possible or desirable, but a combination of them might appeal to the visitor's desire for authenticity. A visitor adds up the positive believable qualities and accepts or rejects authenticity. The greater the sum the more quickly and intensely the visitor will accept the site or interpretive efforts as authentic. Kohl noted, "Through interpretation, a heritage site can indicate a place's natural qualities, how original are the objects, how exceptionally the work has been done; connect the heritage to past figures and periods (referential); and make apparent new ideas and opportunities to improve the visitor experience, as well as strategies to conserve Heritage (Influential). In short, interpretation is the single-most important tool to influence all forms of authenticity."

Once visitors accept a place's authenticity, then they allow their imaginations to enter the place's story. In this state, visitors identify with its characters, transport to another time and place, and understand sympathetically assumptions and beliefs of those who lived there, all goals of history interpretation (Kohl, 2014).

In summary, visitors perceive authenticity when an experience is well-interpreted in multiple facets of authenticity. Interpreters need to thoughtfully encourage factors that affect the perceptions of authenticity and minimize anything that will distract from these five genres of authenticities. These might include new facilities, modern conveniences and fashions, and even the presence or behaviors of other visitors.

> **Interpreters need to thoughtfully encourage factors that affect the perceptions of authenticity.**

Authentic interpretation may require presenting challenging topics such as slavery, the Holocaust, and the impacts of European colonization of the Western Hemisphere. Traditionally these topics were thought to be inherently difficult to interpret in a truly authentic, yet honorable and respectful way. First-person and costumed living history are particularly challenging when dealing with sensitive issues, controversial sites, or tragic events. However, in light of the typologies of authenticity given above by Gilmore and Pine (2007), it is certainly possible to create authentic experiences associated with challenging topics through a mix of influential, referential, exceptional, and original and natural objects. Likewise, in the context of the Hill and Cable (2006) objective authenticity and constructed authenticity in presentations of difficult topics can lead to profoundly personal authentic experiences.

Perfect replicas of uniforms, weapons, and tools are expensive and modern distractions almost impossible to eliminate. Given these challenges, is there ever a time when an interpreter might accept less than fully authentic programming? Mast (2014) answered in the affirmative. For example, he noted that safety trumps authenticity and so he, like many interpreters, carry a radio under the costume or as hidden as possible among the props. And, although modern interruptions to an authentic ambiance might occur, he notes that it won't cause the visitors to misunderstand the program's content. Moreover, often the interpreter can share a laugh with the audience over the intrusion. Although Mast (2014) recognizes the important goal of authenticity he concluded that "we must be careful in our quest for perfection not to sacrifice the true goal of interpretive programming; ... our true goal is connecting people with the past..." The key is to be as authentic as possible in every interpretive effort, and honestly admit when certain aspects of the presentation are less than "perfect." If an acceptable degree of authenticity is too difficult to achieve through costumed interpretation, then the approach should be changed rather than foregoing opportunities to interpret the site's history.

> **The key is to be as authentic as possible in every interpretive effort.**

Controversy

Even when striving for accuracy and authenticity there will always be controversy when interpreting history. Audiences will regularly ask of interpreters, "Whose interpretation is it?" Visitors will come to sites with feelings ranging from infatuation with the past, to fear and even anger at the past. The scope of these controversies can be international (e.g., was Christopher Columbus a villain or hero), national (e.g., how to present the Enola Gay and honor the pilots), or local (e.g., disputes over a place name). Even the word "heritage" is controversial (Hewison, 1989). As Saxe (2009) noted, "heritage is an active phenomenon with two stages: (1) the recovery of something left to us from the past, and (2) our decision to do something about it (options include: to ignore, reject, or destroy it and/or to embrace, restore, and preserve it for others). As such, controversy ... can and does evolve from even the most benign topics ..."

Controversy not only swirls around what stories to interpret, but also in how to present emotionally charged interpretation. Saxe (2009) made the case that interpretation should occasionally be "shocking, moving and provide a cathartic experience." Holocaust sites and war museums contemplate controversial decisions about how graphic and shocking to make their presentations, and how to portray humanely "the enemy."

On the other hand, the use of heritage interpretation as value-added to tourism destinations requires a more commercial and entertaining approach to presenting history. Scripted theatrical performances entertain the crowds at the aforementioned Colonial Williamsburg, Mount Vernon, and similar sites. These presentations of history have proven to be profitable and successful in enhancing the visitor experience and yet commercialization of history creates controversy.

Good entertainment can evoke powerful emotions in audience members. The goal of living history interpreters, and all interpreters, is to explore and discover knowledge and wisdom and present accurately in entertaining and emotionally moving ways.

> *"We have always tried to be guided by the basic idea that, in the discovery of knowledge, there is great entertainment—as, conversely, in all good entertainment, there is always some grain of wisdom, humanity, or enlightenment to be gained."*
> –Walt Disney

Interpreting Indigenous Peoples

To thoughtful readers, it may seem odd that we discuss interpreting indigenous cultures in a chapter on history. After all, Native Americans, Canada's First Nations, Australia's Aborigines, Mayans in Mexico, and other such indigenous peoples and their cultures still exist today. They are not historical curiosities. However, we include the following advice about interpreting these cultures in this chapter because interpreters often work at places that have a rich indigenous history. Telling stories of the land would not be complete without interpreting the histories of the earlier cultures. Interpreters at almost any site have the opportunity, and obligation, to illuminate the stories of peoples who previously lived at that place. Interpreters of history often find themselves talking in the past, but the best interpreters bring the past alive, make connections to the present, and propose possible futures. This is never truer than when interpreting native cultures. The following are important principles when interpreting indigenous cultures.

- Do not say "*When* Native Americans (or other such group) lived here." They still do!
- Whenever possible, involve members of the indigenous community to help plan and carry out the interpretive program. This greatly enhances authenticity and credibility.
- Be as specific as possible regarding which tribe or nation you are talking about when interpreting (e.g., not all Native Americans lived in teepees and hunted bison).
- Don't dress up in the clothing of indigenous people without their cooperation and approval. It can be offensive. This is another reason to invite members of the indigenous community to participate.
- If possible, seek the approval of the native people before repeating their stories, particularly if you are doing so in first-person, and always acknowledge the source of the story. At times, it may be inappropriate to share indigenous knowledge. Often, however, they want their stories told. Usually it is most effective to have them tell their own stories.
- Be sensitive to the fact that specific places or landscapes can hold spiritual or religious meanings to indigenous groups. Interpreters should recognize these sites as special places, and interpret and manage them in light of those meanings.

The American Association for State and Local History publishes a series of books, the Interpreting History Series, which includes excellent titles for interpreting Native American history, American military history, and slavery at museums and historic sites. A broad coverage of such topics, also in the series, is Julia Rose's (2016) *Interpreting Difficult History at Museums and Historic Sites*. Addressing difficult histories encourages people to reconcile with the past, to grieve, to commemorate monuments or memorials—and other acts of remembrance—and to learn from the past. "By exposing and elevating the stories of the oppressed and the victimized, difficult histories in museums and historical sites become tools for advocacy, civility, and education" (Rose, 2016).

> "Addressing difficult histories encourages people to reconcile with the past."

Summary

"We are deceiving ourselves if we think that when we stand in front of a case of medals, or guns, or photographs of mutilated bodies, we are looking at the past. We are looking also at the present and the future. If interpretation is to be a source of social good, then it must recognize the continuity of history and alert us to the future through the past."

–David Uzzell

Most history interpreters and venues focus on illuminating the lifestyles of common folk, telling the stories of traditional communities and cultures, or recreating and interpreting important battles. However, increasingly individual interpreters and public agencies are focusing on exploring social justice issues and the struggles of specific groups to achieve freedom and acceptance. A healthy society has a vivid and accurate memory of all of these things. Therefore, for reasons of both celebration and introspection, we must not forget our past (Beck & Cable, 2011).

While interpreting history can entertain and delight audiences, it also can promote a better understanding of present challenges and help people navigate perilous times. Interpreters play an essential role in preserving memories and stories that can promote human rights, increase understanding, reduce conflict, and work toward peace. Interpretive sites increasingly serve as advocates for social justice and responsible citizenship. History interpretation helps us understand ourselves; where we have been and why we are the way we are. Interpreters preserve a legacy for future generations and a foundation upon which citizens can build a better world.

Literature Cited

Basman, V. (2016). The seventh principle. *Legacy, 27*(2), 10.

Beck, L., & Cable, T. (2011). *The gifts of interpretation: Fifteen guiding principles for interpreting nature and culture.* Urbana, IL: Sagamore.

Gilmore, J. H., & Pine II, B. J. (2007). *Authenticity: what consumers really want.* Boston, MA: Harvard Business School Press.

Hewison, R. (1989). Heritage: An Interpretation. In D. Uzzell (Ed.), *Heritage Interpretation Vol. 1: The Natural and Built Environment.* (pp. 15-23). London. Belhaven Press.

Hill, S., & Cable T. (2006). The concept of authenticity: Implications for interpretation. *Journal of Interpretation Research, 11*(1), 55–65.

Kohl, J. (2014). What is really real? A new vision of authenticity and its role in interpretation and alternative tourism. *Legacy, 25*(6), 6–9.

Luzader, J. C. F. (2016). The ethics of living history and of quality costumed interpretation. *Legacy, 27*(2), 18–21.

Luzader, J. C. F., & Spellman, J. S. (2003) Curing the CBS syndrome: Living history without demonstrations. *2003 NAI sourcebook.* Ft. Collins, CO: National Association for Interpretation.

Magee, R. (2009). A fork in the river: Experiencing the change from first- to third-person interpretation at Historic Fort Snelling. *Legacy, 20*(6), 12–14.

Mast, B. (2014). Why so serious? Authenticity in living history. *Legacy, 25*(6),16–17.

Rose, J. (2016). *Interpreting difficult history at museums and historic sites.* New York, NY: Rowman & Littlefield.

Saxe, D.W. (2009). Living heritage: An experimental model mixing heritage and entertainment. *Journal of Interpretation Research,* 14(1), 33-46.

Williams, P. S., & Floress, K. (2003). Sparking the flame at history through oral histories. *2003 NAI sourcebook.* Ft. Collins, CO: National Association for Interpretation.

SECTION V

Managing Interpretation

CHAPTER 16
A Business Approach to Interpretation

According to Jay Miller, former Chief of Interpretation for Arkansas State Parks, the gift shop is an important part of the interpretive site experience. There interpreters have the opportunity to "clinch the sale," not of random gifts, but of the message and experience through memory-laden items. People look for items that remind them of what they did, saw, and learned at the site. Interpretive gift shop sales reinforce the site's themes and messages. Products include simple messages that generate memories, restate themes, and provide talking points for storytelling back home. Souvenirs generate word-of-mouth advertising because they relate to the site experience. This leads to remarks such as "Look at this, and let me tell you the story behind it."

The interpreter should work closely with the gift shop manager to select the best items and to interpret those for the visitor through display organization, photos, and tags to accompany the items. Good examples include a gold pin made in the pattern of the iron work on the gate to a historic home in Charleston, South Carolina, note cards with illustrations and recipes from early residents of an area, plush animal toys of local wildlife with cards noting their habitat/value at the site, or even a bar of soap made from the milk of sheep visitors have just been petting in the field. Stocking strategic gift shop products allows visitors to re-live the experience, a critical component in the interpretive process.

In fact, Miller notes that interpretive programs can be built around the gift shop. Davidsonville Historic State Park in Arkansas built a new visitor center in 2016, including an enlarged gift shop. The park superintendent wanted to capitalize on this. She turned to books—history books. Everyone knows those won't sell, but they did because they related to the story of this site and the experience visitors had at this site. The park uses interpretation to solidify the connection by creating and advertising simple events of readings and book signings by authors of the books for sale. This attracted attention to the park, to the new visitor center, and to the books. The interpretive effort was successful on many levels, not the least of which was generating revenue. It also contributed to the learning experience of visitors and provided tangible mementos that spark memories.

> *"Much ingenuity with a little money is vastly more profitable and amusing than much money without ingenuity."*
>
> –Arnold Bennett

Although making money is seldom the primary goal of interpretation, interpretation is indeed a business. This chapter focuses on managing interpretive services to provide a quality product that effectively delivers customer satisfaction. It discusses administrative philosophy and methods to achieve high-quality service that benefits the public and the organizations involved. A business-like approach makes interpretation more effective and more available to the public at the best times and places.

> **Interpretation is indeed a business.**

Nonprofit interpretive centers and museums live with the necessity of marketing their programs directly to clients and donors. Public sector interpreters must engender support from taxpayers and politicians, and supplement that support with private donations and user fees. The commercial interpretive business sector has to make money to keep operating. Those few who naively thought being a naturalist or historian would allow them a career of solitary contemplation of nature or history, or got into the field precisely to escape people or business environments soon learn that museums, zoos, and nature centers must operate like a business if they are going to be successful and survive (Figure 16.1). And, like all successful businesses, the focus must be on serving the customers; the guests.

Figure 16.1. The gift shop at the Cheyenne Bottoms Wetland Education Center serves as the only bookstore in a multi-county region of rural Kansas. Residents travel considerable distances just to shop at the visitor center. (TC)

The concepts presented here draw from classic writings on business management, marketing, and leadership. These ideas will serve as guidelines for any place that interpreters work whether they be governmental agencies, nonprofit organizations, or private for-profit companies. In addition, interpretation organizations offer their members publications and training on fundraising, organization management, and other topics found in this chapter. Additional help is often available from local colleges or the Chamber of Commerce in a nearby community.

A Business Framework for Interpretive Organizations

Peters and Austin (1985), in their classic book, *A Passion for Excellence,* present these model components as a framework for strong organizations: *care of customers, constant innovation,* and *turned-on people* all connected by the critical element of *lead-*

ership (Figure 16.2). The following discussion uses this model as its basis and illustrates how interpreters can use these factors to do their jobs effectively. This framework continues to be relevant today and is reinforced by other leading business books (e.g., Christensen, Allworth, & Dillon, 2012; Collins, 2005; Collins, 2011; Goleman, Boyatzis & McKee, 2013; Sinek, 2014).

Leadership

"Management is doing things right; leadership is doing the right things."
—Peter Drucker

Figure 16.2. The three components of strong organizations (Source: Peters & Austin, 1985).

Leadership copes with change. It sets a direction, motivates and inspires, aligns people in coalitions, and keeps them moving in the right direction. Management, on the other hand, copes with complexity. It plans and budgets, organizes and staffs, controls and solves problems, and monitors results (Kotter, 1999). Collins (2005) adds that effective leaders stimulate a commitment to and vigorous pursuit of a clear and compelling vision, whereas a competent manager organizes people and resources toward the effective and efficient pursuit of predetermined objectives.

Leadership is not the same as the exercise of power. True leadership exists only if people follow when they have the freedom not to. If people follow because they have no choice, then you are not leading, you are dictating (Collins, 2005).

Leadership and management skills may seem mysterious qualities that only a few possess. However, most people can learn and practice the principle attributes needed to lead and manage. Collins (2005), in his influential books on making *good* organizations *great*, defines the attributes of excellent leaders in the public sector as a "paradoxical blend of personal humility and professional will" that creates legitimacy and influence. Great leaders are primarily ambitious for the cause or the mission, rather than focusing on themselves and their own advancement. If people know that the leader is motivated by making the organization great, rather than a self-serving focus, they are more likely to follow. That doesn't mean always being soft or nice or inclusive or even consensus-building. Leadership can be tough work. This unerring focus on what's best for the organization means making sure the right things happen no matter how painful or difficult. Leadership artfully motivates people to accept or even thrive in the leader's chosen course of action.

Habits to Develop for Managers and Leaders

Stephen Covey's classic book *7 Habits of Highly Effective People* (1989) was one of the most influential books of the late 20th century. It promoted acting on a Character Ethic (based upon our habits and who we really are) rather than a Personality Ethic (based upon public image and behaviors). This book even influenced language as words like "proactive" and "win-win" are now part of the daily lexicon. Covey concluded that effective managers and leaders practice the following seven habits:

1. **Be proactive.** Recognize that you have the responsibility to make things happen. Initiate, create a vision, empower others, take responsibility for your own actions. This key characteristic distinguishes a supervisor from an employee.
2. **Begin with the end in mind.** Think of how you want to be remembered at your funeral. This will help you decide what is really important. Develop a personal mission statement to identify your core values that will guide your decisions at work and home.
3. **Put first things first**. Prioritize, delegate, and adjust if priorities change. Say no—you cannot do everything yourself. Find those who can do it for you; give them jobs. We don't manage time, we only manage ourselves. Devote time to what is important, not only to what is urgent.
4. **Think win-win.** Think with an abundance mentality; avoid the scarcity syndrome (winners-losers). Seek the best alternative for mutual benefit. In fact, the full description of this principle is "Win-win or no deal." Sincerely wanting the other party to win, too, fosters trust that will pay off in both the short and long term.
5. **Seek first to understand and then to be understood.** Listen to understand, not to reply. Listen not only with the ears, but empathetically with the eyes and heart to understand the other person emotionally and intellectually.
6. **Synergize.** Make the whole greater than the sum of its parts. Put talents together, giving value to differences between people's skills and interests.
7. **Renew yourself; sharpen your skills.** The basis of what we do is enthusiasm. Strength comes from renewal of the physical, mental, emotional, social, and spiritual areas of life.

Leadership defined by these habits provides a foundation for meeting standards of excellence in interpretation facilities. Enthusiastic, effective leadership manifests itself in passionate employees and quality service offered through interpretive programs. Finally, a popular business book by Simon Sinek (2014) summed up the proper mentality of the best leaders: *Leaders Eat Last*.

Constant Innovation

"Creativity is thinking up new things; innovation is doing new things."
–Theodore Levitt

One part of the model of successful organizations is "constant innovation." Interpreters usually fall into the category of highly creative people. Many also use their innovative abilities (Figure 16.3). Society suffers no shortage of creative people.

The shortage is one of innovators. Creativity does not automatically lead to innovation. Some creative people prefer to pass the brass tacks work to others. The creative idea person may even create inertia problems. They pepper everybody with proposals, just enticing enough to arouse interest but too brief to address how to use them or how to implement them. Rare are the people who have the know-how, energy, and persistence to implement ideas. Successful interpretation requires innovation. Sites that have had the same displays for decades or have been offering the same old programs may be neither successfully fulfilling their mission nor garnering much public support.

Encouraging Innovation

How can interpretive managers stimulate innovation? The key is to promote autonomy and entrepreneurship by giving employees independence, the freedom to take risks, and a stake in the outcome. Innovators are individuals who take an idea and run. A new idea will die if nobody champions it. The person passively saying that the idea would be "nice," probably will not become its champion. It takes special energy to implement new ideas and overcome the resistance that change provokes among an agency's many non-innovators. It also requires patience, persistence, and an ability to express ideas persuasively to the organization.

Figure 16.3. Interpreters developed an innovative way to welcome visitors to a museum in Mexico City. Photos of visitors are taken as they enter. People are pleasantly surprised when they notice themselves displayed in the ever-changing, myriad faces on the wall. (TC)

Small autonomous teams usually work better than committees. Generally, the larger the committee, the slower the pace of action and often the pressure to make multiple compromises to satisfy committee members squelches innovation or derails initially exciting proposals. The oft-repeated quips that "A camel is a horse designed by committee" and "a committee keeps minutes, but loses hours" reflect the frustration felt by ineffective committees.

Managers of successful companies have rich support systems for innovation that allow innovative pioneers to flourish and even compete with one another. They do not just give them "enough rope to hang themselves with" but, instead, supply assistance so the innovators can survive to get the job done—to try and fail and try again until they succeed.

Dealing with Failures

Good failures are misdirected quality efforts or well-thought-out missteps, not blind stabs in the dark. Striving for interpretive innovation offers no excuse for sloppiness, inaccuracy, or poor quality work. Therefore, innovation requires discipline, definition of aims, and evaluation of past efforts. It also requires action. The best managers love experiments and are as intrigued with the ones that fail as they are with the successes. Successful organizations are willing to accept failure. Innovation resembles a game of chance in some ways, with odds that many new ideas will fail, but the successes are worth it. An interpreter who makes no mistakes probably has not tried much that is new or different.

> Good failures are misdirected quality efforts.

The idea of rewarding failure is too challenging for some bureaucratic minds. They fear failure rather than aspiring to achievement. Successful interpreters, like successful businesses, have to take risks. Innovative progress comes from those who move ahead, not by those who wait for a smooth, well-marked road. Along the way, risk can be minimized with frequent evaluation, and frank and friendly communication. The best interpretive managers have a contempt for inaction—whatever the excuse. Rather, they are characterized by an adventuresome spirit that keeps the organization moving ahead.

The National Association for Interpretation's *Legacy* magazine devoted an entire issue to the theme of "Interpretive Failures." John Miller, one of the authors in this issue noted, "Sadly, many of us are afraid to fail early in our careers and so we sometimes avoid taking those risks that can pay off both in success or even more valuable life lessons" (Miller, 2016).

Customer Care

A second part of the model for successful organizations is *Customer Care*. Business leaders put a lot of emphasis on customers or clients. As noted in Chapter 5 and throughout this text, interpreters too must focus on meeting the needs of their clientele (i.e., their audiences). At too many public parks and historic sites, visitors are treated as a nuisance rather than as the lifeblood of the organization. Often zoos, museums, and private attractions perform better in this regard than governmental agencies, as the link between satisfied customers and the financial well-being is more direct. However, all agencies benefit by the customer-service approach (Figure 16.4).

Excellent organizations all define themselves as customer service businesses, regardless of what product or service they actually provide. Most excellent companies seem to be

Figure 16.4. Customer care is shown at the Runge Nature Center in Missouri when guests are greeted by a volunteer with a big smile and juicy watermelon. (MDC)

obsessed with service, often to a seemingly unjustifiable degree of commitment. If a provider of an interpretive service fails to understand the customer, he or she fails to understand the interpretive profession. Thinking first of the visitor applies directly to every interpretive sign or program. The first principle of interpretation, as well as of marketing and advertising, says to relate the subject matter to something within the personality or experience of the customer. Treat people accordingly with courtesy, perception, and listening.

Practicing Courtesy

Any organization can act courteously to its clientele. However, surprisingly few actually *commit* to courtesy. Today, common courtesy seems uncommon! The administrator who provides little funding, training, or supervision of young interpreters declares disregard for a key customer service (LaPage, 2002). The naturalist, historian, or volunteer who is impatient with visitors interrupting work on "important" projects or who refers to visitors in less than complimentary terms such as the "mindless masses," or even "tourists," demonstrates a lack of commitment to customer care.

> "Excellent organizations all define themselves as customer service businesses."

By contrast, at the Disney Corporation, every person who comes on a property is a Guest. An employee or executive who writes the word at Disney had best capitalize the "G." A typical Guest interacts with 73 Disney employees per day. That puts Disney's reputation on the line 10 million or more times per day, just in the U.S. theme parks. Likewise, interpreters often provide the only meaningful personal contact for the visitor to a museum or park. Negative impressions come from the interpreter who argues with a visitor, who shows impatience in answering "stupid" questions, or who presents a careless physical appearance. All signal a lack of customer care.

Sincere courtesy makes a powerful positive impression. Courtesy in interpretation reflects directly on an organization. The enthusiastic interpreter will want to stay visible where visitors congregate: circulating through a campground or standing unobtrusively at key points in a museum or park to be easily available to greet and help visitors, and develop a positive impression of the place. Customer-focused interpreters eagerly interpret "beyond the program" by being available to serve guests. This can mean adding signs, exhibits, brochures, and other media to assist guests. When it comes time for guests to leave an interpretive site, courteous interpreters say good-bye and invite them to visit again soon (Box 16.1).

Box 16.1
Take the Time to Say Goodbye

Schaneé Anderson, Curator of Education and Farms, Sedgwick County Zoo, Kansas

You greet a guest at the front door of your home and thank them for visiting when they leave. Do you do the same for guests visiting your interpretive facility? A friendly thanks for visiting or a "We hope you join us for next week's program," to someone leaving your site can make a lasting impression. Therefore, make saying goodbye just as important as saying hello.

Box 16.1 continued

The last thing people see or experience as they leave your facility is generally what they remember most clearly. At Sedgwick County Zoo, staff greet our guests at the entry for all programs and walk back with them after the program. This gives us a chance to say goodbye and offers guests time to ask questions individually. When they leave feeling that someone cares about them and their questions, they are more likely to visit again and, just as importantly, they will also be more likely to tell others about the great experience they had.

This same philosophy holds true as the zoo closes each night. When the weather is nice, people often stay as long as possible, making it difficult to close the zoo at the appointed hour. Instead of a monotone message over a loudspeaker stating that the zoo is now closing, a staff member walks the zoo grounds and talks with groups individually. Phrases like "thanks for visiting today" or "I hope you enjoyed your day at the zoo" are generally enough to encourage guests to leave without feeling as if they are being pushed out the door. For those guests who do not leave, I have found that bringing a passenger golf cart to them and offering a ride to the parking lot works wonders. It gives me time to visit with the guests; they get something special, and I get the facility closed on time.

Treating the guests at our facilities as we would treat guests in our homes makes great business sense. For many local interpretive sites, word of mouth is the best advertising around. Make sure that the words coming out of your guests' mouths are friendly by saying goodbye and inviting them back.

Perhaps the most widely quoted philosophy of customer service is the following series of statements in answer to the question, "What is a customer?" These statements have been attributed to people ranging from Ghandi to L.L. Bean. Regardless of who said it first, interpreters would do well to replace the word "customer" with the word "visitor" or "guest" and then take this philosophy to heart.

What is a customer (visitor)?
A Customer (visitor) is the most important person ever in this office.
A Customer (visitor) is not dependent on us, we are dependent on customers (visitors).
A Customer (visitor) is not an interruption of our work.
Customers (visitors) are the reason for it. We are not doing them a favor by serving them.
They are doing us a favor by giving us the opportunity to serve them.
A Customer (visitor) is not somebody to match wits with.
Nobody has ever won an argument with a customer (visitor).
A Customer (visitor) is a person who brings us their wants.
It is our job to handle them profitably to the customer (visitor) and ourselves.

Handling Controversial Issues

Customer care also involves the delicate and respectful handling of controversial issues. Controversial issues abound in interpretation as discussed throughout this book. It could be evolution vs. creationism, hunting vs. anti-hunting, timber harvest vs. forest preservation, or the various perspectives associated with the American Civil War or Spanish explorers. Remember that you might hold a minority view on the issue. Or, at least recognize that many people in your audience may hold different views than you. Finally, as mentioned above with customers, recognize that you never win an argument with visitors. You might have won a debate if somebody was keeping score, but you will have alienated that person, and lost their political and economic support and the opportunity to serve them in the future. Life (and your career) is too short, and opportunities to enrich lives too few to waste time and energy engaged in ego-based sparring with visitors.

A good place to start when dealing with controversial issues is by applying the previously presented principles of interpretation. For example, the first principle of interpretation prescribes that interpreters must relate their presentation to the audience. In doing so interpreters can find common ground from which they can achieve their interpretive goals. A beautiful example of this is illustrated by the following quote from esteemed conservation biologist Edward O. Wilson. "Those committed by religion to believe that life was put on earth in one divine stroke will recognize that we are destroying the Creation, and those who perceive biodiversity to be the product of blind evolution will agree."

Box 16.2 offers additional tips on handling sensitive or controversial subjects in a way that will serve, rather than offend people.

Box 16.2
Ten Tips for Dealing with Controversial Issues

1. Be nice! Be ladies and gentlemen interpreting to ladies and gentlemen.
2. Be humble, not arrogant.
3. Be credible. Do your own research, including researching the alternative points of view.
4. Present multiple points of view. Encourage visitors to make their own choices and applications.
5. Use the controversy as an entry point into your theme.
6. Interpret the controversy. People love hearing about controversy, but not necessarily engaging in it.
7. Be conditional. Say you could do this, or you could think this way, rather than how they must think or act.
8. Focus on universals such as beauty or courage, rather than focusing on often disputed facts.
9. Find common ground by applying the first principle of interpretation, relating to your audience.
10. Carefully consider why you want to present specific controversial information. Is it essential to your theme? Is it mission-based? Why do guests need to know this? Does it matter enough to risk alienating people? If the answers are affirmative, then move forward.

Customer Care Caveat

"If the person who works at your company is 100% proud of the job they're doing, if you give them the tools to do a good job, if they're proud of the brand, if they're treated well, they're going to be happy... Happy employees equal happy customers."
–Richard Branson

> Happy employees translate into happy customers.

A final note on customer care is warranted. Although the customer is king, he or she is not an absolute tyrant. Leaders at many successful companies say, "The customers come *second*." They put the employees first. Researchers have found that leaders should demonstrate that their loyalty is to employees first, trusting that their employees will then be more loyal and caring to their customers. Happy employees translate into happy customers. Furthermore, an unhappy employee can have a negative impact of *many* customers. Jay Steinfeld (2016) noted, "Your team will never exceed the expectations of your customers until you first exceed the expectations of your team. ... Policies and processes matter, but it's the way you treat people that counts." Box 16.3 suggests ways Steinfeld's company shows employees that the company cares about them.

This caveat leads us to the final attribute of successful organizations—passionate people.

Box 16.3
Ideas for Showing Employees that They Are the Organization's Most Important Resource

These approaches are used at Jay Steinfeld's company to show employees in a large organization that the company cares about them (Adapted from Steinfeld, 2016).

- **Turn your Employees into Heroes**. Use digital signage around the office or site displaying standout employees for the month. The displays look like a sports channel and the employees are shown in video next to their stats. Photoshop every employee into their favorite movie poster, whether it's *The Godfather, Indiana Jones,* or *You've Got Mail*.
- **Share Information**. Have a weekly all-hands-on-deck meeting (even if some attend remotely via technology) to make sure that nobody is surprised with any company news and that a human connection is maintained. Have employees introduce themselves with a song, dance, or joke. It's a great way to get personal and understand more than someone's skill, but a little of who they are.
- **Feed the Masses**. One way that our culture shows we care is to provide food for everyone. When things get busy, lunch shows up (and sometimes dinner). There's always snacks and often a lot of cake laying around. Another way that you "feed" your employees is to remember personal information and have better conversations than "good morning" and "how was your weekend?" People instantly recognize when effort is put into getting to know them.
- **Create Interaction Opportunities**. Every new employee is sent on a scavenger hunt the first day around the office, armed with a list of seemingly difficult questions about the company and its employees, and they can only ask each person two questions. By the end of the afternoon, they've met 20–25 employees and know a lot about the organization's culture and history. We also hold quick chats (think speed dating!), where leadership from different departments is available to meet and get to know employees in other departments.
- **Recognize and Nurture Talent**. Recognize employees who have the makings of a rising star and focus on talent development. Each manager holds one-to-one meetings with their employees every month to focus on their growth and development.
- **Remember to have fun!** One of our core values is to "enjoy the ride." Our Culture Committee and our Employee Engagement Director regularly plan activities to have fun around the office, whether it's flag football, Pajama Day, or a charity event. Almost every week we celebrate life, each other, or our gratitude. It can be infectious.

Passionate People

"Nothing great was ever accomplished without enthusiasm."
–Ralph Waldo Emerson

In the parlance of the 1980s, Peters and Austin in the above model referred to the importance of having "turned-on" employees. Beck and Cable (2011) refer to them as passionate, in that interpreters show passion for the resource and those people who come to be inspired by it.

How do leaders create and nurture passionate employees? By giving them autonomy to create ideas and the authority to implement them. Then by giving them a sense of ownership in the organization's success and acknowledging and rewarding those successes. Keep them feeling positive and hopeful. Keep them up to date by giving them opportunities for professional development. If interpreters are excited about their work and their organization, they will produce visitors who feel they've been served well and enriched by their experiences.

In Covey's list of seven desirable habits, the fifth item focuses on listening, which plays an important role in growing passionate employees and customers. The business literature often speaks of "managing by walking around" or doing regular "walk-abouts." Managers learn most by listening and recording feedback that they get directly from the staff and customers. Getting out from behind the desk to visit the front lines is essential to understanding the work environment and operations. Often managers would be ignorant of important details unless they listened and saw for themselves. These listening and learning sessions not only educate the manager, but the process of listening builds relationships and the morale of those carrying out the organization's mission. This, in turn, fosters better service to the clientele. Mark Goulston (2009) wrote a business book titled, *Just Listen*. He suggested, "Be more interested than interesting."

Finally, it is impossible to feel passion for work if you do not see it as purposeful. Without a purpose, there can be no passion. The best leaders insure that everybody in the organization understands the important purpose and value of their work so that they can become passionate about it. Well-thought out, focused, and widely-articulated mission statements for the organization, site, and even individual, help interpreters focus on their worth and purpose.

> "Without a purpose, there can be no passion."

Supervision

Supervision involves overseeing and directing the work of other people. Collins (2005) identified "having the right people on the bus" as one of the keys to great companies. In other words, hiring and keeping the best people. Supervising people is much easier and more fulfilling if "the right people are on the bus" and that they are in the right seats.

In most interpretive settings, unlike the business world, you cannot use big sums of money to buy and keep talent. Rather, interpretive supervisors generally must hire people that are underpaid relative to the private sector, or unpaid if volunteers. They don't have the financial resources to provide incentives to motivate otherwise unmotivated or undisciplined employees. Moreover, it is more difficult to remove people from the bus in the public sector than in the private sector. These factors make it even more vital that the right people are hired in public agency interpretive settings. According to Collins, great companies in the social sector prioritize hiring the most self-motivated and self-disciplined candidates; people compulsively dedicated to doing the best that they can because they believe in the cause or simply because hard work is in their DNA. Because they lack resources to buy talent, interpretive supervisors seek out and tap into idealistic passions, nobility of service, and meaning over money.

A supervisor serves as the agent of those supervised—organizing them, coaching them, and most importantly, protecting them. To be productive, employees must feel safe (Sinek, 2014). In his book *Leaders Eat Last,* Sinek notes that, "Trust is like lubrication. It reduces friction and creates conditions much more conducive to performance." The wise supervisor garners employees' trust, respects their work, and advocates for them to others in the agency and to the public, and makes them feel safe within the workplace culture. Supervision also requires conscientious concern for the agency's goals and a desire for superior public service. This balancing act requires sensitivity to the administrative policy and agency mission, and the aforementioned commitment to the staff's welfare.

Supervisors have to be more than worn-out field interpreters. Seniority hardly qualifies as a good criterion for giving someone supervisory duty. It should not be a gold watch job. The job requires imagination, creativity, and contagious enthusiasm for attaining excellence through the work of fellow professionals.

Often, supervisors of interpretation feel loaded down by paperwork, scheduling, evaluating, and reporting at meetings. They wish for more contact with people, more time to be in the real museum or park or refuge environment rather than sitting on chairs in cubicles with little public contact. Yet one of their main roles involves coordination and guidance of the work of other interpreters. They achieve productivity through other people's efforts.

The best supervisors aim for a happy medium between being totally hands-off, thereby isolating themselves from subordinates and letting them do all the real work or the other extreme of wanting to do everything themselves (and their way). Both extremes make employees feel less than valuable. As mentioned above in the discussion of leadership, frequent listening by the supervisor to the interpretive staff and the visitors will prevent misguided actions and decisions and maintain healthy morale.

Supervisory Functions

A supervisor's duties include planning, organizing, evaluating, and reporting.

Planning. Planning at the operational level involves preparing schedules, training, and content for the programs; gathering and organizing supplies and equipment for the programs; announcing and advertising the programs. Effective communication of the specific plans, the reasons supporting those plans, and the roles of individuals in carrying out those plans is critical for implementation and "buy-in." Chapter 18 provides detailed information on planning. Sometimes people lose sight of the big picture and forget why routine tasks are critical to the interpretation program's success. As noted before, it pays to remind people that their job performance is important.

Organizing. Organizing interpretive work involves coordinating and scheduling people, spaces, equipment, and materials. This can be complex, especially when it involves many interpreters, volunteers, and programs. The key skill needed is delegation. Delegation of interpretive work requires constant, conscious effort. It demands more than handing out orders or tasks. It involves empowerment and equipping. The supervisor gives the employee authority to perform, responsibility for the program, freedom of action, and freedom from unwanted interference.

Along with delegation comes the job of identifying limits. When staff time becomes fully committed, the supervisor must help the staff members say *no* to additional opportunities and tasks.

Evaluating. Evaluating employees requires regularly scheduled meetings to track the performance of employees over time. These meetings between the supervisor and each interpreter should occur annually or more frequently. They should not threaten the employees, but serve as a tool for professional growth and goal setting. Employees should see the evaluation interview as a chance to discuss what resources they can use to increase their satisfaction and effectiveness. The supervisor should act as a coach to encourage the employee and improve their work.

The following steps are recommended for supervisory evaluations of employees.
- Set up a formal appointment for the supervisor and employee to meet, allowing plenty of time for preparation.
- Review the person's records and performance in advance. Presumably, the supervisor will have records of personal observations of programs and products of each interpreter.
- Concentrate on performance and results, not personality or personal events, as the latter can be used as a club by either side.
- Listen to the employee actively to hear his or her successes, self-identified needs, and feelings about selected issues or programs.
- Focus on the individual's contributions, innovations, and achievements to encourage continued positive production building on the individual's strengths. Do not dwell on negative factors nor treat them as unchangeable.
- Face any problems as *opportunities*, discussing them rationally and openly, not as criticism. Try to separate the problem from the person.
- Agree on a realistic plan of action that defines improvements and how to go about them. Set targets that build on past achievements. Include training and professional association participation in the plan.
- Put into writing the decisions and goals agreed upon and allow the employee to review the report before filing it.
- Track growth, development, and productivity over the years through records that emphasize achievement, growth, and contributions to the agency and profession.

Occasionally, supervisors must deal with a chronically unproductive employee or volunteer. It may be difficult to "get them off the bus." Staff morale makes it imperative to assertively confront the problem. Wise supervisors start with inspiring the person to work more effectively. This may require weekly or monthly coaching sessions, accompanied by thorough documentation, objectivity, honesty, and a sense of humor. However, if you cannot inspire, then you might have to fire. If it comes to firing, first, learn the personnel rules of your organization. Then, true to your supervisory calling, confront the problem and deal with it. Document everything honestly and fairly. It consumes time but has value. Treat the employee with dignity, being calm but forthright. Don't beat around the bush, yet remain compassionate, discreet, and inspirational. Keep your human resources department fully informed throughout the process.

Reporting. Reporting is a necessary responsibility of supervisors. Agency accountability demands reports on budgets and finances, program outcomes and their impacts, and such items as visitor contact hours, personnel training and staff evaluations. The job may also require safety reports and reports about the status of the site's resources. One happy task of a supervisor is to report about awards won, public compliments, donations and other measures of success and support. A related task for supervisors is to write thank you notes and communicate congratulations as necessary.

In reporting to the public or agency administrators, the gracious supervisor always spreads the credit for successes around and never indulges in self-glorification. Moreover, wise supervisors take responsibility for the failures or short-comings of subordinates and do not make excuses or cast blame on others.

A Final Note on Supervision of Interpretation

Some agencies send out their poorest paid, youngest, least experienced, least knowledgeable interpreters to meet the "owners of the company" (i.e., the public). Why not, in the name of customer service, put the most experienced interpreters, those who develop and enhance the visitor experience (the real product), forward and pay them as the essential providers of interpretive services? Unfortunately, to have upward mobility in some agencies the most experienced interpreters must move into administration. When talented interpreters switch to administrative work they often move away from their competency. Why shouldn't the visitors see the top professionals—the best the agency has to offer—when they come to a museum or park? Promoting excellent interpreters to sit behind the scenes does not suggest a "customer first" philosophy. If the organization hopes to give its visitors star treatment, it makes sense to use its star performers. A reward system in interpretation that pays the best-qualified people to *not* interpret, suffers from misguided priorities.

> "Why not put the most experienced interpreters forward?"

Does Money Matter?

Yes, money always matters, but it matters in different ways depending on whether the interpreter is working for a government agency, nonprofit organization or private for-profit company. The key is that an *abundance* of money is not necessary for interpretation to be effective as noted by the quote by Arnold Bennett that began this chapter.

> "Good results often arise out of improvisation and low budgets."

Many interpreters could claim they do not have the time or resources to be innovative. Most do claim to be underfunded. However, many interpreters have become good at scrounging, scraping, and improvising. Perhaps the interpretive ground is then fertile for innovation. Professional organizations such as NAI host regional and national workshops that often feature sessions on practical low-cost approaches to effective programs.

In both business and interpretation, good results often arise out of improvisation and low budgets. For example, many interpreters have discovered that by using cardboard scenery—and costumes and masks made of paper plates, pie pans, coat hangers, and paper bags—they can produce an amusing, educational skit. An added benefit of such simple inexpensive programs is that they model what can be done with children and grandchildren at home using materials found around the house. More expensive facilities and events may not produce greater value. Creating a quality program at virtually no cost is one type of innovation produced by passionate interpreters. Meeting budget crises with energy and imagination produces better, more stable interpretive services.

This does not imply that the people who are grindingly underpaid will be the most productive. It simply suggests that the latest in equipment, fancy offices, and help may dull the use of creative imaginations. On the other hand, constant concern and tension about low pay, short-handedness, and tight budgets can distract from focusing on doing the best job.

Business Plans

Because money matters, regardless if you are a public agency, private company, or nonprofit organization, it is advisable to have a business plan. Obviously, business plans are required for private companies, but Vasarhelyi (2007) made a compelling case that business plans play a key role in strengthening and implementing interpretive plans for nonprofit and governmental agencies. Business plans are documents that specify how an organization will work and why it will be profitable. Profitability is defined as benefits exceeding costs, but those benefits do not necessarily have to be monetary. Business plans meld well with interpretive plans because they begin with understanding the audience and their wants. Business plans include surveying the "industry" and analyzing the competition. Market research on the industry looks to identify trends in products and customers, how much people are willing to pay, how others find these people, and whether demand is shrinking or growing. Competition analyses includes finding out what other sites are offering, and their pricing and sales volume. For interpretive sites this would be looking at other museums, zoos, or parks and determining how you would compete with their products and why people would choose to visit your site instead of or in addition to theirs. Based upon all of this market research, a business plan lays out a strategy for success. The strategy addresses the four Ps: Product, Price, Place, and Promotion (Vasarhelyi, 2007). For interpretive sites this means defining the interpretive product,

> Thoughtful marketing helps to achieve the site's mission.

assigning a price to it that people are willing to pay, determining how the public is going to access it, and then how you are going to tell them about it. The remaining parts of a business plan are items that should already be in an interpretive plan (e.g., details on staffing and operations). Vasarhelyi points out that a business plan is the logical extension of implementing an interpretive plan (See Chapter 18).

Marketing

"The aim of marketing is to know and understand the customer so well the product or service fits him and sells itself."

–Peter Drucker

A large part of a business plan is marketing. Marketing requires interpreters to seek first to understand their potential customers' needs and desires, then design the programs to best fit the market's demands. In other words, they study the demand side of the equation first (i.e., what the customers seek or use) rather than starting with the supply side (i.e., what you want to offer). In a sense, marketing is another application of the principles of interpretation to know your audience, tell your story, and provoke favorable attitudes and behaviors.

Thoughtful marketing helps to achieve the site's mission. Marketing searches for ways to match the organization's mission and interpretive services to the changing desires of patrons and potential patrons. Marketing includes, but goes beyond, demographic information about visitors and non-visitors. Regular client surveys provide the agency with critical information about customer's needs, preferences, and attitudes, as well as ideas about why some feel dissatisfied or have been lost as customers, and information about current and future patterns of repeat visits. This information allows administrators to broaden and diversify the base of clients and potential supporters.

Market segmentation provides a way to analyze the interpretive consumer base. Basically, it separates a total population into subgroups or market segments by interests, abilities, and age groups, for example. Once the market segments are delineated, interpretive services and programs can be tailored to each one. For example, a site might want to offer different programs for local day users and for long-distance travelers who are just passing through the area. Chapter 7 presents ideas about serving different audiences which make up market segments at interpretive sites.

Marketing Activities

An interpretation marketing effort typically would include the following seven components:

1. **Consumer (visitor) analysis.** Identify the consumer population and key target audiences. Get to know their attitudes, opinions, and familiarity with the facility. Find out which media reaches them best.
2. **Internal analyses.** Identify the agency mission, policies, values, and expectations. Determine strengths and weaknesses (budgetary and personnel) through surveys and focus groups of staff and staff of related organizations.
3. **Resource analyses.** Study the site's history and resources thoroughly, including their condition, and the stories and intangible meanings associated with them.
4. **Marketplace analyses.** Study the local social and economic environment including competing sites, opportunities, and risks.
5. **Plan the range of interpretive efforts** to meet the desires of potential or current customers while achieving the organization's mission.
6. **Use various targeted media to inform the public** about these interpretive experiences, programs, and products.
7. **Study the effectiveness, efficiency, and breadth of the programs.** Collect quantitative and qualitative feedback from consumers and interpreters to refine and further develop the interpretive services (See Chapter 19).

Commercial Interpretation

Private interpretation for profit has been going on for centuries in the tourism sector. Enos Mills (1917) stated, "Scenery is the most profitable resource that we have." Enos Mills was one of the first American commercial guides who earned his income from the tourist trade. He added value to his hotel, cabins, and restaurant with guided hikes into what is now Rocky Mountain National Park.

Modern ecotourism and heritage tourism show that people will pay for interpretation on trains, cruise ships, buses, whitewater rafts, or safari vehicles (Figure 16.5). Guided museum tours, city walking tours, and sightseeing bus tours bring profitable interpretation to urban audiences in all major cities. Chapter 2 described many private- for-profit companies and venues.

Research indicates that interpretation can enhance tourist experiences. Ham and Weiler (2002) studied tourists on cruise ships in the Galapagos Islands and Alaska and found that tours led by guides who exhibited characteristics such as being passionate, insightful, enjoyable, relevant, and easy to follow were evaluated as higher quality than tours led by guides without these attributes. They also found that the global satisfaction of tourists in the Panama Canal area was due primarily to their satisfaction with the interpretive services (Ham & Weiler, 2007).

Figure 16.5. A Maasai guide is ready to lead a commercial interpretive ecotour of Kenyan National Parks. (TC)

More broadly, Australian researchers Weiler and Black (2015) provided a comprehensive review of tour guiding literature and concluded that, "Visitors and stakeholders view interpretation as one of the key defining roles of a quality tour guide and a distinguishing feature of a quality tour." Moreover, they summarized the body of literature dealing with customer satisfaction by stating that "to date, all the studies indicate that tour guide performance has a positive effect on visitor satisfaction and in some studies this correlation is statistically significant." Attributes of a good guide as reported by Weiler and Black from the literature include clear communication, knowledge of the destination, interpersonal skills, presentation, and commentary skills; all of which are characteristics of good interpretation.

It is noteworthy that interpretation in the commercial sector can be profitable to the company, while also generating revenue for nonprofit organizations through increased philanthropy. Powell and Ham (2008) found that well-designed thematic interpretation on Lindblad Expedition cruise ships increased passengers' willingness to donate money to the Galapagos Conservation Fund.

Funding Public Sector and Nonprofit Interpretation

Many government agencies provide interpretive material for sale through nonprofit cooperating associations. Many charge fees for participating in special programs, thus gaining financial flexibility. Fees and other revenue-generating strategies have saved programs and allowed them to thrive.

Although some nonprofits also sell interpretive products and programs, most nonprofit organizations rely heavily on donations of time and money to survive. Applying for competitive grants also is commonly done by nonprofits. The Public Lands Alliance (www.publiclandsalliance.org) provides leadership and tremendous educational resources to help nonprofit organizations of all sizes to thrive financially and politically.

> "Fees and other revenue-generating strategies have saved programs."

The rest of this chapter explores various funding mechanisms for interpretation. Although the chapter focuses on the public and private nonprofit sectors from here on, many ideas apply as well to the private interpretive businesses.

User Fees

Many interpretive sites depend on user fees to generate revenue. However, the pricing of interpretive services is controversial. Interpretation has a long tradition of being a free service for the visitor's education, enrichment, and enjoyment of public natural and cultural sites. However, fiscal reality dictates that revenues must come in, one way or another, or programs will disappear.

The implementation of user fees at public sites provides perhaps the most straightforward solution to budget woes. Certain drawbacks exist for this approach:

- Fees deny access to programs for some who cannot afford to pay.
- Fees discourage people who are reluctant to pay from attending programs.
- A cost arises from collecting the fees.

Yet the precedent of people paying for interpretation exists in many private enterprises that collect fees with few problems. Public agency interpreters frequently turn down offers of pay or tips for their good work. They may seek donations for the interpretive division, however.

Fees can provide a minimum base of revenue which assures continuity in services. Furthermore, paying produces psychological investment on the part of consumers to get more out of a service. It also may cause interpreters to push themselves to levels of excellence and productivity if they see direct connection between their efforts and the willingness of visitors to pay.

Despite concerns about equity and access, wise administrators use fees to achieve the organization's mission. For example, at Ernie Miller Nature Center in Kansas, fee-based preschool programs are considered "Gateway" programs because they are a great introduction to the facility and non-fee interpretive programs, and they develop participants for years to come. Successful "Gateway" programs include "Animal Tales" a 30-minute preschool storytime for adults and children that features stories, songs, movement, and live animals. This pay at-the-door program led by park naturalists averages 50 participants per presentation. Another successful "Gateway" program is "Nature Time Yoga." Using music, movement, and imagination, parents and preschoolers act out stories with animal and yoga moves. This program also features a live animal. The fee charged for these programs is only $2.00 per person, but they lead to customers that return for many years to participate in income-producing special events, adventure camps, birthday parties, and hayrides. These higher priced activities support less profitable or free programs and assist with administrative expenses like animal care, registration, and marketing. The income from fee programs totals about $300,000 annually, thereby reducing the dependency on public tax dollars.

Pricing Strategy

Successful pricing sets a fee that both the agency and patrons find acceptable. Several ways to facilitate public acceptance of fees exist. First, the agency can seek to learn, through first-hand interaction with the clients, what level of fees they would accept. A fee survey can help determine how much to charge without incurring considerable resistance.

> Several ways to facilitate public acceptance of fees exist.

McCarville (1992) suggested three principles for ensuring that pricing policies are acceptable. First, participants usually want fairness in a price. Let them know the costs of commercial alternatives. Point out that the charge covers only part of the cost, making them aware of the costs to present the programs that they attend. Often it helps to put the fee in the context of other products/programs or reference other common purchases such as comparing the fee to the cost of a hamburger or can of soda.

Second, participants-seek values or benefits from interpretive services. Attractive program names should convey what the program offers. Make explicit the benefits and values of participation in written and verbal program descriptions. Describe the quality of the staff delivering the service. If the staff interpreters are among the best (e.g., winning professional awards) let the public know.

Third, participants seek choices. Offer a variety of services with a range of prices, from free to expensive. A program that gets heavy use during certain days or hours might be offered for reduced fees at less popular times. Price alternatives may distribute demand. McCarville (1992) concluded that the success of a fee comes not only from the revenue generated or how little outcry it creates, but "the test for a 'good' price must be measured in terms of the perceptions of those involved in the exchange." Successful fee strategies result in increased visitor return rates, greater participant satisfaction, more extensive word-of-mouth promotion, and increased revenue from paying customers.

Again, communication is the key. Let customers know *why* there is a fee, *what* it is being used for, and *what* they are getting from it. Box 16.4 presents Arkansas State Parks' approach to fee vs. free.

Box 16.4
Remove Barriers and Value What is "Free": Pricing Interpretation at Arkansas State Parks

Jay Miller, President, National Association for Interpretation; former Chief of Interpretation, Arkansas State Parks

We know that if we want people to do something the first thing to do is identify barriers and remove them. One instant barrier to attending our programs is charging a fee. Fees keep people away, especially low income families. Add to this that it's been recognized that certain words like sex, fire, and free grab attention. "Free" is one of the most powerful words. Use it!

Know when to charge for programs and when to use the power word: free. Typical programs, such as guided trail walks, visitor center exhibits, and normal 30-minute to an hour interpretive programs are important introductions to our sites' resources. In those programs we present our most important messages. Management wants our visitors to hear those messages; therefore, we want the largest audience possible. We want everyone to receive these messages and have these experiences. Use the word: FREE, and mean it! When to charge for programs? When you have extra-large investments of time or expense. The key is to connect the free program to the fee program, and all must relate to your mission, message and resource. For example:

- Follow a free guided walk with a fee backpacking workshop in which the participant receives the workshop, a book, and a water bottle.
- Follow a free guided kayak tour followed by the opportunity to rent kayaks.
- Follow free camping techniques program with a fee camping trip.
- Follow a free pioneer cooking program with a fee Dutch oven cooking workshop in which the participant receives a recipe book and a Dutch oven.

This approach of offering free interpretation but linking it to fee interpretation has served our parks well.

Value Added

The worth of interpretation may or may not be best expressed in the open market. Many argue that the public should support interpretation because of its social values as well as intangible individual benefits to clients (See Chapter 3). Moreover, sometimes the economic impact of interpretation is indirect and unappreciated. For example, DeGray Lodge in Arkansas' DeGray Lake Resort State Park is a high-quality operation that is busy from spring through fall and generates revenue that helps fund operation of the entire state park system. However, in January this lodge is almost empty and would operate in the red but for one thing: interpretation. During the "Eagles, Etc." event people come from all over Arkansas and surrounding states to see live eagles, go to programs, and wrap in blankets to go out on cruises on the lake to look for bald eagles (Figure 16.6). This event fills the lodge rooms, restaurant, and convention center. The state park is buzzing with people and the month of January moves from being a loss financially to being a profitable success. People are there solely because of interpretation. Yet, when auditors look at the books they see rooms booked, meals sold, cruises filled, gift shop sales, and much more, but none of it is attributed to interpretation (Jay Miller, pers. comm., 2016).

Figure 16.6. Pontoon boat rides with interpreters to see eagles are a popular activity that generates income for Arkansas State Parks. (TC)

Interpretation has added value to the experience of riding selected Amtrak trains in the U.S. The National Park Service (NPS) developed a partnership with Amtrak in 1994 to offer interpretive programming for train passengers on selected routes. Well over a million passengers have attended these presentations. A study by Morgan and Dong (2008) found that passengers were satisfied with all aspects of the presentations, including interpreter characteristics, message quality, and program benefits.

Whether it is in an underutilized lodge or a railroad, interpreters must communicate up the entire chain of command about the many valuable facets of a strong interpretive program and call attention to the economic impacts of interpretation in situations where they are not formally linked to interpretation by auditors and administrators.

Making Friends: Associations, Partnerships, and Friends Groups

The long-term success of interpretive services is dependent on public support. It behooves interpreters to seek out and make friends with people who are not already in their audiences or who share similar goals. Interpreters should strategically reach out to community leaders and other influential people to garner their support. Make friends with groups that can be important allies such as teachers and healthcare professionals and partner with them to achieve mutually beneficial goals. Most of all be aware of the large numbers of individuals and families in your community who perceive your work as nice, but not necessarily essential, and invite their support and friendship.

Inter-Agency Partnerships

Partnerships bring together skills and funds from several sources to create a synergistic operation that can be greater than the sum of its parts. Although any partnership runs the risk of administrative complications and slower decision-making, often cost savings and other efficiencies can be achieved by collaborating with other agencies. For example, the U.S. Bureau of Land Management manages 18 interpretive and visitor centers, but it is a *partner* in 47 others. One such center is the Northwest New Mexico Visitor Center in Grants, New Mexico. Here the BLM shares the facility responsibilities with the National Park Service. The visitor center includes a 60-seat theater showing an award-winning film, *Remembered Earth*, a 27-minute documentary that summarizes the high desert legacy of northwest New Mexico. It also features an exhibit hall, bookstore operated by the Western National Parks Association (see discussion below) and a lobby with a wide view of the El Malpais National Monument grasslands (Figure 16.7). The Public Lands Interpretive Center in Fairbanks, Alaska takes this concept to an extreme with a collaboration of eight state and federal agencies: the state's Division of Tourism, Department of Natural Resources, and Department of Fish and Game; and the U.S. Bureau of Land Management, U.S. Forest Service, U.S. Fish and Wildlife Service, National Park Service, and U.S. Geological Survey. This center serves visitors as a central distribution point for information and interpretation of state and national parks, refuges, forests, and recreation areas.

> Partnerships bring together skills and funds from several sources.

In some cases, interpretive facilities have local, state, and federal partners. At the Great Plains Nature Center (GPNC), in Wichita, Kansas the U.S. Fish and Wildlife Service owns the building and has offices there. The Kansas Department of Wildlife, Parks, and Tourism also uses the building as a district office and supervises and maintains the physical plant. The city of Wichita owns the land and is responsible for the interpretation programming, exhibit hall, and trails. The Friends of the GPNC hire a coordinator of volunteers, a gift/book store manager, and attract scores of volunteers. The interpreters variously get their paychecks from the city, the state, the federal government, or the Friends group. Together this conglomeration of agencies efficiently serves 160,000 visitors each year.

Figure 16.7. As the logos on this sign illustrate, the Northwest New Mexico Visitor Center is shared by the U.S. Forest Service, Bureau of Land Management, and National Park Service. (TC)

Interpretive Associations

Cooperating associations allow flexibility in fund-raising, book sales, and other services that governmental procedures make clumsy or impossible. The agency interpretive staff approves sales items and helps operate the sales counter. A percentage of the receipts go into producing or purchasing books or gift items that help interpret the area. Often, the association donates sales surpluses to finance interpretive exhibits, purchase valuable artifacts, and subsidize special events.

If the public agency owned the stores, it would normally have to turn the money into the government's general fund. This would prevent the profits from being applied directly to interpretive services and to keeping the gift shop stocked.

> "Cooperating associations allow flexibility in fund-raising, book sales, and other services."

The long history of cooperating associations may have started in 1901 with the Society for the Protection of New Hampshire Forests. In the National Park Service, the Yosemite Museum Association organized as a Friends group in 1920. Ansel F. Hall led this private group to raise $9,000 to start the museum. The park naturalist became director of the association and editor of its publications. In 1924, this group became the Yosemite Natural History Association. Other early associations, formed in the 1930s, served the following U.S. national parks: Zion and Bryce, Rocky Mountain, Grand Canyon, Yellowstone, Mesa Verde, Shenandoah Nature Society, Hot Springs, and Grand Teton (Burns, 1941).

A group now called Eastern National operates in 175 of the nation's most significant cultural, historical, and recreational destinations in 33 states, the District of Columbia, Puerto Rico, and the United States Virgin Islands. It works primarily with the National Park Service, but also other federal, state, and local entities, including the U.S. Forest Service, the U.S. Army Corps of Engineers, and state and local park and museum organizations. It operates retail outlets with interpretive books, maps, and gifts all reviewed and approved by park staffs. Since 1947, this association has donated more than $135 million to the National Park Service for research, underwriting of new film projects, purchase of important historical artifacts, and funding special interpretive projects. It also sells materials online at www.easternnational.org.

In a similar way, the Western National Parks Association, Inc. supports 71 western national parks with educational materials, interpretive programs and other products aimed at enriching visitor experience (www.wnpa.org/).

Figure 16.8. Friends of Nevada Wilderness partners with the U.S. Forest Service for a National Public Lands Day Event at the Spring Mountains National Recreation Area near Las Vegas. (JW-FNW)

Another organization, the Eastern National Forests Interpretive Association (ENFIA) sells interpretive materials and educational items to enhance the experience of National Forest visitors. ENFIA also sells books and related material electronically (www.fs.fed.us/r9). ENFIA tries to return 10% or more of the gross sales for visitor information and interpretive services at the contracted eastern national forests.

Friends Groups

A Friends Group is a tremendous resource in that they often include individuals with expertise in history or natural resources. Usually some members will have experience in local or state politics or influential civic groups. They are also a source of photographs, personal stories, and other valuable resources. Friends Groups work much like the interpretive associations and often run the gift shop or bookstore. Beyond handling those duties, Friends Groups provide political advocacy, preservation, or enhancement of historic or natural sites. They also provide volunteer services to the agency by donating thousands of hours assisting in interpretation programs and other visitor services. In some cases, typically at small local sites, they *are* the interpreters. Friends Groups are especially important in conducting special fund-raising events as they not only volunteer the time to pull it off, but use their collective community contacts and influence to solicit support for the event. Friends groups in the U.S. are typically 501c3 nonprofit organizations that accept tax deductible donations that in turn support membership services, community advocacy, resource protection, fundraising events, and the development and maintenance of exhibits and trails (Figure 16.8). Members of Friends organizations usually receive reduced entrance fees, store discounts, behind-the-scenes access, members-only special events or field trips, and a magazine or newsletter.

Friends groups can have considerable economic impacts. For example, each year Friends of Virgin Islands National Park contributes between $500,000 and $600,000 in funding to support projects in the park. Most funding (60%) comes from individual donations whereas the remainder comes from corporations, private foundations, special events, and proceeds from the Friends park store. Every year the Virgin Islands National Park Superintendent submits a request to the Friends' Board of Directors. The Board carefully evaluates and prioritizes each request. Activities involving volunteers and previously funded projects are favored. In recent years, the Friends have funded the following projects:

> Friends groups can have considerable economic impacts.

- SCA Trail Crews—Teams of young conservationists improved more than 65 miles of Park trails.
- Boat Moorings—The Friends installed several hundred moorings to protect turtle habitat and coral reefs from anchors' damage.
- Eco-Camps—Hundreds of 7- to 16-year-old Virgin Islands' youth have spent two to four nights at a camp in the Park learning about the island's terrestrial and marine eco-systems at Eco-Camp, Science Camp, and Ranger-in-Training Camp.
- Archeology Program—Prehistoric Taino and St. John plantation era artifacts were uncovered and the archeology labs were renovated to create a museum.

At a local park level, Friends of the Wabash in Indiana bore the main advocacy role for the establishment of a new state park called Prophetstown State Park. After the park was created, they shifted work under the new name "Museums at Prophetstown, Inc." to provide interpretive facilities and programs and vegetation restoration. Box 16.5 shows the impacts Friends groups can have at a zoo.

Box 16.5
Tulsa Zoo Friends, Inc.

The Tulsa Zoo and Living Museum, a city parks division, works with Tulsa Zoo Friends, Inc. to make this a top tourist attraction in northeast Oklahoma. Friends, staff, and volunteers help receive and handle all visitors. Some key facts about this nonprofit corporation:

Membership: 15,400 member households providing $1.1 million in revenue for zoo operations.

Activities:
- collect all admissions
- manage all food concessions
- help train docents
- operate overnight stays
- sell publications
- sponsor special exhibits
- manage "The Wild Bunch" volunteers
- solicit donations and grants
- back a new exhibit or major development each year
- operate gift shops
- collect for and operate group visits
- operate teacher training
- run the zoo train
- help with school visits
- sponsor travel programs
- testify for city budget support
- sponsor special events

In 2013, nearly 300 volunteers worked more than 23,000 hours, helping with events such as WALTZ on the Wild Side and HallowZOOeen; serving as Rainforest guides; working as zookeeper aides; teaching educational outreach programs; and providing on-grounds programs with animals and bio-facts. With the help of more than 100 docents, the Education department was able to teach a much larger, more diverse audience about the wildlife and the wild places where they live.

Obviously not every park, historic site, zoo, or museum will have a Friends group that can bring in these levels of support, but any level of additional financial and political support is welcome at interpretive sites. The key to having a flourishing Friends group is constant and consistent *communication*. Sometimes active Friends groups take on a life of their own. Vigilance is required to make sure *their* passions are matched with *your* needs. Friends groups are filled with knowledgeable and influential people. Powerful groups might intimidate younger interpreters. Again, communication is a key in building trust. Friends help give perspective, information, vision, and advice as they collaborate with paid staff. The most important part of continual communication is to publically acknowledge and thank Friends for their help.

> The key to having a flourishing Friends group is constant and consistent communication.

Fund-Raising

Fund-raising activities supplement agency resources at many museums and nature centers. Traditional fund-raising projects include on-site craft or book sales, membership programs, newsletters or websites with advertising, and donation boxes (Figure 16.9).

Off-site funding sources include grants, endowments, and corporate contributions. These funds often come with a caveat that they go to specific purposes, such as for capital expenditures on new facilities or they require naming rights for whatever is being funded. As mentioned above, Friends groups play a key role in fund-raising.

Corporate sponsors and large donations from individuals are an important source of support. Raising donations from these sources requires a *continual* search of prospective donors, and *constant* research of promising ones. To avoid the perception of being "owned" by a big donor, it is best if an organization nurtures several funding sources. This not only avoids the appearance of undue influence or favoritism, it also provides a safety net if one of the sources ceases support. All of this requires detailed record-keeping listing who gave how much, and most importantly *why* they gave. It is also to keep track of why some did not give. When approaching donors it is critical to be able to articulate a succinct statement of mission and vision, and then link that mission and vision to the donor's passions. Corporations, charitable foundations, and individuals have funded everything from simple interpretive posters to entire buildings to achieve *their* goals while helping interpreters.

Figure 16.9. A historic safe is repurposed into a donation collection box at Hobbs State Park in Arkansas. (TC)

The opposite of courting large corporate donors is "crowd-funding." Crowd-funding is funding a project through many small monetary donations from a large number of people. It is not a new approach; for example, the Statue of Liberty installation in New York was funded by 160,000 small donations raised through a newspaper ad. Now it is done through the Internet. It is a popular way to raise money because it takes relatively little effort, is inexpensive, and using the internet provides tremendous reach to potential donors. As with all fund-raising you must appeal to the interests of potential donors, such as documenting how a new park provides healthy opportunities for their children or enhances their community, or how a new wing in the museum will provide support for local school children and teachers.

Special Events and Trips

Special events are another way of raising money. A 2015 issue of NAI's *Legacy* magazine featured stories about successful events and celebrations ranging from International Migratory Birds Day, to International Observe the Moon Night, to Alcatraz Island Art Exhibition, to Honor Flights to Washington, D.C. for Veterans. Holidays like Halloween, Earth Day, Christmas, and others give annual opportunities for festivals and events.

Planning special events has become a recognized profession, but most interpretive sites cannot afford to hire an event planner. Often the interpretive staffs have the responsibility for planning special events. Planning a successful event involves the following steps generally in this order over a period of at least several months and in some cases a year or more (Taylor, 2012):

- Plan theme, objectives, target audience, and set the date.
- Call around to vendors to get cost estimates to establish a budget and identify alternatives at various costs.
- Create a map or layout of the site, including considerations for volunteer check in, control centers, and traffic flow.
- Plan for security and sanitation needs.
- Plan an event schedule that allows for flexibility while achieving the event goals.
- Based upon the above, determine how many volunteers or staff are needed, where they will be stationed, and for how long.
- Take this detailed plan to potential sponsors and partners, giving them options for ways they can support and participate, emphasizing their "return on investment" (e.g., their name and logo will be seen by 25,000 people over the weekend).
- In addition to the advertising benefits, offer ticket discounts, shirts or hats, VIP-only access, or other perks of sponsorship.
- Start publicity campaign including an event website or dedicated page on the agency website, and social media messages using Facebook, Twitter, among other outlets and link these back to the website.
- Use traditional media like putting posters and brochures around town and contacting local radio and television to get the word out (See Chapter 8).
- During the event shoot videos to document it and post them on social media to promote next year's event.
- After the event, thank your sponsors and volunteers, and even the paid staff for their support.
- Survey participants and those who worked at or sponsored the event to get feedback on how to improve it.

> Special events are another way of raising money.

Zoos have a long history of hosting successful special fund-raising events. For example, at Sedgwick County Zoo's (Wichita) Zoobilee, dozens of restaurants set up food booths for publicity. Up to 20 drink stations and "pampering stations" (manicures and pedicures by local businesses) produce income. Both silent and live auctions also raise funds to support the zoo. And while all of this is happening a half-dozen bands keep people who paid $150 per ticket happily moving and spending.

Sponsored travel provides opportunities to generate enthusiasm and support. Ecological and archaeological tours organized and conducted by staff interpreters and scientists draw many museum, nature center, and zoo patrons to help with research and observations in remote places. Using staff interpreters as tour leaders gives them a chance to enrich their own knowledge base. Traveling in small groups allows the leaders to bond with the participants as they learn more about the organization's merits and services. Trips can be priced above costs to raise funds. More importantly, upon returning from what often turns out to be a life-changing trip, some participants will become generous donors of time and money, and supporters of the organization's mission.

Summary

Money seldom comprises the major goal of interpretation, but it provides the means for reaching the major goals. A business approach makes more interpretation available to the public at the right times and places. Some interpretive programs rely on revenue generation ranging from user fees to fund-raising. Even when visitors do not pay, their numbers and satisfaction indicated the value of the service. Support for interpretation is often linked to attendance numbers. This fact requires interpreters to address issues such as marketing, customer relations, and product evaluation. Interpreters need to analyze their customers, delivery schedules, and cost-effectiveness. Excellent leadership, efficient management, passionate people, and innovative planning have permitted many agencies to thrive financially.

The business-savvy interpreter serves the profession well. Application of proven business and marketing strategies, along with a strong philosophical grounding in the values of cultural and natural history interpretation, can build stronger and more autonomous interpretive agencies, even in difficult times, all of which contributes to a better world.

> "Sponsored travel provides opportunities to generate enthusiasm and support."

"A wise person should have money in their head, but not in their heart."
—Jonathan Swift

Literature Cited

Beck, L., & Cable, T. (2011). *The gifts of interpretation: Fifteen principles of interpreting nature and culture.* Urbana, IL: Sagamore.

Burns, N. J. (1941). *Field manual for museums.* Washington, DC: National Park Service.

Christensen, C., Allworth, J., & Dillon, K. (2012). *How will you measure your life?* New York, NY: Harper Business.

Collins, J. (2005). *Good to great and the social sectors. A monograph to accompany Good to Great.* Boulder, CO: Collins.

Collins, J. (2011). *Great by choice.* New York, NY: HarperCollins.

Covey, S. R. (1989). *The seven habits of highly effective people: Restoring the character ethic.* New York, NY: Fireside/Simon & Schuster.

Drucker, P. F. (1980). *Managing in turbulent times.* New York, NY: Harper & Row.

Goleman, D., Boyatzis, R., & McKee, A. (2013). *Primal leadership.* Boston, MA: Harvard Business Review Press.

Goulston, M. (2009). *Just listen.* New York, NY: American Management Association.

Ham, S., & Weiler, B. (2002). Toward a theory of quality in cruise-based interpretive guiding. *Journal of Interpretation Research, 7*(2), 29–49.

Ham, S., & Weiler, B. (2007). Isolating the role of on-site interpretation in a satisfying experience. *Journal of Interpretation Research, 12*(2), 5–24.

Kotter, J. P. (1999). On what leaders really do. Cambridge, MA: *Harvard Business Review.*

LaPage, W. (2002). If not us, who? If not now, when? *Legacy, 13*(1), 29–32.

McCarville, R. (1992). Successful pricing. *Parks & Recreation, 27*(12), 36–40.

Miller, Jay. (2016). Personal communication with Jay Miller (Arkansas State Parks).

Miller, J. (2016). Failure is not the end of the world. *Legacy, 27*(4), 6–9.

Mills, E. (1917). Comments. In *Proceedings,* National Parks Conference (January 2-6).

Morgan, M., & Dong, X. (2008). Measuring passenger satisfaction of interpretive programming on two Amtrak trains in the Midwest: Testing the expectancy disconfirmation theory. *Journal of Interpretation Research, 13*(2), 43–58.

Peters, T. J., & Austin, N. (1985). *A passion for excellence: The leadership difference.* New York, NY: Random House.

Powell, R., & Ham, S. (2008). Can ecotourism interpretation really lead to proconservation knowledge, attitudes, and behavior? Evidence from the Galapagos Islands. *Journal of Sustainable Tourism, 16*(4), 467–489.

Sinek, S. (2014). *Leaders eat last.* New York, NY: Penguin.

Steinfeld, J. (2016). 5 reasons your customers are not king. Retrieved from inc.com/jay-steinfeld/5-reasons-your-customers-are-bnot/b-king.html

Taylor, D. (2012). Playing to the crowd. *Parks & Recreation Magazine.* Retrieved from parksandrecreation.org/2012/September/Playing-to-the-Crowd/

Vasarhelyi, J. (2007). Creating business plans for success. *2007 NAI Sourcebook,* Ft. Collins, CO: National Association for Interpretation.

Weiler, B., & Black, R. (2015). *Tour guiding research: Insights, issues, and implications.* Tonawanda, NY: Channel View Publications.

CHAPTER 17
Training and Professional Growth

Honduran tour guide Victor Galvez had it pretty good even before he had interpretive training. Víctor had a business that was thriving. Because he was charismatic and an excellent birder, he had a long list of clients, continual referrals, and had built a solid name. His approach to guiding had brought results.

But when he received the invitation from Jon Kohl, Coordinator of PUP Global Heritage Consortium, to attend PUP's training program, he wondered if he could improve his offerings. After all, a primary market was high school and university students, and often he noticed that they weren't always learning what he had hoped.

Victor kicked off the basic interpretation workshop with high confidence, certain it would be easy. He was the conventional guide who just talked about whatever came to mind, even searched for things to say along the way. However, fear gushed in when instructors asked students to create interpretive themes, objectives, and structure presentations to generate learning and behavior outcomes. Victor realized that maybe he had been guiding wrong all this time, despite his success. His guiding paradigm now faced direct challenge. As Victor said, his "conventional disorder was being replaced with interpretive order."

At first Victor grew depressed, and despite his extroverted, affable personality, he fell into silence. Were it not for many action-oriented activities such as telling stories, interpreting objects, and writing themes, his depression might have ended his course. Part way through training, instructors, in fact, doubted whether he would transition at all to the new interpretive paradigm.

But instructors also taught that depression and negative thoughts signal resistance to change and are normal when students engage in new thinking. Although Victor worried about giving up successful old practices for uncertain new ones, he considered his own resistance, deciding that with his competitive spirit he would rise to this challenge.

"I destroyed my fear of change," Victor said. When he gave his final 30-minute tour, he earned the highest peer evaluation. He marvelously integrated a structure and interpretive theme with his interpersonal skills and professionalism. He now is developing structured interpretive tours for the entire watershed where he works, and he trains local guides in—his words—"the new guiding paradigm."

"Interpretation is a voyage of discovery in the field of human emotions and intellectual growth, and it is hard to foresee that time when the interpreter can confidently say, 'Now we are wholly adequate to our task.'"

–Freeman Tilden

This chapter discusses education and training for professionals and volunteers. Although some interpreters seem to have a natural aptitude for interpretation and excel right from the start, outstanding interpreters usually develop slowly as they pursue careful study, gain experience, and receive training. Just as virtuoso musicians never cease practicing their technique, expanding their skills, and exploring new artistic avenues, interpreters should never quit pursuing higher levels of creativity, interpretive artistry, and performing excellence.

The National Park Service (NPS) recognized the need for training their interpreters early in its history. It set up a seven-week summer school in 1925 (Bryant, 1960). Well before any organized interpretive division existed in the NPS, the Yosemite School of Field Natural History trained naturalists who studied living things in their natural environment. This early training program, centered in a circle of tents, focused on the natural sciences. The 20 students received intensive field work on the Yosemite trees, shrubs, wildflowers, insects, fishes, amphibians, reptiles, birds, and mammals. The course had university rigor but gave a certificate instead of college credit (Bryant & Atwood, 1932).

> Interpreters should never quit pursuing higher levels of creativity, interpretive artistry, and performing excellence.

Today interpreters can receive training from universities, public agencies, and a host of professional organizations. The reasons why training and continued professional growth are important include: 1) the need to maintain credibility with visitors, community-members, and other professionals within the organization; 2) the need to develop different skill sets to function more effectively within the organization; and 3) to improve personal effectiveness, and the organization's effectiveness through better practices.

University Preparation

Lackey (2008) reviewed the state of interpretation in academia and reported an estimate from Tom Mullin, Director of NAI's College and University Academics Section, that 87 universities in North America taught at least one interpretation course. However, few colleges or universities offered a full degree specifically in interpretation. Most respondents to Lackey's survey only offered one or two interpretation courses. Universities in several European countries, as well as in Australia, New Zealand, and Asia also offer formal courses and even degrees in interpretation (See Chapter 20). In some cases, courses with interpretation content are labeled as tour guiding, museum studies, natural resource communications, park design, or public history.

Some have raised the issue of accrediting university programs that teach interpretation. However, since the 1970s, the interpretation profession has struggled with what should be included in such a curriculum and organizational challenges within academic departments would make accreditation difficult, if not impossible, on most campuses (Ham & Hall, 2008). Because of the breadth and diversity of interpretation activities and sites there has been little consensus about core knowledge and skills. Beyond the core competencies, there has been great debate about the peripheral knowledge that supports interpretation. The interpretive profession has long debated whether a strong grounding in communication or expertise in specific resource subject matter (e.g., history, biology, forestry, geology, anthropology, and archaeology) is more critical.

Interpretation requires depth in both subject matter and delivery skills. Interpreters trained in communications may convey a message well, but if they lack expertise about the resource, they have little to say and no foundation of knowledge on which to build, and may even present erroneous information. Interpreters with expertise only in natural or cultural history have much to say, but may transmit the message ineffectively. They may bore audiences with too many facts and technical trivia. Therefore, both communications and subject matter should be integrated into university coursework in the preparation of interpreters. Field experiences and seasonal work during university study will speed the development process. As noted previously in this text, to be an excellent interpreter no amount of "book learning" is enough without a strong passion for both the resource and for people.

> "Field experiences and seasonal work during university study will speed the development process."

Typically, students wanting to become park naturalists would pursue degrees in forestry, wildlife management, biological conservation, park or wildland management, or outdoor recreation. Specific coursework in these areas include basic sciences, and field courses in ecology, geology, soils, botany, ornithology, ichthyology, and entomology, among others. Those students with a specific interest in working at a historical or cultural site typically take courses in history, archaeology, museum studies, and anthropology.

All prospective interpreters benefit from elective courses in the humanities, social sciences, communication, and the performing arts (e.g., drama, speech, music, creative writing) as these help them relate and communicate to their audiences. To these majors and courses, add whatever interpretation and informal education courses the university offers to have a well-rounded preparation for the interpretive profession.

Applied field courses are severely lacking at North American universities. A study by Tweaksbury et. al. (2014) compared natural history requirements in biology programs and contents of introductory biology textbooks in the 1950s to those of today. They found all of the schools required natural history courses for a biology degree and introductory biology texts were dominated by natural history in the 1950s. Today, most universities have no natural history requirements for a biology degree, and the emphasis on natural history in introductory biology texts has dropped by 40%. The trend is to teach more theory and modeling and eliminate the teaching of field identification of plants and wildlife.

What does this mean for interpreters? Bixler, James, and Vadala (2011) concluded that this vacuum places more responsibility on interpreters to educate the public. However, it also has implications for training interpreters who may be entering the field without knowing a blue jay from a bluebird, or bluebonnets from bluestem. If potential interpreters don't learn this information in college where will they learn it? Alternative training opportunities for students are discussed below as are opportunities for the many individuals who come across this field of work later in life.

Agency Training

Most agencies, both public and private, offer introductory trainings to expose the new employee to agency philosophy, policies, and resources. But training doesn't cease after the orientation. Continued training throughout individual careers has become the norm in most organizations. Many organizations cover costs of professional society membership and for attendance at workshops. Several agencies have built their own training centers. California State Parks, for example, offer extensive training at its full-time training center. The National Park Service has the Mather Employee Development Center at Harpers Ferry, West Virginia. The U.S. Fish and Wildlife Service's National Conservation Training Center in Shepherdstown, West Virginia, offers professional facilities for natural resource training programs for both public and private sectors.

> "Continued training throughout individual careers has become the norm."

Perhaps the most comprehensive and dynamic agency training program is the U.S. National Park Service's Interpretive Development Program (IDP). IDP was developed by and for interpretive rangers, but it is also available to law enforcement rangers, volunteers, park managers, superintendents, agency media specialists, and park planners. The training includes such topics as foundations and principles of interpretation, informal visitor contacts, interpretive talks, interpretive writing, and coaching interpreters.

In the early 2000s, the NPS developed online courses in interpretation with the Eppley Institute for Parks and Public Lands at Indiana University. These courses reinforced the previous benchmark skills and helped interpreters design media and other important skills. In 2016, the Eppley Institute formalized a partnership with the National Association for Interpretation to offer the training on a broader scale (Jacobs, pers. comm., 2017). Part of the new partnership agreement resulted in an effort to update and revise the interpretation e-courses for a broader audience of interpreters and to create professional certificate courses for interpretation available online unlike the classroom-based NAI certifications (see provalenslearning.com).

Some agencies bring in experts from universities or professional associations to lead in-service training programs. Several interpretive consulting firms, such as PUP featured in the introductory story, offer excellent training sessions on contract.

> "Organizations serious about interpretation will train seasonal interpreters."

In addition to training employees, it behooves organizations to train and cultivate relationships with allies such as tourism officials, preservation groups, librarians, and other nearby historic site or park staffs. These colleagues should receive some "training" each year, such as special quick orientations, short field trips, and information packets.

Training Seasonal Employees

Organizations serious about interpretation will train seasonal interpreters to provide a quality interpretive product. Seasonal interpreters often face the challenge of arriving at a new site where they find unfamiliar resources, unfamiliar audiences, and an unfamiliar organization. Yet, they often have to begin interpreting almost immediately upon arrival. This leaves them little time to learn about what they interpret, to whom they interpret, and why they interpret in an assigned manner. And, unless it is love at first sight, they have no time to develop and nurture their own appreciation and passion for the site's resources and audiences before the interpretive programs begin.

For these reasons, the training should start even before arrival on the site. Newly hired seasonal interpreters should eagerly seek out online resources to learn about the agency's mission and policies, the site's resources, and the approaches and programs to interpret those resources. If these documents are not readily available online, the agency should demonstrate its interest and investment in the seasonal interpreters by providing books and other resources prior to arrival.

The goals of seasonal training should be to: 1) provide an understanding of agency history and mission, 2) develop good camaraderie and mutual respect, 3) learn basic interpretive techniques and build confidence in using those techniques.

The structure and organization of different seasonal training programs varies considerably. One of the best seasonal training programs is conducted by Missouri State Parks. Their Seasonal Interpretive Training program runs for several days at the beginning of the summer season. It covers the breadth of information and skills needed by a seasonal interpreter in a compact time frame (Box 17.1).

During the intense four days, participants can complete the National Association for Interpretation's Certified Interpretive Guide training, which will be discussed later in this chapter. In addition to the interpretation skills training, the seasonal interpreters rotate through practical sessions on such topics as interpreting rocks, how to transport and care for program animals, and conducting programs about pollinators, macroinvertebrates, water safety, archeology, interpreting cemeteries, and historic uses of plants and animals.

Most sessions are taught by the full-time state park interpreters who are brought in to assist with the training. One full day is devoted to break-out topics where participants choose in-depth training on topics such as beekeeping, astronomy, primitive outdoor skills, or proper archival techniques for cultural resources. This training is so thorough that neighboring states and even some federal agencies send their staff to take advantage of it or to learn how to conduct training in their home agencies.

> Without structure and training, volunteers can cost organizations.

Training Volunteers

> "There is only one thing worse than training your volunteers and having them leave—
> and that's not training them and having them stay."
>
> –Studs Terkel

Most museums, zoos, historical sites, nature centers, and archaeological sites rely heavily on volunteer guides or docents. The first thing to know about volunteers is that they do not provide free labor. They can be helpful, convenient and even essential, but they are never *free*. Volunteer programs require a formal structure and a significant financial investment in training and support. Without structure and training, volunteers can cost organizations much in terms of wasted time and worse, negative visitor experiences and a harmed reputation.

Box 17.1
Objectives of Missouri State Parks Seasonal Interpreter Training Program

A new seasonal interpreter learns the following during Missouri State Parks' intensive seasonal training program (provided by Kendra Swee, MDNR):

1. Become familiar with the mission of the Department of Natural Resources and Division of State Parks.
2. Recognize the importance of interpretation leading to resource protection in Missouri State Parks.
3. Become familiar with the philosophy and history of interpretation and how it differs from environmental education.
4. Understand how to develop a theme and an interpretive program.
5. Become familiar with the various program formats, logistics and presentation techniques.
6. Develop your own program presentation.
7. Become familiar with basic history methods and techniques for living history presentations.
8. Become familiar with and distinguish between living history and costumed interpretive presentations.
9. Become familiar with various cultural history program formats, logistics, and presentation techniques.
10. Become aware of resources for information, clothing, and equipment for cultural interpretation.
11. Be certified to receive and to use Project Wet resources.
12. Become familiar with Missouri's varied cultural and natural resources and how they relate to your interpretive programming.
13. Sharpen program presentation skills and assist others as they sharpen theirs.
14. Recognize the needs of visitors with disabilities as you design and present interpretive programs.
15. Consider safety issues for both yourself and the visitor in interpretive program planning and presentation.
16. Recognize the importance of your role as an interpreter, with support from central office staff, in accomplishing the state park mission.

Often volunteers staff the information desk in the visitor center or interpretive stations scattered throughout the museum or zoo. At many sites, they are the first employee that visitors encounter. At busy sites, volunteers may have responsibility for delivering school or summer camp programs. Volunteers can assist in not only giving programs and working the welcome desk, but also provide an important cadre for doing labor intensive tasks in maintenance (e.g., trails, exhibits, gardens) and research. Their role as citizen scientists can be significant as they conduct time-consuming oral histories from elderly folks, conduct a systematic survey of frogs, birds or plants, or assist with archeological digs. The data gathered informs the development of interpretive programs. What do volunteers receive in return? The joy of learning new things and sharing that knowledge with others. The challenge of developing new skills and the rewards of applying those skills. The knowledge that they are involved in a noble and worthwhile endeavor as they make a difference in the lives of others as well as their own.

A well-run volunteer program will have 1) an established budget for promoting, recruiting, training, and recognizing the work of volunteers, 2) a specific staff person identified as the "volunteer coordinator" and formally assigned those coordination duties as part of their job description, 3) detailed job descriptions for volunteer positions with the required time commitment clearly stated (See Box 17.2), and 4) designated work space.

Box 17.2
Sample Volunteer Position Description

Runge Volunteer Position Description

Position Title: Volunteer Naturalist

Time Required:
A minimum of 24 hours every two months for adult volunteers, and a minimum of 12 hours every two months for youth volunteers for one year. This includes a monthly meeting with continuing education.

General Purpose:
The Volunteer Naturalist provides educational programs, opportunities, and experiences to connect Missourians to their natural resources. They develop, assist, and conduct indoor/outdoor public programs, trail hikes, and special events.

Specific Responsibilities:
- Providing visitors with information regarding the nature center and its facilities.
- Answering questions visitors have about forest, fish, wildlife, and other natural history resources of Missouri.
- Organize, prepare, and present interpretive programs to school classes, youth groups, other organized groups, and families based on outlines developed or approved by Department of Conservation interpretive staff.
- Carry out or assist with projects which require specific expertise or talent. These projects could include a wide variety of skills depending on the needs of the nature center, i.e., photography, gardening, etc.
- In addition, after graduation, new volunteers are required during their first 6 months to:
  - Spend 2 hours greeting at the nature center with an experienced volunteer.
  - Observe 2 interpretive programs presented by a staff naturalist and 1 interpretive program presented by a volunteer.
  - Attend and help at one off-site event.

Qualifications/Requirements:
- 14 years of age or older
- Public speaking skills are helpful.
- Knowledge of Missouri flora, fauna, and ecosystems strongly desired.
- Able to work outdoors in a variety of weather conditions
- Own transportation

Benefits:
- Monthly continuing education in Missouri natural resources, issues, and related topics
- Incentive awards upon completion of service hours
- Educate and connect people to Missouri's natural resources for future generations
- Opportunities to further your own education and interest in the outdoors
- Change lives!

The Runge Conservation Nature Center in Jefferson City, Missouri runs a model volunteer program (Figure 17.1). According to volunteer coordinator Robin Grumm, interested individuals are invited to an open house prior to the start of a new volunteer class. During the open house, prospective volunteers meet current volunteers and learn more about the program. Potential volunteers will be interviewed soon after the open house. Individuals are chosen based on the current needs of the nature center. Chosen volunteers then embark on a 30-hour training program over the course of seven weeks. This training covers agency history, mission and workplace policies, natural resources of the site, and interpretive techniques. It also emphasizes the importance of the volunteer work to the agency and the benefits to participants. The need to perform faithfully and punctually is emphasized.

Figure 17.1. Missouri Department of Conservation volunteers are well trained to serve guests young and old. (MDC)

Board members of a museum or nature association often get overlooked in the training plans. Interpreters need to advocate and plan for educating those supposedly in the know. Board members need to receive regular and special information about the history/nature of the place being interpreted. They need to know the methods, rationale, and special stories behind programs and exhibits. Special field trips combined with board meetings can bring some practical familiarity. A seminar with a board dinner can bring members up to date on technical developments. These people volunteer their time, dignity, and reputation to govern a society or museum. They deserve to be able to talk intelligently about the activities that they govern.

Although volunteers are often indispensable, professional interpreters should serve as the main staff offering public programs. A strong interpretive program requires strong commitment to rigorous training and support of professional employees and volunteers alike.

Professional Development

"To keep a lamp burning, we have to keep putting oil in it."
–St. Theresa of Calcutta

Upon entry into the profession, an interpreter should pursue continual training throughout his or her career. The individual interpreter bears responsibility for initiating and carrying out self-training and for seeking resources to take advantage of membership in professional organizations and attendance at conferences (Figure 17.2).

Often these resources are available from employers because they recognize the benefit of having well-trained personnel with cutting-edge skills and a high level of motivation.

Professional Associations

Interpreters can learn much and grow professionally through participation in professional societies and their interpretation networks. Interpretation Canada, the Association for Heritage Interpretation (UK), Interpretation Australia, Interpret Europe: The European Association for Heritage Interpretation, Interpretation Network New Zealand, and the National Association for Interpretation (NAI) are some of the organizations that provide opportunities to exchange ideas, sharpen skills, and gain a sense of affirmation of interpretive work.

Figure 17.2. Interpreters continue to learn and be inspired through attendance at professional conferences. (MSP)

These groups hold annual regional, national, and sometimes international workshops with sessions aimed at both beginners and advanced interpreters. The proceedings of these conferences contribute valuable practical, theoretical, and research information to the interpretation literature. Likewise, these organizations issue newsletters and journals, which allow interpreters to maintain contact and exchange ideas. These organizations maintain a web presence through their websites and social media Facebook pages to share information and exchange ideas with interpreters. See Chapter 20 for a list of many of these organizations and their web addresses.

Attendance at conferences offered by organizations such as those listed above is especially important for professional development. Participation can broaden interpreters' knowledge by introducing new trends in the field, providing active exchange of ideas, and sharing new interpretive methods. Participation at conferences allows interpreters to network with experts and leaders in the field along with peers. Most of all, these gatherings enhance pride in the profession, and instill a sense of camaraderie and encouragement from a sense of belonging to a larger group. Outstanding interpretive work is recognized at award ceremonies (Figure 17.3). Interpreters return from conferences with a sense of purpose, worth, and renewed enthusiasm for interpretive work.

Figure 17.3. Professional organizations recognize and reward achievements in the field of interpretation. (ASP)

The National Association for Interpretation (NAI) is the largest of these organizations with more than 6,000 members in more than 30 countries. NAI was founded in 1988 with the merger of the Association of Interpretive Naturalists (founded in 1954) and the Western Interpreters Association (founded in 1965). NAI produces a magazine called *Legacy*, the *Journal of Interpretation Research*, and several e-newsletters aimed at special interest sub-groups of members (e.g., zoos, history, naturalists, nature center directors, native peoples, and interpretive media). Webinars dealing with current issues and cutting edge techniques are offered regularly throughout the year.

NAI also offers certification programs throughout the U.S. and internationally. NAI's two *training certifications* are Certified Interpretive Guide (CIG) and Certified Interpretive Host (CIH). The CIG certification is for individuals who present interpretive programs and covers the history and principles of interpretation as well as presentation skills (Figure 17.4). The CIH certification is for front desk, maintenance, retail, food and beverage staff, and others who are in contact with visitors and informally provide interpretation at a site. The CIH course includes customer service and informal interpretation skill development. NAI also offers the following *professional certifications*: Certified Interpretive Manager, Certified Interpretive Planner, Certified Heritage Interpreter, and Certified Interpretive Trainer.

The most widely received of these certifications is the Certified Interpretive Guide, which is designed for individuals who deliver interpretive programs to the public. This 32-hour course includes history, definition, theory and principles of interpretation, and presentation and communication skills. Each participant takes a literature review test, creates a program outline, and gives a 10-minute presentation. NAI's certification program is periodically reviewed and updated (Jacobs, 2016).

Figure 17.4. University students taking the NAI Certified Interpretive Guide training create the NAI definition of interpretation. (TC)

As of 2016, NAI had certified more than 30,000 individuals, mostly in North America but also in Africa, Europe and Latin America. Certification in interpretation, as in any profession, raises standards of performance throughout the profession and provides assurance of quality to employers. Several organizations, including at least one cruise ship line and several national park concession employers, hire only NAI Certified Interpreters (Jacobs, pers. comm., 2017).

Much like NAI, Interpret Europe also offers training and certification courses including a 40-hour Interpretive Guide course (also called CIG). The materials for this course are available in 14 languages, and since the program started in 2015, it has been offered in eight languages. Other certifications offered by Interpret Europe include Certified Interpretive Host, Certified Interpretive Writer, Certified Live Interpreter, and Certified Interpretive Planner. A separate trainer course is required to teach these certification courses.

Other Professional Organizations

Interpreters work in certain settings or industries that have their own specific organizations to contribute to professional development and training. For example, interpreters at zoos and aquariums will be professionally connected to the American Zoo and Aquarium Association (AZA). AZA focuses on accreditation and advancement of its more than 230 member institutions. Interpretation by zoo educators is a high priority at AZA facilities as they draw more than 183 million visitors every year, 50 million of whom are children. AZA-accredited facilities also train 40,000 teachers each year, thereby extending opportunities for interpreters to influence students who otherwise might not get first-hand experience with animals. Annual conventions and publications keep members up to date on issues such as animal rights, conservation of endangered species, proper care of captive animals, and public education and interpretation.

A more focused group is the International Zoo Educators Association. This organization started as a small group of European educators, but now has more than 300 members worldwide who are involved in conservation education at zoos and aquariums.

Among museum associations, the largest is the American Alliance of Museums (AAM). AAM represents more than 30,000 museum professionals, volunteers, and institutional members that include art, military, history, science, maritime, and children's museums. AAM also serves arboretums, botanical gardens, and historic sites. Museum educators and interpreters benefit from helpful articles in *Museum* magazine and from annual conferences. Its counterpart to the north is the Canadian Museums Association which serves museums in Canada.

Other professional groups in the United States focus on specialized interpretive museums including the Association for Living History, Farms, and Agricultural Museums, an international organization that promotes living history, especially of farms and in agricultural settings.

Association of Science and Technology Centers is a global organization providing professional support for science centers, museums, planetariums, natural history and children's museums, and related institutions. It represents more than 600 members in nearly 50 countries who share an interest in informal science education.

Perhaps the organization that serves cultural heritage interpreters more than any other is the American Association for State and Local History (AASLH). AASLH has long been a leader in heritage interpretation through its published studies and training programs that include webinars, online courses, and workshops to enhance local and state history interpretation.

Interpreters working at camps benefit from membership in the American Camp Association (ACA). For more than 100 years ACA has provided guidance, accreditation standards, and publications about interpretation to private and public youth camps throughout North America. Its *Camping* magazine carries occasional articles on environmental education and nature programming.

The World Federation of Tourist Guides Associations offers guide training and promotes professionalism among guides in the tourism industry. However, most tour guide training is provided by private tourism firms or local, regional or national tourism organizations (Figure 17.5). For example, one of the most famous professional guide training programs is found in the United Kingdom where the Institute of Tourist Guiding is responsible for administering training courses and testing to attain a coveted Blue, Green, or White Badge. Blue Badge holders are qualified for conducting guided walks, guiding at specific sites, and guiding from a moving vehicle in their specified region. Green Badge guides can do guided walks and guide at sites in their specified town or area of countryside. White Badge holders are qualified for guiding either at a specific site (e.g., museum, cathedral, historic home) or conducting a guided walk along one fixed route.

Figure 17.5. Trained and certified private tour guides offer walking tours around cities including this tour in Krakow, Poland. (TC)

Other cities and countries have their own tour guide certification programs but the Blue Badge is the most prestigious symbol of professionalism in tourist guiding and presents opportunities to do everything from walking tours in London, to working on cruise ships, and even to guiding famous celebrities. To earn a London Blue Badge students are assessed on the following: background knowledge of the UK, in-depth London knowledge, and regional knowledge which covers sites frequently visited from London in a day. Practical training and assessment take place in the National Gallery, the British Museum, Westminster Abbey, St Paul's Cathedral, the Tower of London, a City of London walk and a panoramic coach tour. Students are also required to write a 3000-word Tour Planning Project.

Such professional certifications are not only found in the world's major cities. For example, Savannah Guides Ltd. provides intensive training and certifies ecoguides working in northern Australia. The Costa Rica Tourism Board offers a Certification of Sustainable Tourism that requires guides be trained in sustainable practices and community development.

Private Training/Consulting Firms

Many consulting companies offer interpretation training for a fee. Such firms are widely available especially in Europe, Australia, and North America (see Chapter 20). Some individuals and firms offer workshops in exhibit design or interpretive writing. Many firms offer interpretive planning training as they assist in planning projects at a specific site. Other firms and individuals focus on museum education or tour guide training. In short, almost any kind of training related to interpretation is available, at least in developed countries. Interpreters can find these firms online or through conferences and publications of the professional organizations mentioned above. Hiring private-sector professional interpretation trainers has the advantages of getting targeted teaching or planning for a particular site and specialized training for specific staff members.

Approaches to Training

Over the years, organizations such as NAI and Interpret Europe have convened committees and task forces to specify best practices for interpreters. Skibins, Powell, and Stern (2012) analyzed the literature and gleaned 17 "best practices" for interpreters. This list included such things as theme development, actively engaging the audience, relating to the audience, using multisensory presentations, and other techniques and approaches found in this book. IDP, CIG, Blue Badge, and most other trainings and certifications focus on teaching best practices and developing competencies in applying these skills.

> "Holistic training recognizes that if students don't continue their learning they will regress."

Although these techniques are essential for excellent interpretation, Jon Kohl of the aforementioned PUP Global Heritage Consortium, warns that teaching only skills can be insufficient for lasting change (Kohl, 2015). PUP recommends a holistic training approach rather than trainings that focus too much on individuals, memorization, and short-term interventions. Holistic training takes into account the context where the interpreters work because without addressing context, interpreters are less likely to implement what they have learned when they return to their sites.

Holistic training also seeks to improve actual performance, not merely the potential for improvement. It involves the trainees in the co-creation and critically reflective evaluation of their instruction. Finally, holistic training recognizes that if students don't continue their learning, they will regress and not implement what they learned. For this reason, trainees find an ongoing support network of colleagues who can provide motivation, support, and helpful insights.

Weiler and Black (2015) provide a thorough review of the tour guide training literature. They concluded that as the tourism industry evolves from a service industry to an experience industry, tour guide training becomes more important and can be an effective quality assurance mechanism. However, they offer the following cautions that need to be addressed, particularly in developing countries:

- Delivery of training may vary across regions and among educational institutions.
- Training may set minimum standards only. If guides are only assessed as competent or not competent there may not be an incentive to strive for excellence.
- Training may be less accessible to guides in remote regions as is often the case with ecotourism guides.
- Prerequisites to enter training may limit access to those with relevant qualifications or experience.
- Because many tour guides in developing countries are illiterate or nearly illiterate, written assessment methods may be inappropriate.

Although the degree to which these concerns exist vary between countries, they should be addressed in any training program, even in developed countries.

In conclusion, regardless of whether the training involves tour guides, nature center volunteers, museum docents, or paid staff, the training itself should follow a "practice what we preach" approach. That is, interpretive principles should be employed and practiced as the training itself is conducted. Ironically, Grenier (2008) studied docent training at an art museum and history museum and although both institutions espoused inquiry-based learning, self-reflection, and other engaging techniques for interpreting to visitors, the docent training consisted only of passive learning from lectures. Training of volunteers and staff should mirror the creative communications espoused for visitors.

> "Training of volunteers and staff should mirror the creative communications espoused for visitors."

Becoming Better Interpreters by Self-Improvement

Formal training by agencies, professional conferences, and knowledgeable colleagues provide wonderful and useful lifelong learning. However, interpreters can supplement those opportunities with their own self-improvement efforts. Lopez (1998), in his book *About This Life,* advises that young writers become great writers through reading, traveling, and becoming someone. Cable (1999) noted that this same advice applies to interpreters seeking personal and professional growth.

First, reading opens the interpreter's mind to new ideas and perspectives, especially if they read the words of voices different from their own. Reading good literature has the added benefit of making the alert reader into a better writer. Good literature can provide a model for composition and style as well as a fountain of inspiration. Good writers are usually good readers and vice versa. Intellectually, we are what we read.

Second, interpreters can travel. Sometimes this entails travel to distant places and sometimes without leaving home. Interpreters can explore new foods, sample new music, and get to know new people in the immediate community. They can wander in their own park or museum, watching people in places seldom visited by interpreters. They can explore new worlds via the Internet, telescopes, microscopes, and all sorts of new technologies. These new experiences will help as interpreters relate to more diverse audiences and enrich their interpretation. As interpreters travel, even through their own "backyards," they will encounter magnificent and miraculous things.

Third, to become a better interpreter, "become someone." Gandhi said, "My life is my message." Interpreters should find out what they truly believe about the world and, with humility, share those beliefs with others. They should make their message and life meaningful and consistent—an identifiable *somebody*. This can produce professional and personal contentment. Heartfelt sincerity, consistent with personal convictions, brings forth enthusiasm and passion, hallmarks of effective interpretation. Thoughtful interpreters put these values in writing as a professional mission statement that motivates and guides their work. Being *someone* allows interpreters to go beyond merely passing on information to presenting interpretive themes with personal conviction. When conviction shows through the interpretive effort, it makes messages credible and persuasive.

> All of this takes time—time to travel, time to read, and time to be introspective about one's life and work.

All of this takes time—time to travel, time to read, and time to be introspective about one's life and work. Slow down and your roots will grow deeper and your interpretation will bloom with vivid colors and abundance.

"Nobody sees a flower—really—it is so small it takes time—we haven't time—and to see takes time, like to have a friend takes time."
–Georgia O'Keefe

Summary

The best interpreters have rigorous education in cultural or natural history as well as training in communications techniques. Interpreter excellence requires expertise in the subjects being presented as well as talent in conveying the message. In addition to formal university training, the best interpreters embark upon lifelong learning through customized in-service training provided by the agency and/or through professional associations and conferences. On the job, they learn on a daily basis by observing successes and failures, and from informal discussions with colleagues. Participation in professional development activities indicates to peers and potential employers that you are serious about professionalism and hold yourself accountable for achieving and maintaining excellence in your interpretive work. Life-long learning is a sign of a personal work ethic and a desire for continuous growth and improvement.

Volunteers, Friends Groups, and Board members contribute significantly to many organizations. Training these individuals requires shared responsibilities among the agency administrators, the interpretive supervisors, and the interpretive staff. However, as with employee training, if effective, it produces knowledgeable, up-to-date, and motivated individuals. This results in higher morale within the agency and better service to the public.

Fundamentally, interpretation involves one individual serving other individuals. An interpreter shares his or her knowledge, convictions, enthusiasm, insight, and inspiration with other people. This individual endeavor is shaped by formal and informal training, groomed by careful supervision, assisted by friends and supporters, and driven by the desire to serve others with excellence. Disciplined reading related to the field, traveling and personal visits to other interpretive settings, development of personal beliefs and articulation of a personal mission statement enhance the interpreter's ability to create and share the art of interpretation. A commitment to personal growth ultimately makes for a better professional, collectively a better organization, a better visitor experience… and a better world.

Literature Cited

Bixler, R., James, J., & Vadala, C. (2011). Environmental socialization incidents with implications for the expanded role of interpretive naturalists in providing natural history experiences. *Journal of Interpretation Research, 16*(1), 35–64.

Bryant, H. C. (1960). The beginning of Yosemite's educational program. *Yosemite, 39*(7), 161–165.

Bryant, H. C., & Atwood, W. W., Jr. (1932). *Research and education in the national parks.* Washington, DC: National Park Service.

Cable, T. (1999). Becoming better interpreters. *Legacy, 10*(6), 14–16.

Grenier, R. (2008). Practicing what we preach. *Journal of Interpretation Research, 13*(1), 7-25.

Ham, S., & Hall, T. (2008). Should NAI develop a program to accredit university curricula? (Probably not just yet). *Journal of Interpretation Research, 13*(1), 39–46.

Jacobs, E. (2016). Can interpretation be taught? Building on the foundations of NAI's training program. *Legacy, 27*(1),15.

Jacobs, E. (2017). Personal communication with Emily Jacobs, Certification and Training Program Manager for the National Association for Interpretation.

Kohl, J. (2015). Training and Performance-Building: Principles of the PUP Global Heritage Consortium. April 2015 Unpublished Report. (http://pupconsortium.net/)

Lackey, B. (2008). The state of interpretation in academia. *Journal of Interpretation Research, 13*(1), 27–36.

Lopez, B. (1998) *About this life.* New York, NY: Knopf.

Skibins, J., Powell, R., & Stern, M. (2012). Exploring empirical support for interpretation's best practices. *Journal of Interpretation Research, 17*(1), 25–44.

Tweaksbury, J., Anderson, J., Bakker, J., Billo, T., Dunwiddie, P., Groom, M., ... & Wheeler, T. (2014). Natural history's place in science and society. *BioScience, 64* (4), 300–310.

Weiler, B., & Black, R. (2015). *Tour guiding research: Insights, issues, and implications.* Bristol, UK: Channel View Publications.

CHAPTER 18

Interpretive Planning

"A goal without a plan is just a wish."
–Antoine de Saint-Exupéry

School tours of a casual walk-and-talk nature using a spontaneous "teachable moments" approach had served the Morton Arboretum for 20 years. But there were no formal goals and objectives, no curriculum-based standards, no plan. Tour numbers declined precipitously and schools indicated withdrawal intents.

New supervisory interpreters came in during the crisis year of 2000. They met with teachers and guides, evaluated the situation, and proposed the following changes as a plan to move ahead: goals and objectives, themes with curriculum relevance, guide job descriptions and schedules, guide training and certification, a guide manual, and teacher training, among other innovations.

The guides revolted. One predicted, "The doors will be locked in six months if these changes occur." However, teachers and principals agreed with the program. The new plan received approval from the board of directors. But the guides continued to resist. Of the original cadre of 53, most quit, leaving only 18 guides. Recruitment added six more for a total of 24.

The plan turned out to be a success. Partnerships with school districts grew in numbers, evaluation became a habit, and grants for teacher training came in. Some of the teachers involved went on to win education awards for integrating field participation with classroom studies. The guides that stayed or were recruited, less than half the original number, went on to serve *more* students with a 47% increase in just two years.

Careful planning paid off despite a tense period of change. Rather than "closing doors," the Arboretum's supporting membership rose to a record 39,250 households and total visitation exceeded one million visitors by 2015 (Leonard & Hootman, 2001; mortonarb.org, 2017).

Interpretive planning discerns strategies to help interpreters connect the visitor to the resource and its caretakers. Interpretive plans guide the sustainable use of facilities and features so that visitors can find meaning in the cultural, natural, and historic values of a place and its significance to their lives. Interpretive planners provide a vision for the future of interpretation (Gross, Zimmerman, & Buchholz, 2006) and produce rich, memorable experiences for interpretive clients.

> Interpretive plans guide the sustainable use of facilities and features so that visitors can find meaning in the cultural, natural, and historic values of a place and its significance to their lives.

This chapter will help readers understand the interpretive plans used by consultants and various agencies. For example, the U.S. Forest Service provides several reasons for developing a plan which may include greater continuity among programs that are offered, improve a forest's public image, generate public understanding and appreciation for national forest resources and management of those resources, facilitate public involvement, create new partnerships, and/or develop a heightened sense of individual stewardship (USFS, 2014).

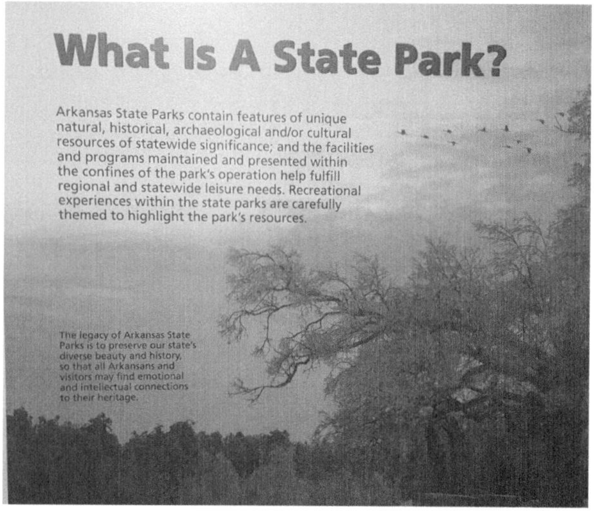

The key message of the chapter is that interpretive facilities and programs should proceed from careful planning and include all stakeholders. An interpretive plan considers the mission and goals of the institution (Figure 18.1), focuses on the clients, states themes, prescribes interpretive methods and media, and details an implementation strategy. For protected areas and cultural heritage sites, plans should be developed by strengthening the involvement of the constituent community so that the plans don't "end on shelves and remain unimplemented" (Kohl & McCool, 2016).

Figure 18.1. Plans start with understanding the mission statement of the site and then charting a course at achieving that mission. How to effectively communicate the mission to the visitors is part of an interpretive plan. (TC)

An Overview of Different Plans

To begin, and for context, we point out that there are many different kinds of agency plans, and the interpretive plan is only one type. Various types of other plans are discussed in the literature (i.e., Brochu, 2014; Merriman & Brochu, 2005; Wells, Butler, & Koke, 2013; Wells, Lovejoy, & Welch, 2009) and are summarized below.

Master Plans

Master plans take into account the entire site and list significant resources, a mission statement, goals and objectives, and details about all aspects of the site including facilities. Other types of plans that focus on the entire institution are the strategic plan and long-range plan.

Business Plans

As discussed in Chapter 16, business plans focus on marketing, finances, and fundraising. Elements generally provided in such plans describe the product or service, a pricing strategy, promotion, and budget. Business-related plans may include a capital campaign plan, marketing plan, and financial plan and can be a critical part of the interpretive plan.

Operational Plans

Plans that focus on management and operations may include a staffing plan, diversity plan, and docent/volunteer plan.

Facility Plans

Specific plans that are related to facilities may include the maintenance plan, emergency response plan, historic structure plan, and landscape plan.

Interpretive Plans

Although the various plans listed above are important, they extend beyond the scope of this chapter. These other types of plans are provided for context and because there is often overlap among various planning documents. In this chapter, we focus on interpretive planning. Note, however, that there is complexity and overlap here as well. Interpretive plans may focus on building new facilities or on improving existing ones (such as museums or visitor centers), outdoor resources (which could include plans for trails or wayside exhibits), new exhibitions, and/or interpretive programs depending on the interpretive site. We offer a broad discussion of interpretive planning that recognizes that each site will have particular nuances unique to that site and that planning situation.

Definitions of Interpretive Planning

Taking into account various references to interpretive planning as an approach, a document, or a process the following comprehensive definition was conceived (Wells, Butler, & Koke, 2013):

> Interpretive planning is a deliberate and systematic process for thinking about, deciding on, and recording in a written format or plan educational and interpretive initiatives for the purpose of facilitating meaningful and effective experiences for visitors, learning institutions, and communities.

This definition notes that interpretive planning is a process that results in a written document and is developed to enhance the experience of the visitor. As this chapter continues, there will be a strong focus on the visitor experience.

In her book, *Interpretive Planning*, Lisa Brochu (2014) provides the following definition:

> Interpretive planning, then, is the decision-making process that blends management needs and resource considerations with visitor desire and ability to pay (with time, interest, and/or dollars) to determine the most effective way to communicate the message to targeted markets.

Brochu continued by noting that such planning prompts agencies to deliver messages through the creation of experiences; some carefully structured and others that may be serendipitous. This is a critical point. Visitors should be encouraged to experience and discover certain aspects of the interpretive site themselves. For example, visitor surveys at Hovenweep National Monument indicate that discovery is one of the qualities park visitors value the most about their experience (National Park Service, 2010).

> "Visitors should be encouraged to experience and discover certain aspects of the interpretive site themselves."

Matching Resources and Customers

The first lesson of interpretive planning is to learn about and plan for the customer. In interpretation, demand comes from the visitors and other potential clientele and supply comes from the cultural and natural resources and the people who interpret them. The following market-focused processes deal with specific planning for how visitors will be able to interact with the resource in ways they will enjoy and that will produce memorable experiences.

Plan to Learn About Who Comes and Who Doesn't

Agencies associated with natural and cultural heritage areas have made impressive progress in using social and behavioral sciences. Economics and marketing now focus first on consumers and the products they desire, rather than focusing first on the products.

Likewise, interpreters define recreational needs and interpretive opportunities in terms of what the visitors desire from the recreational experiences they seek. To discover this requires more than just leaving it up to the interpretive planner to somehow know or divine. It requires public input at early stages of planning.

Before writing down planning assumptions, ask visitors what they would like, usually in a formal way. The consumer-oriented outcome can be called the desired experiences or the experience opportunities. Then follow up by seeking specific input from visitors at various stages of planning. An interpretive planning team could serve itself well by including one permanent member who acts as a visitor advocate.

An early step defines the visitors that are presently involved as well as the ones that are expected or targeted. Important characteristics include the following:

- Are they local and/or regional, national, international?
- What languages do they speak?
- What cultural context and interests do they bring?
- How do they arrive?
- How long and where do (or can) they stay?
- How do they now use the facility in terms of activities and group size?
- To take advantage of the resource more fully, what should visitors do?
- To get a fully immersed experience—the real value of the place—what would interpreters offer/require in terms of time, movement, specialized equipment if any, and guided services?

- What barriers or trepidations might these activities produce to different groups?
- How can communities that have not traditionally been served be included?

Planners can ask front-line staff for their observations of visitor needs and desires. They can conduct interviews with visitors or request responses to questionnaires that focus on what the site does for them and what more it might do. Information can also be gathered through surveys by phone, mail, or online. In addition, guest registers can be studied to find patterns of visitor comments. Observations of visitors can be made to provide information about movement patterns or existing interest in the site amenities. Ultimately, all sources of information can be compiled to provide a useful foundation for planning. Beware of compiling a list of minor complaints; search for the big picture that will lead to more powerful experiences. When alternatives are first developed, visitors might be asked to comment or vote in an advisory capacity. (See Chapter 19 for a broader discussion of the complexities of evaluation.)

Many agencies are seeking to embrace a broader segment of the communities they serve, beyond those who have traditionally been visitors to the site. A leading proponent of this approach, Nina Simon, has been described as a "museum visionary" by *Smithsonian Magazine*. Simon authored *The Participatory Museum* (2010) and *The Art of Relevance* (2016). She wrote, "The more you start to matter to people, the more they will desire opportunities to go deeper into the room of what you offer" (Simon, 2016).

> "Many agencies are seeking to embrace a broader segment of the communities they serve, beyond those who have traditionally been visitors to the site."

Still, many potential visitors do not feel welcome in our parks and cultural centers. At the 2014 reopening of the Whitney Museum, in New York City, Michelle Obama said:

There are so many kids in this country who look at places like museums and concert halls and other cultural centers and they think to themselves, well, that's not a place for me, for someone who looks like me, for someone who comes from my neighborhood. In fact, I guarantee you that right now, there are kids living less than a mile from here who would never in a million years dream that they would be welcome in this museum. And growing up on the South Side of Chicago, I was one of those kids myself. So I know that feeling of not belonging in a place like this.

To make welcome visitors beyond those who have traditionally been served interpreters should invite them on their own terms, "with generosity, humility, and a nod to what speaks to them" (Simon, 2016). The first step is to get people through the front door. However, if they don't have a good experience then the opportunity for connection has been squandered. They key is to see that the visitor does have a powerful experience. And wants to share it. And come again. And become further involved.

Plan for Visitor Experiences

Experiential marketing plans recognize that visitors seek experience (Figure 18.2). The experience may occur even before (or in lieu of) an actual visit. When customers look at the park or museum website they should note depictions of experiences that originate from the cultural and natural wonders of the site. Then, they want follow-up when they arrive. They may seek a package that includes several interpretive programs, a self-guided trail, and birdwatching. They will seek a set of activities that is personalized based on their own background and desires.

Figure 18.2. Planning for visitor experiences may start with fundamental decisions such as whether to renovate a California ranch house into a visitor center (upper) or build a modern building with native limestone and colored glass to evoke a prairie fire (lower). (LB/TC)

The planner needs to customize plans for the visitors (Veverka, 2015). *Mass customization* recognizes the advantages of mass producing services and programs while building in the flexibility to meet individual or group needs. Personal interpretation, if done by professionals, fits this flexible model easily. Nonpersonal interpretation requires packaging combinations of various options and media such as smartphone tours, apps, and wayside exhibits.

The essence of the interpretive plan, first and foremost, is to focus on the visitor experience. The approach to interpreting a museum, forest, park, or reserve starts with what the clients seek and hope for. Then, this should lead to alternative techniques of presenting the interpretation. Value as a planner arises from how one helps to define the interpretive philosophy, sets the strategy, and identifies the type of themes and messages that will help the agency achieve its interpretive goals. The visitor experience boils down to how the visitor will interact with the resource or museum. Interpreters provide brochures, exhibits, talks, walks, podcasts, and videos to help make the interaction possible.

> "The essence of the interpretive plan, first and foremost, is to focus on the visitor experience."

Nina Simon (referred to above) is the museum director of the Santa Cruz Museum of Art & History (MAH) and a consultant for parks, museums, libraries, and historic sites. She relates the story of Sangye Hawke who first came into the MAH as a visitor and added a personal memory to a participatory exhibit. Sangye next visited the historical archive to make an inquiry and the archivist invited her to become involved in local research projects. This led to Sangye joining a committee and becoming a volunteer. She donates time, money, snacks, and has involved her entire family as volunteers. She has become one of the "most valued participants at the museum" (Simon, 2016). As in this, and similar cases, the visitor experience can continue to evolve in ways that benefit the individual, the institution, and the community.

In describing the "community first program design" Simon (2016) indicated how her museum (MAH) does it as follows:

- Define the community or communities to whom you wish to be relevant. The more specific the definition the better.
- Find representatives of this community—staff, volunteers, visitors, trusted partners—and learn more about their experiences. If you don't know many people in this community, this is a red flag moment. Don't assume that programs that are relevant to you or your existing audiences will be relevant to people from other backgrounds.
- Spend more time in the community to whom you wish to be relevant. Explore their events. Meet their leaders. Get to know their dreams, points of pride, and fears. Share yours, too.
- Develop collaborations and programs, keeping in mind what you have learned.

Furthermore, the MAH uses a strategy called social bridging in which they intentionally bring together unlikely partners such as opera singers and ukulele players, Guggenheim fellows and amateur artists, history buffs and homeless adults. The goal is to bring people together "across differences and build a more connected community"

(Simon, 2016). The result is that at the MAH programs that bring diverse people together have become more popular than those that serve homogenous groups. Long-time insiders of the museum now declare, "I come to the museum and see people I wouldn't meet anywhere else" (Simon, 2016).

Plan for Feelings

In planning for visitor experiences, recognize that one of the defining aspects is how the visitor felt during and after the visit. Interpretive plans routinely target learning objectives and behavioral objectives. However, some resist the notion of planning for emotional objectives because of difficulties in measuring success and the controversial idea of prescribing specific emotional responses. Yet, clearly at places such as the Holocaust Museum in Washington, DC or the National 9/11 Memorial and Museum in New York City, and at Civil Rights sites, battlefields, and memorials worldwide, interpretive planners unapologetically aim to evoke certain emotional responses with their interpretive efforts. As noted in Chapter 11, entire museums have been devoted to nurturing emotional responses such as empathy. To expand this approach, it is interesting to speculate on what nature centers, historical sites, and museums would be like if they were organized around uplifting emotional responses. A museum's exhibit area could have a Joy Room or a Hall of Hope with all of the exhibits aimed at evoking those feelings. A nature center could have a Trail of Tranquility. What if an interpretive site scheduled a literal "Happy Hour" devoted to happy celebration of something beautiful or unique? Efforts to evoke emotional responses in a planned and systematic way could have powerful and profound effects on both the audience and the staff.

Plan for Memories

During the planning process, think about post experience memories (Pine & Gilmore, 2011). Planners could map the site for making memories. While planning, think ahead to memories people will take, and the memory enhancers that will recall those interpretive experiences.

First, look for and plan the best and most powerful memories that a visit can provide. This may involve a spectacular scene, a particular historic site or document, a special demonstration, the oldest tree, or some personal achievement such as reaching the highest peak. Identify places and features where visitors will take pictures

> Look for and plan the best and most powerful memories that a visit can provide.

and make it possible to put themselves in the picture (safely). Identify the places that will evoke memories that visitors discuss as they drive home, and in the days ahead with family and friends, and as they recall even years later. One of the key indicators that visitors' experiences are monumental will be the degree to which they talk about them with others. Help create memories that visitors can cherish for a lifetime.

Second, provide memory enhancements related to the experience. Sale items such as compasses, binoculars, magnifying glasses, and nature journals help children and parents make the most of their visit, and remember and extend the park visit when they get home. Other common sales items include videos, T-shirts, and postcards that extend memories of the visit. However, there can be many other intriguing, site-specific souvenirs such as simple art pieces or certificates for completing something associated with the site. Among the most meaningful are crafts made by the indigenous culture or artwork that comes from local artists. These may be displayed at one's home or office to reinforce and remind the visitors of the interpretive themes at the site and rewarding experiences that occurred there. Also, recall the clever gift shop items detailed at Arkansas State Parks and specifically the emphasis on books at Davidsonville Historic State Park (Chapter 16).

Ideally, memorabilia consist of high-quality merchandise that represents the compelling story of the site. Themed, quality memorabilia can enrich the visitor's experience and the bottom line. For example, the Metropolitan Museum of Art grosses about $90 million a year from its stores and catalog sales and without this revenue admission would have to be about $75 per person (Weaver, 2007).

> Themed, quality memorabilia can enrich the visitor's experience and the bottom line.

As visitors become more and more involved with an institution they may create memories for a lifetime *and*, if they continue to stay involved, experiences for a lifetime.

Planning Approaches

Interpretive plans are typically written with five- to seven-year planning horizons (Wells, Lovejoy, & Welch, 2009), although some plans may range up to 15 and even 20 years. Plans should be flexible and responsive to changing conditions.

Experience teaches that if you give a planning group a clear process to follow, things go faster. The interpretive planner can use one of several approaches to planning. As written they seem linear, but that is for simplicity of explanation. Most people do not function in straight lines during creative moments. One experienced planner

> Plans should be flexible and responsive to changing conditions.

says he operates in linear fashion with occasional holistic bursts of inspiration. These inspirational bursts of energy drive the planning team along its somewhat linear path toward completion. They may "set back" earlier progress or even reverse directions. Many planning teams of even two or three people report changes of pace, from a fast start to long slow periods of little apparent progress, to sudden whirlwind sprints, then long tedious writing and editing periods, then a quick spurt at the end of the process.

Many different planning practices exist. For example, the National Association for Interpretation (NAI, 2008) issued *Standards and Practices for Interpretive Planning* that listed these 14 benchmarks as keys to development of an interpretive plan, listed alphabetically, as follows:

1. Advocacy
2. Audience Analysis
3. Civic Engagement
4. Evaluation
5. Management Objectives
6. Marketing Factors
7. Media Descriptions
8. Message Elements

9. Operational Commitment
10. Partnerships
11. Staff/Volunteer Training
12. Stakeholder Involvement
13. Terminology
14. Visitor Experience

All of these benchmarks, incorporated into a process, culminate in the visitor experience. The key outcome is the delivery of the visitor experience, based on the plan that defines it.

Nonetheless, recommended processes may differ. Lisa Brochu specializes in interpretive master planning and training. She served as associate director for the National Association for Interpretation for a decade. She also wrote a seminal work, now in its second edition, titled *Interpretive Planning* (2014). In this book, Brochu provides the 5-M Model for successful interpretive planning projects. See Box 18.1.

Box 18.1
Interpretive Planning
Lisa Brochu, Principal, Heartfelt Associates

Interpretive planning is a process that provides guidance for selection of the most effective interpretive media to communicate a message, given resource considerations and the needs and desires of management and target markets. Interpretive plans can be prepared for individual projects (such as a single exhibit or brochure, a gallery with multiple exhibits and mixed media, or a special event), or they can be prepared as master plans for long-term development and implementation of all interpretive activities and media for a site, facility, community or region.

No matter what the scale of the project, the 5-M model discussed in detail in *Interpretive Planning: the 5-M Model for Successful Planning Projects* provides one way to approach the process. The model is not intended to serve as a table of contents for an interpretive plan, nor should it be considered the only or the "right" way to approach interpretive planning. Rather, it suggests the many variables a planner must consider when determining the most effective solution for a specific situation, lumped into five main categories that conveniently begin with the letter "M" as a memory aid. These categories and a few of the variables in each are as follows:

- Management (mission, vision, core values, goals, objectives; operational resources such as staffing, budget, maintenance capability; current or future issues; previous plans)
- Marketing (primary, secondary and target audiences; pricing strategies; promotional considerations)
- Mechanics (holistic visitor experience; design balance between architecture, site planning, and interpretation; placement; space planning; flow patterns; resource considerations)
- Message (theme, subthemes, storylines)
- Media (anything that helps to communicate the message)

In this model, none of the categories or variables should be considered alone. Each of them influences and is influenced by the others. For example, management objectives may determine what message is desirable, but audience expectations may suggest that there is a specific way in which that message will be better received. Likewise, space considerations, resource sensitivity, or available budget may put a reality check on specific choices that can be made, requiring the planner to work within certain constraints when determining media. In any case, media selection should be the final step in the process after all other "M" categories have been considered to avoid making costly mistakes.

Box 18.1 continued

How to proceed with putting each of the variables into context will depend on the individual project. Some projects will already have some variables clearly identified while others may require additional research or discussion during the process. As you work through the process, keeping these five principles in mind will help you move forward productively, whether you use the 5-M model or another approach:

1. **Listen at multiple levels.**

The interests of key stakeholders (donors, managers, guides, etc.) and the audiences that will be using the media are equally important. Sometimes those involved in the process may not voice all their concerns, so the planner must become adept at listening to "subtext" and body language as well as the words being spoken.

2. **Pay attention to every detail, using all your senses.**

Sometimes the best information comes from personal observation of a situation, noting how people move through a site or react to a particular experience. Listen for intrusive sounds that may need to be overcome and look at wear patterns on the ground. Notice how smells or blowing breezes may add to or detract from an experience.

3. **Nothing exists in isolation.**

Consider the whole; whatever you are planning will either affect or be affected by other parts of a larger experience. Always keep the relationships between the five "Ms" in mind.

4. **Every project is different, so every process is unique.**

Many people are tempted to approach interpretive planning as a recipe that yields consistent results because the ingredients may be similar. Unfortunately, there is no recipe for successful interpretation. The mix of media, message, and audience to achieve specific objectives with available resources will almost certainly be different for different circumstances. Consequently, the process by which the planning team approaches the project will need to be different to accommodate all the unique factors involved in any specific project.

5. **Everybody at the table must be a winner, but the ultimate winner must be the resource.**

The planner's responsibility is to find ways in which everyone can benefit, even if each individual does not always get exactly what he or she wants. The ultimate success of the process and the products that result from it should be measured in continued support and protection of the resource, whatever that may be.

Finally, unless you have an accomplished interpretive planner on staff, it is usually advisable to bring in qualified outside help for this process. Interpretive planning is not the same skill set as providing interpretive programs or designing interpretive products, and although some people have some combination of planning, program delivery, or design skills, the combination of two or three in one person or one firm is not a given. A Certified Interpretive Planner (certified by National Association for Interpretation) should be skilled in facilitating a successful planning process that yields the most appropriate and effective recommendations for the project's owner.

Marcella Wells and her associates (Wells, Butler, & Koke, 2013) developed an interpretive planning sequence for museums. They noted that the interpretive plan is useful as a decision tool, a development tool, a monitoring tool, a marketing tool, and an implementation tool. The authors note "there is no single, universally accepted or approved process of interpretive planning for museums." Nonetheless, these authors offer a thoughtful framework for thinking about planning that is useful for a broad range of interpretive sites beyond museums as follows (Wells, Butler, & Koke, 2013):

- Situation and Need
- Purpose and Goals
- Inventory (supply and demand)
- Analysis (supply and demand)
- Themes and Visitor Experiences
- Recommendations
- Implementation Guidelines

Apparent throughout their model is the integration of visitor perspectives from the outset and throughout the decision making process. The authors note, "The impetus is accountability, and the desired result is more successful (i.e., engaging and meaningful) informal learning experiences" (Wells, Butler, & Koke, 2013).

The Essential Element: Vision

National Park Service planner Fred Babb used five key words to define planning work. *Vision* requires that interpreters design and paint a picture that people can understand and buy into. A need for *change* precedes a need for a plan; plans call for some kind of alteration of the interpretive mix or methods and they direct how to go about it. *Risk* and *conflict* come with any change; planners must learn to work with them. The *challenge* is to facilitate and coordinate the planning process, then to present a plan and to implement it with the staff.

A vision guides the planning process to achieve an end—a target. Too often, planners start their work hearing about problems rather than a vision or target. The problems include things as mundane as how to change the typeface on the brochures. Other more serious problems may involve building an amphitheater or reducing accidents at the overlooks—all which are important items, but not the vision. If the problems get top billing, the planner becomes a short-term troubleshooter. This can kill the planning process. The leader of the team must keep bringing the focus back to accomplishing the vision.

> A vision guides the planning process to achieve an end.

To develop a site vision, the team can wipe the slate clean. For a moment, ignore the mentality that "we've always done this" and avoid focusing on barriers and limitations. Instead, ask questions such as the following:

- What does/should this site really mean?
- What significant stories does/can it tell?
- What of great value does/could a visitor gain and take from here?
- How can the visitor experience be better?
- How do we become more relevant to all possible audiences?

Dream imaginatively, think analytically, believe in what the organization and its partners can do, and dare to take a risk. Only after defining that unfettered vision, then work on practical ways to achieve it with creative imagination.

Dynamics of Practical Planning

To define a vision requires a team, including representation by management staff and interpreters. The team should also include or meet with upper administrators, perhaps a political leader, and current and potential visitors. An outside planner often chairs the team and coordinates the process to prevent suppression of thought among staff or local citizens due to hierarchy status.

The core team is often 5 to 10 individuals, although the team can be flexible in size as the work progresses. At some steps, local or general public input may swell the number of people involved. When writing, a core team will do most of the work with assigned sections and plenty of revisions.

An efficient approach keeps the core team small and active but open to many ideas. With the complex processes required for an interpretive plan, involving a lot of creativity, a small group taking input and review from others provides an expeditious way to proceed. With the emphasis on government citizen interaction, large planning groups often get unwieldy and even simple group decisions take a lot of time.

The group needs a facilitator with compassion but a firm sense of accomplishing the mission on time. It needs visionaries who can see the big interpretive picture, who can comprehend current and potential users, the resource significance, the interpretive methodologies, and the practicalities as one big whole.

A team completely from inside the organization has limitations, unless it is a large organization. A few independent planners who come from outside the tradition may bring fresh perspectives of great utility. On the other hand, a team composed of only outside consultants may deliver a plan astutely and quickly, but may ignore important agency policy or traditions. Astute consulting planners insist that key agency personnel (e.g., interpreters) and local leaders participate fully in the planning process. They structure the steps to optimize local "buy-in" opportunities and subsequent advocacy of implementation.

The Interpretive Plan

An interpretive plan arises from analysis of two key components in parallel: (a) the *resources* and/or *facility* and (b) the *consumers* or likely visitors and other clients. The plan identifies significant resource features and it suggests how to relate them to the visitors, based on their characteristics, needs, and desires. It defines the interpretive vision of how the facility should best serve those consumers given its natural and cultural resources.

The plan proposes the themes and key stories that serve as the core messages of site interpretation (Figure 18.3). It then prescribes the techniques and media to use in different parts of the site, with consideration of financial and physical limitations, to enhance the experiences of visitors. The plan sets a style for the facility: the signs, the publications, the correlation of personal and nonpersonal services, and the balance of on-site and off-site efforts. It also considers timing and financing targets for the new developments.

The key document produced for site-based interpretive planning bears the name of *interpretive prospectus* or *interpretive plan*, which are terms that have been used interchangeably. However, since a prospectus is by definition a summary document (Brochu, 2014), we will refer to the full document as the interpretive plan. From the interpretive plan flow other documents, such as exhibit plans, trail or byway plans, signage specifications, specific media development plans, sales plans, program plans, and others.

A plan may also cover more than one property—what John Veverka (2015) has referred to as a *system plan*. The system may involve several parks of one agency or may cross agency lines in a regional tourism plan, linking themes and interpretive opportunities to give the visitors some integration among federal, state, local, and private interpretive sites. This encourages cooperation and operates in line with the way visitors act and perceive a tourist destination.

Figure 18.3. This planner armed with a scope, notepad, and recorder is "searching for stories" in the landscape. (TC)

> Visitors' needs, perceptions, and expectations contribute to the planning process.

An example of a cooperative venture is the "Great Trinity Forest" in Texas. What was once an illegal construction dumping site is now evolving into a major recreation area. The City of Dallas was court ordered to close the illegal dumping site along the Trinity River and clean up the land that had long been used as a landfill. The "Great Trinity Forest" is a collaborative effort between the City and the Texas Audubon Society. The Trinity River Audubon Center is a $37 million environmental remediation, restoration, and capital improvement project funded and built by the City. This is an important success story of land restoration that led to recreational and interpretive offerings within a major city. The "Great Trinity Forest" harbors groves of hardwood trees and is said to rival New York City's Central Park in terms of recreational potential. Indeed, Dallas' 6,000 acre forest overshadows the 840 acre Central Park. As they like to say in Texas, everything is bigger in Texas. This collaborative effort generates many possibilities for recreation and interpretation for residents and visitors alike, making Dallas a better city (Goodwyn, 2015; Great Trinity Forest, 2016).

Building the Plan

The procedures for developing a plan vary with the agency and its guidelines. Each site will have different needs so it is "virtually impossible to provide a template for interpretive planning" (Merriman & Brochu, 2005). Nonetheless, an overview of the process can be helpful and is provided with five steps that comprise the principal elements of interpretive planning. For each of these five steps we provide examples from the Martin Luther King, Jr. National Historic Site.

Consider the Clients

Visitors' needs, perceptions, and expectations contribute to the planning process. Visitors may arrive in many categories, such as families with diverse interests, passengers on tour buses, and school groups seeking structured lessons that match their curricula. Beyond the visitors, the facility may serve many who seldom visit but who learn remotely through the park or museum website, publications, social media, newspaper columns, or talks and activities in schools led by the interpreters from the site. The planner also may seek to broaden the community served beyond traditional horizons as discussed previously.

The interpretive planner seeks to learn who the clients are, how they experience the place, and what they want in the future. In an existing facility, visitors will suggest how to improve visitation experiences and how to better manage facilities and activities. The simplest way to do this involves handing out brief questionnaires or directly interviewing visitors at random times, then statistically analyzing and segmenting the responses. Focus groups of citizens and advisory committees of experts can also provide ideas. Public meetings may be required by agency rules. Note that these strategies may come with limitations (see Chapter 19).

> Cultural resource analysis identifies the significant human stories of the area.

The challenge consists of using client information to plan interpretation for clients and potential clients so they tune into the vibrancy from what is going on now and in the future. Planners help the interpreters to make the significance of the place come alive for each visitor.

As one example, staff members at Martin Luther King, Jr. National Historic Site received many different responses when they asked visitors "Why are you visiting the site?" Although there is some overlap in the response categories, the following listing provides an overview of why people are attracted to visiting this historic site and provides a background for the planning process (National Park Service, 2011):

- To pay respect to an American hero
- As a pilgrimage
- To seek hope or encouragement
- To learn more about Dr. King
- To connect Dr. King's story to daily experiences
- Because of a personal connection to the civil rights movement
- To personally see the places where Dr. King was born, where he worked, and where he is buried
- To see where Dr. King preached ("a spiritual experience")
- To celebrate the National King Holiday (King Week)
- Because it's free. (Note: there is no fee for visiting Martin Luther King, Jr. National Historic Site.)

Define the Resource: Interpretive Inventory

Planners list and identify the significance of the features, resources, and history available for interpretation at the site. Separating cultural and natural resources at first helps to simplify the task. Later, the two get woven together.

Cultural resource analysis identifies the significant human stories of the area. In some cases this can be a record of people spending the day at one spot, such as some sites on the Lewis and Clark Trail and many battlefields. In other cases, the significance may cover part of a lifetime or generations spent at a location, such as the "this is our traditional home" focus of much interpretation by native peoples in Australia, Canada, and the United States.

Natural resource identification and listing leads to coordinating and prioritizing those aspects by their significance. Statements of significance suggest why certain resources are "special" or "representative" and how they might guide the theme. Among natural resources, the interpretive planners generally deal with water as glaciers, rivers, lakes, or seas; geology and topographic features; flora and fauna; and soils, atmosphere, and climate. The unifying ecosystem approach relates or contrasts one place with the rest of the nation or continent.

An abbreviated inventory of resources at the Martin Luther King, Jr. National Historic Site include the following (National Park Service, 2011):

- 501 Auburn Avenue, the home where Martin Luther King, Jr. was born on January 15, 1929.
- Ebenezer Baptist Church, Dr. King's spiritual home and where he preached his first sermon at the age of 17.
- The Martin Luther King, Jr. Center for Nonviolent Social Change ("The King Center").
- The Birth Home Block, includes portions of the historically African American Sweet Auburn residential community, which was, by law, a racially segregated community during Dr. King's childhood.
- Historic Fire Station No. 6, historically where white firefighters operated within the predominantly African American Sweet Auburn community; it was one of the first racially integrated fire stations in Atlanta.

For those not familiar with this historic site, these physical resources all exist within several blocks of each other. In his childhood, the young Martin Luther King, Jr. spent a great deal of time within the confines of this small area, and yet his work in later years expanded to national and international influence.

Develop the Themes

Identifying the dominant themes helps to focus the entire interpretive program and provides a way to tie diverse characteristics of the site together. Themes are those ideas so important that visitors leave with them imbedded in the mind. Selecting the best, most important, most relevant, most interesting, and most appropriate themes usually requires a narrowing or focusing process. The *genius loci*—the essence of the place, its character, its special qualities, its significance—should direct the selection of themes.

> Selection of the themes may start with founding purposes or legislation.

Selection of the themes may start with founding purposes or legislation. They often have written down the purpose and special values of a place; the *raison d'être*. For example, national parks and other institutions will have a mission statement. At Martin Luther King, Jr. National Historic Site the mission statement is as follows:

...to preserve, protect, and interpret for the benefit, inspiration, and education of present and future generations the places where Martin Luther King, Jr. was born, where he lived, worked, and worshiped, and where he is buried, while also interpreting the life experiences and significance of one of the most influential Americans in the twentieth century (National Park Service, 2011).

The themes of the site differ from and are more focused than the mission statement as follows:

- **Segregation and Struggle.** The life of Martin Luther King, Jr. and his death were central to the transformation of America's segregated past and the promise of equality and justice for all citizens.
- **Childhood and Character.** The development of Martin Luther King, Jr.'s character was the result of a solid family structure and spiritual commitment that began in the home and was influenced by the Sweet Auburn community.
- **Church and Community.** Ebenezer Baptist Church and the Sweet Auburn community embodied the persona, spirituality, passion, and career of Dr. King.
- **Leadership and Legacy.** Dr. King's visionary leadership of the modern American Civil Rights Movement, as shown through his philosophy, words, and works, changed the course of American history and redefined the American promise to include all citizens, and continues to have national and international influence today (National Park Service, 2011).

Once the themes are stated, the team can focus on the mix between personal interpretation and nonpersonal services. The balance of these alternatives derives from study of costs, staffing required, and the nature of the messages. Where the messages should be available day and night, or when the messages are located in remote or little-used places, nonpersonal interpretation seems appropriate. Personal interpretation has its role where guiding, questions and answers, flexible learning, and encouraging visitor action are desired. The planners may wish to present several alternative mixes.

Prescribe the Interpretive Methods and Media

This step defines how to communicate the themes to the public. The interpretive methods and media take into consideration when visitors come, how long they stay, and what they hope to do. The prescription should define the type of logistical visitor experience and its facility implications. For example, tracking a typical interpretive museum visit from a purely functional view might show this sequence:

> The interpretive methods and media take into consideration when visitors come, how long they stay, and what they hope to do.

Arrive by car—park—walk to the museum or visitor center—outdoor and indoor orientation—encounter major theme statements to set up the context and principal messages—flow through the museum/visitor center exhibits and to the outside—move around the site to major features and satellite facilities—return to museum/visitor center—visit gift shop—exit the building and premises.

At each of the locations, consider signage necessary to orient and direct visitors, as well as interpretive signs and exhibits, location of personnel, and provisions for handling lines (e.g., information desk, cash registers, restroom entries, interactive exhibits).

A similar sequential path may be developed for the visitor. It would define the strategy of arranging "interpretive incidents" (signs, exhibits, introductory talks, smartphone tours, immersion programs, field walks and explorations, synthesis sessions, review, and final revelations) so they allow visitors to build a meaningful experience. Two or more packages of incidents could be developed, one for a short stay and others for longer stays.

Satellite interpretive areas and facilities provide further interpretive services that develop and complement the exhibits in the visitor center. The planner defines where interpretive trails lead, what themes will connect to their stories, where signs or outdoor exhibits shall go, and how overlooks of special features will accommodate groups while presenting both personal and nonpersonal interpretation. Sometimes, the details of trail design and other satellite interpretation facilities appear in a separate trail plan.

Visitor experience goals are derived from the prescribed interpretive media and methods. These will include opportunities for physical, intellectual, emotional, and sensory experiences and should be available to visitors of all abilities. At Martin Luther King, Jr. National Historic Site it was determined that visitors have the following opportunities (National Park Service, 2011):

- Pre-visit information
- Availability of public transportation
- Easy navigation throughout the park
- Accessible facilities
- Restrooms, water availability, and a gift shop
- Information on nearby places to have lunch
- A safe visit (the park is in an urban environment with some crime)
- Park orientation film
- Interactions with park staff formally and informally
- A guided tour of the Birth Home
- A visit to Dr. and Mrs. King's Tomb
- Learning about and experiencing the Sweet Auburn community
- An Ebenezer Baptist Church experience to meditate and reflect
- Relate to Dr. King's life experiences and be inspired to share with others

Describe How to Implement the Plan

An exciting aspect of interpretive planning is actually implementing the plan. However, things change. Conditions unanticipated in the plan require new responses. Therefore, the plan should be flexible with opportunity to shift directions if necessary. For example, there may be new information, changing technologies, new research on how people learn in informal settings, and/or a shift in funding opportunities (Wells, Butler, & Koke, 2013). Evaluation is also important and may suggest a shift in direction. (In the following chapter we discuss various types, and some complexities, of evaluation.)

At Martin Luther King, Jr. National Historic Site, the long-range interpretive plan is intended to be fulfilled in the range of 10 to 15 years. The plan includes the following recommendations (of many) for implementation (National Park Service, 2011):

- Incorporate in all new staff training, across divisions, instruction regarding how to handle crucial conversations with park visitors regarding race.
- Encourage all visitors to experience the Visitor Center first before exploring other parts of the park, so the balance of the park can be experienced in context after physical orientation and an interpretive overview.
- Institute visitor experience planning to identify by half-hour, one, two, and three-hour intervals what visitors can experience based upon their available time.
- Keep the park website accurate with a professional look, clear trip planning information, up-to-date content, and exciting features.
- Create an electronic kiosk for all arrival destinations that provides information, orientation, and timing of current activities in multiple languages.
- Work with City of Atlanta officials to remove panhandlers from the site.
- Expand interpretive coverage through the development of cell phone tours, based on different themes. Also, provide translated cell phone tours for the park's primary international visitor groups.
- Work with Eastern National to develop a historic site handbook (interpretive sales item) that includes information about all points of interest.
- Work with Eastern National to create an interactive video and board game for people of all ages about strategies used by Dr. King during the Civil Rights Movement.
- Develop a new Birth Home virtual tour on the website and kiosk in the Visitor Center.
- Develop a social media strategy to engage the greater community including the use of Twitter for announcing news, events, and programs.
- Collaboratively update and pilot-test educational materials with teachers to ensure optimal effectiveness.
- Develop programs to be called "A Day in the Life of Dr. King" for different stages of his life.

The Long-Range Interpretive Plan for Martin Luther King, Jr. National Historic Site concludes as follows (National Park Service, 2011):

And during the course of the next fifteen years, have fun working together as a team—internally and externally—to provide a high-caliber, memorable, and meaningful visitor experience at Martin Luther King, Jr. National Historic Site; in the words of Dr. King, a "Mountaintop" experience.

Summary

"I have a dream."
    –Martin Luther King, Jr.

The best interpretive planners have the skill and imagination to get and use the best information. They know how to gather, comprehend, analyze, and evaluate the information and transmit it in ways that lead to effective plans. The various guidelines presented in this chapter encourage the planner to ask the right questions. These guidelines also allow for clear communication of the planning process to those who fund and implement the decisions.

Interpretive planning now focuses on the visitor experience. The planner ultimately creates opportunities for enjoyable and enriching experiences, as well as fond memories about those experiences.

Interpreters have dreams, too. Interpretive plans make those dreams come true. In this way, the interpretive planning process makes for a better visitor experience—one in which people may see things differently, think about things differently, want to do things differently—and a better world.

"Plans are the dreams of the wise."
    –German proverb

Literature Cited

Brochu, L. (2014). *Interpretive planning: The 5-M model for successful planning projects.* Fort Collins, CO: National Association for Interpretation.

Goodwyn, W. (2015). One of the nation's biggest urban forests isn't where you'd expect. NPR Morning Edition. August 6, 2015.

Great Trinity Forest: trinityrivercorridor.com

Gross, M., Zimmerman, R., & Buchholz, J. (2006). *Signs, trails, and wayside exhibits* (3rd ed.). Stevens Point, WI: UW-SP Foundation Press.

Kohl, J., & McCool, S. (2016). *The future has other plans.* Golden, CO: Fulcrum Publishing.

Leonard, S., & Hootman, L. (2001). Lessons learned: Bringing the Morton Arboretum's school tours into the 21st century. Unpublished presentation at National Interpreters Workshop. Des Moines, IA.

Merriman, T., & Brochu, L. (2005). *Management of interpretive sites.* Fort Collins, CO: Interpress.

Morton Arboretum: mortonarb.org

National Association for Interpretation. (2008). *Standards and practices for interpretive planning.* Retrieved from interpnet.com/docs/BP-planning.

National Park Service. (2010). *Hovenweep National Monument Long-Range Interpretive Plan.* Prepared by Department of Interpretive Planning, Harpers Ferry Center and Hovenweep National Monument. (February 2010).

National Park Service. (2011). *Martin Luther King, Jr. National Historic Site Long-Range Interpretive Plan.* Harpers Ferry Center Interpretive Planning and Martin Luther King, Jr. National Historic Site. (December 2011).

Pine, J., & Gilmore, J. (2011). *The experience economy* (updated ed.). Boston, MA: Harvard Business Review Press.

Simon, N. (2010). *The participatory museum.* Santa Cruz, CA: Museum 2.0.

Simon, N. (2016). *The art of relevance.* Santa Cruz, CA: Museum 2.0.

U.S. Forest Service. (2012). *Regional Wilderness Interpretation and Education Plan.* Forest Service, Pacific Northwest Region. (February 2012)

U.S. Forest Service. (2014). *Interpretive Plans, Version 2.* Center for Design and Interpretation, Rocky Mountain Region, Golden, Colorado (September 2014).

Veverka, J. (2015). *Interpretive master planning: Strategies for the new millennium: Philosophy, theory and practice.* Cambridge, MA: MuseumsEtc, Ltd.

Weaver, S. (2007). *Creating great visitor experiences: A guide for museums, parks, zoos, gardens, and libraries.* Walnut Creek, CA: Left Coast Press.

Wells, M., Butler, B., & Koke, J. (2013). *Interpretive planning for museums: Integrating visitor perspectives in decision making.* Walnut Creek, CA: Left Coast Press.

Wells, M., Lovejoy, V., & Welch, D. (2009). *Creating more meaningful visitor experiences: Planning for interpretation and education.* United States Department of the Interior, Bureau of Reclamation, Policy and Program Services, Denver Federal Center, Denver, Colorado.

CHAPTER 19
Evaluating Interpretation

"Evaluation is about making improvements. If all you want is praise, skip evaluation...But if you want to do a better job, and you can face a little constructive criticism, evaluation can lead to making a better match between what you want to achieve and what actually might happen."
—Beverly Serrell (2015)

For more than four decades, Beverly Serrell has been an evaluation consultant with art, history, and science museums in addition to zoos and aquariums. Early in her career, she worked at the Field Museum in Chicago as a part-time exhibit developer. She had learned about evaluation at a Visitor Studies Association meeting. The small, temporary exhibition she was working on was to be of photographs from the vast museum collection. Beverly selected photos with visitor input and wrote brief captions for each. She made mock-ups of the images and labels and invited the staff to review her work in a written questionnaire. Beverly relates, "After reading the filled-out questionnaires after everyone had left, I drove home crying. I was wounded by my critics' comments, personally crushed by their lack of praise." But she vowed through her tears, "I believe in the PROCESS!" Her moral of the story is to not let your ego get too invested. Beverly concludes, "You are perfect, but the work can always be improved" (Serrell, 2015).

Evaluation is defined as "the systematic collection and analysis of data to address the worth or improvement of something" (Henderson, Bialeschki & Browne, 2017). Evaluation consists of a set of powerful tools to make interpretation better serve its clientele. It is the process of collecting and analyzing information about interpretive effectiveness. It considers message content and delivery on one hand, and visitor responsiveness on the other. Evaluation keeps programs and exhibits fresh. It prevents stagnation. It guides interpreters in honing their skills. Most importantly, evaluation enriches the value of the service to the clients of an interpretive institution.

Interpreters use evaluation before and during the development of a program or exhibit—front-end and formative evaluation. They also evaluate after the program and after exhibit completion—performance and post-occupancy or summative evaluation.

An organization that fails to evaluate indicates disrespect for its interpreters and disregard for the products of their work. This translates into little concern for the quality of visitor experiences.

This chapter discusses what, why, how, and when interpreters evaluate. Practical and academic attention to evaluation has produced a rich and sometimes controversial literature. From the abundance of information, the approaches presented here show how an individual interpreter or organization can get involved in evaluation on a consistent yet *simple* basis.

What We Evaluate

Evaluation of interpretation helps determine "the worth, merit, or significance of a product or service" and refers to the systematic collection and analysis of information to make decisions about exhibits, programs, or media and the effects of these on the participants (Wells, Lovejoy, & Welch, 2009).

Evaluation falls into at least four major categories of whom or what professional interpreters assess in an evaluation. First, and immediately useful to interpreters, is to evaluate "performances" so that they may find ways to improve their delivery methods, messages, and interpretive approach in future presentations. Second, nonpersonal installations such as exhibits and trails can be evaluated to ascertain use levels and learn whether they achieve intended objectives and to guide modifications for greater effectiveness (Figure 19.1). Third, attempts are made to evaluate visitors, their interests and needs, and their behaviors and reactions, to determine the potential and end results of interpretation.

Finally, it is helpful to evaluate overall productivity of the program mix and facilities, to determine whether money and effort are spent efficiently. This evaluation guides adjustments in the interpretive mix and may

Figure 19.1. Trail signs can be evaluated by collecting data on whether people actually stop and read them, including important observations about the preferences of their dogs. (JF)

also offer suggested measures to improve the visitor experience. It also demonstrates and documents benefits (the "products" of interpretation) useful in presenting a case for funding a program or the agency.

Why We Evaluate

If an interpretive program hopes to survive, it must produce a service that draws, pleases, and affects people. Evaluation helps in designing and adjusting programs and exhibits to best serve and expand the clientele. Evaluation puts a value on interpretation. It should indicate not just the faults in the program, but its strengths and the satisfactions produced. The goal of evaluation is to make reliable decisions by determining the value of products or services.

> "Evaluation helps in designing and adjusting programs and exhibits to best serve and expand the clientele."

In some places, professionals are afraid of evaluation because they fear what they may find (Henderson, Bialeschki, & Browne, 2017). However, at the best parks and museums, evaluation comes almost automatically. It helps to justify studying visitor experiences—what they do and what they wish they could do, what they learned and what they'd like to know more of, how interpreters did and how they might do better.

According to Henderson, Bialeschki, and Browne (2017), societal trends and changing attitudes toward accountability offer opportunities for evaluation: "Many organizations are seeking ways to show that what they do really makes a difference." Evaluation helps interpreters to check how closely they meet objectives, to determine cost-effectiveness, to provide evidence of interpretation's impact, and to guide policy and program planning. Evaluation stimulates improved interpretive programming to the public. Interpreters can demonstrate the value of their work in a systematic, convincing manner.

How To Evaluate

Evaluation may occur at all phases of the interpretive effort—before, during, and after the preparation of exhibits and signs, as well as talks, hikes, or special events. Evaluation can combine many approaches, using both qualitative and quantitative methods.

Qualitative evaluation describes what people might say or feel; the quantitative summarize results with numbers, scores, or costs. Both approaches may prove useful and many evaluations contain both, the strengths of one method complementing the other (Bitgood, 1988; Henderson, Bialeschki, & Browne, 2017).

> "Evaluation goes beyond intuitive assessment or self-serving guesses."

Evaluation goes beyond intuitive assessment or self-serving guesses, identified by indefinite phrases such as "well used," or "visitors seemed to enjoy it." The process of evaluation goes on constantly (Box 19.1). It can be done in-house and/or with the collaboration of an outside specialist at relatively low cost. Evaluation has little value unless it can result in some modification of the services provided.

Box 19.1
A Vision for Effective Interpretive Evaluation

1. Evaluation is an integral part of the management process.
2. All interpretive efforts should be evaluated.
3. The results of evaluation (both positive and negative) contribute to better achievement of an organization's mission.
4. Evaluation should be a continuous process.
5. Evaluation techniques are effective when appropriate for the environment, organization, and visitors.
6. Evaluation requires clear standards or goals.
7. Evaluation should occur at all levels and between levels.
8. Evaluation itself should be continuously assessed and modified where appropriate.

Source: National Association for Interpretation

Methods of Evaluation

This section presents several methods: insights from "becoming a visitor," evaluating individual performances, and audience or client-based evaluation techniques. The agents of evaluations include supervisors, peers or outside experts, self-evaluation, and audience responses. Each has advantages and problems, so combining them makes a more complete package to improve interpretive effectiveness.

Become A Visitor

Become a Visitor to Your Own Facility

One way to evaluate your service to your customers is to play the role as one of them. Put yourself in the shoes of the visitor *and* the nonvisitor. Temporarily erase your work perspective and see your site as a visitor might, as an unfamiliar place. Try to remember your first impressions, before you became part of the agency or company culture. Think about driving into the general region and not knowing about the interpretive opportunities available. Will the family in a private resort know about the state forest hikes and campfires just down the road?

> Put yourself in the shoes of the visitor *and* the nonvisitor.

Drive into your site and park in the *visitors'* parking lot; start from there. Ponder questions such as, where does the visit and interpretive experience begin? Does it begin in the parking lot? Or does the interpretive experience begin inside the visitor center, and if so, how far inside the building and why? Are visitors well oriented to the themes and how to experience the place intelligently? Do they encounter interpreters easily, at different times of the day? Where and how does the interpretive experience end? Wear the visitors' shoes for as long as you can. Take notes and use them to make changes to enhance service and reduce confusion.

Become a Visitor to Other Facilities

You also gain insight by becoming a visitor to similar interpretive sites. Go not as a professional interpreter but as an anonymous visitor seeking answers and experiences. Ask natural, normal questions about activities and programs, about features of the facility, about the big story. Take notes on what pleased you and what disappointed you. Review your own operation with these concerns in mind.

One state park interpreter made 15 such visits to other interpretive facilities. Only once did a staff person greet her. This quickly reinforced her own staff policy of greeting every group that enters her center and inviting them to ask questions. Most often, however, the results of visiting other places will come in the form of witnessing good, positive practices that will transfer easily to your site and provide better visitor service.

Evaluating Individual Performance

Supervisory Feedback

The most frequent and systematic evaluations occur in the area of personal performance evaluations. Auditing, critiquing, and coaching of an individual's talks occur routinely in most large museums, the National Park Service, many interpretive villages and parks, and some major county organizations, among many others. In some smaller organizations, direct auditing by supervisors or peers (attending the program and discussing it) occurs only rarely.

Some interpretive supervisors come from an interpretive background. Supervisors in many museums, parks, forests, and refuges, however, may have little interpretive experience and may have many other responsibilities. Whatever their background or job focus, their interest in a strong product requires them to evaluate the performance of the organization's interpreters—the paid professionals and the volunteers. Whatever the supervisor's workload, the interpretive performance deserves careful attention and evaluation; it represents the "sales force" and direct consumer contact part of the organization.

A supervisor's evaluation provides feedback to the interpreter for the improvement of individual programs. Supervisors also use this type of evaluation to determine the overall performance of the employee for continued employment or advancement. Therefore, the supervisor should plan frequent attendance at programs and regularly provide objective feedback to the interpreters with a set of notes or rating system complimented by notes.

> The supervisor should plan frequent attendance at programs and regularly provide objective feedback.

During job orientation and training sessions, supervisors should explain and discuss the criteria and system for evaluation. A list of supervisory evaluation points appears in Box 19.2. To make them easy to use, supervisors could make up a simple rating sheet. Rate each item on a 1-to-5 Likert scale and add written comments or explanations for some or all items. Itemizing this way helps to avoid sweeping generalized judgments. It helps the interpreter find specific strengths and areas to improve.

Box 19.2
Supervisory Evaluation Criteria for a Presentation

Interpreter
- Professional demeanor and appearance
- Arrives early for program
- Mixes with audience
- Establishes rapport
- Enthusiasm
- Depth of knowledge
- Poise and confidence
- Communicates with entire audience
- Appropriate use of humor
- Nonverbal communication
- Appropriate technical level
- Delivery (e.g., volume, pace, pronunciation)
- Reaction to unexpected situations
- Ability to answer questions

Program
- Interesting introduction
- Clear theme
- Organization (e.g., effective sequence, transitions, subtopics)
- Effective use of visuals
- Application of interpretive principles
- Diversity of communication strategies
- Accuracy of information
- Memorable, effective conclusion
- Audience reaction and involvement

In critiquing, supervisors should emphasize the positive. Reinforce what was done well, for example: "You did the introduction very well. Keep it up. Your identification skills are excellent. Both the audience and I sensed your interest in careful research of the plants and birds of this area."

As either the supervisor or the person being evaluated, concentrate on performance and results. Discuss the program, not the person. Avoid attacks or doubts about personality, physical attributes, or personal habits (unless they disrupt performance or disturb visitors).

Critiquing requires diplomacy and humility when one asks another person to change. The interpreter being critiqued has presumably spent some time and energy preparing the best presentation possible. The evaluator merely represents one response (hopefully an educated and sensitive one) to the message as heard. The evaluator can remind the interpreter that the views expressed may represent only one person in the audience.

Before the supervisor attends the event, an "involving interchange" might occur between the interpreter and the "critic" (Lewis, 1989). The supervisor might ask the interpreter, "On what aspects of your presentation do you most want feedback? How can I evaluate most usefully for you?" This can create a mood of collaboration that will drain off some of the dread and prepare for a calm and constructive post event meeting.

Interpreters need to accept that most supervisors have a level of education or experience that qualifies them to evaluate the work of subordinates. Even if they are not experts in interpretation, they can present helpful points of view. However, few supervisors have training in auditing or critiquing. Many of them have not practiced the diplomacy of positive evaluation. Therefore, interpreters need the emotional stability to react positively and analytically to an evaluation. They need to interpret the words as well-intentioned and appreciate the effort made by someone to help them improve their skills and service.

Few supervisors relish the role of critic. They do not want to argue with an interpreter about their appraisal of a program. They have little interest in hearing excuses. They do not want to deal with an individual who contests each suggestion or criticism. Rather, an auditor/evaluator will appreciate openness to feedback and desire to improve. Most supervisors prefer to act as coaches, not critics. Coaches teach and encourage as they critique. They seek to help the interpreter to grow. Although they may not say so, they will assume that the interpreter worked hard to prepare the presentation. When the supervisor's feedback proves insightful and useful, the interpreter does well to politely express appreciation for a high-quality evaluation that should help produce more polished, better service to the visitors.

Peer Evaluation

Another assessment may come by asking other interpreters to evaluate programs. They may come from the same organization or a neighboring organization. Sometimes, an outside subject-matter expert may prove to be valuable, especially when a program uses relatively new material.

> Critiquing others' programs gives insight regarding one's own.

Interpreters often evaluate programs of their peers. Critiquing others' programs gives insight regarding one's own. Noting effective strategies in the work of others as well as habits and approaches to avoid often become clear lessons for personal application. If an interpreter wants to get better, he or she will have to change.

Self-Evaluation

Frequently, interpreters have to rely on self-evaluation. This can work well, as the most efficient and least threatening method of evaluation. When possible record the presentation and play it back to find flaws of delivery. This technique dramatically reveals nervous tics, bad habits, and timing peculiarities.

With or without a recording, after each session ask yourself some key questions and record the answers on your own simple rating sheet (Box 19.3). Keep it simple, neutral, and nonthreatening. Study the answers. Watch the improvement.

This level of quick evaluation occurs shortly after each program. Interpreters can note key impressions in a journal or self-improvement notebook. Keep a list of topics that require more research or preparation. Then reinforce and reuse what worked best, drop problem segments from the presentation, and introduce or strengthen material where gaps or confusion existed. Avoid two contrasting tendencies that do *not* count as evaluation. One focuses only on negative faults and resigned, lament: "I'm a failure; I'll never be any good." The other asserts, unwaveringly, that "It went really well; they really like it, there is nothing more to be done"—the cheerleading self-delusion. Neither helps to improve the product and service. Improvement comes in small positive steps, sharpening the tools stroke by stroke. Make notes of the improvements.

> Personal evaluations will supplement supervisory and peer evaluations.

Interpreters should evaluate after every talk, hike, or other interpretive activity. Self-evaluation assigns value to the work. Many professional athletes and performers do this in their chosen crafts.

Box 19.3
Self-Evaluation Questions

After each presentation, ask yourself a short set of questions and record the answers with the title, date, and audience data. Keep a file and review regularly. Talk over problem areas with a supervisor.

In what ways did I show the following:
- Friendliness to visitors?
- High regard for resources, artifacts, exhibits?
- Concern for safety and welfare of visitors?
- Enthusiasm for the topic and audience?
- A high degree of preparation for the program?
- Application of interpretive principles?

How did I stimulate the curiosity of visitors?
How did I relate information to visitors' lives?
How did I reveal the essence of the theme with a unique perspective?
How did I treat the topic within a whole, broad context?
What kinds of active audience participation occurred?
What were the strengths that I will want to continue?
What weaknesses should I work on?
What are two things I can do to improve by tomorrow?

Personal evaluations will supplement supervisory and peer evaluations. Sometimes one will criticize oneself harder than will a supervisor. Nevertheless, the peer or supervisor will have insights and suggestions that may not occur to the individual being evaluated.

Observing The Visitors

Getting evaluation from the audience ranges from observing their reactions during a program and making instantaneous adjustments to gathering trend data over a season or several years. How the audience responds during a program provides instant feedback that an interpreter can put to immediate use. Direct observation shows attentiveness through smiles, laughter, intellectual response, and alert eyes. Careful observation of the audience during a walk or talk can reveal whether people are paying attention.

If visitors talk with each other, fidget, or leave the program, then something may be wrong. Adjust. If participants are tired or too cold on a hike to listen to the message, change the pace or the number and length of stops. Given the ubiquitous use of smartphones, it may be necessary to enforce a gentle policy of turning them off during a program in order to have a more rewarding overall experience and so as not to distract others (Beck & Dustin, 2016). Another possibility would be to include periodic "breaks" in which people can take selfies on the trail or at exhibits (as advocated by Museum Hack in Chapter 11) and check texts and social media, then once again focus on the activity at hand. Or fully make use of technologies throughout in such a way that also fosters engagement with the resource.

Three Periods of Evaluation

The museum exhibit field commonly recognizes three periods of evaluation (Serrell, 2015). These periods of evaluation may be effective when applied to zoo exhibits and other interpretive program activities as well. Traditionally, many exhibit or program evaluation decisions have been based on qualitative information gathered from interviews, focus groups, and questionnaires, although such methods have limitations and some controversy within the profession exists as indicated later in this chapter.

Front-End Evaluation

The period of evaluation that occurs *before* the program or debut of an exhibition is called front-end evaluation and generally occurs during the planning stages (Ward & Wilkinson, 2006). Front-end evaluation seeks information about the potential visitors—what they know, expect, and their level of experience with a topic. Furthermore, Serrell (2015) noted, "This information will be useful for creating interpretive opportunities for visitors to make new connections and to recollect old ones—what visitors are concerned about, what knowledge they feel confident about, what they are less certain of, or what misconceptions they have."

This type of evaluation can take the form of front-end interviews with a small, diverse sample of visitors. It may also take the form of focus groups in which facilitators can probe for more depth and breadth to extract rich, detailed data. However, in either case, there are limitations. Participants may provide answers they think the interviewer wants to hear. Furthermore, they don't necessarily always tell the truth or follow through and do what they say (Serrell, 2015).

Formative Evaluation

Formative evaluation is "conducted during the creation process to work out the bugs in content and presentation" (Falk & Dierking, 2013). Formative evaluation allows for change in the program during preparation or while an exhibit goes up. Staff and selected clients can study and rate alternate placements of rough drafts and large sketches of exhibits to assess receptivity and understanding. The same process could work for interpretive hikes that may involve dry runs with a few visitors to test the length of the route, key concepts, and alternative types of interactive activities.

Summative Evaluation

Summative evaluation focuses on how to make adjustments in the final product or to do it better next time. This also carries the names postperformance or postoccupancy evaluation (POE). Summative evaluation provides information about whether a new program or exhibit is indeed meeting educational and related goals. It informs how visitors understand and make use of the interpretation. Where change is feasible, it guides alterations.

The accuracy, timeliness, and effectiveness of programs within the overall interpretive mix benefits from periodic evaluation. This should result in updating some events or exhibits by deleting, adding, or altering the content. Current research findings may prompt changes in the content of certain programs. In other instances, new or different methods may replace the way programs or exhibits have been presented. For example, visitor attendance and interest evaluations may show a positive response when theater, music, and storytelling replace more traditional programs.

Assessment by staff experts can be supplemented by outside content specialists from universities, public agencies, or consulting firms. Outsiders serve a valuable role for topics of rapid technological or social change and highly controversial or technical topics.

Participant Evaluations

> "Assessment by staff experts can be supplemented by outside content specialists."

Several methods, such as suggestion boxes and verbal comments, give occasional and usually incomplete information, but *may* identify otherwise unforeseen issues. Similarly, participant evaluation has often come from individual responses to written questionnaires or formal interviews. If conducted in a scientifically valid way, these *may* provide useful feedback to interpreters and managers. Researchers at nearby universities or private sector research firms can assist with making these quantitative research approaches into more precise, valid and powerful tools (Figure 19.2). Although concerns exist over disrupting visitor experiences, *brief* questioning methods did not appear to interfere with normal activities of participants of a study focused on health issues for outdoor recreationists in resorts and parks throughout North America (Beck et. al., 2016).

Evaluating the real output—the impact of interpretive programs on visitors—often prompts considerable debate. More than three decades ago, Dustin and McAvoy (1985) suggested that deeper contributions of interpreters to the participant experience are intangible and beyond the bounds of measurement practices. Some aspects of the interpretive experience are indeed ineffable and defy evaluation of outcomes. Nonetheless, researchers have strived to determine various participant responses to interpretive experiences. Qualitative structured interviews have *potential* for exploring some of the deeper meanings. Questions traditionally used the following open-ended style:

Figure 19.2. University researcher armed with clipboards and questionnaires awaits visitors to Cumberland Island National Seashore. (RS)

- Explain what this setting means to you.
- Was that meaning enriched by interpretive efforts?
- Which of the interpretive facilities did you use?
- Explain what you liked most and least about each.
- How valuable were the interpretive services to your enjoyment of the area?
- How could your experience at this site be a life-enriching one, if at all?

Respondents answer such subjective questions in their own words. Condensed transcriptions of the recorded narratives and content analysis summarize the responses. Enumeration counts the frequency of key words or phrases, which can be supplemented by representative respondent testimony. The popular phenomenological or qualitative evaluation has greatest value in documenting the richness of experience that interpretation can produce.

Focus Groups

Another tool used to assess reactions of visitors to programs and facilities provides qualitative information through the focus group approach. This amounts to structured or unstructured group interviews with about 10 participants. Discussion focuses on interpretive services. Visitors who are willing to participate meet in a group and respond to questions about what they did and did not like about various interpretive services.

> "Some aspects of the interpretive experience are indeed ineffable and defy evaluation of outcomes."

Before conducting a focus group, a *sampling plan* should be created to allow researchers to meticulously choose "sources" for the data collection process. These willing participants can be employed from a multitude of recruitment efforts. The first type, *random sampling*, allows all potential participants to have an equal chance of being selected and therefore the findings from the focus group may be generalizable to larger populations. The second type of sampling is a *convenience* or *opportunistic sample* that offers researchers a fairly inexpensive way to gather data in a timely manner. Additionally, researchers may collect data using *maximum variation samples* where outliers, underrepresented, or marginalized data are represented to ensure the inclusion of ideas, notions, and topics by a wide range of individuals (Tracy, 2013).

Focus groups tend to foster an informative type conversation by using structured or unstructured interviews. A structured interview often uses an *interview schedule* that reads exactly the same across all focus group sessions, in the same order, similar to that of a script in which the facilitator does not deviate from the set of questions provided. An unstructured interview allows for more organic conversation and allows for side-conversations and focus group flexibility. Generally, an *interview guide* promotes conversation rather than dictating it (Tracy, 2013). Although frequently used, a focus group is not *usually* a representative sample of visitors and has other limitations (Graves, 2013). Its strength is in identifying potential preferences, existing issues or concerns, and potential solutions.

Cautions About Evaluation

"If I'd asked people what they wanted, they would have said a faster horse."
–Henry Ford

Robert Bixler is a professor and researcher at Clemson University. In a thematic issue of *Legacy* (the magazine of the National Association for Interpretation) Bixler (2014) wrote a provocative article titled "Evaluation? Don't Bother!" as the concluding feature story. According to Bixler, "Skeptical social scientists, with the help of neuroscientists working with fMRI, a brain scanner that measures what parts of the brain become active and in what order when a stimulus or problem are presented, are documenting that many results of surveys are not valid" (Box 19.4).

Box 19.4
Cautions About Evaluation Methods
Robert Bixler, Associate Professor, Clemson University

A common rationale for conducting evaluations is that human perception and judgment are flawed in so many ways. Typically, research and evaluation are recommended as checks and balances on our biases. Yet, in the last 20 years scrutiny of social science research has shown itself also to be of questionable accuracy. ATM machines and Red Bull were rejected by focus groups. Managers followed their supposedly flawed gut instincts and launched these successful products anyway. Coca Cola tested new Coke with 200,000 people before launching that colossal marketing failure. Over 80% of new products and services fail, even though most were tested by the best marketing researchers major corporations can buy.

While evaluations of interpretive programs may produce useful information, each project must be carefully designed. Unfortunately, most evaluations depend on surveys, interviews and focus groups. When an evaluator asks someone a question about something they have not already thought about, the evaluator is evoking thoughts that would not have naturally occurred within the participant. The results of closed-ended questions from survey research and much of the results of interviews are "artifacts" of the questions asked. Unless the evaluator can show that the explicit questions asked are the same types of discussion the program attendee would *naturally* have had with friends, relatives or children, then the evaluation results were fabricated by the research process.

One area where research on interpretation has been supremely effective is exhibit design. Evaluations of exhibits have disproportionately used covert observation of visitor behavior. Changes in the exhibits are progressively made until they are working as designed. Evaluations of interpretive services are at their best when actual behavior is measured.

The following example of an interpretive program designed to reduce littering illustrates a reasonable design, even though it failed in the end. The interpretive program was designed to test messages designed to reduce littering in parks by school children. After the anti-littering message (the treatment) was delivered to half the school groups, both the treatment and control groups were given candy in paper wrappers. The measure of success was the number of wrappers thrown on the ground.

This design met the first design criterion for a realistic evaluation as it measured actual behavior. Secondly, the audience was unaware they were being studied. When people know they are being studied, they engage in much higher self-monitoring than they would otherwise. The third design issue is whether the desired behavior was measured in the same time frame that it would naturally occur. Littering behaviors occur in a matter of a second. Observing whether littering occurred did not require taking several minutes to complete a questionnaire or an in-depth interview. The fourth design criterion is whether the behavior is likely to naturally occur where it is being measured. Here the evaluation design failed.

By first grade, a vast majority of children know that littering is unacceptable. Littering is generally done inconspicuously to avoid being caught. In the presence of rangers, teachers, chaperones, and tattle-tale peers, children are unlikely to litter. This evaluation design, while stronger than most, failed because the behavior to be observed does not commonly occur in the setting it was measured: Neither the treatment or the control groups littered!

Any organization with several staff should designate a person to take responsibility for developing evaluation protocols. Along with learning standard program evaluation techniques the issues raised above should be well understood. In *The Illusion of Public Opinion*, George Bishop (2005) provides extensive evidence that surveys fabricate the attitudes they purport to measure. In *Consumer.ology*, Philip Graves (2013) provides a scathing critique of marketing research methods that is both entertaining and troubling. *Realistic Evaluation* by Ray Pawson and Nick Tilley (1997) provides extensive discussion of how to design behavior-based, context-sensitive evaluations. In addition, *Fooled by Randomness* by Nassim Nicholas Taleb (2004), *Thinking, Fast and Slow* by Daniel Kahneman (2011), and *You Are Not So Smart* by David McRaney (2011) are excellent resources. [Full citations for these books are provided at the end of the chapter under *Literature Cited*.]

With certain cautions in mind, Bixler (2014) suggested many possible ways to gauge the success of interpretive programs based on actual visitor behavior:

> Evaluators may want to explore the use of videotaping audiences for changes in attention and emotional reactions during programs, tracking the percentage of audience members who retrieve relevant handouts at the end of a program, facial coding, eye tracking, number of visitors electing to attend additional programs or events, number and types of questions asked, implicit association tests, and some types of experimental designs.

With a fuller understanding of current concerns related to evaluation methods, interpreters and administrators are better prepared to recognize limitations of some methods and pursue evaluation accordingly.

Observations of Actual Behavior

Going all the way back to the 1970s, the Forest Service developed and tested various methods for taping or observing visitor behavior during a presentation. This allowed post program analysis of both positive and negative actions. A similar "eye on the visitor" has traditionally recorded visitor actions in exhibit halls in museum settings. The benefit of such methods, as noted above, is that they track actual visitor behavior. For example, the Muir Woods National Monument gathered video camera footage at wayside exhibits to provide valuable insight on visitor preferences and visitor learning behaviors (Koenen, Legg, & Darville, 2007). More recently the advent of GPS tracking in phones and other hand-held devices allows researchers to monitor traffic patterns and time spent at specific locations within an interpretive site. These can produce a visual "heat map" of visitor movements and indicate where people congregate and linger, thereby informing the evaluation interpretive effectiveness.

Unobtrusive observation has traditionally occurred in exhibit halls to provide information about the attraction and holding power of exhibits and labels. That is, the use of exhibits by visitors lends itself to straightforward observations of their actual behavior. Bixler (2014) noted, "Changes made based on findings from these observation-based evaluations can be rapidly made, allowing us to see if evaluation results actually improve visitors' use of exhibits."

Cost-Effectiveness for Program Evaluation

A few interpreters have reacted to messages about evaluating productivity as if they were threats of some kind—almost as if revealing attendance figures would jeopardize their job or future funding. Others argue that "the numbers game" (as some would put it) will automatically dilute quality. These arguments aside, the manager must live with quantitative measures. Scarce resources often get allocated to programs and individuals with *growing* numbers.

> "Unobtrusive observation has traditionally occurred in exhibit halls to provide information about the attraction and holding power of exhibits and labels."

Counts of attendance help the interpreter first by signaling needs to adjust the timing of events, the content, or the activity mixes. Cost-effectiveness data allow comparisons among program efforts, to guide selection of more productive use of interpreters' time. Most interpreters seek to spread the message of the importance and meaning of their resources to as many as possible.

> "Counts of attendance help the interpreter first by signaling needs to adjust the timing of events, the content, or the activity mixes."

Cost-effectiveness evaluation presents comparative information. This calculates the costs per visitor contact hour for all types of programs (Yarde & Knudson, 1989).

For example, a sunrise hike may cost $200 to prepare and conduct (staff time). If 50 people attend for one hour, the cost is $4 per visitor contact hour. This can compare to an evening illustrated talk with 150 participants for one hour that costs $300 to prepare and conduct. This program's cost adds up to $2 per visitor contact hour.

Simple recordkeeping allows this method to operate over an entire season at low cost, thus smoothing out the vicissitudes of weather and flux in visitor numbers. This system allows the interpreters themselves to evaluate the effectiveness of the various types of programs, at least in comparative monetary terms. Cost-effectiveness allows comparisons among the various personal services, determining whether one or another merits some extra attention. For example, if 1 p.m. museum tours or nature hikes draw only a few visitors, the interpreters can try different times and keep track of the response.

Cost-effectiveness data, based on real attendance figures, permit comparisons that go beyond anecdotal memories. They allow analysis of the whole programming effort, through a season or the year. The systematic, numerical counts, with the hours spent in the program in preparation, and in travel, will give interpreters and programmers much more to go on than a "lots of people came and liked it" type of report. It gives interpreters facts to help develop the optimal mix of program types and schedules, based on visitor attendance.

Cost-effectiveness data provide administrators with a firm base for support of interpretive programs. They can cite facts such as "Our interpretive program served 100,000 people at a cost of 49¢ per visitor contact hour." As one of several measures, it helps comprise evaluation at its best.

Total Program Analysis

A basic step involves gathering year-to-year data for the agency or park program. This often comes from annual reports. For example, an annual activity report might show total attendance of 250,000 at 3,500 activities. Breaking this down, perhaps exhibit center visits accounted for more visits than any other type of offering, followed by interpretive walks, special events, campfire programs, and Junior Naturalist sessions.

> "Cost-effectiveness data provide administrators with a firm base for support of interpretive programs."

The data can show how many programs each interpreter (or team) gave, and the average attendance. The numbers can break into activity categories. Data on attendance at each of these activities provides further information for evaluation and future strategy planning.

Several criteria figure into the total program analysis, including the following:

- Number and kinds of services offered
- Number of visitors contacted
- Reactions of visitors to facilities and programs
- Some measure of actual impact on the visitors
- Benefits of the overall interpretive program
- Cost-effectiveness measures

Total program analysis can lead to discussions in staff meetings. Giving the whole process over to a small committee leaves others feeling excluded and therefore not particularly ready to accept the results. A mix of informal and formal (written) discussion and questioning should include the whole staff. Then, a few people can compile data and opinions on the tough issues, bringing them back to the whole staff for discussion.

A small group of five or fewer people can operate as a committee of the whole, developing and responding to a set of questions and then making positive, constructive suggestions. In some cases, any size group may benefit from outside intervention. An outside observer and facilitator can depersonalize the discussion and solicit opinions from everyone, especially the less assertive people who seldom express themselves.

Summary

Interpreters and managers evaluate interpretation for support and survival, and to provide better service. They evaluate to assign value to the work. They evaluate to know whom they reach and how well. Interpreters evaluate to identify and retain what works best for their clients as well as what needs improvement. They measure strengths as well as weaknesses. In sum, the entire interpretive program merits serious, systematic, open, fair analysis. Purposeful evaluation can uplift the individual interpreter and the institution, while providing better service to the interpretive customers.

Without evaluation as recommended in this chapter, interpreters have little basis for asking for new funding, new positions, and continuing support. Likewise, without evaluation, the interpreters and curators have only a vague sense of how effectively their programs serve the public—or even what portion of the public is being served.

With evaluation, however, interpreters can put a value on their work and astutely improve it. Since the intent of evaluation is to improve circumstances, then, by definition, quality interpretive evaluation methods and the interpretation that follows makes for a better world.

"The test of the artist does not lie in the will with which he goes to work, but in the excellence of the work he produces."
–Thomas Aquinas

Note to reader: We felt that a chapter on evaluation needed some levity. Therefore, the latter part of the caption for Figure 19.1 isn't entirely serious.

Literature Cited

Beck, L., & Dustin, D. (2016). Technology on the trails. *Legacy, 27*(6), 20–22.

Beck, L., Walkosz, B., Andersen, P., Abbott, A., Buller, D., Scott, M., & Eye, R. (2016). Communication strategies to promote health: Sun safety in outdoor recreation settings. *Journal of Interpretation Research, 20*(2), 41–50.

Bishop, G. (2005). *The illusion of public opinion.* Lanham, MD: Rowman & Littlefield.

Bitgood, S. (1988). Visitor evaluation: What is it? *Visitor Behavior, 3*(3), 6–7.

Bixler, R. (2014). Evaluation? Don't bother! *Legacy, 25*(4), 21–23.

Dustin, D., & McAvoy, L. (1985). Interpretation as a management tool: A dissenting opinion. *The Interpreter, 16,* 18–20.

Falk, J., & Dierking, L. (2013). *The museum experience revisited.* Walnut Creek, CA: Left Coast Press.

Graves, P. (2013). *Consumer.ology.* Boston, MA: Nicholas Brealey Publishing.

Henderson, K., Bialeschki, M. D., & Browne, L. (2017). *Evaluating recreation services* (4th ed.). Urbana, IL: Sagamore-Venture.

Kahneman, D. (2011). *Thinking, fast and slow.* New York, NY: Farrar, Straus and Giroux.

Koenen, S., Legg, M., & Darville, R. (2007). Monitoring visitor behavior at interpretive waysides at Muir Woods National Monument. *2007 interpretive sourcebook.* NAI National Workshop, Wichita, KS.

Lewis, W. (1989). Some thoughts on critiquing. *Journal of Interpretation, 13*(1), 19–20.

McRaney, D. (2011). *You are not so smart.* New York, NY: Penguin Random House.

National Association for Interpretation. (1990). *Preparing for the 21st Century: Solving management problems through interpretation.* Ft. Collins, CO: NAI.

Pawson, R., & Tilley, N. (1997). *Realistic evaluation.* Thousand Oaks, CA: SAGE Publications.

Serrell, B. (2015). *Exhibit labels: An interpretive approach.* Lanham, MD: Rowman & Littlefield.

Taleb, N. (2004). *Fooled by randomness.* New York, NY: Random House.

Tracy, S. J. (2013). *Qualitative research methods.* West Sussex, UK: Wiley-Blackwell.

Ward, C., & Wilkinson, A. (2006). *Conducting meaningful interpretation.* Golden, CO: Fulcrum Publishing.

Wells, M., Lovejoy, V., & Welch, D. (2009). *Creating more meaningful visitor experiences: Planning for interpretation and education.* United States Department of the Interior, Bureau of Reclamation, Policy and Program Services, Denver Federal Center, Denver, Colorado.

Yarde, N., & Knudson, D. (1989). Cost effectiveness of interpretive programs. In *Proceedings, National Interpreters Workshop.* Ft. Collins, CO: National Association for Interpretation.

SECTION VI

Growth of the Profession

CHAPTER 20

Global Interpretation

Can interpretation increase literacy among children? It is doing just that in Mexico. Teaching interpretive principles and best practices is usually done with college students and adult volunteers or professionals. But in Baja California Sur, Mexico, high school students receive interpretation training to prepare for careers in ecotourism. An NGO called Social and Environmental Formation and Innovation (SEFI) works with local schools in poor fishing villages where most young children join their fathers in fishing rather than continuing their education. Director Mario Escalera uses approaches he learned in the NAI Certified Interpretive Guide curriculum to train young people for alternative careers in ecotourism. He teaches these children to develop program outlines and themes, and includes periods of personal reflection on meanings and relevancy. Storytelling is also taught to these young people. Training these students for a career in ecotourism has conservation implications because when children join their fathers in fishing, they eventually branch off on their own and fish illegally without the proper permits and limits. This results in overfishing and destruction of the fisheries.

However, Mario's program is more than merely a vocational training program. Generally, people think of interpretation as provoking conservation of cultural or natural heritage. But this program uses interpretation to provoke reading of classic books and to foster a setting where children will be changed by those books. Weekend campouts are organized by SEFI around a book such as *The Little Prince, Lord of the Flies, Diary of Anne Frank,* or *20,000 Leagues under the Sea.* The high school students use the interpretive principles, techniques, and activities (e.g., games, skits, hands-on crafts) they learned to interpret themes and passages from these books to elementary school children. This program has been a tremendous success in getting children to read classics and in giving the older students valuable experience in developing their interpretive techniques. Perhaps the most significant result of these camping trips is personal growth. On these book-based camping trips, shy students gain confidence. Problem students often become more cooperative and sociable. Through the readings students learn about themselves, their passions and potential to contribute to their communities. After a weekend camping trip centered on the *Lord of the Flies*, one student said, "We came as a divided group, but we are going home as one entire group." That message of unity is one that will be brought back to their schools and communities and carried with them throughout their lives.

Interpretation is not only a *noble* profession; it is a *global* profession. From cruise ships skirting the icebergs of Antarctica to icebreaker cruises in the Arctic, interpreters share knowledge and inspiration with audiences at the ends of the earth. Between these extremes, opportunities for interpretation abound. The International Union for the Conservation of Nature (IUCN) recognizes 209,000 designated protected areas in 193 countries and territories. These include national parks, wilderness areas, and wildlife refuges. The United Nations Educational, Scientific and Cultural Organization (UNESCO) has designated 1,052 World Heritage Sites of which 814 are cultural sites. Most of these protected areas and World Heritage Sites benefit from written or personal interpretation. Add to those the incalculable number of local, regional, or national sites worldwide that benefit from interpretation and it is apparent interpretation covers the globe.

International Interpretation: Innovations and Inspirations

The global spread of interpretation has resulted in thousands of bright and creative individuals being added to the growing cadre of interpreters and these people have made tremendous contributions toward advancing the profession. Here are just a few examples:

- In Germany, Dr. Anna Chatel may have been the first professor of interpretation to have students create interpretive apps for trails and parks. Student-designed apps direct visitors into and through the Black Forest (Figure 20.1). Additionally, she and her colleagues have used GPS monitoring to evaluate the use of interpretive trails and kiosks in the Black Forest. These data indicate which interpretive kiosks hikers stop at and how long they stay there. Dr. Chatel and her colleagues at the University of Freiburg have been leaders in taking digital interpretation into the field.

Figure 20.1. Dr. Anna Chatel and her colleague Monika Nethe at the University of Freiburg, Germany teach their students how to create their own interpretive apps for the Black Forest and then evaluate them. (AC)

- Aotearoa New Zealand—the full name often used for the country—is a country that has woven its indigenous people's culture throughout the fabric of 21st century life. Maori language, art, and customs are celebrated across all dimensions of public life in New Zealand. Here Maori culture is incorporated into most mainstream interpretive efforts regardless if the subject is nature or history. The Maori are interpreted at world-class museums such at the Museum of New Zealand Te Papa Tongarewa in Wellington and at important tourist destinations such as Rotorua where tourists experience and learn about Maori culture. Interpretive programs often honor Maori traditions by beginning with a *pōwhiri*, a central part of Māori protocol. It is a ceremony of welcome between *tangata whenua* (hosts) and *manuhiri* (visitors). The *pōwhiri* signifies the two groups coming together as one. Interpretive programs for youth include Auckland Council's innovative Maori and the Forest: Learning through Experience Program. This school-based curriculum takes children outdoors to teach them traditional Maori uses of the forest, how they hunted, what they ate, traditional fire-making, and their medicinal uses of plants. Children also learn vocabulary in the Maori language about these subjects and activities. In Aotearoa New Zealand, indigenous interpretation is seen as a critically important and growing component of quality interpretation (Figure 20.2).

Figure 20.2. In New Zealand, Maori interpreter Joe Harawira sometimes begins by interpreting the stories in tattoos on his face. (TC)

- Situated in southeast Siberia, Lake Baikal is the oldest and deepest lake in the world. Containing 20% of the world's freshwater, the lake is known as the "Galapagos of Russia" with many endemic species including the nerpa—a freshwater seal. Here in Siberia, professional interpretation is thriving with Certified Interpretive Guides and passionate interpreters working to build a tourism industry based upon experiences that are both sustainable and interpretive (Figure 20.3). Box 20.1 tells the story of interpretation's presence in this remote, yet stunningly beautiful, region.

Figure 20.3. A father and daughter, who is a NAI-Certified Interpretive Guide, explain the work that went into developing the interpretive trail across the Siberian landscape. (CL)

Box 20.1
Interpretation Enhancing Ecotourism Around Lake Baikal
Chuck Lennox, Founder and Owner, Lennox Insites

Soon after Lake Baikal was designated as a World Heritage Site in 1996, Ariadna Reida came from Siberia to the United States to earn a graduate degree in environmental studies at The Evergreen State College in Washington State with a special focus on ecotourism development at Lake Baikal.

Upon her return to Russia, Ariadna met at length with Andrei Suknev, a local expert on ecotourism. Together they sat down with local national park directors and other friends from around the lake to plan The Great Baikal Trail. This new NGO would bring together local volunteers and leaders from all corners of Russia (and from around the world) to build trails for use by residents and visiting tourists and to help provide environmental education opportunities for village schools and local communities.

Box 20.1 continued

In 2010, during a trip to the area that included extended time in the field with local guides, Jean MacGregor (a faculty member at Evergreen State whom Ariadna had met during her graduate studies) realized that heritage interpretation and its principles were unfamiliar to her Russian hosts. Jean, Ariadna and their Russian colleagues hatched the idea of bringing multiple delegations of tour guides and park staff to the U.S. to experience the National Association of Interpretation's (NAI's) Certified Interpretive Guide Course (CIG). Several delegations over the years have been part of this course and its subsequent tours.

The CIG Course was an opportunity for the Russians to learn about interpretation alongside their American colleagues. And, in turn, it gave the American CIG participants the chance to learn more about a very different country, its outstanding natural beauty, and ways of life. Following this CIG training, each Russian delegation would travel with their American leaders around the U.S. Pacific Northwest and/or Southwest, to observe interpretation on the ground in parks, zoos, museums, forests and other settings. Through these field experiences, they saw first-hand the value of interpretation and its potential for supporting the important work of protected areas, government ministries, museums, and tour operations.

Participants in these training and study tours were chosen carefully with the hope that they would return home to share interpretive principles with their networks around Russia. In return, American experts including government agency personnel were invited to Lake Baikal to help lead seminars and promote the value of interpretation to a variety of audiences including students of tourism and recreation at regional universities, museum staff, and educators, as well as many other aspiring guides and interpreters.

As ecotourism has grown around Lake Baikal, interpretation has emerged as a communication strategy for guiding visitors around parks and protected areas and at the historical sites in the larger cities and villages in the region. Our Russian colleagues have discovered that they need to work with grassroots communities—in tandem with those at a management level—to explain the value of interpretation. Due to the difference in our cultures, the new leaders of Russian interpretive programs have made sure to adjust how interpretation is explained and practiced. Direct translation from English to Russian cannot always suffice. For example, the English word "interpretation" as we know it does not have an equivalent in Russian.

As interest has grown in interpretation around Russia, more and more groups and individuals are now curious about this new communication strategy. Both the Russians and Americans have learned a lot about themselves, their respective cultures, and above all, about interpretation in international settings. With support and encouragement from their American colleagues, the alumni from these U.S.-based training courses have formed a Siberian Association for Interpretation (SAI). The cooperation of different organizations, agencies, ministries, universities, and foundations has helped this once nascent movement to grow steadily over the last 15 years, where everyone is supporting each other to expand the reach of interpretation around the world.

The Global Spread of Professionalism

The history of the profession of interpretation has been covered previously, but a review of professional interpretation organizations illustrates the spread of the profession from the United States to other countries and continents. The earliest professional organization strictly focused on interpretation was the Association of Interpretive Naturalists (AIN). AIN grew out of informal meetings with state park naturalists in the mid-1950s. Over the next 50 years,

> A review of professional interpretation organizations illustrates the spread of the profession from the United States to other countries and continents.

professional organizations sprouted up in developed countries around the world. (See Box 20.2). These professional organizations are supplemented with many informal associations such as the Slovenian Interpretation Association (interpretacija.si) and networks built primarily around Facebook pages such as Interpretazione Ambientale-Professione Futuro in Italy administered by Maurilio Ciapparone a leading figure in Italian heritage interpretation. Opening each of the links in Box 20.2 will give the reader an inspirational and informative tour of the wide world of interpretation.

Box 20.2
Professional Interpretation Organizations

Note how dates of establishment illustrate the spread of the interpretation profession around the world.

* Organization no longer exists

1961	Association of Interpretive Naturalists (AIN) (informal meetings started in 1954)*
1969	Western Interpreters Association (WIA)*
1970	Association for Living History, Farm and Agricultural Museums http://alhfam.org/
1973	Interpretation Canada www.interpscan.ca
1975	Association for Heritage Interpretation (originally Society for the Interpretation of Britain's Heritage) www.ahi.org.uk
1983	Association of Missouri Interpreters www.mointerp.net
1985	Heritage Interpretation International*
1988	National Association for Interpretation (from merger of AIN and WIA) www.interpnet.com
1992	Interpretation Australia Association www.interpretationaustralia.asn.au
1997	Interpret Scotland www.interpretscotland.org.uk
1997	Mountain Parks Heritage Interpretation Association (now Interpretive Guides Association (Canada) interpretiveguides.org
2001	Interpret Wales www.interpretwales.org
2002	Association for the Interpretation of Heritage (Spain) www.interpretaciondelpatrimonio.com
2007	Interpretation Network New Zealand www.innz.net.nz
2010	Interpret Europe: European Association for Heritage Interpretation (began as an informal network in 2000) www.interpret-europe.net
2011	SIMID, the Czech Association for Heritage Interpretation http://www.dobrainterpretace.cz/
2016	Portuguese Interpretation Association for Natural and Cultural Heritage www.interpretare.pt
2016	The Siberian Association for Interpretation of Natural and Cultural Heritage https://www.facebook.com/siberian.association.for.interpretation/
2017	Interpret Croatia www.interpretirajmo-hrvatsku.hr
2017	Interpret Switzerland–The Swiss Association for Heritage Interpretation www.interpret-europe.net (see contacts links)

The first interpretation organization with an international scope was Heritage Interpretation International (HII) founded in Canada in the early 1980s. HII's mission was to bring global perspectives to the support of national and regional interpretive organizations, offer an international congress every third year, and create a global network of professional interpreters and interpretation organizations for the exchange of information or assistance. In 1985, HII held the First World Congress on Heritage Presentation and Interpretation in Banff. The Second World Congress was held in 1988 in Warwick, England, and resulted in the publication of a noteworthy two-volume set of books based on the papers given at the Congress (Uzzell, 1989). At HII's Third Global Congress in 1991, attendees from 35 countries drafted a Charter and submitted it to the

United Nations. This "Honolulu Charter" called attention to "the indispensable roles of heritage interpretation and preservation in the provision of quality tourism experiences" and stated "unique local heritages must be interpreted, not only to visiting guests, but to community residents themselves." The United Nations charter stated "heritage interpretation principles, practices, and heritage identity preservation, are at the very core of tourism development approaches such as cultural tourism and ecotourism." (Tabata, Yamashiro, & Cherem, 1992). The last HII Global Congress was held in Sydney Australia in 1996.

The effort to connect interpreters internationally continued into the 21st century with NAI providing leadership. In the early 2000s, NAI organized volunteer interpretive planning and design consultancy trips to China. Then in 2006 NAI organized their first International Interpretation Conference in Puerto Rico. This conference attracted attendees from more than 30 countries. Since then NAI has offered international conferences annually in partnership with local interpretation groups in such diverse locations as Panama, Korea, Mexico, and Sweden (Figure 20.4). By 2006, NAI had members from 32 countries and had conducted certification courses in numerous countries from Kenya to China. Beginning in 2008, Canadian Duane Fast provided leadership for an International Section of NAI and a website and online network called International Interpretation.

Figure 20.4. A first-person living history portrayal of botanist Carl Linnaeus in his garden delights attendees of a joint NAI and Interpret Europe conference in Sweden. (TC)

Interpreters in the United Kingdom and on the European continent have a long history of excellence in interpretation, particularly in museums and cultural heritage sites. NAI played a supportive role in helping coalesce an existing network of European interpreters into a single group called Interpret Europe. In 2009, NAI organized an international conference in Greece. An initiative group was formed, and the following year, Interpret Europe: The European Association for Heritage Interpretation was founded at an assembly in Slovenia. At its first annual conference held in Freiburg, Germany, in 2011, participants drafted and signed the Freiburg Declaration, a strong statement guiding the interpretive profession in Europe and elsewhere (Box 20.3). Interpret Europe has become an active and strong organization bringing together interpreters from all over the world for formal training (as described in Chapter 17), collegiality, and inspiration.

Global Challenges: Professional Recognition and Training

In many countries, heritage interpretation is not considered a profession. This hampers government recognition and associated government benefits such as health care and education. Indeed, often interpretation is carried out in an unprofessional manner. At some of the world's most important heritage sites, interpretive guides are illiterate local people who while growing up near the site may have learned foreign languages from tourists. Sometimes local children serve as the only tour guides. In many places, these local interpreters must take a knowledge test about the site to become an official guide licensed by local, regional, or national tourism agencies, but sometimes that is the only requirement to serve visitors.

Box 20.3
The Freiburg Declaration on Heritage Interpretation

We, the participants at the first annual conference of Interpret Europe, held in Freiburg in July 2011, address this declaration to:
- Governmental and nongovernmental policy making bodies at international, European, national, regional, and local levels
- Owners and operators responsible for the conservation, management, and presentation of natural and cultural heritage sites, including museums
- Tourism industry organizations and host destinations
- Local, minority, and shared-interest communities
- Educational and training institutions and organizations
- Professional and voluntary heritage interpreters

We believe that:
- Natural and cultural heritage play an essential part, in terms of biodiversity, history, sense of place, and community inheritance, in the life and development of the people of Europe as a whole and of their own regions and localities.
- Heritage interpretation plays an important role in presenting and explaining this heritage and encouraging people across Europe to appreciate both the distinct and the common elements of their shared and continually developing heritage.
- Heritage interpretation acts as a force for the greater good and can make a substantial contribution to education for sustainable development, to sustainable tourism, and to increased economic and social benefits for host communities.
- There is an urgent need, throughout Europe, for increased knowledge about the value of heritage interpretation among responsible bodies, and the promotion of good practice in heritage interpretation through the training of professional and volunteer interpreters.
- Heritage interpretation contributes to the cultural and environmental aims of international agreements, including the ICOMOS Charter on Interpretation and Presentation of Cultural Heritage.

In support of this declaration, we advocate a number of actions:

We advocate that governmental and nongovernmental policy-making bodies:
- Formulate policies that recognize the role of heritage interpretation, ensure the provision of resources to implement these policies, and foster appropriate professional standards among site operators and interpretation practitioners.
- Ensure that these policies are consistent with the demands of heritage conservation and sustainable development through consultation with, and involvement of, heritage professionals, site operators, and local communities.

Box 20.3 continued

- Encourage and support cooperation in the promotion and realization of more professional heritage interpretation and ensure that it is socially, culturally, and intellectually responsible, and recognizes the importance of minorities of all kinds.
- Support and promote the development and implementation of international guidelines, codes of ethics, and principles of good practice for interpretation.
- Support and promote educational and training programs for heritage professionals and volunteers to establish and enhance their knowledge of heritage interpretation philosophy and their skills in delivery.
- Support and promote academic and social research into the effectiveness and impact of heritage interpretation on sites and communities.

We advocate that owners and operators of heritage sites:
- Operate their sites using accepted principles of good heritage interpretation so that they contribute to the conservation of heritage to visitors' understanding and to the social and economic well-being of host communities.
- Recognize that good interpretive facilities and activities make a substantial contribution to the ethical, social, cultural, and financial success of their sites.
- Ensure that the design, development, and operation of interpretive facilities and activities achieve high standards, including those related to sense of place, host community interests and aspirations, lack of discrimination, and accessibility to all.
- Cooperate with research institutions to develop adequate and practical means of providing quality interpretation at heritage sites to ensure their sustainability.

We advocate that tourism promotion organizations and host destinations:
- Support and accurately promote heritage sites which make best use of interpretation to ensure authentic and satisfying visitor experiences and to enhance the social and economic benefits to host communities.
- Provide educational institutions with relevant data and information to support research into the effectiveness and impact of heritage interpretation.

We advocate that local, minority, and shared-interest communities:
- Sustain and interpret their unique tangible and intangible heritage to create an increased sense of worth and share it widely to develop greater mutual understanding.

We advocate that education and training institutions and organizations:
- Develop courses, programs, and vocational training courses to educate and train heritage professionals and interpreters and to disseminate knowledge of the principles and practice of heritage interpretation and its good practice.
- Develop and promote academic and social research into the effectiveness and impact of heritage interpretation on natural and cultural heritage sites, tourism destinations and local communities.

We advocate that professional and voluntary heritage interpreters:
- Employ the principles and good practice of interpretation to present and explain the significance of natural and cultural heritage generally and specifically and to encourage the understanding and appreciation of local cultural and social beliefs and traditions, skills, arts, and crafts.

The lack of professional recognition results in a lack of opportunities for professional training, particularly in developing countries. In Grant Sharpe's classic 20th century textbook, Sutton (1982) noted regarding nature interpretation, "Since protection against poaching, vested interests, political pressures, and other threats is the first order of business in new national park systems, interpretive installations are not generally as advanced in developing countries..." He added, "The need for interpretation is especially acute in countries where national consciousness of conservation has not fully manifested itself." Unfortunately, the observation made by Sutton is still true many decades later. If interpretation training happens at all in these underdeveloped countries, it happens in the broader context of park ranger or wildlife tour guide training.

> "The need for interpretation is especially acute in countries where national consciousness of conservation has not fully manifested itself."

This lack of recognition of nature interpretation being a distinct profession manifests itself even in developed countries such as South Africa and Argentina. In South Africa the Field Guides Association of South Africa is devoted to training guides who take people into game reserves on foot or in safari vehicles. Private training providers such as The Nature College (naturecollege.co.za) and the Limpopo Field Guide Training South Africa (limpopotraining.co.za) help potential guides achieve national guiding qualifications. They provide training in "bush knowledge," wildlife management, and animal behavior. These programs to varying degrees have elements of interpretive principles or approaches, but interpretation is not recognized as a distinct field with its own qualifications or competencies. Similarly, in Argentina, interpreters are trained in park ranger schools such as the National Center for Training in Protected Areas (Figure 20.5) or in tour guide training programs such as the one at the Instituto Tecnológico Iguazú rather than in university interpretation programs.

In Ecuador where the international nature tourism industry is booming, the government is strictly requiring all guides to be certified and to carry their credentials with them at all times. Because of the flourishing economy and ecotourism industry, individuals from Cuba, Spain, and Venezuela were coming to Ecuador and offering their services at a rate that undercut the prices of local Ecuadorian guides. They also lacked the knowledge to provide excellent service to tourists. Another problem was Americans being hired because of their excellent English in areas where locals

Figure 20.5. An artfully designed sign in Spanish with English translation interprets the creatures found on a beach in a Protected Area in Argentina. (VF)

did not have those language skills. Clients from North America were disappointed upon arrival to find an American guide with little first-hand knowledge of local customs or culture. Today to get certified, the candidate must study in a Tourism Institute for about two years. In these institutes, as a capstone course, most professors require students to prepare and carry out tourism itineraries with the faculty. They need to prepare all of the logistics, be prepared to interpret the places and resources, and make a tourism experience that will be financially attractive for a tourism agency. In addition to interpretation-related training, students are required to take etiquette classes so that clients are not offended by their different table manners. In National Parks and Indigenous communities, the certified guide needs to work with a local guide, as these locals sometimes don't have much training dealing with tourists and lack foreign language skills. To get a local certification, they need to prove they live in the area and have completed at least elementary school.

In some countries, such as India, most of the interpretation training is done by the tourism industry itself. In India with 1.2 billion people and millions of tourist visits each year, the interpretation needs are served mostly by individuals trained by a few private tourism firms, if they are trained at all. Although the Archeological Survey of India licenses guides at differing levels based upon the subject matter and significance of the site, these certifications are based upon content knowledge and do not involve training in message presentation or delivery.

The good news is that the situation may be improving. The International Council on Monuments and Sites (ICOMOS) and other heritage interpretation organizations and consultants are getting more involved in India and assisting with site design and message delivery. Moreover, firms such as those associated with Travel Operators for Tigers (toftigers.org) are now offering professional interpretation training for their guides to fill this need. Such private sector tour guide training also provides a significant amount of the interpretation training in many European, African, and Asian countries.

Global Progress

In spite of regional gaps in professional recognition and training, interpretation has a widespread international presence in governments, universities, and nongovernmental organizations, the largest of which is ICOMOS with expert and institutional members in 151 countries. ICOMOS has an International Committee on Interpretation and Presentation (ICIP) which supports interpretation at cultural heritage sites. In 2008, ICOMOS, ratified the Ename Charter, which includes seven principles of interpretation for cultural heritage sites (Box 20.4).

Box 20.4
ICOMOS's Ename Charter for the Interpretation of Cultural Heritage Sites: Seven Principles

(Each of these principles is elaborated on at enamecharter.org.)

Principle 1–Access and Understanding
Interpretation and presentation programs, in whatever form deemed appropriate and sustainable, should facilitate physical and intellectual access by the public to cultural heritage sites.

Principle 2–Information Sources
Interpretation and presentation should be based on evidence gathered through accepted scientific and scholarly methods as well as from living cultural traditions.

Box 20.4 continued

Principle 3–Context and setting
The interpretation and presentation of cultural heritage sites should relate to their wider social, cultural, historical, and natural contexts and settings.

Principle 4–Authenticity
The interpretation and presentation of cultural heritage sites must respect the basic tenets of authenticity in the spirit of the Nara Document.

Principle 5–Sustainability
The interpretive plan for a cultural heritage site must be sensitive to its natural and cultural environment, with social, financial, and environmental sustainability among its central goals.

Principle 6–Inclusiveness
The interpretation and presentation of cultural heritage sites must be the result of meaningful collaboration between heritage professionals, associated communities, and other stakeholders.

Principle 7–Research, Evaluation, and Training
Continuing research, training, and evaluation are essential components of the interpretation of a cultural heritage site.

Over the past 20 years, the European Union has financially supported several multinational heritage interpretation training projects (e.g., InHerit, HeriQ) related to heritage interpretation. These projects were carried out by a mix of professional associations and organization partners. Unlike North America, where much training is done by national and state park agencies or other public entities, in Europe, many private firms conduct professional training of interpreters, sometimes as part of these EU projects.

Many firms are also doing excellent planning and design work at interpretive sites throughout Europe and on other continents. Principals of such firms as TellTale (telltale.co.uk), Bill Taylor Associates (billtaylorassociates.co.uk), Touchstone Heritage Management Consultants/QuiteWrite (touchstone-heritage.co.uk), Barker Langham (barkerlangham.co.uk), and Bildungswerk Interpretation (interp.de) have a long history of leadership within professional organizations and are key contributors at interpretation conferences.

Outside of Europe, principals at such firms as Sue Hodges Productions (shp.net.au), Lennox Insites (lennoxinsites.com), Nomad Studio (nomad-studio.net), John Pastorelli (johnpastorelli.com.au), Tuhura Communications (tuhuracommunications.com) and John Veverka and Associates (heritageinterp.com), have played an active role internationally in interpretation training, design, planning and evaluation projects. Many other excellent interpretation companies working internationally can be found in the membership directories of NAI and other interpretation organizations as well as exhibiting their work at workshops and conferences.

University and Academic Activity

Dozens of universities on every continent offer programs in heritage studies, tourism, museum studies and disciplines related to interpretation. Heritage studies and museum studies programs are especially common in Europe, Australia, and the Middle East. To illustrate the widespread nature of interpretation training and research, Box 20.5 offers a listing of some of the universities, research centers, and consortia outside of North America involved in interpretation research and offering courses in interpretation.

Box 20.5
Sampling of Schools, Institutes and Centers Outside North America Currently Engaged with Interpretation Research or Offering Courses in Interpretation

Note university interpretation programs are housed within tourism, history, anthropology, environmental education, forestry, or allied departments

Centers and Institutes Outside of Universities
Andalusian Historical Heritage Institute, Seville, Spain
CENEAM–National Environmental Education Centre, Valsaín, Spain
CEIDA–Center of University Extension and Environmental Disclosure of Galicia, Santa Cruz de Oleiros, Spain
Central Institute for Conservation, Belgrade, Serbia
Heritage Interpretation Center, Sofia, Bulgaria
Mediterranean Centre of Environment, Athens, Greece
National Institute of Anthropology and History, Mexico City, Mexico
PANGEA Institute, European Institute for Environmental Education, Interpretation and Training, Sabaudia, Italy
Satul Verde' Association, Sibiu, Romania

Universities
Academia Istropolitana Nova, Svätý Jur, Slovak Republic
Autonomous University of Barcelona, Cerdanyola del Vallès, Spain
Belarusian State University, Minsk, Belarus
Bournemouth University, Poole, England
Center for Outdoor Recreation and Nature Interpretation at Forest and Landscape College, Copenhagen University, Nødebo, Denmark.
Central University of Venezuela, Caracas, Venezuela
CURSA, University Consortium for Socio-Economic Research and Environment, the Universities of Molise, Tuscia, and Ferrara, Italy
Eberswalde University for Sustainable Development, Eberswalde, Germany
Environment and Heritage Interpretation Center, Beijing Normal University, Beijing, China
Institute for Environmental Communication, Leuphana University of Lüneburg, Lüneburg Germany
International Center for Interpretation and Environmental Education, Kunming Agriculture and Forestry College, Kunming, China
Italian Association of Nature Interpreters and Environmental Educators
James Cook University, Brisbane, Australia
Klaipeda State University of Applied Sciences, Klaipeda, Lithuania
Lincoln University, Canterbury, New Zealand
Manchester Metropolitan University, Manchester, England
Masaryk University, Brno, Czech Replublic
National Distance Learning University of Costa Rica (UNED), San Jose, Costa Rica
National School of Conservation, Restoration and Museology, Mexico City, Mexico
National Taichung University, Taichung, Taiwan
Newcastle University, Newcastle upon Tyne, England

Box 20.5 continued

Nottingham Trent University, Nottingham, England
Southern Cross University, Gold Coast, Australia
Sunchon National University, Suncheon, Korea
Swedish Center for Nature Interpretation, Swedish University of Agricultural Sciences, Uppsala, Sweden
University of Almería, Almería, Spain
University of Balearic Islands, Palma, Majorca
University of Birmingham, Birmingham, England
University of Beograd, Beograd, Serbia
University of Beograd, Beograd, Serbia
University of Bucharest, Bucharest, Romania
University of Clermont Auvergne, Clermont-Ferrand, France
University of Chester, Chester, England
University of Coruña, La Coruña, Spain
University of Costa Rica, San Jose Costa Rica
University of Freiburg, Freiburg, Germany
University of Highlands and Islands, Perth College. Perth, Scotland
University of L'Aquila, L'Aquila, Italy
University de La Laguna, Tenerife (Canary Islands), Spain
University of Leicester, Leicester, England
University of Ljubljana, Ljubljana, Slovenia
University of Malta, Msida, Malta
University of Primorska, Slovenia
University of Queensland, Brisbane, Australia
University of Science and Culture, Tehran, Iran
University of Zagreb, Zagreb, Croatia
Victoria University, Wellington, New Zealand

Just as professional interpretation organizations seem to have originated in the United States and then spread to other countries, American interpretive texts have been translated and used in other countries. For decades, Tilden (1977) was available and widely read by European interpreters. It is now available in German. Dr. Sam Ham's book, *Environmental Interpretation: A Practical Guide for People with Big Ideas and Small Budgets* (Ham, 1992), was published first in Spanish. It has been the most widely used and influential text in Spanish-speaking countries around the world since its publication. His more recent book, *Interpretation: Making a Difference on Purpose* (2013), has also been published in Spanish as well as in Russian.

Interpretation of Cultural and Natural Resources (Knudson, Cable, & Beck, 2003), was translated at Beijing Normal University and published in China. Likewise, the first edition of Beck and Cable's *Interpretation for the 21st Century* (Beck & Cable, 1998) was translated and published in China and also in Taiwan. Portions of that book have been translated into French and used in Francophone countries including France, Mali, and Laos. The most recent edition, with the revised title *The Gifts of Interpretation* (Beck & Cable, 2011), has been translated into Persian and is used in Iran to train interpreters at Iran's 21 world heritage sites (Nekouie-Sadry pers. comm., 2017). Beck and Cable's

15 principles of interpretation also are part of the Iranian government's university curriculum called "Defense Heritage Tourism." This program trains "Holy Defense Storytellers" (called Ravian *defae moghadas* in Persian) who work as heritage interpreters at battle sites, including sites from the eight-year war with Iraq.

In the past two decades, professionals in other countries have been producing their own excellent interpretation texts. Scholars in Australia and the United Kingdom have been particularly prolific (e.g., Ballantyne, Hughes, & Moscardo, 2007; Black & Weiler, 2003; Hems & Blockley, 2006; Howard, 2003; Pastorelli, 2003; Uzzell & Ballantyne, 1998; Weiler & Black, 2015). James Carter's *Sense of Place: An Interpretive Planning Handbook* (Carter, 1997) has been published in Czech, French, and Chinese. Thorsten Ludwig has published course workbooks and sets of interpretive training materials in German (e.g., Ludwig, 2003; Ludwig, 2012; Ludwig, 2015). The latter publication, *The Interpretive Guide*, is available in 14 languages and it can be downloaded for free, making it the most widely used interpretation publication in Europe. In 2015, Dr. Valeria Klitsounova and the Belarusian Association of Rural and Ecotourism published the first interpretation textbook in Russian (Klitsounova, 2015). In Costa Rica, Mayorga and Kohl (in press) have authored an interpretation textbook in Spanish.

From this brief and partial review of interpretation texts, it is obvious interpretation scholars work in many countries and their scholarship is impacting the interpretation profession worldwide.

A Global Opportunity

"In facilitating more authentic social relationships between individuals, tourism can help overcome many real prejudices and foster new bonds of fraternity.
In this sense, tourism has become a real force for world peace."

–Pope John Paul II

The wide-ranging and profound benefits of interpretation are presented in Chapters 3 and 4 in this book. As noted in those chapters and elsewhere in this book, interpretation can be educational and inspirational. It can contribute to conservation of natural and cultural resources and foster increased appreciation of our heritage. These benefits play out wherever excellent interpretation is found. For example, in Singapore interpretation efforts over several decades have contributed to the greening of the city. What was once a city of trash, animals, and mud is now called "The City in a Garden" thanks in large part to the establishment of parks with nature trails and guided forest walks (Auger, 2013).

Most importantly perhaps, interpreters working at sites with foreign travelers have an opportunity to play the role of peacemaker (Figure 20.7). Tourism has been called "The World's Peace Industry." In 1988, The First Global Conference: "Tourism—A Vital Force for Peace" was held in Vancouver, Canada, to explore "new initiatives to further the goal of global peace through tourism." Since then "peace through tourism" initiatives have expanded across the world, including the founding of the International Institute for Peace Through Tourism (iipt.org).

> "Interpreters working at sites with foreign travelers have an opportunity to play the role of peacemaker."

Figure 20.7. Young men from the war-torn mountainous border region between Afghanistan and Pakistan visit a wildlife refuge in Kansas as part of a U.S. State Department peace-making program allowing them to spend time in the U.S. (TC)

As interpreters shape and enhance travelers' experiences they are well positioned to promote understanding of the different cultures, environments, and heritage.

Knowing the International Audience

To maximize interpretation's effectiveness, interpreters should know how foreign visitors expect to be treated and served at interpretive sites. We have noted many times in this book how important it is to know the audience. In this case interpreters should be especially aware of cultural nuances and norms. These may be very different than the customs of the interpreter. Interpretation consultant Chuck Lennox trains tour guides in countries around the world and often trains them to serve *American* tourists. Here are his tips along with advice from other tourism professionals for serving American tourists in foreign countries (Weed, 2016).

- Americans do not appreciate comments about their weight. Pointing out a person's size is a compliment in many countries where a large girth is a sign of success and prosperity, but not in the U.S.
- Americans like "give-and-take" discussion and serious dialogue with guides. American guides are taught to know their audience, study their body language, and tailor the talk to the interests of the audience (as recommended in this book). This is different than in many countries where tourists expect a more formal didactic one-way presentation. For example, many Europeans prefer an

"academic" tour, with much information provided, unlike Americans who want entertainment with their facts.
- Americans want to relate personally to their guide and often ask about the guide's family, education, interests, and living conditions. Guides in many countries find that level of interaction odd or even rude. Sometimes Americans expect to be treated as the guide's family member, which is not appropriate in many places.
- Americans say "thank you" excessively for every small action, making guides feel more indebted to them.
- Americans expect their children to be heard and just as involved as an adult on the tour or hike. In some places, the children will be ignored completely by the guide (particularly male guides).
- Americans generally do not understand history and art as well as Europeans do. Guides at cultural sites in Europe must start with more basic information for most Americans.

These training points illustrate how it behooves interpreters everywhere to learn more about the cultures of travelers who visit their sites. Only by knowing international visitors can interpreters relate to them, meet their needs, and exceed their expectations. Of many books that focus on characterizing the diverse cultures of the world, a classic resource still useful to interpreters is *When Cultures Collide* by Richard Lewis (2006). This source provides descriptions of the cultural nuances of more than 60 countries and every major region of the world. Also useful are the many databases found in university and major libraries such as *CountryWatch* that provide background information and cultural etiquette on countries around the world. Finally, we recommend Melanie Smith's (2016) *Issues in Cultural Tourism Studies*, which includes coverage of heritage, tourism, and museums.

A Future Federation?

No umbrella organization links and supports the organizations mentioned in Box 20.1. For many years, interpreters have discussed ways to promote international collaboration. When this topic was formally addressed at the International Interpretation Conference in Montreal in 2015 the consensus of participants was that a worldwide federation of interpretation organizations could 1) advocate and promote interpretation to legitimize it as a profession, 2) increase awareness and enhance recognition of interpretation, 3) support national or regional heritage interpretation organizations, and 4) serve individuals in countries without a national professional organization. Another potential benefit identified of having such a federation was to aide in the dissemination of research findings and promote collaboration on research projects. After additional discussions at subsequent NAI workshops and international interpretation conferences, in 2016 representatives from AHI, NAI and IE drafted a charter for a Global Alliance for Heritage Interpretation. Jon Kohl who is deeply involved with interpretation internationally makes a strong case for such an alliance or federation (See Box 20.6). With or without a formal federation, diverse groups of interpreters on every continent have an opportunity and obligation to work together for a better world.

Box 20.6
Uniting Heritage Interpretation to Save the World
Jon Kohl, Director, PUP Global Heritage Consortium

For heritage interpretation, the developed-developing world divide has proven much wider than for other fields. All the interpretation associations, publications, and most professionals operate in developed countries, whereas the principal manifestation of interpretation in developing countries centers on tour guides (see Weiler & Black, 2015). Since regions such as Africa and Latin America have almost no academic programs, established professional communities, or government jobs that define interpretation as an official competence area, interpretation in these regions has a steep hill to climb.

Sometimes, however, interpretation mixes with environmental education and practitioners use this combination in the field with communities to promote local development, environmental protection, and conservation (Ham, Sutherland, & Meganck, 1993). And this application of interpretation, ironically, may become the most consequential function of interpretation internationally, aside from its improving visitor experiences. In recent years, the importance of interpretation to community development has been made violently clear by ISIS which in Iraq and Syria has intentionally destroyed World Heritage, not to punish per se, but with the explicit intention of wiping out the collective history and culture of peoples ("culturecide"), rendering them vulnerable to the forceful insertion of a new narrative based on ISIS's belief system (Sarah, 2015; Silberman, 2013). As Napoleon said, history is written by the winners.

UNESCO is well aware of this strategy so the director general, Irina Bokova, responded to ISIS's destruction of Syria's Palmyra World Heritage Site with a proclamation which could be interpreted as a clarion call for interpretation in international community development (UNESCO, 2013):

> At UNESCO, we believe there is no choice to make between saving lives and saving cultural heritage. Protecting heritage is inseparable from protecting populations, because heritage enshrines people's identities. Heritage gives people strength and confidence to look to the future — it is a force for social cohesion and recovery. This is why protection of heritage must be an integral part of all humanitarian efforts.

Though Bokova never explicitly mentions heritage interpretation, it is not difficult to interpret interpretation as a vital discipline in preserving cultural heritage, so essential for community development (Kohl, 2015). Interpretation facilitates communities' examination of their past in shaping their current identity (Silberman, 2015). If heritage meanings so infuse community self-esteem and self-image which can motivate community progress (such as long-term site sustainability) or cement forlorn doubt (dependency on outsiders), then interpreters can play a role in crystallizing those meanings of collective memory and leveraging them for both internal community audiences as well as external visiting audiences, if only the interpretation field built links with international heritage and development organizations as well as the more traditional protected area and tourism organizations.

If one considers, aside from cultural cleansing, the threats of globalization and climate change (Markham et al., 2016) to the integrity of heritage, then interpretation, especially in the developing world, has much potential work ahead, well beyond embellishing experiences of transient tourists.

To do this requires, however, that a long dream of the interpretation community actually materializes: establishment of an international federation for heritage interpretation. Such has been attempted several times without enduring success.

The idea calls for the union of the various associations around the world, almost all of which can be found in developed countries (USA, UK, Canada, Europe, Australia, Korea, Spain, Portugal, and Croatia). Together, they could leverage their combined influence to support interpretation in developing countries or regions where heritage often finds itself under greatest threat, reminiscent of Interpret Europe's work in supporting interpretation in southeastern Europe such as the establishment of Interpret Croatia (Babic, 2016). Such a federation could tighten ties not just with protected areas and tourism communities, but also with heritage and community development organizations.

Box 20.6 continued

Such a federation would seed and support associations in developing countries, set up academic programs, and the consequent definition of interpretation as a formal competency if not profession so that people could work in public agencies beyond just tour operators, zoos, botanical gardens, and as freelancers. Indeed, such a view of international interpretation would fuse the more visitor-oriented approach of developed countries with a community-centered necessity of developing countries. Such a melding, however, requires what has been a sticking point in past efforts to build a federation: involvement of developing countries in the conversation when they have no associations to represent them in an emerging federation of interpretation associations. To transcend this barrier demands additional creativity to engage the entire international interpretation community with and without association representation.

Summary

*"Travel is fatal to prejudice, bigotry, and narrow-mindedness,
all foes of real understanding."*

–Mark Twain

The interpretive profession is spreading widely. As seen in this chapter, the global spread of professionalism in interpretation has been steady and significant. Although challenges remain, especially in developing countries, tremendous advances have been made throughout the world and this can be expected to continue. On a broad scale, these advances offer great promise in the realm of global tourism.

With reference to the quote by Mark Twain, travel *is* fatal to narrow-mindedness. However, it is not merely the movement of travel that reaps these benefits, but rather the *connections* made by the traveler to foreign people and places. These connections make up precisely the role of interpreters and so interpreters have an extraordinary opportunity to promote peace and understanding. Interpreters illuminate the meanings and beauty of places and peoples, which eliminates not only prejudice and bigotry, but also complacency. Humans care more about places and people they get to know. Interpreters introduce travelers to new landscapes and cultures. Interpreters touching emotional chords in the hearts of travelers evoke empathy for the local people and appreciation for their culture and their land. In this way interpreters foster the spread of stewardship and fellowship, and contribute to tourism's potential for peace. It is the privilege and the responsibility of interpreters to be peacemakers. This clearly makes for a better world.

> The global spread of professionalism in interpretation has been steady and significant.

Literature Cited

Auger, T. (2013). *Living in a garden: The greening of Singapore.* Singapore: National Parks Board.

Babic, D. (2016). What has been cooked in Croatia — Interpret Croatia. *Interpret Europe Newsletter.* Retrieved from http://www.interpret-europe.net/de/top/news/singlepage-news/archive/2016/october/article/what-has-been-cooked-in-croatia-interpret-croatia.html

Ballantyne, R., Hughes, K. & Moscardo, G. (2007). *Designing interpretive signs: Principles in practice.* Golden, CO: Fulcrum.

Beck, L., & Cable, T. (1998). *Interpretation for the 21st century: Fifteen guiding principles for interpreting nature and culture.* Champaign, IL: Sagamore.

Beck, L., & Cable, T. (2011). *The gifts of interpretation: Fifteen guiding principles for interpreting nature and culture* (3rd ed.). Urbana, IL: Sagamore.

Black, R., & Weiler, B. (Eds.) (2003). *Interpreting the land down under: Australian heritage interpretation and tour guiding.* Boulder, CO:Fulcrum.

Carter, J. (Ed). (1997). *A sense of place: An interpretive planning handbook.* Inverness, Scotland: Tourism and Environment Initiative.

Ham, S. H. (1993). *Environmental interpretation: A practical guide for people with big ideas and small budgets.* Golden, CO. Fulcrum Publishing.

Ham, S. H. (2013). *Interpretation. Making a difference on purpose.* Golden, CO: Fulcrum Publishing.

Ham, S. H., Sutherland, D. S., & Meganck, R. A. (1993). Applying environmental interpretation in protected areas of developing countries: Problems in exporting a US model. *Environmental Conservation, 20*(3), 232–242.

Hems, A., & Blockley, M. (Eds.). (2006). *Heritage interpretation.* London, UK: Routledge.

Howard, P. (2003) *Heritage: Management, interpretation, identity.* London, UK: Continuum.

Klitsounova, V. (2015). *Heritage interpretation in tourism: New approaches in experience economy era.* Minsk, Belarus: Ekoperspektiva.

Knudson, D. M., Cable, T. T., & Beck, L. (2003). *Interpretation of cultural and natural resources* (2nd ed.). State College, PA: Venture.

Kohl, J. (2014). Achieving self-identity and self-worth. *Journal of the Association for Heritage Interpretation, 19*(1), 24–26.

Lewis, R. (2006). *When cultures collide* (3rd ed.) Boston, MA: Nicholas Brealey Publishing.

Ludwig, T. (2003). Grundlagen der interpretation:Kurshandbuch *[Basic interpretive skills].* Werleshausen, Germany: Bildungswerk interpretation.

Ludwig, T. (2012). *Basiskurs natur und kulturinterpretation: Trainerhandbuch* [Basic course heritage interpretation: Trainer manual]. Werleshausen, Germany: Bildungswerk interpretation.

Ludwig, T. (2015). *The interpretive guide* (2nd ed.). Werleshausen, Germany: Bildungswerk interpretation.

Markham, A., Osipova, E., Lafrenz-Samuels, K., & Caldas, A. (2016). World heritage and tourism in a changing climate. United Nations Environment Programme, Nairobi, Kenya and United Nations Educational, Scientific and Cultural Organization, Paris, France. Retrieved from http://whc.unesco.org/document/139944

Mayorga, M., & Kohl, J. M. (In Press). *Esencia de la interpretación del patrimonio: Una visión holística para experimentar y conservar el patrimonio natural y cultural de América Latina.* San José, Costa Rica: Editorial Universidad Estatal a Distancia (EUNED).

Nekouie-Sadry, B. (2017). Personal communication with Bahram Nekouie-Sadry, Professor of Geotourism at the University of Science and Culture, Tehran, Iran.

Pastorelli, J. (2003). *Enriching the experience: An interpretive approach to tour guiding.* Frenchs Forest. Australia: Hospitality Press.

Sarah, A. A. (2015). Why is ISIS destroying Iraq's heritage? *Haaretz.* Retrieved from http://www.haaretz.com/opinion/.premium-1.646517

Silberman, N. (2013). The tyranny of narrative history, heritage, and hatred in the modern Middle East. *Journal of Eastern Mediterranean Archaeology and Heritage Studies* 1:2. http://works.bepress.com/neil_silberman/47/

Silberman, N. (2015). Remembrance of things past: Collective memory, sensory perception, and the emergence of new interpretive paradigms. *2nd International Conference on Best Practices in World Heritage: People and Communities.* https://works.bepress.com/neil_silberman/51/

Smith, M. (2016). *Issues in cultural tourism studies* (3rd ed.). New York, NY: Routledge.

Sutton, M. D. (1982). Interpretation around the world. In G. Sharpe (Ed.), *Interpreting the environment* (2nd ed., pp. 644–663). New York, NY: John Wiley & Sons.

Tabata, R. S., Yamashiro, J., & Cherem, G. (Eds.). (1992). Joining hands for quality tourism: Interpretation, preservation, and the travel industry. *Proceedings of the Heritage Interpretation International Third Global Congress.* Honolulu: University of Hawaii.

Tilden, F. (1977). *Interpreting our heritage* (3rd ed.). Chapel Hill, NC: The University of North Carolina Press.

UNESCO. (2013). Emergency red list of Syrian antiquities at risk is launched in New York. Retrieved from http://whc.unesco.org/en/news/1073

Uzzell, D. (Ed). (1989). *Heritage interpretation. Volume 1-The natural and built environment and Volume 2-The visitor experience.* London, UK: Belhaven Press.

Uzzell, D. & Ballantyne, R. (Eds.). (1998). *Contemporary issues in heritage and environmental interpretation: Problems and prospects.* London: The Stationery Office.

Weed, J. (2016). How tour guides abroad learn to cater to exotic Americans. Retrieved from https://www.nytimes.com/2016/11/28/business/how-tour-guides-abroad-learn-to-cater-to-exotic-americans.html

Weiler, B., & Black, R. (2015). *Tour guiding research: Insights, issues, and implications.* Bristol, UK: Channel View Publications.

CHAPTER 21
The Bright Future of Interpretation

Each chapter has begun with a story. One last story has been saved as we come full circle back to the first and provide an indication of the future that lies ahead for those who understand the power of interpretation. In the preface we proved that interpretation is worth a million dollars, and actually a whole lot more—it is priceless. The book began with a story from the Museum of Art in San Diego's Balboa Park. Now we end with a story from the same location.

In 1915, San Diego hosted the Panama-California Exposition (much like a World's Fair). In 2015, the centennial of that expo was celebrated, and the concession contract was opened up for the sculpture garden courtyard of the Museum of Art. The owners of two local alehouses secured the contract with an outdoor restaurant that features local food and drink they named "Panama 66."

As reported by Quintero (2014), Jeff Motch, one of the founders of Panama 66, has a degree in fine art. The ownership group pays rent to the San Diego Museum of Art. Motch noted, "If we are successful, we will be paying thousands of dollars to a museum! How many bars and restaurants have that kind of landlord?"

To secure the contract, Motch focused on interpreting the San Diego culture through locally sourced food and drink, and promoting the art of the museum, including the sculpture garden. Panama 66 offers local beer from craft breweries along with food sourced from local farms. The emphasis is on sustainability, a goal for all 17 museums, and the San Diego Zoo, located in Balboa Park. As with other progressive museums, Panama 66 has hosted special evening events at the Museum of Art that include food and drink, such as a celebration of Valentine's Day highlighting works of art on the theme of love.

San Diego is arguably the most prominent craft beer region in the nation. For this reason, many people are traveling to San Diego to experience this aspect of the culture. Motch was asked how he wanted to make people feel when they visit Panama 66. He said:

> To feel inspired by the city. To taste [food and drink] they came to San Diego explicitly for…We want to add big picnic tables where travelers, locals, and regulars all interact and share their stories, where the picnic table becomes a hub of information. If we can make something like that, then we will have made something that we can be proud of.

His intent is to not only provide meaningful experiences in the Museum of Art sculpture garden, but to accentuate the experience by providing opportunities to taste San Diego through local food and drink, and provide a forum for locals, travelers, and his staff to interact and learn from one another.

Such a set up can result in people spending more time in the sculpture garden, attending a museum program (at the art museum itself or any of the other museums in Balboa Park), learning more about other opportunities to pursue in San Diego (hiking at Torrey Pines State Reserve or Mission Trails Regional Park), telling friends and family about what they experienced, buying a book or memorabilia, coming back for return visits, and/or donating to the cause.

In this case, then, as we look at the broadest intent of interpretation, perhaps every place can be interpreted in unique and innovative ways that spur *further* interest and action. Clientele can be served with thoughtful, creative, effective, progressive, meaningful interpretation. Doing so benefits individuals, communities, the organization or business, society in general, and ultimately the integrity of the planet. A better nation and a better world, with people leading richer lives.

> Clientele can be served with thoughtful, creative, effective, progressive, meaningful interpretation.

Along with stories that have introduced each chapter, this book has featured "boxes" by experts on various facets of interpretation. For this last chapter we asked Tim Merriman for his input about the future of the profession. Merriman has been involved with interpretation at many levels over a career that spans more than four decades. He was a ranger/interpreter at Giant City State Park; the executive director of The Greenway and Nature Center of Pueblo, Colorado; and executive director of the National Association for Interpretation. He has taught as an adjunct professor at three universities, written several books on interpretation, and is an avid reader. As a principal of Heartfelt Associates he continues to lead seminars and trainings all around the world. With this background, Tim Merriman shares his thoughts on a profession with a future (Box 21.1).

Interpretation Everywhere

"A nature guide in every locality who, around his home or in the nearest park could show with fitting stories the wild places, birds, flowers, and animals, would add to the enjoyment of everyone who lives in the region or who visits it."

–Enos Mills (1920)

Every place in which interpretation could occur should include some element of interpretation. This means traditional sites such as parks and museums, but could be expanded to include…almost anything from playgrounds to wineries. For example, playgrounds (and wineries) could have something as simple as a plaque or sign that explains the history of the site and some of the natural features. Beyond that, there might be an exhibit or two. Furthermore, an app might provide more information about the site and its history via one's smartphone.

Box 21.1
A Profession with a Future
Tim Merriman, Principal, Heartfelt Associates

We have come a long way these past 100 years since Enos Mills wrote *Adventures of a Nature Guide* in 1920. Interpretation has become more recognized as a profession, with its own body of research, great teaching texts like this book, training materials, and unique video resources. National Association for Interpretation's (NAI) *Journal of Interpretation Research* and certification programs have added important dimensions to professionalism in interpretation.

As we grapple with the complex challenges facing the planet in the coming years, I think those engaged in the interpretive profession can continue to make a positive difference in the world by keeping abreast of these important areas of concern.

Interpretation is management. I first heard Mike Watson say that ("interpretation is management") when he served in the lead role for interpretation with the National Park Service years ago. The Definitions Project led by NAI in 2006 added the term "mission-based" to the most broadly accepted definition of interpretation. Effective interpretation can help achieve management goals but both managers and interpreters must be at the planning table, setting objectives and looking for creative ways to achieve them.

Climate change looms as a threat to communities, safety, and food production on many fronts. Messages from the vast majority of climate scientists calling for more strict control of carbon emissions have fallen on deaf ears in some legislative bodies. We still need to help the world's decision-makers understand the vital importance of the effects we have on the Earth's atmosphere and ocean, and we must continue to help all people understand how individual behavior contributes to both the problems and the solutions.

Oceans are the lifeblood of the planet, but they have become the "commons" of the new millennium, enjoyed and harvested by all, but poorly protected on most fronts. While aquariums around the world generally do an amazing job of interpreting these rich ecosystems, we need more efforts in diverse settings with skilled interpreters crafting the messages and delivering effective products, services and experiences, helping people understand the connection between their actions on land and sea with the overall health of the oceans.

Emerging high-tech technologies are ripe for exploration by interpreters. Many of us regard virtual reality, robotics, and the Internet with suspicion. Will it trap all future generations indoors with headsets and digital imagery, when we hope to lure them into more authentic experiences on hikes and museum visits? We need more young interpreters who love technology to get an interpretive education and innovate with digital media. Social media offers the opportunity to deliver our messages to millions of people with a simple keystroke. How might we use these powerful new technologies in a variety of settings to help people understand and connect with history, science, cultures, and the natural world?

Tourism is one of the most powerful economic drivers for nations rich and poor around the world. Interpreters are on the front line at natural and cultural history sites, and science museums, but not so commonly in communities. Community cultural tours, agritourism and even traditional farmers markets are emerging as important tourism experiences around the world. Interpretation can have an important role with these movements, but we need to become more proactive in making an interpretive approach an integral part of tourism experiences.

Box 21.1 continued

The Internet has brought us closer to our colleagues around the world. I chat almost daily with colleagues in dozens of nations, many of whom have only a smartphone and Internet purchased by the hour. We are hungry to know each other, share ideas and techniques, and embrace the global profession. Social media outlets carry our messages and thoughts to each other every day. In 2006, the first NAI-sponsored international conference convened in San Juan, Puerto Rico, encouraging an ongoing global discussion about the profession that continues today. The challenges of distance can be bridged by technology, opening the door to increasing and more diverse digital training resources.

What is the upper limit for human population? As the world's population approaches eight billion, we have made minimal efforts to interpret carrying capacity of the planet in most interpretive venues. Paul Ehrlich tackled the challenge with his 1968 book, *The Population Bomb*. It was a popular subject in interpretive circles in the early 1970s, but faded as future population problems seemed less compelling than immediate conservation issues of desertification, deforestation, and destruction of cultural heritage sites. The Earth is still finite and the need to share that story and its implications is ours to tackle.

The future is rich with opportunities for the profession. To take full advantage of those opportunities, professional organizations, universities with programs related to the profession, and major employers of interpreters must continue to find new ways to invest in appropriate training so that interpreters can continue to make a positive difference in the world.

Enos Mills, (1920) as a founder of the modern interpretive profession, foresaw the connection between interpretation and the general welfare of people (Figure 21.1). As the quote above suggests, Mills' dream seems more realistic now, about a hundred years later. Most city, county, state, and federal parks support interpreters as do museums, zoos, camps, nature centers, aquariums, and historic sites. Still the goal of an interpreter in every locality has not quite arrived, although the trend remains positive. As noted in the introductory story it is possible to further interpretive efforts, formally or informally, almost anywhere.

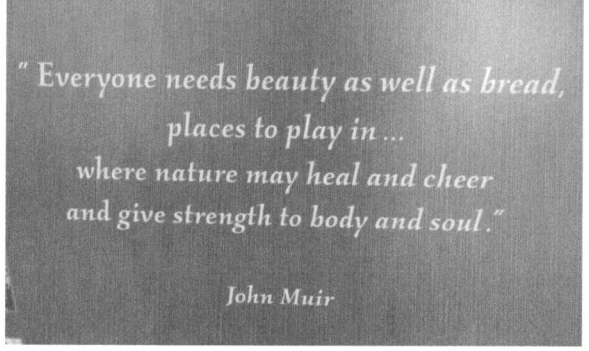

Figure 21.1. Interpreters reveal beauty and provide strategic and focused access to places where nature can heal and strengthen people. (TC)

Interpretation for Everyone

Local interpreters can set a goal to help all residents of a locality, and visitors, to learn the historical and natural features of the area and to sense how they relate to the community, the nation, and the rest of the world. As a community leader, the interpreter expresses concerns for environmental quality and human equality. Interpreters may also serve in a prophetic role taking into account projections from science about

> It is possible to further interpretive efforts, formally or informally, almost anywhere.

how things might be in the future if we aren't careful in the present. Part of the job entails equipping and provoking others to turn their consciences to action.

Interpreters make themselves vital social implements when they connect the information from the park or the museum collection to what is going on in the world, to what the consequences of certain action (or non-action) may be, and how society can improve life quality and the wellbeing of all other species we co-inhabit the planet with. By concentrating on the possible, positive, and practical alternatives; by focusing on facts; and by seeing through the myths and politics; the interpreter can gently provoke clients to confidently build a better future.

> Taking into account diversity is critical to success.

Furthermore, taking into account diversity is critical to success. National Association for Interpretation president Jay Miller (2017) shares NAI's commitment to diversity as follows:

NAI is dedicated to advancing the profession of heritage interpretation. Interpreters are the keepers, tellers, and facilitators of stories for our natural and cultural resources. As such, interpreters hold a tremendous responsibility to really understand the stories that we tell, and to richly represent all people, all backgrounds, and all perspectives.

Lifelong Learning

Art museums have been involved for years with adult skill education. Their approach offers three or four levels of art lessons, from beginning to advanced, in each of the different media. Those taking classes pay a reasonable fee for the instruction and the materials.

Few natural history centers apply this approach, however. Much of the programming remains at the beginner or first-time visitor level. More could be offered to improve and hone skills and knowledge, so visitors become clients who keep developing their expertise in nature study and/or history. Advanced adults could shift into roles as volunteer leaders or independent contractors.

Putting together lifetime learning curricula that help residents to develop and to sharpen their skills in several areas will make interpretive centers repeat destinations—places identified as valuable in personal life, places of growth and achievement. Programs through the life cycle could include the following:

> Putting together lifetime learning curricula will make interpretive centers repeat destinations.

- Preschool and school programs, seasonally or throughout the year.
- Scout badge and 4-H projects, with interpreters and volunteers to assist in advising and certifying accomplishments. Junior Naturalist or Historian projects could be offered for other young people.
- Summer and vacation day camps for various age ranges.
- High school local history projects, science experiment research center, and clubs for students interested in the environment and/or history could be coordinated with guidance from the interpretive staff.

- Facilities used as a college resource center, tied in with student volunteer groups, work projects with fraternities and sororities or other campus groups, leading to interpreter training and seasonal employment.
- Young adult programs that focus on gardening, landscaping for birds, xeriscaping, edible plants, environmental awareness, and history of local neighborhoods.
- Young parents (and grandparents) sessions on how to teach children about nature and cultural traditions to avoid nature deficit disorder.
- Outdoor/cultural adult skills development over the span of several years to provide progressive learning on topics such as birds, trees, local history, photography, or insects.
- "Empty nest" nature and history could offer many sociable means for individuals and couples to enjoy the center or museum with others. Special programming for vigorous, interested people can enhance stewardship, encourage sustained support of the facility, and make use of their expertise in many ways, including volunteer work and fund-raising.
- Road Scholar programs attract older adults for a week or so of classes and field trips. These programs bring a facility and its community to people from all over the country. Staff personnel and local experts can be used as faculty.

Growing the Profession

Interpretation produces many personal, social, and economic benefits as discussed throughout this book. Some refer to it as a value-added service. Interpretation certainly does add great value to tourism, recreation, and community welfare, but it has a greater integral value than just a tag-on activity. Interpretation is increasingly regarded as an integrated component of many organizations, much as sales or marketing divisions serve an essential core function of any customer-oriented business. Interpretation is an integral aspect of the organization from national parks to innovative museum restaurants. As Jay Miller (2016) suggested, it should be "what we are known for, and be recognized as a significant reason people come…"

Throughout this book, we have used the terms *profession* and *professional* to describe the people and work of interpretation because we believe this work truly functions as one of the noblest of professions.

Interpretive professionals uphold several characteristics and responsibilities, both personally and collectively, that contribute to the acceptance of professional status (Brochu & Merriman, 2008):

- They make the effort to gain relevant specialized education and training.
- They provide public service with social responsibility.
- They participate in accreditation and certification programs.
- They keep current with a research-based foundation of knowledge.
- They lay out and follow a program of life-long learning.
- They accept and practice the discipline of an established code of ethics within their workplace.

Strong curricula in colleges and universities; certification programs through the National Association for Interpretation; formal training through agencies, traditional on-site workshops, webinars, and technological learning opportunities; as well as possibilities for global interactions will continue to advance the profession of interpretation (Figure 21.2).

> *Interpretive professionals uphold several characteristics that contribute to the acceptance of professional status.*

As discussed in Chapter 17, the certification activities of NAI have helped improve quality in all levels of public and private interpretation. The popularity and growth of certification indicates increasing financial and professional commitment of those who pay for the training. The professionally certified status of employees boosts agency and public respect for interpretation.

Interpreters and Their Charges as Scientists

Larger agencies such as the National Park Service and U.S. Forest Service, as well as large museums and aquariums, employ a science staff. Smaller operations will often engage the interpreters with inventorying and monitoring resources that exist at the site. Interpreters generally inform visitors to the site about key features and resources of the property. They can also engage them in citizen science initiatives. Citizen science can include locals and school groups at small nature centers to day visitors at large destination parks.

Figure 21.2. Interpretation students from the U.S. learn about cutting-edge exhibit design as they do land use simulations with an interactive exhibit at UNESCO's World Nature Forum Visitor Center in Naters, Switzerland. (TC)

Regular citizens have traditionally participated in activities such as the Audubon Society's Christmas bird counts. To help manage park resources and to inform science, bird counts have taken place in national parks for decades.

Now, with more accessible technology and easier coordination through the Internet and social media, more people can contribute to scientific endeavors. Smartphones are equipped with increasingly sophisticated microphones, cameras, and sensors. With a smartphone and various apps citizen scientists can contribute to science as follows:

- Keep records on plant and animal species, in particular those that may be endangered.
- Inventory cultural resources that exist on the site.
- Document the effects of disasters such as toxic spills in rivers or seas.
- Measure changes in vegetation and recovery rates after fires.
- Follow animal migration patterns.
- Measure environmental noise and pollution.

Participation in science is democratized through the range and quality of data that ordinary citizens can collect. GPS, clocks, and sensors assure that the observations that people collect have scientific value. Furthermore, Cavalier and Kennedy (2016) noted that social media is used to coordinate group observations, publicize new findings, or share enthusiasm for scientific pursuits. Open-access publications make dissemination of the information more efficient so that citizen scientists can publish their findings and make their data available to others.

Furthermore, when necessary, citizen science enters the realm of political advocacy with "members of the public educating other citizens about scientific findings and opportunities for participation, pushing for particular regulatory changes on the basis of scientific arguments, or confronting the actions of companies that may be causing harm" (Cavalier & Kennedy, 2016).

Citizen science programs that warrant special mention include: iNaturalist (iNaturalist.org), the Cornell Lab of Ornithology and National Audubon Society ebird program (ebird.org), the Association of Zoos and Aquarium's FrogWatch USA program (aza.org/frogwatch), and Galaxy Zoo (galaxyzoo.org). This latter program, in which volunteers classify galaxies, has contributed more scientific publications than any other citizen science project, and it spawned another site (zooniverse.org) where people can participate in more than 50 ongoing research projects dealing with everything from notes from Shakespeare's contemporaries to sea lions and chimpanzees. Interpretive sites can promote and facilitate such participation in citizen science.

The Potential of Crowdsourcing in Interpretation

Similarly, crowdsourcing facilitates opportunities for citizens to share their expertise and augment the knowledge of professionals. Brabham (2015) defines crowdsourcing as an "online, distributed problem-solving, and production model that leverages the collective intelligence or energy of an online community to serve an organizational goal." An agency or organization provides an open call, online, for people to voluntarily undertake a task, which involves that online community to seek a solution. This idea builds on the Jeffersonian democratic tradition in which government capitalizes on the knowledge of its citizens to connect government with the governed, in this case through advanced technologies. For example, in cooperation with the U.S. Department of Agriculture, former First Lady Michelle Obama backed the Apps for Healthy Kids contest to crowdsource the development of a new phone app to encourage youth to eat healthy foods and exercise more frequently.

> Innovative interpreters may generate ways to involve the community for the benefit of the agency, the resource, and the online community itself.

Crowdsourcing occurs in both the pubic sector and the business sector. Brabham (2015) noted that a variation of crowdsourcing is the Peer-Vetted Creative Production (PVCP) approach in which a challenge is issued to the online community, the community responds with solutions, and the community is empowered to choose among the solutions, often through a commenting and voting mechanism.

The classic business case of PVCP is a clothing company (Threadless) whose members submit graphic t-shirt designs that are voted on by their peers. The company then prints the winning designs and sells them to the online community. Similarly, innovative interpreters may generate ways to involve the community for the benefit of the agency, the resource, and the online community itself.

Technology: Friend and Foe

"But if the trance induced by electronic gadgets makes us oblivious to the wood, the wildflowers, and the songs and smells of resurgent spring, then we have suffered a grievous loss."

–Scott Russell Sanders, 2016

As discussed throughout this book we recognize and value many of the novel uses of technology from parks and museums to aquariums and zoos that help illuminate things in ways that reveal meanings (Figure 21.3). Various technologies can assist in conveying interpretive messages at sites, helping visitors to learn more about the place, and encouraging visitors to further explore other possibilities at the site.

Such technologies include relevant and meaningful websites that promote places in ways that encourage people to visit firsthand. To allow broader audiences to appreciate spectacles of nature we recognize the values of live web cams that show nesting bald eagles at Channel Islands National Park or brown bears fishing for salmon at Katmai National Park in Alaska.

Figure 21.3. At UNESCO's World Nature Forum Visitor Center technology allows exhibits to engage all of the senses as visitors: (a) find labels and artifacts in a drawer with glacial ice, (b) experience good and bad smells of the Alpine landscape, and (c) see tiny details that would be too small for the naked eye. (TC)

Jessica Moore (2016) described Microsoft Skype in the Classroom as a free virtual education program that connects more than 1.2 million educators from around the world with host site partners. The virtual field trip aspect of the program offers tours of Yellowstone National Park, of Abraham Lincoln's home, fur trade travels at the Canadian Canoe Museum, Skype with a Holocaust survivor, or a behind-the-scenes tour about native Pacific Northwest raptors at the Northwest Trek Wildlife Park in the state of Washington, where Moore is the education and conservation curator.

Using this technology, host site partners can remove potential barriers and reach out to underserved audiences. As Moore (2016) noted, "As of now, our reach has extended around the world. However, we want to use this technology to reach out to our local communities and underserved populations." In addition to educating many who may never have a chance to see Northwest Trek, the intent is that the virtual experiences will result in local communities visiting on-site and participating in conservation programs such as habitat restoration.

Social media, websites, apps, and other technologies assist in informing people of opportunities and becoming more deeply involved. One way to extend sphere of influence is blogging in which any interpreter can create a following by sharing expertise on a particular topic. For success with a blog, Omar (2015) suggests that people consider the following: 1) What do you have knowledge or personal experience in? Confidence in the subject matter is essential. Knowing the subject makes for easier, smoother, and more natural writing. 2) What do you love to talk about and discuss with other people; what do you have a passion for? 3) What would you like to learn more about? These criteria are precisely what interpreters do naturally.

Technology is also used, such as webinars, to assist with interpretive training. Furthermore, John Veverka initiated an e-Magazine, *InterpNews*, sent out via email to three hundred thousand interpreters, in more than 60 countries worldwide.

Although there are many benefits associated with our advancing technologies, there are also concerns. Part of the problem is that by relying too greatly on technology our engagement with the world is compromised and our skills, both mental and physical erode (Figure 21.4). As Nicholas Carr (2014) suggested, "The mounting evidence of an erosion of skills, a dulling of perceptions, and a slowing of reactions should give us all pause." For one thing, the ubiquitous availability of information online weakens our memories and attention spans. Some estimates indicate that "when browsing the web, our attention span can be the same as a goldfish—9 seconds" (Scott, 2010). And with ever-more frequency, children and adults are checking their smartphones (Turkle, 2015).

> Information overload and constant connectivity is changing how we interact with one another *and* how we interact with nature.

Furthermore, our relationships with others are being compromised. Robert Moor (2016) noted, "Many people currently worry that digital technology is making us less connected to the people and things in our immediate environment."

Information overload and constant connectivity is changing how we interact with one another *and* how we interact with nature. Beck and Dustin (2016) suggested that among the greatest gifts of the natural world and extended time spent there is being able to think clearly without distraction. "And that is precisely what people are giving up, obsessed with their smartphones."

Richard Louv (2016) stated, "Today, children and adults who work and learn in a dominating digital environment expend enormous energy blocking out many of the human senses…in order to focus narrowly on the screen in front of the eyes. That's the very definition of being less alive."

Concern here is mostly for our youth, those who have grown up in the digital age. Young urbanites are, in part, products of their social and cultural habitats, all of which have "defined, constrained, and/or exacerbated tendencies toward a sense of technological dependency" (Dustin, Beck, & Rose, 2017). These connections to technology may also interfere with their ability to connect with their biological moorings.

Figure 21.4. A simple laminated photograph in the hands of a helpful interpreter may develop observation skills and relationships better than an impersonal technological approach. (TC)

For example, millennials visit the national parks in numbers well below their share of the population. In recounting the dilemma the National Park Service faces, Egan (2016) noted the Service embraced the digital age to find a younger audience by using a constantly updated website, extensive social media outreach, and temporary kiosks in cities such as New York, where users can take a brief virtual tour of the national parks. Egan concluded, "In other words, they decided to use screens to try to get young people off their screens."

Beck and Dustin (2016) concluded:

Perhaps more so than anyplace else, taking to our nation's trails offers a respite from the technology that surrounds us everywhere else. The value of leaving technology behind, in at least this one last instance, leads to freedom of thought, deeper awareness of what is directly in front of us (including species other than our own), and ultimately being more alive.

The advantage of sometimes leaving technology behind is revealed in an undiminished encounter with nature and the kaleidoscope of wonders that can be experienced when we are finely tuned to the present moment and all that is going on around us (Dustin, Beck, & Rose, 2017). Toward the conclusion of *The Hour of Land*, Terry Tempest Williams (2016) reasoned that it is "time to reimagine our public lands as sanctuaries, refuges, and sacred lands. Time to rethink what is acceptable and what is not."

The Next Generation of Interpreters

In a book titled *Permanent Vacation: Twenty Writers on Work and Life in Our National Parks*, one of the contributors, Robert Cornelius (2011), recounts an encounter he had with a father and his young son. The boy was eager to leave one of the trails in Gunnison National Park, but Cornelius offered to take the pair to the top of a ravine to point out a bighorn ram. The boy, who had been so anxious to leave the trail before, now wanted to stay. When his father finally told the boy it was time to leave, he continuously looked back over his shoulder for one more glimpse of the majestic animal. Further down the trail, Cornelius heard the boy exclaim to his father, "I'll never forget this for the rest of my life!" Cornelius, at the time, was only a couple months away from retirement after a long career with the National Park Service. But he wondered if this brief encounter might somehow influence the boy to later consider a career in the parks. It wasn't a far-fetched notion. When Cornelius was a boy, his father took him to Yosemite, and they joined a nature hike near El Capitan. A park naturalist introduced him to the "meadows, forests, waterfalls, and wildlife," and he marveled at the wonders of Yosemite (Cornelius, 2011). Indeed, it was this encounter with nature and an interpreter that sparked his desire to someday work for the National Park Service and a career that ultimately spanned 33 years (Figure 21.5).

Figure 21.5. This roving interpreter at Acadia National Park interprets to families with children who may remember this encounter and grow up to be part of the next generation of interpreters. (TC)

More than a hundred years ago, Anna Botsford Comstock first published *The Handbook of Nature Study*. At nearly 900 pages long, it was a book written for educators to assist students to learn more about their environment. One schoolteacher of the era, Maria Carson, embraced Comstock's theories. She taught her own daughter how to identify birds and learn more about the plants and animals in the fields and woods where they lived. Maria was the mother of Rachel Carson, biologist and best-selling author of *Silent Spring*, who was instrumental in sparking the environmental movement.

In addition to *exposure* to the outdoors, pillars of the environmental movement such as Aldo Leopold, and contemporary spokespersons such as Barry Lopez and Terry Tempest Williams, relate the importance of *learning about* the outdoors as a form of field study. Knowledge of natural history breeds a "fond familiarity" with nature leading people to deeper and more enjoyable experiences and a sense of stewardship for these places so special to them (Smith, 2016). This ecological literacy is also critical for understanding pollution of our lands and waters, climate change, extinction, and other environmental problems.

Nature study goes beyond memorizing facts about the natural world. As Amanda Giracca (2016) observed, "It's not just our ability to name plants and birds, to 'know our neighbors,' as significant as that might be, but the opportunity to question and grow, to be moved, to be momentarily stunned—or flummoxed—by something you couldn't have anticipated."

Many observers are concerned that with ubiquitous technologies and a trend toward less nature-oriented curricula in schools that there will be fewer youth attracted to environmental careers, such as those found in the interpretive profession. Bixler and Joy (2016) noted the importance of "mentoring children and youth such that later, as young adults, they desire to participate in nature-dependent recreation on their own or even seek careers working in wild settings." These same authors suggest that involvement with nature doesn't begin in adulthood, but rather during early-to-middle-childhood, "beginning a developmental process that shapes later perceptions of nature and wild places."

Lopez (2002) discussed the naturalist of the modern era as "among the best informed of the American electorate when it comes to the potentially catastrophic environmental effects of political decisions." Lopez continued, "The contemporary naturalist, it has turned out—again, scientifically grounded, politically attuned, field experienced, library enriched—is no custodian of irrelevant knowledge..." Lopez

> Involvement with nature doesn't begin in adulthood, but rather during early- to middle-childhood.

(2002) noted the importance of firsthand knowledge that is attained by the naturalist. And then suggested, "Historically, tyrants have sought selectively to eliminate firsthand knowledge when its sources lay outside their control. By silencing those with problematic firsthand experiences, they reduced the number of potential contradictions in their political or social designs, and so they felt safer."

Advocacy in Action

Simon (2016) noted that being relevant means "taking action—publicly—on the issues that matter" the most to the organization. Of course, public advocacy can be risky, and not always possible everywhere, but for the right organizations there can be enormous opportunities to more deeply connect with their clientele and make a difference in the world. This is the case with the Monterey Bay Aquarium, in California, when they more purposefully shifted toward advocacy.

As documented by Simon (2016), the Aquarium created an exhibit in the late 1990s, *Fishing for Solutions*, which focused on ocean conservation and seafood sustainability. The exhibit coordinated with their in-house café to feature sustainable seafood. Many visitors asked for a take-home list of the seafood rankings, and the Aquarium responded.

Through its Seafood Watch program, the Aquarium assists consumers and businesses to choose seafood that is sustainable. Public awareness is raised through use

> Public advocacy for the right organizations can make a difference.

of Seafood Guides that list ocean-friendly seafood choices as "Best Choices," "Good Alternatives," and what choices for consumers to "Avoid." Those seafood items to avoid are those that are overfished, or caught or farmed in ways that harm other marine life or the environment.

Their website (montereybayaquarium.org), notes since 1999 the Aquarium has distributed more than 56 million consumer guides. Their free Seafood Watch app has been downloaded more than 1.6 million times. In addition, more than a thousand businesses with more than 100,000 locations across North America reference Seafood Watch science to guide their purchasing decisions.

With this success into their foray of advocacy the Aquarium continued to delve deeper into strong actions on behalf of oceans. The Aquarium now states its mission simply: "to inspire conservation of the ocean." This nonprofit goes on to solicit membership support as follows (montereybayaquarium.org):

> Overfishing, pollution, and climate change have put the ocean in a precarious position, endangering not just marine life, but all life on Earth. But, together, we can turn the tide if we act now. Your support will help us create positive change for the ocean and the animals that call it home—not just today, but for generations to come.

The Aquarium takes a stand on political issues. In 2016, the Aquarium urged California voters to vote "Yes" on Proposition 67, which passed, making California the first state in the nation to ban single-use carryout plastic bags. This law will help to protect oceans from plastic pollution. The Aquarium website offers six podcasts on addressing different aspects of ocean plastic pollution. Supporters are urged to make a commitment to reusable bags, to buy products with nonplastic packaging, and to ask elected representatives to reduce the sources of plastic pollution. As one of the podcasts notes, "If nothing is done, researchers predict there will be more plastic than fish in the ocean by 2050."

The Aquarium's professional staff, through its Ocean Conservation Policy Program, engages with elected officials and advocates science-based policy action. Aquarium staff reach out at local, state, national, and international levels to advance policies that protect key species such as sea otters, and address global threats that include overfishing, pollution, and climate change.

At the Aquarium itself the staff strives to reduce its own carbon footprint. Staff and volunteers communicate to aquarium visitors through exhibits and programs what can be done to help solve the problems, including writing letters to Congress from the aquarium floor. Offsite, the Aquarium prompts interest about climate change and other issues among its three million social media followers on Twitter, Facebook, and other channels.

Specifically, the Aquarium advocates (montereybayaquarium.org) the following:

- Elect leaders who commit to take climate action. Tell candidates for public office—from your city council to United States president—that climate change is important to you.
- Urge elected officials to take action on climate change. Call, write, or tweet your representatives. Ask them to reduce carbon emissions, protect marine habitats, and help us adapt to the changes in motion.
- Encourage climate-friendly practices at work and in your community.

The Monterey Bay Aquarium has clearly made its conservation mission public. Policies are advanced to protect key species such as sharks and tuna and to address global threats to the oceans such as climate change. And the Aquarium encourages their visitors to become involved in this advocacy as well.

Simon (2016) suggests that the "pretty fish" are certainly an important component of the visitor experience at an aquarium, just as the large animals are important at a zoo. However, these features are a portal to something deeper and more meaningful—the fate of certain species and the quality of their habitats and what that means for the rest of us and the fate of the planet (Figure 21.6).

The most important aspect of an interpretive site should be front and center even if, and perhaps most importantly if, the mission of the site touches on difficult subjects or controversial issues. There is some risk, but the benefit is that the site's mission will be clearer, and most people will care more, when the site itself is committed to social justice and environmental integrity.

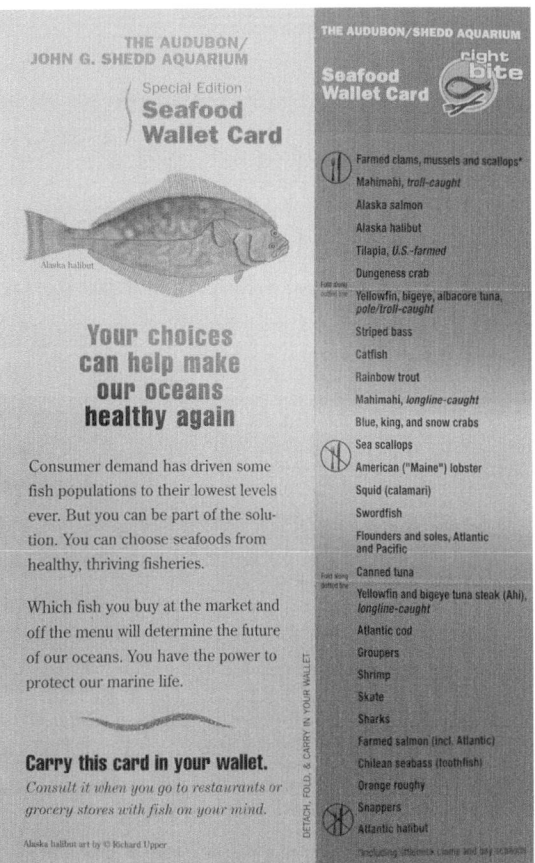

Figure 21.6. Chicago's John G. Shedd Aquarium distribute helpful Rite Bite Wallet cards that helps restaurant diners choose seafood harvested from healthy, sustainable populations. (TC)

Authenticity and Awe

"In various studies we've asked people, "What's running through your mind when you feel awe, and they'll say things like, 'I want to make the world better.'"
–Dacher Keltner

The defining aspect—the backdrop—of almost any interpretive site relates to its authenticity. In a world that seeps more and more toward the inauthentic, the field of interpretation relies on the authentic. As those things, those places, those experiences elsewhere become less authentic, the demand for the authentic increases. Looking to the future, since the interpretive enterprise *is* authentic, there is little question that it will be increasingly sought.

> The defining aspect—the backdrop—of almost any interpretive site relates to its authenticity.

In their book, *Authenticity*, Gilmore and Pine (2007) stated that in an increasingly *unreal* world "consumers choose to buy or not buy based on how *real* they perceive an offering to be. Business today, therefore, is all about being real. Original. Genuine. Sincere. *Authentic*." This real world is what interpretation is all about. Interpretation is rooted in reality: fact, truth, science. Interpreters *are* genuine and sincere. Authenticity is foundational, indeed requisite for effective interpretation to occur. Furthermore, authentic places, artifacts, buildings, wildlife, and the arts can elicit the emotion of awe (Figure 21.7 and Figure 21.8).

Up until the turn of the 21st century, there was little empirical or theoretical work in psychology on the emotion of awe (Keltner & Haidt, 2003). Since then, a growing body of studies has shown the positive effects on people when they encounter a vast and often unexpected stimulus. According to Keltner and Haidt (2003), "Fleeting and rare, experiences of awe can change the course of a life in profound and permanent ways." For example, people tend to act more kindly, ethically, and generously (Abrahamson, 2014). After experiencing awe, people tend to focus more outward and less inward. In other words, a person will redefine the self in terms of the collective and orient toward the interest of others. In an evolutionary sense, awe leads people to cooperate and share resources all of which are necessary for the collective life of the human species (Keltner, 2016).

In addition, experiences of awe stimulate wonder, curiosity, perspective, purpose, and creativity. Current research on the relationship to the immune system has suggested physical health benefits (Keltner, 2016). In regard to mental health, experiences of awe can reduce stress and improve mood (Green & Keltner, 2017).

Experiences of awe occur precisely in the authentic settings where interpreters work: natural landscapes, museums, and historic sites. According to Keltner (2016), awe is "elicited especially by nature, art, and impressive individuals or feats." Sometimes just being at a park or museum and soaking in the experience is enough, and no interpretation is required.

As an example, in the summer of 2015, one of the authors was at Bryce Canyon National Park. Late in the day at the Sunset Point overlook, the low sun cast its rich golden light over the "hoodoos" of Bryce: the bronze, chestnut, and vanilla hues of the rock formations. Rain had fallen earlier, resulting in even deeper tones of the wondrous geological features. Arching over the landscape was a rainbow that touched down on both sides and framed the sacred Navajo Mountain, far off. A rainstorm was brewing in the distance, the rain descending in a small pocket of sky, miles away. And reflecting up from the landscape, in the center of the rainbow, were fingers of light, like the spokes of a wheel, shooting into the darkened clouds above. This was an awe-inspiring sight, really beyond words, that evolved over the course of about an hour. Here was not a time to learn more about the geological strata and erosive forces that carved this remarkable landscape. This was a time to simply bask in the glory of the moment. A color photograph that attempts to capture the magic of that spectacle can be found on the back cover.

> Experiences of awe occur precisely in the authentic settings where interpreters work.

Figure 21.7. The awe-inspiring beauty of the rugged coast of Channel Islands National Park (BB) above, and reflections on May Lake in the high country of Yosemite National Park (LB) below.

Figure 21.8. The awe-inspiring beauty of a sunset over the Pacific Ocean in Olympic National Park (LB) above, and a rare "super-bloom" in Anza-Borrego Desert State Park, California (VGF) below.

Similar moments may happen in the numerous places that interpreters work every day from national parks to art museums. These moments of awe could occur when looking at a million-dollar piece of art, perhaps "St. Francis in Prayer in a Grotto," donated by a philanthropist who, himself, was awed by an interpretive experience viewing masterpieces in the museum. Or perhaps that awe may arrive outside the museum, exploring the sculpture garden, under a full moon on a warm summer evening, beneath the ornate and subtly lit California Tower and luminous dome of the Museum of Man, while enjoying locally sourced food and drink, and listening to local jazz musicians (Figure 21.9).

Or perhaps awe may be inspired at any other interpretive site on the planet where a moment turns to magic and you want to—and you think you can—change the world.

Conclusion

Figure 21.9. Evening at Balboa Park; California Tower and Museum of Man. (LB)

Interpretation's future role will bring greater vitality to society. Interpretation promotes living with a lighter impact on the earth and with stronger ties to our cultural heritage. It produces a more harmonious relationship between the individual and the environment—physically, mentally, emotionally and spiritually. Interpretive experiences help people grow into caring stewards of the land and their heritage.

To serve the present and the future, the profession has the opportunity to help guide humanity toward more thoughtful and generous living within the natural world, to learn the lessons of history that shed light on how we treat people in the future, and to share human and spiritual values of diverse cultures in ways that broaden the horizons of everyone.

Interpretation must exercise vigorous, proactive, and sensible leadership. In a gracious and winsome manner, it must challenge individuals, communities, and nations to consider their impact on the earth, their historical context, and the solutions to the problems of living well with each other, and other species, in this our only home.

An informed citizenry with respect and love for its resources and culture can make better decisions. People who understand the interconnectedness of things can foresee consequences and long-term impacts of their actions on this and future generations.

Interpreters face the responsibility to lead in stimulating love for the earth and humanity and the myriad creatures we share the planet with. Interpreters must grasp the opportunity provided by society and continue to try new ways that lead to greater outreach and greater productivity. Any sense of despair or narrow, small thinking must subside under an energetic, positive thrust. This thrust must focus on real issues and affirmative strategies to stir others to perceive cultural and natural resources as not just our past heritage, but also as our current treasure to use wisely and perpetuate for the future. The goal is to uplift perceptions and thereby enrich life and sustain its support system throughout the world.

Interpretation enriches experiences, advances physical and mental health, benefits the environment, promotes cultural heritage, enhances community welfare, and recognizes the importance of diversity, equality, sustainability, science, and truth.

Thus a better world.

Literature Cited

Abrahamson, J. (2014). The science of awe. *Sierra, 99*(6), 36–39, 54.

Beck, L., & Dustin, D. (2016). Technology on the trails. *Legacy, 27*(6), 20–22.

Bixler, R., & James, J. (2016). *Where the sidewalk ends: Pathways to nature-dependent leisure activities.* In D. Klieber & F. McGuire (Eds.), *Leisure and human development* (pp. 107–131). Urbana, IL: Sagamore.

Brabham, D. (2016). *Crowdsourcing in the public sector.* Washington, DC: Georgetown University Press.

Brochu, L., & Merriman, T. (2008). *Personal interpretation: Connecting your audience to heritage resources* (2nd ed.). Fort Collins, CO: InterpPress.

Carr, N. (2014). *The glass cage: How our computers are changing us.* New York, NY: W. W. Norton & Company, Inc.

Cavalier, D., & Kennedy, E. (Eds). (2016). *The rightful place of science: Citizen science.* Tempe, AZ: Consortium for Science, Policy & Outcomes.

Dustin, D., Beck, L., & Rose, J. (2017). From landscape to techscape. *International Journal of Wilderness,* Spring, 2017.

Dustin, D., Bricker, K., Negley, S., Brownlee, M., Schwab, K. & Lundberg, N. (Eds.). (2016). *This land is your land.* Urbana, IL: Sagamore.

Egan, T. (2016). Unplugging the selfie generation. *National Geographic, 230*(4), 32–55.

Gilmore, J., & Pine, J. (2007). *Authenticity.* Boston, MA: Harvard Business School Press.

Giracca, A. (2016). Into the field: Why science education needs to leave the classroom. *Orion, 35*(3), 46–53.

Green, K., & Keltner, D. (2017). What happens when we reconnect with nature. *Greater Good: The Science of a Meaningful Life.* March 1, 2017.

Keltner, D. (2016). Why do we feel awe? *Greater good: The science of a meaningful life.* May 10, 2016.

Keltner, D., & Haidt, J. (2003). Approaching awe, a moral, spiritual, and aesthetic emotion. *Cognition and Emotion,* 17, 297–314.

Kohl, J., & McCool, S. (2016). *The future has other plans: Planning holistically to conserve natural and cultural heritage.* Golden, CO: Fulcrum Publishing.

Lopez, B. (2002). The naturalist. In The Orion Society, *Patriotism and the American land, 25–38.* Great Barrington, MA: The Orion Society.

Louv, R. (2016). *Vitamin N.* Chapel Hill, NC: Algonquin Books.

Miller, J. (2016). Valuing interpretation. *Legacy, 27*(5), 15–19.

Miller, J. (2017). Great things to come. *Legacy, 28*(1), 40.

Monterey Bay Aquarium: montereybayaquarium.org.

Moor, R. (2016). *On trails: An exploration.* New York, NY: Simon & Schuster.

Moore, J. (2016). Virtual trips to the zoo. *Legacy, 27*(5), 26–29.

Omar, M. (2015). *How to start a blog that people will read.* In association with makemoneyfromhomelionsclub.com.

Quintero, G. (2014). Panama 66: Balboa Park's newest addition. *WestCoasterSD.* September, 33–34.

Sanders, S. (2016). Kinship and kindness: On deepening our connection with our fellow beings. *Orion, 35*(3), 26–37.

Scott, P. (2010). Getting a squirrel to focus: How to communicate with and persuade today's listeners. *Proceedings of the Conference on Corporate Communication*, 307–318.

Simon, N. (2016). *The art of relevance*. Santa Cruz, CA: Museum 2.0.

Smith, W. (2016). Observational ecology: Renewing the study of nature. *Legacy, 27*(2), 30–33.

Turkle, S. (2015). *Reclaiming conversation: The power of talk in a digital age*. New York, NY: Penguin Press.

Williams, T. (2016). *The hour of land*. New York, NY: Sarah Crichton Books.

Appendix A

The Interpreter's Creed

As a Practicing Interpreter, I Shall:

- Seek to serve visitors; to be an ambassador for the place I work; to instill in visitors the ability and desire to sense beauty in their surroundings.

- Seek to respect all the visitors with whom I come in contact and welcome them as I would welcome guests in my home; and to share equally my knowledge and passion regardless of the visitor's age, gender, interests, physical abilities, or cultural differences.

- Seek to be agreeable, look good, have a polished presence, speak in a well-modulated voice, and be genuinely friendly.

- Seek to see the good, or the humor, in any situation and answer repetitious questions with enthusiasm, as if they were asked for the first time.

- Seek to convey only well-documented, accurate information.

- Seek to be an exemplary role model for environmentally responsible behavior by word and example.

- Seek to structure interpretive design and programming in such a way as to minimize the impact on cultural and environmental resources.

- Seek to improve my mind, continue learning about the resource, and expand my learning about the principles and processes of interpretation that will ultimately benefit visitors to the site.

- Seek to help other interpreters achieve their interpretive goals, particularly assisting new interpreters to develop confidence and abilities.

- Believe in myself; give my best to the world and expect that the world will give its best to me.

From Beck, L. and Cable, T. (1998). *Interpretation for the 21st Century: Fifteen Guiding Principles for Interpreting Nature and Culture.* Urbana, IL: Sagamore.

Acknowledgments

In addition to those individuals who contributed introductory stories and boxes, listed separately, we want to acknowledge the following individuals who assisted with the collection of photos or who provided editorial assistance by reviewing sections of the book: Jeffery Aarnio, Schaneé Anderson, Melissa Bean, Heather Brown, LuAnn Cadden, Kathy Cavender, Anna Chatel, Cyndi Cogbill, John Cunning, Steven Espiner, Duane Fast, Jill Firmin, Susan Forgrave, Victor Fratto, Diane Golden, Matthew Graves, Robin Grumm, Emily Jacobs, Ashley Kelly, Valeria Klitsounova, Chuck Lennox, Andres Leon, Amy Lethbridge, Thorsten Ludwig, Joe Harawira, George Kastler, Jon Kohl, Pam Martin, Marisol Mayorga, Bill McGowan, Catherine Morgan-Proux, Janet Price, Nancy Russell, Bahram Nekouie-Sadry, Rebecca Sellers, Ryan Sharp, Pat Silvosky, Jeffrey Skibins, Debby Smith, Gerry Snyder, Kendra Swee, John Veverka, Paul Weidhaas, Neal Wollenberg, and Erica Wheeler. The following graduate teaching assistants at San Diego State University, all from the School of Communication, assisted with typing and research assistance: Kelly Christerson, Allie Doherty, and Anuja Majmundar. Finally, appreciation to Vicki Fielden who provided valuable input every step of the way over the course of this project.

About the Contributors

The following have contributed either "boxes" or stories featured throughout the text. All have won various awards for their work, and many have received the Fellow Award, the National Association for Interpretation's highest honor.

Schaneé Anderson is Curator of Education and Farms at Sedgwick County Zoo in Wichita, Kansas. She is a certified interpretive trainer and conducts regular certified interpretive guide trainings for the National Association for Interpretation. Schaneé also teaches an interpretation course at Friends University in Wichita.

J. Patrick Barry is the director of The Corps Foundation. He retired from the U.S. Army Corps of Engineers after 35 years of federal service. During 25 of those years he supervised the Bonneville Lock and Dam Visitor Center. He served as lead instructor for the Corps' Interpretive Services and Outreach courses.

Robert Bixler is an associate professor of Parks, Recreation, and Tourism Management at Clemson University (2017 College Football Playoff National Champions). His research involves advocating the role of local and regional parks in cultivating the next generation of enthusiasts for heritage resources.

Andy Bleckinger is an interpretive naturalist at the Mountains Recreation and Conservation Authority in southern California. He does inspiring work with youth from the urban Los Angeles area.

Lisa Brochu is a certified interpretive planner. She is the author of *Interpretive Planning: The 5-M Model for Successful Planning Projects* and has co-authored other interpretive books. She is a principal of Heartfelt Associates and was previously the associate director of the National Association for Interpretation.

LuAnn Cadden was Outreach and Education District Supervisor for the Missouri Department of Conservation where she supervised a naturalist, the outdoor skills coordinator, and conservation educators. She is currently a freelance author, editor, and librarian based in St. Joseph, Missouri.

Rita Cantu is a singer/songwriter whose albums include *Canyon Lifesongs* and *Desert Lifesongs*. She has worked in the interpretive profession with the National Park Service and U.S. Forest Service.

Paul Caputo is deputy director of the National Association for Interpretation and editor of *Legacy* magazine. He co-authored *Interpretation by Design: Graphic Design Basics for Heritage Interpreters*. He is a certified interpretive trainer and has presented sessions on graphic design nationally and internationally.

Daniel Dustin is a professor of Outdoor Recreation Planning and Policy at the University of Utah. He has chaired programs at San Diego State University, Florida International University, and the University of Utah. He has written extensively (10 books) in the fields of planning and policy, environmental ethics, and professional issues.

Mario A. Escalera is the director of an organization in La Paz, Mexico, called Social and Environmental Formation and Innovation. He is pursuing a master's degree in Administration for Social-Environmental Business (known as the Green MBA) at the Universidad del Medio Ambiente. Mario is a certified interpretive guide and is pursuing NAI certification as a trainer.

Ted Eubanks is president/CEO of Fermata, Inc. For more than 25 years he has worked nationally and internationally in sustainable tourism, park planning, and interpretation of the travel experience. He has designed numerous scenic byways and was instrumental in establishing the concept of a birding trail road tour.

Robin Grumm spent 18 years working for the Missouri Department of Conservation. Her first eight years was as a frontline interpreter, and her final 10 years was as Assistant Nature Center Manager and volunteer coordinator at Runge Nature Center in Jefferson City, Missouri.

Sam Ham is professor emeritus of Communication Psychology and Conservation Social Sciences at the University of Idaho. He is the author of *Environmental Interpretation* and *Interpretation—Making A Difference on Purpose*. He has taught thematic communication throughout the U.S. and in nearly 50 other countries.

Jonathan Kohl is the president and founder of the PUP Global Heritage Consortium, a nonprofit global network of people and organizations dedicated to the heritage management and planning field. He co-authored *The Future Has Other Plans: Planning Holistically to Conserve Natural and Cultural Heritage*.

Alan Leftridge spent 25 years teaching interpretation and environmental studies courses at Miami University, Ohio, and Humboldt State University, California. He served as editor of interpretive publications, including *The Interpreter* and *Legacy*. He is the author of *Interpretive Writing* and *The Best of Glacier National Park*.

Chuck Lennox is founder and owner of Lennox Insites. His firm develops strategic interpretive master plans, educational plans and curricula, and conducts interpretive training sessions. Prior to establishing his consulting firm, he worked for the National Park Service, Woodland Park Zoo, and King County Department of Natural Resources and Parks.

John C. F. Luzader has been a leader in living history interpretation since 1961. As a principal at Living Museums of the West, he provided training for historic sites and museums across the United States and internationally. John has held several high offices in the National Association for Interpretation.

Tim Merriman served as executive director of the National Association for Interpretation, and The Greenway and Nature Center of Pueblo, Colorado. He co-authored several interpretive books, including *Personal Interpretation: Connecting Your Audience to Heritage Resources.* He is a principal of Heartfelt Associates.

Jay Miller is president of the National Association for Interpretation. He served as Chief of Interpretation for Arkansas State Parks for three decades. He teaches interpretation at Arkansas Tech University, and is a speaker, planner, and trainer.

Lisa Nagurny is a park ranger with the National Park Service at Great Smoky Mountains National Park. She has worked with the International Coalition of Sites of Conscience on trainings for Facilitated Dialogue. She has also worked at the Flint Hills Discovery Center and *Brown v. Board of Education* National Historic Site.

Jess Reese is the interpretive programs supervisor at the Brookfield Zoo near Chicago. She supervises all interpretive programing institution-wide for quality and consistency. Jess provides coaching, direction, and instruction to the staff. She is also a climate change education consultant and is a presenter for The Climate Project.

Roger Riolo is an independent interpretive trainer and NAI Master Trainer. He is the former interpretive program manager of Newberry Volcanic National Monument and has taught resource interpretation at the college level. He was previously a U.S. Air Force pilot and commercial pilot.

Irene N. Rodríguez is the executive director of the Cabot's Pueblo Museum in Desert Hot Springs, California. In her role as administrator, she oversees all school programs, public tours, media relations, artisans, and the gift shop and gallery.

Jeremy Shellhorn is a professor of graphic design and associate dean for Strategic Initiatives in the School of Architecture, Design and Planning at the University of Kansas. Jeremy and his students recently designed new wayside exhibits at Rocky Mountain National Park.

Gerry Snyder is a multimedia specialist at Kansas State University. He has worked on several media projects involving interpretation at Kansas State and the University of Idaho. He has assisted in teaching interpretation courses at both of these universities.

Photography Credits Key

The following individuals and agencies contributed photographs to the book as indicated by the initials that accompanied each photograph.

ASP	Arkansas State Parks
BB	Benjamin Beck
LB	Larry Beck
SB	Spencer Beck
TC	Ted Cable
LC	LuAnn Cadden
KC	Kathy Cavender (Missouri Department of Conservation)
AC	Anna Chatel
JF	Jill Firmin
SF	Susan Forgrave
VF	Victor Fratto
VGF	Vicki Fielden
CHSC-GWJ	George Wharton James (California Historical Society Collection)
KDWPT	Kansas Department of Wildlife, Parks and Tourism
DK	Douglas Knudson
JK	Jon Kohl
CL	Chuck Lennox
NPS-NL	Neal Lewis (National Park Service)
MDC	Missouri Department of Conservation
MSP	Missouri State Parks
NPS	National Park Service
NPS-HMAC	National Park Service History Collection, Horace M. Albright Collection (HPC-000487)
PM	Pam Martin
GPNC-RS	Rebecca Sellers (Great Plains Nature Center)
USFS - CMS	Cynthia M. Sandeno (USDA Forest Service)
RS	Ryan Sharp
AS	Alan Stolfus
USACOE	U.S. Army Corps of Engineers
USFS	USDA Forest Service
NPS-MWW	M. Woodbridge Williams (National Park Service)
FNW	Jose Witt (Friends of Nevada Wilderness)

Index

7 Habits of Highly Effective People (Covey), 350

A

Abbey, Edward, 193
About This Life (Lopez), 390
Abram, David, 230
Acadia National Park, 468
accuracy of interpreting history, 336–338
activities and demonstrations, 205–206
Adams, Ansel, vii
administration, museum, 251–253
adventure cruising interpreters, 34
Adventures of a Nature Guide, The (Mills), 7, 459
advocacy, 469–471
Ady, Janet, 120
affective domain, 106
after-hours information, 189
age groups, serving different, 144–154
agency training, 380–384
agricultural museums, 243–244
Alaska Zoo, Anchorage, 33
Alexander, Lamar, 53
Alexander the Great, 33
Algonquin Provincial Park, Ontario, Canada, 62
All-American Road Plans, 293
American Alliance of Museums 2016-2020 Strategic Plan, 235, 255
American Alliance of Museums (AAM), 266, 387
American Association for State and Local History (AASLH), 326, 342, 387
American Association of Museums, 266
American Camp Association (ACA), 388
American Forest & Paper Association (AFPA), 36
American Forest Foundation, 36
American Indian Movement, 241
American Museum of Natural History, 246, 275
American Zoo and Aquarium Association (AZA), 387
Americans with Disabilities Act (ADA), 139–141
Anasazi Cultural Heritage Center, Colorado, 28–29
Anderson, Schaneé, 353–354, 481
angry visitors, 187
animals, dead or alive, 272–273
Anza-Borrego Desert State Park, California, 474
Aotearoa New Zealand, 437
Apple's iPad, 277
Apps for Healthy Kids, 464
aquariums, 32–33, 273, 276
Arango, Eduardo, 172
Arches National Park, Utah, 201
Aristotle, 43
Arkansas State Parks, 175, 403
Armstrong, John, 244
Army Corps of Engineers (COE), 59, 62
    Bonneville Lock & Dam Visitor Center, 190
    Grand Ecore Visitor Center, 236
    interpreters, 27–38
    promotion of water safety, 228
art museums, 244
Arthus-Bertrand, Yann, 233
arts in interpretation
    dance, 226–227
    interpretive theater, 217–222
    introduction, 215
    music, 225–226
    storytelling and poetry, 222–225
    the use of, 216–217
    visual arts, 227–230
Association for Living History, Farm and Agricultural Museums (ALHFAM), 335–336
Association of Interpretive Naturalists (AIN), 386, 439–440
attitudes
    should interpreters change, 71–72
    in Theory of Planned Behavior (TPB), 66
audiences
    approaching, 154–158
    connecting to diverse, 131–139
    connecting to sovereign, 130–131
    getting to know your, 128–130
    serving different age groups, 144–154
    serving guests with disabilities, 139–144
audio-enhanced interpretations, 291
auditoriums, 250
Audubon, John James, 239, 320
augmented reality (AR), 299
Augustine, Saint, 292
Auschwitz Concentration Camp, Poland, 328
Authenticity (Gilmore & Pine), 471–472
authenticity of interpreting history, 338–339, 471–475
Authority of the Resource Technique (ART), 61
Autry Museum of Western Heritage, 245

B

Babb, Fred, 406
Balboa Park, San Diego, California, 233, 237
Bambi (Walt Disney), 22
Banana Slug String Band, the, 225, 226
Banff National Park, Canada, 219
Barnum, P.T., 239
Barry, Patrick, 59, 481
Basman, Cem, 336
Bass, Rick, 193
Bat Conservation International's website, 167
Batts, Dr. H. Lewis, 35
Baumer, Michele, 152
Beck, Larry, vii, x, 11, 448
beehives, 276
Beghetto, Ronald, 253
behavioral control in Theory of Planned Behavior (TPB), 66
benefits
    of interpretation to individuals, 42–46
    of interpretation to society, 49–55
Bennett, Arnold, 348, 360
Beyond Ecophobia: Reclaiming the Heart in Nature Education (Sobel), 149

Big Bend National Park, 202
bike paths, 300–301
bird observation rooms, 252
Bishop, George, 428
Bitgood, Stephen, 260, 264, 265
Bixler, Robert, 427, 428–429, 481
Black Forest, Germany, 157
Bleckinger, Andy, 138–139, 481
Blehm, Eric, vii, viii, xiii
BLM's Yaquina Head Outstanding Natural Area, Newport, Oregon, 28
Blue Star Museums Initiative, 31
boards of directors, 253
Bonneville Lock & Dam Project, 28
bookstore/gift shops for museum facilities and services, 251
Boone, Daniel, 244
Boonsboro, Kentucky, 244
Botton, Alain de, 244
Boundary Waters Canoe Area Wilderness, 65
Boys & Girls Club of Mar Vista Gardens, California, 127
Braille Trails, 141
Branson, Richard, 355
broadcast media, 174–177
Brochu, Lisa, 88, 397, 404, 481
brochures, 61–62, 317–318
Bronx Zoo, 151–152, 260
Brook, Paul, 221
Brookfield Zoo, 97
Brown, John, 222
Brown, William, 132
brown bears, 165
Brown v. Board of Education National Historic Site, Topeka, Kansas, 327
Bryant, Dr. Harold C., 7
Bryce Canyon National Park, 211, 472
Buffalo Soldiers National Museum, 135
Burbank, Luther, 146
Burdee, John, 88
Burden, Chris, 278
Bureau of Land Management's interpreters, 28–29
Burroughs, John, 46
Bush, Barbara, 245
business plans, 361, 397

C

Cable, Ted, vii, x, 11, 448
cable television, 176–177
Cabot Yerxa Elementary School, Desert Hot Springs, California, 325
Cabrillo, Juan Rodriquez, ix
Cabrillo National Monument, California, 190
Cadden, LuAnn, 303, 481
Cades Cove, Smoky Mountain National Park, 329
California State Parks training, 380
Callaway Gardens, Pine Mountain, Georgia, 34
Calloway, Cab, 127
camp interpreters, 33–34
Caneday, Lowell, xi–xii
Cantu, Rita, 218, 481

Canyon de Chelly, 223
Canyonlands National Park, 47
Capulin Volcano National Monument, 98
Caputo, Paul, 169–170, 481
Carlock, Margo, 255
Carnegie Museum of Natural History, 269
Carr, Nicholas, 466
Carson, Maria, 468
Carson, Rachel, 118, 149, 221, 304, 319, 468
Carter, Rosalynn, 245
Caterpillar, Peoria, Illinois, 36
Catlin, George, 239
certifications, interpreter, 386
chamber pots, 272
Channel Island National Park, 63, 465, 473
chaotic patterns, 90
Chatel, Dr. Anna, 436
Cheyenne Bottoms Wetland Education Center, Kansas, 348
Chicago Historical Society Museum, 254
children, tips for working with very young, 147–148
Chincoteague NWR, 27
Chittenden, Hiram, 41
Christiansen, Tina, x
Chugach National Forest, 25
Cialdini, Robert, 68
Ciapparone, Maurilio, 440
Cicero, 144
Cimarron National Grasslands Road Tour, 292
citizen science programs, 464
civics and interpretation, 52–54
Clark, Roy Peter, 316
Cleveland Museum of Art, 277
climate change, 24, 96–99, 222
cognitive development theory, 107–109
cognitive domain, 106
cognitive map theory, 111–112
Colonial Williamsburg, Virginia, 243, 330, 331
Columbus, Christopher, 341
communication theory and education theory, 91–93
compassionate intelligence, 114–115
Comstock, Anna Botsford, 468
concrete operations stage, Piaget's model, 109
"constructivist" approach, 91–92
constructivist learning, 112–113
Consumer.ology (Graves), 428
controversy in interpreting history, 341, 354–356
Cornelius, Robert, 468
Cornell, Joseph, 118, 120
Corps of Engineers. *See* Army Corps of Engineers
courtesy, practicing, 353
Covey, Stephen, 350, 357
CPR, 189
Craig, Steve, 220
Creole Nature Trail, Louisiana, 296
Cumberland Island National Seashore, 426
customer care, 352–356
customers, matching resources to, 398–403
cycloramas, 275

D

Dabney, Walt, 81, 96
dance, 226–227
Dark Skies Parks, 174
"Darkened Waters" exhibit, Pratt Museum, Homer, Alaska, 269–271
Davidsonville Historic State Park, Arkansas, 347
Declaration of Independence, the, 43, 271
DeGray Lake Resort State Park, Arkansas, 366
Delaware Bay Schooner Project, 35
demonstrations and activities, 205–206
Denali National Park and Preserve, Alaska, 89–90, 204, 205
Denver Museum of Nature and Science, 275
design
    of exhibits, 273–275
    of museums, 249–251
    trails, 285–288
    of visitor centers, 249–251
    wayside road tours, 296–300
dialogue, facilitated, 208–210
digital media, 166–171
dioramas, 275
disabilities, serving guests with, 139–144
Disney, Walt, 341
Disney Corporation, 353
Doctorow, E.L., 322
Doering, Zahava, 235
Drake Well Museum & Old Economy Village, 29
Drucker, Peter, 349, 361
Dry Tortugas National Park, 98
Dunmire, William, 60
Dustin, Dan, 49–50, 51, 482

E

Eastern National Forests Interpretive Association (ENFIA), 369, 370
ECHO Lake Aquarium & Science Center, Burlington, Vermont, 277
ecological model of health promotion, 52
ecotourism, 363
Edelstein, Barry, 217
Edison, Thomas, 330
education
    See also training and professional growth
    defined, 8
    educational benefits of interpretation, 42–43
    lifelong learning, 461–462
    theory and communication theory, 91–93
Edwards, Yorke, 5
Effigy Mounds National Monument, 241
Eisenhower, President Dwight D., 242
Elaboration Likelihood Model (ELM) of persuasion, 64–65
emergency response, 189
Emerson, Ralph Waldo, 356
Empathy Museum, London, England, 245
Ename Charter for Interpretation of Cultural Heritage Sites, 445–446

Environmental Interpretation (Ham), 86, 448
Eppley Institute for Parks and Public Lands, Indiana University, 380
Ernie Miller Nature Center, Kansas, 364–365
Escalera, Mario, 435, 482
etiquette, disability, 141–142
Eubanks, Ted, 295, 482
European Association for Heritage Interpretation, 441
evaluation
    become a visitor, 420–421
    cautions about, 427–429
    cost-effectiveness for program, 429–430
    of employees, 359
    evaluating individual performance, 421–424
    focus groups, 427
    methods of, 420
    observations of actual behavior, 429
    observing the visitors, 424
    participant, 426–427
    three periods of, 425–426
    total program analysis, 430–431
    what, how, and why evaluate, 418–420
evening programs, 199–201
Everglades National Park, 94
exhibit plans, 279
exhibitions, 250
exhibits
    design principles, 298–300
    function of, 260–262
    how people visit, 262–268
    planning and design, 273–275
    types of, 275–279
    and visitors, 268
experiences
    enriching, 10–11
    interpretation as visitor, 12–13
    museum, 253–255
Exxon Valdez oil tanker, 270–271

F

facilitated dialogue, 208–210
facility plans, 397
failure, dealing with, 352
Falk, John, 253, 273
farms' interpreters, 32
Fast, Duane, 441
federal agencies' interpreters, 18
Field Museum of Natural History, Chicago, 275, 417
Figari, Elyssa, 252
first aid, 189
Fishing for Solutions (Monterey Bay Aquarium, California), 469–470
Fleming, David, 242
Flesch Index, 315
Flint Hills Prairie Discovery Center, Kansas, 143, 276
flow learning, 118–119
focus groups, 427
Fog Index, 315–316
Fontenelle Nature Association, Nebraska, 154
Fooled by Randomness (Taleb), 428

Ford, Betty, 245
Ford, Henry, 330, 427
Forestry Service's Petawawa National Forestry Institute, Canada, 145
forest interpreters, 29
Forgrave, Susan, 325
formal operations stage, Piaget's model, 109
Fowler, Susan, 56
fractal relationships, 90
Frames of Mind: The Theory of Multiple Intelligences (Gardner), 110
Freiburg Declaration on Heritage Interpretation, 441, 442–443
Friedman, Jonathan, 59
friends groups, 370–371
Friends of the Wabash, Indiana, 371
Friends of Virgin Islands National Park, 370
Frost, Robert, 321
Fudge, Robert, 131
fund-raising, 371–374

G

Galapagos Islands, 63, 363
Galaxy Zoo, 464
Galvez, Victor, 377
gaming, 277
Gander, Newfoundland, 215
Gandhi, Mahatma, 391
Gardner, Howard, 110
Gates, Bill, 105
genius of place, 89–90
Gettysburg National Military Park, 111, 211
Gibran, Kahlil, 114
Gifford Pinchot National Forest, 25, 26
Gifts of Interpretation, The (Beck & Cable), 448
Gilligan, Carol, 116
Gilman, Benjamin, 247
Giracca, Amanda, 469
Glacier Bay National Park, 98
Glacier National Park, 98, 222
Glen Canyon, 14
Glen Canyon National Recreation Area, 30
global interpretation
    global progress, 445–449
    global spread of professionalism, 439–441
    international interpretation, innovations, inspirations, 436–439
    introduction, 435–436
    professional recognition and training, 442–445
    tourism and peace, 449–453
Goethe, Mr. and Mrs. Charles M., 7
Golden Gate National Recreation Area, California, 134, 137
Goode, George Brown, 235
Gospel of Nature, The (Burroughs), 46
Goulston, Mark, 357
government, local, interpreters, 30–31
GPS-linked content, 296
Grand Canyon, 14
Grand Canyon National Park, 24, 93–94, 174, 211, 317

Graves, Philip, 428
Great Basin Desert, Mojave Desert, 295
Great Plains Nature Center, Wichita, Kansas, 229, 368
Great Smoky Mountains National Park, 129, 208
"Great Trinity Forest," Texas, 408
Green Mountain Conservation Camps, 33
Greenfield Village & Henry Ford Museum, Dearborn, Michigan, 32
Greenfield Village, Michigan, 330
"Greening Health" (Dustin), 51
Griffiths, Jay, 216
Gross, Michael, 237, 248
Grosvenor, Gilbert, 53
group singing, 201
Grumm, Robin, 148, 283, 482
Guide, The (Grand Canyon National Park), 174
Guide to the Lampshades of Paradise Inn (WNPF), 259–260
guided travel, 204
guided travel for museum facilities and services, 251
Gunning's Fog Index, 315–316

H

habitat groups, 275
Haida Nation, 34
Hall, Ansel, 7, 240, 369
Hall of Northwest Coast Indians, Canada, 276
Ham, Sam, 6, 60, 63, 86, 89, 192, 195, 448, 482
Hamill, Pete, 307
Hana Road tour, Maui, Hawaii, 294
Hanauma Bay, Hawaii, 62
Handbook of Nature Study, The (Comstock), 468
handouts, 189
hands-on exhibits, 275–276
Harper's Ferry Center, 81
Harpers Ferry National Historical Park, 151, 230
Harrison, President Benjamin, 23
Hart, Leslie, 112
Hartz, Julia, 172
Hartzog, George, 9
Hawke, Sangye, 401
Hazelius, Arthur, 330
Hazelius, Artur, 243
Heacox, Kim, 98
health, values of interpretation, 49–50
Healthy Parks, Healthy People (NPS), 49
Hein, David, 215
Hennepin County Park District, Minnesota, 31
Heritage Interpretation International (HII), 440
historic agencies' interpreters, 29
historic buildings, 242–243
Historic Fort Snelling, Minnesota, 334, 335
history, interpreting. *See* interpreting history
history museums, 242
Hobbs State Park Visitor Center, Arkansas, 247
Holocaust Museum, Washington DC, 402
Holocaust museums, 242
holographs, 276
Hoover, President Herbert, 330
Hope Diamond at the Smithsonian, 261

Hour of Land, The: A Personal Topography of America's National Parks (Williams), 98, 467
Houston Zoos' preschool programs, 144, 146
Hovenweep National Monument, 398

I

Ickes, Harold, 83–84
Illusion of Public Opinion (Bishop), 428
illustrated talks, 198–199
Indiana Dunes National Lakeshore, 94
indigenous peoples, interpreting, 341–342
industrial interpreters, 36–37
information desks in museum facilities and services, 250–251
information duty, 186–187
information personnel duties, 188–190
information technologies, 122
innovation, encouraging, 351
inspirational benefits of interpreters, 44–45
Instagram, 169
Institute of Tourist Guiding, United Kingdom, 388
inter-agency partnerships, 368–370
International Coalition of Sites of Conscience (ICSC), 327
International Council on Monuments & Sites (ICOMOS), 445–446
International Dark Skies Parks, 174
International Surfing Museum, Huntington Beach, California, 245
International Union for the Conservation of Nature (IUCN), 436
Interpret Europe, 387, 389
interpretation
    applying appropriately, 71–72
    arts in. *See* arts in interpretation
    benefits to individuals, 42–46
    best practices research, 211
    business approach to, 347–374
    civics and, 52–54
    definitions, 5–6, 60
    a dynamic profession, xv
    essence of, 100–101
    evaluating, 417–431
    future of, 457–476
    global. *See* global interpretation
    growing the profession, 462–463
    guiding principles of, 81–101
    ideals of, 12–13
    interpreters and, xiii
    introduction, 3–5
    as management tool in practice, 68–70
    as management tool in theory, 64–68
    as part of recreation, 12
    personal, 185–212
    philosophy of, 13–14
    principal terms, 8–9
    public sector and nonprofit, 364–367
    purposes of, 9–12
    quality, xiii–xiv
    roots, 6–8
    roving, 156–157, 251
    thematic, 86–88
    training and professional growth, 378–392
Interpretation by Design (National Association for Interpretation), 318
Interpretation for the 21st Century (Knudson, Cable & Beck), 448
Interpretation: Making a Difference on Purpose (Ham), 86, 195, 448
Interpretation of Cultural and Natural Resources (Knudson, Cable & Beck), 448
interpreters
    defined, 8–9
    Interpreter's Creed, 479
    next generation of, 468–469
    self-improvement, 390–391
    should they change attitudes, 71–72
    tasks of, 13
    where they work, 18–29
interpreting
    for individual growth, 46–49
    history. *See* interpreting history
    in visitor centers, 235–238
Interpreting Difficult History at Museums and Historic Sites (Rose), 342
Interpreting for Park Visitors (Lewis), 86
interpreting history
    accuracy and authenticity, 336–341
    approaches to, 327–336
    interpreting indigenous peoples, 341–342
    introduction, 325
    living history, 330–336
    why interpret history, 326–327
Interpreting Our Heritage (Mills), 9
interpretive associations, 368–370
interpretive planning
    building the plan, 408–413
    definitions, 397–398
    dynamics of practical planning, 407
    interpretive plans, 407–408
    introduction, 395
    matching resources and customers, 398–403
    planning approaches, 403–406
    plans overview, 396–397
    vision, 406
Interpretive Planning (Brochu), 397
interpretive programming, 91
interpretive road tours
    beyond the park or historic park, 293–294
    generally, 292–293
    media options, 295–296
    special interest road tours, 294–295
    wayside design, 296–298
interpretive services, organizations providing (table), 19
interpretive sign materials, 298
interpretive talks, 192, 194–197
interpretive theater, 216–217
interpretive trails. *See* trails

interpretive villages' interpreters, 32
interpretive writing
    introduction, 304–306
    journaling and poetry, 319–322
    the process, 307–310
    proofreading, 309
    style, 313–316
    techniques, tips for effective writing, 310–313
    written media, 316–319
Interpretive Writing (Leftridge), 304
interviewing, being interviewed, 180–182
"Iron Crosses of the Great Plains," 45
Issues in Cultural Tourism Studies (Smith), 451

J

James Whitcomb Riley House, 242
Jarvis, Jon, 5, 98
Jefferson, Thomas, 43, 53, 239, 243
Jefferson County (CO) Open Space parks, 157
Jobs, Steve, 193
John Deere, Moline, Illinois, 36
John G. Shedd Aquarium, Chicago, Illinois, 471
John Pennekamp Reef State Park, Florida, 292
Johnson, Lady Bird, 245
Johnson, Samuel, 303
Joshua Tree National Park, 98, 99, 306
journaling and poetry, 319–322

K

Kahneman, Daniel, 428
Kalamazoo Nature Center, Michigan, 35
Katmai National Park & Preserve, King Salmon, Alaska, 165, 465
Keitner, Dacher, 471
Kellert, Stephen, 50
Kenai Fjords National Park, 98
Kenai NWR, 27
Kenyan National Parks, 363
Kiltner, Dacher, 47
kinesthetic domain, 106
King, Stephen, 306, 307
King Jr., Martin Luther, 94, 197, 410–414, 452–453
King Tut exhibit, 261
Kingsley Plantation, 130
Knopf, Richard, 111
Knudson, Doug, vii, 448
Kohl, Jon, 11, 377, 389, 451, 482
Kohlberg's Six Stages of Moral Development (table), 117

L

La Jolla Playhouse, California, 215, 216
La Mesa, California, 17
LaBar, Wayne, 277
labels, 316–317
Lake Baikal, Russia, 438
Lake Mead National Recreation Area, 157
L'Amour, Louis, 283
Laona, Wisconsin's timber train, 246
Larsen, David, 130
Lashmet, Jeff and Chris, 190
Lassoing the Sun: A Year in America's National Parks (Woods), 98
Last Child in the Woods (Louv), 120
Last Season, The (Blehm), vii
layouts of trails, 287
Lazansky, Nadja, 269
Leaders Eat Last (Sinek), 358
leadership, 349–350
learning styles, 110
learning theories and useful strategies, 107–117
lecturers described, 8
Lee, Kaiulani, 221
Leftridge, Alan, 304, 305–306, 482
Lennox, Chuck, 438–439, 450, 482
Leopold, Aldo, 45, 90, 118, 218, 468
Lessons from the World of Theater (Missouri State Parks and Historic Sites), 219
Levitt, Theodore, 350
Lewis, Bill, 86, 195
Lewis, Meriwether, 259
Lewis, Richard, 451
libraries for museum facilities and services, 251
lifelong learning, 461–462
"Lifelong Learning Day," 121
lighthouse metaphor, ix
Lillie, Ben, 224
Limpopo Field Guide Training South Africa, 444
Lincoln, Abraham, 14, 20–21, 305, 309, 337, 466
Lindblad Expedition cruise ships, 363
Linnaeus, Carl, 441
Little Rock Central High School National Historic Site, Arkansas, 327
Living Memorial Project, Forest Service, 25–26
local service information list (table), 188
Logan Pass Visitor Center, 222
Lopez, Barry, 468, 469
Louv, Richard, 50, 120, 467
low wattage radio, 176
Lumber Museum, Pennsylvania, 29
luxury cruising interpreters, 34
Luzader, John C.F., 332, 483

M

MacGregor, Jean, 439–440
magazines, 173
Makah Cultural & Research Center, Washington, 30
Makah Museum, Neah Bay, Washington, 269–270
managers, habits to develop for, 350
Mandelbrot, Benoit, 90
Manhattan, Kansas, 44
maps, 189, 289
marketing
    and business plans, 361–362
    introducing, 11–12
Martin Luther King, Jr., National Historic Site, 94, 95, 409, 410–414
Maslow, Abraham, 46, 47, 187
mass customization, 401
master plans, 396–397

Mather, Stephen, 7–8, 60, 185, 240
McCavitt, Brian, 59
McCullough, David, 326
McKibben, Bill, 230
McLean, Kathleen, 270
McLuhan, Marshall, 93
McPhee, John, 307–308
McPhee Reservoir, Colorado, 28
McRaney, David, 428
Meaningful Interpretation (Larsen), 88
mechanics of apperception, 114
media
    broadcast, 174–177
    digital, 166–171
    interpretive road tours, 295–296
    print, 173–174
    social, 168–170
    trail, 289–291
    written, 316–319
media relations, 172–173
Merriman, Tim, 88, 458, 459, 482
Mesa Verde National Park, 63, 211, 242
messages, tips for more powerful (table), 69
Metropolitan Museum of Art, New York City, 50–51, 246
Michener, James, 313
Midwest Open Air Coordinating Council (MOACC), 336
Miller, Dr. Loye, 7
Miller, Jay, 347, 366, 461, 482
Miller, John, 352
Mills, Enos, 6–7, 8, 45, 82, 83, 112, 193, 321, 363, 458, 459, 460, 462
Minidoka Internment National Monument, Idaho, 327
Mini-Indonesia park near Jakarta, Indonesia, 53
Minnesota Zoo, 43
minorities, why they don't come to national parks, 133–134
mission statements, 253
Missouri Department of Conservation (MDC), 152, 177
Missouri State Parks and Historic Sites, 219
Missouri State Parks seasonal interpreter training program, 382
Monet, Charles, 229
Monterey Bay Aquarium, California, 156–157, 219–220, 469–471
Montessori, Dr. Maria, 92
Monument Valley Navajo Park, Arizona, 30
Moor, Robert, 466
Moore, Jessica, 466
moral development theory, 115–117
Morgenson, Randy, vii
Mormon Pioneer National Historic Trail, 95
Morton Arboretum, Illinois, 395
Morwellham Quay, Devon, England, 244
Moses, James, 121
Motch, Jeff, 457
Mott, William Penn, 74
Mount Rainier National Park, 20, 24, 259
Mount St. Helens National Volcanic Monument, 25

Mountains Recreation & Conservation Authority (MRCA), 127, 137
Mt. McKinley, 89–90
Muir, John, 10, 22, 118, 193, 220, 230
Muir Woods National Monument, 429
Mulllin, Tom, 378
multiple intelligences, 110–112
Muses of Greek mythology, 238
Museum Hack, 246–248
Museum of Art, Balboa Park, San Diego, California, 457
"Museum of Memory," Paraguay, 327
Museum of Natural History, 239
museums
    administration, 251–253
    design, 249–251
    different, for different purposes, 241–245
    focus on the museum experience, 253–255
    function of, 234–235
    history of, 238–241
    interpreters, 31
    interpreting in, 235–238
    programming, 245–248
music, 225–226

N

Nabokov, Vladimir, 309
Nagurny, Lisa, 208, 483
Nash, Roderick, 230
National Aquarium of Baltimore, Maryland, 272
National Association for Interpretation (NAI), 18, 255, 385–387
National Association for Interpretation (NAI) Master Trainers, 206
National Audubon Society (NAS), 36
National Back Country Byways, 294
National Cemetery, 3
National Conservation Training Center, Shepherdstown, West Virginia, 27
national forests' interpreters, 22–26
National Mall, the, 211
National Museum of African American History & Culture, National Mall, 241
National Museum of American History, Smithsonian Institution's *The Time Trial of John Brown* program, 222
national park interpreters, 18–22
National Park Rx Day Celebration (NPS), 50
National Park Service Climate Change Response Program, 96
National Park Service (NPS), 7, 60, 63, 129, 135
    interpreters in, 20–22
    interpretive associations, 369
    partnership with Amtrak, 367
    training at, 378
    website, 167
National Parks, The An Illustrated History (Heacox), 98
National Scenic Byways, 293
National Trails, 294
National Wildlife Refuges (NWR), and interpreters, 26–27

Native American Graves Protection & Repatriation Act of 1990, 241
"Native People" interpreters, 34
Nature College, the, 444
"nature deficit disorder," 50
"nature literacy," 119–120
Nature Literacy Series (Orion Society), 119–120
nature trails, 284
Navajo Nation, 30
Nebuchadnezzar, King, 33
Nelson, Steve, 23
New Zealand, Maori interpreters, 437
news releases, 177–179
news story diagram (fig.), 178
newsletters, 318–319
nonprofit interpretation, 364–367
North Olympic Library System, 225
Northwest Interpretive Association, 25
Northwest New Mexico Visitor Center, 186, 368
Northwest Trek Wildlife Park, Washington, 466
NPS Interpretive Development Program, 209

O

Oakland Museum of California (OMCA) Gallery of California Natural Sciences, 269
Obama, Michelle, 399, 464
Obama, President Barack, 241
O'Keefe, Georgia, 391
Okutama-Kohan Park, Japan, 130
Old Point Loma Lighthouse, Cabrillo National Monument, San Diego, ix, x
Old Spanish Missions, Texas, 151
Old Sturbridge Village, Massachusetts, 244, 335
Oliver, Mary, 225
Olympic National Park, 225, 474
Omaha Zoo, Nebraska, 229
operational plans, 397
organizations, business framework for interpretive, 348–349
Orion Society, 119–120
outdoor dramas, 221–222
OWLS (Older, Wiser, Livelier Seniors), 153
Ozark Folk Center State Park, Arkansas, 175
Ozark Highlands Radio, 175

P

Panama Canal tours, 363
Paradise Inn, Mount Rainier National Park, 259
park newspapers, 174, 317–318
parking for museum facilities and services, 250
park interpreters, 29
participation, promoting, 210–211
Pascal, Blaise, 322
Passion for Excellence, A (Peters & Austin), 348–349
Paul II, Pope John, 449
Pawling, Richard N., 34–35
Pawson, Ray, 428
peak experiences, 10–11
Peale, Charles Wilson, 239

peer evaluation, 423
Peer-Vetted Creative Production (PVCP), 464–465
Pennsylvania Historical & Museum Commission, 29
Permanent Vacation...National Parks (Cornelius), 468
Personal Interpretation (Brochu & Merriman), 88
Petrified Forest National Park, 62
Petrified Wood National Park, 4
phone, taking better pictures with your, 171
photography credits key, 484
photos
    taking better pictures with your phone, 171
    taking for social media, 170–171
Piaget, Jean, 107
Pinchot III, Gifford, 26
Pinkley, Frank, 240
Pioneer, Arizona, 32
planetariums, 276
planning
    and designing trails, 285–292
    interpretive, 395–414
    road tours, 293
    special events, 373
    supervisor's function, 358
plans
    All-American Road Plans, 293
    exhibit, 279
    interpretive, 396–397
    sampling, 427
Plimoth Plantation, 243–244, 331
poetry and journaling, 319–322
poetry and storytelling, 222–225
politics and religion, 94–95
pollinator protection, 24
Pools of 'Ohe'o, Haleakala National Park, 66
Pope John Paul II, 449
Porter, Eliot, 90
postconventional morality, 115
Pratt Museum, Homer, Alaska, 250, 270, 271
Prebys, Conrad, x
preconventional morality, 115
preoperational stage, Piaget's model, 108
presentations, supervisory evaluation criteria for, 422
pricing strategy, 365–367
print media, 173–174
private commercial interpreters, 34
private museums, 252
private nonprofit interpreters, 35–36
private sector
    interpretation, 34–36
    partnerships, and Forest Service, 25
professional associations, 385–387
professional development, 384–389
professionalism, global spread of, 439–441
programming
    evaluation, 429–430
    museum, 245–248
    total, 91
programs, evening, 199–201
Project Learning Tree, Project Wild, 117
promoting participation, 210–211

proofreading, 309
Prophetstown State Park, Indiana, 371
"proster" theory, 112
Public History, 327, 329
public sector interpretation, 364–367
public service announcements (PSAs), 180
public support and interpreters, 63
Pueblo Museum, 325
Pulitzer, Joseph, 166
PUP Global Heritage Consortium, 377

Q

questioning strategies, 206–207

R

radio, 174–175
railroads and bike paths, 300–301
Reagan, Nancy, 245
recreational benefits of interpretation, 43–44
Recreational Equipment, Inc. (REI), 25
Red Rock Canyon Visitor Center, Nevada, 28
Redmond-Jones, Beth, 269
Reese, Jess, 97, 482
Reida, Ariadna, 438
relief models/maps, 275
religion and politics, 94–95
Remembered Earth documentary, 368
Renegade Museum Tours, 248
reporting, 360
resource protection, 61–62
resources, matching to customers, 398–403
restaurants for museum facilities and services, 251
Rice, Isaac, 330
Ridge, Mia, 246
Riley, James Whitcomb, 242
Riolo, Roger, 107, 206, 207, 482
Risk, Paul, 202
road tours
    interpretive, 292–296
    wayside, 296–300
Roadside Heritage program, 295
Robinson, Edward Stevens, 262
Rockefeller family, 243
Rocky Mountain National Park, 6, 83, 135
Rodriguez, Irene N., 325
Rollins, Jack, 23
Roosevelt, President Theodore, 22
Rose, Charlie, 105
Rose, Julia, 342
Route du Fromage (Trail of Cheese), Auvergne, France, 294
roving interpretation, 156–157, 251
Runge Nature Center, Missouri, 152, 283, 352, 384
rural museums, 243–244

S

Sabino Canyon Tours, 34
safety
    and interpreters, 62
    of interpretive waysides, 297
Saint Augustine, 292
Saint-Exupéry, Antoine, 395
Salamanca National Park, Columbia, 172
sampling plans, 427
San Diego Natural History Museum, 253
San Jose Tech Museum of Innovation, California, 278
Sanders, Scott Russell, 230, 465
Sankoff, Irene, 215
Savannah Guides Ltd., 388
Schaefer, Norman, 230
School for Environmental Studies at the Minnesota Zoo," 43
schools outside North America engaged with interpretation research or offering courses in interpretation, 447–448
Seabourn Cruise Line, 34
Seafood Watch program, 469–470
seasonal employees, training, 381
Seattle City Parks, 30
Sedgwick County Zoo, Kansas, 354
self-actualization, 46, 47
self-evaluation, 423–424
self-improvement, 390–391
"self-perception theory," 67
Senior Wednesdays, Wichita, Kansas, 154
seniors, serving, 152–154
sense of place, developing, 10
sensorimotor stage, Piaget's model, 108
Sequoia & Kings Canyon National Park, 62
Serrell, Beverly, 265, 277, 316, 417
Service, Robert, 197
Sharp, Dr. Ryan, 165
Sharpe, Grant, 443, 444
Shellhorn, Jeremy, 299, 483
Shenandoah National Park, 62, 136, 154–155
Silent Spring (Carson), 304, 468
Simon, Nina, 399, 401
simulated immersions, 276
Skibins, Dr. Jeff, 165
Skönsen Fdkk Museum, Sweden, 243
slavery, 339
Smith, Melanie, 451
Smith, Wren, 88
Smithsonian museums, 240
Smokey Bear, 22–23, 180
Smoky Mountain National Park, 130
Snyder, Gerry, 171, 482
Sobel, David, 149, 150
Social and Environmental Formation and Innovation (SEFI), 435
social media, 168–170
Society for the Protection of New Hampshire Forests, 369
Solomon, King, 33
speaking, basic qualities for effective, 192–194

specialized museums, 244–245
special interest road tours, 294–295
Speth, James Gustave, 53
spittons, 272
St. Lawrence Islands National Park, Canada, 62
St. Theresa of Calcutta, 384
Standard Practices for Interpretive Planning (NAI), 403–404
"Standards of Excellence for Urban National Wildlife Refuges" (FWR), 27
Standish, Miles, 243–244
Statue of Liberty, NYC, 372
Stegner, Wallace, vii, 20
Steinfeld, Jay, 355–356
Stern, Marc, 211
Stetson, Lee, 216, 220–221, 230
Stevens, Jason Jay, 277, 278
Stevenson, Robert Lewis, 72
Stone, Julia, 59
Stonewall National Monument, 241
Story Collider, 224
storytelling and poetry, 222–225
Straits of Mackinac Underwater Preserve, Michigan, 291
Strauss, Susan, 223–224
Stroud, Joseph, 230
subjective norms in Theory of Planned Behavior (TPB), 66
Suknev, Andrei, 439–440
Sunset Zoo, Manhattan, Kansas, 229
supervision, 357–360, 421–423
Syrigos, Jan and George, 225–226

T

Taleb, Nassim Nicholas, 428
talks
    illustrated, 198–199
    interpretive, 192, 194–197
Tama'stslikt Cultural Institute, Oregon, 30
Tanki, China's Empress, 33
Te Papa Museum, New Zealand, 107
TEAMS (Talent, Expertise, Agility, Mobility & Simplicity) Enterprise Unit, Forest Service, 25–26
technology, and the future of interpretation, 465–467
television, 176–177
Terkel, Studs, 381
Texas Museum of Natural History, 275
Theory of Planned Behavior (TPB), 65–67
Thinking, Fast and Slow (Kahneman), 428
Thompson, Dale, 259
Thoreau, Henry David, 284
Tidwell, Chief Tom, 26
Tilden, Freeman, xiii, 5, 9, 60, 72, 81, 82, 84, 96, 100, 111, 131, 144, 186, 223, 276, 306, 321, 334, 378, 448
Tilden's Principles of Interpretation (fig.), 84
Tilley, Nick, 428
Tippecanoe Battlefield, 14
Tolkien, J.R.R., 301
Tongass National Forest, 25
TORE (Thematic, Organized, Relevant, Enjoyable) Model of thematic communication, 86–88
tourism
    ecotourism, 363
    future of, 449–453
tourist information centers, 236–237
traffic considerations in designing trails, 293
trails
    design, 285–288
    generally, 283–284
    interpretive considerations, 288–289
    railroads and bike paths, 300–301
    that teach and touch, 284–285
    trail media, 289–291
    vandalism of, 288
    water, 291–292
training and professional growth
    agency training, 380–384
    approaches to training, 389–390
    introduction, 377
    professional development, 384–389
    professional recognition and, 442–445
    self-improvement, 390–391
    university preparation, 378–380
travel, guided, 204
travel interpretation, and Forest Service, 25
Travelers' Information Stations (TIS), 176
Trees for Tomorrow Natural Resource Education Center, Eagle River, Wisconsin, 36
tribal interpretation, 30
Trunk Bay, Virgin Islands, underwater interpretive trail, 292
Tulsa Zoo Friends, Inc., 371
Turnbull, Colin, 100
Turner, Jack, 230
Tuttle Creek Reservoir, Kansas, 28
Twain, Mark, 453
Twitter, 169

U

Ulrich, Roger, 51–52
Umatilla Indian Reservation, Oregon, 30
UNESCO's World Nature Forum Visitor Center, Naters, Switzerland, 463
United National Educational, Scientific and Cultural Organization (UNESCO), 436, 452
university preparation, 378–380
U.S. Federal Reserve money museum, Chicago, 272
U.S. Fish & Wildlife Service, 61
U.S. Forest Service, 22–26
U.S. Government Museum Department, 240
U.S. National Park Service. See National Park Service (NPS)
U.S. National Park Service's Interpretive Development Program (IDP), 380
U.S. National Trail System, 294
user fees, 364–365
Uzzell, David, 342

V

vandalism of trails, 288
Velásquez, Roxana, x

Vermont Fish & Wildlife department, 33
Veverka, John, 268, 408, 466
videos for social media, 170–171
visitor centers
    design, 249–251
    interpreting in, 235–238
    museums and, 233
visitors
    angry, 187
    appropriate behavior, barriers to (table), 70
    becoming, for evaluation, 420–421
    with disabilities, serving, 139–144
    and exhibits, 268
    needs, and how interpreters can meet them (table), 48
    observing the, in evaluation, 424
    serving, 12
"Visitor's Bill of Rights, The," 131
visual arts, 227–230
Vitamin N: The Essential Guide to a Nature-Rich Life (Louv), 120
Vizcaíno, Sebastián, ix
volunteers, 253, 383

W

Wallis, Marc, 330
Walmart, Bentonville, Arkansas, 36
Walsh, Patricia, 98
Wang, Wen, 33
Washington Crossing, Pennsylvania, 29
Washington's National Park Fund (WNPF), 259
water trails, 291–292
Watkins, Carleton, 21
Watson, Larry, 306
Watson, Mike, 459
wayside road tours, 296–300
waysides, 293–300
webcams, 165
WebRangers program, National Park Service, 21
websites, 166–168
Weil, Stephen, 234
Weilbacher, Michael, 150
Wells, Marcella, 405
Western Interpreters Association, 386
Western National Parks Association, 369
whale watch ships, 34
whaling, 270
When Cultures Collide (Lewis), 451
Whitney Museum, New York City, 399
wildlife parks' interpreters, 32–33
wildlife rehabilitation, 95–96
wildlife windows, 276
Williams, Terry Tempest, vi, 18, 56, 98, 193, 230, 307, 467, 468
Wilson, Edward O., 355
Wilson's Creek National Battlefield, Missouri, 88–89
Wisconsin State Museum, Madison, 263
Women of the West museum, 245
Women's Rights National Historic Park, 95
Woods, Mark, 98

World Federation of Tourist Guides Associations, 388
World Heritage Sites, 338, 436
Wright Brothers Memorial, Kitty Hawk, North Carolina, 250
writing, interpretive. See interpretive writing
WWII Holocaust Museums and concentration camps in Europe, 327

Y

Yale School of Forestry & Environmental Studies' Park/School Program, 149
Yeats, William Butler, 130
Yellowstone National Park, 7, 20, 41, 63, 81, 82, 91, 466
Yerxa, Cabot, 325, 326
Yosemite Museum Association, 369
Yosemite National Park, 4, 7, 8, 20, 22, 185, 192, 220, 229–230, 240, 267, 473
Yosemite Park Act of 1864, 20–21
Yosemite School of Field Natural History, 378
You Are Not So Smart (McRaney), 428
Youth Conservation Corps (YCC), 33–34

Z

Zimmerman, Ron, 237, 248
Zinsser, William, 309, 315
Zion National Park, 202, 204
Zoo Educators Association, 387
Zoological Society of San Diego, 33
zoos, 32–33, 273, 373
Zurbanán, Francisco de, x

Related Books

BUY DIRECT & SAVE — MOST E-BOOKS 50% OFF PRINTED PRICE
INSTANT ACCESS | INSTANT SAVINGS

www.sagamorepublishing.com   1-800-327-5557

SAGAMORE PUBLISHING